New UK GAAP Supplement 2016

Generally Accepted Accounting Practice
under UK and Irish GAAP

Larissa Connor   Dean Lockhart   Amanda Marrion

Tim Rogerson   Claire Taylor

EY
Building a better
working world

WILEY

About this book

This book is a supplement to the EY publication New UK GAAP 2015 which was published in 2015. New UK GAAP 2015 provides a comprehensive guide to interpreting and implementing the new UK accounting standards. This book provides a guide to understanding the changes made to those new UK accounting standards between August 2014 and September 2015, particularly the changes to:

- FRS 100 – *Application of Financial Reporting Requirements*;
- FRS 101 – *Reduced Disclosure Framework – Disclosure exemptions from EU-adopted IFRS for qualifying entities*; and
- FRS 102 – *The Financial Reporting Standard applicable in the UK and Republic of Ireland*.

In addition, this supplement provides a guide to a new UK accounting standard, FRS 104 – *Interim Financial Reporting*.

In summary, this publication updates New UK GAAP 2015 for the following:

- *Amendments to FRS 100* issued in July 2015;
- *Amendments to FRS 101 Reduced Disclosure Framework (2014/15 Cycle and other minor amendments)* issued in July 2015;
- the editorial amendment to Section 12 – *Other Financial instruments Issues* of FRS 102 in relation to examples of hedge accounting issued in September 2014;
- *Amendments to FRS 102 – Pension Obligations* issued in February 2015;
- consequential amendments to FRS 102 included in FRS 104 issued in March 2015;
- *Amendments to FRS 102 – Small entities and other minor amendments* issued in July 2015;
- some minor typographical or presentational corrections made to FRSs 100-102; and
- FRS 104, which was issued in March 2015.

This publication contains six chapters which cover the above changes as follows:

- Chapter 1 – a revised chapter on the application of FRS 100 reflecting the amendments made in July 2015;
- Chapter 2 – a revised chapter on the application of FRS 101 reflecting the amendments made in July 2015;
- Chapter 3 – a new chapter on the small entities regime within FRS 102 which was introduced by the changes made to the standard in July 2015;
- Chapter 4 – a revised chapter on the presentation requirements of FRS 102 including the ability to use 'adapted' balance sheet and profit and loss account

formats for certain companies (which was introduced by the changes made to the standard in July 2015);

- Chapter 5 – a chapter detailing the other amendments made to FRS 102 in February and July 2015 (not otherwise covered above); and
- Chapter 6 – a new chapter on FRS 104.

Preface

Over the last few years the Financial Reporting Council (FRC) has fundamentally changed its financial reporting standards in the UK and Ireland. Existing requirements have been replaced with new Financial Reporting Standards, including: FRS 100 – *Application of Financial Reporting Requirements*, FRS 101 – *Reduced Disclosure Framework*, FRS 102 – *The Financial Reporting Standard applicable in the UK and Republic of Ireland* and FRS 104 – *Interim Financial Reporting*. We refer to these standards, which are mandatory for accounting periods beginning on or after 1 January 2015, along with the associated accounting requirements of the Companies Act 2006, as new UK GAAP.

The FRC has also changed the financial reporting regime for small and micro-entities. For accounting periods beginning on or after 1 January 2016, the *Financial Reporting Standard for Smaller Entities* (FRSSE) is withdrawn. Instead, small entities that choose to apply the small entities regime will be subject to the recognition and measurement requirements of FRS 102 but with separate, reduced, disclosure requirements. A micro-entity that chooses to apply the micro-entities regime will apply a new accounting standard, FRS 105 – *The Financial Reporting Standard applicable to the Micro-entities Regime* although the requirements and proposals for micro-entities are not covered in detail in this publication.

This publication is a supplement to our 2015 publication, New UK GAAP 2015, and covers the changes made to FRSs 100-102 since August 2014 up to and including the new editions of those standards issued in September 2015.

A number of significant changes have been made to the new standards prior to the end of the first accounting period in which they are mandatory. Many of these changes derive from the need to implement the new Accounting Directive into UK Company Law. However, in response to the identification of a number of implementation issues, the FRC has taken the opportunity to make other improvements to the standards, particularly to FRS 102. Most of these changes, including the new small entities regime within FRS 102 and the option to use IFRS-style balance sheet and profit and loss account formats (where available), are not mandatory before accounting periods beginning on or after 1 January 2016 but can be early-adopted for accounting periods beginning on or after 1 January 2015. The result of this, as we explain in this publication, is that entities which have not early-adopted FRS 101 and FRS 102, have the opportunity to apply these changes on conversion from previous UK GAAP.

This publication explains these changes to the new reporting requirements in a way that is intended to help entities deal with everyday issues as well as more complex issues as they arise. This publication includes our views on the judgemental areas we believe are likely to be most common in practice. Our views are based on our experience of similar issues under IFRS and previous UK GAAP. As experience of applying the new standards grows over time, we expect our views will continue to evolve.

In addition to the changes discussed in this publication, it is possible that further amendments and clarifications will be issued prior to the first application of FRS 102. Reporters are therefore advised to stay alert to further developments.

Guidance on International Financial Reporting Standards can be found in EY's publication International GAAP 2016®.

****

We are deeply indebted to many of our colleagues within the UK organisation of EY for their selfless assistance and support in the publication of this book.

Our thanks go particularly to those who reviewed, edited and assisted in the preparation of drafts, most notably: Tony Clifford, Marianne Dudareva and Michael Pratt.

Our thanks also go to everyone who directly or indirectly contributed to the book's creation, including the following members of the Financial Reporting Group: Mike Bonham, Denise Brand, Rob Carrington, Wei Li Chan, Mike Davies, Pieter Dekker, Tim Denton, Jane Hurworth, Rabin Jogarajan, Ted Jones, Bernd Kremp, Andrea Maylor, Robert McCracken, Sharon MacIntyre, Richard Moore, Margaret Pankhurst and Michael Varila.

We also thank Jeremy Gugenheim for his assistance with the production technology throughout the period of writing.

London,   *Larissa Connor*   *Amanda Marrion*   *Claire Taylor*

October 2015   *Dean Lockhart*   *Tim Rogerson*

Lists of chapters

References and abbreviations

The following references and abbreviations are used in this book:

References:

FRS 100.4	Paragraph 4 of FRS 100
FRS 100.AG7	Paragraph 7 of the Application Guidance to FRS 100
FRS 100 Appendix I	Appendix I of FRS 100
FRS 101.10	Paragraph 10 of FRS 101
FRS 101 Appendix I Table 1	Table 1 of Appendix I of FRS 101
FRS 102.23.9	Paragraph 9 of Section 23 of FRS 102
FRS 104.1	Paragraph 1 of FRS 104
FRS 11.9	Paragraph 9 of FRS 11
SSAP 9.10	Paragraph 10 of SSAP 9
UITF 26.4	Paragraph 4 of UITF 26
S395(2)	Section 395 of the Companies Act 2006 subsection (2)
Regulations 6(2)	Paragraph 6(2) of the Large and Medium-sized Companies and Groups (Accounts and Reports) Regulations 2008
1 Sch 55	Paragraph 55 of Schedule 1 to the Large and Medium-sized Companies and Groups (Accounts and Reports) Regulations 2008
1 Sch 1 (LLP)	Paragraph 1 of Schedule 1 of The Large and Medium-sized Limited Liability Partnerships (Accounts) Regulations 2008
I Sch 1C (SC)	Paragraph 1C of Schedule 1 to the Small Companies and Groups (Accounts and Directors' Report) Regulations 2008
S 399, LLP SI 2008/1911	Section 399 of The Limited Liability Partnerships (Accounts and Audit) (Application of Companies Act 2006) Regulations 2008
LLP Regulations 3	Paragraph 3 of The Large and Medium-sized Limited Liability Partnerships (Accounts) Regulations 2008

LLP SC Regulations 3	Paragraph 3 of The Small Limited Liability Partnerships (Accounts) Regulations 2008
1 Sch 10(2) (LLP SC)	Paragraph 10 of Schedule 1 to the Small Limited Liability Partnerships (Accounts) Regulations 2008
TECH 02/10	Technical Release 02/10 issued by the ICAEW and ICAS
FRED 56.3B	Paragraph 3B of Financial Reporting Exposure Draft 56
DTR 4.2.10	Paragraph 4.2.10 of the Disclosure and Transparency Rules
IFRS 1.D16	Paragraph D16 of IFRS 1
IAS 1.12	Paragraph 12 of IAS 1
IFRIC 18.BC22	Paragraph 22 of the Basis for Conclusions to IFRIC 18
Foreword to Accounting Standards.19	Paragraph 19 of the Foreword to Accounting Standards issued by the FRC

Professional and regulatory bodies:

ASB	Accounting Standards Board in the UK
BIS	Department for Business, Innovation and Skills
FRC	Financial Reporting Council
IASB	International Accounting Standards Board
ICAEW	Institute of Chartered Accountants in England and Wales
ICAS	Institute of Chartered Accountants of Scotland
IFRIC	International Financial Reporting Interpretations Committee

Accounting related terms:

Accounting Directive	Directive 2013/34/EU
AIM	Alternative Investment Market
CA 2006	Companies Act 2006
CGU	Cash-generating Unit
E&E	Exploration and Evaluation
EBIT	Earnings Before Interest and Taxes
EBITDA	Earnings Before Interest, Taxes, Depreciation and Amortisation
EBT	Employee Benefit Trust
EIR	Effective Interest Rate

EPS	Earnings per Share
FC	Foreign currency
FIFO	First-In, First-Out basis of valuation
FRED	Financial Reporting Exposure Draft
FRS	Financial Reporting Standard (issued by the ASB)
FRSSE	Financial Reporting Standard for smaller Entities
FTA	First-time Adoption
FVLCD	Fair value less costs of disposal
FVLCS	Fair value less costs to sell
GAAP	Generally Accepted Accounting Practice
IAS	International Accounting Standard (issued by the former board of the IASC)
IFRS	International Financial Reporting Standard (issued by the IASB)
IRR	Internal Rate of Return
JA	Joint Arrangement
JANE	Joint arrangement that is not an entity
JCA	Jointly Controlled Asset
JCE	Jointly Controlled Entity
JV	Joint Venture
LIBOR	London Inter Bank Offered Rate
LIFO	Last-In, First-Out basis of valuation
LLP	Limited liability partnership
LLP Regulations	Large and Medium-sized Limited Liability Partnerships (Accounts) Regulations 2008 (SI 2008/1912)
LLP (SC)	Small Limited Liability Partnerships (Accounts) Regulations 2008 (SI 2008/1913)
NCI	Non-controlling Interest
NBV	Net Book Value
NPV	Net Present Value
NRV	Net Realisable Value
OCI	Other Comprehensive Income
PP&E	Property, Plant and Equipment
R&D	Research and Development
Regulations	Large and Medium-sized Companies and Groups (Accounts and Reports) Regulations 2008 (SI 2008/410)
SCA	Service Concession Arrangement

SE	Structured Entity
SI 2008/1911	The Limited Liability Partnerships (Accounts and Audit) (Application of Companies Act 2006) Regulations 2008
SI 2015/980	The Companies, Partnerships and Groups (Accounts and Reports) Regulations 2015 (SI 2015/980)
Small Companies Regulations	Small Companies and Groups (Accounts and Directors' Report) Regulations 2008 (SI 2008/409)
SME	Small or medium-sized entity
SORP	Statement of Recommended Practice
SPE	Special Purpose Entity
SSAP	Statement of Standard Accounting Practice
SV	Separate Vehicle
TSR	Total Shareholder Return
UITF	Urgent Issues Task Force
UK	United Kingdom
VIU	Value In Use
WACC	Weighted Average Cost of Capital

Authoritative literature

The content of this book takes into account all accounting standards and other relevant rules issued up to September 2015.

New UK and Ireland Reporting Standards

FRS 100	Application of Financial Reporting Requirements (September 2015)
FRS 101	Reduced Disclosure Framework – Disclosure exemptions from EU-adopted IFRS for qualifying entities (September 2015)
FRS 102	The Financial Reporting Standard applicable in the UK and Republic of Ireland (September 2015)
FRS 104	Interim financial reporting (March 2015)
FRS 105	The Financial Reporting Standard applicable to the Micro-entities Regime (July 2015)

Financial Reporting Standard for Smaller Entities (effective January 2015 but withdrawn for accounting periods beginning on or after 1 January 2016)

Previous UK GAAP

FRS 1	Cash flow statements (revised 1996)
FRS 2	Accounting for subsidiary undertakings
FRS 3	Reporting financial performance
FRS 4	Capital instruments
FRS 5	Reporting the substance of transactions
FRS 6	Acquisitions and mergers
FRS 7	Fair values in acquisition accounting
FRS 8	Related party disclosures
FRS 9	Associates and joint ventures
FRS 10	Goodwill and intangible assets
FRS 11	Impairment of fixed assets and goodwill
FRS 12	Provisions, contingent liabilities and contingent assets
FRS 13	Derivatives and other financial instruments: Disclosures
FRS 14	Earnings per share
FRS 15	Tangible fixed assets
FRS 16	Current tax
FRS 17	Retirement benefits
FRS 18	Accounting policies
FRS 19	Deferred tax
FRS 20 (IFRS 2)	Share-based payment
FRS 21 (IAS 10)	Events after the balance sheet date

FRS 20 (IAS 33)   Earnings per share
FRS 23 (IAS 21)   The effects of changes in foreign exchange rates
FRS 25 (IAS 32)   Financial instruments: Presentation
FRS 26 (IAS 39)   Financial instruments: recognition and measurement
FRS 27   Life Assurance
FRS 28   Corresponding amounts
FRS 29   Financial instruments: disclosures
FRS 30   Heritage assets

Financial Reporting Standard for Smaller Entities (effective April 2008)

Amendments to the FRSSE (effective April 2008)

UITF Abstracts (under previous UK GAAP)

UITF 4	Presentation of long-term debtors in current assets
UITF 5	Transfers from current assets to fixed assets
UITF 9	Accounting for operations in hyper-inflationary economies
UITF 11	Capital instruments: issuer call options
UITF 15	(revised 1999) Disclosure of substantial acquisitions
UITF 19	Tax gains and losses on foreign currency borrowings that hedge an investment in a foreign operation
UITF 21	Accounting issues arising from the proposed introduction of the euro
UITF 22	The acquisition of a Lloyd's business
UITF 23	Application of the transitional rules in FRS 15
UITF 24	Accounting for start-up costs
UITF 25	National insurance contributions on share option gains
UITF 26	Barter transactions for advertising
UITF 27	Revision to estimates of the useful economic life of goodwill and intangible assets
UITF 28	Operating lease incentives
UITF 29	Website development costs
UITF 31	Exchanges of businesses or other non-monetary assets for an interest in a subsidiary, joint venture or associate
UITF 32	Employee benefit trusts and other intermediate payment arrangements
UITF 34	Pre-contract costs
UITF 35	Death-in-service and incapacity benefits
UITF 36	Contracts for sale of capacity
UITF 38	Accounting for ESOP trusts
UITF 39	(IFRIC Interpretation 2) Member's shares in co-operative entities and similar instruments
UITF 40	Revenue recognition and service contracts
UITF 41	Scope of FRS 20 (IFRS 2)
UITF 42	Reassessment of embedded derivatives
UITF 43	The interpretation of equivalence for the purposes of section 228A of the Companies Act 1985

UITF 44	(IFRIC Interpretation 11) FRS 20 (IFRS 2) Group and Treasury Share Transactions
UITF 45	(IFRIC Interpretation 6) Liabilities arising from participating in a specific market – Waste electrical and electronic equipment
UITF 46	(IFRIC Interpretation 16) Hedges of a net investment in a foreign operation
UITF 47	(IFRIC Interpretation 19) Extinguishing Financial Liabilities with Equity Instruments
UITF 48	Accounting implications of the replacement of the retail prices index with the consumer prices index for retirement benefits

Chapter 1   FRS 100 – Application of financial reporting requirements

Chapter 1

List of examples

Chapter 1   FRS 100 – Application of financial reporting requirements

1   INTRODUCTION

In 2012, 2013 and 2014 the Financial Reporting Council (FRC), following a lengthy period of consultation (between 2002 and 2012), changed financial reporting standards in the United Kingdom and the Republic of Ireland. Evidence from consultation supported a move towards an international-based framework for financial reporting that was proportionate to the needs of preparers and users. *[FRS 102 Summary (i), (ii), (v)]*.

The new financial reporting framework, 'new UK and Irish GAAP' replaces almost all extant previous UK GAAP (see 4.3 below) with the following Financial Reporting Standards:

- FRS 100 – *Application of Financial Reporting Requirements*;
- FRS 101 – *Reduced Disclosure Framework: Disclosure exemptions from EU-adopted IFRS for qualifying entities* (see Chapter 2);
- FRS 102 – *The Financial Reporting Standard Applicable in the UK and Republic of Ireland* (see EY New UK GAAP 2015 and Chapters 3 to 5);
- FRS 103 – *Insurance Contracts – Consolidated accounting and reporting requirements for entities in the UK and Republic of Ireland issuing insurance contracts*;
- FRS 104 – *Interim Financial Reporting* (see Chapter 6); and
- FRS 105 – *The Financial Reporting Standard applicable to the Micro-entities regime.*

An entity that applies FRS 102 must apply FRS 103, published in March 2014, to insurance contracts (including reinsurance contracts) that it issues, reinsurance contracts that it holds and financial instruments that it issues with a discretionary participation feature.

FRS 104 applies only to interim financial reports and does not apply to the annual financial statements of an entity. It is intended for use by entities that prepare annual financial statements in accordance with FRS 102 but can also be used by entities that prepare annual financial statements in accordance with FRS 101.

The FRC issued amendments to FRS 101, FRS 102 and the FRSSE (now withdrawn) in both 2014 and 2015 as discussed below. These amendments have varying effective dates so their adoption by an entity may depend on their date of transition to the new standards.

This chapter deals only with the application of FRS 100. This standard, which was issued originally in November 2012, sets out the new financial reporting framework and applies to entities preparing financial statements in accordance with legislation, regulation or accounting standards applicable in the UK and the Republic of Ireland. *[FRS 100.1]*. FRS 101, FRS 102 (and FRS 103) are mandatory for accounting periods beginning on or after 1 January 2015, but permit early application (subject to the requirements of the applicable standards). FRS 101 and FRS 102 were amended in July 2015, principally to reflect implementation of the new Accounting Directive. FRS 105 is mandatory for accounting periods beginning on or after 1 January 2016, but early application is permitted for accounting periods beginning on or after 1 January 2015, see 4.2 below.

Amendments to FRS 100 (with early application subject to the early application provisions in FRS 101 (amended July 2015), FRS 102 (amended July 2015) or FRS 105   – see 4.2.1 below) were issued in July 2015 to reflect the implementation of the *EU Accounting Directive*, with the amended standard effective for accounting periods beginning on or after 1 January 2016 (with early application subject to the early application provisions in the applicable standards – see 4.2 below). A revised edition of FRS 100 was issued in September 2015 incorporating the July 2015 amendments. The revised standard changes the financial reporting framework for small entities and micro-entities, by withdrawing the *Financial Reporting Standard for Smaller Entities* (FRSSE) (effective January 2015), and introducing a new accounting standard for micro entities – FRS 105. *[FRS 100.15A]*.

This chapter deals only with the September 2015 edition of FRS 100, which incorporates the July 2015 amendments. For a discussion of FRS 100, prior to the July 2015 amendments, refer to Chapter 1 of EY New UK GAAP 2015.

Under the Companies Act 2006 the choice of financial reporting framework is closely related to the requirements of company law or other regulatory requirements. UK companies with transferable securities admitted to trading on a regulated market (at the financial year end) are required under the IAS Regulation to prepare their consolidated financial statements using EU-adopted IFRS. A list of regulated markets is available online.[1]

In addition, entities that are not required by UK company law to prepare financial statements using EU-adopted IFRS may be required to do so by other regulatory requirements, such as the AIM Rules (see 4.4.1 below) or by other agreements (e.g. shareholders' or partnership agreements).

However, other UK companies are permitted to prepare their consolidated and/or individual financial statements as IAS accounts (using EU-adopted IFRS) or Companies Act accounts (using 'applicable accounting standards' – see 4.6.1 below), subject to company law restrictions concerning the 'consistency of financial reporting framework' used in the individual accounts of group undertakings and over changes in financial reporting framework from IAS accounts to Companies Act accounts. See 6.1 below.

Prior to the implementation of FRS 100 to FRS 102, Companies Act accounts were prepared in accordance with 'previous UK GAAP'. In essence, under the new financial reporting framework, previous UK GAAP is replaced by FRS 100, FRS 101 and FRS 102 and FRS 105. The requirements for preparation of financial statements under the CA 2006 are addressed at 6 below. Except where otherwise stated, the rest of this chapter will refer to the requirements for UK companies, and therefore will refer to UK GAAP (prior to implementation of FRS 100 to FRS 103 and FRS 105) as 'previous UK GAAP'. UK LLPs and other entities preparing financial statements in accordance with Part 15 of the CA 2006 are subject to similar requirements, modified as necessary by the regulations that govern the content of their financial statements.

2   SUMMARY OF FRS 100

The following is a summary of FRS 100:

* FRS 100 sets out the application of the financial reporting framework for UK and Republic of Ireland entities (see 4 below). The detailed accounting requirements are included in EU-adopted IFRS, FRS 101, FRS 102 and FRS 105, depending on the choice of GAAP made by the entity. FRS 103 applies to financial statements prepared in accordance with FRS 102. FRS 104 applies to interim financial statements and can be applied by entities preparing annual financial statements under FRS 101 or FRS 102.

* FRS 100 sets out the effective date of the new standards. All are mandatory, effective for accounting periods beginning on or after 1 January 2015, except for FRS 105 which is mandatory for accounting periods beginning on or after 1 January 2016. However, the July 2015 amendments to FRS 100-102 are mandatory, effective for accounting periods beginning on or after 1 January 2016. Early application of FRS 100 is permitted subject to the early application provisions in the applicable standards but must be stated (see 4.2 below).

* FRS 100 sets out the application of SORPs (see 4.7 below).

* FRS 100 sets out the transition arrangements to FRS 101, FRS 102, and FRS 105 (see 5 below).

* FRS 100 withdraws virtually all existing UK and Irish GAAP ('previous UK GAAP'), with effect from its application date. Some parts of previous

UK GAAP have been retained by incorporation of their requirements into FRS 101, FRS 102 or FRS 103 (see 4.3 below).

- FRS 100 includes application guidance on the interpretation of 'equivalence' for the purposes of:

  (i)   the exemption from preparation of consolidated financial statements in s401, Companies Act 2006. This is discussed in Chapter 2 at 2.1.6 (FRS 101) and Chapter 6 at 3.1.1.C of EY New UK GAAP 2015 (FRS 102) but the same requirements apply to IAS accounts; and

  (ii)   the reduced disclosure framework discussed in Chapter 2 at 6.2 (FRS 101) and in Chapter 5 at 2.3 and Chapter 2 at 3 of EY New UK GAAP 2015 (FRS 102) respectively.

- FRS 100 sets out the definition of a 'financial institution' (which is replicated in FRS 101 and FRS 102). A financial institution:

  (i)   that applies FRS 102 needs to give the additional disclosures required by Section 34 – *Specialised Activities* – of FRS 102 in its individual financial statements; and

  (ii)   is not eligible for certain disclosure exemptions in its individual financial statements under the FRS 101 or FRS 102 reduced disclosure frameworks for qualifying entities.

The definition of a financial institution and the disclosure requirements for financial institutions are addressed in Chapter 2 at 6.4 (for FRS 101) and in Chapter 2 at 2.4.1 and 3.5 of EY New UK GAAP 2015 (for FRS 102).

3   DEFINITIONS

The following terms used in FRS 100 are as defined in the Glossary (included as Appendix I to FRS 100):

- *Accounting Directive* – Directive 2013/34/EU of the European Parliament and of the Council of 26 June 2013;

- *CA 2006* – the Companies Act 2006;

- *Date of transition* – the beginning of the earliest period for which an entity presents full comparative information under a given standard in its first financial statements that comply with that standard;

- *EU-adopted IFRS* – IFRSs adopted in the European Union in accordance with EU Regulation 1606/2002 (IAS Regulation);

- *Financial institution* – see the definition included in Chapter 2 at 6.4 (for FRS 101) and Chapter 2 of EY New UK GAAP 2015 at 2.4.1 (for FRS 102). The definition is the same for both FRS 101 and FRS 102;

- *FRS 100, FRS 101, FRS 102 and FRS 105* – see 1 above;

- *IAS Regulation* – EU Regulation 1606/2002;

- *IFRS (or IFRSs)* – standards and interpretations issued or (adopted) by the International Accounting Standards Board (IASB). They comprise International Financial Reporting Standards, International Accounting

Standards, Interpretations developed by the IFRS Interpretations Committee (the Interpretations Committee) or the former Standing Interpretations Committee (SIC);

- *Individual financial statements* – accounts that are required to be prepared by an entity in accordance with the CA 2006 or relevant legislation.

  For example, this term includes 'individual accounts' as set out in section 394 of the CA 2006, a 'statement of accounts' as set out in section 132 of the Charities Act 2011, or 'individual accounts' as set out in section 72A of the Building Societies Act 1986.

  Separate financial statements are included in the meaning of the term individual financial statements;

- *Public benefit entity* – an entity whose primary objective is to provide goods or services for the general public, community or social benefit and where any equity is provided with a view to supporting the entity's primary objectives rather than with a view to providing a financial return to equity providers, shareholders or members. Footnote 28 to FRS 102's Glossary includes further guidance on the definition of a public benefit entity;

- *Qualifying entity* – a member of a group where the parent of that group prepares publicly available consolidated financial statements, which are intended to give a true and fair view (of the assets, liabilities, financial position and profit or loss) and that member is included in the consolidation. For the purposes of FRS 101 only, a charity cannot be a qualifying entity. *[FRS 101.Glossary]*. See Chapter 2 at 2.1 (for FRS 101) and Chapter 2 at 3.1 of EY New UK GAAP 2015 (for FRS 102);

- *Regulations – The Large and Medium-sized Companies and Groups (Accounts and Reports) Regulations 2008* (SI 2008/410); and

- *Small entity* – (a) a company meeting the definition of a small company as set out in section 382 or 383 of the Act and not excluded from the small companies regime by section 348; (b) an LLP qualifying as small and not excluded from the small LLPs regime, as set out in the LLP Regulations; or (c) any other entity that would have met the criteria in (a) had it been a company incorporated under company law (see Chapter 3 at 4.1); and

- *SORP* – an extant Statement of Recommended Practice (SORP) developed in accordance with the FRC's *SORPs: Policy and Code of Practice*. SORPs recommend accounting practices for specialised industries or sectors, and supplement accounting standards and other legal and regulatory requirements in light of the special factors prevailing or transactions undertaken in a particular industry or sector.

Consistent with the FRS 102 Glossary, this chapter refers to *The Small Companies and Groups (Accounts and Directors' Report) Regulations 2008* (SI 2008/409) as the Small Companies Regulations.

4   FRS 100 – APPLICATION OF FINANCIAL REPORTING REQUIREMENTS

The publication of FRS 100 to FRS 105 followed a lengthy period of consultation (from 2002 to 2012) on changes to financial reporting in the UK and Republic of Ireland (the 'Future of UK and Irish GAAP'). The consultations supported a move towards an international-based framework proportionate to the needs of preparers and users. Further background on these consultations and the evolution of the FRC's approach leading up to the development of the new standards is included in Appendix III to FRS 100. *[FRS 100.Summary (ii)]*.

In developing the new standards, the FRC has set out an overriding objective to enable users of accounts to receive high-quality understandable financial reporting proportionate to the size and complexity of the entity and users' information needs. *[FRS 100.Summary (iii)]*.

In meeting this objective, the FRC has stated that it aims to provide succinct financial reporting standards that:

- provide an IFRS-based solution (unless an alternative clearly better meets the overriding objective);
- are based on up-to-date thinking and developments in the way entities operate and the transactions they undertake;
- balance consistent principles for accounting by UK and Republic of Ireland entities with practical solutions based on size, complexity, public interest and users' information needs;
- promote efficiency in groups; and
- are cost effective to apply. *[FRS 100.Summary (iv)]*.

The financial reporting framework set out in FRS 100 is summarised in the diagram below:

Figure 1.1 The UK Financial Reporting Framework

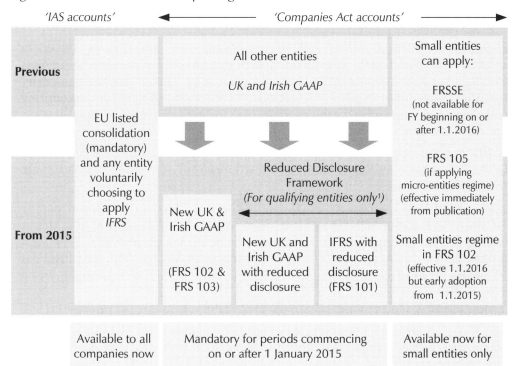

1: A qualifying entry (i.e. a parent or subsidiary undertaking) which is consolidated in publicly available consolidated financial statements that give a true and fair view can take advantage of the reduced disclosure framework. Applies to individual financial statements only and shareholders must be notified in writing about and not object to the disclosure exemptions. There are restrictions over IFRS 7, IFRS 13 and capital management disclosure exemptions (and in FRS 102, financial instruments-related disclosure exemptions) for financial institutions.

4.1   Scope of FRS 100

The objective of FRS 100 is to set out the applicable financial reporting framework for entities presenting financial statements in accordance with legislation, regulations or accounting standards applicable in the UK and Republic of Ireland. *[FRS 100.1]*.

FRS 100 applies to financial statements intended to give a true and fair view of assets, liabilities, financial position and profit for a period. *[FRS 100.2]*.

FRS 100 to FRS 102 can be applied by an entity that is not a UK or Irish company, preparing financial statements that are intended to give a true and fair view. However, Appendix II to FRS 100 states that the FRC sets accounting standards within the framework of the CA 2006 and therefore it is the company law requirements that the FRC primarily considered when developing FRS 102. See 4.4 below.

4.2   Effective date

The original editions of FRS 100 to FRS 103 are mandatory for accounting periods beginning on or after 1 January 2015, but were available for early application subject to the transitional rules set out in those standards. Early application must be disclosed in the notes to the financial statements. *[FRS 100.10, FRS 101.11, FRS 102.1.14, FRS 103.1.11]*.

This chapter only deals with the September 2015 edition of FRS 100. See Chapter 1 at 4.2 of EY New UK GAAP 2015 for a discussion of the effective date of the original edition of FRS 100.

The September 2015 edition of FRS 100 incorporates the amendments issued in July 2015. The July 2015 amendments are mandatory for accounting periods beginning on or after 1 January 2016. Early adoption is permitted providing an entity also applies the edition of FRS 101, FRS 102 or FRS 105 effective for accounting periods beginning on or after 1 January 2016, and the early application provisions set out in those standards. *[FRS 100.10]*.

FRS 101 can be applied by a qualifying entity (see Chapter 2 at 2.1) in its individual financial statements subject to restrictions on early application that are set out in the standard.

FRS 102 specifies that an entity may apply FRS 102 for accounting periods ending on or after 31 December 2012 but for entities within the scope of a SORP, this is providing it does not conflict with the requirements of a current SORP or legal requirements for the preparation of financial statements. *[FRS 102.1.14]*. The FRC has clarified the meaning of 'providing it does not conflict with the requirements of a current SORP' (see Chapter 2 at 1.3.1 of EY New UK GAAP 2015).

FRS 103 applies to financial statements prepared in accordance with FRS 102 and so may similarly be applied for accounting periods ending on or after 31 December 2012 provided that FRS 102 is applied from the same date (and that the entity is not subject to the transitional arrangements in paragraph 1.14 of FRS 102 relating to entities within scope of a SORP). *[FRS 103.1.1, 1.11]*.

FRS 105 is mandatory for accounting periods beginning on or after 1 January 2016.

4.2.1   *Amendments to FRS 100 issued in July 2015*

In July 2015, the FRC issued amendments to FRS 100 and these amendments have been included in the revised edition of FRS 100 issued in September 2015. The revised standard is mandatory for accounting periods beginning on or after 1 January 2016. Early application of the revised standard is permitted, providing an entity also applies the edition of FRS 101, FRS 102 and FRS 105 effective for accounting periods beginning on or after 1 January 2016 and is subject to the early application provisions set out in those standards. *[FRS 100.10]*.

An entity that chooses not to early adopt these amendments to FRS 100 to accounting periods beginning before 1 January 2016 shall not adopt the associated amendments to FRS 101, FRS 102 or FRS 105 to accounting periods beginning before 1 January 2016. *[FRS 100.10]*.

If an entity adopts the revised version of FRS 100 before 1 January 2016 it must disclose that fact, unless it is a micro-entity or a small entity (since the FRC does not have the power to require small entities to make disclosures in excess of those required by company law – see Chapter 3 at 11). However, a small entity is encouraged to make this disclosure.

4.3   Withdrawal of previous UK and Irish GAAP

FRS 100 withdraws all previously extant UK and Irish SSAPs, FRSs, and UITF extracts (i.e. previous UK and Irish GAAP) with effect from its application date. *[FRS 100.14]*. However, some parts of previous UK and Irish GAAP are retained by direct incorporation of their requirements into FRS 100 or FRS 102.

The following statements are also withdrawn when FRS 100 is applied: *[FRS 100.15]*

- *Statement of Principles for Financial Reporting*;

- *Statement of Principles for Financial Reporting – Interpretation for Public Benefit Entities*; and

- *Reporting Statement: Retirement Benefits – Disclosures*.

Also, separately:

- in June 2014, the FRC issued *Guidance on the Strategic Report* which superseded *Reporting Statement: Operating and Financial Review*; and

- in March 2015, the FRC issued FRS 104 which replaced *Reporting Statement – Half-Yearly Reports* and *Reporting Statement – Preliminary announcements*. FRS 104 is discussed in Chapter 6.

Additionally, *The Financial Reporting Standard for Smaller Entities* (effective January 2015) (FRSSE) is superseded on the early application of the July 2015 amendments to FRS 100 (and the related amendments to other accounting standards, particularly FRS 102 and FRS 105) and the early application of *The Companies, Partnerships and Groups (Accounts and Reports) Regulations 2015* (SI 2015/980), and is withdrawn for accounting periods beginning on or after 1 January 2016. *[FRS 100.15A]*. See 4.4.6 below.

4.4   Basis of preparation of financial statements

FRS 100 does not address which entities must prepare financial statements, but sets out the applicable financial reporting framework for entities presenting financial statements in accordance with legislation, regulations or accounting standards applicable in the UK and Republic of Ireland. *[FRS 100.1]*.

The individual or consolidated financial statements of any entity within the scope of FRS 100 (that is not required by the IAS Regulation or other legislation or regulation to be prepared in accordance with EU-adopted IFRS) must be prepared in accordance with either:

- EU-adopted IFRS (see 4.4.3 below);

- FRS 102 (see 4.4.4 below) and, where applicable, FRS 103 (see Chapter 2 at 1.2.4 of EY New UK GAAP 2015);

- FRS 101 (if the financial statements are individual financial statements of a qualifying entity) (see 4.4.5 below) *[FRS 100.4]*; or

- FRS 105 (if the entity is a micro entity eligible to apply that standard and chooses to do so – see 4.4.7 and 6.4 below).

The above choices are also available for the individual financial statements of an entity that is required to prepare consolidated financial statements in accordance with EU-adopted IFRS. *[FRS 100.4, FRS 102.1.3]*.

An entity's choice of financial reporting framework must be permitted by the legal framework or other regulations or requirements that govern the preparation of the entity's financial statements. Other agreements or arrangements (such as shareholders' agreements, banking agreements) may also restrict the choice of financial reporting framework.

4.4.1 *Company law and regulatory requirements governing financial reporting framework*

As required by Article 4 of the IAS Regulation, a UK parent company with transferable securities admitted to trading on a regulated market at its financial year end must prepare its consolidated financial statements as IAS group accounts. *[s403(1)]*. The individual financial statements of such a parent company may be either Companies Act individual accounts or IAS individual accounts. *[s395(1)]*.

AIM is not a regulated market. An 'AIM company' (i.e. a company with a class of security admitted to AIM) incorporated in an EEA country (including, for this purpose, a company incorporated in the Channel Islands or the Isle of Man) must prepare and present its annual accounts in accordance with EU-adopted IFRS. However, an AIM company incorporated in an EEA country that is *not* a parent company at the end of the relevant financial period may prepare and present its annual accounts *either* in accordance with EU-adopted IFRS *or* in accordance with the accounting and company legislation and regulations that are applicable to that company due to its country of incorporation (which, under the new UK and Irish financial reporting framework, could include EU-adopted IFRS, FRS 101 – if a qualifying entity – and FRS 102). While the AIM Rules do not specifically differentiate between consolidated and individual financial statements, many AIM companies incorporated in the UK use EU-adopted IFRS in their consolidated financial statements but national GAAP in their individual financial statements. However, a parent company that only prepares individual financial statements, e.g. it is exempt from preparing consolidated financial statements, must prepare these in accordance with EU-adopted IFRS.[2]

For a UK company, the choice of framework, discussed at 4.4 above, is subject to the requirements in the CA 2006 on change in financial reporting framework (from IAS accounts to Companies Act accounts) (see 6.1.2 below) and consistency of financial reporting framework in individual accounts of group undertakings (see 6.1.3 below).

For the purposes of the CA 2006, only statutory accounts prepared in accordance with full EU-adopted IFRS are IAS accounts, whereas statutory accounts prepared in accordance with FRS 102, FRS 101, or FRS 105 are Companies Act accounts. *[s395(1), s403(2)]*.

UK charitable companies are not permitted to prepare IAS accounts under the CA 2006, *[s395(2), s403(3)]*, and charities are not permitted to apply FRS 101 (as excluded from its definition of a qualifying entity) *[FRS 101.Glossary]*. UK charitable companies preparing financial statements under the CA 2006 must, therefore, apply

FRS 102. Other charities in England and Wales and Scotland preparing financial statements under charities legislation must also apply FRS 102 (see Chapter 2 at 1.3.1.A of EY New UK GAAP 2015).

There is further detail on the requirements of the CA 2006 in relation to annual reports and accounts at 6 below.

FRS 100, FRS 101, FRS 102 and FRS 105 may also be used by entities preparing financial statements intended to give a true and fair view but that are not subject to the CA 2006 (or Irish law). Entities preparing such financial statements intended to give a true and fair view within other legal frameworks will need to satisfy themselves that the standard being applied does not conflict with any relevant legal obligations. *[FRS 100.A2.20, FRS 102.A4.41]*. Appendix II to FRS 100 and Appendix IV to FRS 102 include observations on the requirements of specific UK and Northern Ireland legislation. Where an entity is subject to a SORP, the relevant SORP will provide more details on the relevant legislation. *[FRS 100.A2.21, FRS 102.A4.2, A4.42]*.

4.4.2 New EU Accounting Directive

In July 2013, the new Accounting Directive was published in the EU's Official Journal. This consolidates the 4th and 7th Company Law Directives into a single document. It also repeals and incorporates the requirements of Directive 2012/6/EU (the Micros Directive) and amends Directive 2006/43/EC on statutory audits of individual and consolidated accounts.

The Accounting Directive was required to be transposed into EU Member State law by 20 July 2015. In the UK, this was achieved by The Companies, Partnerships and Groups (Accounts and Reports) Regulations 2015 (SI 2015/980) which came into force on 6 April 2015. However, there were two exceptions, one relating to disclosure of information about related undertakings and the second relating to the availability of the small company audit exemption when an entity early adopts the amendments in SI 2015/980. The changes made by SI 2015/980 come into force for financial years beginning on or after 1 January 2016 although there is an option to apply them for a financial year beginning on or after 1 January 2015 if the directors of the company so decide.

The principal changes made by SI 2015/980 are to:

- increase the size limits for the small companies regime and for medium-sized companies, and change the eligibility conditions for many auditing and accounting exemptions. In general, more companies will fall within these regimes because of the increase in size limits and changes in the eligibility criteria. In particular, a company that is not a public limited company (PLC) itself but is a member of a group containing a PLC will now be able to use the small companies regime, unless it is a member of a group which includes a 'traded company' (i.e. a company any of whose transferable securities are admitted to trading on a regulated market (in the EEA));

- simplify significantly the disclosures for small companies. There are new abridged formats available for small companies (subject to annual member consent) but the separate abbreviated accounts regime for small companies (and medium-sized companies) is withdrawn;

- introduce more flexible formats for the balance sheet and profit and loss account, for both small companies and large and medium-sized companies subject to Schedule 1 of the Regulations and the Small Companies Regulations. This change has allowed the FRC to introduce formats in FRS 101 and FRS 102 based on the formats in IAS 1 – *Presentation of Financial Statements*;

- allow a company that would be subject to the small companies regime, but for being a PLC, an exemption from preparing group accounts (so long as it is not a 'traded company');

- change certain statutory disclosures, recognition and measurement requirements (discussed in Chapter 4 and 5);

- require information on subsidiary undertakings to be presented in full in the financial statements rather than just for principal undertakings (with full details provided in the annual return). This change took effect for annual accounts approved on or after 1 July 2015; and

- change the wording of auditor's reports.

SI 2015/980 impacts companies and qualifying partnerships. SI 2015/980 does not apply to LLPs (as these are not covered by the new Accounting Directive) but it is likely that similar changes for LLPs will be implemented in the future.

As a consequence of the new Accounting Directive, the FRSSE was withdrawn, effective for financial years beginning on or after 1 January 2016 (or on earlier application of the new financial reporting framework). In its place:

- micro-entities can apply a new financial reporting standard for micro-entities, FRS 105; and

- small entities are permitted to apply FRS 102, but with a new Section 1A – *Small entities* – covering the presentation and disclosure requirements applicable to small entities (based on the new company law requirements, as amended by SI 2015/980) replacing the presentation and disclosure requirements of FRS 102.

As a result of the above, amendments to FRS 100, FRS 101 and FRS 102 were required and these amendments were issued in July 2015.

Otherwise the scope of FRS 102 remains the same, i.e. FRS 102 is applied by entities other than those applying EU-adopted IFRS, FRS 101 or FRS 105. Entities required by the IAS Regulation or other legislation or regulation to prepare financial statements in accordance with EU-adopted IFRS will continue to do so.

An entity will continue to have the option to apply a more comprehensive accounting standard, e.g. a micro-entity can choose FRS 105, the small companies regime within FRS 102, FRS 102 in full or EU-adopted IFRS. A qualifying entity will continue to have the option to apply FRS 101. See 4.4 above.

4.4.3   EU-adopted IFRS

EU-adopted IFRS means IFRSs as adopted by the EU pursuant to the IAS Regulation. *[s474]*.

4.4.4   FRS 102 – The Financial Reporting Standard applicable in the UK and Republic of Ireland

FRS 102 is a single, largely stand-alone, financial reporting standard based on a significantly modified version of the IFRS for SMEs issued by the IASB in 2009. FRS 102 was originally issued in March 2013 but has had several subsequent amendments. The August 2014 edition of FRS 102 is discussed in EY New UK GAAP 2015. Amendments made subsequently to the August 2014 edition up to and including the September 2015 edition (see 4.2.1 above) are discussed in Chapters 3, 4 and 5 respectively of this publication.

FRS 102 is arranged into sections: Section 1 addresses scope, Sections 2 to 33 each address a separate accounting topic, Section 34 addresses specialised activities, and Section 35 addresses transition. There is a reduced disclosure framework available for qualifying entities (see 4.5 below) in their individual financial statements and also a separate disclosure framework for small entities introduced in July 2015 (see Chapter 3).

The IFRS for SMEs is in the main a simplified version of IFRSs (with fewer accounting options and disclosures) although in a number of areas, e.g. requiring amortisation of goodwill or the treatment of deferred tax, its requirements depart from IFRSs. Use of the IFRS for SMEs met many of the FRC's objectives (see 4 above). However in the writing of FRS 102, the FRC made further amendments to the IFRS for SMEs for application in the UK and Republic of Ireland in order to meet its objectives (discussed further in Chapter 2 at 1.2 of EY New UK GAAP 2015).

4.4.5   FRS 101 – Reduced Disclosure Framework

FRS 101 was originally issued in November 2012 and revised editions were subsequently issued in August 2014 and September 2015. FRS 101 is discussed in Chapter 2, with the amendments made by the revised editions discussed at 1.2 of that chapter. The standard sets out a framework which addresses the financial reporting requirements and disclosure exemptions for the individual financial statements of qualifying entities (see 4.5 below) that otherwise apply the recognition, measurement and disclosure requirements of standards and interpretations issued by the International Accounting Standards Board (IASB) that have been adopted in the European Union (EU-adopted IFRS).

An entity reporting under FRS 101 complies with EU-adopted IFRS except as modified by the standard. FRS 101 contains various recognition and measurement modifications to EU-adopted IFRS, primarily to ensure compliance with UK company law.

The Accounting Council advised the FRC to ensure that the disclosure framework remains consistent with EU-adopted IFRS. *[FRS 101.AC.20]*. It is therefore expected that the standard will be reviewed regularly as EU-adopted IFRS changes.

4.4.6   *Small entities*

Under previous UK GAAP, small entities (as defined in the FRSSE) were eligible to apply the Financial Reporting Standard for Small Entities (FRSSE) as an alternative to full UK GAAP.

The FRSSE is superseded on the early application of the amendments set out in *Amendments to FRS 100* (and the related amendments to other accounting standards, particularly FRS 102 and FRS 105) issued in July 2015 and the early application of SI 2015/980, and is withdrawn for accounting periods beginning on or after 1 January 2016. In its place, the FRC has published a new standard, FRS 105 and introduced a new small entities regime, Section 1A into FRS 102. Section 1A requires small entities to apply the recognition and measurement requirements of FRS 102 in full. However, the presentation and disclosure requirements required by Section 1A are based on those required by the CA 2006 and Small Companies Regulations for companies subject to the small companies regime.

The small entities regime of FRS 102 is discussed in Chapter 3.

4.4.7   *FRS 105 – The Financial Reporting Standard applicable to the Micro-entities Regime*

An entity that chooses to prepare its financial statements in accordance with the micro-entities regime (see 6.4 below) as set out in *The Small Companies (Micro-entities' Accounts) Regulations 2013 (SI 2013/3008)* is required to apply FRS 105 for periods beginning on or after 1 January 2016. Early application is permitted.

FRS 105 is outside the scope of this publication.

4.4.8   *Considerations on choice of financial reporting framework*

Entities will need to carefully consider their choice of financial reporting framework, based on their individual circumstances. In doing so, entities may need to consider the implications of a new financial reporting framework for other aspects of their business, such as covenants in loan agreements, employee remuneration (e.g. performance-related bonuses), the effect on key performance indicators, accounting systems, taxation and distributable profits.

Factors influencing the choice of financial reporting framework might include:

- whether the entity is a member of a group, and if so, what GAAP is used for group reporting. In particular, subsidiaries of groups reporting under IFRS or in multinational groups may prefer to apply IFRS or FRS 101 rather than FRS 102;

- the level of disclosures required in the financial statements.

    FRS 101 and FRS 102 financial statements prepared by a UK company are Companies Act accounts and therefore must comply with the requirements of the CA 2006 and all applicable schedules of the Regulations (as well as accounting standards). Financial statements prepared under EU-adopted IFRS do not need to comply with Schedules 1, 2 or 3 to the Regulations but must comply with the extensive disclosure requirements in IFRSs (see 6.7 below).

The level of disclosure also depends on whether the entity is a qualifying entity and can make use of a reduced disclosure framework (under FRS 101 or FRS 102) in its individual financial statements (see 4.5 below). While FRS 102 has fewer disclosures than IFRS, the level of disclosure required may sometimes not be significantly different from FRS 101, but this will depend on the entity's individual circumstances.

- stability of the financial reporting framework (in general, there are more frequent changes to IFRSs than to FRS 102);

- the implications of new IFRSs (such as IFRS 9 – *Financial Instruments* – or IFRS 15 – *Revenue from Contracts with Customers*) or expected changes to IFRSs (e.g. arising from the IASB's leases project) that will be implemented or expected to be finalised in future periods;

- IFRSs provide detailed and sometimes complex guidance, whereas the requirements in FRS 102 are much shorter (but lack the same level of application guidance as in IFRSs, and are likely to involve increased application of management judgement in applying the standard); and

- the implications of different GAAPs for distributable profits (see 5.5 below) and taxation, in particular cash tax. This will also depend on the interaction with tax legislation, and whether tax elections are made.

4.5   Reduced disclosure framework

Both FRS 101 and FRS 102 provide for a reduced disclosure framework for qualifying entities in individual financial statements. The shareholders of the qualifying entity must be notified in writing and not object to use of the disclosure exemptions. While a charity cannot be a qualifying entity for FRS 101, there is no such restriction for use of the reduced disclosure framework in FRS 102. *[FRS 101.5, FRS 102.1.11]*.

A 'qualifying entity' is a member of a group (i.e. a parent or subsidiary) where the parent of that group prepares publicly available consolidated financial statements which are intended to give a true and fair view (of the assets, liabilities, financial position and profit or loss) and that member is included in the consolidation. *[FRS 100.Appendix 1, FRS 101.Appendix 1, FRS 102 Appendix I]*. The term 'included in the consolidation' has the meaning set out in section 474(1) of the CA 2006, i.e. that the qualifying entity is consolidated in the financial statements by full (and not proportional) consolidation.

The disclosure exemptions available in FRS 102 are more limited than in FRS 101, which provides a reduced disclosure framework for qualifying entities under EU-adopted IFRS. However, this reflects the fact that FRS 102 (as a starting point) has much simpler disclosures than EU-adopted IFRS. Under the reduced disclosure framework in both standards, there are fewer disclosure exemptions available for the individual financial statements of financial institutions.

Certain disclosures require 'equivalent' disclosures to be included in the publicly available consolidated financial statements of the parent in which the qualifying entity is consolidated (i.e. of the parent referred to in the definition of qualifying entity). FRS 100 provides guidance on the concept of 'equivalence' for these purposes. *[FRS 100.AG8-10].*

Chapter 2 has further discussion of the reduced disclosure framework under FRS 101 and Chapter 2 of EY New UK GAAP 2015 at 3 and Chapter 5 at 2.3 discuss further the reduced disclosure framework under FRS 102, including the detailed requirements for its use, the definitions of 'qualifying entity' and 'financial institution', the disclosure exemptions available, and guidance on 'equivalence' for the purpose of the reduced disclosure framework.

4.6   Statement of compliance

FRS 100 requires that an entity preparing its financial statements in accordance with FRS 101 or FRS 102 (and where applicable, FRS 103) includes a statement of compliance in the notes to the financial statements in accordance with the requirements of the relevant standard. This requirement is not mandatory for a small entity applying the small entities regime in FRS 102 (Section 1A), although including a statement of compliance in the notes to the accounts is encouraged. *[FRS 100.9, FRS 103.1.12, FRS 102.1AD.1(a), FRS 102.3.3, FRS 101.10, FRS 102.3.3].* See Chapter 2 at 1.3 (for FRS 101 financial statements) and Chapter 4 at 3.8 (for FRS 102 financial statements).

This requirement is similar to that in IAS 1 for an entity preparing its financial statements using EU-adopted IFRS to give an explicit and unreserved statement of compliance with IFRSs.

In the same way as required for IFRS financial statements, financial statements should not be described as complying with FRS 101, FRS 102 or the FRSSE, unless they comply with *all* of the requirements of the relevant standard. Indeed, FRS 102 includes an explicit requirement to this effect. *[FRS 102.3.3].*

4.6.1   *Related Companies Act 2006 requirements*

Where the directors of a large or medium-sized company (i.e. a company not subject to the micro-entity provisions or the small companies regime – see 6.4 and 6.5 below) prepare Companies Act individual or group accounts (such as those prepared under FRS 101 and FRS 102), the notes to the accounts must include a statement as to whether the accounts have been prepared in accordance with applicable accounting standards. Particulars of any material departure from those standards and the reasons for the departure must be given. This statement is not required in the individual accounts of medium-sized companies (see 6.6 below). *[Regulations 4(2), 1 Sch 45].*

'Applicable accounting standards' means statements of standard accounting practice issued by the FRC (and SSAPs, FRSs issued by the Accounting Standard Board and UITF Abstracts, until withdrawn).[3] Therefore, FRS 100 to FRS 103 (and FRS 105 for companies applying the micro-entity provisions only) are 'applicable accounting standards'.[4]

Where the directors of a company prepare IAS individual or IAS group accounts (see 6.1 below), the notes to the accounts must include a statement that the accounts have been prepared in accordance with international accounting standards (i.e. EU-adopted IFRS). *[s397, s406, s474].*

4.7   SORPs

References to a SORP are to an extant Statement of Recommended Practice developed in accordance with the FRC's *Policy and Code of Practice on SORPs*. SORPs recommend accounting practices for specialised industries or sectors. They supplement accounting standards and other legal and regulatory requirements in the light of the special factors prevailing or transactions undertaken in a particular industry or sector. *[FRS 102 Appendix I]*.

SORPs may only be developed and issued by 'SORP-making bodies', being bodies recognised by the FRC for the purpose of producing the SORP for a particular industry or sector. SORP-making bodies have a responsibility to act in the public interest when developing a SORP. The FRC's Codes & Standards Committee will recognise a body as a SORP-making body on the advice of the Accounting Council.

SORPs recommend particular accounting treatments and disclosures with the aim of narrowing areas of difference and variety between comparable entities. Compliance with a SORP that has been generally accepted by an industry or sector leads to enhanced comparability between the financial statements of entities in that industry or sector. Comparability is further enhanced if users are made aware of the extent to which an entity complies with a SORP, and the reasons for any departures. *[FRS 100.7]*.

FRS 100 states that if an entity's financial statements are prepared in accordance with FRS 102, SORPs apply in the circumstances set out in that standard. *[FRS 100.5]*.

The application of SORPs under FRS 102 is discussed at Chapter 2 at 2.2 of EY New UK GAAP 2015. There are certain constraints on early application of FRS 102 (see Chapter 2 at 1.3.1 of EY New UK GAAP 2015) where an entity is subject to a SORP and that standard also makes reference to extant SORPs as part of the hierarchy for management to consider when developing and applying accounting policies (see Chapter 7 at 3.2 of EY New UK GAAP 2015).

When a SORP applies, an entity, other than a small entity applying the small entities regime in FRS 102, must state in the financial statements the title of the SORP and whether the financial statements have been prepared in accordance with the SORP's provisions currently in effect. The provisions of a SORP cease to have effect, for example, to the extent they conflict with a more recent financial reporting standard. *[FRS 100.6]*.

Paragraph 6 of the FRC's Policy and Code of Practice explains that SORPs should be developed in line with current accounting standards and best practice. A SORP's provisions cannot override provisions of the law, regulatory requirements or accounting standards. Therefore, where at the time of issue, the SORP's provisions conflict with accounting standards or legal or regulatory requirements, these take precedence over the SORP and the FRC's Statement on the SORP will usually be varied to refer to this. When a more recently issued accounting standard or change in legislation leads to conflict with the provisions of an existing SORP, the relevant provisions of the SORP cease to have effect. The SORP-making body is responsible for updating the relevant provisions of the SORP on a timely basis to bring them in line with new legislation or accounting standards, or to withdraw them, as appropriate.

Chapter 1

Where an entity departs from the SORP's provisions, it must give a brief description of how the financial statements depart from the recommended practice set out in the SORP, which must include:

- for any treatment that is not in accordance with the SORP, the reasons why the treatment adopted is judged more appropriate to the entity's particular circumstances; and

- brief details of any disclosures recommended by the SORP that have not been provided, together with the reasons why not. *[FRS 100.6].*

A small entity applying the small entities regime in FRS 102 is encouraged to provide these disclosures. *[FRS 100.6].*

The effect of a departure from a SORP need not be quantified, except in those rare cases where such quantification is necessary for the entity's financial statements to give a true and fair view. *[FRS 100.7].*

Entities whose financial statements do not fall within the scope of a SORP may, if the SORP is otherwise relevant to them, nevertheless choose to comply with the SORP's recommendations when preparing financial statements, providing that the SORP does not conflict with the requirements of the framework adopted. Where this is the case, entities are encouraged to disclose this fact. *[FRS 100.8].*

FRS 100, therefore, does not require an entity preparing its financial statements in accordance with FRS 101, or EU-adopted IFRS, to disclose whether it has applied the relevant SORP. However, FRS 100 does not preclude such an entity from following a SORP (provided its requirements do not conflict with EU-adopted IFRS) but encourages the entity to disclose that it has done so.

4.7.1   *Status of SORPs*

Certain of the current SORPs are withdrawn on implementation of the new UK and Irish GAAP framework. Other SORPs have been updated to conform with FRS 102 (although two Charities SORPs have been issued, one for use with the FRSSE and one for use with FRS 102).

The following SORPs have been updated to conform with FRS 102 for which the FRC has given its statement:

- *Further and Higher Education* (March 2014);

- *UK Authorised Funds* (May 2014);

- *Charities* (July 2014);

- *Limited Liability Partnerships* (July 2014);

- *Registered Social Housing Providers* (September 2014);

- *Investment Trust Companies and Venture Capital Trusts* (November 2014); and

- *Pension Schemes* (November 2014).

The withdrawal of the FRSSE and the amendments to FRS 102 in July 2015 mean that the Charities SORP (FRSSE) will not apply for financial years beginning on or after 1 January 2016, and that changes will be required to be made to the Charities

SORP (FRS 102) effective for periods beginning on or after 1 January 2016. The Charity Commission for England and Wales and the Office for the Scottish Charity Regulator have published an Exposure Draft dealing with these changes and the consultation period closed on 18 September 2015. At the time of writing no results of the consultation had been announced.

The *Banking Segments SORP* is to be withdrawn and the *Leasing* SORP has been withdrawn. The SORP on *Accounting for Insurance Business* (December 2005 and amended December 2006) is withdrawn on implementation of FRS 103. *[FRS 103.1.13]*.

The SORP on *Accounting for Oil and Gas Exploration, Development, Production and Decommissioning Activities* (updated June 2001) was not updated. The OIAC website explains that the SORP remains applicable for non-listed UK entities until such time as those entities adopt FRS 100 to FRS 102 and therefore is not applicable to any entity for accounting periods beginning on or after 1 January 2015.[5]

5 TRANSITION

FRS 100 sets out the requirements for transition to FRS 101, FRS 102 and FRS 105. The requirements differ depending on the standard transitioned to and whether the entity previously reported under EU-adopted IFRS or other GAAP (such as previous UK GAAP).

The date of transition is the beginning of the earliest period for which an entity presents full comparative information under a given standard in its first financial statements which comply with that standard. *[FRS 100.Glossary]*. Therefore, 1 January 2014 is the date of transition for an entity with a 31 December year-end which prepares its first IFRS (or FRS 101 or FRS 102) financial statements for the financial year ended 31 December 2015.

Before deciding to transition to a particular standard in the new UK and Irish GAAP framework, entities should assess whether this is permitted by the statutory framework or other regulation that applies to them. See 6.1 and 6.2.1.D below for considerations applicable to the CA 2006.

On first-time application of FRS 100 or when an entity changes its basis of preparation of its financial statements within the requirements of FRS 100, it shall apply the transitional arrangements relevant to its circumstances as explained at 5.1 to 5.3 below.

There is no requirement to change the GAAP applied by a UK parent and its UK subsidiaries at the same time. However, the CA 2006 sets out restrictions over changes in financial reporting framework (in both individual and group accounts) and over consistency of financial reporting framework in individual accounts of group undertakings (see 6.1.2 and 6.1.3 below).

5.1 Transition to EU-adopted IFRS

An entity transitioning to EU-adopted IFRS must apply the transitional requirements of IFRS 1 – *First-time Adoption of International Financial Reporting Standards*, as adopted by the EU. *[FRS 100.11(a)]*.

An entity's first IFRS financial statements (to which IFRS 1 must be applied) are the first annual financial statements in which the entity adopts EU-adopted IFRS, by an explicit and unreserved statement in those financial statements of compliance with EU-adopted IFRS. *[IFRS 1.2-3]*.

An entity that has applied EU-adopted IFRS in a previous reporting period, but whose most recent previous annual financial statements did not contain an explicit and unreserved statement of compliance with EU-adopted IFRS must either apply IFRS 1 or else apply EU-adopted IFRS retrospectively in accordance with IAS 8 – *Accounting Policies, Changes in Accounting Estimates and Errors* – as if the entity had never stopped applying IFRSs. *[IFRS 1.4A]*.

The requirements of IFRS 1 are discussed in Chapter 5 of EY International GAAP 2016.

5.2   Transition to FRS 101

A qualifying entity can transition to FRS 101 from either EU-adopted IFRS or another form of UK GAAP. In this context, another form of UK GAAP means FRS 102, the FRSSE or previous UK GAAP. The transition requirements differ depending on whether the qualifying entity is applying EU-adopted IFRS or not prior to the date of transition. *[FRS 100.11(b), 12-13]*. The transition requirements to FRS 101 are explained in Chapter 2 at 3.

5.3   Transition to FRS 102

A first-time adopter of FRS 102 is an entity that presents its first annual financial statements that conform to FRS 102, regardless of whether its previous accounting framework was EU-adopted IFRS or another set of GAAP such as its national accounting standards, or another framework such as the local income tax basis. *[FRS 102.35.1, FRS 102 Appendix I]*. In practice, most first time adopters of FRS 102 will have applied previous UK GAAP. An entity transitioning to FRS 102 must apply the transitional arrangements set out in Section 35 – *Transition to this FRS* – of the standard. *[FRS 100.11(c), FRS 102.35.1]*. Chapter 30 of EY New UK GAAP 2015 addresses the transition arrangements to FRS 102. The new transitional exemptions for small entities and the clarification of the share based payments exemption included in the July 2015 amendments to FRS 102 are discussed in Chapter 3 at 6.3.

FRS 102 also addresses the situation where an entity has previously applied FRS 102, and then applies a different GAAP for a period before re-applying FRS 102. An entity that adopted FRS 102 in a previous reporting period but whose most recent annual financial statements did not contain an explicit and unreserved statement of compliance with FRS 102 must either apply Section 35 or else apply FRS 102 retrospectively in accordance with Section 10 – *Accounting Policies, Estimates and Errors*, as if the entity had never stopped applying the standard. *[FRS 102.35.2]*.

An entity applying FRS 102 is required to apply FRS 103 to insurance contracts (including reinsurance contracts) that the entity issues and reinsurance contracts that the entity holds, and to financial instruments (other than insurance contracts) that the entity issues with a discretionary participation feature (see Chapter 2 at 1.2.4 of EY New UK GAAP 2015). *[FRS 103.1.2]*. An entity may, therefore, apply FRS 103 at the same time as it adopts FRS 102 or after it has adopted FRS 102, depending on whether it has transactions within scope of FRS 103 on adoption of FRS 102. It is not, however possible to apply FRS 103 without also applying FRS 102. *[FRS 103.1.11-12]*. The detailed requirements of FRS 103 are outside the scope of this publication.

5.4   Transition to FRS 105

A first time adopter of FRS 105 is an entity that presents its first annual financial statements that conform to FRS 105, regardless of its previous accounting framework. *[FRS 105 Appendix I]*. In practice, most first time adopters of FRS 105 will have applied the FRSSE. An entity transitioning to FRS 105 must apply the transitional arrangements set out in Section 28 – *Transition to this FRS* – of FRS 105. *[FRS 100.11(d), FRS 105.28.3]*.

As noted in 4.4.7 above, the application of FRS 105 is outside the scope of this publication.

5.5   Impact of transition on distributable profits

There may be circumstances where a conversion to FRS 101, FRS 102, FRS 105 or EU-adopted IFRS eliminates an entity's realised profits or even turns those realised profits into a realised loss. TECH 02/10 – *Guidance on Realised and Distributable Profits under the Companies Act 2006*, issued by the ICAEW and ICAS, states that the change in the treatment of a retained profit or loss as realised (or unrealised) as a result of a change in the law or in accounting standards or interpretations would not render unlawful a distribution already made out of realised profits determined by reference to 'relevant accounts' which had been prepared in accordance with generally acceptable accounting principles applicable to those accounts (subject to the considerations below). This is because the CA 2006 defines realised profits and realised losses for determining the lawfulness of a distribution as 'such profits or losses of the company as fall to be treated as realised in accordance with principles generally accepted at the time when the accounts are prepared, with respect to the determination for accounting purposes of realised profits or losses'.[6]

The effects of the introduction of a new accounting standard or of the adoption of IFRSs (or FRS 101, FRS 102 or FRS 105) become relevant to the application of the common law capital maintenance rule only in relation to distributions accounted for in periods in which the change will first be recognised in the accounts. This means that a change in accounting policy known to be adopted in a financial year needs to be taken into account in determining the dividend to be approved by shareholders in that year. Therefore, for example, an entity converting to a new financial reporting framework (FRS 101, FRS 102, FRS 105 (if adopted early), or EU-adopted IFRS) in 2015 must have regard to the effect of adoption of the new financial reporting framework in respect of all dividends payable in 2015, including any final dividends in respect of 2014, even though the 'relevant accounts' may still be those for 2014 prepared under another GAAP. These considerations apply to all dividends whether in respect of shares classified as equity or as debt (or partly equity or debt).[7]

Statutory 'interim accounts' are required to be prepared under sections 836(2) and 838 of the CA 2006 (and delivered to the Registrar if the company is a public company) if a proposed distribution cannot be justified by reference to the relevant accounts. However, under common law, a company cannot lawfully make a distribution out of capital and the directors may therefore consider preparing non-statutory 'interim accounts' using the new financial framework to ascertain that there are sufficient distributable profits and, if the company is a public company, that the net asset restriction in section 831 of the CA 2006 is not breached.[8] In some cases, however, the directors may be satisfied that no material adjustments arise from transition to the new financial framework (and therefore that there are sufficient distributable profits) without preparing such 'interim accounts'. Statutory 'interim accounts' would be required if transition to a new financial reporting framework increases distributable profits and the directors wish to make a distribution not justified by reference to the relevant accounts.[9] TECH 02/10 states that if the directors have not yet decided whether to adopt EU-adopted IFRS, say, for the current financial year, the company's accounting policies are those that it has previously applied until a decision is made to change them. Therefore, in applying the above, it is not necessary to have regard to possible changes of policy that are being considered but have not yet been agreed.[10] TECH 02/10, however, was written at a time where UK companies had a choice, subject to certain constraints in the CA 2006 (see 6.1 below), of whether to change to EU-adopted IFRS or remain under previous UK GAAP; for financial years beginning on or after 1 January 2015, previous UK GAAP is withdrawn. It is possible for example that adoption of any of the financial reporting frameworks might have an adverse effect on the profits available for distribution.

6   COMPANIES ACT 2006

6.1   Basis of preparation of financial statements

The directors of every company (except certain dormant subsidiary undertakings that qualify for exemption from preparation of accounts – the criteria are set out in sections 394A to C, amended by SI 2015/980) must prepare individual accounts for the company for each financial year (see 6.2 below). *[s394]*. The directors of a parent company must prepare group accounts, unless there is an exemption available from preparation of group accounts (see 6.3 below).

Directors must not approve accounts unless they are satisfied that they give a true and fair view of the assets, liabilities, financial position and profit or loss of the company and in the case of group accounts, of the undertakings included in the consolidation as a whole, so far as concerns members of the company. *[s393]*. See 7.2 below for a discussion of accounting standards and 'true and fair'.

This section does not deal with LLPs. SI 2015/980 amends the requirements for companies and qualifying partnerships, but not for Limited Liability Partnerships (LLPs), although a change to LLP law is expected to be consulted on in due course. The Republic of Ireland is yet to issue its equivalent version of SI 2015/980 and Irish law is expected to be updated later in 2015 to implement the new Accounting Directive. Consequently, LLPs and other entities that are not UK companies need to consider carefully the statutory requirements that apply. For example, LLPs have different size and eligibility conditions to qualify for the small LLPs regime compared to companies subject to the small companies regime.

6.1.1   Choice of IAS accounts and Companies Act accounts under the Companies Act 2006

The Companies Act 2006 (CA 2006) distinguishes between IAS accounts and Companies Act accounts. Financial statements prepared in accordance with the CA 2006 using EU-adopted IFRS are IAS accounts. Financial statements prepared in accordance with the CA 2006 using FRS 101, FRS 102 or FRS 105 are Companies Act accounts.

See 6.2 below for the requirements for IAS accounts and Companies Act accounts.

A company's individual accounts may be prepared:

- in accordance with section 396 (Companies Act individual accounts); or

- in accordance with EU-adopted IFRS (IAS individual accounts). *[s395(1)]*.

This is subject to the restrictions on changes of financial reporting framework and the requirements for consistency of financial reporting framework within the individual accounts of group undertakings (see 6.1.2 and 6.1.3 below).

The group accounts of certain parent companies are required by Article 4 of the IAS Regulation to be prepared in accordance with EU-adopted IFRS. *[s403(1)]*. Article 4 of the IAS Regulation requires an EEA-incorporated company with securities admitted to trading on a regulated market (as at its financial year end) to prepare its consolidated financial statements in accordance with EU-adopted IFRS.

The group accounts of other companies may be prepared:

- in accordance with section 404 (Companies Act group accounts); or

- in accordance with EU-adopted IFRS (IAS group accounts). *[s403(2)]*.

This is subject to the restrictions on changes of financial reporting framework (see 6.1.2 below).

The individual and any group accounts of a company that is a charity must be Companies Act accounts. *[s395(2), s403(3)]*.

6.1.2   Companies Act 2006 restrictions on changes of financial reporting framework

Under the CA 2006, a company which wishes to change from preparing IAS individual accounts to preparing Companies Act individual accounts (such as financial statements prepared under previous UK GAAP, FRS 101, FRS 102 or FRS 105) may do so only:

- if there is a relevant change of circumstance (see below); or

- for financial years ending on or after 1 October 2012, for a reason other than a relevant change of circumstance, provided the company has not changed to Companies Act individual accounts in the period of five years preceding the first day of that financial year. In calculating the five year period, no account is taken of a change made due to a relevant change of circumstance. *[s395(3)-(5)]*.

The same requirements apply where a company wishes to change from preparing IAS group accounts to preparing Companies Act group accounts, except that the references to individual accounts above are to group accounts. *[s403(4)-(6)]*.

These requirements enable a group where the parent and subsidiary undertakings prepare IAS individual accounts to instead prepare FRS 101 financial statements or even FRS 102 financial statements (as these are both Companies Act individual accounts) where the above criteria are met.

A relevant change of circumstance in respect of individual accounts occurs if, at any time during or after the first financial year in which the directors of a company prepare IAS individual accounts:

- the company becomes a subsidiary undertaking of another undertaking that does not prepare IAS individual accounts;
- the company ceases to be a subsidiary undertaking;
- the company ceases to be a company with securities admitted to trading on a regulated market in an EEA State; or
- a parent undertaking of the company ceases to be an undertaking with securities admitted to trading on a regulated market in an EEA State. *[s395(4)]*.

A relevant change of circumstance for the purposes of group accounts occurs if, at any time during or after the first financial year in which the directors of a parent company prepare IAS group accounts:

- the company becomes a subsidiary undertaking of another undertaking that does not prepare IAS group accounts;
- the company ceases to be a company with securities admitted to trading on a regulated market in an EEA State; or
- a parent undertaking of the company ceases to be an undertaking with securities admitted to trading on a regulated market in an EEA State. *[s403(5)]*.

Section 395's requirements in respect of individual accounts and section 403's requirements in respect of group accounts operate independently of each other. Therefore, an IFRS reporter would be permitted to move from IAS accounts to Companies Act accounts in its individual accounts, while continuing to prepare IAS group accounts.

Paragraph 9.18 of the June 2008 BERR document *Guidance for UK Companies on Accounting and Reporting: Requirements under the Companies Act 2006 and the application of the IAS regulation* notes that the first example of a relevant change in circumstance in the lists above is 'intended to deal with situations where a subsidiary undertaking is sold by a group generally using IAS, to another group or entity not generally using IAS. It is not intended that companies switch between accounting regimes on the basis of an internal group restructuring.'

The restriction is 'one-way' only from IAS accounts to Companies Act accounts. There is no restriction on the number of times a company can move from Companies Act accounts to IAS accounts or *vice versa* so theoretically a company could 'flip' from IAS accounts to Companies Act accounts and back again several times without a relevant change of circumstance provided it reverted back to Companies Act accounts no more than once every five years.

The CA 2006 does not restrict changes made between previous UK GAAP, FRS 105, FRS 102 or FRS 101 since these are all Companies Act accounts.

6.1.3   Consistency of financial reporting framework in individual accounts of group undertakings

The CA 2006 requires that the directors of a UK parent company must secure that the individual accounts of the parent company and of each of its subsidiary undertakings are prepared under the same financial reporting framework, be it IAS accounts or Companies Act accounts, except to the extent that in the directors' opinion there are 'good reasons' for not doing so. *[s407(1)]*. However, this requirement does not apply:

- where the UK parent company does not prepare group accounts under the CA 2006; *[s407(2)]*

- to accounts of subsidiary undertakings not required to be prepared under Part 15 of the CA 2006 (e.g. accounts of a foreign subsidiary undertaking); *[s407(3)]* or

- to accounts of any subsidiary undertakings that are charities, *[s407(4)]*, (so charities and non-charities within a group are not required to use the same financial reporting framework in their accounts). Charities are not permitted to prepare either IAS group or IAS individual accounts. *[s395(2), s403(3)]*.

Additionally, a parent company that prepares both consolidated and separate financial statements under EU-adopted IFRS (i.e. IAS group accounts and IAS individual accounts) is not required to ensure that its subsidiary undertakings all prepare IAS individual accounts. However, it must ensure that its subsidiary undertakings use the same financial reporting framework (i.e. all prepare IAS accounts or all prepare Companies Act accounts) in their individual accounts unless there are 'good reasons' for not doing so. *[s407(5)]*.

Although not explicitly stated by FRS 100, there appears to be no requirement that all subsidiary undertakings in a group must use the same GAAP for their Companies Act individual accounts. Some could use, for example, FRS 101, and others could use FRS 102 since all are Companies Act individual accounts and therefore part of the same financial reporting framework. This approach would comply with the statutory requirements of Section 407. However, groups that use a 'mix' of GAAP in the individual financial statements may be challenged by HMRC, particularly if this results in tax arbitrage. Examples of 'good reasons' for not preparing all individual accounts within a group using the same financial reporting framework are contained in the June 2008 BERR document *Guidance for UK Companies On Accounting and Reporting: Requirements under the Companies Act 2006 and the application of the IAS regulation*. Paragraph 9.17 of the Guidance notes that this provision is intended to provide a degree of flexibility where there are genuine (including cost/benefit) grounds for using different accounting frameworks within a group of companies and identifies the following examples:

- 'A group using IAS acquired a subsidiary undertaking that had not been using IAS; in the first year of acquisition, it might not be practical for the newly acquired company to switch to IAS straight away.

- The group contains subsidiary undertakings that are themselves publicly traded, in which case market pressures or regulatory requirements to use IAS might come into play, without necessarily justifying a switch to IAS by the non-publicly traded subsidiaries.

- A subsidiary undertaking or the parent were planning to apply for a listing and so might wish to convert to IAS in advance, but the rest of the group was not planning to apply for a listing.

- The group contains minor or dormant subsidiaries where the costs of switching accounting framework would outweigh the benefits.

The key point is that the directors of the parent company must be able to justify any inconsistency to shareholders, regulators or other interested parties'.

6.2   Companies Act requirements for the annual report and accounts

Part 15 of the CA 2006 sets out the requirements for the annual report and accounts for UK companies.

The company's 'annual accounts' are the company's individual accounts for that year and any group accounts prepared by the company for that year.

Section 408 permits a parent company preparing group accounts (whether as IAS group accounts or Companies Act group accounts) to omit the individual profit and loss account from the annual accounts, where the conditions for this exemption are met (see 6.3.2 below). *[s471(1)]*.

References in Part 15 to the annual accounts (or to a balance sheet or profit and loss account) include notes to the accounts giving information required by any provision of the Companies Act 2006 or EU-adopted IFRS, and that is required or allowed by any such provision to be given in a note to the company's accounts. *[s472]*.

The principal Companies Act requirements for annual accounts are set out at 6.2.1 below and for the annual report at 6.2.2 below. While this chapter focuses on the disclosure requirements for UK companies, LLPs and other types of entities other than companies are also subject to similar statutory requirements. Reference should be made to the legislation that applies to such entities.

The Listing Rules, Disclosure and Transparency Rules or rules of the relevant securities market may require additional information beyond that required by the CA 2006 (and related regulations) to be included in the annual reports. For example, premium listed companies must state how they apply the main principles of, and present a statement of compliance or otherwise with the provisions of the UK Corporate Governance Code.[11] It is beyond the scope of this publication to cover such regulatory requirements.

6.2.1   Companies Act requirements for annual accounts

6.2.1.A   Companies Act accounts

Companies Act individual accounts and Companies Act group accounts are prepared in accordance with sections 396 and 404 of the CA 2006 respectively. Companies Act accounts comprise:

*   a balance sheet as at the last day of the financial year that gives a true and fair view of the state of affairs of the company (and in respect of group accounts, of the parent company and its subsidiary undertakings included in the consolidation as a whole, so far as concerns members of the company) as at the end of the financial year; and

*   a profit and loss account that gives a true and fair view of the profit or loss of the company (and in respect of group accounts, of the parent company and its subsidiary undertakings included in the consolidation as a whole, so far as concerns members of the company) for the financial year. *[s396(1)-(2), s404(1)-(2)]*.

The accounts must comply with regulations as to the form and content of the company balance sheet and profit and loss account (and in respect of group accounts, of the consolidated balance sheet and consolidated profit and loss account) and additional information provided by way of notes to the accounts. *[s396(3), s404(3)]*.

These regulations are principally *The Large and Medium-sized Companies and Groups (Accounts and Reports) Regulations 2008* (Regulations) as amended by SI 2015/980. Companies subject to the small companies regime (see 6.5 below) are entitled to apply *The Small Companies and Groups (Accounts and Directors' Report) Regulations 2008* (Small Companies Regulations) as amended by SI 2015/980. Micro-entities (see 6.4 below) are entitled to apply *The Small Companies (Micro Entities' Accounts) Regulations 2013* (Micro-entity Regulations), as amended by SI 2015/980 (see 4.4.2 above).

If compliance with the regulations and any other provisions made by or under the CA 2006 as to the matters to be included in the accounts or notes to those accounts would not be sufficient to give a true and fair view, the necessary additional information must be given in the accounts or notes to the accounts. *[s396(4), s404(4)]*. If in special circumstances, compliance with any of those provisions is inconsistent with the requirement to give a true and fair view, the directors must depart from that provision to the extent necessary to give a true and fair view. Particulars of any such departure, the reasons for it and its effect must be given in a note to the accounts. *[s396(5), s404(5)]*. See Chapter 4 at 9.2 for further discussion of the 'true and fair override' provided for in the CA 2006 and FRS 102's requirements for a true and fair view.

A company's annual accounts must be approved by the board of directors and signed on behalf of the board by a director of the company, with the signature included on the company's balance sheet. *[s414(1)]*.

Financial statements prepared in accordance with FRS 101, FRS 102 or FRS 105 are Companies Act accounts, and are therefore required to comply with the applicable provisions of Parts 15 and 16 of the CA 2006 and with the Regulations. *[FRS 102.A4.7]*.

6.2.1.B   IAS accounts

Where the directors prepare IAS individual and/or IAS group accounts, they must state in the notes to those accounts that they have been prepared in accordance with EU-adopted IFRS. *[s397(2), s406(2), s474]*.

Where the section 408 exemption to omit the individual profit and loss account is taken where group accounts are prepared, the notes to IAS individual accounts must state that they have been prepared in accordance with EU-adopted IFRS as applied in accordance with the provisions of the CA 2006. See 6.3.2 below.

6.2.1.C   General – Companies Act accounts and IAS accounts

There are two types of CA 2006 disclosures required for a UK company:

(a)   those required by the Regulations (or other applicable regulations, as discussed below) for an entity preparing Companies Act accounts but not for an entity preparing IAS accounts (see 6.7.1 below); and

(b)   those required for both IAS accounts and Companies Act accounts (see 6.7.2 below).

The CA 2006 distinguishes between companies that are micro-entities (see 6.4 below), companies subject to the small companies regime (see 6.5 below), and medium-sized companies (see 6.6 below).

The above categories of company are all based on meeting certain size criteria and not being excluded from the applicable regime. These companies benefit from a lighter disclosure regime in their financial statements than for large companies, i.e. the default category of companies that are not medium-sized companies, subject to the small companies regime or the micro-entities regime. Certain disclosure exemptions are available to companies preparing IAS accounts or Companies Act accounts, whereas others are only available to companies preparing Companies Act accounts. Companies subject to the small companies regime are entitled to follow the Small Companies Regulations and companies subject to the micro-entities regime are entitled to follow the Micro-entities Regulations (rather than the Regulations).

The CA 2006 also distinguishes between quoted and unquoted companies. While there is no difference in the disclosures required in the financial statements by the CA 2006 and the Regulations for quoted and unquoted companies, there are significant additional disclosures for quoted companies in the annual report (see 6.2.2 below). There are also disclosures only required to be given by companies with securities admitted to trading on a regulated market (see 6.2.2. below).

The CA 2006 now requires that both Companies Act and IAS accounts group and individual accounts must give disclosures to explain the status of a company. A company must state:

- the part of the United Kingdom in which the company is registered;
- the company's registered number;
- whether the company is a public or private company and whether it is limited by shares or by guarantee;
- the address of the company's registered office; and
- where appropriate, the fact that the company is being wound-up. *[s396(A1), s397(1), s404(A1), s406(1)].*

6.2.1.D *Interaction of the Small Companies Regulations with FRS 101 and FRS 102*

FRS 101 and FRS 102 (unless Section 1A is applied) do not permit use of the formats included in the Small Companies Regulations (see 6.5 below). *[FRS 101.5(b), AG1(h)-(i), FRS 102.4.2, 5.5, 5.7].* However, a small entity that applies Section 1A of FRS 102 must present a statement of financial position and profit or loss in accordance with the requirements set out in Part 1 of Schedule 1 to the Small Companies Regulations or Part 1 of Schedule 1 to the Small LLP Regulations (except to the extent that these requirements are not permitted by any statutory framework under which such entities report). *[FRS 102.1A.4, 1A.12, 1A.14].*

In our view, a company subject to the small companies regime which chooses to apply FRS 101, or which chooses to apply FRS 102 without applying Section 1A, is not precluded from taking advantage of other exemptions applicable to companies subject to the small companies regime. See Chapter 2 at 2 and Chapter 2 of EY New UK GAAP 2015 at 4.1.1.

Companies applying the micro-entity provisions (see 6.4 below) must apply FRS 105 (see 4.4.7 above).

6.2.2 *Companies Act requirements for annual reports*

The content of the annual report depends principally on whether the company is an unquoted company or a quoted company.

A quoted company means a company whose equity share capital:

- has been included in the Official List (as defined in section 103(1) of the Financial Services and Markets Act 2000) in accordance with the provisions of Part 6 of the Financial Services and Markets Act 2000; or
- is officially listed in an EEA State; or
- is admitted to dealing on either the New York Stock Exchange or the exchange known as Nasdaq.

A company is a quoted company in relation to a financial year if it is a quoted company immediately before the end of the accounting reference period (defined in section 391 of the Companies Act 2006) by reference to which that financial year was determined. An unquoted company means a company that is not a quoted company. *[s385(1)-(3)].*

The content of the annual reports and accounts of an unquoted and a quoted company are as follows:

- an unquoted company's annual accounts and reports comprise its annual accounts, strategic report (if required – see 6.2.2.A below), directors' report (unless a micro-entity – see 6.2.2.A below), any separate corporate governance statement and the auditor's report (unless the company is exempt from audit); and

- a quoted company's annual accounts and reports comprise its annual accounts, directors' remuneration report, strategic report, directors' report, any separate corporate governance statement, and the auditor's report.

Where the company is a parent company preparing group accounts, the directors' and strategic reports must be consolidated reports (i.e. a 'group directors' report' and 'group strategic report') relating to the undertakings included in the consolidation. These group reports may, when appropriate, give greater emphasis to the matters that are significant to the undertakings included in the consolidation. *[s414A-s414D, s415-s419, 7 Sch].*

Small and medium-sized companies are entitled to certain exemptions (see 6.2.2.A below). Companies with securities admitted to a regulated market must make statutory corporate governance disclosures in the annual report and quoted companies have extended disclosures (see 6.2.2.B below). These include the Takeovers Directive disclosures required in the Directors' Report for companies with securities carrying voting rights admitted to trading on a regulated market at the financial year end. *[7 Sch 13].*

A company's strategic report (if any), directors' report, directors' remuneration report (if any), and separate corporate governance statement (if any) must be approved by the board of directors and signed on behalf of the board by a director or the secretary of the company. *[s414D(1), s419(1), s419A, s422(1)].*

It is beyond the scope of this publication to set out the content of the directors' report, strategic report, directors' remuneration report or corporate governance statement. In June 2014, the FRC published best practice *Guidance on the Strategic Report.* This is intended to be persuasive rather than have mandatory force. In September 2013, the GC 100 and Investor Group published *Directors' Remuneration Report Guidance* which provides best practice guidance on the directors' remuneration report prepared by quoted companies. The GC 100 and Investor Group subsequently issued *Directors Remuneration Reporting Guidance: 2014 Statement* providing supplementary guidance.

6.2.2.A   *Exemptions for micro, small and medium-sized companies*

The directors of a company must prepare a strategic report for the financial year unless the company is entitled to the small companies exemption (see 6.5 below). *[s414A(2), s414B].* There are certain disclosure exemptions available in respect of the strategic report for a medium-sized company (see 6.6 below).

All companies, except for micro entities (where SI 2015/980 is applied), must prepare a directors' report for the financial year. *[s415].* The exemption for micro entities was introduced following the implementation of the Accounting Directive (see 4.4.2 above). *[s415(1A)].* A company subject to the small companies regime (see 6.5 below) is entitled to prepare the directors' report in accordance with the

Small Companies Regulations which has significantly fewer disclosures than a directors' report prepared in accordance with the Regulations. *[s382-s384, para 2 (SC), 5 Sch (SC)]*. There are also certain disclosure exemptions available in respect of the directors' report for a company entitled to the small companies exemption.

6.2.2.B   *Additional requirements for quoted companies and companies with transferable securities admitted to trading on a regulated market*

The directors of a quoted company must prepare a directors' remuneration report for the financial year. *[s420-s422, 8 Sch 11]*.

A quoted company must also include additional disclosures in the directors' report (greenhouse gas disclosures) and strategic report compared to those required for an unquoted company. Additional disclosures for quoted companies in the strategic report include:

*   the company's strategy and business model;

*   gender diversity disclosures; and

*   to the extent necessary for an understanding of the development, performance or position of the company's business:

    *   the main trends and factors likely to affect the future development, performance and position of the company's business; and

    *   certain information about environmental matters (including the impact of the company's business on the environment), the company's employees and social, community and human rights issues). *[s414C(7)-(10)]*.

Where group accounts are prepared, the information required relates to the undertakings included in the consolidation (i.e. the consolidated group) rather than the company, except that there are detailed requirements on the gender diversity disclosures required. *[s417(10), (13)]*.

UK companies with transferable securities admitted to trading on a regulated market are required to prepare a statutory corporate governance statement. *[s472A]*. The requirements for the statutory corporate governance statement are included in the FCA's Disclosure and Transparency Rules (DTR) for a UK company, although the DTR extend the requirement to prepare a corporate governance statement to certain overseas listed companies, *[DTR 1B.1.4-1.6, DTR 7.2]*, and there may be corresponding requirements in other EEA states.

UK and overseas premium listed companies are also required to state how they apply the main principles of, and present a statement of compliance or otherwise with the provisions of the UK Corporate Governance Code.[12] This UK Corporate Governance Code statement overlaps with certain of the content requirements in DTR 7.2 for the statutory corporate governance statement (and with the required statement on audit committees included in DTR 7.1 which applies to issuers with securities admitted to trading on a regulated market required to appoint a statutory auditor, unless exempted from the requirements). *[DTR 1B.1.1-1.3, DTR 7.1]*.

The statutory corporate governance statement can be included as part of the directors' report or as a separate corporate governance statement published together with and in the same manner as its annual report or on a website. *[DTR 7.2.9-11]*. A 'separate corporate governance statement' is defined as one not included in the directors' report, and therefore has its own approval and publication requirements. *[s472A(3)]*.

The directors' report of a company with securities carrying voting rights admitted to trading on a regulated market at the financial year end must include certain disclosures concerning the company's capital and control (Takeovers Directive disclosures). *[7 Sch 13]*. These disclosures are also required by DTR 7.2 as part of the statutory corporate governance statement.

6.3 Preparation of consolidated financial statements

The CA 2006 requires a UK company, that is a parent company at its financial year end, to prepare group accounts (i.e. consolidated financial statements) unless otherwise exempt (see below). *[s399]*. A company that is exempt from the requirement to prepare group accounts may still do so. *[s398, s399(4)]*.

A company that is subject to the small companies regime (or would be subject to the small companies regime except for it being a public company – for financial years beginning on or after 1 January 2016 or on earlier adoption of SI 2015/980) is not required to prepare group accounts, but may do so. *[s398, s399(1), s399(2A)]*.

The other CA 2006 exemptions from preparation of group accounts comprise:

- Section 400 – parent company is a majority or wholly owned subsidiary undertaking whose immediate parent undertaking is established under the law of an EEA State, and is consolidated in group accounts of a larger group drawn up by an EEA parent undertaking (see Chapter 6 at 3.1.1.A of EY New UK GAAP 2015 supplemented by Chapter 5 at 3.1);

- Section 401 – parent company is a majority or wholly owned subsidiary undertaking whose parent undertaking is not established under the law of an EEA State, and which is consolidated in group accounts of a larger group drawn up by a parent undertaking (see Chapter 6 at 3.1.1.B of EY New UK GAAP 2015 supplemented by Chapter 5 at 3.2); and

- Section 402 – parent company, none of whose subsidiary undertakings need be included in the consolidation (see Chapter 6 at 3.1.1.E of EY New UK GAAP 2015).

FRS 102 has been developed to be consistent with the requirements for group accounts (and exemptions) included in Part 15 of the CA 2006. Consequently, the detailed conditions for the above exemptions from preparing group accounts under the CA 2006 are discussed further in Chapter 6 at 3.1.1 of EY New UK GAAP 2015 as supplemented by Chapter 5 at 3 of this publication.

The application guidance to FRS 100 explains the use of equivalence in the context of the exemption from preparing consolidated financial statements under s401. This is discussed in Chapter 2 at 2.1.6 (FRS 101) and Chapter 5 at 3.2.2 (FRS 102).

6.3.1   Requirements of accounting standards to prepare consolidated financial statements

FRS 100 does not address the requirements to prepare consolidated financial statements (nor do FRS 101 or FRS 105, since these standards only address individual financial statements).

EU-adopted IFRS and FRS 102 both include requirements on which entities should prepare consolidated financial statements, and how these should be prepared. Their requirements need to be read in conjunction with the requirements of the relevant statutory framework for preparation of the entity's financial statements.

FRS 102 requires an entity, that is a parent at its year end, to present consolidated financial statements in which it consolidates all its investments in subsidiaries in accordance with the standard (except those permitted or required to be excluded from consolidation) unless it is exempt from the requirement to prepare consolidated financial statements provided in the standard. *[FRS 102.9.2-9.3]*. As noted above, FRS 102's requirements to prepare group accounts (and exemptions) are consistent with the requirements of the CA 2006. See Chapter 6 at 3.1 of EY New UK GAAP 2015. The July 2015 amendments to FRS 102 update Section 9 for the changes made to UK company law by SI 2015/980. See Chapter 5 at 3.

A small entity that is a parent entity is not required to prepare consolidated financial statements under Section 1 of FRS 102 (see Chapter 3 at 6.2). *[FRS 102.1A.21]*.

6.3.2   Exemption from publishing the individual profit and loss account where group accounts are prepared

When SI 2015/980 is implemented, where a company prepares group accounts in accordance with the CA 2006,

*   the company's individual profit and loss account need not contain the information specified in paragraphs 65 to 69 of Schedule 1 to the Regulations (specified information supplementing the profit and loss account); and

*   the company's individual profit and loss account must be approved by the directors in accordance with section 414(1) but may be omitted from the company's annual accounts.

This exemption is conditional on the company's individual balance sheet showing the company's profit or loss for the financial year (determined in accordance with the CA 2006) and use of the exemption conferred by section 408 being disclosed in the annual accounts. *[s408, Regulations 3(2)]*.

Example 1.1:   *Example of a s408 exemption statement following implementation of SI 2015/980.*

Basis of preparation
The group accounts consolidate the financial statements of ABC Limited (the company) and all its subsidiary undertakings drawn up to 31 December each year. No individual profit and loss account is presented for ABC Limited as permitted by section 408 of the Companies Act 2006.
[...]
Parent company balance sheet
The profit for the financial year of the company is £130,000 (2015 £111,000).

For companies that have not implemented SI 2015/980, the company profit and loss account is required to be shown in the notes to the balance sheet and the information required by s411 concerning staff costs and staff numbers need not be given for the company in the individual accounts. See Chapter 1 at 6.3.2 of EY New UK GAAP 2015 which also contains an illustrative example of a s408 exemption statement under the previous requirements.

The exemption is available for both Companies Act and IAS group accounts. Paragraph 9.24 of the June 2008 BERR document *Guidance for UK Companies on Accounting and Reporting: Requirements under the Companies Act 2006 and the application of the IAS regulation* clarifies that:

'The omission of the profit and loss account (referred to within IAS as the income statement) might be considered to be inconsistent with certain aspects of IAS, for example, the requirement in IAS 1 *Presentation of Financial Statements* in relation to a fair presentation. However, IAS does not in itself require the preparation of separate financial statements but permits the omission of certain elements. In other words, the separate financial statements required to be published under the 2006 Act are an extract of the full IAS separate financial statements. This exemption should not affect the ability of a parent company to be treated as a "first-time adopter" and hence to take advantage of exemptions for first time use under the provisions of IFRS 1. The company will need to provide the disclosure required by section 408(4) i.e. that advantage has been taken of the publication exemption in section 408(1). The auditor will also need to describe the accounting framework that has been used within its audit reports. In respect of individual accounts, the reference to the framework will need to make clear that its basis is IAS as adopted by the EU as applied in accordance with the provisions of the 2006 Act.'

Paragraph 9.25 of the BERR guidance further notes that:

'The exemption in the 2006 Act relates only to the profit and loss account. By virtue of section 472(2), the exemption also extends to the notes to the profit and loss account. The individual IAS accounts would, however, still need to include the other primary statements and note disclosures required by IAS, including a cash flow statement and a statement of changes in shareholders' equity.'

6.4   Micro-entities regime

A new voluntary regime for companies that are micro-entities was introduced into UK companies legislation by *The Small Companies (Micro-Entities' Accounts) Regulations 2013* (SI 2013/3008) (Micro-entities Regulations), and is effective for financial years ending on or after 30 September 2013 for companies filing their accounts on or after 1 December 2013. These regulations implement the provisions of the new EU Accounting Directive, which sets out certain minimum requirements for micro-entities into UK company law (see 4.4.2 above). There is no similar legislation currently applicable in the Republic of Ireland. *[FRSSE.Appendix I.18].*

In response to the introduction of the Micro-entities Regulations and the new financial reporting framework (see 1 above) the FRC issued FRS 105 (see 4.4.7 above). FRS 105 is outside the scope of this publication and 6.4.1 and 6.4.2 below only address the Companies Act requirements for micro-entities.

6.4.1   Scope of the micro-entities regime

A company can only use the micro-entity provisions if it meets the size criteria and is not excluded from being treated as a micro-entity. The size criteria operate in the same way as for the small companies regime (see 6.5 below and Chapter 3 at 4.3).

The micro-entity provisions are not available to LLPs, qualifying partnerships, overseas companies and other entities. The Explanatory Note to the Micro-entities Regulations confirms that the regime is only available to companies formed and registered (or treated as formed and registered) under the CA 2006.

The qualifying conditions are met in a year in which the company satisfies two or more of the following requirements: *[s384A(4)-(7)]*

- turnover must not exceed £632,000;
- balance sheet total (gross assets) must not exceed £316,000; and
- the number of employees must not exceed 10.

In the case of a company which is a parent company, the company qualifies as a micro-entity in relation to a financial year only if the company qualifies as a micro-entity in relation to that year and the group headed by the company qualifies as a small group. *[s384A(8)]*.

The micro-entity provisions do not apply to a company's accounts for a particular financial year if the company was at any time within that year: *[s384B(1)]*

- a company excluded from the small companies regime by section 384;
- an investment undertaking as defined in Article 2(14) of the EU Accounting Directive (Directive 2013/34/EU);
- a financial holding undertaking as defined in Article 2(15) of the EU Accounting Directive;
- a credit institution as defined in Article 4 of Directive 2006/48/EC (other than one referred to in Article 2 of that directive);
- an insurance undertaking as defined in Article 2(1) of Directive 91/674/EEC; or
- a charity.

The micro-entity provisions also do not apply in relation to a company's accounts for a financial year if the company is a parent company which prepares group accounts for that year as permitted by section 398, or is not a parent company but its accounts are included in consolidated group accounts for that year. *[s384B(2)]*.

6.4.2   Companies Act requirements for micro-entities

The Micro-entities Regulations provide extensive presentation and disclosure exemptions for micro-entities (known as the micro-entity provisions). In summary, a micro-entity applies one of two abridged formats for the balance sheet and one abridged format for the profit and loss account, as set out in the Section C formats included in the Small Companies Regulations and presents limited prescribed notes which must be included at the foot of the balance sheet. The formats and related notes disclosures are known as the 'micro-entity minimum accounting items'. *[s472(1A)]*.

The prescribed notes comprise: information on directors' advances, credits and guarantees (required by s413); and on financial guarantees and commitments (required by 1 Sch 57 to the Small Companies Regulations). The micro-entity is not required to give any of the other information required by way of notes to the accounts set out in Schedules 1 to 3 to the Small Companies Regulations. This means there is no requirement to give the information on related undertakings set out in Schedule 2 or the disclosures on directors' remuneration set out in Schedule 3. *[Regulations (SC) 4, 5, 5A].*

Following the amendments to the Companies Act as a consequence of implementing the new Accounting Directive, for financial years commencing on or after 1 January 2016 (or on early application of SI 2015/980), micro-entities are no longer required to prepare a directors' report. As a result the disclosure requirements on acquisition of own shares currently required in the directors' report will become a mandatory balance sheet note. *[s415(1A)].*

The alternative accounting rules and fair value accounting rules (explained further in Chapter 4 at 10) do not apply where the micro-entity provisions are applied; therefore a micro-entity applying the micro-entity provisions is not permitted to revalue tangible fixed assets, investment properties or financial instruments.

In considering whether the individual accounts give a true and fair view, the directors apply the following provisions:

- where the accounts comprise only micro-entity minimum accounting items, the directors must disregard any provision of an accounting standard which would require the accounts to contain information additional to those items;

- in relation to a micro-entity minimum accounting item contained in the accounts, the directors must disregard any provision of an accounting standard which would require the accounts to contain further information in relation to that item; and

- where the accounts contain an item of information additional to the micro-entity minimum accounting items, the directors must have regard to any provision of an accounting standard which relates to that item. *[s393(1A)].*

Even though the presentation and disclosure requirements are minimal, 'the micro-entity minimum accounting items' included in the company's accounts for the year are presumed to give the true and fair view required (the usual requirements to give additional information where the matters required to be included in the accounts are not sufficient to give a true and fair view and the provisions on 'true and fair override' do not apply in relation to the micro-entity minimum accounting items included in the company's accounts for the year).

The auditor of a company which qualifies as a micro-entity in relation to a financial year applies the same provisions above in considering whether the individual accounts of the company for that year give a true and fair view. *[s495(3A)].*

If the accounts are prepared in accordance with the micro-entity provisions, the balance sheet must contain a statement to this effect in a prominent place above the signature(s) of the director(s). *[s414(3)(a)].*

Companies using the micro-entity provisions must file a copy of their accounts at Companies House (but are not permitted to file abbreviated accounts). *[s444(3)-(3B)]*. However, micro-entities can use the other filing exemptions for companies subject to the small companies regime (subject to making the statement that the accounts (and reports) have been delivered in accordance with the provisions applicable to companies subject to the small companies regime). *[s444(1)-(2), (5)]*.

6.5   Small companies

There are two sets of exemptions available for small companies:

*   the small companies regime – which applies to the preparation and/or filing of the financial statements; and

*   the small companies exemption – which applies to the preparation and/or filing of the strategic report and directors' report.

The small companies regime and small companies exemption under the Companies Act are discussed in Chapter 3. Chapter 3 also addresses the requirements in Section 1A of FRS 102 for entities subject to the small entities regime. Chapter 3 reflects the requirements for an entity applying SI 2015/980 which is effective for financial years beginning on or after 1 January 2016, although there is an option to early apply SI 2015/980 for a financial year beginning on or after 1 January 2015 if the directors of the company so decide.

For entities not applying the new small companies requirements in SI 2015/980 for financial years beginning before 1 January 2016, see Chapter 1 at 6.5 of EY New UK GAAP 2015.

6.6   Medium-sized companies and groups

Medium-sized companies and groups must apply the Regulations in preparing their annual reports and accounts. A medium-sized company may take advantage of certain disclosure exemptions in its annual reports and accounts for a financial year in which the company qualifies as medium-sized and is not an excluded company. *[s465-467]*

The guidance below on medium-sized companies and groups reflects the requirements for an entity applying SI 2015/980 which is effective for financial years beginning on or after 1 January 2016, although there is an option to early apply SI 2015/980 for financial years beginning on or after 1 January 2015 if the directors of the company so decide. For entities not applying SI 2015/980 for financial years beginning before 1 January 2016, see Chapter 1 of EY New UK GAAP 2015.

There is no requirement for the annual reports and accounts of a medium-sized company to state use of the disclosure exemptions.

6.6.1   *Qualification as medium-sized company*

The medium-sized companies regime works in the same way as the small companies regime (described in Chapter 3 at 4.3). The size criteria and excluded companies (as amended by SI 2015/980) are detailed below.

6.6.1.A   Size criteria for medium-sized companies and groups

A company qualifies as medium-sized in relation to its first financial year if the qualifying conditions are met in that year *[s465(1)]*.

A group qualifies as medium-sized in relation to a subsequent financial year if the qualifying conditions are met in that year. *[s465(2)]*. In relation to a subsequent financial year, where on its balance sheet date a company meets or cease to meet the qualifying conditions, then that will affect its qualification as a medium-sized company only if it occurs in two consecutive years. *[s465(3)]*.

Where the company itself is a parent undertaking, then it only qualifies as medium-sized if the group that it heads qualifies as a medium-sized group. This is the case whether or not group accounts are prepared. A group qualifies as medium-sized in relation to its first financial year if the qualifying conditions (as set out below) are met in that year. In relation to a subsequent financial year, where on its balance sheet date a group meets or ceases to meet the qualifying conditions, then that will affect its qualification as a medium-sized company only if it occurs in two consecutive years. *[s466]*.

The qualifying conditions for a medium-sized company are met in a year in which the company satisfies two or more of the following requirements: *[s465]*

- turnover must not exceed £36 million;
- balance sheet total (gross assets) must not exceed £18 million; and
- the number of employees must not exceed 250.

The qualifying conditions for a medium-sized group are met in a year in which the group headed by the company satisfies two or more of the following requirements: *[s466(3)]*

- turnover must not exceed £36 million net (or £43.2 million gross);
- balance sheet total must not exceed £18 million (or £21.6 million gross); and
- the number of employees must not exceed 250.

The aggregate figures for the above limits are ascertained by aggregating the relevant figures determined in accordance with s466 for each member of the group. The figures used for each subsidiary undertaking are those included in its individual accounts for the relevant financial year. That is, where its financial year is coterminous with that of the parent company, the financial year that ends at the same date as the parent company, or where its financial year is not coterminous, the financial year ending last before the end of the financial year of the parent company. If those figures are not obtainable without disproportionate expense or undue delay, the latest available figures are used.

The turnover and balance sheet total criteria may be satisfied on either the gross or net of consolidation adjustments basis. For Companies Act accounts (such as FRS 102 financial statements), the consolidation adjustments are determined in accordance with regulations made under s404, i.e. the Regulations. For IAS accounts, the consolidation adjustments are determined in accordance with EU-adopted IFRS. It is permissible to satisfy one limit on the 'net' basis and the other on the 'gross' basis. *[s466(4)-(7)]*.

SI 2015/980 raises the thresholds for turnover and balance sheet total. In determining whether a company or group qualifies as medium-sized under s465(2) or s466(3) (see above) in relation to a financial year for which the amendments made by SI 2015/980 have effect, the company or group is treated as having qualified as medium-sized in any previous financial year in which it would have so qualified if the amendments to the same effect as the amendments made in SI 2015/980 had had effect in relation to that previous year. This means that if SI 2015/980 is first applied in calendar year 2016, the new size thresholds are applied to 2016 and the preceding financial years (to see whether the company qualifies as medium-sized in 2016).

6.6.1.B   Companies excluded from medium-sized companies

A company is not entitled to take advantage of any of the provisions available for companies qualifying as medium-sized if it was at any time within the financial year to which the accounts relate:

- a public company;
- a company that has permission under Part 4 of the Financial Services and Markets Act 2000 to carry on a regulated activity;
- a company that carries on an insurance market activity;
- an e-money issuer; or
- a member of an ineligible group. *[s467(1)]*.

A group is ineligible if any of its members is:

- a traded company;
- a body corporate (other than a company) whose shares are admitted to trading on a regulated market in an EEA State (as defined in Directive 2004/39/EC);
- a person (other than a small company) who has permission under Part 4 of the Financial Services and Markets Act 2000 to carry on a regulated activity;
- an e-money issuer;
- a small company that is an authorised insurance company, banking company, a MiFID investment firm or a UCITS management company; or
- a person who carries on an insurance market activity. *[s467(2)]*.

A company is a small company for the purposes of section 467(2) if it qualified as small in relation to its last financial year ending on or before the end of the financial years to which the accounts relate. *[s467(3)]*.

The reference to a 'company' above is to a company formed and registered (or treated as formed and registered) under the CA 2006. This means a company formed and registered under the CA 2006, or prior to 1 October 2009 under the Companies Act 1985, Companies (Northern Ireland) Order 1986 or former Companies Acts (i.e. an 'existing company' for the purposes of that Act and Order). *[s1]*.

A public company means a company limited by shares or limited by guarantee and having a share capital (a) whose certificate of incorporation states that it is a public company and (b) in relation to which the requirements of the CA 2006 or former

Companies Acts as to registration or re-registration as a public company have been complied with (on or after the relevant date, being 22 December 1980 in Great Britain and 1 July 1983 in Northern Ireland). *[s4]*. Therefore, a public company means a UK-incorporated company that is a 'plc' or 'PLC' rather than a publicly traded company.

A traded company means a company any of whose transferable securities are admitted to trading on a regulated market. *[s474]*.

An authorised insurance company is defined in section 1165(2), a banking company in section 1164(2)-(3) and insurance market activity in section 1165(7). See Chapter 4 at 4.2.2 and 4.2.3.

The terms e-money issuer, MiFID investment firm, regulated activity, and UCITS management company are defined in section 474 of the CA 2006. The term 'e-money issuer' means an electronic money institution within the meaning of *The Electronic Money Regulations 2011* (SI 2011/99). *[s474]*.

A body corporate includes a body incorporated outside the UK but does not include (a) a corporation sole or (b) a partnership that, whether or not a legal person, is not regarded as a body corporate under the law by which it is governed. *[s1173(1)]*. Therefore, a body corporate would include an overseas company or a UK LLP.

SI 2015/980 also changes the exclusions. The key change is that previously a company that was a member of an ineligible group containing a public company (i.e. a PLC) was excluded whereas now the exclusion applies to a company that is a member of an ineligible group containing a 'traded company' (i.e. a company any of whose transferable securities are admitted to trading on a regulated market). A medium-sized company that is itself a public company remains excluded.

6.6.1.C   Medium-sized LLPs regime

SI 2015/980 does not apply to LLPs. The size limits and exclusions for medium-sized LLPs have not changed and consequently differ to those of medium-sized companies.

6.6.2   Disclosure exemptions available for medium-sized companies

6.6.2.A   Disclosure exemptions available in the accounts and reports prepared for members

The disclosure exemptions for medium-sized companies include:

* no requirement to disclose non-financial key performance indicators, including information relating to environmental matters and employee matters, in the strategic report; *[s414C(6)]*

* no requirement for Companies Act individual accounts to disclose the information required by paragraph 45 (the statement that the accounts have been prepared in accordance with applicable accounting standards, giving particulars and reasons for any material departures from these standards) or paragraph 72 (related party disclosures) of Schedule 1 to the Regulations (see 4.6.1 above); *[s4]* and

- no requirement to disclose auditor's remuneration in respect of non-audit services. Like companies subject to the small companies regime, only remuneration for the auditing of the annual accounts receivable by the company's auditor (but not the associates of the auditor) is required to be disclosed. *[s494].*[13] TECH 14/13 FRF – *Disclosure of auditor information* – provides guidance on disclosure of auditor remuneration.

Medium-sized entities preparing financial statements in accordance with FRS 101 or FRS 102 must still give the disclosures required by accounting standards, e.g. medium-sized companies still need to give the related party disclosures required by accounting standards.

6.6.2.B   *Abbreviated accounts*

As a result of the Accounting Directive implementation, for financial years beginning on or after 1 January 2016 (or on early adoption of SI 2015/980), the option to deliver abbreviated accounts to the Registrar has been removed.

6.7   Disclosures

The CA 2006 (particularly Part 15), the Regulations and other statutory instruments include disclosure requirements which apply to Companies Act accounts and IAS accounts. As discussed at 6.7.1 below, only some parts of the Regulations apply to IAS accounts. See 6.7.2 for a list of Companies Act disclosures applicable to both IAS accounts and Companies Act accounts.

The disclosure exemptions for companies subject to the small companies regime in the CA 2006 and the Small Companies Regulations are addressed in Chapter 3.

6.7.1   *Disclosures required by the Regulations*

The Regulations contain the following schedules:

- Schedule 1 (Companies Act individual accounts – companies other than banking and insurance companies);
- Schedule 2 (Companies Act individual accounts: banking companies);
- Schedule 3 (Companies Act individual accounts: insurance companies);
- Schedule 4 (Information about related undertakings – Companies Act or IAS accounts);
- Schedule 5 (Information about directors' benefits: remuneration – Companies Act or IAS accounts);
- Schedule 6 (Companies Act group accounts);
- Schedule 7 (Matters to be dealt with in directors' report);
- Schedule 8 (Directors' remuneration report – quoted companies);
- Schedule 9 (Definition of 'provision'); and
- Schedule 10 (General interpretation).

A company preparing IAS individual accounts in accordance with section 397 (or IAS group accounts in accordance with section 406) does not apply Schedules 1 to 3, or Schedule 6 to the Regulations.

A company preparing Companies Act accounts must comply with all the requirements of the Regulations, including Schedules 1 to 3 (as applicable) and, where group accounts are prepared, Schedule 6. Schedules 1 to 3 include the formats for the profit and loss account and balance sheet, recognition and measurement principles, and disclosure requirements. Schedule 1 applies to all companies (other than banking companies and insurance companies), Schedule 2 to banking companies and groups, and Schedule 3 to insurance companies and groups. See Chapter 4 at 4.2.2 and 4.2.3 for definitions of banking and insurance companies and groups respectively.

The Regulations require various disclosures to be given in the financial statements. In particular, Parts 3 of Schedules 1 to 3 for Companies Act accounts require certain disclosures to be made in the notes to the financial statements if not given in the primary statements. The relevant paragraphs are as follows:

- Schedule 1 paragraphs 42 to 72B;
- Schedule 2 paragraphs 52 to 92B;
- Schedule 3 paragraphs 60 to 90B; and
- Schedule 6 various paragraphs.

Although some of these disclosure requirements are replicated in EU-adopted IFRS, others are not. Entities that move to FRS 101 or FRS 102 from previous UK GAAP will have been required to provide the statutory disclosures required for Companies Act accounts previously and therefore these requirements will not increase their reporting burden. Entities that move to FRS 101 or FRS 102 from EU-adopted IFRS are required to provide the additional statutory disclosures for Companies Act accounts and should consider carefully the impact of these new requirements against the benefits of the reduced disclosures under those standards.

6.7.2   *Existing Companies Act disclosures in the accounts and reports applicable to IAS accounts and Companies Act accounts*

Companies preparing IAS accounts or Companies Act accounts are subject to the following disclosures:

- s396(A1) and 397(1) – information about the status of the company where individual accounts are prepared. See 6.2.1.C above;
- s404(A1) and section 406(1) – information about the status of the company where group accounts are prepared See 6.2.1.C above; and
- s409 (and Schedule 4 to the Regulations) – information about related undertakings.

  The alternative compliance in s410(2) of the CA 2006 has been removed for annual accounts of companies and qualifying partnerships approved on or after 1 July 2015. Therefore, UK companies must present these disclosures under s409 in full in the financial statements. Section 410(2) previously allowed companies, where the information required in the notes to the accounts would be of excessive length, to give information in the notes to the accounts in respect of the undertakings whose results or financial position, in the opinion of the directors, principally affected the figures shown in the company's annual accounts and, where group accounts are prepared, in respect of subsidiary undertakings excluded from consolidation under s405(3) (i.e. other than materiality grounds). Where the exemption was used, a statement was required in the notes to the accounts that the information was only given in respect to such undertakings and the full information (both that disclosed in the notes to the accounts and that which is not) was annexed to the next annual return delivered to the Registrar after the accounts were approved;

- s410A – off-balance sheet arrangements (unless subject to the small companies regime). See Chapter 4 at 8.7;

- s411 – employee numbers and costs (unless subject to the small companies regime). See Chapter 4 at 8.6;

- s412 (and Schedule 5 and paragraph 22A of Schedule 6 to the Regulations) – directors' benefits: remuneration;

- s413 – directors' benefits: advances, credits and guarantees. See Chapter 4 at 8.8;

- s414A-D – strategic report. The FRC's *Guidance on the Strategic Report* (June 2014) provides best practice guidance. This is intended to be persuasive rather than have mandatory force;

- s236, 415 to 419 (and Schedule 7 to the Regulations) – directors' report;

- s420 to 421 (and Schedule 8 to the Regulations) – directors' remuneration report (quoted companies only). The GC 100 and Investor Group's *Directors' Remuneration Report Guidance* (September 2013), as updated in 2014 (see 6.2.2. above), provides best practice guidance on the directors' remuneration report prepared by quoted companies; and

- s494 (and *Companies (Disclosure of Auditor Remuneration and Liability Limitation Agreements) Regulations 2008*) – services provided by auditor and associates and related remuneration.

  Medium-sized companies are only required to disclose remuneration for the audit of the annual accounts receivable by the company's auditor (but not the associates of the auditor) and are not required to disclose remuneration for non-audit services. *[s494]*.[14]

TECH 14/13 FRF provides guidance on disclosure of auditor remuneration. In addition, other CA 2006 or related disclosures may apply depending on individual circumstances such as the disclosures required for a parent taking advantage of the exemption from preparing consolidated accounts under either s400 or 401 of the CA 2006.

7   FINANCIAL REPORTING COUNCIL (FRC) AND ACCOUNTING STANDARD SETTING

The structure of the FRC was reformed with effect from 2 July 2012, and the FRC was given new statutory powers including assuming responsibility for accounting standards (see 7.1 below). The Accounting Standards Board, previously responsible for issuing accounting standards and the Urgent Issues Task Force have ceased to exist.

This section draws on information concerning the new FRC structure that is included on the FRC website.

The FRC Board is now supported by three business committees:

- the Codes & Standards Committee;
- the Conduct Committee; and
- the Executive Committee.

This chapter discusses the role of the FRC in accounting standard setting.

7.1   Accounting standards setting

Accounting standards are statements of standard accounting practice issued by such body or bodies prescribed by regulations.[15] *[s464(1)]*. Prior to 2 July 2012, this body was the Accounting Standards Board and from 2 July 2012, the Financial Reporting Council. New accounting standards, or amendments to or withdrawal of existing accounting standards must be approved by the FRC Board, having received advice from the Accounting Council and/or the Codes and Standards Committee (see below).

The FRC's objective in setting accounting standards is to enable users of accounts to receive high quality, understandable financial reporting proportionate to the size and complexity of the entity and users' information needs. *[Foreword to Accounting Standards.8]*. The FRC collaborates with accounting standard setters from other countries and the IASB to influence the development of international accounting standards and to ensure that its standards are developed with due regard for international developments. The FRC works closely with the European Financial Reporting Advisory Group (EFRAG), which advises the European Commission on IFRSs in Europe and with the International Forum of Accounting Standard Setters (IFASS).

The Codes & Standards Committee, which contains both FRC Board members and others with particular technical expertise (including practising professionals) is responsible, *inter alia*, for advising the FRC Board on maintaining an effective framework of UK codes and standards for Corporate Governance, Stewardship, Accounting, Auditing and Assurance, and Actuarial technical standards. In relation to accounting standard setting, the FRC Board and the Codes & Standards Committee are advised by the Accounting Council (which is appointed by the Codes & Standards Committee). Its advice is put fully to the FRC Board, with the Board member chairing the Council responsible for submitting the Council's advice to the Board. The Accounting Council, which is appointed by the Codes & Standards Committee:

- provides strategic input and thought leadership, in the fields of accounting and financial reporting and in the work-plan of the FRC as a whole. This involves 'horizon-scanning' and consulting with practitioners or users;
- considers and advises the FRC Board upon draft codes and standards (or amendments thereto) to ensure that a high quality, effective and proportionate approach is taken;
- considers and comments on proposed developments in relation to international codes and standards and regulations; and
- considers and advises on research proposals and other initiatives undertaken to inform the FRC on matters material to its remit and any resultant publications.

In June 2013, the FRC established a UK GAAP Technical Advisory Group (TAG) to assist the Accounting Council. The TAG advises the Accounting Council on all issues relating to UK accounting standards, including areas where unsatisfactory or conflicting interpretations of accounting standards or Companies Act provisions have developed or seem likely to develop, as well as those relating to smaller entities.

The TAG and Committee for Accounting on Public Benefit Entities (CAPE) are advisory committees to assist the Accounting Council in relation to the development of SORPs by SORP-making bodies by carrying out a limited review of a SORP (see 4.7 above). An Academic Panel also meets regularly to discuss issues relating to the FRC's work. The Accounting Council may also establish short-term advisory groups to provide input to specific projects.

The FRC's procedure for issuing accounting standards is set out in the *FRC Codes & Standards: Procedures.*[16]

7.2   Scope and authority of accounting standards

The *Foreword to Accounting Standards*, last updated in March 2015, explains the authority, scope and application of accounting standards, known as Financial Reporting Standards (FRSs) issued by the FRC. The March 2015 version of the Foreword withdraws the November 2012 version. The Foreword addresses accounting standards applicable in Companies Act accounts. Some key points included in the Foreword are addressed below.

Previous UK GAAP is withdrawn for financial years beginning on or after 1 January 2015 or on early application of FRS 100. For financial years beginning on or after 1 January 2015 (or on earlier adoption of FRS 100 and the new financial reporting framework), FRS 101, FRS 102, FRS 103, FRS 105 and FRC Abstracts (none have been issued to date) apply.

Accounting standards are applicable to the financial statements of a reporting entity that are intended to give a true and fair view of the assets, liabilities and financial position of the company and, where relevant, the group at the end of the reporting period; and the profit or loss of the company and, where relevant, the group for the reporting period. *[Foreword to Accounting Standard.4]*.

Accounting standards developed by the FRC will be designated Financial Reporting Standards (FRSs). The FRC may issue FRSs that relate to other aspects of financial reporting, but which are not accounting standards. Each FRS will indicate its status, i.e. that it is an accounting standard or, if not, the circumstances in which it may be applied. *[Foreword to Accounting Standards.9-11]*. FRS 100 to FRS 103 and FRS 105 (but not FRS 104) are accounting standards for the purpose of company law.

Where exposure drafts are issued for comment and are subject to revision, until it is finalised as an accounting standard the requirements of any existing accounting standard that would be affected by proposals in the exposure draft remain in force. *[Foreword to Accounting Standards.13]*.

7.2.1   *Accounting standards and true and fair*

Section 393 of the CA 2006 requires that the directors of a company must not approve accounts unless they are satisfied that they give a true and fair view of the assets, liabilities, financial position and profit or loss. *[s393]*.

Predecessor bodies to the FRC obtained legal opinions that have confirmed the centrality of the true and fair concept to the preparation and audit of financial statements, whether prepared in accordance with UK accounting standards or international accounting standards. The latest Opinion written by Martin Moore QC (2008) followed the enactment of the CA 2006 and the introduction of international accounting standards and endorsed the analysis in the earlier Opinions of Leonard Hoffman QC (1983) and Mary Arden (1984) and Mary Arden QC (1993) as to the approach that Courts would take to accounting standards when considering whether accounts show a true and fair view.

In October 2013, the Department of Business, Skills and Innovation (BIS) published a ministerial statement:

'The Department of Business has given serious consideration to concerns raised by some stakeholders that accounts prepared over the past 30 years, in accordance with UK or international financial reporting standards, have not been properly prepared under UK and EU law.

'However, it is entirely satisfied that the concerns expressed are misconceived and that the existing legal framework, including international financial reporting standards, is binding under European Law.

'In preparing financial statements, achieving a true and fair view is and remains the overriding objective (and legal requirement). In the vast majority of cases, compliance with accounting standards will result in a true and fair view. However, where compliance with an accounting standard may not achieve that objective, accounting standards expressly provide that that standard may be overridden. [...]'

The FRC published its independent legal advice, available on the FRC website. The Opinion written by Martin Moore QC (3 October 2013) – *International Accounting Standards and the true and fair view* – considered issues addressed in an Opinion written by George Bompas QC (8 April 2013), in particular the interaction of International Accounting Standards and the legal requirement that directors must not approve accounts that do not show a true and fair view, and the place of prudence.

However, both the FRC (in its Press Notice of 3 October 2013) and the BIS ministerial statement noted scope for improvements in aspects of international financial reporting standards and the IASB's Conceptual Framework, for example:

- stewardship reporting (i.e. holding directors to account for their management of the company's property) should be regarded as a primary objective of financial reporting;
- prudence (i.e. the exercise of caution), should be explicitly acknowledged in the Conceptual Framework; and
- there should be clear principles to describe when specific measurement bases, such as fair value (which needs to be appropriately defined) should be

used. Performance reporting should present movements in fair value clearly and appropriately.

The FRC noted that investors raised other concerns and that it looked forward to working with investors and other stakeholders to address the full range of issues.

In June 2014, the FRC issued updated guidance – *True and Fair*. This confirms the fundamental importance of the true and fair requirement in both IFRSs and UK GAAP, whether applying FRS 100 to FRS 103 or previous UK GAAP. This guidance emphasises the application of objective professional judgement, which applies at all stages of preparation of the financial statements, to ensure the financial statements give a true and fair view. The guidance specifically addresses the concept of prudence and reflecting the substance of transactions under both IFRSs and UK GAAP.

The FRC expects preparers, those charged with governance and auditors to stand back and ensure that the financial statements as a whole give a true and fair view, provide additional disclosures where compliance with an accounting standard is insufficient to present a true and fair view, to use the true and fair override where compliance with the standards does not result in the presentation of a true and fair view and to ensure that the consideration they give to these matters is evident in their deliberations and documentation. See Chapter 4 at 9.2.

7.3   UK GAAP

UK GAAP is a wider concept than accounting standards, as defined at 7.2 above. For example, UK GAAP can include:

*   SORPs (where an entity is within the scope of a SORP – see 4.7 above);

*   other pronouncements issued by the FRC or its predecessor bodies (such as FREDs or best practice Reporting Statements) – providing these do not conflict with an extant accounting standard;

*   pronouncements by authoritative bodies, such as Technical Releases issued by the Institute of Chartered Accountants in England and Wales and/or the Institute of Chartered Accountants in Scotland (examples include TECH 02/10); and

*   generally accepted accounting practice where areas are not covered by specific accounting standards. This could include reference to the requirements of other bodies of GAAP where it addresses an issue, but does not conflict with accounting standards. For example, FRS 102 permits but does not require management to refer to the requirements of EU-adopted IFRS dealing with similar and related issues in developing and applying a reliable and relevant accounting policy *[FRS 102.10.6]*. Generally accepted accounting practice can also include established industry practice in accounting for transactions.

In addition, an entity must comply with any legal or regulatory requirements applicable to its annual report and financial statements, including the overall requirement for directors of a company to prepare accounts that give a true and fair view.

References

1 http://ec.europa.eu/internal_market/
securities/isd/mifid/index_en.htm
2 AIM Rules, para. 19, Glossary.
3 s464, *The Statutory Auditors (Amendment
of Companies Act 2006 and Delegation of
Functions etc.) Order 2012* (SI 2012/1741).
4 *The Accounting Standards (Prescribed
Bodies) (United States of America and
Japan) Regulations 2015* (SI 2015/1675)
permits companies with securities registered
with the SEC or publicly traded on specified
Japanese exchanges (but that do not have
securities admitted to trading on an (EEA)
regulated market) to prepare consolidated
financial statements (but not individual
financial statements) using US GAAP or
JGAAP. Such consolidated financial
statements would also be Companies Act
accounts. The Regulations, which replace a
similar Statutory Instrument, come into force
on 1 October 2015 and apply for financial
years beginning on or after 1 January 2015.
However, the dispensation applies only in
respect of the group financial statements of a
parent company for the first 4 financial years
following incorporation of that company. It
ceases to have effect on 30 September 2022.
5 http://oiac.co.uk/sorp-current-status
6 *TECH 02/10 Guidance on the
determination of realised profits and losses
in the context of distributions under the
Companies Act 2006*, ICAEW/ICAS,
February 2010, paras. 3.28 and 3.29. Also
section 853(4) of Companies Act 2006.
7 *TECH 02/10 Guidance on the
determination of realised profits and losses
in the context of distributions under the
Companies Act 2006*, ICAEW/ICAS,
February 2010, paras. 3.30 to 3.33.
8 *TECH 02/10 Guidance on the
determination of realised profits and
losses in the context of distributions
under the Companies Act 2006*,
ICAEW/ICAS, February 2010, paras. 3.35.
9 *TECH 02/10 Guidance on the
determination of realised profits and losses
in the context of distributions under the
Companies Act 2006*, ICAEW/ICAS,
February 2010, paras. 3.34 and 3.37.
10 *TECH 02/10 Guidance on the
determination of realised profits and losses
in the context of distributions under the
Companies Act 2006*, ICAEW/ICAS,
February 2010, para. 3.36.
11 Listing Rules, FCA, para. 9.8.6(5), (6).
12 Listing Rules, FCA, para. 9.8.6(5), (6).
13 Para 4, SI 2008/489.
14 Para 4, SI 2008/489.
15 See footnote 5 above. *The Accounting
Standards (Prescribed Bodies) (United
States of America and Japan)
Regulations 2015* extend the prescribed
bodies for issuing accounting standards to
include the FASB and the Accounting
Standards Board of Japan for group accounts
of parent companies with securities
registered with the Securities Exchange
Commission of the United States of
America and specified Japanese exchanges
respectively, with the restrictions set out in
the statutory instrument.
16 https://www.frc.org.uk/About-the-FRC/
Procedures/Regulatory-policies.aspx

Chapter 2 — FRS 101 – Reduced disclosure framework

Chapter 2

Chapter 2

FRS 101 – Reduced disclosure framework

1 INTRODUCTION

This chapter deals only with the application of FRS 101 – *Reduced Disclosure Framework: Disclosure exemptions from EU-adopted IFRS for qualifying entities* – as amended in September 2015. References made to FRS 101 throughout this chapter are to the September 2015 edition of the standard unless otherwise indicated.

FRS 101 is a voluntary framework, which can be applied by 'qualifying' entities that previously used either EU-adopted IFRS or UK GAAP (including the FRSSE, FRS 102 – *The Financial Reporting Standard applicable in the UK and Republic of Ireland* – and FRS 105 – *The Financial Reporting Standard applicable to the Micro-entities Regime*). This chapter discusses FRS 101 only as it applies to UK companies, LLPs and other entities preparing financial statements under Part 15 of the Companies Act 2006 (CA 2006). However, FRS 101 may also be adopted by non-UK entities currently applying IFRS as issued by the IASB or another GAAP although application would depend on local legislation.

FRS 101 sets out a framework which addresses the financial reporting requirements and disclosure exemptions for the financial statements of subsidiaries and parents that otherwise apply the recognition, measurement and disclosure requirements of standards and interpretations issued (or adopted) by the International Accounting Standards Board (IASB) that have been adopted in the European Union (EU-adopted IFRS). To use the framework, an entity needs to be a 'qualifying entity' (see section 2.1 below) which is included in publicly available consolidated financial statements of its parent which are intended to give a true and fair view. The shareholders of the qualifying entity must be notified about and not object to the use of the FRS 101 disclosure exemptions.

An entity reporting under FRS 101 complies with EU-adopted IFRS except as modified in accordance with this FRS. This chapter does not discuss EU-adopted IFRS, which is covered in EY International GAAP 2016. The FRC's overriding objective is to enable users of accounts to receive high-quality, understandable financial reporting proportionate to the size and complexity of the entity and the users' information needs. In other words, the objective of FRS 101 is to enable subsidiary and parent company financial statements to be prepared under the recognition and measurement rules of EU-adopted IFRS, without the need for some of the copious disclosures which are perceived to act as a barrier to those entities preparing those financial statements under EU-adopted IFRS.

An entity using the reduced disclosure framework of FRS 101 is unable to make the explicit and unreserved statement that its financial statements comply with EU-adopted IFRS. This is because an accounting framework that allows such reduced disclosures cannot be described as EU-adopted IFRS. UK companies and other entities that prepare financial statements in accordance with Part 15 of CA 2006 under FRS 101 prepare Companies Act individual accounts as defined in s395(1)(a) of the Companies Act. Those entities must comply with the Companies Act and The Large and Medium-sized Companies and Groups (Accounts and Reports) Regulations 2008 ('the Regulations'). This means that financial statements prepared under FRS 101 are subject to different CA 2006 requirements than financial statements prepared under EU-adopted IFRS which are IAS accounts prepared under s395(1)(b) of the CA 2006.

1.1   Summary of FRS 101

Application of FRS 101 can be summarised as follows:

- Adoption of FRS 101 is voluntary.

- FRS 101 can only be applied in individual financial statements (see 2 below).

- FRS 101 can only be applied by a 'qualifying entity' (see 2.1 below).

- Approval of shareholders must be obtained in order to use FRS 101 (see 2.2 below).

- Entities can transition to FRS 101 from either UK GAAP or IFRS (see 3 below).

- Entities using FRS 101 apply the recognition and measurement principles of EU-adopted IFRS, except as amended by this standard (see 4 below).

- Entities using FRS 101 must prepare a balance sheet and profit and loss account section of the statement of comprehensive income in accordance with the Regulations (see 5 below).

- Entities using FRS 101 can take advantage of various disclosure exemptions from EU-adopted IFRS. Entities defined as 'financial institutions' have fewer exemptions than entities that are not financial institutions. Some of these disclosure exemptions are conditional on equivalent disclosures being included in the publicly available consolidated financial statements of a parent of the entity which are intended to give a true and fair view and in which the entity is consolidated (see 6 below).

- In addition to IFRS disclosures, entities using FRS 101 must comply with disclosures required by Company Law and the Regulations if subject to those requirements (see 7 below).

1.2   Effective date of FRS 101

FRS 101 was issued originally on 22 November 2012. The FRC reviews FRS 101 annually to ensure that the reduced disclosure framework maintains consistency with

EU-adopted IFRS. In addition, FRS 101 also requires limited other amendments for compliance with company law following the implementation of the new Accounting Directive. So far, amended versions of FRS 101 have been issued in August 2014 (reflecting the July 2014 amendments discussed at 1.2.1 below) and September 2015 (reflecting the July 2015 amendments discussed at 1.2.2 below), respectively.

A qualifying entity (see 2.1 below) may apply FRS 101 for accounting periods beginning on or after 1 January 2015. FRS 101 can also be applied early. Entities that wish to transition to FRS 101 from UK GAAP or any other GAAP can do so in respect of any financial statements not issued as at 22 November 2012. If an entity applies FRS 101 before 1 January 2015, it shall disclose that fact. *[FRS 101.11]*.

Transitional rules and eligibility to adopt FRS 101 are discussed at 3 below.

1.2.1 Amendments to FRS 101 issued in July 2014

Amendments to FRS 101 Reduced Disclosure Framework (2013/14 Cycle) sets out changes to FRS 101 and its appendices for amendments made to:

- IFRS 10 – *Consolidated Financial Statements* – and IAS 27 – *Separate Financial Statements* – as a result of the IASB's project *Investment Entities (Amendments to IFRS 10, IFRS 12 and IAS 27)*; and

- IAS 36 – *Impairment of Assets* – as a result of the IASB's project *Recoverable Amount Disclosures for Non-Financial Assets (Amendment to IAS 36)*.

In addition, the amendments include a number of editorial changes to clarify the company law requirements applicable to UK companies applying FRS 101 that hold financial instruments at fair value subject to paragraph 36(4) of Schedule 1 to the Regulations.

These amendments had the same effective date as the original version of FRS 101 issued in November 2012 (i.e. accounting periods beginning on or after 1 January 2015) and early adoption is permitted to the extent that a qualifying entity can apply the underlying IFRSs (i.e. IFRS 10 and IAS 36). If a qualifying entity has adopted FRS 101 early, then the amendments in respect of IFRS 10 and IAS 36 must be applied for accounting periods beginning on or after 1 January 2014.

1.2.2 Amendments to FRS 101 issued in July 2015

Amendments to FRS 101 – Reduced Disclosure Framework 2014/15 cycle and other minor amendments sets out changes made to FRS 101 and its appendices to:

- provide exemptions in respect of disclosures required by paragraph 18A of IAS 24 – *Related Party Disclosures* – and the requirements of paragraphs 6 and 21 of IFRS 1 – *First-time Adoption of International Financial Reporting Standards* (see 6 below); and

- maintain consistency between FRS 101 and UK company law as a result of the new EU Accounting Directive – *Directive 2013/34/EU on the annual financial statements, consolidated financial statements and related reports of certain types of undertakings* – which has been implemented in the UK through *The Companies, Partnerships and Groups (Accounts and Reports) Regulations 2015 (SI 2015/980)* ('SI 2015/980').

The amendments relating to the disclosure exemptions in respect of IAS 24 and IFRS 1 must be applied for accounting periods beginning on or after 1 January 2015. Early application is permitted (i.e. the amendments can be applied to accounting periods beginning before 1 January 2015). *[FRS 101.12(a)]*.

The amendments arising for consistency with company law must be applied for accounting periods beginning on or after 1 January 2016. Early application is permitted for accounting periods beginning on or after 1 January 2015, (i.e. these amendments cannot be applied to accounting periods beginning before 1 January 2015 because SI 2015/980 prohibits such application). When these amendments are applied the SI 2015/980 is applied from the same date. Early application is also required if a qualifying entity applies SI 2015/980 to a reporting period beginning before 1 January 2016 (i.e. a qualifying entity cannot apply the changes resulting from SI 2015/980 without also applying the related changes made to FRS 101). *[FRS 101.12(b)]*.

If the amendments above are adopted early, an entity is required to disclose that fact. *[FRS 101.12(a)-(b)]*.

1.3   Statement of compliance with FRS 101

A set of financial statements prepared in accordance with FRS 101 must contain a statement in the notes to the financial statements that '*These financial statements were prepared in accordance with Financial Reporting Standard 101 "Reduced Disclosure Framework*"'. FRS 101 also clarifies that because FRS 101 does not comply with all of the requirements of EU-adopted IFRS it shall not therefore contain the unreserved statement of compliance referred to in paragraph 3 of IFRS 1 and otherwise required by paragraph 16 of IAS 1 – *Presentation of Financial Statements.* *[FRS 101.10]*.

2   SCOPE OF FRS 101

FRS 101 may be applied to the individual financial statements of a 'qualifying entity' (see 2.1 below), that are intended to give a true and fair view of the assets, liabilities, financial position and profit or loss for a period. *[FRS 101.2]*.

Individual financial statements to which FRS 101 applies are individual accounts as set out in s394 of the Companies Act or as set out in s72A of the Building Societies Act 1986. Separate financial statements, as defined by IAS 27, are included in the meaning of the term individual financial statements. *[FRS 101.Appendix I]*.

This means that FRS 101 can be used in:

- individual financial statements of subsidiaries;
- separate financial statements of an intermediate parent which does not prepare consolidated financial statements; and
- separate financial statements of a parent which does prepare consolidated financial statements.

However, the entity applying FRS 101 must be included in a set of consolidated financial statements intended to give a true and fair view (see 2.1.6 below).

A parent that prepares consolidated financial statements but applies FRS 101 in its separate financial statements can also use the exemption in s408 of the Companies Act from presenting a profit and loss account and related notes in the individual financial statements, as well as taking advantage of the reduced disclosures from EU-adopted IFRS.

FRS 101 cannot be applied in consolidated financial statements even if the entity preparing consolidated financial statements is a qualifying entity. *[FRS 101.3]*.

Financial statements prepared by qualifying entities in accordance with FRS 101 are not accounts prepared in accordance with EU-adopted IFRS. A qualifying entity must ensure it complies with any relevant legal requirements applicable to it. Therefore, individual financial statements prepared by UK companies in accordance with FRS 101 are Companies Act accounts rather than IAS accounts as set out in section 395(1) of the Companies Act. Accordingly, UK companies that apply FRS 101 must comply with the Regulations including the rules on recognition and measurement, the Companies Act accounts formats and note disclosures. *[FRS 101.4A]*. SI 2015/980, when adopted, has modified the requirements of the CA 2006 and the Regulations in certain respects. The presentation requirements of the Regulations, including the requirements modified as a result of SI 2015/980, are discussed in Chapter 4 – *Presentation of financial statements*.

In order to ensure that financial statements prepared in accordance with FRS 101 comply with the Companies Act and the Regulations, some limited recognition, measurement and presentational changes have been made by FRS 101 to EU-adopted IFRS. FRS 101 iterates that, for the avoidance of doubt, the amendments set out in paragraph AG1 of the Application guidance to FRS 101 are an integral part of the standard and necessary to remove conflicts between EU-adopted IFRS and the Companies Act and the Regulations. These amendments to EU-adopted IFRS are applicable to any qualifying entity applying FRS 101 not just to UK companies. *[FRS 101.5(b)]*. These amendments are discussed at 4 and 5 below.

FRS 101 does not permit the company law formats included in Part 1 'General Rules and Formats' of the Small Companies Regulations applicable to small companies to be applied. However, our view is that companies subject to the Small Companies regime can still apply FRS 101, and, in doing so, are not prevented from taking advantage of other Companies Act exemptions applicable to companies subject to the Small Companies Regime. Likewise, medium-sized entities applying FRS 101 can still take advantage of applicable CA 2006 disclosure exemptions for medium-sized entities.

A charity may not be a qualifying entity and therefore may not apply FRS 101. *[FRS 101.Appendix I]*.

2.1   Definition of a qualifying entity

FRS 101 defines a qualifying entity as 'a member of a group where the parent of that group prepares publicly available consolidated financial statements, which are intended to give a true and fair view (of the assets, liabilities, financial position and profit or loss) and that member is included in the consolidation'. *[FRS 101.Appendix I]*.

There is no requirement that a qualifying entity is a member of the group in which it is consolidated for its entire reporting period. The use of the present tense implies that the intention is only that the qualifying entity is a subsidiary of the parent at its reporting date. This is consistent with UK company law which requires that an entity which is a parent at the end of a financial year must prepare group accounts unless it is exempted from the requirement. *[s399(2)]*.

The phrase 'included in the consolidation' is referenced to s474(1) of the Companies Act which means that 'the undertaking is included in the accounts by the method of full (and not proportional) consolidation and references to an undertaking excluded from consolidation shall be construed accordingly'. Therefore, entities that are not fully consolidated in the group financial statements, such as subsidiaries of investment entities which are accounted for at fair value through profit and loss as allowed by IFRS 10, cannot use FRS 101. Associates and joint ventures are not qualifying entities.

2.1.1   *Reporting date of the consolidated financial statements of the parent*

The requirement for the qualifying entity to be included in the consolidation implies that the consolidated financial statements of the parent must be approved before, or at the same time as, the FRS 101 individual financial statements of the qualifying entity are approved. FRS 101 is silent on whether the reporting date and period of those consolidated financial statements has to be identical to that of the qualifying entity. In contrast, both s400 and s401 of the Companies Act require that the exemption from preparing group accounts for a parent that is a subsidiary is conditional on the inclusion of the subsidiary in the consolidated financial statements of the parent drawn up to the same date or to an earlier date in the same financial year. It would seem logical that the reporting date criteria in s400 and s401 should also be used for FRS 101.

However, when the consolidated financial statements are prepared as at an earlier date than the date of the qualifying entity's financial statements, some of the disclosure exemptions may not be available to the qualifying entity because the consolidated financial statements may not contain the 'equivalent' disclosures (see 6.2 below).

2.1.2   *Definition of group and subsidiary*

The definition of a qualifying entity contains a footnote that refers to s474(1) of the Companies Act which defines a 'group' as 'a parent undertaking and its subsidiary undertakings'. EU-adopted IFRS defines a group as 'a parent and its subsidiaries'. *[IFRS 10.Appendix A, s474(1)]*.

EU-adopted IFRS defines a parent as 'an entity that controls one or more entities' and a subsidiary as 'an entity that is controlled by another entity'. *[IFRS 10.Appendix A]*.

The Companies Act states that an undertaking is a parent undertaking in relation to another undertaking, a subsidiary undertaking, if:

(a)   it holds a majority of the voting rights in the undertaking; or

(b)   it is a member of the undertaking and has the right to appoint or remove a majority of its board of directors; or

(c)   it has the right to exercise a dominant influence over the undertaking by virtue of provisions in the undertaking's articles or by virtue of a control contract; or

(d)   it is a member of the undertaking and controls alone, pursuant to an agreement with other shareholders or members, a majority of the voting rights in the undertaking.

An undertaking is also a parent undertaking in relation to another undertaking, a subsidiary undertaking, if it has the power to exercise, or actually exercises, dominant control or influence over it, or it and the subsidiary undertaking are managed on a unified basis.

A parent undertaking shall be treated as the parent undertaking of undertakings in relation to which any of its subsidiary undertakings are, or are to be treated as, parent undertakings; and references to its subsidiary undertakings shall be construed accordingly. *[s1162]*.

These differences in definition make it possible for an entity to be a subsidiary undertaking under the Companies Act but not under EU-adopted IFRS, for example an entity in which a parent owns a majority of the voting rights but does not have control over the subsidiary. However, the key issue for the application of FRS 101 is whether the subsidiary is included in the consolidation of the parent's consolidated financial statements. A company that meets the definition of a subsidiary undertaking under the Companies Act but is not included in the consolidation of the consolidated financial statements of its parent cannot apply FRS 101.

2.1.3   Publicly available consolidated financial statements

By 'publicly available', we believe that FRS 101 requires that the consolidated financial statements can be accessed by the public as the use of the EU-adopted IFRS disclosure exemptions is conditional on a disclosure by the qualifying entity indicating from where those consolidated financial statements can be obtained (see 2.2 below). This does not mandate that the consolidated financial statements must be filed with a regulator. However, it does mean that UK consolidated financial statements that have not been filed with the Registrar of Companies, at the date the subsidiary's financial statements prepared in accordance with FRS 101 are approved, must be publicly available via some other medium.

2.1.4   Non-UK qualifying entities

There is no requirement that a qualifying entity is a UK entity. Therefore, overseas entities can apply FRS 101 in their individual or separate financial statements subject to meeting the criteria and subject to FRS 101 being allowed in their own jurisdiction.

There is also no requirement that the parent that prepares publicly available consolidated financial statements, in which the qualifying entity is included, is a UK parent (see 2.1.6 below).

2.1.5   Non-controlling interests

There is no ownership threshold for a subsidiary to apply FRS 101. Therefore, a qualifying entity can apply FRS 101 even if its parent holds less than a majority of

Chapter 2

the voting rights. However, other shareholders are permitted to object to the use of FRS 101 (see 2.2 below).

2.1.6   *Intended to give a true and fair view*

In the definition of a qualifying entity (see 2.1 above), the consolidated financial statements in which the qualifying entity is included are not required to give an explicit true and fair view of the assets, liabilities, financial position and profit or loss. Rather, they are '*intended* to give a true and fair view' (our emphasis). This means that the consolidated financial statements in which the qualifying entity is consolidated need not contain an explicit opinion that they give a 'true and fair view' (for example, US GAAP financial statements do not have such an opinion) but, in substance, they should be intended to give such a view. The FRC obtained a Queen's Counsel's (QC) opinion in 2008 which stated that 'the requirement set out in international accounting standards to present fairly is not a different requirement to that of showing a true and fair view but is a different articulation of the same concept'.[1]

In our view, a set of consolidated financial statements drawn up in a manner equivalent to consolidated financial statements that are in accordance with the Accounting Directive (i.e. a set of consolidated financial statements that meets the 'equivalence' test of s401 of the Companies Act) is intended to give a true and fair view. The Application Guidance to FRS 100 states that consolidated financial statements of a higher parent will meet the exemption or the test of equivalence in the Accounting Directive if they are intended to give a true and fair view and:

- are prepared in accordance with FRS 102;
- are prepared in accordance with EU-adopted IFRS;
- are prepared in accordance with IFRS, subject to the consideration of the reasons for any failure by the European Commission to adopt a standard or interpretation; or
- are prepared using other GAAPs which are closely related to IFRS, subject to the consideration of the effect of any differences from EU-adopted IFRS.

Consolidated financial statements of the higher parent prepared using other GAAPs or the IFRS for SMEs should be assessed for equivalence with the Accounting Directive based on the particular facts, including the similarities to and differences from the Accounting Directive. *[FRS 100.AG6]*.

The EU established a mechanism to determine the equivalence to IFRS of GAAP from other countries in 2007. Subsequently, the EU Commission has identified the following as equivalent to IFRS: *[FRS 100.AG7]*

Equivalent GAAP	*Applicable From*
GAAP of Japan	1 January 2009
GAAP of the United States of America	I January 2009
GAAP of the People's Republic of China	1 January 2012
GAAP of Canada	1 January 2012
GAAP of the Republic of Korea	1 January 2012

In addition, third country issuers were permitted to prepare their annual consolidated financial statements and half-yearly consolidated financial statements in accordance with the Generally Accepted Accounting Principles of the Republic of India for financial years starting before 1 January 2015. For reporting periods beginning on or after 1 January 2015, in relation to GAAP of the Republic of India, equivalence should be assessed on the basis of the particular facts. *[FRS 100.AG7]*.

In theory, there is no reason why consolidated financial statements of a parent prepared under a GAAP that is not 'equivalent' to the Accounting Directive cannot be used provided those consolidated financial statements in which the entity is included are publicly available and are intended to give a true and fair view.

However, a parent company that wishes to claim an exemption from preparing consolidated accounts under either s400 or s401 of the Companies Act must be a subsidiary of a parent that prepares consolidated accounts in accordance with the provisions of the Accounting Directive or in a manner so equivalent. *[s400(2)(b), s401(2)(b)]*.

In addition, a number of the disclosure exemptions from EU-adopted IFRS in FRS 101 are conditional on 'equivalent' disclosures being made in those consolidated financial statements. Where the equivalent disclosure is not made, the relevant disclosure exemptions cannot be applied in the qualifying entity's financial statements prepared under FRS 101 (see 6.2 below). A GAAP that is not 'equivalent' to the Accounting Directive is less likely to have those 'equivalent' disclosures.

One issue not addressed by FRS 101 is the impact of a qualified audit opinion on the parent's consolidated financial statements on a qualifying entity's ability to use FRS 101. The QC's opinion obtained by the FRC in 2008 stated that 'the scope for arguing that financial statements which do not comply with relevant accounting standards nevertheless give a true and fair view is very limited'.[2]

2.2 Use of the disclosure exemptions

The use of the disclosure exemptions in FRS 101 (see 6 below) is conditional on all of the following criteria being met:

* the shareholders have been notified in writing about the use of the disclosure exemptions;

* the shareholders have not objected to the use of the disclosure exemptions;

* the reporting entity applies the recognition, measurement and disclosure requirements of EU-adopted IFRS but makes amendments to those requirements where necessary in order to comply with the Companies Act and the Regulations because the financial statements it prepares are Companies Act individual accounts as defined in s395(1) of the Companies Act (see 4 below);

* the reporting entity discloses in the notes to its financial statements a brief narrative summary of the disclosure exemptions adopted; and

* the reporting entity discloses the name of the parent of the group in whose consolidated financial statements its financial statements are consolidated and from where those financial statements may be obtained. *[FRS 101.5]*.

FRS 101 does not state whether the requirement of the reporting entity to notify its shareholders about the use of the disclosure exemptions is an annual requirement or whether a more open-ended notification can be provided. In addition, no timescale is mentioned. Therefore, there is no requirement that notification occurs in the period covered by the financial statements; it could be earlier or later. It is also not clear what an entity should do in the event of changes in its shareholders (i.e. whether new shareholders must be notified separately). In the absence of clear guidance, we would recommend that entities obtain legal advice as to the form in which they should notify shareholders of their intention to use FRS 101.

Objections to the use of FRS 101's disclosure exemptions may be served on the qualifying entity in accordance with reasonable specified timeframes and format requirements by a shareholder that is the immediate parent of the entity, or by a shareholder or shareholders holding in aggregate 5% or more of the allotted shares in the entity or more than half of the allotted shares in the entity that are not held by the immediate parent. *[FRS 101.5(a)]*. FRS 101 does not explain what is meant by 'reasonable specified timeframes and format requirements' in respect of any shareholder objection. Entities may wish to obtain legal advice as to what 'reasonable specified timeframes and format requirements' should be contained in any notice provided to shareholders.

An objection by a shareholder or shareholders holding in aggregate 5% or more of the total allotted shares or more than half of the allotted shares that are not held by the immediate parent (which could be less than 5% of the total allotted shares) automatically means that FRS 101 cannot be applied by the entity. A shareholder is not required to supply a reason for any objection.

2.3   The impact of s400 and s401 of the Companies Act on FRS 101

FRS 101 does not override either s400 or s401 of the Companies Act. Section 400 exempts a UK parent company from preparing consolidated accounts if it is a subsidiary undertaking and is included in the consolidated accounts of a larger group drawn up to the same date, or to an earlier date in the same financial year, by a parent undertaking established under the law of an EEA State. Section 401 exempts a UK parent company from preparing consolidated accounts if it is a subsidiary undertaking of a parent undertaking *not* established under the law of an EEA State and is included in the consolidated accounts of a larger group drawn up to the same date, or to an earlier date in the same financial year, by that parent undertaking. The exemptions from preparing consolidated accounts in both s400 and s401 are subject to various conditions including 'equivalence' (in respect of s401) which is discussed at 2.1.6 above. The detailed conditions for the above exemptions from preparing group accounts under the CA 2006 are discussed further in Chapter 6 at 3.1.1 of EY New UK GAAP 2015 as supplemented by Chapter 5 at 2 of this publication.

If a UK parent company does not meet all of the conditions set out in either s400 or s401 (and is not otherwise exempt under the Companies Act) then it must prepare consolidated financial statements. Such consolidated financial statements cannot be prepared under FRS 101. However, the parent entity could still prepare its individual financial statements under FRS 101.

2.4   Interim financial statements

FRS 101 does not address the preparation of interim financial statements. However, entities applying FRS 101 to annual financial statements may use FRS 104 – *Interim Financial Reporting* – as a basis for their interim financial reports. FRS 104 is discussed in Chapter 6.

3   TRANSITION TO FRS 101

An entity can transition to FRS 101 from either EU-adopted IFRS or another form of GAAP (e.g. another form of UK GAAP). In this context, another form of UK GAAP means either FRS 102, the FRSSE (for accounting periods beginning before 1 January 2016), FRS 105 or previous UK GAAP.

FRS 101 is adopted in the first accounting period for which a reporting entity has notified its shareholders in writing about the use of the disclosure exemptions (see 2.2 above). When this occurs, the date of transition to FRS 101 is the beginning of the earliest period for which an entity presents full comparative information under a given standard in its first financial statements that comply with that standard, e.g. 1 January 2014 for an entity with a 31 December year-end adopting FRS 101 in its 2015 financial statements. *[FRS 100.Appendix I].*

3.1   Companies Act restrictions on changes to FRS 101

Under the Companies Act, a company that wishes to change from preparing IAS individual accounts to preparing individual accounts under FRS 101 may do so either:

- if there is a 'relevant change of circumstance' as defined in s395(4) of the Companies Act; or
- for financial years ending on or after 1 October 2012, for a reason other than a relevant change of circumstance, once in a five year period. *[FRS 100.A2.14].*

There is no restriction on the number of times an entity can move from Companies Act accounts to IAS accounts or *vice versa*. Theoretically, an entity could 'flip' from IAS accounts to FRS 101 and back again several times without a 'relevant change in circumstance' provided such flips are done no more than once every five years and provided that the entity is also complying with the requirements of the Companies Act, such as those relating to consistency of financial reporting within groups (see 3.2 below).

There are no Companies Act restrictions on a change from FRS 102, FRS 105 or the FRSSE (for accounting periods beginning before 1 January 2016) to FRS 101 and back again or *vice versa* since these are all Companies Act accounts.

3.2   Consistency of financial statements within the group

The Companies Act requires that the directors of a UK parent company secure that the individual accounts of the parent company and of each of its subsidiary undertakings are prepared under the same financial reporting framework, be it IAS accounts or Companies Act accounts, except to the extent that in the directors' opinion there are good reasons for not doing so. *[s407(1)]*. However, this rule does not apply:

- if the parent company does not prepare group accounts; *[s407(2)]*

- if the accounts of the subsidiary undertaking are not required to be prepared under Part 15 of the Companies Act (for example foreign subsidiary undertakings); *[s407(3)]* or

- to any subsidiary undertakings that are charities (charities and non-charities within a group are not required to use the same accounting framework). *[s407(4)]*. This is because charities are not permitted to prepare either IAS group or individual accounts. *[s395(2), s403(3)]*.

Additionally, a parent company that prepares both consolidated and separate financial statements under EU-adopted IFRS (i.e. IAS group accounts and IAS individual accounts) is not required to ensure that its subsidiary undertakings all prepare IAS individual accounts. However, it must ensure that its subsidiary undertakings use the same accounting framework in their individual accounts unless there are good reasons for not doing so. *[s407(5)]*.

Therefore, a group that decides to use FRS 101 for any of its qualifying subsidiaries, must ensure, unless there are good reasons for not doing so, that all UK subsidiaries prepare Companies Act individual accounts (i.e. the same financial reporting framework). Although not explicitly stated by FRS 100, there appears to be no requirement that all subsidiaries in a group must use FRS 101 for their Companies Act individual accounts. Some subsidiaries could also use FRS 102, the FRSSE (for accounting periods beginning before 1 January 2016) or FRS 105, since these are all Companies Act individual accounts and therefore they are all under the the same financial reporting framework. However, while this approach would comply with the statutory requirements, groups that use a 'mix' of GAAP in the individual financial statements may be challenged by HMRC, particularly if this results in tax arbitrage.

Examples of 'good reasons' for not preparing all individual accounts within a group using the same reporting framework are contained in the document *Guidance for UK Companies on Accounting and Reporting: Requirements under the Companies Act 2006 and the application of the IAS regulation* issued by the Department for Business Enterprise and Regulatory Reform (BERR) in June 2008.

3.3   Transition from EU-adopted IFRS to FRS 101

In substance, the transition requirements for entities that have been applying EU-adopted IFRS prior to conversion to FRS 101 treat the qualifying entity as not having changed its financial reporting framework. Disclosure is required only where changes are made on transition, because FRS 101 modifies EU-adopted IFRS in certain respects, in order to comply with the Companies Act and the Regulations.

A qualifying entity that is applying EU-adopted IFRS at the date of transition to FRS 101 must consider whether amendments are required to comply with paragraph 5(b) of FRS 101 – see 4 and 5 below – but it does not reapply the provisions of IFRS 1. Where amendments in accordance with paragraph 5(b) of FRS 101 are required, the entity shall determine whether the amendments have a material effect on the first FRS 101 financial statements presented. *[FRS 100.12]*. Details of measurement differences between EU-adopted IFRS and FRS 101 which might result in a material effect on the financial statements are discussed at 4 below.

Where there is no material effect of such changes, the qualifying entity shall disclose that it has undergone transition to FRS 101 and give a brief narrative of the disclosure exemptions taken for all periods presented in the financial statements. *[FRS 100.12(a)]*.

Where there is a material effect caused by such changes, the qualifying entity's first FRS 101 financial statements shall include:

- a description of the nature of each material change in accounting policy;

- reconciliations of its equity determined in accordance with EU-adopted IFRS to its equity determined in accordance with FRS 101 for both the date of transition to FRS 101 and for the end of the latest period presented in the entity's most recent annual financial statements prepared in accordance with EU-adopted IFRS; and

- a reconciliation of the profit or loss determined in accordance with EU-adopted IFRS to the profit or loss determined in accordance with FRS 101 for the latest period presented in the entity's most recent annual financial statements prepared in accordance with EU-adopted IFRS. *[FRS 100.12(b)]*.

This means that, for an entity adopting FRS 101 for the first time in its annual financial statements ending on 31 December 2015 (and presenting one comparative period), reconciliations will be required of:

- equity as at 1 January 2014 and 31 December 2014; and

- profit or loss for the year ended 31 December 2014.

There is no requirement for a transition balance sheet to be prepared presumably on the grounds that IFRS 1 is not being reapplied.

Material amendments must be applied retrospectively on transition unless impracticable. Where a retrospective amendment is impracticable, the qualifying entity shall apply the amendment to the earliest period for which it is practicable to do so and it shall identify the data presented for prior periods that are not comparable with the data for the period for which it prepares its first financial statements that conform to FRS 101. *[FRS 100.13]*. 'Impracticable' is defined in IAS 8 – *Accounting Policies, Changes in Accounting Estimates and Errors.*

Paragraph 5(b) of FRS 101 cross-refers to application guidance that includes presentational changes to the financial statements as well as corresponding amendments due to recognition and measurement differences. The transitional rules contain no explicit requirement to disclose material presentational changes such as the use of balance sheet and profit and loss formats in accordance with the Regulations. However, we recommend that entities explain any material presentational changes compared to EU-adopted IFRS arising from adoption of FRS 101 in order to assist readers' understanding of the financial statements.

Chapter 2

3.4   Transition from another version of UK GAAP or another GAAP to FRS 101

In substance, the transition requirements treat conversion to FRS 101 from another version of UK GAAP (FRS 102, the FRSSE, FRS 105 or previous UK GAAP) or another GAAP as a full first time conversion to EU-adopted IFRS (as modified by FRS 101).

A qualifying entity that transitions to FRS 101 shall, unless it is applying EU-adopted IFRS prior to the date of transition (see 3.3 above), apply the requirements of paragraphs 6 to 33 of IFRS 1 including the relevant appendices, except for the requirement of paragraphs 6 and 21 to present an opening statement of financial position at the date of transition. *[FRS 100.11(b)]*. This means that all of the recognition, measurement and disclosure rules for an IFRS first-time adopter apply (except for the requirement to present an opening statement of financial position) to the extent they do not conflict with EU-adopted IFRS as amended by paragraph 5(b) of FRS 101. First-time adoption of IFRS is discussed in Chapter 5 of EY International GAAP 2016.

IFRS 1 sets out requirements for where a subsidiary becomes a first-time adopter later than its parent or where a parent becomes a first-time adopter later than its subsidiary (or it becomes a first-time adopter in its separate financial statements earlier or later than in its consolidated financial statements).

IFRS 1 permits a subsidiary that becomes a first-time adopter later than its parent to measure its assets and liabilities at either the carrying amounts required by IFRS 1, based on the subsidiary's date of transition, or the carrying amounts that would be included in the parent's consolidated financial statements, based on the parent's date of transition if no adjustments were to be made for the effects of consolidation procedures or the business combination in which the parent acquired the subsidiary (the D16 election). There is a similar election available for an associate or joint venture that becomes a first-time adopter later than an entity that has significant influence or joint control over it. *[IFRS 1.D16]*.

When an entity becomes a first-time adopter later than its subsidiary it shall, in the consolidated financial statements, measure the assets and liabilities of the subsidiary after adjusting for consolidation and equity accounting adjustments and for the effects of the business combination in which the entity acquired the subsidiary. Similarly, if a parent becomes a first-time adopter for its separate financial statements earlier or later than for its consolidated financial statements, it shall measure its assets and liabilities at the same amounts in both financial statements, except for consolidation adjustments (the D17 requirements). *[IFRS 1.D17]*.

Although FRS 101 retains the D16 election and the D17 requirements, the qualifying entity must ensure it measures its assets and liabilities in accordance with FRS 101 (where application of these paragraphs conflicts with EU-adopted IFRS). *[FRS 101.AG1(a)-(b)]*.

3.5   The impact of transition on realised profits

There may be circumstances where a conversion to FRS 101 eliminates a qualifying entity's realised profits or turns those realised profits into a realised loss. TECH 02/10 *– Guidance on the Determination of Realised Profits and Losses in the Context of*

Distributions under the Companies Act 2006 issued by the ICAEW and ICAS, states that the change in the treatment of a retained profit or loss as a result of a change in the law or in accounting standards or interpretations would not render unlawful a distribution already made out of realised profits determined by reference to 'relevant accounts' which had been prepared in accordance with generally acceptable accounting principles applicable to those accounts. This is because the Companies Act defines realised profits or losses for determining the lawfulness of a distribution as 'such profits and loss of the company as fall to be treated as realised in accordance with principles generally accepted at the time when the accounts are prepared, with respect to the determination for accounting purposes of realised profits or losses'.[3]

The effects of the introduction of a new accounting standard or on the adoption of IFRSs become relevant to the application of the common law capital maintenance rule only in relation to distributions accounted for in periods in which the change will first be recognised in the accounts. This means that a change in accounting policy known to be adopted in a financial year needs to be taken into account in determining the dividend to be approved by shareholders in that year. Therefore, for example, an entity converting to FRS 101 in 2015 must have regard to the effect of adoption of FRS 101 in respect of all dividends payable in 2015 (including any final dividends in respect of 2014) even though the 'relevant accounts' may still be those for 2014 prepared under another GAAP.[4]

4 MEASUREMENT DIFFERENCES BETWEEN FRS 101 AND EU-ADOPTED IFRS

As noted at 2 above, entities applying FRS 101 use EU-adopted IFRS as amended by the standard in order to comply with the Companies Act and the Regulations. This is because financial statements prepared under FRS 101 are Companies Act individual accounts and not IAS individual accounts. There are several conflicts between the recognition and measurement rules of EU-adopted IFRS and those required by the Regulations. Consequently, entities applying FRS 101 apply a modified version of EU-adopted IFRS designed to eliminate these differences.

FRS 101 changes EU-adopted IFRS in respect of the following matters:

- negative goodwill (see 4.2 below);
- reversal of goodwill impairments (see 4.3 below);
- contingent consideration balances arising from business combinations (see 4.4 below);
- government grants deducted from the cost of fixed assets (see 4.5 below);
- provisions, contingent assets and contingent liabilities (see 4.6 below);
- realised profits (see 4.7 below);
- equalisation provisions (see 4.8 below);
- investments in subsidiaries, associates and joint ventures (see 4.9 below);
- investment entities (see 4.10 below); and
- limited liability partnerships (LLPs) (see 4.11 below).

4.1   Positive goodwill and indefinite-life intangible assets

No changes have been made to EU-adopted IFRS in respect of positive goodwill that is not amortised. Instead, FRS 101 states that paragraph B63(a) of IFRS 3 – *Business Combinations*, which requires that goodwill is measured at cost less impairment, should be read in accordance with paragraph A2.8 of FRS 101. *[FRS 101.AG1(f)]*. The non-amortisation of goodwill required by IFRS 3 conflicts with paragraph 22 of Schedule 1 to the Regulations (and its equivalents in Schedules 2 and 3) which requires that an intangible asset (including goodwill) must be written off over its useful economic life.

Paragraph A2.8 of FRS 101 notes that the non-amortisation of goodwill will usually be a departure, for the overriding purpose of giving a true and fair view, from the requirements of the Regulations. FRS 101 goes on to state that this is not a new instance of the use of the 'true and fair override' and it would have been required for companies reporting under previous UK GAAP which used an indefinite life for goodwill as permitted by FRS 10 – *Goodwill and intangible assets. [FRS 101.A2.8]*. This means that the FRC expects that entities with positive goodwill should continue not to amortise that goodwill. Those entities should invoke a true and fair override as permitted by paragraph 10(2) of Schedule 1 to the Regulations (or its equivalents in Schedules 2 and 3) to overcome the prohibition on amortisation of goodwill required by paragraph 22 of Schedule 1 to the Regulations. The use of the true and fair override would require disclosure of the particulars of the departure from the Regulations, the reasons for it and its effect. *[1 Sch 10(2)]*. Continuation of goodwill amortisation, if permitted under previous GAAP, is not allowed by FRS 101.

It is anticipated that the use of a true and fair override in respect of goodwill amortisation will be limited in application since, in individual financial statements, there will only be goodwill where a business that is not an entity has been acquired.

FRS 101 goes on to state that similar considerations (i.e. the need for a true and fair override) may apply to other intangible assets that are not amortised because they have an indefinite life and intangible assets that have a residual value that is not zero (i.e. intangible assets that are not written off over their useful economic life). *[FRS 101.A2.8A]*.

As FRS 101 specifically amends EU-adopted IFRS to alter the accounting for the matters discussed at 4.2 to 4.11 below, to remove conflicts identified between EU-adopted IFRS and the Regulations, the issue of invoking a 'true and fair override' does not arise in respect of these matters.

4.2   Negative goodwill

FRS 101 changes paragraph 34 of IFRS 3 so that any gain arising from a bargain purchase (i.e. negative goodwill) is not recognised immediately in profit and loss. Instead, any amount of the negative goodwill up to the fair values of the non-monetary assets acquired should be recognised in profit and loss in the periods in which the non-monetary assets are recovered, whether through depreciation or sale.

Any amount of the negative goodwill in excess of the fair values of the non-monetary assets acquired should be recognised in profit or loss in the periods expected to be benefited. *[FRS 101.AG1(c)].*

This change to EU-adopted IFRS was necessary because the Accounting Directive (on which the requirements in the Regulations are based) may be inconsistent with the recognition requirements for negative goodwill under EU-adopted IFRS. *[FRS 101.A2 Table 1].*

Monetary assets are defined in EU-adopted IFRS as 'money held and assets to be received in fixed or determinable amounts of money'. *[IAS 38.8].* Conversely, an essential feature of a non-monetary asset is the absence of a right to receive a fixed or determinable number of units of currency. IAS 21 – *The Effects of Changes in Foreign Exchange Rates* – gives examples of non-monetary assets as amounts prepaid for goods and services, goodwill, intangible assets, inventories and property, plant and equipment. *[IAS 21.16].* IAS 39 – *Financial Instruments: Recognition and Measurement* – indicates (and IFRS 9 – *Financial Instruments* – states) that investments in equity instruments are non-monetary items. *[IAS 39.AG83, IFRS 9.B5.7.3].* This suggests that equity investments in subsidiaries, associates or joint ventures are also non-monetary items.

Negative goodwill must be presented in the statement of financial position immediately below goodwill and followed by a subtotal showing the net amount of the goodwill assets and the excess. The excess shall be attributed to the acquirer. *[FRS 101.AG1(c)].*

4.3   Reversal of goodwill impairments

Prior to the July 2015 amendments, FRS 101 changed paragraph 124 of IAS 36 to permit a goodwill impairment loss to be reversed in a subsequent period if, and only if, the reasons for the impairment loss have ceased to apply. *[FRS 101(2014).AG1(s)].* EU-adopted IFRS does not permit the reversal of a goodwill impairment. This change to EU-adopted IFRS was necessary because the Regulations required the reversal of a provision for diminution in value of a fixed asset, if the reason for the provision has ceased to exist. *[FRS 101(2014).A 2 Table 1].*

The new Accounting Directive prohibits the reversal of a goodwill impairment loss and hence the amendments to FRS 101 have deleted the original paragraph AG1(s) and aligned the accounting for reversal of goodwill impairment under FRS 101 with IFRS.

4.4   Contingent consideration balances arising from business combinations

Prior to the July 2015 amendments, FRS 101 required that an adjustment to the cost of a business combination contingent on future events be recognised only if the estimated amount of the adjustment was probable and could be measured reliably. If the potential adjustment was not recognised at the acquisition date but subsequently became probable and could be measured reliably, the additional consideration was treated as an adjustment to the cost of the combination (i.e. goodwill).

Chapter 2

The new Accounting Directive now permits measurement of contingent consideration at fair value because it allows measurement of certain financial instruments at fair value where it is in accordance with EU-adopted IFRS; previously this was restricted to IFRS adopted on or before 5 September 2006. Consequently, the July 2015 amendments to FRS 101 state that contingent consideration balances arising from business combinations whose acquisition dates preceded the date when an entity first applies the amendments to company law set out in the SI 2015/980 (i.e. usually the start of accounting periods beginning on or after 1 January 2016 when SI 2015/980 has not been early adopted) shall not be adjusted as a result of the change in company law. Instead, the entity's previous accounting policies for contingent consideration shall continue to apply.

Contingent consideration balances arising from business combinations whose acquisition dates are on or after the date an entity first applies the amendments to company law set out in SI 2015/980, shall be accounted for in accordance with IFRS 3 (i.e. initially recognised at fair value with subsequent changes in the fair value of any liabilities recognised in profit or loss). *[FRS 101.AG1(d)].*

The accounting impact of these requirements on an entity – assuming it has contingent consideration balances arising from business combinations - will depend on the previous GAAP used by the entity (before conversion to FRS 101), the date at which the entity converted from previous GAAP to FRS 101 and the date that the entity first applies SI 2015/980. Therefore:

- a UK company that adopts FRS 101 before applying SI 2015/980 will apply the old rules in FRS 101 until SI 2015/980 is applied. Once SI 2015/980 is applied, the IFRS 3 requirements on contingent consideration will apply prospectively to business combinations from the beginning of the accounting period in which SI 2015/980 is first applied;

- a UK company that adopts the FRS 101 July 2015 amendments and SI 2015/980 at the same time and did not previously apply FRS 101 (e.g. a company that early-adopted the July 2015 amendments in the first year in which it applied FRS 101) will apply the IFRS 3 requirements on contingent consideration from the date of transition to FRS 101 and apply the transitional rules for business combinations prior to transition in IFRS 1.

The situation for entities that do not apply SI 2015/980 (e.g. overseas entities) is less clear but the intention appears to be that these entities will apply the old rules until such time as they adopt the July 2015 amendments.

FRS 101 is silent on accounting for contingent consideration on the acquisition of a subsidiary, associate or joint venture which is accounted for as an investment under IAS 27. However, in practice, if contingent consideration is included in the initial measurement of the asset, subsequent payments are either recognised in profit or loss or capitalised as part of the cost of the asset. We believe that, consistent with the view expressed in Chapter 8 of EY International GAAP 2016, until the Interpretations Committee or IASB issue further guidance, differing views remain about the circumstances in which, and to what extent, variable payments, such as contingent consideration should be recognised when initially recognising the underlying asset. There are also differing views about the extent to which subsequent changes should be recognised through profit or loss or capitalised as part of the cost of the asset. Where entities have made an accounting policy choice regarding recognition of contingent consideration and subsequent changes in accounting for the cost of investments in subsidiaries, associates or joint ventures in separate financial statements, the policy should be disclosed and consistently applied.

4.5   Government grants deducted from the cost of fixed assets

FRS 101 changes paragraph 28 of IAS 16 – *Property, Plant and Equipment* – and paragraphs 24 to 29 of IAS 20 – *Accounting for Government Grants and Disclosure of Government Assistance* – in order to eliminate the option in IFRS that permits a government grant relating to an asset to be deducted in arriving at the carrying amount of the asset. Consequently, all government grants related to assets must be presented in the financial statements by setting up the grant as deferred income and recognising the grant as deferred income in profit or loss on a systematic basis over the useful life of the asset. In addition, the option in paragraph 29 of IAS 20 that permits grants related to income to be deducted in reporting the related expense has been deleted. *[FRS 101.AG1(l)-(r)]*.

These changes to EU-adopted IFRS have been necessary because the Regulations prohibit off-setting of items that represent assets against items that represent liabilities unless specifically permitted or required. *[FRS 101.A2 Table 1]*.

SSAP 4 – *Accounting for Government Grants* – permitted entities to deduct a government grant from the purchase price or production cost of an asset where the grant was made as a contribution towards expenditure on that asset. This was despite the fact that this accounting was not permitted by the Regulations. *[SSAP 4.25]*. Consequently, under SSAP 4, some entities deducted government grants from the cost of assets and used a 'true and fair override' to overcome the prohibition in the Regulations. As FRS 101 has specifically amended EU-adopted IFRS to remove the option to reduce assets with the value of government grants, we do not consider that entities are permitted to use this accounting with a true and fair override under FRS 101 since the accounting standard does not permit this treatment.

4.6   Provisions, contingent assets and contingent liabilities

The July 2015 amendments to FRS 101 have amended paragraph 92 of IAS 37 – *Provisions, Contingent Liabilities and Contingent Assets* – to state that when disclosure of some or all of the information required by paragraphs 84-89 of IAS 37 can be expected to prejudice seriously the position of the entity in a dispute with other parties, the entity need not disclosure all of the information required by those paragraphs insofar as it relates to the dispute, but shall disclosure at least the following: *[FRS 101.AG1(s)]*

- in relation to provisions:
  - a table showing the reconciliation required by paragraph 84 in aggregate, including the source and application of any amounts transferred to or from provisions during the reporting period;

- particulars of each provision in any case where the amount of the provision is material; and
- the fact that, and reason why, the information required by paragraphs 84 and 85 has not been disclosed.

- in relation to contingent liabilities:
  - particulars and the total amount of contingent liabilities (excluding those which arise out of insurance contracts) that are not included in the statement of financial position;
  - the total amount of contingent liabilities which are undertaken on behalf of or for the benefit of:
    - any parent or fellow subsidiary of the entity;
    - any subsidiary of the entity;
    - any entity in which the reporting entity has a participating interest,

    shall each be stated separately; and
  - the fact that, and reason why, the information required by paragraph 86 has not been disclosed.

    In relation to contingent assets, the entity shall disclosure the general nature of the dispute, together with the fact that, and reason why, the information required by paragraph 89 has not been disclosed.

This amendment was made because the seriously prejudicial exemption in IAS 37 does not apply to disclosures required by Schedules 1-3 of the Regulations. Although this matter is implicitly covered by the paragraph 4A of FRS 101, which requires that the requirements of the Regulations must be complied with (see 2 above), the Accounting Council decided to specifically highlight this constraint on the IAS 37 exemption in a new paragraph. *[FRS 101.AC advice 2014/1015 cycle.35]*.

4.7   Realised profits under FRS 101

FRS 101 has changed paragraph 88 of IAS 1 to clarify the precedence of the Regulations over IFRS in this matter by adding the words 'or unless prohibited by the Act' after 'an entity shall recognise all items of income and expense arising in a period in profit or loss unless an IFRS requires or permits otherwise'. *[FRS 101.AG1(k)]*.

Paragraph 13(a) of Schedule 1 to the Regulations (and its equivalents in Schedules 2 and 3 and the LLP Regulations) require that only profits realised at the balance sheet date are included in the profit or loss account. *[FRS 101.A2.12]*. Paragraph 39 of Schedule 1 to the Regulations (and its equivalents in Schedules 2 and 3 and the LLP Regulations) allows stocks, investment property and living animals and plants to be held at fair value in Companies Act accounts. *[FRS 101.A2.13]*. Paragraph 40(2) of Schedule 1 to the Regulations (and its equivalents in Schedules 2 and 3 and the LLP Regulations) require that, in general, movements in the fair value of financial instruments, stocks, investment properties or living animals and plants are recognised in the profit and loss account notwithstanding the usual restrictions allowing only realised profits and losses to be included in the profit and loss account. Therefore, in the opinion of the FRC, paragraph 40 of Schedule 1 overrides paragraph 13(a) of Schedule 1 and such fair value gains can be recognised in profit and loss under FRS 101. *[FRS 101.A2.14]*.

The legal appendix to FRS 101 states that entities measuring investment properties, living animals or plants, or financial instruments at fair value may transfer such amounts to a separate non-distributable reserve instead of carrying them forward in retained earnings but are not required to do so. The FRC suggests that presenting fair value movements that are not distributable profits in a separate reserve may assist with the identification of profits available for that purpose. *[FRS 101.A2.15]*.

Whether profits are available for distribution must be determined in accordance with applicable law. Entities may also refer to TECH 02/10 to determine the profits available for distribution. *[FRS 101.A2.16]*.

4.8   Equalisation provisions

FRS 101 has changed paragraph 14(a) of IFRS 4 – *Insurance Contracts* – to insert the words 'unless otherwise required by the regulatory framework that applies to the entity' at the beginning of the sentence which prohibits the recognition of catastrophe provisions and equalisation provisions. In addition, the following sentence has been added to the end of the paragraph, 'the presentation of any such liabilities shall follow the requirements of the Regulations (or other legal framework that applies to the entity).' *[FRS 101.AG1.f(A)]*.

These amendments remove a conflict between IFRS 4 (which does not permit the recognition of equalisation and catastrophe provisions for claims that have not been incurred) and Schedule 3 of the Regulations (which requires the recognition of equalisation provisions as a liability). Consequently, equalisation provisions are recognised as a liability under FRS 101 when the Regulations require their recognition.

4.9   Investments in subsidiaries, associates and joint ventures

SI 2015/980 amends Schedule 1 of the Regulations to permit the use of equity accounting for participating interests (e.g. subsidiaries, associates and joint ventures) for accounting periods beginning on or after 1 January 2016 (with early adoption permitted in 2015 as discussed at 1.2.2 above). This will enable FRS 101 reporters applying Schedule 1 to the Regulations to make use of the new option in IAS 27 to apply the equity method once this amendment to IAS 27 is adopted by the EU and is effective.

In addition, there may be some entities that are not parents but have used the equity method for associates, joint ventures or jointly controlled entities under EU-adopted IFRS on the grounds that they are not preparing separate financial statements as defined by IAS 27. The amendments to SI 2015/980 also eliminate this potential measurement difference between FRS 101 and EU-adopted IFRS for Schedule 1 entities.

Chapter 2

However, Schedule 2 and 3 reporters and Limited Liability Partnerships are not permitted to use equity accounting for participating interests. FRS 101 does not identify this as a potential measurement difference with EU-adopted IFRS.

4.10   Investment entities

As FRS 101 does not apply to consolidated financial statements, the Group Accounts Regulations, 1992, or other legislative provisions pertaining to group accounts should not apply. However, where a parent meets the definition of an investment entity under IFRS 10, and is therefore required to measure its investment in a subsidiary at fair value through profit or loss, it must measure that investment in the same way in its separate financial statements (i.e. at fair value through profit or loss) as required by paragraph 11A of IAS 27. In other words, a qualifying entity that meets the definition of an investment entity must measure its investment in subsidiaries at fair value through profit or loss in its individual financial statements. *[FRS 101.A2.17]*.

An investment entity which measures its investments in subsidiaries at fair value through profit or loss will be required to make the additional disclosures required by paragraph 36(4) of Schedule 1 to the Regulations (see 6.3 below). *[FRS 101.A2.20]*.

4.11   Limited liability partnerships (LLPs)

The note of legal requirements to the July 2015 amendments to FRS 101 observes that LLPs applying FRS 101 will be doing so in conjunction with the LLP Regulations. In many cases, these LLP Regulations are similar to the Regulations, limiting the situations in which legal matters relevant to the financial statements of LLPs are not addressed. However, amendments made to the Regulations by the 2015 Regulations have not been reflected in the LLP Regulations. This gives rise to some differences for LLPs which may have an impact including:

*   the flexibility in relation to the format of the balance sheet and profit and loss account (see 5.1 below);

*   the scope of financial instruments that can be measured at fair value through profit or loss (see 4.4 above and 6.3 below);

*   the reversal of impairment losses in relation to goodwill (see 4.3 above); and

*   the application of merger accounting. *[FRS 101.A2.21]*.

In addition to the matters identified above, there may also be differences in respect of equity accounting for participating interests (see 4.9 above).

The FRC advise that, if following the requirements of FRS 101 would lead to a conflict with applicable legislation, an LLP shall instead apply its own legal requirements and consider whether disclosure of a departure from FRS 101 is required. *[FRS 101.A2.21]*.

5 PRESENTATIONAL DIFFERENCES BETWEEN FRS 101 AND EU-ADOPTED IFRS

As noted at 2 above, entities applying FRS 101 must prepare their financial statements in accordance with the Companies Act and the Regulations. This is because financial statements prepared under FRS 101 are Companies Act individual accounts and not IAS individual accounts as set out in section 395 of the Companies Act. *[FRS 101.A2.3]*. The presentation requirements of the Companies Act and the Regulations are discussed in Chapter 4.

Prior to the issuance of the 2015 Regulations, there were several conflicts between the presentational requirements of EU-adopted IFRS and those required by the Regulations. As a result, the FRC amended EU-adopted IFRS to ensure that financial statements prepared under FRS 101 comply with the Regulations. The 2015 Regulations removed most of these conflicts, or offered entities a choice as to whether or not to avoid a conflict, and these changes have been reflected in the July 2015 amendments to FRS 101. The following presentational matters are discussed below:

- balance sheet and profit and loss account formats required by FRS 101 (see 5.1 below);
- presentation of extraordinary activities (see 5.2 below); and
- presentation of discontinued operations on the face of the profit and loss account (see 5.3 below).

5.1 Balance sheet and profit and loss formats required by FRS 101

As a result of SI 2015/980, qualifying entities subject to Schedule 1 of the Regulations have an accounting policy choice regarding the presentation of the balance sheet and the profit and loss account. These entities can either:

- comply with the balance sheet and profit and loss format requirements of the Regulations; or
- adapt one of the balance sheet or profit and loss account formats in Section B of Schedule 1 to the Regulations so as (in the case of the balance sheet) to distinguish between current and non-current items in a different way provided that (for both the balance sheet and profit and loss account) the information given in the adapted format is at least equivalent to that which would have been required by use of such format has it not been thus adapted and the presentation is in accordance with generally accepted accounting principles or practice. *[1 Sch.1A.SI980/2015]*.

Consequently, FRS 101 states that when an entity chooses to use the adapted balance sheet and profit and loss account formats as described above, it shall apply the relevant presentation requirements of IAS 1 i.e. paragraphs 54 to 76, 82 and 85-86) and, in addition, disclose 'profit or loss before taxation'. *[FRS 101.AG1(h)-(i)]*. The presentation requirements of IAS 1 are discussed in Chapter 3 – *Presentation of financial statements and accounting policies* – of EY International GAAP 2016.

The choice of applying the adapted balance sheet and profit and loss formats (i.e. the presentation requirements of IAS 1) is available only for those entities subject to Schedule 1 to the Regulations. The choice is not available to entities subject to

Schedule 2 to the Regulations (banking entities), Schedule 3 of the Regulations (insurance entities) or to those subject to the LLP Regulations. These entities, as well as those Schedule 1 entities not choosing to use the adapted formats, must use the Companies Act balance sheet and profit and loss account formats. They must therefore apply either Part 1 'General Rules and Formats' of Schedule 1 to the Regulations; Part 1 'General Rules and Formats' of Schedule 2 to the Regulations; Part 1 'General Rules and Formats' of Schedule 3 to the Regulations; or Part 1 'General Rules and Formats' of Schedule 1 to the LLP Regulations. *[FRS101.AG1(h)-(i)]*. The FRS 101 legal appendix confirms that the requirements of paragraphs 54 to 76, 82 and 84 to 86 of IAS 1 disapply unless the adapted formats in Schedule 1 to the Regulations (i.e. the option to use the IAS formats) are chosen. *[FRS 101.A 2 Table1]*. The choice of applying the adapted formats (i.e. the presentation requirements of IAS 1) is available only to a Schedule 1 entity that adopts the July 2015 amendments (which are not mandatory until accounting periods beginning on or after 1 January 2016 but can be early-adopted for accounting periods beginning on or after 1 January 2015). Prior to application of the July 2015 amendments, all Schedule 1 entities must prepare balance sheet and profit and loss account in accordance with the Companies Act formats, and the IAS 1 formats were permitted, only if they still complied with the Regulations. The Companies Act formats are discussed in Chapter 4.

FRS 101 is silent on how an entity would implement a change from a Companies Act balance sheet and profit and loss account format to an IAS 1 format (or *vice versa*) in an accounting period subsequent to adoption of FRS 101. In our view, this is a voluntary change in accounting policy to which IAS 8 applies. Consequently, the change shall be applied retrospectively, prior periods should be restated and the disclosures required by paragraph 29 of IAS 8 must be made. Consistent with all voluntary changes in accounting policy, the change must satisfy the criteria in paragraph 14(b) of IAS 8 that it results in the financial statements providing reliable and more relevant information about the effects of transactions, other events or conditions on the entity's financial position, financial performance or cash flows. We would normally expect an entity to be able to justify such a change in presentation formats.

A UK parent company presenting both consolidated financial statements (either IAS group accounts or Companies Act group accounts) and Companies Act individual financial statements under FRS 101 can take advantage of the exemption in s408 of the Companies Act from presenting a profit and loss account and related notes in respect of its individual profit and loss account.

FRS 101 makes no amendments to the requirement in IAS 1 to present a statement of changes in equity for the reporting period.

There is no requirement to present a statement of cash flows where the reduced disclosure exemption is taken (see 6.1.8 below).

5.1.1 Additional presentation requirements needed to comply with Company Law by a Schedule 1 entity using the adapted (IAS 1) balance sheet and profit and loss account formats

The appendix on legal requirements to FRS 101 clarifies that a Schedule 1 entity applying the adapted balance sheet and profit and loss account formats – see 5.1 above – shall apply the relevant presentation requirements of IAS 1 subject to: *[FRS 101.A2.9A]*

- disclosure of profit or loss before taxation and the amendment to IFRS 5 – *Non-current Assets Held for Sale and Discontinued Operations* – set out at 5.3 below; and

- a further disaggregation of the statement of financial position, for example in relation to trade and other receivables and trade and other payables (which may be provided in the notes to the financial statements) that is necessary to meet the requirement to give the equivalent information.

The appendix on legal requirements does not elaborate what is meant by a 'further disaggregation of the statement of financial position' other than provide the examples above. It reiterates that the option to apply the presentation requirements of IAS 1 is not available to a qualifying entity applying Schedule 2 or Schedule 3 to the Regulations or Schedule 1 to the LLP Regulations. *[FRS 101.A2.9A]*.

5.1.2 Additional presentation requirements needed to comply with IFRS by an entity using the Companies Act balance sheet and profit and loss account formats

The appendix on legal requirements to FRS 101 clarifies that for a qualifying entity not permitted or not choosing to apply the adapted (i.e. IAS) balance sheet or profit and loss account formats – see 5.1 above – the format and presentation requirements of IAS 1 may conflict with those of company law because of the following: *[FRS 101.A2.9B]*

- differences in the definition of 'fixed assets' (the term used in the Regulations) and 'non-current assets' (the term used in EU-adopted IFRS);

- differences in the definition of 'current assets' as the term is used in the Regulations and EU-adopted IFRS. See Chapter 4 at 5.1.1;

- differences in the definition of 'creditors falling due within or after one year' (the term used in the Regulations) and 'current and non-current liabilities' (the term used in EU-adopted IFRS). Under the Act a loan is treated as due for repayment on the earliest date on which a lender could require repayment, whilst under EU adopted IFRS the due date is based on when the entity expects to settle the liability or has no unconditional right to defer payment; and

- the Act requires presentation of debtors falling due after more than one year within current assets. Under EU-adopted IFRS these items will be presented in non-current assets. UITF 4 – *Presentation of long-term debtors in current assets* – addresses the inclusion of debtors due after more than one year with 'current assets' – see 5.1.2.A below.

Chapter 2

5.1.2.A   Debtors due after more than one year

The legal appendix to FRS 101 reproduces the consensus of UITF 4 that 'in most cases it will be satisfactory to disclose the size of debtors due after more than one year in the notes to the accounts. There will be some instances, however, where the amount is so material in the context of the total net current assets that in the absence of disclosure of debtors due after more than one year on the face of the balance sheet readers may misinterpret the accounts. In such circumstances, the amount should be disclosed on the face of the balance sheet within current assets'. *[FRS 101.A2.10]*.

5.1.2.B   Non-current assets or disposal groups held for sale

Paragraph 38 of IFRS 5 requires an entity to present a non-current asset classified as held for sale and the assets of a disposal group held for sale separately from other assets in the statement of financial position, and the liabilities of a disposal group separately from other liabilities in the statement of financial position. Paragraph 54 of IAS 1 requires a single line approach in the balance sheet for both assets and liabilities held for sale. Detailed analysis of the components of the assets and liabilities held for sale is required in the notes to the financial statements.

A one-line presentation approach in the balance sheet is not allowed by FRS 101 when a qualifying entity is not permitted or chooses not to apply the adapted (i.e. IAS 1) balance sheet formats – see 5.1 above – because the Regulations do not otherwise permit the aggregation of different types of assets or liabilities in this way. In addition, paragraph 54 of IAS 1 cannot be applied if it conflicts with the Regulations (see 5.1 above). One practical solution to this matter could be to present aggregate assets and aggregate liabilities held for sale as a memorandum on the statement of financial position, cross-referenced to the detailed analysis in the notes.

5.2   Extraordinary items

IFRS has no concept of 'extraordinary items'. Prior to SI 2015/980, the Regulations required the separate disclosure of extraordinary items in the profit and loss account and a qualifying entity was required to disclose items that were deemed to be extraordinary items separately in the statement of comprehensive income. Therefore, prior to the July 2015 amendments, FRS 101 changed paragraph 87 of IAS 1, and introduced a new paragraph 87A which required an entity to distinguish between ordinary activities and extraordinary items.

SI 2015/980 abolished the concept of extraordinary items for entities reporting under Schedule 1 to the Regulations. This change has also been reflected in the July 2015 amendments to FRS 101 which now prohibit a Schedule 1 entity from presenting or describing any items of income or expenses as 'extraordinary items' in either the primary statements or the notes.

Consequently, once the July 2015 amendments are applied, only entities reporting under Schedule 2, Schedule 3 and the LLP Regulations are allowed to present extraordinary items separately in the profit and loss account. However, we would expect this requirement to have no practical impact as we would not expect to see any extraordinary items under FRS 101. This is because the legal appendix of FRS 101 states that 'entities should note that extraordinary items are extremely rare as they relate to highly abnormal events or transactions'. *[FRS 101.A2.11].*

Ordinary activities are defined as 'any activities which are undertaken by a reporting entity as part of its business and such related activities in which the reporting entity engages in furtherance of, or incidental to, or arising from, these activities. Ordinary activities include any effects on the reporting entity of any event in the various environments in which it operates, including the political, regulatory, economic and geographical environments, irrespective of the frequency or unusual nature of the events'. *[FRS 101.AG1(j)].*

Extraordinary activities are 'material items possessing a high degree of abnormality which arise from events or transactions that fall outside the ordinary activities of the reporting entity and which are not expected to recur. They do not include items occurring within the entity's ordinary activities that are required to be disclosed by paragraph 97 of IAS 1 nor do they include prior period items merely because they relate to a prior period'. *[FRS 101.AG1(j)].*

5.3   Presentation of discontinued operations

FRS 101 amends IFRS 5 to:

*   remove the option to present the analysis of discontinued operations into its component parts (e.g. revenue, expenses, tax) in the notes to the accounts. This analysis must be presented on the face of the statement of comprehensive income;

*   require the analysis above to be shown on the face of the statement of comprehensive income in a column identified as related to discontinued operations (i.e. separately from continuing operations);

*   require a total column (i.e. the sum of continuing and discontinued operations) to be presented on the face of the statement of comprehensive income; and

*   remove the option to present income from continuing operations and from discontinued operations attributable to owners of the parent in the notes to the accounts. *[FRS 101.AG1(g)].*

This amended presentation is required for all entities applying FRS 101, even those who have chosen to apply the adapted (i.e. IAS 1) balance sheet and profit and loss account presentation formats (see 5.1 above) as a result of the July 2015 amendments.

In substance, this means that the single line presentation of discontinued operations is replaced by a three-column approach with the detailed analysis of the results from the discontinued operation shown on the face of the statement of comprehensive income. This is illustrated in the following example:

Chapter 2

Example 1:   *Presentation of discontinued operations*

Statement of comprehensive income
For the year ended 31 December 2016

	Continuing operations 2016 £000	Dis-continued operations 2016 £000	Total 2016 £000	Continuing operations 2015 £000	Dis-continued operations 2015 £000	Total 2015 £000
Turnover	4,200	1,232	5,432	3,201	1,500	4,701
Cost of Sales	(2,591)	(1,104)	(3,695)	(2,281)	(1,430)	(3,711)
Gross profit	1,609	128	1,737	920	70	990
Administrative expenses	(452)	(110)	(562)	(418)	(120)	(538)
Other operating income	212	–	212	198	–	198
Profit on disposal of operations	–	301	301	–	–	–
Operating profit	1,369	319	1,688	700	(50)	650
Interest receivable and similar income	14	–	14	16	–	16
Interest payable and similar charges	(208)	–	(208)	(208)	–	(208)
Profit on ordinary activities before tax	1,175	319	1,494	508	(50)	458
Taxation	(390)	(4)	(394)	(261)	3	(258)
Profit on ordinary activities after taxation and profit for the financial year	785	315	1,100	247	(47)	200

Other comprehensive income

	Total 20X5	Total 20X4
Actuarial losses on defined benefit pension plans	(108)	(68)
Deferred tax movement relating to actuarial losses	28	18
Total Comprehensive income for the year	1,020	150

6   DISCLOSURE EXEMPTIONS FOR QUALIFYING ENTITIES

Qualifying entities may take advantage in their financial statements of a number of disclosure exemptions from EU-adopted IFRS (see 6.1 below).

Financial institutions, as defined by FRS 101, that are qualifying entities are not entitled to some disclosure exemptions (see 6.4 below).

Some, but not all, of these exemptions are conditional on 'equivalent' disclosures in the consolidated financial statements of the group in which the entity is consolidated (see 6.2 below).

In addition, some disclosures required by the Regulations for certain financial instruments that are held at fair value must be made even if the qualifying entity takes advantage of the disclosure exemptions from the disclosure requirements of IFRS 7 – *Financial Instruments: Disclosures* – and IFRS 13 – *Fair Value Measurement* (see 6.3 below). *[FRS 101.A2.5A].*

6.1   Disclosure exemptions

Qualifying entities are permitted the following disclosure exemptions from EU-adopted IFRS: *[FRS 101.7-8]*

- the requirement of paragraphs 6 and 21 of IFRS 1 to present an opening statement of financial position at the date of transition on first-time adoption of FRS 101 and related notes (see 3.4 above);

- the requirements of paragraphs 45(b) and 46 to 52 of IFRS 2 – *Share-based Payment* – provided that for a qualifying entity that is:

    - a subsidiary, the share-based payment arrangement concerns equity instruments of another group entity;

    - an ultimate parent, the share-based payment arrangement concerns its own equity instruments and its separate financial statements are presented alongside the consolidated financial statements of the group;

    and, in both cases, provided that equivalent disclosures are included in the consolidated financial statements of the group in which the entity is consolidated (see 6.1.1 below);

- the requirements of paragraphs 62, B64(d) to (e), (g) to (h), (j) to (m), n(ii), (o)(ii), (p), (q)(ii), B66 and B67 of IFRS 3 provided that equivalent disclosures are included in the consolidated financial statements of the group in which the entity is consolidated (see 6.1.2 below);

- the requirements of paragraph 33(c) of IFRS 5 provided that equivalent disclosures are included in the consolidated financial statements of the group in which the entity is consolidated (see 6.1.3 below);

- the requirements of IFRS 7 provided that equivalent disclosures are included in the financial statements of the group in which the entity is consolidated (see 6.1.4 below). However, entities which are subject to the UK Companies Act and Regulations are legally required to provide disclosures related to financial instruments including those measured at fair value (see 6.3 below). Qualifying entities that are financial institutions do not receive this exemption and must apply the disclosure requirements of IFRS 7 in full (see 6.4 below);

- the requirements of paragraphs 91 to 99 of IFRS 13 provided that equivalent disclosures are included in the consolidated financial statements of the group in which the entity is consolidated (see 6.1.5 below). However, entities which are subject to the UK Companies Act and Regulations are legally required to provide disclosures related to financial instruments including those measured at fair value (see 6.3 below). Qualifying entities that are financial institutions can only take advantage of the exemptions to the extent that they apply to assets and liabilities other than financial instruments (see 6.4 below);

- the requirement in paragraph 38 of IAS 1 to present comparative information in respect of:

    - paragraph 79(a)(iv) of IAS 1;

    - paragraph 73(e) of IAS 16;

    - paragraph 118(e) of IAS 38 – *Intangible Assets*;

Chapter 2

- paragraphs 76 and 79(d) of IAS 40 – *Investment Property*; and

- paragraph 50 of IAS 41 – *Agriculture* (see 6.1.6 below);

- the requirements of paragraphs 10(d), 10(f), 16, 38A to 38D, 40A to 40D, 111 and 134 to 136 of IAS 1. (see 6.1.7 below). However, qualifying entities that are financial institutions are not permitted to take advantage of the exemptions in paragraphs 134 to 136 of IAS 1(see 6.4 below);

- the requirements of IAS 7 – *Statement of Cash Flows* (see 6.1.8 below);

- the requirements of paragraphs 30 and 31 of IAS 8 (see 6.1.9 below);

- the requirements of paragraphs 17 and 18A of IAS 24 and the requirements in IAS 24 to disclose related party transactions entered into between two or more members of a group, provided that any subsidiary which is a party to the transaction is wholly owned by such a member (see 6.1.10 below); and

- the requirements of paragraphs 130(f)(ii), 130(f)(iii), 134(d) to 134(f) and 135(c) to 135(e) of IAS 36 provided that equivalent disclosures are included in the consolidated financial statements of the group in which the entity is consolidated (see 6.1.11 below).

Use of the disclosure exemptions is conditional on the following disclosures in the notes to the financial statements:

(a)   a brief narrative summary of the exemptions adopted; and

(b)   the name of the parent of the group in whose consolidated financial statements the reporting entity is consolidated and from where those financial statements may be obtained (i.e. the parent identified in the term 'qualifying entity'). *[FRS 101.5(c)].*

There is no requirement to list all of the disclosure exemptions in detail. Reporting entities can also choose to apply the disclosure exemptions on a selective basis. This may be necessary, for example, where not all of the relevant 'equivalent' disclosures are made in the consolidated financial statements of the parent on the grounds of materiality (see 6.2 below).

Each of the disclosure exemptions listed above is discussed below.

6.1.1   Share-based payment (IFRS 2)

The disclosure exemption eliminates all IFRS 2 disclosures apart from those required by paragraphs 44 and 45(a), (c) and (d) of IFRS 2. In substance, this reduces the disclosure requirements of IFRS 2 to:

- a description of the type of share-based payment arrangements that existed during the reporting period, including general terms and conditions, maximum terms of options granted, and the method of entitlement (e.g. whether in cash or equity);

- weighted average share price information in respect of options exercised during the reporting period; and

- the range of exercise prices and weighted average remaining contractual life of share options outstanding at the end of the reporting period.

6.1.2   Business combinations (IFRS 3)

In substance, this disclosure exemption eliminates the qualitative disclosures required on a business combination. However, a number of factual or quantitative disclosures are still required for each business combination including:

- the name and description of the acquiree, acquisition date and percentage of voting equity interests acquired;

- the acquisition date fair value of total consideration transferred split by major class;

- the amount recognised at the acquisition date for each major class of assets acquired and liabilities assumed;

- the amount of any negative goodwill recognised and the line item in the statement of comprehensive income in which it is recognised;

- the amount of any non-controlling interest recognised and the measurement basis for the amount (although there should be no non-controlling interests for acquisitions in individual financial statements);

- revenue and profit or loss of the acquiree since acquisition date included in comprehensive income for the period; and

- the information above (except for the details of the acquirees) in aggregate for individually immaterial business combinations that are collectively material.

In addition, an acquirer is still subject to the general requirements of paragraphs 59 to 61 of IFRS 3. These require disclosure of information that enables users of the financial statements to evaluate the nature and effect of a business combination that occurs, either during the current reporting period or at the end of the financial reporting period but before the financial statements are authorised for issue. These paragraphs also require disclosure of the financial effects of adjustments recognised in the current reporting period relating to business combinations that occurred in the current or previous periods.

6.1.3   Discontinued operations (IFRS 5)

This exemption eliminates the requirement to disclose cash flows attributable to discontinued operations. This cash flow disclosure exemption is contingent on equivalent disclosures in the consolidated financial statements of the parent, although equivalent disclosures in the parent are not necessary to make use of the exemption not to prepare a cash flow statement.

6.1.4   Financial instruments (IFRS 7)

This exemption removes all of the disclosure requirements of IFRS 7. However, notwithstanding this exemption, some IFRS 7 disclosures are still required for certain financial instruments measured at fair value (see 6.3 below). In addition, some specific financial instruments disclosures are required by the Regulations (see 7.2 below).

Financial institutions are not permitted to use this exemption (see 6.4 below).

Chapter 2

6.1.5   Fair values (IFRS 13)

This exemption removes all of the disclosure requirements of IFRS 13. However, notwithstanding this exemption, some IFRS 13 disclosures are still required for certain financial instruments measured at fair value (see 6.3 below). In addition, specific disclosures in respect of the fair value of stocks, financial instruments, investment property and living animals and plants carried at fair value are required by the Regulations (see 7.2 below).

Financial institutions are not permitted to use this IFRS 13 disclosure exemption in respect of financial instruments. However, they can use this exemption in respect of disclosures of non-financial assets and liabilities (see 6.4 below).

6.1.6   Comparatives (IAS 1, IAS 16, IAS 38, IAS 40, IAS 41)

This exemption eliminates the requirement for comparatives to be presented for reconciliations of:

- outstanding shares at the beginning and end of the current period (IAS 1);
- the carrying amount of property, plant and equipment at the beginning and end of the current period (IAS 16);
- the carrying amount of intangible assets at the beginning and end of the current period (IAS 38);
- the carrying amount of investment property held at either fair value or cost at the beginning and end of the current period (IAS 40); and
- the carrying amount of biological assets at the beginning and end of the current period (IAS 41).

These comparative disclosures were also not required under previous UK GAAP.

6.1.7   Presentation (IAS 1)

This exemption removes:

- the requirement to present a cash flow statement (see 6.1.8 below);
- the requirement to present a statement of financial position and related notes at the beginning of the earliest comparative period whenever an entity applies an accounting policy retrospectively, makes a retrospective restatement, or when it reclassifies items in its financial statements;
- the requirement to make an explicit statement of compliance with IFRS. Indeed, FRS 101 prohibits such a statement of compliance and an FRS 101 statement of compliance is required instead (see 1.3 above); and
- the requirement to disclose information about capital and how it is managed.

Financial institutions are not permitted to use the exemption in respect of the disclosure of information about capital and how it is managed. This is because financial institutions are usually subject to externally imposed capital requirements.

6.1.8   Cash flows (IAS 7)

The exemption removes the requirement for a cash flow statement for any qualifying entity. This exemption therefore goes beyond the exemption in

FRS 1 – *Cash flow statements* – which provided an exemption for presenting a cash flow statement for only those subsidiary undertakings where 90% or more of the voting rights were controlled within the group, provided the consolidated financial statements in which the subsidiary undertakings are included were publicly available.

6.1.9   Standards issued but not effective (IAS 8)

This exemption removes the requirement to provide information about the impact of IFRSs that have been issued but are not yet effective.

6.1.10   Related party transactions (IAS 24)

The exemptions in respect of IAS 24 remove:

- the requirement to disclose information about key management personnel compensation;

- the requirement to disclose amounts incurred for the provision of key management personnel services that are provided by a separate management entity; and

- the requirements to disclose related party transactions between two or more members of a group, provided that any subsidiary which is a party to the transaction is wholly owned by such a member.

Although the requirement to disclose information about key management personnel compensation required by IAS 24 is eliminated, UK companies are required separately by the Companies Act to disclose information in respect of directors' remuneration. Additionally, quoted companies must prepare a directors' remuneration report. There is no exemption from other IAS 24 disclosure requirements, so disclosure of other transactions with key management personnel (e.g. loans) is still required.

In this context of FRS 101, we believe that there are two possible interpretations of the 'group' being referred to in respect of the exemption from disclosure of transactions with other wholly owned subsidiaries. These are:

- the 'group' is that headed by the ultimate controlling entity (which may not necessarily be the same entity as the entity that is preparing the publicly available consolidated accounts intended to give a true and fair view in which the qualifying entity is included). This interpretation follows paragraph 38 of Appendix IV of FRS 8 – *Related party disclosures* – which clarified the meaning of the identical disclosure exemption in FRS 8. However, this explanatory wording has not been carried into FRS 101 and should not, therefore, be seen as a constraint in applying FRS 101; or

- the 'group' is the sub-group involved in the transaction (i.e. the exemption is available within part of a group where the entities participating in the transaction are wholly-owned).

6.1.11   Impairment of assets (IAS 36)

This exemption eliminates all requirements to disclose information about estimates used to measure recoverable amounts of cash-generating units containing goodwill or intangible assets with indefinite useful lives, including details of fair value measurements where the recoverable amount is fair value less costs of disposal other than:

- the carrying amounts of goodwill and indefinite life intangibles allocated to cash generating units; and

- the basis on which the recoverable amount of those units has been determined (i.e. value in use or fair value less costs to sell).

Qualifying entities are also still required to make the disclosures required by paragraphs 126 to 133 of IAS 36 in respect of impairment losses (and reversal of impairment losses) recognised in the period.

6.2   'Equivalent' disclosures

Certain of the disclosure exemptions in FRS 101 are dependent on the provision of 'equivalent' disclosures in the publicly available consolidated financial statements of the parent in which the entity is included.

The following table summarises which disclosure exemptions need 'equivalent' disclosures in the consolidated financial statements of the parent and which do not.

Disclosure exemption	*Equivalent disclosures required in parent consolidated financial statements*
First-time adoption exemption (see 6 above)	No
Share-based payment (see 6.1.1 above)	Yes
Business combinations (see 6.1.2 above)	Yes
Discontinued operations (see 6.1.3 above)	Yes
Financial instruments (see 6.1.4 above)	Yes
Fair values (see 6.1.5 above)	Yes
Comparatives (see 6.1.6 above)	No
Presentation (see 6.1.7 above)	No
Cash flows (see 6.1.8 above)	No
Standards issued but not effective (see 6.1.9 above)	No
Related party transactions (see 6.1.10 above)	No
Impairment of assets (see 6.1.11 above)	Yes

FRS 101 refers to the Application Guidance in FRS 100 in deciding whether the consolidated financial statements of the group in which the reporting entity is included provides disclosures that are 'equivalent' to the requirements of IFRS from which relief is provided. *[FRS 101.9]*.

The Application Guidance in FRS 100 states that:

- it is necessary to consider whether the publicly available consolidated financial statements of the parent provide disclosures that meet the basic disclosure requirements of the relevant standard or interpretation without regarding strict conformity with each and every disclosure. This assessment should be based on the particular facts, including the similarities to and differences from the requirements of the relevant standard from which relief is provided. 'Equivalence' is intended to be aligned to that described in s401 of the Act; *[FRS 100.AG8-9]* and

- disclosure exemptions for subsidiaries are permitted where the relevant disclosure requirements are met in the consolidated financial statements, even where the disclosures are made in aggregate or abbreviated form, or in relation to intra-group balances, those intra-group balances have been eliminated on consolidation. If, however, no disclosure is made in the consolidated financial statements on the grounds of materiality, the relevant disclosures should be made at the subsidiary level if material in those financial statements. *[FRS 100.AG10]*.

This means that a qualifying entity must review the consolidated financial statements of its parent to ensure that 'equivalent' disclosures have been made for each of the above exemptions that it intends to use. Where a particular 'equivalent' disclosure has not been made (unless the disclosure relates to an intra-group balance eliminated on consolidation) then the qualifying subsidiary cannot use the exemption in respect of that disclosure.

6.3   Disclosures required by the Regulations in the financial statements of non-financial institutions for certain financial instruments which may be held at fair value

Paragraph 36 of Schedule 1 to the Regulations (and its equivalents in Schedule 2 and Schedule 3 to the Regulations and the LLP Regulations) states that financial instruments which under IFRS may be included in accounts at fair value may be so included provided that the disclosures required by such accounting standards are made. *[FRS 101.A2.6]*.

The legal appendix to FRS 101 confirms that a qualifying entity that has financial instruments measured at fair value in accordance with the requirements of paragraph 36(4) of Schedule 1 to the Regulations (or equivalent) is legally required to provide the relevant disclosures set out in International Accounting Standards adopted by the European Commission (for entities that have not adopted the July 2015 amendments to FRS 101 the words 'on or before 5 September 2006' are added). *[FRS 101.A2.6]*.

The financial instruments referred to by paragraph 36(4) of Schedule 1 of the Regulations (and its equivalents) are those in paragraphs 36(2)(c) and 36(3) of Schedule 1 to the Regulations (and its equivalents). These are:

- any financial liability which is not held for trading or a derivative (i.e. a financial liability designated at fair value through profit or loss (FVPL) under paragraph 9 of IAS 39);

- loans and receivables originated by the reporting entity, not held for trading purposes, and designated at either available-for-sale (AFS) or FVPL under paragraph 9 of IAS 39;

- interests in subsidiary undertakings, associated undertakings and joint ventures designated at either AFS or FVPL under paragraph 10 of IAS 27;

- contracts for contingent consideration in a business combination measured at FVPL; or

- other financial instruments with such special characteristics that the instruments according to generally accepted accounting principles or practice, should be accounted for differently from other financial instruments. *[1 Sch 36]*.

FRS 101 does not elaborate what 'the relevant disclosures set out in International Accounting Standards adopted by the European commission' means other than to note that 'such disclosures should be based on extant standards'. *[FRS 101.A2.20]*. The most logical interpretation of this is that an entity should make all material disclosures required by IFRS 7 and IFRS 13 in respect of such instruments.

In addition, qualifying entities that are preparing Companies Act accounts must provide the disclosures required by paragraph 55 of Schedule 1 to the Regulations (and its equivalents in Schedules 2 and 3 of the Regulations and the LLP Regulations) which sets out requirements relating to financial instruments at fair value. *[FRS 100.A2.7D]*. These disclosures relate to financial instruments held at fair value generally and not just to those financial instruments measured at fair value in accordance with paragraph 36(4) as discussed above. Disclosures are required of: *[1 Sch 55]*

- significant assumptions underlying the valuation models and techniques used when determining fair value of the instruments;

- fair value of each category of financial instrument or other asset and the changes in value included directly in the profit and loss account or credited to or debited from the fair value reserve;

- for each class of derivatives, the extent and nature of the instruments, including significant terms and conditions that may affect the timing and certainty of future cash flows; and

- a tabular disclosure of amounts transferred to or from the fair value reserve reconciling the opening and closing balance of the reserve, showing the amount transferred to or from the reserve during the year and the source and application of the amounts so transferred.

6.4   Disclosure exemptions for financial institutions

Financial institutions are permitted to apply FRS 101 but receive fewer disclosure exemptions. A qualifying entity which is a financial institution may take advantage in its individual financial statements of the disclosure exemptions set out at 6.1 above except for:

- the disclosure exemptions from IFRS 7;

- the disclosure exemptions from paragraphs 91 to 99 of IFRS 13 to the extent that they apply to financial instruments. Therefore, a financial institution can take advantage of the disclosure exemptions from paragraphs 91 to 99 of IFRS 13 for assets and liabilities other than financial instruments (e.g. property plant and equipment, intangible assets, and investment property); and

- the capital disclosures of paragraphs 134 to 136 of IAS 1. *[FRS 101.7]*.

The FRC has opted not to provide a generic definition of a financial institution. Instead, it has provided a list of entities that are stated to be financial institutions. A 'financial institution' is stated to be any of the following: *[FRS 101.Appendix I]*

(a)   a bank which is:

    (i)   a firm with a Part IV permission (as defined in s40(4) of the Financial Services and Markets Act 2000) which includes accepting deposits and:

        (a)   which is a credit institution; or

        (b)   whose Part IV permission includes a requirement that it complies with the rules in the General Prudential sourcebook and the Prudential sourcebook for Banks, Building Societies and Investment Firms relating to banks, but which is not a building society, a friendly society or a credit union;

    (ii)   an EEA bank which is a full credit institution;

(b)   a building society which is defined in s119(1) of the Building Societies Act 1986 as a building society incorporated (or deemed to be incorporated) under that Act;

(c)   a credit union, being a body corporate registered under the Industrial and Provident Societies Act 1965 as a credit union in accordance with the Credit Unions Act 1979, which is an authorised person;

(d)   custodian bank, broker-dealer or stockbroker;

(e)   an entity that undertakes the business of effecting or carrying out insurance contracts, including general and life assurance entities;

(f)   an incorporated friendly society incorporated under the Friendly Societies Act 1992 or a registered friendly society registered under section 7(1)(a) of the Friendly Societies Act 1974 or any enactment which it replaced, including any registered branches;

(g)   an investment trust, Irish investment company, venture capital trust, mutual fund, exchange traded fund, unit trust, open-ended investment company (OEIC);

(h)   a retirement benefit plan; or

(i)   any other entity whose principal activity is to generate wealth or manage risk through financial instruments. This is intended to cover entities that have business activities similar to those listed above but are not specifically included in the list above.

    A parent entity whose sole activity is to hold investments in other group entities is not a financial institution.

Category (i) is potentially wide-ranging since the first sentence has a different emphasis from (a) to (h) which focus on entities that hold assets in a fiduciary capacity on behalf of others rather than wealth generation or risk management through the use of financial instruments. However, we believe that the second sentence is supposed to limit the application of the first sentence to those entities similar to (a) to (h) and that a general extension of the definition of a financial institution is not intended by the wording in category (i).

The Accounting Council has advised that 'a parent entity whose sole activity is to hold investments in other group entities is not a financial institution, but notes that a subsidiary entity engaged solely in treasury activities for the group as a whole is likely to meet the definition of a financial institution'. *[FRS 102.AC.37].*

Chapter 2

In many groups, there will be entities whether it is not clear whether a qualifying entity is a financial institution and judgement will need to be applied based on the facts and circumstances.

7   ADDITIONAL COMPANIES ACT DISCLOSURES

FRS 101 individual financial statements are subject to disclosures required by the Regulations as well as other disclosures required by the Companies Act or other related regulations. These disclosures are in addition to those required by EU-adopted IFRS.

There are two types of Companies Act disclosures that are required for a UK entity applying FRS 101:

(a)   those already required for IAS accounts prepared under EU-adopted IFRS and Companies Act accounts prepared under UK GAAP (see 7.1 below); and

(b)   those required by the Regulations which would have been applied by an entity preparing Companies Act accounts under previous UK GAAP (or FRS 102) but not by an entity preparing IAS accounts under EU-adopted IFRS (see 7.2 below).

This means that, in certain scenarios, a move from EU-adopted IFRS to FRS 101 would result in increased disclosures for an entity despite the use of the disclosure exemptions described at 6 above.

There may also be additional disclosures for an entity other than a company where that entity is subject to separate regulations.

7.1   Existing Companies Act disclosures in the financial statements for EU-adopted IFRS and UK GAAP reporters that also apply under FRS 101

FRS 100 identifies the following required disclosures: *[FRS 100.A2.19]*

*   s410A – off-balance sheet arrangements (entities subject to the Small Companies regime are no longer exempt when SI 2015/980 is applied although no disclosure of the financial effect is required);

*   s411 – employee numbers and costs (unless subject to the Small Companies regime where employee numbers are required when SI 2015/980 is applied);

*   s412 – directors' benefits: remuneration;

*   s413 – directors' benefits: advances, credit and guarantees;

*   s415 to 419 – directors' report;

*   s420 to 421 – directors' remuneration report; and

*   s494 – services provided by auditor and associates and related remuneration (disclosures of non-audit services are not required for companies subject to the Small Companies Regime or medium-sized companies).

The list of disclosures identified by FRS 100 is not complete and omits, for example, the information about related undertakings required by s409 and the requirement to prepare a strategic report required by s414A.

In addition, other Companies Act or related disclosures may apply depending on individual circumstances such as the disclosures required for a parent taking advantage of the exemption from preparing consolidated accounts under either s400 or s401 of the Companies Act.

7.2 Disclosures required by the Regulations and the LLP Regulations in FRS 101 financial statements but not required under EU-adopted IFRS

The Regulations and the LLP Regulations require various disclosures in financial statements. In particular, Part 3 of Schedules 1 to 3 require certain disclosures to be made in the notes to the financial statements if not given in the primary statements. The relevant paragraphs are as follows:

- Schedule 1 paragraphs 42 to 72;
- Schedule 2 paragraphs 52 to 92;
- Schedule 3 paragraphs 60 to 90; or
- the LLP Regulations paragraphs 42 to 71.

Although some of these disclosure requirements are replicated in EU-adopted IFRS, others are not. Entities that move to FRS 101 from previous UK GAAP will have made these disclosures previously and therefore these requirements will not increase their reporting burden. Entities that move to FRS 101 from EU-adopted IFRS will not have made these disclosures previously or any other disclosures required by the applicable Schedule above and should consider carefully the impact of these new requirements against the benefits of the reduced disclosures discussed at 6 above.

Some examples of disclosures not required under EU-adopted IFRS in individual or separate financial statements are:

(a) Schedule 1 companies (i.e. companies other than banking and insurance companies):

- a statement required by large companies that the accounts have been prepared in accordance with applicable accounting policies; *[1 Sch 45]*

- disclosures in respect of share capital and debentures; *[1 Sch 47-50]*

- disclosure of the split of land between freehold and leasehold and the leasehold land between that held on a long lease and that held on a short lease; *[1 Sch 53]*

- disclosure of information about listed investments; *[1 Sch 54]*

- disclosure of information about the fair value of financial assets and liabilities which, in substance, 'reinstates' some parts of IFRS 7 and IFRS 13. In particular, there are requirements to disclose significant assumptions underlying the valuation models and techniques used when determining fair value of the instruments, details of the fair value of financial instruments by category and details concerning significant terms and conditions of derivatives (see 6.3 above); *[1 Sch 55]*

- disclosure of information about creditors due after five years; *[1 Sch 61]*

- disclosure of information about loans made in connection with the purchase of own shares; *[1 Sch 64]*

Chapter 2

- disclosure of particulars of taxation; *[1 Sch 67]* and

- disclosure of information about turnover by class of business and geographical markets. IFRS 8 – *Operating Segments* – does not require segmental information if an entity's debt or equity instruments are not traded in a public market or the entity is not in the process of filing financial statements for that purpose. *[1 Sch 68]*.

The profit and loss account of a company that falls within s408 of the Act (individual profit and loss account where group accounts prepared) need not contain the information specified in paragraphs 65 to 69 of Schedule 1. *[Regulations 3(2)]*.

(b)   Schedule 2 companies (i.e. banking companies)

- a statement that the accounts have been prepared in accordance with applicable accounting policies; *[2 Sch 54]*

- disclosures in respect of share capital and debentures; *[2 Sch 58-61]*

- disclosure of the split of land between freehold and leasehold and the leasehold land between that held on a long lease and that held on a short lease; *[2 Sch 64]*

- disclosure of a specific maturity analysis for loans and advances and liabilities; *[2 Sch 72]*

- disclosure of arrears of fixed cumulative dividends; *[2 Sch 75]*

- disclosure of details of transferable securities; *[2 Sch 79]*

- disclosure of leasing transactions; *[2 Sch 80]*

- disclosure of assets and liabilities denominated in a currency other than the presentational currency; *[2 Sch 81]*

- disclosure of details of unmatured forward transactions; *[2 Sch 83]*

- disclosure of loans made in connection with the purchase of own shares; *[2 Sch 84]*

- disclosure of particulars of taxation; *[2 Sch 86]* and

- disclosure of certain profit and loss account information by geographical markets. IFRS 8 does not require segmental information if an entity's debt or equity instruments are not traded in a public market or the entity is not in the process of filing financial statements for that purpose. *[2 Sch 87]*.

The profit and loss account of a banking company that falls within s408 of the Act (individual profit and loss account where group accounts prepared) need not contain the information specified in paragraphs 85 to 91 of Schedule 2. *[Regulations 5(2)]*.

(c)   Schedule 3 companies (i.e. insurance companies)

- a statement that the accounts have been prepared in accordance with applicable accounting policies; *[3 Sch 62]*

- disclosures in respect of share capital and debentures; *[3 Sch 65-68]*

- disclosure of the split of land between freehold and leasehold and the leasehold land between that held on a long lease and that held on a short lease; *[3 Sch 71]*

- disclosure of information about listed investments; *[3 Sch 72]*
- disclosure of creditors due after five years; *[3 Sch 79]*
- disclosure of loans made in connection with the purchase of own shares; *[3 Sch 82]*
- disclosure of particulars of taxation; *[3 Sch 84]*
- disclosure of certain profit and loss account information by type of business and by geographical area. IFRS 8 does not require segmental information if an entity's debt or equity instruments are not traded in a public market or the entity is not in the process of filing financial statements for that purpose; *[3 Sch 85-87]* and
- disclosure of total commissions for direct insurance business. *[3 Sch 88]*.

The profit and loss account of an insurance company that falls within s408 of the Act (individual profit and loss account where group accounts prepared) need not contain the information specified in paragraphs 83 to 89 of Schedule 3. *[Regulations 6(2)]*.

Banking and insurance companies are financial institutions (see section 6.4 above) and therefore must comply with IFRS 7 disclosures in full and IFRS 13 disclosures in respect of financial instruments, including disclosures about the fair value of financial assets and liabilities.

(d)   LLPs (i.e. entities subject to the *Large and Medium-sized LLPs (Accounts) Regulations 2008*)

- a statement required by large companies that the accounts have been prepared in accordance with applicable accounting policies; *[LLP Regs 45]*
- disclosures in respect of loans and debts due to members; *[LLP Regs 47]*
- disclosures in respect of debentures; *[LLP Regs 48]*
- disclosure of the split of land between freehold and leasehold and the leasehold land between that held on a long lease and that held on a short lease; *[LLP Regs 51]*
- disclosure of information about listed investments; *[LLP Regs 52]*
- disclosure of information about the fair value of financial assets and liabilities which, in substance, 'reinstates' some parts of IFRS 7 and IFRS 13. In particular, there are requirements to disclose information about significant assumptions where the fair value of a financial instrument results from generally accepted valuation models and techniques, details of the fair value of financial instruments by category and details concerning significant terms and conditions of derivatives (see 6.3 above); *[LLP Regs 53]*
- disclosure of information about creditors due after five years; *[LLP Regs 59]*
- disclosure of particulars of taxation; *[LLP Regs 64]*
- disclosure of information about turnover by class of business and geographical markets. IFRS 8 – *Operating Segments* – does not require segmental information if an entity's debt or equity instruments are not traded in a public market or the entity is not in the process of filing financial statements for that purpose; *[LLP Regs 65]* and
- disclosure of particulars of members. *[LLP Regs 66]*.

Chapter 2

The disclosures illustrated above are not intended to be an exhaustive list of additional disclosures required by the Regulations and LLP Regulations for entities applying FRS 101 that have previously reported under EU-adopted IFRS.

8.   FUTURE CHANGES TO IFRS AND THEIR IMPACT ON FRS 101

Although not specifically addressed by FRS 101, future changes to EU-adopted IFRS would appear to be automatically incorporated into FRS 101 unless they are modified by the FRC.

The Accounting Council has advised the FRC to update FRS 101 at regular intervals, to ensure that the disclosure framework maintains consistency with EU-adopted IFRS. *[FRS 101.AC.20]*. As a result, the FRC has so far reviewed FRS 101 annually to ensure that the reduced disclosure framework remains effective as EU-adopted IFRS develops. Amendments to FRS 101 have been issued in July 2014 and July 2015 (see 1.2 above).

Whenever a new IFRS is issued or an amendment is made to an existing EU-adopted IFRS, the FRC has to:

- consider whether any proposed requirements are prohibited by the Companies Act or the Regulations; and

- consider whether exemptions should be provided in respect of any disclosures required by the change.

The principles established are that UK financial reporting standards should:

- have consistency with global accounting standards through the application of an IFRS-based solution unless an alternative clearly better meets the overriding objective;

- reflect up-to-date thinking and developments in the way businesses operate and the transactions they undertake;

- balance consistent principles for accounting by all UK and Republic of Ireland entities with practical solutions, based on size, complexity, public interest and users information needs;

- promote efficiency within groups; and

- be cost-effective to apply. *[FRS 100.AC.8]*.

8.1   IFRS 9 – *Financial Instruments*

IFRS 9 was issued in July 2014 and is effective for accounting periods beginning on or after 1 January 2018. The Accounting Council observes that IFRS 9 has not yet been endorsed by the EU and therefore is not applicable to an entity applying FRS 101. However, the Accounting Council has noted that recording fair value gains and losses attributable to changes in credit risk in other comprehensive income on financial liabilities measured at fair value will usually be a departure from the requirement of paragraph 40 of Schedule 1 of the Regulations for the overriding purpose of giving a true and fair view. *[FRS 101.AC Advice 2014/2015 cycle.36]*.

The Accounting Council advice is silent about the other two circumstances in IFRS 9 in which accounting for fair value gains and losses are required in other comprehensive income. In our view:

- accounting for changes in the fair value of an equity instrument through other comprehensive income (without recycling of fair value changes to profit and loss) makes use of the alternative accounting rules in the Regulations, the Small Company Regulations, the LLP Regulations and the Small Company LLP Regulations and does not therefore require the use of a true and fair override (see Chapter 4 at 10.2); and

- the model used for accounting for changes in the fair value of a debt instrument through other comprehensive income is similar, but not identical, to the available-for-sale asset model under IAS 39. In our view, it is inferred from the Accounting Council's silence on the matter that this model is included within the fair value accounting rules in the Regulations the Small Company Regulations, the LLP Regulations and the Small Company LLP Regulations (see Chapter 4 at 10.3) and does not therefore require the use of a true and fair override to apply.

8.2 IFRS 15 – *Revenue from Contracts with Customers*

IFRS 15 was issued in May 2014 and is effective for accounting periods beginning on or after 1 January 2018. The disclosure requirements of IFRS 15 are significantly more detailed than those currently required by IAS 18 – *Revenue* – and IAS 11 – *Construction Contracts*. At the date of issuing the July 2015 amendments to FRS 101, the effective date of IFRS 15 was some way off and the EU endorsement process was not complete.

Currently, the Accounting Council advises that no exemptions from the disclosure requirements of IFRS 15 should be added to FRS 101. However, the Accounting Council advises the FRC that IFRS 15 should be revisited as part of the 2015/2016 amendments cycle in order to consider whether any disclosure exemptions are appropriate in FRS 101 and notes that two respondents to FRED 57 (of which EY were one) commented that, in their view, exemptions would be appropriate. *[FRS 101.AC Advice 2014/2015 cycle.22]*.

References

1 *The Financial Reporting Council: The True and Fair Requirement Revised – Opinion*, Martin Moore QC, May 2008, para. 4(C).

2 *The Financial Reporting Council: The True and Fair Requirement Revised – Opinion*, Martin Moore QC, May 2008, para. 4(F).

3 TECH 02/10 – *Guidance on the determination of realised profits and losses in the context of distributions under the Companies Act 2006*, ICAEW/ICAS, February 2010, paras. 3.28 and 3.29.

4 TECH 02/10 – *Guidance on the determination of realised profits and losses in the context of distributions under the Companies Act 2006*, ICAEW/ICAS, February 2010, paras. 3.30 to 3.32.

Chapter 2

Chapter 3   FRS 102 – Small entities

Chapter 3

List of examples

Chapter 3   FRS 102 – Small entities

1   INTRODUCTION

1.1   Background

In March 2015, *The Companies, Partnerships and Groups (Accounts and Reports) Regulations 2015* (SI 2015/980), which implement the new Accounting Directive (Directive 2013/34/EU) in the UK, were issued. SI 2015/980 amends the Companies Act 2006 ('CA 2006'), the *Small Companies and Groups (Accounts and Directors' Report) Regulations 2008* ('Small Companies Regulations'), the *Large and Medium-sized Companies and Groups (Accounts and Reports) Regulations 2008* ('Regulations') and *Partnership (Accounts) Regulations 2008*. SI 2015/980 therefore changes the requirements for statutory accounts and reports for UK companies and qualifying partnerships (but not LLPs).

A change to LLP law to implement the new Accounting Directive is expected to be consulted on in due course. Irish law is expected to be updated later in 2015 to implement the new Accounting Directive.

One key theme of the new Accounting Directive is to simplify accounting requirements and reduce the associated administrative burden (particularly for small companies) through:

- increasing levels of disclosure dependent on the size of undertaking;

- raising the size thresholds for small and medium-sized undertakings;

- reducing the number of options available for preparers in respect of recognition and measurement and presentation;

- introducing a small number of mandatory accounting changes that will affect Companies Act accounts (such as FRS 101 – *Reduced Disclosure Framework* – and FRS 102 – *The Financial Reporting Standard applicable in the UK and Republic of Ireland* – financial statements) and providing a Member State option (taken up in the UK) for more flexibility over company law layouts which could facilitate use of IAS 1 – *Presentation of Financial Statements* – layouts in Companies Act accounts;

- creating a largely harmonised small companies regime (which excludes public interest entities (PIEs)). The Accounting Directive limits the amount of information that Member States are permitted to require small undertakings to place in their annual statutory accounts (although statutory accounts prepared by small companies must still give a true and fair view); and

- excluding all small undertakings (except PIEs) from the audit requirement. However, Member States can require an audit as a matter for national law.

PIEs must report as large companies unless the new Accounting Directive explicitly provides otherwise. PIEs include companies with transferable securities admitted to trading on a regulated market, credit institutions and insurance undertakings. However, Member States can designate other undertakings as PIEs, e.g. undertakings that are of significant public relevance because of the nature of their business, their size or the number of their employees (in the UK, the small companies regime and medium-sized companies exclude certain types of companies).

The key changes made in SI 2015/980 affecting small companies are to:

- extend the scope of the small companies regime, with a significant increase in size limits to the maximum permitted by the new Accounting Directive (and changes to the types of excluded companies) (see 4 below);

- introduce new simpler presentation and disclosure requirements for the small companies regime;

- amend the Small Companies Regulations to permit the use of statutory formats (with some minor amendments to previous statutory formats), new 'abridged formats', or new 'adapted formats' (see 8 below);

- make a small number of accounting changes affecting Companies Act accounts;

- remove the separate abbreviated accounts regime available to small companies to file Companies Act individual accounts (see 12.3 below); and

- extend the exemption from preparing group accounts to a company that would be subject to the small companies regime if it was not a public company (so long as it is not a 'traded company', being a company any of whose transferable securities are admitted to trading on a regulated market) (see 6.2 below).

Under previous UK GAAP, small entities (as defined in the *Financial Reporting Standard for Small Entities* ('FRSSE')) were eligible to apply the FRSSE as an alternative to full UK GAAP. In November 2012, amendments to the FRSSE (effective January 2015) were issued. However, it was recognised that this was only a short-term solution, given the forthcoming changes arising from the new Accounting Directive.

In particular, as Member States (including national accounting standard setters) were not permitted to extend disclosure requirements beyond those permitted by the new Accounting Directive, a replacement to the FRSSE was required.

The FRC has now withdrawn the FRSSE, effective for accounting periods beginning on or after 1 January 2016. In its place, the FRC has published a new standard, FRS 105 – *The Financial Reporting Standard for Micro-entities*, and introduced a new small entities regime, Section 1A – *Small Entities* – into FRS 102. Section 1A requires small entities to apply the recognition and measurement requirements of FRS 102 in full. However, the presentation and disclosure requirements required by Section 1A are based on those required by the CA 2006 and Small Companies

Regulations (as amended by SI 2015/980) for companies subject to the small companies regime.

The FRS 100 (July 2015) amendments give effect to the new accounting framework (see Chapter 1 at 4) as follows:

• companies that qualify for and choose to apply the micro-entities regime apply FRS 105;

• other entities have a choice of applying EU-adopted IFRS, FRS 101 (individual financial statements of a qualifying entity only) or FRS 102; and

• an entity qualifying for the small entities regime that adopts FRS 102 can choose to apply Section 1A or the full standard.

1.2   Scope of this Chapter

This Chapter principally addresses the requirements of Section 1A and the related company law requirements (as amended by SI 2015/980, for companies subject to the small companies regime). A summary of Section 1A is included at 2 below, and its content is discussed at 6 to 11 below. Key definitions used in this chapter are included at 3 below.

A company subject to the small companies regime, an LLP subject to the small LLPs regime and an entity that would have qualified for the small companies regime had it been a company are permitted to use Section 1A. The small companies regime and small LLPs regime are defined in the CA 2006 (as amended by SI 2015/980) and the *Limited Liability Partnerships (Accounts and Audit) (Application of Companies Act 2006) Regulations 2008* (SI 2008/1911). See 4 below.

The requirements on effective date (see 5 below) have the consequence that a company subject to the small companies regime applying Section 1A will also be applying SI 2015/980.

Companies subject to the small companies regime and LLPs subject to the small LLPs regime apply the Small Companies Regulations and Small LLP Regulations (which have lighter disclosures than the Regulations and LLP Regulations) and are eligible for certain disclosure exemptions in the CA 2006 or SI 2008/1911. In general, the Small Companies Regulations (as amended by SI 2015/980) contain significantly fewer disclosures than previously but some new disclosures have been added or existing disclosures amended. The disclosure requirements in Companies Act accounts for companies subject to the small companies regime and some of the changes made by SI 2015/980 are set out at 11 below.

If a small entity chooses not to apply Section 1A (or presents additional primary statements), refer to Chapter 4 which addresses the presentation requirements of full FRS 102, both before and after applying the FRS 102 (July 2015) amendments. The presentation requirements of full FRS 102 that are mandatory for entities applying Section 1A are covered in 7 below.

FRS 102 (amended July 2015) introduces new transition exemptions for small entities (see 6.3 below) and exempts small entities from preparing a cash flow statement (see 7.1 below). These exemptions apply whether or not Section 1A is applied.

This Chapter has been cross referred from Chapter 1 – FRS 100 because it discusses the qualifying criteria for the small companies regime and small LLPs regime (see 4 below). The statutory disclosure exemptions available to companies subject to the small companies regime and to companies taking advantage of the small companies exemption are addressed at 12 below. This section sets out the disclosure exemptions available in Companies Act accounts (FRS 101, full FRS 102, FRS 102 applying Section 1A) and IAS accounts prepared by companies subject to the small companies regime for financial years beginning on or after 1.1.2016 (or where SI 2015/980 is early applied). As small companies statutory exemptions discussed at 12 below have a wider scope than FRS 102 financial statements applying Section 1A, it has been located at the end of the Chapter. Chapter 1 of EY New UK GAAP 2015 addresses company law requirements for small companies (preparing IAS accounts or Companies Act accounts) prior to SI 2015/980. SI 2015/980 amends the requirements for companies and qualifying partnerships, but not Limited Liability Partnerships (LLPs). As noted at 1 above, a change to LLP law is expected to be consulted on in due course and Irish law is expected to be updated later in 2015 to implement the new Accounting Directive. Consequently, LLPs and other entities that are not UK companies need to consider carefully the statutory requirements that apply. In particular, LLPs have different size and eligibility conditions to qualify for the small LLPs regime compared to companies subject to the small companies regime. Small LLPs need to comply with the requirements of Section 1A, where applied, and LLP law. Appendix IV to FRS 102 – *Note on Legal Requirements* – notes that if following the requirements of FRS 102 would lead to a conflict with applicable legislation, an LLP shall instead apply its own legal requirements and consider whether disclosure of a departure from FRS 102 is required. *[FRS 102.A4.43-47]*. For this reason, where appropriate, this chapter highlights key changes made by SI 2015/980.

2   SUMMARY OF SECTION 1A (AND OTHER SMALL ENTITY ACCOUNTS REQUIREMENTS)

- Section 1A sets out accounting requirements for entities subject to the small entities regime (see 4 below). Section 1A can be applied by a company qualifying for the small companies regime (see 4.3 below), an LLP qualifying for the small LLPs regime (see 4.4 below) or an entity that would have qualified for the small companies regime had it been a company. It is optional and small entities can choose to apply the full standard, FRS 102.

- Section 1A, like the other FRS 102 (July 2015) amendments (excepting the change to share-based payment classification), is effective for accounting periods beginning on or after 1 January 2016. Early application is permitted for accounting periods beginning on or after 1 January 2015 provided that SI 2015/980 is applied from the same date, and required if the reporting entity applies SI 2015/980 to an accounting period beginning before 1 January 2016. For entities not subject to company law, early application is permitted from 1 January 2015. See 5 below.

- Section 1A requires that small entities apply the recognition and measurement requirements of FRS 102 in full and exempts small entities from most of the existing presentation requirements of FRS 102 (except for general principles). See 5 and 7 below.

- Where Section 1A is applied by a small entity, a complete set of financial statements comprises: a statement of financial position, an income statement, and notes. Small entities are encouraged to but not required to present a statement of comprehensive income, or statement of changes in equity (or statement of income and retained earnings). See 8 below.

- Small entities applying FRS 102 are not required to prepare a cash flow statement (even if they do not apply Section 1A). See 7.1 below.

- Section 1A requires the statement of financial position and income statement to be presented in accordance with Schedule 1 to the Small Companies Regulations (as amended by SI 2015/980) (which permits the use of abridged formats, adapted formats or statutory formats) or Schedule 1 to the Small LLP Regulations (which permits use of statutory formats only, unless LLP law is subsequently changed). See 8 to 10 below.

- Small entities must provide the disclosures set out in Appendix C to Section 1A, which are based on the statutory requirements in the CA 2006 and Small Companies Regulations (as amended by SI 2015/980) for companies subject to the small companies regime. Appendix C covers the vast majority of statutory disclosures applicable to companies subject to the small companies regime. Small LLPs need to comply with both the disclosures in Section 1A and those in LLP law (which differ). See 11 below.

- Financial statements prepared by small entities are required to give a true and fair view; consequently, additional disclosures beyond those specifically mandated may be required (see 7.2 and 11 below). Appendix D to Section 1A sets out additional disclosures specifically encouraged for small entities. See 11.3 below.

- A small entity that is a parent entity (see the conditions for a small parent company at 4.3.2 and 4.3.3 and for a small parent LLP at 4.4 below) is not required to prepare consolidated financial statements. Section 1A sets out requirements for voluntary preparation of consolidated financial statements. See 6.2.1 below.

- FRS 102 includes new transitional exemptions for small entities (whether or not applying Section 1A). See 6.2 below.

- SI 2015/980 increases the size limits for companies subject to the small companies regime – the thresholds are: turnover £10.2m, balance sheet total £5.1m and 50 employees. SI 2015/980 also changes the types of companies excluded from the small companies regime. These changes do not apply to LLPs (unless LLP law is subsequently changed). See 4 below.

- SI 2015/980 removes the option for companies subject to the small companies regime to prepare abbreviated accounts for filing purposes that are separate from the accounts prepared for members. The accounts for members must instead be filed; however, small companies and LLPs do benefit from certain filing exemptions. See 12.3 below.

Chapter 3

3   KEY DEFINITIONS

See Chapter 4 of EY New UK GAAP 2015 at 3.1. Definitions relevant to qualification for the small companies regime (and small LLPs regime) are included at 4 below.

4   SCOPE OF SMALL ENTITIES REGIME

This section defines a small entity and explains how Section 1A applies. It also explains the definition of the small companies regime (as amended by SI 2015/980) and small LLPs regime because this is relevant to the scope of which small entities can apply Section 1A. The definitions below reflect the amendments in *The Small Companies (Micro-Entities' Accounts) Regulations 2013* (SI 2013/3008) for financial years ending on or after 30 September 2013 and *The Companies and Partnerships (Accounts and Audit) Regulations 2013* (SI 2013/2005) for financial years beginning on or after 1 October 2013.

4.1   Definition of a small entity

A small entity is defined as:

(a)   a company meeting the definition of a small company as set out in section 382 or 383 of the CA 2006 and not excluded from the small companies regime by section 384 (see 4.3 below);

(b)   an LLP qualifying as small and not excluded from the small LLPs regime, as set out in LLP Regulations (see 4.4 below); or

(c)   any other entity that would have met the criteria in (a) had it been a company incorporated under company law. *[FRS 102.Appendix I]*.

4.2   Application of Section 1A

Section 1A applies to all small entities applying the small entities regime, whether or not they report under the CA 2006. Small entities that do not report under the CA 2006 must comply with Section 1A and with the Small Companies Regulations (or where applicable, the Small LLP Regulations) where referred to by Section 1A, except to the extent that these requirements are not permitted by any statutory framework under which such entities report. *[FRS 102.1A.4]*.

Note that one of the requirements of the CA 2006, included in Section 1A, is for the financial statements of a small entity to give a true and fair view. *[FRS 102.1A.5]*. The requirement to comply with the CA 2006, Small Companies Regulations, Small LLP Regulations or other statutory framework may mean that additional disclosures to those listed in Section 1A may be required. *[FRS 102.1A.6]*. See 7.2 and 11 below for further guidance.

Section 1A sets out the information to be presented and disclosed in the financial statements of a small entity that chooses to apply the small entities regime. Unless specifically excluded (see 7.1 below), all of the requirements of FRS 102, including the recognition and measurement requirements, apply to a small entity applying Section 1A. *[FRS 102.1A.1]*.

References to a small entity in paragraphs 1A.4 to 1A.22 of Section 1A (and its appendices), i.e. all its remaining requirements, are to a small entity that chooses to apply the small entities regime. *[FRS 102.1A.3]*.

Unless a small entity chooses to apply EU-adopted IFRS or, if eligible, FRS 101, a small entity that chooses not to apply the small entities regime shall apply FRS 102, excluding Section 1A. *[FRS 102.1A.2]*. Section 1A is therefore optional for small entities.

4.3   Small companies regime

The small companies regime applies to a company for a financial year in relation to which the company qualifies as small (see 4.3.1 and 4.3.2 below) and is not excluded from the regime (see 4.3.3 below). *[s381]*.

The size criteria and exclusions below are those set out in SI 2015/980, because if a UK company applies Section 1A it will also be applying SI 2015/980. See 5 below for effective dates of both Section 1A and SI 2015/980.

SI 2015/980 raises the size thresholds for turnover and balance sheet total. Note that in determining whether a company or group qualifies as small under sections 382(2) or 383(3) (qualification in relation to subsequent financial year by reference to circumstances in preceding financial years) in relation to a financial year for which the amendments made by SI 2015/980 have effect, the company or group is treated as having qualified as small in any previous financial year in which it would have so qualified if the amendments to the same effect as the amendments made in SI 2015/980 had had effect in relation to that previous year.[1] This means that if SI 2015/980 is first applied in calendar year 2016, the new size thresholds are applied to 2016 and the preceding financial years (to see whether the company qualifies as small in 2016).

SI 2015/980 also changes the exclusions (see 4.3.3 below). The key change is that previously a company that was a member of an ineligible group containing a public company (i.e. a PLC) was excluded whereas now the exclusion applies to a company that is a member of an ineligible group containing a 'traded company' (i.e. a company any of whose transferable securities are admitted to trading on a regulated market). A small company that is itself a public company remains excluded.

4.3.1   *Companies qualifying as small – company is not a parent undertaking (size criteria)*

A company qualifies as small in relation to its first financial year if the qualifying conditions (as set out below) are met in that year.

A company qualifies as small in relation to a subsequent financial year if the qualifying conditions are met in that year. In relation to a subsequent financial year, where on its balance sheet date a company meets or ceases to meet the qualifying conditions, then that will affect its qualification as a small company only if it occurs in two consecutive years. *[s382(1), (1A), (2)]*.

This provision is designed to assist companies which fluctuate in and out of the qualifying conditions. However, if a company fails to meet the criteria in two consecutive years, it will cease to qualify, and then would need to meet the criteria in two later consecutive years to re-qualify for the exemptions.

The qualifying conditions are met in a year in which the company satisfies two or more of the following requirements:

- turnover must not exceed £10.2 million;
- balance sheet total must not exceed £5.1 million; and
- the number of employees must not exceed 50.

If the company's financial year is not in fact a full year, the turnover figure should be adjusted proportionately. The 'balance sheet total' means the aggregate of the amounts shown as assets in the balance sheet, i.e. total assets. The number of employees means the average number of persons employed under contracts of service by the company in the year (determined on a monthly basis, with the monthly totals added together and then divided by the number of months in the financial year). *[s382(3)-(6)]*.

4.3.2   *Companies qualifying as small – company is a parent undertaking (size criteria)*

Where the company is itself a parent undertaking, then it only qualifies as small if the group that it heads qualifies as a small group *[s382(7), 383(1)]*. This is the case whether or not group accounts are prepared.

A group qualifies as small in relation to the parent's first financial year if the qualifying conditions (as set out below) are met in that year.

A group qualifies as small in relation to a subsequent financial year if the qualifying conditions are met in that year. In relation to a subsequent financial year, where on its balance sheet date the group meets or ceases to meet the qualifying conditions, then that will affect the group's qualification as small only if it occurs in two consecutive years. *[s383(2), (2A), (3)]*.

The qualifying conditions for a small group are met in a year in which the group headed by the company satisfies two or more of the following requirements:

- turnover must not exceed £10.2 million net (or £12.2 million gross);
- balance sheet total must not exceed £5.1 million (or £6.1 million gross); and
- the number of employees must not exceed 50.

The aggregate figures for the above limits are ascertained by aggregating the relevant figures determined in accordance with section 382 for each member of the group. The figures used for each subsidiary undertaking are those included in its individual accounts for the relevant financial year, i.e. where its financial year is coterminous with that of the parent company, the financial year that ends at the same date as the parent company, or where its financial year is not coterminous, the financial year ending last before the end of the financial year of the parent company. If those figures are not obtainable without disproportionate expense or undue delay, the latest available figures are used. The turnover and balance sheet total criteria may be satisfied on either the gross or net of consolidation adjustments basis. For Companies Act accounts (such as FRS 102 financial statements), the consolidation adjustments are determined in accordance with regulations made under section 404, i.e. the Regulations or the Small Companies Regulations. For IAS accounts, the consolidation adjustments are determined in accordance with EU-adopted IFRS. It is permissible to satisfy one limit on the 'net' basis and the other on the 'gross' basis. *[s383(4)-(7)]*.

4.3.3 Companies excluded from the small companies regime

A company is excluded from the small companies regime if it was at any time in the financial year to which the accounts relate:

- a public company;
- a company that is an authorised insurance company, a banking company, an e-money issuer, a MiFID investment firm or a UCITS management company;
- a company that carries on an insurance market activity; or
- a member of an ineligible group. *[s384(1)]*.

A group is ineligible if any of its members is:

- a traded company;
- a body corporate (other than a company) whose shares are admitted to trading on a regulated market in an EEA State;
- a person (other than a small company) who has permission under Part 4 of the Financial Services and Markets Act 2000 to carry on a regulated activity;
- an e-money issuer;
- a small company that is an authorised insurance company, banking company, a MiFID investment firm or a UCITS management company; or
- a person who carries on an insurance market activity. *[s384(2)]*.

A company is a small company for the purposes of section 384(2) if it qualified as small in relation to its last financial year ending on or before the end of the financial year to which the accounts relate. *[s384(3)]*.

4.3.3.A Relevant definitions for small companies regime

The reference to a 'company' above is to a company formed and registered (or treated as formed and registered) under the CA 2006. This means a company formed and registered under the CA 2006, or prior to 1 October 2009 under the Companies Act 1985, Companies (Northern Ireland) Order 1986 or former Companies Acts (i.e. was an existing company for the purposes of that Act and Order). *[s1]*.

A traded company is a company any of whose transferable securities are admitted to trading on a regulated market. *[s474(1)]*.

A regulated market is a regulated market (as defined in Directive 2004/39/EC). A list of regulated markets is obtainable from the ESMA website.[2] *[s1173(1)]*.

A public company means a company limited by shares or limited by guarantee and having a share capital (a) whose certificate of incorporation states that it is a public company and (b) in relation to which the requirements of the CA 2006 or the former

Companies Acts as to registration or re-registration as a public company have been complied with (on or after the relevant date, being 22 December 1980 in Great Britain and 1 July 1983 in Northern Ireland). *[s4]*. Therefore, a public company means any UK-incorporated company that is a 'plc' or 'PLC' rather than a publicly traded company.

An authorised insurance company is defined in section 1165(2), a banking company in section 1164(2)-(3) and insurance market activity in section 1165(7). See Chapter 4 at 4.2.2 and 4.2.3

The terms e-money issuer, MiFID investment firm, regulated activity, and UCITS management company are defined in section 474 of the CA 2006. The term 'e-money issuer' means an electronic money institution within the meaning of *The Electronic Money Regulations 2011* (SI 2011/99). *[s474]*.

A body corporate includes a body incorporated outside the UK but does not include (a) a corporation sole or (b) a partnership that, whether or not a legal person, is not regarded as a body corporate under the law by which it is governed. *[s1173(1)]*. Therefore, a body corporate would include an overseas company or a UK LLP.

A group means a parent and its subsidiary undertakings. *[s474(1)]*.

4.4   Small LLPs regime

Because SI 2015/980 does not apply to LLPs, the size limits and exclusions applying to the small LLPs regime have not changed and consequently differ to the small companies regime. A change to LLP law to implement the new Accounting Directive is expected to be consulted on in due course.

4.4.1   Size criteria

The qualifying conditions are the same as for small companies regime except that the size criteria for an LLP (that is not a parent) are that:

- turnover must not exceed £6.5 million;
- balance sheet total must not exceed £3.26 million; and
- the number of employees must not exceed 50.

Similarly, the small size criteria for an LLP (that is a parent) are that for the group headed by that LLP:

- turnover must not exceed £6.5 million net (or £7.8 million gross);
- balance sheet total must not exceed £3.26 million (or £3.9 million gross); and
- the number of employees must not exceed 50.

These size criteria operate in the same way as described for companies above. *[s382, SI 2008/1911]*.

4.4.2   Excluded LLPs

An LLP is excluded from the small LLPs regime if it is (or was at any time in the financial year to which the accounts relate):

- an LLP whose securities are admitted to trading on a regulated market in an EEA State;

- an LLP that is an authorised insurance company, a banking LLP, an e-money issuer, a MiFID investment firm or a UCITS management company;

- an LLP that carries on an insurance market activity; or

- a member of an ineligible group. *[s384(1), LLP SI 2008/1911].*

A group is ineligible if any of its members is:

- a public company;

- a body corporate (other than a company) whose shares are admitted to trading on a regulated market in an EEA State;

- a person (other than a small company or small LLP) who has permission under Part 4 of the Financial Services and Markets Act 2000 to carry on a regulated activity;

- an e-money issuer;

- a small company or small LLP that is an authorised insurance company, banking company or banking LLP, a MiFID investment firm or a UCITS management company; or

- a person who carries on an insurance market activity. *[s384(2), LLP SI 2008/1911].*

A company or LLP is a small company or small LLP for the purposes of section 384(2) if it qualified as small in relation to its last financial year ending on or before the end of the financial year to which the accounts relate. *[s384(3), LLP SI 2008/1911].*

5 EFFECTIVE DATE

The FRS 102 (July 2015) amendments which introduce Section 1A are effective for accounting periods beginning on or after 1 January 2016. These amendments have been included in the September 2015 edition of FRS 102.

Early application is permitted for accounting periods beginning on or after 1 January 2015 provided that SI 2015/980 is applied from the same date and required if an entity applies SI 2015/980 for an accounting period beginning before 1 January 2016. For entities not subject to company law, early application is permitted from 1 January 2015.

If an entity applies the FRS 102 (July 2015) amendments before 1 January 2016, it shall disclose that fact, unless it is a small entity in which case it is encouraged to disclose that fact. *[FRS 102.1.15].*

These effective dates are clearly intended to align with application of SI 2015/980 (which is required for financial years beginning on or after 1 January 2016 but may be applied for financial years beginning on or after 1 January 2015 but before 1 January 2016, if the directors so decide).[3]

There is a lack of clarity over early application of the FRS 102 (July 2015) amendments for entities not applying SI 2015/980. We presume that, for entities not subject to company law, the reference to 'early application is permitted from 1 January 2015' is intended to mean for accounting periods beginning on or after 1 January 2015.

The reference to 'entities not subject to company law' is unclear. Appendix IV to FRS 102 – *Note on Legal Requirements*, however, may support the view that LLPs may apply early since it discusses areas of inconsistency between FRS 102 (amended July 2015) and LLP law, including the flexibility available in relation to the format of the balance sheet and of the profit and loss account. *[FRS 102.A4.43-A4.47]*. This particular example is, however, not so much an inconsistency as a restriction meaning LLPs may not take advantage of the new 'adapted formats' (unless LLP law is subsequently changed to allow this). We expect that Irish companies will implement FRS 102 (amended July 2015) from the same date that Irish company law implementing the new Accounting Directive (once in place) is applied, in order to align the legal and accounting requirements.

6   ACCOUNTING REQUIREMENTS

Section 1A does not set out a separate recognition and measurement regime for small entities, instead requiring that small entities follow the recognition and measurement requirements of full FRS 102 (see 6.1 below). It also addresses the requirements where a small entity prepares consolidated financial statements (see 6.2 below). Section 35 of the standard includes certain transition exemptions for small entities (which apply whether or not the small entity applies Section 1A) (see 6.3 below).

6.1   Recognition and measurement requirements of FRS 102

All the recognition and measurement requirements of FRS 102 apply to a small entity applying Section 1A. The only exclusions from the remainder of FRS 102 relate to certain presentation and disclosure requirements. *[FRS 102.1A.1, 1A.7]*.

6.2   Preparation of consolidated financial statements under Section 1A

A small entity that is a parent entity is not required to prepare consolidated financial statements. *[FRS 102.1A.21]*.

This is consistent with the requirements of the CA 2006 as a parent company subject to the small companies regime (see 4.3 above) is not required to prepare group accounts but may do so. *[s398, s399]*.

The group accounts exemption in CA 2006 has been extended by SI 2015/980 to a small parent company that would qualify for the small companies regime but for being a public company, so long as it is not a traded company (see definitions at 4.3.3.A above). This exemption has been included in Section 9 – *Consolidated and Separate Financial Statements* – of the standard. *[s399(2A), FRS 102.9.3(e)]*. Unless LLP law is subsequently changed, this extension of the exemption for preparation of group accounts does not apply to LLPs. *[s399, LLP SI 2008/1911]*.

6.2.1 Voluntary preparation of consolidated financial statements

If a small entity that is a parent voluntarily chooses to prepare consolidated financial statements, it:

(a) shall apply the consolidation procedures set out in Section 9 (see Chapter 6 of EY New UK GAAP 2015);

(b) is encouraged to provide the disclosures set out in paragraph 9.23 (see 11.4.1 below);

(c) shall comply so far as practicable with the requirements of Section 1A as if it were a single entity (Schedule 6 of the Small Companies Regulations, paragraph 1(1)), subject to any restrictions or exemptions set out in legislation; and

(d) shall provide any disclosures required by Schedule 6 of the Small Companies Regulations (see 11.4.3 and 11.4.4 below). *[FRS 102.1A.22].*

6.2.2 Interaction with statutory requirements

Group accounts are drawn up as at the same date as the accounts of the parent company. *[6 Sch 2(1A) (SC)].* Only the 'adapted formats' or statutory formats can be applied in group accounts. The abridged formats are not available in group accounts. *[6 Sch 1(1A) (SC)].* See 8.1 below for further discussion of these formats.

Small companies must comply with Schedule 6 to the Small Companies Regulations (and small LLPs with Schedule 4 to the Small LLP Regulations) which set out further requirements over consolidation procedures, the acquisition method, the conditions for merger accounting and disclosures. The requirements for consolidated financial statements in the Small Companies Regulations are the same as in the Regulations, as discussed in Chapter 15 at 5.2.1 of EY New UK GAAP 2015.

SI 2015/980 changes the group accounts exemptions and the conditions where merger accounting is permitted when a parent company acquires a subsidiary undertaking. *[s400, s401, 6 Sch 10 (SC)].* The change to the law affects companies rather than LLPs (unless there is a subsequent change to LLP law). In the event of a conflict between the requirements of FRS 102 and applicable legislation, an LLP is required to apply its own legal requirements and consider, if applicable, whether disclosure of a departure with FRS 102 is required. *[FRS 102.A4.47].* See Chapter 5 at 7.2 and 13.

6.3 Transition

The FRS 102 (July 2015) amendments introduce three new transitional exemptions that apply specifically to small entities. These are time limited and apply where a small entity first adopts FRS 102 for an accounting period that commences before 1 January 2017.

The exemptions relate to share-based payment transactions (see 6.3.1 below), fair value measurement of financial instruments (see 6.3.2 below) and financing transactions involving related parties (see 6.3.3 below) These are principally areas where additional burdens may be incurred in applying FRS 102 for the first time because an entity's transition date to FRS 102 occurred before the amendments were finalised. The FRSSE remains available for financial years beginning on or after 1 January 2015 so many small entities may only apply FRS 102 for the first time for financial years beginning on or after 1 January 2016.

Note that there is no requirement for Section 1A to be applied for the small entity in order to make use of these exemptions.

6.3.1   Share-based payment transactions

Section 35 – *Transition to this FRS* – already included an exemption for entities not previously applying FRS 20 – *Share-based payment* – or IFRS 2 – *Share-based Payment* – in respect of equity instruments granted before the date of transition to FRS 102 in share-based payment transactions. *[FRS 102.35.10(b)]*. See Chapter 30 at 5.4 of EY New UK GAAP 2015. For a small entity that first adopts FRS 102 for an accounting period that commences before 1 January 2017, the transition exemption relating to equity instruments granted before the date of transition is extended to equity instruments that were granted before the start of the first reporting period that complies with FRS 102, provided that the small entity did not previously apply FRS 20 or IFRS 2. However, a small entity that applies this exemption shall provide disclosures in accordance with paragraph 1AC.31. This paragraph sets out the disclosures for off-balance sheet arrangements so presumably it is intended that disclosures of the share-based payment arrangements are given (see 11.1.5.H below). *[FRS 102.35.10(b)]*.

This enhanced transition exemption would therefore mean that a small entity that first applies FRS 102 for financial statements beginning on or after 1 January 2016 need not apply the requirements of Section 26 – *Share-based Payment* – of the standard to equity instruments granted before 1 January 2016, unless it had previously applied FRS 20 or IFRS 2.

The FRS 102 (July 2015) amendments also clarify that the reference in the transition exemption to equity instruments granted prior to transition in 35.10(b) extends to the equity component of share-based payment transactions previously treated as compound instruments. *[FRS 102.35.10(b)]*.

6.3.2   Small entities – fair value measurement of financial instruments

A small entity that first adopts FRS 102 for an accounting period that commences before 1 January 2017 need not restate comparative information to comply with the fair value measurement requirements of Section 11 – *Basic Financial Instruments* – or Section 12 – *Other Financial Instruments Issues* (see Chapter 8 at 4 of EY New UK GAAP 2015), unless those financial instruments were measured at fair value in accordance with the small entity's previous accounting framework.

A small entity that chooses to present comparative information that does not comply with the fair value measurement requirements of Sections 11 and 12 in its first year of adoption:

*   shall apply its existing accounting policies to the relevant financial instruments in the comparative information and is encouraged to disclose this fact;

- shall disclose the accounting policies applied, in accordance with paragraph 1AC.3 (see 11.1.2 below); and

- shall treat any adjustment between the statement of financial position at the comparative period's reporting date and the statement of financial position at the start of the first reporting period that complies with Sections 11 and 12 as an adjustment, in the current reporting period, to opening equity. *[FRS 102.35.10(u)]*.

6.3.3   Small entities – financing transactions involving related parties

A small entity that first adopts FRS 102 for an accounting period that commences before 1 January 2017 need not restate comparative information to comply with the requirements of paragraph 11.13 only insofar as they related to financing transactions involving related parties.

Related parties are defined in paragraph 33.2 of FRS 102 (which was amended by FRS 102 July 2015 amendments). See Chapter 28 at 3.1 of EY New UK GAAP 2015 and details of the amendment in Chapter 5 at 12.1.

A small entity that chooses to present comparative information that does not comply with the financing transaction requirements of Section 11 in its first year of adoption:

- shall apply its existing accounting policies to the relevant financial instruments in the comparative information and is encouraged to disclose this fact;

- shall disclose the accounting policies applied, in accordance with paragraph 1AC.3 (see 11.1.2 below); and

- shall treat any adjustment between the statement of financial position at the comparative period's reporting date and the statement of financial position at the start of the first reporting period that complies with paragraph 11.13 as an adjustment, in the current reporting period, to opening equity. The present value of the financial asset or financial liability at the start of the first reporting period that complies with FRS 102 may be determined on the basis of the facts and circumstances existing at that date rather than when the arrangement was entered into. *[FRS 102.35.10(v)]*.

Note that the transition exemption only extends to financing transactions involving related parties. It also appears that this exemption is not available where IAS 39 – *Financial Instruments: Recognition and Measurement* – or IFRS 9 – *Financial Instruments* – are applied to recognition and measurement of financial instruments (since it refers to paragraph 11.13 which would not be relevant where IFRSs are being applied).

The transition exception for derecognition of financial instruments (see Chapter 30 at 4.1 of EY New UK GAAP 2015) still applies. *[FRS 102.35.9(a)]*. Therefore, in our view, paragraph 35.10(v) is only relevant to financial instruments that continue to be recognised at the date of transition, after applying the transition exception.

Paragraph 11.13 requires that where an arrangement constitutes, in effect, a financing transaction, the entity shall measure the financial asset or financial liability at the present value of the future payments discounted at a market rate of interest for a similar debt instrument. Paragraph 11.13 further explains that a financing transaction may take place in connection with the sale of goods and services, for example, if payment is deferred beyond normal business terms or is financed at a rate of interest that is not a market rate, and gives examples. *[FRS 102.11.13]*.

An entity (including a small entity) will need to apply Section 11 fully retrospectively to transactions not covered by paragraph 35.10(v), including financing transactions with non-related parties (subject to the exemption for fair value measurement requirements described at 6.3.2 above).

A small entity has a choice of measuring the adjustment required for financing transactions involving related parties at the beginning of the first FRS 102 reporting period:

(a)   by applying FRS 102 retrospectively, which would include applying the market rate of interest for a similar debt instrument as at the date of the original transaction; or

(b)   based on the facts and circumstances existing at the start of the first FRS 102 reporting period.

Where approach (b) to measure the adjustment based on the facts and circumstances existing at the start of the first FRS 102 reporting period is taken, this means that the market rate of interest applied to the future payments would reflect that for a similar debt instrument as at the start of the first FRS 102 reporting period. This provides relief from identifying what market rate of interest would have pertained to a similar debt instrument, as at the date of the original transaction, which may, in some cases, have been many years ago. Approach (b) may still involve practical difficulties in determining a market rate of interest for a similar debt instrument but the potential problems of exercising undue hindsight are resolved.

As discussed below, approach (b) would also appear to allow a financing transaction with a related party that has been previously restructured to be measured based on the circumstances at the beginning of the first FRS 102 reporting period rather than fully retrospectively applying the standard (with an adjustment to opening equity at the beginning of the first FRS 102 reporting period). Using approach (b) means an entity need not determine how any previous restructuring(s) would be accounted for under FRS 102 had it been applied retrospectively, as is required under approach (a). Applying FRS 102 retrospectively may be difficult, requiring, in principle, knowledge of previous contractual terms, details of any changes to contractual terms and the original effective interest rate.

The new transition exemption (which relates to the initial measurement requirements in paragraph 11.13) refers to 'a small entity that chooses to present comparative information that *does not comply with the financing transaction requirements of Section 11 in its first year of adoption*' [emphasis added] and approach (b) allows measurement based on the facts and circumstances as at the first FRS 102 reporting period (so clearly applies to subsequent measurement too). The italicised references would seem to allow an entity not to apply Section 11 in its entirety to related party financing transactions in the comparative period. Even if it did so, we believe that if the transaction qualifies for derecognition (subject to application of the transition exception) under the standard by the start of the first

FRS 102 reporting period, it will need to be derecognised at that date since this reflects the facts and circumstances at that date and the exemption relates to *measurement* of the present value of the financial instrument. However, sometimes a modification of the contractual terms of a financial instrument leads to extinguishment and recognition of a new financial instrument and sometimes to continued recognition of the existing financial instrument. In both cases, where there is still a financial instrument (whether new or the existing financial instrument) to recognise, the transition exemption (under approach (b)) appears to allow it to be measured based on the facts and circumstances existing at the start of the first FRS 102 reporting period rather than retrospectively applying the standard.

Where a financing transaction with a related party is designated at fair value through profit and loss under paragraph 11.14(b), in our view, it would be more appropriate to apply FRS 102 retrospectively or, where available, the transition exemption described at 6.3.2 above.

7   REQUIREMENTS IN SECTION 3 – FINANCIAL STATEMENT PRESENTATION OF FRS 102 THAT STILL APPLY WHERE SECTION 1A IS APPLIED

A small entity applying Section 1A of FRS 102 must comply with Section 3 of the standard, except for certain specified paragraphs (see 7.1 below). This means such an entity must still comply with Section 3's requirements on:

- 'true and fair view'(including overrides) (see 7.2 below); *[FRS 102.3.1-3.2, 3.4-3.6]*

- assessment of the entity's ability to continue as a going concern (see 7.3 below); *[FRS 102.3.8]*

- frequency of reporting (see 7.4 below); *[FRS 102.3.10]*

- consistency of presentation and comparative information (see 7.5 below); *[FRS 102.3.11-3.14, 3.20]*

- materiality and aggregation (see 7.6 below); *[FRS 102.3.15-3.16A]*

- requirements to present each financial statement in a complete set of financial statements with equal prominence, and ability to use other titles for the financial statements as long as they are not misleading; *[FRS 102.3.21-3.22]*

- identification of the financial statements, except for paragraph 3.24(b) (see 7.7 below); *[FRS 102.3.23-3.24(a)]* and

- interim financial reports (see 7.8 below). *[FRS 102.3.25].*

7.1   Exemptions from certain presentation and disclosure requirements in FRS 102 for a small entity applying Section 1A

A small entity applying Section 1A is not required to comply with the following paragraphs of Section 3 (see also discussion below):

- paragraph 3.3 (statement of compliance);
- paragraph PBE 3.3A (statement of compliance by a public benefit entity);
- paragraph 3.9 (disclosure of material uncertainties over going concern);

- paragraph 3.17 (requirements for a complete set of financial statements);
- paragraph 3.18 (option to present a statement of income and retained earnings, where certain conditions are met);
- paragraph 3.19 (option to present only an income statement where there are no items of other comprehensive income, or to label the bottom line of the statement of comprehensive income as 'profit or loss'); and
- paragraph 3.24(b) (description of the nature of the entity's operations and its principal activities, unless disclosed in the business review (or similar statement) accompanying the financial statements). *[FRS 102.1A.7, 3.1A]*.

In addition, a small entity applying Section 1A is not required to comply with Section 4 – *Statement of Financial Position*, Section 5 – *Statement of Comprehensive Income and Income Statement*, Section 6 – *Statement of Changes in Equity and Statement of Income and Retained Earnings* – and Section 7 – *Statement of Cash Flows* (or the disclosure requirements in Sections 8 to 35) of the standard. The cash flow exemption is extended to any small entity, whether or not applying Section 1A. *[FRS 102.1A.7, 1A.17, 3.1A, 4.1A, 5.1A, 6.1A, 7.1B]*. The above requirements have been disapplied because they relate to disclosures not required by the CA 2006 and the Small Companies Regulations (as amended by SI 2015/980) and because company law only requires presentation of a balance sheet and profit and loss account.

As explained further at 8 below, Section 1A states that a complete set of financial statements includes a statement of financial position and income statement, in accordance with the requirements of Part 1 of Schedule 1 to the Small Companies Regulations (as amended by SI 2015/980) or Part 1 of Schedule 1 to the Small LLP Regulations, together with the required notes. *[FRS 102.1A.8, 1A.12, 1A.14]*. However, a small entity is encouraged to present a statement of total comprehensive income, where it has items in other comprehensive income, and to present a statement of changes in equity (or statement of income and retained earnings) where it has transactions with equity holders. *[FRS 102.1A.9, 6.1A]*.

Section 1A requires that a complete set of financial statements prepared by a small entity also includes notes in accordance with paragraphs 1A.16 to 1A.20. *[FRS 102.1A.8]*. The notes to the financial statements contain information in addition to those presented in the primary financial statements and provide narrative descriptions or disaggregations of items presented in those statements and information about items that do not qualify for recognition in those statements. *[FRS 102.Appendix I]*. Consistent with the Small Companies Regulations (as amended by SI 2015/980), the notes must be presented in the order in which, where relevant, the items to which they relate are presented in the statement of financial position and in the income statement. *[FRS 102.1AC.2]*.

Appendix C of Section 1A sets out specific note disclosures to be given by a small entity that are based on the statutory requirements for a small company applying the Small Companies Regulations. However, additional disclosures may be needed in order for the financial statements to give a true and fair view. Section 1A includes a list of FRS 102 disclosures that are specifically encouraged (and which may nevertheless be necessary for the financial statements to give a true and fair view). Small entities are also encouraged to consider and provide other disclosures from the standard that are relevant to material transactions, other events or conditions of the small entity in order for the financial statements to give a true and fair view. Specific disclosures are not required if the information is immaterial. *[FRS 102.1A.16-20]*. See 7.2 and 11 below.

Consequently, the presentation sections of FRS 102, beyond the mandatory paragraphs of Section 3, remain relevant to small entities applying Section 1A that present additional primary statements or disclosures.

7.2   True and fair view

The financial statements of a small entity shall give a true and fair view of the assets, liabilities, financial position and profit or loss of the small entity for the reporting period. *[FRS 102.1A.5]*. The Companies Act 2006 similarly requires that directors of a company must not approve accounts unless satisfied that they give a true and fair view of the assets, liabilities, financial position and profit or loss of the company (and in respect of any group accounts, the undertakings included in the consolidation as a whole, so far as concerns the members of the company). *[s393]*.

Section 3 of FRS 102 provides further guidance on the requirement that financial statements must give a true and fair view. *[FRS 102.3.1]*. Application of FRS 102, with additional disclosure when necessary, is presumed to result in financial statements that give a true and fair view of the financial position, financial performance and, when required to be presented, cash flows of entities within the scope of the standard. Additional disclosures are necessary when compliance with the specific requirements in the standard is insufficient to enable users to understand the effect of particular transactions, other events and conditions on the entity's financial position and performance and, when required to be presented, cash flows of an entity. *[FRS 102.3.2]*.

The requirement for a true and fair view for a small entity applying Section 1A refers to profit or loss (rather than financial performance in paragraph 3.2) and excludes reference to cash flows because small entities are not required to present a statement of comprehensive income or a cash flow statement.

Section 1A's similar requirement to present additional disclosures where necessary to meet the requirement for the financial statements to give a true and fair view *[FRS 102.1A.16]* is consistent with the statutory requirement that if compliance with the regulations, and any other provisions made by or under the Companies Act 2006, as to matters to be included in a company's individual (and/or group) accounts or in notes to those accounts, would not be sufficient to give a true and fair view, the necessary additional information must be given in the accounts or notes to them. *[s396(4), s404(4)]*.

A particular issue for small entities relates to the fact that the statutory disclosures for companies subject to the small companies regime (and hence the disclosures included in Section 1A) are considerably more limited than those required for entities applying full FRS 102. Consequently, a small entity may need to provide disclosures in addition to those set out in Section 1A in order to comply with the requirement in paragraph 1A.5 that the financial statements give a true and fair view of the assets, liabilities, financial position and profit or loss of the small entity. *[FRS 102.1A.6]*. See 11 below for further guidance.

The general principles governing financial statements – going concern, consistency, prudence, accruals basis and rules on offset and that the opening balance sheet for a financial year corresponds to the closing balance sheet for the previous financial year – set out in the Small Companies Regulations are exactly the same as those set out in the Regulations and discussed in Chapter 4 at 9.1. *[1 Sch 11-15A (SC)]*. Similarly, the Small Companies Regulations set out the historical cost accounting rules, alternative accounting rules and fair value accounting rules. *[1 Sch 16-41 (SC)]*. The recognition and measurement requirements are the same as in the Regulations as discussed in Chapter 4 at 10 (although the Small Companies Regulations have simpler disclosures). Small companies that are micro entities preparing accounts in accordance with the micro-entity regime cannot apply the alternative accounting rules or fair value accounting rules (but such companies would apply FRS 105 rather than Section 1A of FRS 102). *[1 Sch 3(1A) (SC)]*.

For LLPs, the Small LLP Regulations omit the new general principle that an opening balance sheet for the financial year corresponds to the closing balance sheet for the previous financial year. *[1 Sch 15A (SC)]*. In addition, the historical cost accounting rules, alternative accounting rules and fair value accounting rules set out in the Small LLP Regulations differ in certain respects to those in the Small Companies Regulations (as amended by SI 2015/980). The requirements of the Small LLP Regulations are the same as those discussed for the Regulations in Chapter 4 at 9 of EY New UK GAAP 2015.

See further discussion on the true and fair view requirement (including its relationship with accounting standards) in Chapter 1 at 7.2 and Chapter 4 at 9.2.

7.2.1   *True and fair override*

In the special circumstances when management concludes that compliance with any requirement of FRS 102 or applicable legislation (only when it allows for a true and fair override) is inconsistent with the requirement to give a true and fair view, the entity shall depart from that requirement in the manner set out in paragraph 3.5 of the standard. *[FRS 102.3.4]*. Paragraphs 3.5 and 3.6 of the standard set out the disclosures required where an entity departs from a requirement of FRS 102 or from a requirement of applicable legislation (see 11.1.4 below). In our view, paragraphs 3.5 and 3.6 should be read with adaptations to refer to profit or loss rather than financial performance, consistent with the concept of 'true and fair view' in Section 1A.

FRS 102's requirements for the disclosures in respect of departures from the standard or legislation for the overriding purpose of the financial statements giving a true and fair view) are consistent with the requirements of the CA 2006. *[s396(5), s404(5)]*. There are similar requirements for LLPs in the *Limited Liability Partnerships (Accounts and Audit) (Application of the Companies Act 2006) Regulations 2008* (SI 2008/1911).

Appendix IV to FRS 102 highlights certain instances where the requirements of FRS 102 result in a departure from the requirements of the Regulations in order to give a 'true and fair view'. These examples, which are not exhaustive, are relevant to UK companies preparing Companies Act accounts (and similarly, LLPs preparing non-IAS accounts).

Where it appears to the directors that there are special reasons for departing from any of the general principles (see 7.2 above) in preparing the accounts for the financial year, the particulars of the departure, reasons and effect should be disclosed in a note to the accounts. *[1 Sch 10(2) (SC), 1 Sch 10(2) (LLP SC)].*

See further discussion of the true and fair override requirement in FRS 102 and company law in Chapter 4 at 9.2.

7.3   Going concern

FRS 102 requires management, when preparing financial statements, to make an assessment of an entity's ability to continue as a going concern. An entity is a going concern unless management either intends to liquidate the entity or to cease trading, or has no realistic alternative but to do so. In assessing whether the going concern assumption is appropriate, management takes into account all available information about the future, which is at least, but is not limited to, twelve months from the date when the financial statements are authorised for issue. *[FRS 102.3.8, Appendix I]*. This review period is a longer minimum period than that specified in IAS 1 and is consistent with that specified for management's assessment of going concern in auditing standards by ISA (UK & Ireland) 570 – *Going Concern.*

When management is aware, in making its assessment, of material uncertainties related to events or conditions that cast significant doubt upon the entity's ability to continue as a going concern, those uncertainties should be disclosed in the financial statements. When financial statements are not prepared on a going concern basis, that fact should be disclosed, together with the basis on which the financial statements are prepared and the reason why the entity is not regarded as a going concern. *[FRS 102.3.9].*

While a small entity is not required to comply with paragraph 3.9, Section 1A specifically encourages a small entity to make this disclosure by its inclusion in Appendix D to Section 1A which sets out disclosures 'which may nevertheless be necessary to give a true and fair view'. *[FRS 102.1A.7, 1A.20, 1AD.1(c)].*

FRS 102 states that an entity shall not prepare its financial statements on a going concern basis if management determines after the reporting period either that it intends to liquidate the entity or to cease trading or that it has no realistic alternative but to do so. Deterioration in operating results and financial position after the reporting period may indicate a need to consider whether the going concern assumption is no longer appropriate. If the going concern assumption is no longer appropriate, a fundamental change in the basis of accounting rather than an adjustment to the amounts recognised within the original basis of accounting is required, and therefore the disclosures in paragraph 3.9 of the standard, as described above, apply. *[FRS 102.32.7A-7B].*

As noted above, a small entity is specifically encouraged to make the disclosures in paragraph 3.9 but, in any event, departure from adoption of the going concern principle is a departure from the general principles, so particulars of the departure, the reasons and effect must be given in the accounts (see 11.1.4 below). *[1 Sch 10(2) (SC), 1 Sch 10(2) (LLP SC)].*

FRS 102 provides no further guidance concerning what impact there should be on the financial statements if it is determined that the going concern basis is not appropriate. Accordingly, entities will need to consider carefully their individual circumstances to arrive at an appropriate basis.

FRS 102's requirements are supplemented by FRC guidance. In September 2014, the FRC issued *Guidance on Risk Management, Internal Control: and Related Financial and Business Reporting*. This guidance integrates and replaces the previous *Internal Control: Revised Guidance for Directors on the Combined Code (2005)* and *Going Concern and Liquidity Risk: Guidance for Directors of UK companies 2009* ('the 2009 Going Concern Guidance') and reflects changes made to the UK Corporate Governance Code. This new guidance is aimed primarily at entities subject to the UK Corporate Governance Code (and applies for such entities for financial years beginning on or after 1 October 2014). The FRC hopes that other entities will find it helpful but expects to issue updated guidance for unlisted entities later in 2015.

While many FRS 102 reporters will not be subject to or voluntarily applying the UK Corporate Governance Code, Section 6, Appendix A and Appendix D of *Guidance on Risk Management, Internal Control: and Related Financial and Business Reporting* include relevant information on adoption of the going concern basis of accounting (including disclosures on material uncertainties) in the financial statements. See Chapter 4 at 9.3.

7.4   Frequency of reporting

A small entity must present a complete set of financial statements (including comparative information) at least annually.

When the end of an entity's reporting period changes and annual financial statements are presented for a period longer or shorter than one year, the entity shall disclose that fact, the reason for using a longer or shorter period, and the fact that comparative amounts presented in the financial statements (including the related notes) are not entirely comparable. *[FRS 102.3.10].*

Normally, financial statements are consistently prepared covering a one year period. Some entities, particularly in the retail sector, present financial statements for a 52-week period. This practice is permitted by the CA 2006 which allows companies to prepare financial statements to a financial year end, not more than 7 days before or after the end of the accounting reference period (based on the accounting reference date notified to the Registrar). *[s390(2)(b), s391].* While the standard does not explicitly address this issue, we consider that FRS 102 financial statements can be prepared to a financial year end, not more than 7 days from the end of the accounting reference period.

7.5   Comparatives

Except when FRS 102 permits or requires otherwise, a small entity presents comparative information in respect of the preceding period for all amounts presented in the current period's financial statements. *[FRS 102.1A.10, 3.14]*. This means that the requirement to present comparative information applies both to mandatory and voluntary information presented for the current period. In certain cases, FRS 102 provides specific exemptions from presenting comparatives (as indicated in the disclosures listed at 11 below). The General Rules to the formats also contain requirements on comparatives (see 8.2 below).

7.5.1   *Comparative information for narrative and descriptive information*

An entity shall include comparative information for narrative and descriptive information when it is relevant to an understanding of the current period's financial statements. *[FRS 102.3.14]*. See further discussion in Chapter 4 at 3.6.1.

7.5.2   *Consistency of, and reclassifications of, comparative information*

The requirements on consistency of, and reclassification of, comparative information where Section 1A is applied are exactly the same as under full FRS 102. See Chapter 4 at 3.6.2.

The General Rules to the formats also address restatements of comparatives and the disclosures required where comparatives are not comparable (see 8.2 below).

7.6   Materiality and aggregation

Financial statements result from processing large numbers of transactions or other events that are aggregated into classes according to their nature or function. The final stage in the process of aggregation and classification is the presentation of condensed and classified data, which form line items in the financial statements. *[FRS 102.3.16]*.

Materiality is defined as follows: 'Omissions or misstatements of items are material if they could, individually or collectively, influence the economic decisions of users taken on the basis of the financial statements. Materiality depends on the size and nature of the omission or misstatement judged in the surrounding circumstances. The size or nature of the item, or a combination of both, could be the determining factor.' However, it is inappropriate to make, or leave uncorrected, immaterial departures from the standard to achieve a particular presentation of an entity's financial position, financial performance or cash flows. *[FRS 102.2.6, Appendix I]*.

FRS 102 requires each material class of similar items to be presented separately and items of a dissimilar nature or function to be presented separately unless they are immaterial. *[FRS 102.3.15]*. If a line item is not individually material, it is aggregated with other items either in those statements or in the notes. An item that may not warrant separate presentation in those financial statements may warrant separate presentation in the notes. *[FRS 102.3.16]*. The principle of materiality and level of aggregation is particularly relevant to small entities in determining whether additional information is required to be presented in the notes to the financial statements in order for the financial statements to give a true and fair view (see 7.2 above). *[FRS 102.1A.16-17]*.

Small companies reporting under FRS 102 must comply with the balance sheet and profit and loss account formats set out in the Small Companies Regulations (or Small LLP Regulations) (see 8.1 below).

The General Rules to the formats (see 8.2 below) allow the directors to combine items denoted with Arabic numbers in the (statutory) balance sheet and profit and loss account formats if their individual amounts are not material to assessing the state of affairs or profit or loss of the company for the financial year in question, or where the combination facilitates that assessment (in which case, the individual amounts of the line items combined must be disclosed in the notes). *[1 Sch 4(2) (SC), 1 Sch 4(2) (LLP SC)]*. In respect of the abridged formats (see 9.2 and 10.2 below), Section 1A of FRS 102 states that disaggregation of gross profit or loss, disclosure of turnover and disaggregation of information in the balance sheet may be necessary in the notes to the financial statements in order to give a true and fair view. *[FRS 102.1AA.2, 1AB.2]*.

FRS 102 states that an entity need not provide a specific disclosure required by the standard if the information is not material. *[FRS 102.1A.17, 3.16A]*. The Small Companies Regulations and Small LLP Regulations, where applied, also permit that 'amounts which in the particular context of any provision of Schedule 1 to these Regulations are not material may be disregarded for the purposes of that provision.' *[8 Sch 7 (SC), 5 Sch 7 (LLP SC)]*.

Chapter 4 at 9.4.1 discusses initiatives on 'clear and concise financial reporting' by the FRC and other bodies.

7.7   Identification of the financial statements

It is commonly the case that financial statements will form only part of a larger annual report, regulatory filing or other document, but FRS 102 only applies to the financial statements (including the notes). The annual report and accounts for a small UK company, for example, comprise the directors' report and the annual accounts. An LLP is not required to prepare a members' report, but the LLP SORP requires certain information to be disclosed which may be included in a separate members' report.[4]

Accordingly, FRS 102 requires that an entity clearly identifies the financial statements and the notes, and distinguishes them from other information in the same document. In addition, the entity must display the following information prominently, and repeat it when necessary, for an understanding of the information presented: *[FRS 102.3.23]*

- the name of the reporting entity and any change in its name from the end of the preceding reporting period;
- whether the financial statements cover the individual entity or a group of entities;
- the date of the end of the reporting period and the period covered by the financial statements;

- the presentation currency, as defined in Section 30 – *Foreign Currency Translation* (discussed in Chapter 25 at 3.7 of EY New UK GAAP 2015); and

- the level of rounding, if any, used in presenting amounts in the financial statements.

In practice, these requirements can be met through the use of appropriate headings for pages, statements, notes and columns. This could include, for example, the inclusion of a basis of preparation note within the accounting policies, the use of appropriate titles for the primary financial statements, distinguishing group and company and the use of appropriate headings in the columns in the primary financial statements (and notes to the financial statements). Entities will need to consider how best to present the required information where financial statements are made available electronically.

Financial statements are usually presented to an appropriate level of rounding, such as thousands or millions of currency units. An appropriate level of rounding can avoid obscuring useful information (and hence 'cut clutter' – see Chapter 4 at 9.4.1) but entities need to ensure that material information is not omitted. The level of rounding used must be clearly disclosed in the primary statements and notes to the financial statements. Entities are not precluded from using lower levels of rounding in certain notes to the financial statements. In all cases, it is important that the units used are clearly stated.

The legal form of the entity, its country of incorporation and the address of its registered office (or principal place of business, if different to the registered office) is required to be disclosed in the note to the financial statements. *[FRS 102.3.24(a)]*. See similar disclosures at 11.1.8 below.

7.8   Interim financial reports

FRS 102 does not address the presentation of interim financial reports. It is unlikely that many small entities will be preparing interim financial reports but if they do such reports must describe the basis for preparing and presenting such information. FRS 104 – *Interim Financial Reporting* – sets out a basis for the preparation and presentation of interim financial reports that an entity may apply. *[FRS 102.3.25]*.

See Chapter 4 at 3.3.1 and Chapter 6 if interim reporting is relevant for a small entity.

8   COMPLETE SET OF FINANCIAL STATEMENTS

A complete set of financial statements of a small entity shall include all of the following (with comparatives – see 7.5 above):

- a statement of financial position as at the reporting date, in accordance with paragraph 1A.12 (see 9 below);

- an income statement for the reporting period in accordance with paragraph 1A.14 (see 10 below); and

- notes in accordance with paragraphs 1A.16 to 1A.20 (see 11 below). *[FRS 102.1A.8]*.

A small entity may use other titles for the financial statements as long as they are not misleading. *[FRS 102.1A.7, 1A.11, 3.22]*. In a complete set of financial statements, an entity shall present each financial statement with equal prominence. *[FRS 102.1A.7, 3.21]*.

While paragraphs 3.18 to 3.21 (covering the requirements for a complete set of financial statements in full FRS 102) do not apply to entities not applying Section 1A, a small entity, however, is not prohibited from applying any or all of Sections 3 to 7. *[FRS 102.1A.7, 3.1, 4.1A, 5.1A, 6.1A, 7.1B]*.

In addition to the primary statements required by company law and set out in paragraph 1A.8 a small entity is encouraged in order to meet the requirements in 1A.5 (i.e. for the financial statements to give a true and fair view) to present a statement of total comprehensive income when it recognises gains or losses in other comprehensive income, and to present a statement of changes in equity or a statement of changes in retained earnings when it has transactions with equity holders. *[FRS 102.1A.9, 6.1A]*.

8.1   Formats

A small entity must present a statement of financial position and its profit or loss in accordance with the requirements set out in Part 1 of Schedule 1 to the Small Companies Regulations or Part 1 of Schedule 1 to the Small LLP Regulations (except to the extent that these requirements are not permitted by any statutory framework under which such entities report). *[FRS 102.1A.4, 1A.12, 1A.14]*.

SI 2015/980 introduces a choice of statutory, abridged and 'adapted' formats where Schedule 1 to the Small Companies Regulations is applied. As LLP law was not amended by SI 2015/980, there is no change to the statutory formats previously applied by LLPs. LLPs cannot apply abridged formats or 'adapted formats' (unless LLP law is subsequently changed).

8.1.1   *Statutory formats*

There is a choice of two balance sheet and two profit and loss account formats. Section B of Part 1 of Schedule 1 to the Small Companies Regulations and Section B of Part 1 of the Small LLP Regulations set out the line items required. *[1 Sch 1 (SC), 1 Sch 1 (LLP SC)]*. The General Rules to the formats (see 8.2 below) apply. SI 2015/980 introduces minor modifications to the statutory formats previously in the Small Companies Regulations.

Statutory formats can also be used in group accounts, as modified by Schedule 6 to the Small Companies Regulations (see 8.1.4 below). *[6 Sch 1 (SC), 4 Sch 1 (LLP SC)]*.

8.1.2   *Abridged formats*

Abridged formats are only available in individual financial statements prepared in accordance with Schedule 1 to the Small Companies Regulations. Abridged formats cannot be applied by a company that was a charity at any time within that year or by LLPs (unless there is a subsequent change to LLP law). *[1 Sch 1A (SC), 6 Sch 1(1A) (SC), 1 Sch 1 (LLP SC)]*. Appendix IV – *Note on legal requirements* – effectively broadens this restriction and states that this option is not available to small entities that are charities. *[FRS 102.A4.11E]*.

To use abridged formats, all of the members of the company must have consented to the drawing up of the abridged balance sheet and / or abridged profit and loss account. Consent may only be given as regards the preparation of, as appropriate, the balance sheet or profit and loss account in respect of the preceding financial year. *[1A(1)-(3) Sch 1 (SC)]*. The implication is that consent is required to be obtained each year in respect of the preceding financial year, before the date of approval of the financial statements for the preceding financial year. The Small Companies Regulations provide no further requirements on how such consent is obtained.

Appendix IV to the standard explains that when a small entity that is not a company chooses to prepare abridged financial statements, it should ensure that:

- similar consent is obtained from the members of its governing body, taking into account its legal form; and

- abridged financial statements would not be prohibited by relevant laws or regulation. *[FRS 102.A4.11E]*.

Where the balance sheet or profit and loss account is abridged pursuant to paragraph 1A of Schedule 1 to the Small Companies Regulations, the directors must deliver to the Registrar a statement by the company that all the members of the company have consented to the abridgement. *[s444(2A)]*.

So far as practicable, the provisions of paragraphs 2 to 9A of the General Rules to the formats (see 8.2 below) apply to the balance sheet or profit or loss account of a company, notwithstanding any such abridgment pursuant to paragraph 1A. *[1 Sch 1C (SC)]*.

8.1.3 *'Adapted formats'*

Paragraph 1B(1) of Schedule 1 to the Small Companies Regulations allows a company's directors to adapt one of the balance sheet formats in Section B to Schedule 1 to the Small Companies Regulations (i.e. the statutory formats) so to distinguish between current and non-current items in a different way, provided that:

(a) the information given is at least equivalent to that which would have been required by the use of such format had it not been thus adapted; and

(b) the presentation of those items is in accordance with generally accepted accounting principles or practice. *[1 Sch 1B(1) (SC)]*.

Similarly, paragraph 1B(2) of Schedule 1 to the Small Companies Regulations, introduced by SI 2015/980, allows a company's directors to adapt, otherwise than pursuant to paragraph 1A(2), one of the profit and loss account formats in Section B to Schedule 1 to the Regulations (i.e. the statutory formats) provided that:

(a) the information given is at least equivalent to that which would have been required by the use of such format had it not been thus adapted, and

(b) the presentation is in accordance with generally accepted accounting principles or practice. *[1 Sch 1B(2) (SC)]*.

The reference to 'otherwise than pursuant to paragraph 1A(2)' means that an entity making an adaptation to combine specified line items as a single line item for 'gross profit' must apply the abridged format requirements in paragraph 1A (including annual member consent).

So far as practicable, the provisions of paragraphs 2 to 9A of the General Rules to the formats (see 8.2 below) apply to the balance sheet or profit or loss account of a company, notwithstanding any such adaptation pursuant to paragraph 1B. *[1 Sch 1C (SC)]*.

Schedule 1 to the Small Companies Regulations provides no further guidance on 'adapted formats', leaving the detail to UK accounting standards. Section 1A of FRS 102 specifies that, at a minimum, certain line items are presented on the face of the statement of financial position and income statement, with further sub-classifications of balance sheet items in the notes to the financial statements (see 9.3 and 10.3 below). In general, few difficulties should arise over classification of line items where 'adapted formats' are applied since the required line items are aligned with the categories of assets and liabilities discussed in FRS 102. Some areas to watch on classification, including potential classification differences to previous UK GAAP, are, however, discussed at Chapter 4 at 5.1.

In addition, the Small Companies Regulations require supplementary information in respect of certain line items to be given in the notes to the accounts. See 11.1 below. One complexity is that this information is in respect of line items required in the statutory formats, which may not align completely with the line items included in the primary statements where the adapted formats are applied. See discussion at 9.3 below.

'Adapted formats', as modified by Schedule 6 to the Small Companies Regulations, can also be used in group accounts (where prepared). In effect, this means that a small entity using the 'adapted formats' must follow the requirements in the Small Companies Regulations on non-controlling interests (see 8.1.4 below).

8.1.4   *Consolidated financial statements*

Part 1 of Schedule 6 to the Small Companies Regulations addresses the balance sheet and profit and loss account formats applicable to group accounts of companies, modifying the formats included in the earlier schedules. The group accounts must comply, so far as practicable with the provisions of Schedule 1 to the Small Companies Regulations (i.e. including the formats) as if the undertakings included in the consolidation were a single company. *[SC Regulations 8, 6 Sch 1(1), 17 (SC)]*. Part 1 of Schedule 4 to the Small Companies LLP Regulations similarly addresses the balance sheet and profit and loss formats applicable to group accounts of LLPs. *[LLP Regulations 6, 4 Sch 1(1) (LLP SC)]*.

Note that Section 1A does not require an entity to prepare group accounts (see 6.2 above). *[FRS 102.1A.21]*.

8.1.4.A   *Modifications to formats for purposes of consolidated financial statements*

The formats required in group accounts (relevant to both 'adapted formats' and statutory formats) must identify non-controlling interests (see 8.1.4.B below).

In addition, in the statutory formats for the group balance sheet, line item B III 'Investments in participating interests' is replaced with the line items in Figure 3.1. *[6 Sch 1(2) (SC)]*. Note that shares and loans to group undertakings will only be relevant in consolidated financial statements for those subsidiary undertakings excluded from consolidation (see Chapter 6 at 3.4 of EY New UK GAAP 2015). Group undertakings, associated undertakings and participating interests are defined at Chapter 4 at 5.3.4.C to 5.3.4.E.

Figure 3.1   Analysis of investments

B	**Fixed assets**	
III	Investments	
	1	Shares in group undertakings
	2	Interests in associated undertakings
	3	Other participating interests
	4	Loans to group undertakings and undertakings in which a participating interest is held
	5	Other investments other than loans
	6	Others

In the statutory formats for the group profit and loss account, the line item 'income from participating interests' is replaced by two items 'Income from interests in associated undertakings' and 'Income from other participating interests'. *[6 Sch 1(3) (SC)]*.

The same modifications are made in the Small LLP Regulations. *[4 Sch 1 (LLP SC)]*.

8.1.4.B   *Non-controlling interest*

Under FRS 102, non-controlling interest is defined as 'the equity in a subsidiary not attributable, directly or indirectly, to a parent'. *[FRS 102.22.19, Appendix I]*. See Chapter 6 at 3.6 of EY New UK GAAP 2015.

The requirements for non-controlling interest in Section 9 apply to a small entity. *[FRS 102.1A.22(a)]*. An entity shall present non-controlling interest in the consolidated statement of financial position within equity, separately from the equity of the owners of the parent *[FRS 102.9.20]* and shall disclose non-controlling interest in the profit or loss of the group separately in the statement of comprehensive income (or income statement if presented). *[FRS 102.9.21]*.

The Small Companies Regulations and Small LLP Regulations contain requirements on presentation of non-controlling interests in the balance sheet and profit and loss account. These requirements must clearly be followed by a small company and small LLP respectively. In our view, the requirement that a small entity that prepares consolidated financial statements shall comply so far as practicable with the requirements of Section 1A as if it were a single entity (Schedule 6 of the Small Companies Regulations, paragraph 1(1)), subject to any restrictions or exemptions set out in legislation, *[FRS 102.1A.22(c)]*, means that the requirements also apply to other small entities applying the formats in the Small Companies Regulations or Small LLP Regulations under the standard. In addition, in our view, paragraph 17 of the Small Companies Regulations also applies to 'adapted formats' because any adaptations made need to be 'at least equivalent' to the information required in the statutory formats (in Part B of Part 1 of Schedule 1 to the Small Companies Regulations). *[1 Sch 1B (SC), 6 Sch 1 (SC)]*.

Paragraph 17 of Schedule 6 to the Small Companies Regulations (as amended by SI 2015/980) requires that the formats set out in Schedule 1 to these regulations have effect in relation to group accounts with the following additions: *[6 Sch 17 (SC)]*

'(2)   In the balance sheet formats there must be shown, as a separate item and *under the heading "non-controlling interests"* [emphasis added], the amount of capital and reserves attributable to shares in subsidiary undertakings included in the consolidation held by or on behalf of persons other than the parent company and its subsidiary undertakings.

(3)   In the profit and loss account formats there must be shown, as a separate item and *under the heading "non-controlling interests"* [emphasis added], *the amount of any profit or loss* [emphasis added] attributable to shares in subsidiary undertakings included in the consolidation held by or on behalf of persons other than the parent company and its subsidiary undertakings.'

Paragraph 17 of the Small LLP Regulations states that: *[4 Sch 17 (LLP SC)]*

'(2)   In the balance sheet formats there must be shown, as a separate item and *under an appropriate heading* [emphasis added], the amount of capital and reserves attributable to shares in subsidiary undertakings included in the consolidation held by or on behalf of persons other than the parent company and its subsidiary undertakings.

(3)   In the profit and loss account formats there must be shown, as a separate item and *under an appropriate heading* [emphasis added] –

(a)   *the amount of any profit or loss on ordinary activities, and*

(b)   *the amount of any profit or loss on extraordinary activities,* [emphasis added]

attributable to shares in subsidiary undertakings included in the consolidation held by or on behalf of persons other than the parent company and its subsidiary undertakings.'

The heading used in the balance sheet is treated as if it has a letter assigned, meaning that it must be included on the face of the balance sheet. However, the heading used in the profit and loss account is treated as if it has an Arabic number assigned (allowing the adaptations permitted by the General Rules to the formats, as described at 8.2 below). *[6 Sch 17(4) (SC), 4 Sch 17(4) (LLP SC)]*. The statutory requirements for presentation of non-controlling interests would permit a presentation consistent with the requirements of FRS 102. In most cases, the amounts shown as non-controlling interest under the standard and the amounts required by the Small Companies Regulations or Small LLP Regulations will be the same. There is a theoretical possibility that the amounts required by the standard and the Small Companies Regulations or Small LLP Regulations may differ. In such a case, two totals are strictly required to be presented to meet the requirements of both FRS 102 and the statutory requirements.

Figure 3.2 below illustrates the presentation of non-controlling interest in the statement of financial position for a company subject to the small companies regime. Figure 3.3 illustrates the allocation of profit or loss to owners of the parent and to non-controlling interest where a separate income statement is presented by a company subject to the small companies regime. The terminology 'non-controlling interests' in the Small Companies Regulations (rather than 'non-controlling interest' in FRS 102) is used.

Figure 3.2   Presentation of non-controlling interest in statement of financial position – UK company

	£'000
Capital and reserves	
Called up share capital	12,075
Share premium account:	493
Capital redemption reserve	500
Merger reserve	6,250
Profit and loss account	27,882
Equity attributable to owners of the parent company	47,200
Non-controlling interests	360
	47,560

Figure 3.3   Presentation of non-controlling interest in income statement (where presented separately) – UK company

	£'000
Profit before taxation	7,786
Tax on profit:	(3,339)
Profit after taxation and profit for the financial year	4,447
Profit for the financial year attributable to:	
Owners of the parent company	4,209
Non-controlling interests	238

A small entity is not required to prepare a statement of changes in equity or a statement of comprehensive income (but see Chapter 4 at 4.5 for guidance on the presentation of non-controlling interest in such statements, if presented).

8.1.5   *Changes in formats*

The General Rules to the formats to Schedule 1 to the Small Companies Regulations state that once a particular format (in Section B of Part 1 to those regulations) for the balance sheet or profit or loss account has been adopted for any financial year, the company's directors must use the same format in preparing Companies Act accounts for subsequent financial years, unless in their opinion there are special reasons for a change. Particulars of any such change must be given in a note to the accounts in which the new format is first used, and the reasons for the change must be explained. *[1 Sch 2 (SC), 6 Sch 1(1) (SC)]*. The members of an LLP applying the Small LLP Regulations are subject to the same requirements for non-IAS accounts. *[1 Sch 2 (LLP SC), 4 Sch 1 (LLP SC)]*.

While the wording refers to the statutory formats, the General Rules apply so far as practicable to abridged formats (which are derived from the statutory formats) and 'adapted formats'. Therefore, the same requirements apply to changes in the statutory format used and also changes between abridged, 'adapted' and statutory formats. *[1 Sch 1C, 2 (SC), 6 Sch 1 (SC)].*

A change in the format applied would be regarded as a change in accounting policy for the purposes of FRS 102 and, therefore, would be retrospectively effected. See Chapter 7 at 3.4 of EY New UK GAAP 2015 for the requirements on changes in accounting policy.

8.2   General Rules to the formats

The following discussion relates to the balance sheet and profit and loss account formats included in Schedule 1 to the Small Companies Regulations. The requirements in Schedule 1 to the Small LLP Regulations are the same, except where noted. See 8.1.5 above on changes in formats.

8.2.1   *General Rules governing the form of the statutory formats*

Subject to paragraph 1A and the following provisions, the General Rules to the formats require that every balance sheet and every profit and loss account of a company must show the items listed in the balance sheet or profit or loss format adopted. Section B of Part 1 of Schedule 1 to the Small Companies Regulations, as amended by SI 2015/980 sets out a choice of two balance sheet (formats 1 and 2, only format 1 is commonly applied) and two profit or loss formats (formats 1 and 2) (referred to below as 'statutory formats'). The Small LLP Regulations have the equivalent requirement but there are some differences in detail in the LLP statutory formats compared to the company formats.

While the Small Companies Regulations refer to 'Subject to paragraph 1A' (which provides for abridged formats), it seems likely that this is a drafting error and should read 'Subject to paragraphs 1A and 1B' to cover both the abridged formats and the 'adapted formats' (see 8.2.2 below). The Small LLP Regulations do not contain paragraphs 1A and 1B.

See Figure 3.4 at 9.1 below for the format 1 balance sheet and see Figures 3.7 to 3.10 at 10.1 below for the format 1 and 2 profit and loss accounts (for a company and LLP) for the individual accounts. Each of the headings and sub-headings denoted with a capital letter or Roman numeral must be presented on the face of the balance sheet. Note that SI 2015/980 now requires a UK company to show the revaluation reserve under that name (previously it had to be shown in the position required in the formats but need not be shown under that name). *[1 Sch 35(2) (SC)].* This change does not apply to an LLP (unless there is a subsequent change to LLP law).

The items in the balance sheet and profit and loss account statutory formats must be shown in the order and under the headings and sub-headings given in the particular format used, but the letters or numbers assigned to that item in the format do not need to be given (and are not in practice). References to items in the formats are to the items listed in the statutory formats read together with the notes to the formats, which may also permit alternative positions for any particular items. *[1 Sch 1 (SC), 1 Sch 1 (LLP SC)].*

The individual line items in the statutory balance sheet and profit and loss account formats (and their related notes), which are similar to those in the Regulations, are discussed respectively in Chapter 4 at 5.3 and 6.6 below.

8.2.2   Abridged formats and 'adapted formats'

Paragraph 1A sets out the requirements for abridged formats (see 8.1.2 above and 9.2 and 10.2 below) and paragraph 1B sets out the requirements for 'adapted formats' (see 8.1.3 above and 9.3 and 10.3 below).

8.2.3   Rules applying to statutory, abridged and 'adapted formats'

The following provisions in the General Rules to the formats apply to the statutory formats *[1 Sch 1 (SC), 1 Sch 1 (LLP SC)]* and, so far as practicable, to the abridged formats and 'adapted formats'. *[1 Sch 1C (SC)]*. The Small Companies Regulations do not provide further guidance on how 'so far as practicable' is to be interpreted, but in our view this phrase is needed because the General Rules have been written from the perspective of the statutory formats, e.g. they refer to items given an Arabic number which may not have a direct counterpart in the abridged formats or 'adapted formats'. In other cases, such as in relation to corresponding amounts, there are no difficulties in applying the requirements. We do not consider that 'so far as practicable' allows small companies flexibility to regard the General Rules to the formats as optional.

Every profit and loss account must show 'profit or loss before taxation' as a line item on the face of the profit and loss account. Prior to applying SI 2015/980 (and in the Small LLP Regulations, unless LLP law is subsequently changed), the line item required is 'profit or loss on ordinary activities before taxation'. *[1 Sch 6 (SC), 1 Sch 6 (LLP SC)]*. This line item is not required for a qualifying partnership preparing statutory accounts.[5]

The General Rules to the formats allow any item to be shown in the company's balance sheet or profit and loss account in greater detail than required by the particular format used. The balance sheet or profit and loss account may include an item representing or covering the amount of any asset or liability, income or expenditure not otherwise covered by any of the items listed in the format used, but preliminary expenses; the expenses of, and commission on, any issue of shares or debentures; and the costs of research may not be treated as assets in the balance sheet. *[1 Sch 3 (SC), 1 Sch 3 (LLP SC)]*. A qualifying partnership preparing statutory accounts is not subject to the above rules on which types of costs may not be treated as assets in the balance sheet.[6]

Where the special nature of the company's (or LLP's) business requires it, the company's directors (for an LLP, the members) *must* adapt the arrangement, headings and sub-headings otherwise required in respect of items given an Arabic number in the balance sheet or profit or loss account format used. The directors (for an LLP, the members) *may* combine items to which Arabic numbers are given in the formats if their individual amounts are not material to assessing the state of affairs or profit or loss of the company for the financial year in question; or the combination facilitates that assessment. In the latter case, the individual amounts of any items combined must be disclosed in a note to the accounts. *[1 Sch 4 (SC), 1 Sch 4 (LLP SC)]*. FRS 102's requirements on materiality and aggregation are discussed at 7.6 above.

Where there is no amount in the current or immediately preceding financial year for a particular item in the balance sheet or profit and loss account format, that heading or sub-heading should be omitted from the balance sheet or profit and loss account, but an amount for an item relating to the immediately preceding year should be included under the required heading or sub-heading (even if there is no such item in the current financial year). *[1 Sch 5 (SC), 1 Sch 5 (LLP SC)]*.

A corresponding amount (i.e. comparative) must be shown for every item shown in the balance sheet or profit and loss account. Where that corresponding amount is not comparable with the amount shown in the current financial year, the corresponding amount may be adjusted. Particulars of the non-comparability and of any adjustment must be disclosed in a note to the accounts. *[1 Sch 7 (SC), 1 Sch 7 (LLP SC)]*. This statutory requirement would permit FRS 102's requirements on restatement of comparatives to be followed. Where amounts are not restated, e.g. due to transitional provisions in accounting policies or where it is impracticable to determine the effects of a change in accounting policies on earlier periods *[FRS 102.10.11-12]*, a note to the accounts will need to disclose the non-comparability. FRS 102's requirements on comparatives are discussed at 7.5 above.

Amounts in respect of items representing assets or income may not be set off against amounts in respect of items representing liabilities or expenditure (as the case may be), or *vice versa*. *[1 Sch 8 (SC), 1 Sch 8 (LLP SC)]*. FRS 102's requirements on offset are discussed in Chapter 4 at 9.1.1.C.

The company's directors (for an LLP, the members) must, in determining how amounts are presented within items in the profit and loss account and balance sheet, have regard to the substance of the reported transaction or arrangement, in accordance with generally accepted accounting principles or practice. *[1 Sch 9 (SC), 1 Sch 9 (LLP SC)]*.

A new requirement, introduced by SI 2015/980 so not relevant to LLPs (unless LLP law is subsequently changed), is that where an asset or liability relates to more than one item in the balance sheet, the relationship of such asset or liability to the relevant items must be disclosed either under those items or in the notes to the accounts. *[1 Sch 9A (SC)]*.

Examples of situations where this may be relevant include:

- items which are partly reported in debtors: amounts falling due within one year and debtors: amounts falling due after more than one year (where reported separately on the balance sheet) in the statutory formats;

- items which are partly reported in creditors: amounts falling due within one year and creditors: amounts falling due after more than one year (in the statutory formats); and

- items which are partly reported as current and non-current assets or liabilities (in the 'adapted formats').

This disclosure requirement does not appear to extend to reporting the relationship between assets and liabilities that derive from a single transaction (e.g. an asset acquired on a finance lease has an impact both on tangible fixed assets and lease creditors) nor, say, to identifying the associated deferred tax consequences of an asset or liability. Where a *single* asset or liability is required to be reported as more than one line item in the statement of financial position, e.g. split accounting for a convertible loan between equity and liability elements, or a loan at off-market rates made by a parent to its subsidiary is split between investment and loan asset, it would seem appropriate, in our view, to disclose the relationship between these line items.

9   STATEMENT OF FINANCIAL POSITION

A small entity must present a statement of financial position in accordance with the requirements for a balance sheet set out in Part 1 *General Rules and Formats* of Schedule 1 to the Small Companies Regulations or Part 1 *General Rules and Formats* of Schedule 1 to the Small LLP Regulations. *[FRS 102.1A.12].*

As noted at 8.1 above, a small entity applying Schedule 1 to the Small Companies Regulations has the following three alternatives:

- apply the required statutory balance sheet formats (subject to any permitted flexibility – see the General Rules to the formats at 8.2 above) – see 9.1 below;

- draw up an abridged balance sheet – see 9.2 below; or

- adapt one of the balance sheet formats – see 9.3 below. *[FRS 102.1AA.1].*

A small LLP must apply the required statutory balance sheet formats (subject to any permitted flexibility).

9.1   Statutory balance sheet (format 1)

Schedule 1 to the Small Companies Regulations provides a choice of two statutory formats for the balance sheet – format 1 is a vertical format and is adopted by virtually all UK companies. Format 2 presents assets separately from liabilities (including capital and reserves) and is rarely used.

This chapter only discusses the format 1 balance sheet in Schedule 1 to the Small Companies Regulations. The statement of financial position in financial statements prepared by a small entity in accordance with the statutory formats will look similar to one prepared under previous UK GAAP, although there is potential for reclassifications of items due to differing accounting requirements in FRS 102. These may particularly impact intangible assets and tangible assets. There is further discussion in Chapter 4 at 5.3.2 and 5.3.3.

SI 2015/980 introduces some minor changes to these formats. There were no modifications made to the individual balance sheet format 1 in SI 2015/980, although some amendments were made to format 2.

Figure 3.4   *Format 1 individual balance sheet - UK small company*

A	**Called up share capital not paid***	
B	**Fixed assets**	
	I	**Intangible assets**
		1 Goodwill
		2 Other intangible assets
	II	**Tangible assets**
		1 Land and buildings
		2 Plant and machinery etc.
	III	**Investments**
		1 Shares in group undertakings and participating interests
		2 Loans to group undertakings and undertakings in which the company has a participating interest
		3 Other investments other than loans
		4 Other investments
C	**Current assets**	
	I	**Stocks**
		1 Stocks
		2 Payments on account
	II	**Debtors**
		1 Trade debtors
		2 Amounts owed by group undertakings and undertakings in which the company has a participating interest
		3 Other debtors
	III	**Investments**
		1 Shares in group undertakings
		2 Other investments
	IV	**Cash at bank and in hand**
D	**Prepayments and accrued income***	
E	**Creditors: amounts falling due within one year**	
		1 Bank loans and overdrafts
		2 Trade creditors
		3 Amounts owed to group undertakings and undertakings in which the company has a participating interest
		4 Other creditors
F	**Net current assets (liabilities)**	
G	**Total assets less current liabilities**	
H	**Creditors: amounts falling due after more than one year**	
		1 Bank loans and overdrafts
		2 Trade creditors
		3 Amounts owed to group undertakings and undertakings in which the company has a participating interest
		4 Other creditors
I	**Provisions for liabilities**	
J	**Accruals and deferred income***	
K	**Capital and reserves**	
	I	Called up share capital not paid*
	II	Share premium account
	III	Revaluation reserve
	IV	Other reserves**
	V	Profit and loss account

*The notes to format 1 provide alternative positions for prepayments and accrued income, and accruals and deferred income. Prepayments and accrued income may be shown within sub-heading C-II.3 and accruals and deferred income may be shown within E.4 and H.4 or both (as the case may require). Called up share capital not paid may also be shown within C-II.3.

**There is no breakdown of 'Other reserves' in the formats in the Small Companies Regulations (unlike the Regulations)

See 9.1.2 below for modification of the format 1 balance sheet for small LLPs.

The main modifications required for the group balance sheet format are the identification of non-controlling interests, where SI 2015/980 amended the requirements, and changes to B III in Figure 2.4 above (see 8.1.4 above).

The balance sheet statutory formats set out in the Small Companies Regulations distinguish between fixed assets and current assets. Under the Small Companies Regulations, fixed assets are defined and current assets are the residual. 'Fixed assets' are assets of an entity which are intended for use on a continuing basis in the company's activities, and 'current assets' are assets not intended for such use. The Small LLP Regulations have the same requirements. *[8 Sch 3 (SC), 5 Sch 3 (LLP SC), FRS 102.Appendix I]*. See Chapter 4 at 5.2.2.

In addition, the balance sheet statutory formats distinguish between creditors: amounts falling due within one year; and creditors: amounts falling due after more than one year. In distinguishing amounts between the two categories of creditor, the deciding factor is the earliest date of payment. The Small Companies Regulations state that a loan is treated as falling due for repayment, and an instalment of a loan is treated as falling due for payment, on the earliest date on which the lender could require repayment or (as the case may be) payment, if the lender exercised all its available options and rights. The Small LLP Regulations have the same requirements. *[8 Sch 6 (SC), 5 Sch 6 (LLP SC)]*. See Chapter 4 at 5.2.3.

The headings for the format 1 balance sheet in the Small Companies Regulations (and Small LLP Regulations) are slightly more simplified than the headings for the format 1 balance sheet in Schedule 1 to the Regulations but the guidance on the headings included in the latter at Chapter 4 at 5.3 remains relevant (although the disclosures required in the notes to the accounts by the Small Companies Regulations are fewer than those required by the Regulations).

Each of the headings and sub-headings denoted with a capital letter or Roman numeral, as set out in Figure 3.4, must be presented on the face of the format 1 balance sheet for the individual accounts of a company in the order and under the headings and sub-headings given. The format 1 balance sheet includes sub-headings, denoted with an Arabic number. The General Rules to the formats (see 8.2 above), which must be complied with, explain further the presentation of line items with an Arabic number.

A new requirement, introduced by SI 2015/980, so not relevant to LLPs (unless LLP law is subsequently changed), is that where an asset or liability relates to more than one item in the balance sheet, the relationship of such asset or liability to the relevant items must be disclosed either under those items or in the notes to the accounts. *[1 Sch 9A]*. See discussion of this requirement at 8.2 above.

FRS 102, like IFRSs, has accounting requirements for various items that do not have separate line items in format 1, but which would be presented separately on the face of the statement of financial position under IAS 1. Such items include investment property, financial assets, biological assets, cash and cash equivalents and deferred tax.

FRS 102's requirement (in Section 4 of the standard) to present additional line items on the face of the statement of financial position where relevant to an understanding of the entity's financial position does not apply to small entities, *[FRS 102.1A.7, 4.3]*, but the General Rules to the formats provide flexibility to present line items in additional detail. So, for example, a property company may distinguish its investment property from other tangible fixed assets. The presentation of additional line items might require use of boxes and subtotals in order to comply with the balance sheet formats.

9.1.1   Notes to the formats

Certain alternative positions for line items are indicated in Figure 3.4 above. In addition, the notes on the balance sheet formats clarify that:

- amounts representing goodwill must only be included to the extent that the goodwill was acquired for valuable consideration. This is consistent with the requirements of FRS 102 that internally generated goodwill is not recognised; *[FRS 102.18.8C(f)]*

- amounts in respect of concessions, patents, licences, trademarks and similar rights and assets must only be included at item B.I.2 if either the assets were acquired for valuable consideration and are not required to be shown under goodwill or the assets in question were created by the company itself. FRS 102 has more restrictive requirements over recognition of internally developed intangible assets (where a policy of capitalisation is adopted, instead of a policy of expensing internally developed intangible assets). See Chapter 14 of EY New UK GAAP 2015;

- amounts falling due after more than one year must be shown separately for each item included under debtors (items C.II.1-3);

- within other creditors (items E4, H4 and J), there must be shown separately:

  (a)   the amount of any convertible loans; and

  (b)   the amount for creditors in respect of taxation and social security.

  Payments received on account of orders must be included in so far as they are not shown as deductions from stocks. In our view, the offset rules in FRS 102 would not permit payments received on account to be shown as deductions from stocks;

- in determining the amount shown as net current assets (liabilities) (item F), any prepayments and accrued income must be taken into account, wherever shown; and

- the amount of allotted share capital and amount of called up share capital which has been paid up must be shown separately (item K1).

The notes to the formats also require that where other investments (at item B.III.4 or C.III.2) include own shares, the nominal value of such shares must be shown separately. This accounting treatment is not permitted by FRS 102, which requires own shares to be accounted as a deduction against equity. *[FRS 102.22.16]*.

9.1.2   Modifications of the format 1 balance sheet for small LLPs

Note that the format 1 balance sheet in the Small LLP Regulations differs in the following respects:

- A – Called up share capital is omitted so the headings above are A – Fixed Assets to I-Accruals and deferred income;

- B.II.2 (C.II.2 in company formats) is amounts owed by group undertakings and undertakings in which the LLP has a participating interest;

- D.3 and G.3 (E.3 and H.3 in company formats) are amounts owed to group undertakings and undertakings in which the LLP has a participating interest;

- There is an additional item J – Loans and other debts due to members. Note (7) to the LLP balance sheet formats requires that the following amounts must be shown separately under this item – the aggregate amount of money advanced to the LLP by the members by way of loan, the aggregate amount of money owed to members by the LLP in respect of profits, and any other amounts; and

- K – Capital and reserves is replaced with K – Members' other interests (with sub-headings: K.I – Members' capital, K.II – Revaluation reserve and K.III – Other reserves).

The notes to the LLP format 1 balance sheet are the same as detailed at 9.1.1 for companies except for the additional requirement to analyse loans and other debts due to members discussed above and the omission of items relating to shares. Note that (unless there is a subsequent change to LLP law), the amount falling due after more than one year must be shown separately for each item included under debtors unless the aggregate amount of debtors falling due after more than one year is disclosed in the notes to the accounts.

The *Statement of Recommended Practice – Accounting by Limited Liability Partnerships* (July 2014) issued by CCAB provides further guidance on members interests' and application of the statutory formats for LLPs. The SORP requires a total for net assets attributable to members, and total members' interests and provides illustrations of LLP balance sheets for different situations. Detailed guidance on issues specific to LLPs is outside the scope of this Chapter.

9.2   Abridged balance sheet (format 1)

Where appropriate to the circumstances of a company's business, the company's directors may, with reference to one of the formats in Section B of Part 1 to Schedule 1 to the Small Companies Regulations, draw up an abridged balance sheet showing only those items in that format preceded by letters and Roman numerals provided that:

(a)   in the case of format 1, note (5) of the notes to the formats is complied with;

(b)   in the case of format 2, notes (5) and (10) of those notes are complied with; and

(c)   all of the members of the company have consented to the drawing up of the abridged balance sheet. *[1 Sch 1A(1) (SC)]*. See 8.1.2 above.

NB Notes (5) and (10) were amended by SI 2015/980.

So far as practicable, the provisions of paragraphs 2 to 9A of the General Rules to the formats (see 8.2 above) apply to the balance sheet or profit or loss account of a company, notwithstanding any such adaptation pursuant to paragraph 1A of Schedule 1 to the Small Companies Regulations. *[1 Sch 1C (SC)].*

Figure 3.5 sets out an abridged format 1 balance sheet for a UK company taking full advantage of the permitted abridgements above. We only discuss the format 1 balance sheet in this publication as format 2 is rarely used.

Figure 3.5   Format 1 abridged balance sheet – UK small company

A	Called up share capital not paid*
B	Fixed assets
	I Intangible assets
	II Tangible assets
	III Investments
C	Current assets
	I Stocks
	II Debtors
	III Investments
	IV Cash at bank and in hand
D	Prepayments and accrued income*
E	Creditors: amounts falling due within one year
F	Net current assets (liabilities)
G	Total assets less current liabilities
H	Creditors: amounts falling due after more than one year
I	Provisions for liabilities
J	Accruals and deferred income*
K	Capital and reserves
	I Called up share capital not paid*
	II Share premium account
	III Revaluation reserve
	IV Other reserves**
	V Profit and loss account

*The notes to format 1 provide alternative positions for prepayments and accrued income, and accruals and deferred income. Prepayments and accrued income may be shown within sub-heading C.II and accruals and deferred income may be shown within E and H or both (as the case may require). Called up share capital not paid may also be shown within C.II.

**There is no breakdown of 'Other reserves' in the formats in the Small Companies Regulations (unlike the Regulations)

Note (5) requires separate disclosure of the amount falling due after more than one year for each item included under debtors (items C.I to C.III).

As all these headings are preceded with a capital letter or Roman numeral, they must be presented on the face of the of the format 1 balance sheet for the individual accounts of a company in the order and under the headings and sub-headings given.

The only difference to the statutory formats is the abridgement. The disclosures required by the Small Companies Regulations are still required. Therefore, the guidance on statutory formats at 9.1 above remains relevant where abridged formats are used.

A small entity choosing to apply paragraph 1A(1) of Schedule 1 to the Small Companies Regulations and draw up an abridged balance sheet must still meet the requirement for the financial statements to give a true and fair view. A small entity must therefore also consider the requirements of paragraph 1A.16 (see 11 below) and provide any additional disclosure that is necessary in the notes to the financial statements, for example in relation to disaggregating the information in the balance sheet. *[FRS 102.1AA.2]*. In considering what level of disaggregation may be appropriate in order for the financial statements to give a true and fair view, in our view, entities should have regard to FRS 102's requirements on materiality and aggregation (see 7.6 above).

9.3   Adapted balance sheet

'Adapted formats' may be used to distinguish between current and non-current items in a different way (to the statutory formats), provided that the information given in the balance sheet is at least equivalent to that which would have been required by the use of the statutory format had it not been thus adapted and the presentation of those items is in accordance with generally accepted accounting principles or practice. *[1 Sch 1B(1) (SC)]*. The detail, however, is left to accounting standards, namely Section 1A.

An entity choosing to apply paragraph 1B(1) of Schedule 1 to the Small Companies Regulations and adapt one of the balance sheet formats shall, as a minimum, include in its statement of financial position the line items presented in Figure 3.6 below, distinguishing between those items that are current and those that are non-current (see 9.3.1 and 9.3.2 below). *[FRS 102.1AA.3]*. To comply with this requirement, an entity must present as separate classifications: current assets, current liabilities, non-current assets and non-current liabilities. *[FRS 102.1AA.6]*.

Figure 3.6   Balance sheet – UK small company applying paragraph 1B(1) of Schedule 1 to the Small Companies Regulations ('adapted formats')

(a)	Property, plant and equipment
(b)	Investment property carried at fair value through profit and loss
(c)	Intangible assets
(d)	Financial assets (excluding amounts shown under (e), (f), (j) and (k)
(e)	Investments in associates
(f)	Investments in jointly controlled entities
(g)	Biological assets carried at cost less accumulated depreciation and impairment
(h)	Biological assets carried at fair value through profit and loss
(i)	Inventories
(j)	Trade and other receivables
(k)	Cash and cash equivalents
(l)	Trade and other payables
(m)	Provisions
(n)	Financial liabilities (excluding amounts shown under (l) and (m))
(o)	Liabilities and assets for current tax
(p)	Deferred tax liabilities and deferred tax assets (classified as non-current)
(q)	Non-controlling interest, presented within equity separately from the equity attributable to the owners of the parent
(r)	Equity attributable to the owners of the parent

The line items required where 'adapted formats' are used where Section 1A is applied *[FRS 102.1AA.3]* are the same line items required where 'adapted formats' under the full standard FRS 102 is applied. *[FRS 102.4.2A]*. See Chapter 4 at 5.1 for implementation issues on the above line items, including classification differences arising from previous UK GAAP. In addition, an example 'adapted' statement of financial position relevant to both Section 1A and Section 4 of the standard is included in Example 3.2 in Chapter 4 at 5.1.14.

Note that while line items (o) and (p) appear to combine liabilities and assets for current tax and deferred tax respectively, the assets will need to be shown separately from the liabilities.

Paragraph 1AA.3 (unlike the statutory formats) makes no adaptations to the line items required for consolidated financial statements (where prepared by a small entity), but a line item for non-controlling interest (see 8.1.4.B above) is relevant where consolidated financial statements are prepared.

So far as practicable, the provisions of paragraphs 2 to 9A of the General Rules to the formats apply to the 'adapted' balance sheet, notwithstanding any such adaptation pursuant to paragraph 1B of Schedule 1 to the Small Companies Regulations. *[1 Sch 1C (SC)]*. A new requirement, introduced by SI 2015/980, so not relevant to LLPs (unless LLP law is subsequently changed), is that where an asset or liability relates to more than one item in the balance sheet, the relationship of such asset or liability to the relevant items must be disclosed either under those items or in the notes to the accounts. *[1 Sch 9A]*. See 8.2 above.

In addition, the following sub-classifications of the line items presented must be disclosed either in the statement of financial position or in the notes:

- property, plant and equipment in classifications appropriate to the entity;
- goodwill and other intangible assets;
- investments, showing separately shares and loans;
- trade and other receivables showing separately amounts due from related parties, amounts due from other parties;
- trade and other payables, showing separately amounts payable to trade suppliers, and amounts payable to related parties; and
- classes of equity, such as share capital, share premium, retained earnings, revaluation reserve, fair value reserve and other reserves. *[FRS 102.1AA.4]*.

Note that the sub-classifications of line items required in the notes to the financial statements are less extensive than required under Section 4.

The descriptions of the line items in the statement of financial position set out in paragraph 1AA.3 (and of the sub-classifications of those line items set out in paragraph 1AA.4) and the ordering of items, or aggregation of similar line items, may be amended according to the nature of the small entity and its transactions, to provide information that is relevant to an understanding of the entity's financial position, providing the information given is at least equivalent to that required by the balance sheet format had it not been adapted. *[FRS 102.1AA.5]*.

Where 'adapted formats' are used, there is no requirement to disclose debtors: amounts falling due after more than one year or to classify creditors: amounts falling due within or after more than one year. *[FRS 102.4.4A, 4.7]*. Section 4 of the standard clarifies this in respect of 'adapted formats' under full FRS 102. While Section 1A is silent on this matter, this will also be the case where 'adapted formats' are used in accordance with Section 1A. 'Adapted formats' instead distinguish instead between current assets, current liabilities, non-current assets and non-current liabilities.

While the 'adapted formats' are closely based on IAS 1 formats, Section 1A does not require IAS 1's disclosure of the amount expected to be recovered or settled after more than 12 months for each asset and liability line that combines amounts expected to be recovered or settled:

(a)   no more than 12 months after the reporting period and

(b)   more than 12 months after the reporting period. *[IAS 1.61]*.

The Small Companies Regulations set out disclosures to be given in the notes to the accounts which apply where statutory formats, abridged formats or the 'adapted formats' are used. One complexity is that the information required sometimes refers to items required in the statutory formats (which may differ to the line items identified where the 'adapted formats' are used). For example, the 'adapted formats' do not refer to fixed assets, creditors: amounts falling due within one year, creditors: amounts falling due after more than one year, investments, land or buildings, or turnover. A UK company using 'adapted formats' in Companies Act accounts will, therefore, need to identify which of its assets, liabilities, revenue streams needs to be included in the required disclosures. While 'adapted formats' require a classification of non-current assets and current assets which differs to the fixed assets and current assets classification required in statutory formats, the statutory definition of 'fixed assets' is relevant for the purposes of disclosures in respect of fixed assets in the Small Companies Regulations. See Chapter 4 at 5.2.2.

In addition, the Small Companies Regulations frequently require analyses and reconciliations to be given for Arabic-numbered sub-headings in the statutory balance sheet formats. Section 1A includes nearly all the statutory disclosures in the Small Companies Regulations but restates these disclosures in a way that can be applied even if statutory formats are not used (see 11 below). Where Section 1A refers to, say, 'In respect of each item which is shown under the general item fixed assets', in our view, it may be appropriate to give the information required for each of the sub-classifications of fixed assets required to be presented by paragraph 1AA.4 of the standard (see above). This is because these sub-classifications in effect stand in place of the Arabic-numbered headings identified in the statutory formats.

9.3.1   *Current and non-current assets*

The definitions of current and non-current assets discussed below apply only where an entity chooses to use 'adapted formats' in accordance with paragraph 1B(1) of Schedule 1 to the Small Companies Regulations.

FRS 102 defines non-current assets, with current assets being 'assets of the entity which are not non-current assets' (i.e. the residual). *[FRS 102.Appendix I]*. This is different to IAS 1 which defines current assets with non-current assets as the residual, although the classification is aligned.

Non-current assets are defined as: 'Assets of the entity which:

(a)   it does not expect to realise, or intend to sell or consume, in its normal operating cycle (see Chapter 4 at 5.1.1.A);

(b)   it does not hold primarily for the purpose of trading (see Chapter 4 at 5.1.1.B below);

(c)   it does not expect to realise within 12 months after the reporting period; or

(d)   are cash or cash equivalents restricted from being exchanged or used to settle a liability for at least 12 months after the reporting period.' *[FRS 102 Appendix I]*.

'Cash or cash equivalents' are defined in the FRS 102 Glossary, and should be interpreted in a manner consistent with Section 7 of the standard (see Chapter 5 at 3.3 of EY New UK GAAP 2015).

Meeting any one of (a) to (d) leads to the asset being required to be classified as non-current.

Note that the 'adapted formats' themselves require that deferred tax assets are always classified as non-current. *[FRS 102.1AA.3]*.

See Chapter 4 at 5.1.1 for further discussion of the classification of current and non-current assets.

9.3.2   *Current and non-current liabilities*

The definitions of current liabilities and non-current liabilities in this section apply only where an entity chooses to apply paragraph 1B(1) of Schedule 1 to the Small Companies Regulations.

FRS 102, consistent with IFRS defines current liabilities, with non-current liabilities being 'liabilities of the entity which are not current liabilities' (i.e. the residual). *[FRS 102.Appendix I]*.

Current liabilities are defined as:

'Liabilities of the entity which

(a)   it expects to settle in its normal operating cycle (see Chapter 4 at 5.1.2.A below);

(b)   it holds primarily for the purpose of trading (see Chapter 4 at 5.1.2.B below);

(c)   are due to be settled within 12 months after the reporting period (see Chapter 4 at 5.1.2.C below); or

(d)   it does not have an unconditional right to defer settlement for at least 12 months after the reporting period (see Chapter 4 at 5.1.2.D below).'

Meeting any one of (a) to (d) leads to the liability being required to be classified as current.

Note that the 'adapted formats' themselves require that deferred tax liabilities are always classified as non-current. *[FRS 102.1AA.3]*.

10 INCOME STATEMENT (OR PROFIT AND LOSS ACCOUNT)

A small entity must present its profit or loss for a period in an income statement in accordance with the requirements for a profit and loss account set out in Part 1 *General Rules and Formats* of Schedule 1 to the Small Companies Regulations or Part 1 *General Rules and Formats* of Schedule 1 to the Small LLP Regulations. *[FRS 102.1A.14]*.

As noted at 8.1 above, a small entity applying Schedule 1 to the Small Companies Regulations has the following three alternatives:

• apply the required statutory profit and loss formats (subject to any permitted flexibility – see the General Rules to the formats at 8.2 above) – see 10.1 below;

• draw up an abridged profit and loss account – see 10.2 below; or

• adapt one of the profit and loss account formats – see 10.3 below. *[FRS 102.1AB.1]*.

A small LLP must apply the required statutory profit and loss account formats (subject to any permitted flexibility).

An income statement presents all items of income and expense recognised in a reporting period excluding the items of other comprehensive income. *[FRS 102 Appendix I]*. Consequently, the income statement must include line items that add down to the profit or loss for the year even if the detailed analysis of certain line items is presented in the notes to the accounts, where this is permitted by the General Rules to the formats (where statutory or abridged formats are used) or the line items are not required on the face of the income statement where 'adapted formats' are used.

FRS 102 includes additional requirements on presentation of the profit and loss account that are relevant whatever format is used. For instance:

• guidance on operating profit, where this is presented (see Chapter 4 at 6.7.3); *[FRS 102.5.9B]*

• incoming dividends and similar income receivable are recognised at an amount that includes any withholding tax but excludes other taxes, such as attributable tax credits. Any withholding tax suffered is shown as part of the tax charge; *[FRS 102.29.19]* and

• Section 28 – *Employee Benefits* – does not specify how the cost of a defined benefit plan should be presented in the income statement. Therefore, entities may present the cost as a single item or disaggregate the cost into components presented separately.

Where Sections 8 to 35 require further analysis of items included in the income statement to be disclosed, these requirements do not apply to financial statements prepared in accordance with Section 1A.

10.1 Statutory profit and loss account (format 1 and format 2)

Schedule 1 to the Small Companies Regulations provides a choice of two statutory formats for the profit and loss account. Format 1 analyses expenses by function and is presented at Figure 3.7 below (where SI 2015/980 has been adopted) and at Figure 3.8 below (format 1 for a small LLP, unless there is a subsequent change to LLP law).

The *Statement of Recommended Practice – Accounting by Limited Liability Partnerships* (July 2014) issued by CCAB provides further guidance on application of the statutory formats for LLPs, and requires that profit or loss for the financial year before members' remuneration and profit shares, members' remuneration charged as an expense and profit or loss for the financial year available for discretionary division among members are presented. The basis on which each element of remuneration has been treated in the accounts should be disclosed and explained by way of note.[7] The SORP provides guidance and illustrations of LLP profit or loss account for different situations. Detailed guidance on issues specific to LLPs is outside the scope of this Chapter.

Figure 3.7   Format 1 profit and loss account – UK small company

1	Turnover
2	Cost of sales
3	Gross profit or loss
4	Distribution costs
5	Administrative expenses
6	Other operating income
7	Income from shares in group undertakings
8	Income from participating interests†
9	Income from other fixed asset investments
10	Other interest receivable and similar income
11	Amounts written off investments
12	Interest payable and similar expenses
	Profit or loss before taxation*
13	Tax on profit or loss
14	Profit or loss after taxation
19	Other taxes not shown under the above items
20	Profit or loss for the financial year

*While not in format 1, every profit and loss account must show the amount of a company's profit or loss before taxation (1 Sch 6, Small Companies Regulations).
† See discussion below for modifications in group accounts.

Figure 3.8   Format 1 profit and loss account – UK small LLP

1	Turnover
2	Cost of sales
3	Gross profit or loss
4	Distribution costs
5	Administrative expenses
6	Other operating income
7	Income from shares in group undertakings
8	Income from participating interests†
9	Income from other fixed asset investments
10	Other interest receivable and similar income
11	Amounts written off investments
12	Interest payable and similar charges
	Profit or loss on ordinary activities before taxation*
13	Tax on profit or loss on ordinary activities

14	Profit or loss on ordinary activities after taxation
15	Extraordinary income
16	Extraordinary charges
17	Extraordinary profit or loss
18	Tax on extraordinary profit or loss
19	Other taxes not shown under the above items
20	Profit or loss for the financial year before members' remuneration and profit shares

*While not in format 1, every profit and loss account must show the amount of an LLP's profit or loss on ordinary activities before taxation (1 Sch 6, Small LLP Regulations).
† See discussion below for modifications in group accounts.

Format 2 analyses expenses by nature and is presented at Figure 3.9 below (where SI 2015/980 has been adopted) and at Figure 3.10 below (format 2 for a small LLP, unless there is a subsequent change to LLP law).

Figure 3.9　　Format 2 for the profit and loss account – UK small company

1		Turnover
2		Change in stocks of finished goods and in work in progress
3		Own work capitalised
4		Other operating income
5	(a)	Raw materials and consumables
	(b)	Other external expenses
6		Staff costs
	(a)	wages and salaries
	(b)	social security costs
	(c)	other pension costs
7	(a)	Depreciation and other amounts written off tangible and intangible fixed assets
	(b)	Amounts written off current assets, to the extent that they exceed write-offs which are normal in the undertaking concerned
8		Other operating expenses
9		Income from shares in group undertakings
10		Income from participating interests†
11		Income from other fixed asset investments
12		Other interest receivable and similar income
13		Amounts written off investments
14		Interest payable and similar expenses
		Profit or loss before taxation*
15		Tax on profit or loss
16		Profit or loss after taxation
21		Other taxes not shown under the above items
22		Profit or loss for the financial year

*While not in format 2, every profit and loss account must show the amount of a company's profit or loss before taxation (1 Sch 6, Small Companies Regulations).
† See discussion below for modifications in group accounts.

Figure 3.10   Format 2 for the profit and loss account – UK small LLP

1		Turnover
2		Change in stocks of finished goods and in work in progress
3		Own work capitalised
4		Other operating income
5	(a)	Raw materials and consumables
	(b)	Other external charges
6		Staff costs
	(a)	wages and salaries
	(b)	social security costs
	(c)	other pension costs
7	(a)	Depreciation and other amounts written off tangible and intangible fixed assets
	(b)	Exceptional amounts written off current assets
8		Other operating charges
9		Income from shares in group undertakings
10		Income from participating interests†
11		Income from other fixed asset investments
12		Other interest receivable and similar income
13		Amounts written off investments
14		Interest payable and similar charges
		Profit or loss on ordinary activities before taxation*
15		Tax on profit or loss on ordinary activities
16		Profit or loss on ordinary activities after taxation
17		Extraordinary income
18		Extraordinary charges
19		Extraordinary profit or loss
20		Tax on extraordinary profit or loss
21		Other taxes not shown under the above items
22		Profit or loss for the financial year before members' remuneration and profit shares

*While not in format 2, every profit and loss account must show the amount of a company's profit or loss on ordinary activities before taxation (1 Sch 6, Small LLP Regulations).
† See discussion below for modifications in group accounts.

The main modifications required for group profit and loss account formats are the identification of non-controlling interests (see 8.1.4.B above) and replacing 'income from participating interests' with 'income from associated undertakings' and 'income from other participating interests'. *[6 Sch 1(3) (SC), 4 Sch 1(3) (LLP SC)].*

The line items in the formats need to be read together with the notes to the formats. *[1 Sch 1(2) (SC), 1 Sch 1(2) (LLP SC)].* These require that:

• cost of sales, distribution costs and administrative expenses (format 1, items 2, 4 and 5) are stated after taking into account any necessary provisions for depreciation or diminution in value of assets;

• in income from other fixed asset investments and other interest receivable and similar income (format 1, items 9 and 10, format 2, items 11 and 12), income and interest derived from group undertakings must be shown separately from income and interest derived from other sources; and

• in interest payable and similar expenses (format 1, item 12 and format 2, item 14), the amount payable to group undertakings must be shown separately.

Where the LLP format 1 profit and loss account is used, the amount of any provisions for depreciation and diminution in value of tangible and intangible fixed assets falling to be shown under item 7(a) in format 2 must be disclosed in a note to the accounts. This requirement was removed by SI 2015/980 from the Small Companies Regulations.

The individual line items in the profit and loss account formats in the Small Companies Regulations are the same as in the Regulations and are discussed at Chapter 4 at 6.6.1 to 6.6.15 (although disclosures in other sections of FRS 102 are generally not mandated).

The General Rules to the formats (see 8.2 above) apply. As all of the line items are denoted with Arabic numbers, these allow a degree of flexibility in the profit and loss account formats.

10.2   Abridged profit and loss account

Where appropriate to the circumstances of a small company's business, the company's directors may, with reference to one of the formats in Section B of Part 1 to Schedule 1 to the Small Companies Regulations, draw up an abridged profit and loss account, combining under one item called 'Gross profit or loss':

(a)   items 1, 2, 3 and 6 in the case of format 1; and

(b)   items 1 to 5 in the case of format 2

provided that, in either case, all of the members of the company have consented to the drawing up of the abridged profit and loss account. *[1 Sch 1A(2) (SC)]*. See 8.1.2 above.

So far as practicable, the provisions of paragraphs 2 to 9A of the General Rules to the formats (see 8.2 above) apply to the profit or loss account, notwithstanding any such adaptation pursuant to paragraph 1A of Schedule 1 to the Small Companies Regulations. *[1 Sch 1C (SC)]*.

Figure 3.11 sets out an abridged format 1 profit and loss account and Figure 3.12 sets out an abridged format 2 profit and loss account for a UK company taking full advantage of the permitted abridgements above.

Chapter 3

Figure 3.11   Format 1 profit and loss account – UK small company

*	[Turnover]
1, 2, 3, 6*	Gross profit or loss (combines: turnover, cost of sales, gross profit or loss, other operating income)
4	Distribution costs
5	Administrative expenses
7	Income from shares in group undertakings
8	Income from participating interests†
9	Income from other fixed asset investments
10	Other interest receivable and similar income
11	Amounts written off investments
12	Interest payable and similar expenses
	Profit or loss before taxation**
13	Tax on profit or loss
14	Profit or loss after taxation
19	Other taxes not shown under the above items
20	Profit or loss for the financial year

*Disaggregation of gross profit or loss and disclosing turnover may be necessary in the notes to the financial statements in order to give a true and fair view(see FRS 102.1AB.2).

**While not in format 1, every profit and loss account must show the amount of a company's profit or loss before taxation (1 Sch 6, Small Companies Regulations).

Format 2 analyses expenses by nature and is presented at Figure 3.12.

Figure 3.12   Format 2 for the profit and loss account – UK small company

*		[Turnover]
1-5*		Gross profit (combines items 1 to 5 in format 2)
6		Staff costs
	(a)	wages and salaries
	(b)	social security costs
	(c)	other pension costs
7	(a)	Depreciation and other amounts written off tangible and intangible fixed assets
	(b)	Amounts written off current assets, to the extent that they exceed write-offs which are normal in the undertaking concerned
8		Other operating charges
9		Income from shares in group undertakings
10		Income from participating interests†
11		Income from other fixed asset investments
12		Other interest receivable and similar income
13		Amounts written off investments
14		Interest payable and similar expenses
		Profit or loss before taxation*
15		Tax on profit or loss
16		Profit or loss after taxation
21		Other taxes not shown under the above items
22		Profit or loss for the financial year

* Disaggregation of gross profit or loss and disclosing turnover may be necessary in the notes to the financial statements in order to give a true and fair view(see FRS 102.1AB.2).

**While not in format 1, every profit and loss account must show the amount of a company's profit or loss before taxation (1 Sch 6, Small Companies Regulations).

The only difference to the statutory formats is the abridgement. The disclosures required by the Regulations are still required. Therefore, the guidance on statutory formats at 10.1 above remains relevant where abridged formats are used.

A small entity choosing to apply paragraph 1A(2) of Schedule 1 to the Small Companies Regulations and draw up an abridged profit and loss account must still meet the requirement for the financial statements to give a true and fair view. A small entity must therefore also consider the requirements of paragraph 1A.16 (see 11 below) and provide any additional disclosure that is necessary in the notes to the financial statements, for example in relation to disaggregating gross profit or loss and disclosing turnover. *[FRS 102.1AB.2].* In considering what level of disaggregation may be appropriate in order for the financial statements to give a true and fair view, in our view, entities should have regard to FRS 102's requirements on materiality and aggregation (see 7.6 above).

10.3   Adapted profit and loss account

'Adapted formats' may be used provided that the information given in the profit and loss account is at least equivalent to that which would have been required by the use of the statutory format had it not been thus adapted and the presentation is in accordance with generally accepted accounting principles or practice. *[1 Sch 1B(1) (SC)].* The detail, however, is left to accounting standards, namely Section 1A. A small entity choosing to apply paragraph 1B(2) of Schedule 1 to the Small Companies Regulations and adapt one of the profit and loss account formats shall, as a minimum, include in its income statement line items that present amounts (a) to (f) for the period (as set out in Table 3.13 below). *[FRS 102.1AB.3].*

The main modification required for group profit and loss account formats is the identification of non-controlling interests (see 8.1.4.B above).

Figure 3.13   Profit and loss account – UK small company applying paragraph 1B(2) of Schedule 1 to the Small Companies Regulations ('adapted formats')

(a)	Revenue
(b)	Finance costs
(c)	Share of the profit or loss of investments in associates and jointly controlled entities accounted for using the equity method
(d)	Profit or loss before taxation
(e)	Tax expense (excluding tax allocated to other comprehensive income or equity)
(f)	Profit or loss

So far as practicable, the provisions of paragraphs 2 to 9A of Section A of the General Rules to the formats (see 8.2 above) apply to the profit or loss account, notwithstanding any such adaptation pursuant to paragraph 1B of Schedule 1 to the Small Companies Regulations. *[1 Sch 1C (SC)].*

A small entity may include additional line items in the income statement and it amends the descriptions used in the line items set out in (a) to (f) in the above figure, and the ordering of items, when this is necessary to explain the elements of financial performance, providing the information given is at least equivalent to that required by the profit and loss account format had it not been adapted. *[FRS 102.1AB.4]*. Line item (f) is only relevant in consolidated financial statements under FRS 102.

Example 4.3 in Chapter 4 at 6.5.2 illustrates a statement of comprehensive income for an entity using 'adapted formats' in the full standard which provides an analysis of expenses. A small entity presenting only an income statement would omit the lines after profit for the year in Example 4.3.

An analysis of expenses is not explicitly required by Section 1A (since Section 5 of the standard does not apply) *[FRS 102.1A.7, 5.11]*, but a small entity may consider additional analysis necessary to explaining elements of financial performance. In this regard, it is notable that, where 'abridged formats' are used, Section 1A requires a small entity to provide any additional disclosure that is necessary for a true and fair view in the notes to the financial statements, for example, in relation to disaggregating gross profit or loss and disclosing turnover (see 10.2 above). *[FRS 102.1AB.2]*. Section 5's requirements to disclose turnover, however, do not appear to apply to 'adapted formats' prepared in accordance with Section 1A (which must instead present revenue as a line item on the face of the income statement). *[FRS 102.5.7D]*.

A significant difference to the items required for a small company on the face of the separate income statement (or profit or loss section of a single statement of comprehensive income) to the 'adapted formats' in full FRS 102 is that a separate line item (and columnar analysis) for discontinued operations is not required. In addition, there is no requirement to present a full statement of comprehensive income.

The Small Companies Regulations set out disclosures to be given in the notes to the financial statements which apply where statutory formats, abridged formats or the 'adapted formats' are used. One complexity is that the information required sometimes refers to items required in the statutory formats (which may differ to the line items identified where the 'adapted formats' are used). See discussion at 9.3 above.

11   INFORMATION TO BE PRESENTED IN THE NOTES TO THE FINANCIAL STATEMENTS

A small entity must present sufficient information in the notes to the financial statements to meet the requirement for the financial statements to give a true and fair view of the assets, liabilities, financial position and profit or loss of the small entity for the reporting period. *[FRS 102.1A.16]*

A small entity is not required to comply with the disclosure requirements of Section 3 (to the extent set out in paragraph 1A.7) and Sections 8 to 35 of FRS 102. However, because those disclosures are usually considered relevant to giving a true and fair view, a small entity is encouraged to consider and provide any of those disclosures that are relevant to material transactions, other events or conditions of the small entity in order to meet the requirement (for the financial statements to give a true and fair view) set out in paragraphs 1A.5 (see 7.2 above) and 1A.16 above. *[FRS 102.1A.17]*.

Appendix C of Section 1A sets out certain minimum requirements, based on the statutory requirements for companies subject to the small companies regime (see 11.1 below). *[FRS 102.1A.18-19]*. The list is not quite exhaustive and additional statutory disclosures are noted at 11.2 below. Section 1A also specifically encourages a small entity to give certain FRS 102 disclosures listed in Appendix D of Section 1A which may nevertheless be necessary to give a true and fair view (see 11.3 below). *[FRS 102.1A.20]*. Statutory disclosures relevant to consolidated financial statements are noted at 11.4 below.

In accordance with paragraph 3.16A, a small entity need not provide a specific disclosure (including those set out in paragraph 1A.18 and Appendix C to Section 1A) if the information is not material. *[FRS 102.1A.17]*.

A small LLP applying Section 1A must provide the following disclosures:

- the disclosures set out in Appendix C to Section 1A and

- any additional disclosures required by LLP law (in particular, the *Limited Liability Partnerships (Accounts and Audit) (Application of the Companies Act 2006) Regulations 2008* and the Small LLP Regulations) and

- any additional disclosures necessary to meet the requirement to give a true and fair view as set out in paragraph 1A.17

in accordance with paragraph 1A.20, a small LLP is encouraged to provide the disclosures set out in Appendix D to Section 1A. *[FRS 102.A4.45]*.

As LLP law has not yet been updated to implement the new Accounting Directive, the statutory disclosures differ from those listed in Section 1A so particular care is needed.

11.1 Minimum requirements – Appendix C

A small entity must provide, at a minimum, where relevant to its transactions, other events or conditions, the disclosures in Appendix C. *[FRS 102.1A.18, 1AC.1]*.

Appendix C sets out the disclosure requirements for small entities based on the requirements of company law, i.e. the statutory requirements in the Small Companies Regulations (as amended by SI 2015/980). The disclosure requirements are shown below in italicised font, consistent with Appendix C. Other than substituting company law terminology with the equivalent terminology used in FRS 102 (as set out in Appendix III to the standard), the drafting is stated to be as close as possible to that set out in company law.

Many of these disclosures are similar to existing FRS 102 disclosures in Sections 8 to 35, and Appendix C highlights the relevant paragraphs in these sections by including an asterisk in the left hand margin by the disclosures. Section 1A notes that in many cases compliance with the similar requirement of FRS 102 will result in compliance with the requirements in Appendix C. *[FRS 102.1A.19, Appendix C to Section 1A]*.

11.1.1 *Structure of notes*

- *The notes must be presented in the order in which, where relevant, the items to which they relate are presented in the statement of financial position and in the income statement.* *[1 Sch 42(2) (SC)]*.

  Paragraphs 8.3 and 8.4 of FRS 102 address similar requirements (see Chapter 4 at 8.1). *[FRS 102.1AC.2]*.

11.1.2   Accounting policies

- *The accounting policies adopted by the small entity in determining the amounts to be included in respect of items shown in the statement of financial position and in determining the profit or loss of the small entity must be stated (including such policies with respect to the depreciation and impairment of assets). [1 Sch 44 (SC)].*

  Paragraph 8.5 of FRS 102 addresses similar requirements. Including information about the judgements made in applying the small entity's accounting policies, as set out in paragraph 8.6 of FRS 102, may be useful to users of the small entity's financial statements (see Chapter 4 at 8.2 and 8.3). *[FRS 102.1AC.3].*

- *If any amount is included in a small entity's statement of financial position in respect of development costs, the note on accounting policies must include the following information:*

  (a) *the period over which the amount of those costs originally capitalised is being or is to be written off; and*

  (b) *the reasons for capitalising the development costs in question. [1 Sch 21(2) (SC)].*

  Paragraph 18.27(a) of FRS 102 addresses similar requirements to paragraph 1AC.4(a) (see Chapter 14 at 3.5.2 of EY New UK GAAP 2015). *[FRS 102.1AC.4].*

- *Where development costs are shown or included as an asset in the small entity's financial statements and the amount is not treated as a realised loss because there are special circumstances justifying this, a note to the financial statements must state the reasons for showing development costs as an asset and that it is not a realised loss. [s844, FRS 102.1AC.5].*

  See Chapter 4 at 10.1.3 for discussion of this disclosure requirement.

- *Where in exceptional cases, the useful life of intangible assets cannot be reliably estimated, there must be disclosed in a note to the financial statements the period over which those intangible assets are being written off and the reasons for choosing that period. [1 Sch 22(4) (SC)].*

  Intangible assets include goodwill. Paragraphs 18.27(a) (see Chapter 14 at 3.5.2 of EY New UK GAAP 2015) and 19.25(g) (see Chapter 5 at 7.1) of FRS 102 address similar disclosure requirements. *[FRS 102.1AC.6].*

11.1.3   Changes in presentation and accounting policies and corrections of prior period errors

- *Where there is a change in the presentation of a small entity's statement of financial position or income statement, particulars of any such change must be given in a note to the financial statements in which the new presentation is first used, and the reasons for the change must be explained. [1 Sch 2(2) (SC)].*

  Paragraphs 3.12 and 3.13 of FRS 102 address similar requirements (see 7.5.2 above). *[FRS 102.1AC.7].* The statutory reference given is for changes in formats (see 8.1.5 above).

- *Where the corresponding amount for the immediately preceding financial year is not comparable with the amount to be shown for the item in question in respect of the reporting period, and the corresponding amount is adjusted, the particulars of the non-comparability and of any adjustment must be disclosed in a note to the financial statements. [1 Sch 7(2) (SC)].*

  This is likely to be relevant where there has either been a change in accounting policy or the correction of a material prior period error. Paragraphs 10.13, 10.14 and 10.23 of FRS 102 address similar requirements (see 7.5.2 above and Chapter 7 at 3.7.1 and 3.7.3 of EY New UK GAAP 2015). *[FRS 102.1AC.8].*

- *Where any amount relating to a preceding reporting period is included in any item in the income statement, the effect must be stated. [1 Sch 61(1) (SC), FRS 102.1AC.9].*

11.1.4   True and fair override

- *If it appears to the small entity that there are special reasons for departing from any of the principles set out in company law in preparing the small entity's financial statements in respect of any reporting period, it may do so, in which case particulars of the departure, the reasons for it, and its effects must be given in the notes to the financial statements. [1 Sch 10(2) (SC)].*

  This is only expected to occur in special circumstances. Paragraphs 3.4 and 3.5 of FRS 102 address similar requirements. *[FRS 102.1AC.10].* See 7.2 above and Chapter 4 at 9.2. The general principles – going concern, consistency, prudence, accruals basis and rules on offset and that the opening balance sheet for a financial year corresponds to the closing balance sheet for the previous financial year – in the Small Companies Regulations are the same as those set out in the Regulations and discussed in Chapter 4 at 9.1. *[1 Sch 11-15A (SC)].*

There is an additional related statutory requirement for companies and LLPs not separately identified in Appendix C to Section 1A. *[s396(5), s404(5)].* However, this appears to be because it is required by paragraphs 3.5 and 3.6 of FRS 102, which are not scoped out for a small entity applying Section 1A. Therefore, the following disclosures of paragraphs 3.5 and 3.6 apply to all entities applying Section 1A making use of the 'true and fair override'. See 7.2 above.

- *When an entity departs from a requirement of FRS 102 (in special circumstances, in order to give a true and fair view – see paragraph 3.4 of the standard) or from a requirement of applicable legislation, it shall disclose:*

  (a)   that management has concluded that the financial statements give a true and fair view of the entity's financial position, financial performance and, when required to be presented, cash flows;

  (b)   that it has complied with FRS 102 or applicable legislation, except that it has departed from a particular requirement of the standard or applicable legislation to the extent necessary to give a true and fair view; and

  (c)   the nature and effect of the departure, including the treatment that FRS 102 or applicable legislation would require, the reason why that treatment would be so misleading in the circumstances that it would conflict with the objective of financial statements set out in Section 2 and the treatment adopted. [FRS 102.3.5].

Chapter 3

- *When an entity has departed from a requirement of FRS 102 or applicable legislation in a prior period and that departure affects the amounts recognised in the financial statements for the current period, it shall make the disclosures set out in (c) above.* [FRS 102.3.6].

11.1.5   Notes supporting the statement of financial position

11.1.5.A   *An asset or liability relating to more than one item in the statement of financial position*
- *Where an asset or liability relates to more than one item in the statement of financial position, the relationship of such asset or liability to the relevant items must be disclosed either under those items or in the notes to the financial statements.* [1 Sch 9A (SC), FRS 102.1AC.11].

See discussion at 8.2 above concerning situations where this disclosure requirement may apply.

11.1.5.B   *Fixed assets (general)*
- *In respect of each item which is shown under the general item 'fixed assets' in the small entity's statement of financial position, the following information must be given:* [FRS 102.1AC.12]

  (a)   *the aggregate amounts (on the basis of cost or revaluation) in respect of that item as at the date of the beginning of the reporting period and as at the reporting date respectively;*

  (b)   *the effect on any amount shown in the statement of financial position in respect of that item of:*

    (i)   *any revision of the amount in respect of any assets included under that item made during the reporting period as a result of revaluation;*

    (ii)   *acquisitions during the reporting period of any assets;*

    (iii)   *disposals during the reporting period of any assets; and*

    (iv)   *any transfers of assets of the small entity to and from that item during the reporting period.* [1 Sch 48(1)-(2) (SC)].

- *In respect of each item within paragraph 1AC.12 above, there must also be stated:* [FRS 102.1AC.13]

  (a)   *the cumulative amount of provisions for depreciation and impairment of assets included under that item as at the date of the beginning of the reporting period and as at the reporting date respectively;*

  (b)   *the amount of any such provisions made in respect of the reporting period;*

  (c)   *the amount of any adjustments made in respect of any such provisions during the reporting period in consequence of the disposal of any such assets; and*

  (d)   *the amount of any other adjustments made in respect of any such provisions during the reporting period.* [1 Sch 48(3) (SC)].

These two paragraphs apply to all fixed assets, including investment property, plant and equipment, intangible assets (including goodwill), fixed asset investments, biological assets and heritage assets recognised in the statement of financial position.

Each item refers to a class of fixed assets shown separately either in the statement of financial position or in the notes to the financial statements. These reconciliations need not be presented for prior periods.

FRS 102 addresses similar requirements for investment property, *[FRS 102.16.10(e)]*, property, plant and equipment, *[FRS 102.17.31(d)-(e)]*, intangible assets other than goodwill, *[FRS 102.18.27(c), (e)]*, biological assets *[FRS 102.34.7(c), 34.10(e)]* and heritage assets *[FRS 102.34.55(e)-(f)]* recognised in the statement of financial position. *[FRS 102.1AC.13]*. These are discussed in Chapter 12 at 3.6.1, Chapter 13 at 3.8.1, Chapter 29 at 2.5.3 and 2.6.2, and Chapter 29 at 5.2.3 respectively of EY New UK GAAP 2015.

'Fixed assets' are assets of an entity which are intended for use on a continuing basis in the company's activities, and 'current assets' are assets not intended for such use. *[10 Sch 4, FRS 102.Appendix I]*. (See 9.1 above and Chapter 4 at 5.2.2). However, note that the above disclosures are still required even if 'adapted formats' with a non-current and current analysis of assets and liabilities are applied (see 9.3 above).

11.1.5.C   Fixed assets (measured at revalued amounts)

Section 1A clarifies that the following disclosure requirements in paragraphs 1AC.14 to 1AC.18 of FRS 102 apply when:

* investments in subsidiaries, associates and joint ventures are measured at fair value with changes in fair value recognised in other comprehensive income. Paragraph 9.27(b) addresses a similar disclosure requirement (see Chapter 6 at 4 and 4.6.1 of EY New UK GAAP 2015);

* property, plant and equipment are revalued using the revaluation model set out in paragraphs 17.15B to 17.15F of FRS 102. Paragraph 17.31(a) of FRS 102 addresses a similar disclosure requirement (see Chapter 13 at 3.8.1 of EY New UK GAAP 2015); and

* intangible assets other than goodwill are revalued using the revaluation model set out in paragraphs 18.18B to 18.18H of FRS 102.

These requirements do not apply to investment property and biological assets measured at fair value through profit or loss. *[FRS 102.1AC.14-18]*. This is because such accounting for investment property and biological assets is in accordance with the fair value accounting rules (see Chapter 4 at 10.4) rather than being a revaluation under the alternative accounting rules (see Chapter 4 at 10.2), which is what this disclosure concerns.

The disclosures in respect of fixed assets (measured at revalued amounts) are as follows:

* *When fixed assets are measured at revalued amounts the items affected and the basis of valuation adopted in determining the amounts of the assets in question in the case of each such item must be disclosed in the note on accounting policies.* *[1 Sch 34(2) (SC), FRS 102.1AC.14]*.

- *Where any fixed assets of the small entity (other than listed investments) are included under any item shown in the small entity's statement of financial position at a revalued amount, the following information must be given:*

  (a) *the years (so far as they are known to the directors) in which the assets were severally valued and the several values;*

  (b) *in the case of assets that have been valued during the reporting period, the names of the persons who valued them or particulars of their qualifications for doing so (and whichever is stated), the bases of valuation used by them.* [1 Sch 49 (SC)].

Paragraphs 17.32A(a) and (c), 18.29A(a) and (c), and 34.55(e)(ii) of FRS 102 address similar requirements (see Chapter 13 at 3.8.1, Chapter 14 at 3.5.4 and Chapter 29 at 5.2.3 of EY New UK GAAP 2015). These paragraphs do not require the names or qualifications of the persons who valued the fixed assets to be disclosed; paragraphs 17.32A(b) and 18.29A(b) address only whether or not the valuer was independent. [FRS 102.1AC.15].

A listed investment is an investment which has been granted a listing on a recognised investment exchange other than an overseas investment exchange (both as defined in Part 18 of the Financial Services and Markets Act 2000) or a stock exchange of repute outside the UK. [8 Sch 5 (SC)]. A list of recognised investment exchanges (and recognised overseas investment exchanges) is available on the Financial Conduct Authority website. AIM is not a recognised investment exchange. Note that this disclosure is referring to use of the alternative accounting rules and not the fair value accounting rules (see Chapter 4 at 10.2 to 10.4).

- *In the case of each item in the statement of financial position measured at a revalued amount, the comparable amounts determined according to the historical cost accounting rules must be shown in a note to the financial statements.* [1 Sch 34(3) (SC)].

The comparable amounts refers to the aggregate amount of cost and the aggregate of accumulated depreciation and accumulated impairment losses that would have been required according to the historical cost accounting rules (see Chapter 4 at 10.1). [1 Sch 34(4) (SC)].

Paragraphs 17.32A(d) and 18.29A(d) of FRS 102 (Chapter 13 at 3.8.1 and Chapter 14 at 3.5.4 of EY New UK GAAP 2015) address similar requirements. [FRS 102.1AC.16].

Note that this disclosure is referring to use of the alternative accounting rules and not the fair value accounting rules (see Chapter 4 at 10.2 to 10.4).

- *Where fixed assets are measured at revalued amounts, the following information must be given in tabular form:*

  (a) *movements in the revaluation reserve in the reporting period, with an explanation of the tax treatment of items therein; and*

  (b) *the carrying amount in the statement of financial position that would have been recognised had the fixed assets not been revalued.* [1 Sch 54(2) (SC)].

Paragraphs 6.3A (see Chapter 4 at 7.1), 17.32A(d), 18.29A(d), and 29.27(a) of FRS 102 (see Chapter 13 at 3.8.1, Chapter 14 at 3.5.4 and Chapter 24 at 11.2 of EY New UK GAAP 2015) address similar requirements. *[FRS 102.1AC.17]*.

- *The treatment for taxation purposes of amounts credited or debited to the revaluation reserve must be disclosed in a note to the financial statements.* *[1 Sch 35(6) (SC)]*.

Paragraph 29.27(a) of FRS 102 (see Chapter 24 at 11.2 of EY New UK GAAP 2015) addresses similar requirements. *[FRS 102.1AC.18]*.

11.1.5.D   Capitalisation of borrowing costs

- *When a small entity adopts a policy of capitalising borrowing costs, the inclusion of interest in determining the cost of the asset and the amount of the interest so included is disclosed in a note to the financial statements.* *[1 Sch 27(3) (SC)]*.

Paragraph 25.3A(a) of FRS 102 addresses a similar requirement to the second part of this (see Chapter 20 at 3.7.1 of EY New UK GAAP 2015). *[FRS 102.1AC.19]*.

11.1.5.E   Impairment of assets

- *Provisions for impairment of fixed assets (including fixed asset investments) must be disclosed separately in a note to the financial statements if not shown separately in the income statement.* *[1 Sch 19(3) (SC))]*.

Paragraph 27.32(a) of FRS 102 (see Chapter 22 at 8 of EY New UK GAAP 2015) addresses similar requirements. *[FRS 102.1AC.20]*.

- *Any provisions for impairment of fixed assets that are reversed because the reasons for which they were made have ceased to apply must be disclosed (either separately or in aggregate) in a note to the financial statements if not shown separately in the income statement.* *[1 Sch 20(2) (SC)]*.

Paragraph 27.32(b) of FRS 102 (see Chapter 22 at 8 of EY New UK GAAP 2015) addresses similar requirements. *[FRS 102.1AC.21]*.

11.1.5.F   Fair value measurement

- *Where financial instruments or other assets have been measured at fair value through profit or loss there must be stated:*
  - *(a) the significant assumptions underlying the valuation models and techniques used to determine the fair values;*
  - *(b) for each category of financial instrument or other asset, the fair value of assets in that category and the change in value*
    - *(i)   included directly in the income statement; or*
    - *(ii) credited to or (as the case may be) debited from the fair value reserve,*
  - *in respect of those assets.* *[1 Sch 51(2)(a)-(b) (SC)]*.

This does not apply where financial instruments or other assets are measured at fair value only on initial recognition. This applies where financial instruments, certain inventories, investment property, and biological assets are subsequently measured at fair value through profit or loss, which is permitted or required by paragraphs 9.26(c), 11.14(b), 12.8, 13.4A, 14.4(d), 15.9(d), 16.7 and 34.4.

Paragraphs 11.41(a), 11.41(d), 11.43, 11.48(a)(i), 11.48(a)(ii), 12.28, 12.29(c) and 12.29(e) of FRS 102 address similar disclosure requirements for financial instruments. See Chapter 8 at 8 of EY New UK GAAP 2015.

Paragraphs 16.10(a) and 16.10(e)(ii) of FRS 102 addresses similar disclosure requirements for investment property. See Chapter 12 at 3.6.1 of EY New UK GAAP 2015.

Paragraphs 34.7(c)(i) and 34.7(b) of FRS 102 address similar disclosure requirements for biological assets. See Chapter 29 at 2.5.3 of EY New UK GAAP 2015. *[FRS 102.1AC.22].*

The requirement in paragraph 51(2)(b) of Schedule 1 to the Small Companies Regulations and Section 1A refers to 'change in value ... in respect of those assets'. This looks like a drafting error, when compared to both Directive 2013/34/EU (the new Accounting Directive) and the previous disclosure requirement for financial instruments. In our view, the disclosure is intended to be in respect of those financial instruments or other assets.

- *Where financial instruments or other assets have been measured at fair value through profit and loss there must be stated for each class of derivatives, the extent and nature of the instruments including significant terms and conditions that may affect the amount, timing and certainty of future cash flows.* [1 Sch 51(2)(c) (SC), FRS 102.1AC.23].

- *Where any amount is transferred to or form the fair value reserve during the reporting period there must be stated in tabular form:*

    (a)   *the amount of the reserve as at the beginning of the reporting period and as at the reporting date respectively; and*

    (b)   *the amount transferred to or from the reserve during that year.* [1 Sch 51(3) (SC)].

Paragraphs 6.3A (see Chapter 4 at 7.1), 12.29(c) and 12.29(d) of FRS 102 (see Chapter 8 at 8.1 of EY New UK GAAP 2015) address similar requirements. *[FRS 102.1AC.24].*

- *The treatment for taxation purposes of amounts credited or debited to the fair value reserve must be disclosed in a note to the financial statements.* [1 Sch 41(2) (SC)].

Paragraph 29.27(a) of FRS 102 (see Chapter 24 at 11.2 of EY New UK GAAP 2015) addresses similar requirements. *[FRS 102.1AC.25].*

11.1.5.G   *Financial instruments measured at fair value*

- *Financial instruments which, under international accounting standards may be included at fair value, may be so included, provided that the disclosures required by such accounting standards are made.* [1 Sch 36(4) (SC)].

This only applies in certain circumstances, for example, it does not apply to derivatives. It applies where investments in subsidiaries, associates and joint ventures are measured at fair value through profit or loss. When it applies, the disclosures required by Section 11 that relate to financial assets and financial liabilities measured at fair value, including paragraph 11.48A shall be given. *[FRS 102.1AC.26]*.

The explanatory guidance above is consistent with our view that this disclosure applies only to financial instruments that are held at fair value subject to the requirements of paragraph 36(4) to Schedule 1 to the Small Companies Regulations. Therefore, the disclosures would not apply to all financial instruments held at fair value but would apply to those financial instruments held at fair value that are listed in paragraphs 36(2) and (3) of Schedule 1 to the Small Companies Regulations. The reference to 'international accounting standards' in paragraph 1AC.26 is to EU-adopted IFRS. *[s474(1)]*.

The Small LLP Regulations have a similar (but not identical requirement, since the Small LLP Regulations were not amended by SI 2015/980). The Small LLP Regulations, unless there is a subsequent change to LLP law, instead refer to 'international accounting standards, adopted by the EU on or before 5 September 2006 in accordance with the IAS Regulation'. This means that it requires the disclosures included in EU-adopted IFRS on or before 5 September 2006 (rather than extant EU-adopted IFRS, as required by paragraph 1AC.26). The disclosures given need to comply with both paragraph 1AC.26 and the Small LLP Regulations.

See Chapter 4 at 10.3.1 for further explanation of this disclosure requirement.

For the avoidance of doubt, this disclosure applies to all small entities applying Section 1A, whether or not subject to statutory requirements.

11.1.5.H   Indebtedness, guarantees and financial commitments
*   *For the aggregate of all items shown under 'creditors' in the small entity's statement of financial position there must be stated the aggregate of the following amounts:* [FRS 102.1AC.27]*

    (a)   the amount of any debts included under 'creditors' which are payable or repayable otherwise than by instalments and fall due for payment or repayment after the end of the period of five years beginning with the day next following the reporting date; and

    (b)   in the case of any debts so included which are payable or repayable by instalments, the amount of any instalments which fall due for payment after the end of that period. [1 Sch 55(1) (SC)]*.

*   *In respect of each item shown under 'creditors' in the small entity's statement of financial position there must be stated the aggregate amount of any debts included under that item in respect of which any security has been given by the small entity with an indication of the nature and form of any such security.* [1 Sch 55(2) (SC)]*.

    Paragraphs 11.46, 13.22(e), 16.10(c), 17.32(a) and 18.28(c) of FRS 102 address similar requirements. *[FRS 102.1AC.28]*. See Chapter 8 at 8.1, Chapter 9 at 3.6.2, Chapter 13 at 3.8.1 and Chapter 14 at 3.5.2 of EY New UK GAAP 2015.

*   *The total amount of any financial commitments, guarantees and contingencies that are not included in the balance sheet must be stated.* [1 Sch 57(1) (SC)]*.

The total amount of any commitments concerning pensions must be separately disclosed. [1 Sch 57(3) (SC)].

The total amount of any commitments which are undertaken on behalf of or for the benefit of:

(b)   *any parent, fellow subsidiary or any subsidiary of the small entity (see definition in Chapter 2 at 3.1.2 of* EY New UK GAAP 2015*); or*

(b)   *any undertaking in which the small entity has a participating interest (see definition in Chapter 4 at 5.3.4.D);*

must be separately stated and those within (a) must also be stated separately from those within (b). [1 Sch 57(4) (SC)].

Such commitments can arise in a variety of situations including in relation to group entities, investments, property, plant and equipment, leases and pension obligations. Paragraphs 15.19(d), 16.10(d), 17.32(b), 18.28(d), 20.16, 21.15, 28.40A(a), 28.40A(b), 28.41A(d), 33.9(b)(ii) and 34.62 address similar requirements. *[FRS 102.1AC.29].* See Chapter 11 at 3.11, Chapter 12 at 3.6.1, Chapter 13 at 3.8.1, Chapter 14 at 3.5.2, Chapter 16 at 3.11.1.B, Chapter 17 at 3.10.3 and 3.10.7, Chapter 23 at 3.12.3 and 3.12.4.B, and Chapter 28 at 3.2.3.A of EY New UK GAAP 2015.

•   *An indication of the nature and form of any valuable security given by the small entity in respect of commitments, guarantees and contingencies within paragraph 1AC.29 must be given.* [1 Sch 57(2)].

Paragraphs 11.46, 13.22(e), 16.10(c), 17.32(a) and 18.28(c) address similar requirements. *[FRS 102.1AC.30].* See Chapter 8 at 8.1, Chapter 9 at 3.6.2, Chapter 13 at 3.8.1 and Chapter 14 at 3.5.2 of EY New UK GAAP 2015.

•   *If in any reporting period a small entity is or has been party to arrangements that are not reflected in its statement of financial position and at the reporting date the risks or benefits arising from those arrangements are material, the nature and business purpose of the arrangements must be given in the notes to the financial statements to the extent necessary for enabling the financial position of the small entity to be assessed.* [s410A].

Examples of off-balance sheet arrangements include risk and benefit-sharing arrangements or obligations arising from a contract such as debt factoring, combined sale and repurchase arrangements, consignment stock arrangements, take or pay arrangements, securitisation arranged through separate entities, pledged assets, operating lease arrangements, outsourcing and the like. In many cases, the disclosures about financial commitments and contingencies required by paragraphs 1AC.29 and 1AC.30 will also address such arrangements. *[FRS 102.1AC.31].*

See Chapter 4 at 8.7 for discussion of off-balance sheet arrangement, and in respect of any consolidated financial statements, 11.4.2.E below.

11.1.6 Notes supporting the income statement

*   *The amount and nature of any individual items of income or expenses of exceptional size or incidence must be stated.* [1 Sch 61(2) (SC)].

    Paragraph 5.9A addresses a similar requirement in relation to material items. *[FRS 102.1AC.32].* See Chapter 4 at 6.7.5.

*   *The notes to a small entity's financial statements must disclose the average number of persons employed by the small entity in the reporting period.* [s411, FRS 102.1AC.33].

    The average number is ascertained by determining the number of persons employed under contracts of service by the company for each month in the financial year (whether throughout the month or not – so including both part- and full-time employees), adding together all the monthly numbers and dividing by the numbers of months in the financial year. *[s411(3)-(4)].* See 11.4.2.C below and Chapter 4 at 8.6.

11.1.7 Related party disclosures

*   *Where the small entity is a subsidiary, the following information must be given in respect of the parent of the smallest group for which consolidated financial statements are drawn up of which the small entity is a member:*

    (a) *the name of the parent which draws up the consolidated financial statements;*

    (b) *the address of the parent's registered office (whether in or outside the UK); or*

    (c) *if it is unincorporated, the address of its principal place of business.* [1 Sch 65 (SC)].

    Paragraph 33.5 of FRS 102 addresses a similar requirement to paragraph (a). *[FRS 102.1AC.34].* See Chapter 28 at 3.2.1 of EY New UK GAAP 2015.

*   *Particulars must be given of material transactions the small entity has entered into that have not been concluded under normal market conditions with:*

    (a) *owners holding a participating interest (see definition at Chapter 4 at 5.3.4.D) in the small entity;*

    (b) *companies in which the small entity itself has a participating interest; and*

    (c) *the small entity's directors [or members of its governing body].*

    Particulars must include:

    (a) *the amount of such transactions;*

    (b) *the nature of the related party relationship; and*

    (c) *other information about the transactions necessary for an understanding of the financial position of the small entity.*

Chapter 3

Information about individual transactions may be aggregated according to their nature, except where separate information is necessary for an understanding of the effects of the related party transactions on the financial position of the small entity.

Particulars need not be given of transactions entered into between two or more members of a group provided that any subsidiary which is a party to the transaction is wholly owned by such a member. [1 Sch 66 (SC)]. See Chapter 28 at 1.1.2 of EY New UK GAAP 2015 for discussion on the meaning of this exemption.

Although disclosure is only required of material transactions with the specified related parties that have not been concluded under normal market conditions, small entities disclosing all transactions with such related parties would still be compliant with company law.

Transactions with directors, or members of an entity's governing body, include directors' remuneration and dividends paid to directors.

Paragraphs 33.9 and 33.14 address similar requirements for all related parties. See Chapter 28 at 3.2.3 of EY New UK GAAP 2015. [FRS 102.1AC.35]. However, the categories of related party that information must be reported for and details required under full FRS 102 differ slightly to the requirements of paragraph 1AC.35.

SI 2015/980 removed the statutory directors' remuneration disclosures previously included in Schedule 3 to the Small Companies Regulations. However, paragraph 1AC.35 confirms that directors' remuneration (or where the entity is not a company, the remuneration of the entity's governing body) still requires disclosure as a related party transaction. This does not mean that the directors' remuneration disclosures are required in the format previously specified by Schedule 3. The statutory disclosures of directors' remuneration sometimes required remuneration to be reported in periods and at amounts that differed to the accounting for the remuneration in the financial statements.

Full FRS 102 requires key management personnel compensation to be given in total. [FRS 102.33.6-7]. This disclosure does not apply to small entities applying Section 1A and differs from directors' remuneration as key management may include persons other than directors of the reporting entity. In addition key management compensation includes all forms of consideration paid, payable or provided by the entity or on behalf of the entity (e.g. by its parent or a shareholder) in exchange for services rendered to the entity. It also includes such consideration paid on behalf of a parent of the entity in respect of goods or services provided to the entity. Consequently, key management personnel captures certain transactions not entered into by the reporting entity itself or where the cost is not borne by the reporting entity. In our view, one approach to disclosing directors' remuneration might be to disclose the element of total key management compensation that relates to the directors, separately disclosing compensation that is not provided by the reporting entity. Where necessary for an understanding of the financial position of the company, other information about the transactions might be required, This might sometimes be the case, for example, where long-term incentive plan or share-based payment awards have been made to a director and the amount of the transaction disclosed (say, the expense recognised) does not fully provide an understanding of the financial position of the company (which could include commitments).

• *Details of advances and credits granted by the small entity to its directors and guarantees of any kind entered into by the small entity on behalf of its directors must be shown in the notes to the financial statements.*

The details required of an advance or credit are:

(a) *its amount;*

(b) *an indication of the interest rate;*

(c) *its main conditions;*

(d) *any amounts repaid;*

(e) *any amounts written off; and*

(f) *any amounts waived.*

There must also be stated in the notes to the financial statements the totals of amounts stated under (a), (d), (e) and (f).

The details required of a guarantee are:

(a) *its main terms;*

(b) *the amount of the maximum liability that may be incurred by the small entity; and*

(c) *any amount paid and any liability incurred by the small entity for the purpose of fulfilling the guarantee (including any loss incurred by reason of enforcement of the guarantee).*

There must also be stated in the notes to the financial statements the totals of amounts stated under (b) and (c). [s413].

Paragraph 33.9 addresses similar requirements for all related parties. See Chapter 28 at 3.2.3 of EY New UK GAAP 2015.

A small entity that is not a company shall provide this disclosure in relation to members of its governing body. *[FRS 102.1AC.36].*

See Chapter 4 at 8.8 for discussion of the scope and content of this disclosure. For the requirements in group accounts, see 11.4.2.D below.

11.1.8 Other requirements

The financial statements must state:

(a) *the part of the UK in which the small entity is registered;*

(b) *the small entity's registered number;*

(c) *whether the small entity is a public or a private company and whether the small entity is limited by shares or by guarantee;*

(d) *the address of the small entity's registered office; and*

(e) *where appropriate, the fact that the entity is being wound up.* [s396].

Chapter 3

Paragraph 3.24(a) addresses similar requirements *[FRS 102.1AC.37]* and is actually scoped in by Section 1A. See 7.7 above which also addresses the requirements of the standard on identification of the financial statements.

- *Where items to which Arabic numbers are given in the formats have been combined, unless they are not material, the individual amounts of any items which have been combined must be disclosed in a note to the financial statements.* *[1 Sch 4(3) (SC), FRS 102.1AC.38].*

  See the discussion on the General Rules to the formats at 8.2 above.

- *The nature and financial effect of material events arising after the reporting date which are not reflected in the income statement or statement of financial position must be stated.* *[1 Sch 64 (SC)].*

  Paragraphs 32.10 and 32.11 address similar requirements. See Chapter 27 at 3.2.2 and 3.5.2 of EY New UK GAAP 2015. *[FRS 102.1AC.39].*

11.2   Statutory disclosures not noted in Section 1A

Financial statements of a small entity will also need to comply with any statutory requirements arising from the CA 2006 and applicable regulations, or other legal framework that applies to the small entity.

Section 1A is not a complete list of all statutory requirements for a small company applying the Small Companies Regime. Some additional disclosures are noted below. The statutory disclosures in group accounts (where voluntarily prepared) are set out at 11.4 below.

The disclosures noted below also apply to LLPs but, as noted at 11 above, LLPs must additionally give the disclosures required by LLP law, which differ. A change to LLP law to implement the new Accounting Directive is expected to be consulted on in due course. The additional LLP disclosures are not listed below.

11.2.1   *Audited financial statements only*

A note to the annual accounts of a company subject to the small companies regime must disclose the amount of remuneration receivable by the company's auditor for the auditing of the annual accounts. Where the remuneration includes benefits in kind, the nature and estimated money value of those benefits must also be disclosed in a note. Where more than one person has been appointed as a company's auditor in respect of the period to which the accounts relate, separate disclosure is required in respect of the remuneration of each such person. *[s494].*[8]

A small company which has entered into a liability limitation agreement (that purports to limit the liability owed to a company by its auditor in respect of any negligence, default, breach of duty or breach of trust, occurring in the course of the audit of the accounts, of which the auditor may be guilty in relation to the company *[s534]*) must disclose its principal terms, the date of the resolution approving the agreement or the agreement's principal terms or, in the case of a private company, the date of the resolution waiving the need for such approval. This disclosure is required in a note to the annual accounts for the financial year to which the agreement relates unless the agreement was entered into too late for it to be reasonably practicable for the disclosure to be made in those accounts (in which case, the disclosure is made in a note to the company's next following accounts).[9]

11.2.2 Audit exemption statement

If the small company is audit exempt, its balance sheet will need to contain a statement by the directors (above the signature of the director required by section 414 of the CA 2006) to the effect that:

(a)   the company is exempt from audit under section 477 (small companies), section 479A (subsidiary companies) or section 480 (dormant companies) or under section 482 (non-profit-making companies subject to public sector audit) of the CA 2006, as applicable;

(b)   the members have not required the company to obtain an audit of its accounts for the year in question in accordance with section 476 of the CA 2006; and

(c)   the directors acknowledge their responsibilities for complying with the requirements of the CA 2006 with respect to accounting records and the preparation of accounts. *[s475]*.

11.2.3 Group accounts not prepared by a parent company

No disclosure of the exemption from preparing group accounts is required in the annual accounts if a parent company applying the small companies regime does not prepare group accounts (nor, where SI 2015/980 is applied, a parent company that would be subject to the small companies regime but for being a public company and is not a traded company does not prepare group accounts). *[s399(1), (2A)]*. See 6.2 above.

As its balance sheet must contain a statement that the annual accounts have been prepared in accordance with the provisions applicable to the small companies regime (see 11.2.5 below), it will be clear that a company subject to the small companies regime is entitled to an exemption from preparing group accounts. However, it may be helpful for a company that does not qualify for the small companies regime (on the grounds that it is a public company that is not a traded company) but takes the exemption from preparing group accounts to disclose that it has done so in a note to its annual accounts.

As companies subject to the small companies regime are exempt from preparing group accounts, the disclosures required where the exemptions from preparing group accounts in sections 400 and 401 of the CA 2006 are taken are not noted here.

11.2.4 Other disclosures

The Small Companies Regulations require that where fixed asset investments (falling under item B.III in the statutory balance sheet format – see 9.1 above) are included at a value determined on any basis which appears to the directors to be appropriate in the circumstances of the company, particulars of the method of valuation adopted and of the reasons for adopting it must be disclosed in a note to the accounts. *[1 Sch 32(3) (SC)]*.

FRS 102 does not permit use of the alternative accounting rules for fixed asset investments, with the exception of investments in subsidiaries, associates and jointly controlled entities carried at fair value through other comprehensive income. *[FRS 102.9.9A, 9.26(b), 14.4, 15.9]*. See Chapter 6 at 3.4.1, 4.1 and 4.2 of EY New UK GAAP 2015. As such investments are carried at fair value, this disclosure would not apply. However, the alternative accounting rules may also be used where such investments are carried using a deemed cost in individual or separate financial statements on transition. *[FRS 102.35.10(f)]*. See Chapter 30 at 5.9 of EY New UK GAAP 2015. In such circumstances, the above disclosure will be required.

11.2.5   *Approval of annual accounts*

The annual accounts of a company must be approved by the board of directors and the company's balance sheet signed on behalf of the board by a director of the company. *[s414(1)-(2)]*. The annual accounts of an LLP are approved by the members and the balance sheet is signed on behalf of all the members by a designated member. *[s414(1)-(2) (LLP)]*.

If the accounts are prepared in accordance with the small companies regime (unless applying the micro-entity provisions – see Chapter 1 at 6.4), the balance sheet must contain, in a prominent position above the signature(s) of the director(s), a statement to the effect that the accounts have been prepared in accordance with the provisions applicable to companies subject to the small companies regime. *[s414(3)(b)]*.

Similarly, if the accounts are prepared in accordance with the provisions applicable to LLPs subject to the small LLPs regime, the balance sheet must contain a statement to that effect in a prominent position above the signature. *[s414(3) (LLP)]*.

This statement will be required if Section 1A is applied but also if any of the statutory exemptions available to the small companies or small LLPs regimes are taken. Example 3.1 provides an example of this statutory statement, adapting wording provided by Companies House, and combines it with the statement of compliance with FRS 102 that small entities applying Section 1A are encouraged to give (see 11.3 below). FRS 102 does not provide a standard form of wording for this statement of compliance.

Example 3.1:   Use of small companies regime and statement of compliance with FRS 102

These financial statements have been prepared in accordance with the provisions applicable to companies subject to the small companies regime and in accordance with Financial Reporting Standard 102 'The Financial Reporting Standard applicable in the UK and Republic of Ireland', applying Section 1A (Small Entities).

11.3   Specifically encouraged disclosure requirements – Appendix D

A small entity is also encouraged to make the disclosures set out in Appendix D to Section 1A, which may nevertheless be necessary to give a true and fair view. *[FRS 102.1A.20]*. While the FRC cannot mandate disclosures not included in the new Accounting Directive (as implemented in SI 2015/980), this statement implies that the disclosures below should generally be given, where relevant, since they may be necessary to give a true and fair view.

Where relevant to its transactions, other events and conditions, a small entity is encouraged to provide the following disclosures:

- a statement of compliance with FRS 102 as set out in paragraph 3.3, adapted to refer to Section 1A (see Chapter 4 at 3.8). An example is given at 11.2.5 above;

- a statement that it is a public benefit entity as set out in paragraph PBE 3.3A (see Chapter 4 at 3.8);

- the disclosures relating to going concern set out in paragraph 3.9 (see 7.3 and Chapter 4 at 9.3);

- dividends declared and paid or payable during the period (for example, as set out in paragraph 6.5(b)); and

- on first-time adoption of FRS 102, an explanation of how the transition has effected its financial position and financial performance as set out in paragraph 35.13 (see Chapter 30 at 6.3 of EY New UK GAAP 2015). *[FRS 102.1AD.1]*.

Note that paragraph 6.5(b) of FRS 102 requires the information on dividends to be presented in the statement of income and retained earnings (which may not be presented by a small entity applying Section 1A). In our view, this disclosure could be presented in the notes to the financial statements.

11.4   Disclosures in consolidated financial statements

FRS 102 does not require a small entity that is a parent entity to prepare consolidated financial statements. *[FRS 102.1A.21]*. However, some small entities may choose to (or may be required, for example, by their statutory framework) to prepare consolidated financial statements.

Section 1A addresses the preparation of consolidated financial statements, including the disclosures required (see 6.2.1 above). A small entity is encouraged to provide the disclosures set out in paragraph 9.23 of FRS 102 (see 11.4.1 below) and must comply with the disclosure requirements specified in Section 1A as if the group were a single entity, subject to any restrictions or exemptions set out in legislation (see 11.1 and 11.3 above, and 11.4.2 below) and any disclosures in Schedule 6 to the Small Companies Regulations (see 11.4.3 and 11.4.4 below). *[FRS 102.1A.22]*.

A company subject to the small companies regime must comply with the statutory disclosure requirements of the CA 2006 (see 11.4.2 below) and Schedule 6 to the Small Companies Regulations (see 11.4.3 and 11.4.4 below). These largely overlap with the disclosures required by Section 1A alone (although some additional disclosures are noted at 11.2 and 11.4.2 below).

An LLP subject to the small LLPs regime must comply with the statutory disclosure requirements in SI 2008/1911 and Schedule 4 to the Small LLP Regulations. The Small LLP Regulations (unless LLP law is subsequently changed) include many additional disclosures to those required for companies subject to the small companies regime, following application of SI 2015/980. However, the effect of paragraph 1A.22 (discussed above) is that LLPs subject to the small LLPs regime must give most of the statutory disclosures required for companies subject to the small companies regime as well.

The modifications made to the formats for group accounts in the Small Companies Regulations and Small LLP Regulations are addressed at 8.1.4 above.

11.4.1   *Disclosures encouraged in consolidated financial statements (FRS 102)*

Section 1A encourages a small entity to provide the following disclosures in consolidated financial statements:

- the fact that the financial statements are consolidated financial statements;

- the basis for concluding that control exists when the parent does not own, directly or indirectly through subsidiaries, more than half of the voting power;

- any difference in the reporting date of the financial statements of the parent and its subsidiaries used in the preparation of the consolidated financial statements;

- the nature and extent of any significant restrictions (e.g. resulting from borrowing arrangements or regulatory requirements) on the ability of subsidiaries to transfer funds to the parent in the form of cash dividends or to repay loans; and

- the name of any subsidiary excluded from consolidation and the reason for exclusion. *[FRS 102.1A.22(b), 9.23]*.

11.4.2   *Statutory disclosures in consolidated financial statements – CA 2006*

11.4.2.A   *General*

Companies Act group accounts must state, in respect of the parent company:

- the part of the UK in which the company is registered;

- the company's registered number;

- whether the company is a public or a private company and whether it is limited by shares or by guarantee;

- the address of the company's registered office, and

- where appropriate, the fact that the company is being wound up. *[s404(A1)]*.

Note that these are the same as the disclosures required by a company preparing Companies Act individual accounts and included in paragraph 1AC.37 for a small entity preparing individual financial statements (see 11.1.8 above).

11.4.2.B   *Section 408 exemption from presenting the individual profit and loss account*

Parent companies preparing group accounts in accordance with the CA 2006 can take advantage of the section 408 exemption not to present the individual profit and loss account and certain related notes (providing the conditions for its use are met). See Chapter 1 at 6.3.2.

SI 2015/980 has made changes to the disclosure of use of the exemption (the company's individual balance sheet must now show the profit or loss of the company; previously, this was disclosed in the notes to the accounts) and to the disclosures required in the individual profit and loss account prepared, where the section 408 exemption is taken.

The individual profit and loss account of a company subject to the small companies regime must now include the disclosures required by section 411 on the average number of persons employed (see 11.4.2.C below). The previous concession to omit certain profit and loss account disclosures in Schedule 1 to the Small Companies Regulations (prior to amendment by SI 2015/980) *[SC Regulations 3(2), 1 Sch 59-61 (SC)]* from the individual profit and loss account has also been removed (although paragraphs 59 and 60 have been deleted and paragraph 61 amended – see 11.1.6 above).

References made to the section 408 exemption in 11.4.2 are as amended by SI 2015/980. There is a similar exemption available for LLPs (but without the amendments made by SI 2015/980, unless there is a subsequent change to LLP law).

This exemption would not extend to individual financial statements prepared under other statutory frameworks, unless permitted by these frameworks.

11.4.2.C   Employee numbers

The notes to the accounts of a company applying the Small Companies Regulations must disclose the average number of persons employed (a) by the company (in the individual accounts – see 11.1.6 for details) and (b) by the company and its consolidated subsidiary undertakings (in the group accounts). *[s411]*.

This is a new statutory disclosure since SI 2015/980 extends the requirement to present employee numbers to companies subject to the small companies regime. In addition, SI 2015/980 removes the previous exemption in section 408(2) from presenting information about employee numbers in the individual accounts, so this information is required both for the company and the consolidated group. While this statutory disclosure requirement does not apply to LLPs, LLPs subject to the small LLP regime must give the same employee number disclosures in group and individual accounts by virtue of paragraph 1AC.33 and paragraph 1A.22(c) (see (c) at 6.1.1 above).

11.4.2.D   Advances, credits and guarantees granted to directors

In the case of a parent company preparing group accounts, the notes to the group accounts must include details of:

- advances and credits granted to the directors of the parent company, by that company or by any of its subsidiary undertakings (as defined in section 1162 of the CA 2006); and
- guarantees of any kind entered into on behalf of the directors of the parent company, by that company or by any of its subsidiary undertakings.

The details required in respect of advances, credits and guarantees are those set out in section 413(3)-(5). The information required is the same as that discussed at 11.1.7 which sets out the equivalent statutory disclosure required in individual accounts (where group accounts are not prepared). Where group accounts are prepared, only the disclosure required in the group accounts is given. *[s413]*.

While paragraph 1AC.36 incorporates the disclosure required in individual accounts into Section 1A, in our view, the reference in paragraph 1A.22(c) to 'subject to any restrictions or exemptions set out in legislation' allows a small entity applying

Section 1A to only give the information required by section 413 in the group accounts. This is particularly because the FRC does not intend to mandate disclosures for companies subject to the small companies regime beyond those required by law.

While this statutory disclosure requirement does not apply to LLPs, the same disclosures are required in respect of the members of an LLP's governing body by virtue of paragraph 1AC.36 and paragraph 1A.22(c) (see (c) at 6.1.1 above). In our view, parent LLPs preparing group accounts need only give the information required in group accounts.

11.4.2.E   Off-balance sheet arrangements

In group accounts, the disclosures required for off balance sheet arrangements (see 11.1.5.H above) apply as if the undertakings included in the consolidation were a single company. Therefore, the disclosures are required for both the consolidated group and the company. *[s410A(5)]*.

11.4.2.F   Audited financial statements

A note to audited group accounts must include auditors' remuneration (see 11.2.1 below) receivable for the annual accounts for the financial year. Since the annual accounts include the individual accounts and any group accounts prepared by the company for the financial year, *[s471(1)]*, no separate figure is required for the audit of the individual accounts, as confirmed by paragraphs 10.1 and 19.2 of the ICAEW Technical Release TECH 14/13 FRF – *Disclosure of auditor remuneration*.

See 11.2.1 below for disclosures of limited liability limitation agreements in individual accounts. *[s538]*. Only the disclosures required in individual accounts are required where group accounts are also prepared.

11.4.2.G   Audit exemption statement

See 11.2.2 for the disclosures required in respect of the audit exemption. *[s475]*. Only the disclosures required in individual accounts are required where group accounts are also prepared.

11.4.3   Statutory disclosures in consolidated financial statements – Part 1 of Schedule 6 to the Small Companies Regulations

Group accounts must comply so far as practicable with the requirements of Schedule 1 to the Small Companies Regulations as if the undertakings included in the consolidation were a single company, *[SC Regulations 8, 6 Sch 1(1) (SC)]*, and so the disclosures required in individual accounts are also given for the parent and its consolidated subsidiary undertakings (as a single unit, the consolidated group). See 11.1 and 11.2.4 for further details on disclosures included in Schedule 1 to the Small Companies Regulations. There is a similar requirement in the Small LLP Regulations, although as noted previously, there are different statutory disclosures for LLPs. *[LLP SC Regulations 6, 4 Sch 1(1) (LLP SC)]*.

Following amendment of the Small Companies Regulations by SI 2015/980, it appears that the section 408 exemption (see 11.4.2.B above) no longer covers the profit and loss account note (i.e. paragraph 61 – see 11.1.3 and 11.1.6 above) still required by Schedule 1 to the Small Companies Regulations so this information is required for the company and the consolidated group.

In relation to LLPs, the section 408 exemption extends to information required by paragraphs 57 to 59 of the Small LLP Regulations. *[LLP SC Regulations 3, 1 Sch 57-59 (LLP SC)]*. These include some paragraphs removed or amended by SI 2015/980 from the Small Companies Regulations (and which therefore do not appear as disclosures noted in 11 below).

Part 1 of Schedule 6 to the Small Companies Regulations includes the following disclosures specific to group accounts (unless not material): *[6 Sch 5 (SC)]*

- Where assets and liabilities to be included in the group accounts have been valued or otherwise determined by undertakings according to accounting rules differing from those used for the group accounts, the values or amounts must be adjusted so as to accord with the rules used for the group accounts. If it appears to the directors of the parent company that there are special reasons for departing from this requirement, particulars of any such departure, the reasons for it and its effect must be given in a note to the accounts. *[6 Sch 3 (SC)]*.

  Since Section 9 requires consolidation adjustments to be made to align with the group accounts, disclosure of departures would not be expected in practice. *[FRS 102.9.17]*.

- Any differences of accounting rules as between a parent company's individual accounts for a financial year and its group accounts must be disclosed in a note to the group accounts and the reasons for the difference given. *[6 Sch 4 (SC)]*.

- Unless the exemption in paragraph 16 of Schedule 6 to the Small Companies Regulations applies (see below), the following information with respect to acquisitions taking place in the financial year must be stated in a note to the accounts:

  (a)   the name of the undertaking acquired or, where a group was acquired, the name of the parent undertaking of that group;

  (b)   whether the acquisition has been accounted for by the acquisition or the merger method of accounting; and

  (c)   in relation to an acquisition which significantly affects the figures shown in the group accounts:

    (i)   the composition and fair value of the consideration for the acquisition given by the parent company and its subsidiary undertakings; and

    (ii)   where the acquisition method of accounting has been adopted, the book values immediately prior to the acquisition and the fair values at the date of the acquisition, of each class of assets and liabilities of the undertaking or group acquired (in tabular form), including the amount of any goodwill or negative consolidation difference arising on the acquisition together with an explanation of any significant adjustments made.

      In respect of an acquired group, the above amounts are disclosed after any set-offs and other adjustments required by Schedule 6 to the Small Companies Regulations in respect of group accounts. *[6 Sch 13 (SC)]*.

Chapter 3

- Unless the exemption in paragraph 16 of Schedule 6 to the Small Companies Regulations applies, a note to the accounts must state the cumulative amount of goodwill (net of any goodwill attributed to subsidiary undertakings or businesses disposed of prior to the balance sheet date) resulting from acquisitions in that and earlier financial years which has been written off otherwise than in the consolidated profit and loss account in that or any earlier financial year. *[6 Sch 14 (SC)]*.

  In our view, this would apply to any cumulative goodwill taken to reserves prior to application of FRS 10 – *Goodwill and intangible assets* – even though the goodwill, in effect, ceases to exist for accounting purposes on transition to FRS 102.

- Unless the exemption in paragraph 16 of Schedule 6 to the Small Companies Regulations applies, where during the financial year there has been a disposal of an undertaking or group which significantly affects the figure shown in the group accounts, a note to the accounts must state:

  (a) the name of that undertaking or, as the case may be, of the parent undertaking of that group, and

  (b) the extent to which the profit or loss shown in the group accounts is attributable to profit or loss of that undertaking or group. *[6 Sch 15 (SC)]*.

The information required by paragraphs 13 to 15 of Schedule 6 to the Small Companies Regulations need not be disclosed with respect to an undertaking which: (a) is established under the law of a country outside the UK, or (b) carries on business outside the UK, if in the opinion of the directors of the parent company the disclosure would be seriously prejudicial to the business of that undertaking or to the business of the parent company or any of its subsidiary undertakings and the Secretary of State agrees that the information should not be disclosed. *[6 Sch 16 (SC)]*.

- Where an acquisition has taken place in the financial year and the merger method of accounting has been adopted, the notes to the accounts must also disclose: *[6 Sch 16A (SC)]*

  (a) the address of the registered office of the undertaking acquired (whether in or outside the UK);

  (b) the name of the party referred to in paragraph 10(a) of Schedule 6 to the Small Companies Regulations, i.e. the ultimate controlling party;

  (c) the address of the registered office of that party in (b) (whether in or outside the UK); and

  (d) the information required by paragraph 11(6) of Schedule 6 to the Small Companies Regulations, i.e. the adjustment to consolidated reserves made in applying the merger accounting method. This adjustment is the difference between:

  (i) the aggregate of (1) the fair value of consideration (except in respect of shares covered by (2)) for the acquisition of shares in the undertaking acquired, determined at the date of acquisition of those shares and (2) the 'appropriate amount' for shares issued by the parent company or its subsidiary undertakings in consideration for the acquisition of shares in the undertaking acquired (where merger relief or group reconstruction relief is taken).

The 'appropriate amount' used in (2) is nominal value (in relation to shares where merger relief is taken) and nominal value together with any minimum premium value (in relation to shares where group reconstruction relief is taken); and

(ii)   the nominal value of the issued share capital of the undertaking acquired held by the parent company and its subsidiary undertakings. *[6 Sch 11(5)-(7) (SC)]*.

Where a group is acquired, references to 'shares of the undertaking acquired' are construed as references to 'shares of the parent undertaking of the group'. *[6 Sch 12 (SC)]*.

- The requirements of paragraphs 17 to 20 and 22 of Schedule 1 to the Regulations apply to any goodwill relating to an interest in an associated undertaking shown by the equity method of accounting. *[6 Sch 21(1) (SC)]*.

In our view, this would include the disclosures of the amortisation period used and the reasons (where the useful life of the goodwill cannot be reliably estimated); and of any provision for diminution or write-back of provision for diminution of goodwill relating to an interest in an associated undertaking (see commentary at 11.4.4.C below on meaning of associated undertaking). See 11.1.2 and 11.1.5.E above for details of the disclosures.

There are additional disclosures in relation to joint ventures (as defined in paragraph 18 of Schedule 6 to the Small Companies Regulations) that are included in the group accounts by the method of proportional consolidation. *[6 Sch 18 (SC)]*. These are not discussed in this Chapter because jointly controlled entities are equity accounted under FRS 102 and accordingly the disclosures are unlikely to apply.

- The Small Companies Regulations also clarify that the new statutory disclosure introduced by SI 2015/980 in paragraph 66 of Schedule 1 to the Small Companies Regulations on related party transactions (see 11.1.7 above) applies in group accounts to transactions which the parent company or other undertakings included in the consolidation have entered into with related parties, unless they are intra-group transactions. *[1 Sch 66 (SC), 6 Sch 20B (SC)]*. This clarification appears to simply be an application of the general requirement to present disclosures required by Schedule 1 in individual accounts for the consolidated group.

While this statutory disclosure requirement does not apply to LLPs, LLPs subject to the small LLPs regime must give the same related party disclosures (as for companies subject to the small companies regime) by virtue of paragraph 1AC.35 and paragraph 1A.22(c) (see (c) at 6.2.1 above).

11.4.4   *Statutory disclosures in consolidated financial statements – Part 2 of Schedule 6 to the Small Companies Regulations – information about related undertakings*

Schedule 2 (information about related undertakings) was removed by SI 2015/980 where a company is not preparing group accounts. However, disclosures in respect of related undertakings are still required in group accounts and are set out in Part 2 of Schedule 6 to the Small Companies Regulations. In respect of below, references to 'group' means 'the parent company and its subsidiary undertakings', and therefore includes subsidiary undertakings excluded from consolidation. *[6 Sch 21 (SC)]*.

References in the disclosure requirements below to shares held by the parent company or the group are to be construed as follows:

- for the purposes of paragraphs 23, 27(4), 27(5), 28 to 30 of Schedule 6 to the Small Companies Regulations (information about holdings in subsidiary and other undertakings), there must be attributed to the parent company shares held on its behalf by any person. Shares held on behalf of a person other than the company must be treated as not held by the parent company;

- references to shares held by the group are to any shares held by or on behalf of the parent company or any of its subsidiary undertakings. Any shares held on behalf of a person other than the parent company or any of its subsidiary undertakings are not to be treated as held by the group; and

- shares held by way of security must be treated as held by the person providing the security:

    (a)   where apart from the right to exercise them for the purpose of preserving the value of the security, or of realising it, the rights attached to the shares are exercisable only in accordance with his instructions, and

    (b)   where the shares are held in connection with the granting of loans as part of normal business activities and apart from the right to exercise them for the purpose of preserving the value of the security, or of realising it, the rights attached to the shares are exercisable only in his interests. *[6 Sch 37 (SC)]*.

Part 2 of Schedule 6 to the Small Companies Regulations requires the following disclosures (at 11.4.4.A to 11.4.4.G below) to be given. The alternative compliance in section 410(2) of the CA 2006 has been removed for annual accounts of companies and qualifying partnerships approved on or after 1 July 2015.[10] Therefore, these disclosures must be presented in full in the financial statements whereas previously, where the disclosure of information required in the notes to the accounts would be of excessive length, certain disclosures were required in the notes to the accounts with full details in the annual return. See Chapter 5 at 3.4

11.4.4.A   Subsidiary undertakings

The following information must be stated with respect to the undertakings that are subsidiary undertakings of the parent company at the end of the financial year:

- the name of each undertaking;

- the address of the undertaking's registered office (whether in or outside the UK);

- if the undertaking is unincorporated, the address of its principal place of business;

- whether the subsidiary undertaking is included in the consolidation (i.e. consolidated [s474(1)]) and, if it is not, the reasons for excluding it from consolidation; and

- by virtue of which of the conditions specified in section 1162(2) or (4) of the CA 2006 it is a subsidiary undertaking of its immediate parent undertaking. This is not required to be given where the relevant condition is section 1162(2)(a) (holding a majority of voting rights) and the immediate parent undertaking holds the same proportion of shares in the undertaking as it holds voting rights. *[6 Sch 22 (SC)].*

The following information must be given with respect to the shares of a subsidiary undertaking held (a) by the parent company and (b) by the group (separately, if the information for (a) and (b) is different):

- the identity of each class of shares held; and

- the proportion of the nominal value of the shares of that class represented by those shares. *[6 Sch 23 (SC)].*

There must be shown with respect to each subsidiary undertaking not included in the consolidation, unless not material:

- the aggregate amount of capital and reserves as at the end of its relevant financial year; and

- its profit or loss for that year.

The relevant financial year is the subsidiary's financial year (where this ends on the same date as the company's financial year); otherwise, it is the subsidiary's financial year that ends last before the end of the company's financial year.

This information need not be given if:

- the group's investment in the undertaking is included in the accounts by way of the equity method of valuation; or

- the undertaking is not required by any provision of the CA 2006 to deliver a copy of its balance sheet for its relevant financial year and does not otherwise publish that balance sheet in the UK or elsewhere and the holding in the group is less than 50% of the nominal value of the shares in the undertaking. *[6 Sch 24 (SC)].*

11.4.4.B   Shares of company held by subsidiary undertakings

The number, description and amount of the shares in the company held by or on behalf of its subsidiary undertakings must be disclosed.

Chapter 3

Note that this does not apply in relation to shares where the subsidiary undertaking is concerned as:

- personal representative; or

- trustee (unless the company or any of its subsidiary undertakings is beneficially interested under the trust, otherwise than by way of security only for the purposes of a transaction entered into by it in the ordinary course of business which includes the lending of money). Part 2 of Schedule 2 to the Small Companies Regulations provides interpretation on a beneficial interest under a trust. *[6 Sch 25 (SC)].*

11.4.4.C   *Associated undertakings*

Where an undertaking included in the consolidation has an associated undertaking, the following information must be stated:

- the name of the associated undertaking;

- the address of the undertaking's registered office (whether in or outside the UK);

- if the undertaking is unincorporated, the address of its principal place of business;

- with respect to the shares of the undertaking held (a) by the parent company and, separately, (b) by the group:

    (i)   the identity of each class of shares held; and

    (ii)   the proportion of the nominal value of the shares of that class represented by those shares

    This information is required even if not material. *[6 Sch 27 (SC)].*

An 'associated undertaking' is defined in paragraph 19 of Schedule 6 to the Small Companies Regulations (see Chapter 4 at 5.3.4.E). This will generally include a jointly controlled entity and an associate under FRS 102. However, the definition includes a requirement for a 'participating interest' (not a feature of the definitions of a jointly controlled entity or associate in FRS 102).

There are additional disclosures in relation to joint ventures (as defined in paragraph 18 of Schedule 6 to the Small Companies Regulations) that are included in the group accounts by the method of proportional consolidation. *[6 Sch 26 (SC)].* These are not discussed in this Chapter because jointly controlled entities are equity accounted under FRS 102 and accordingly the disclosures are unlikely to apply.

11.4.4.D   *Other significant holdings of parent company or group*

A holding is significant for the purpose of the disclosures in paragraphs 29, 30, 32 and 33 of Schedule 6 to the Small Companies Regulations if:

- it amounts to 20% or more of the nominal value of any class of shares in the undertaking; or

- for the disclosures for (a) the parent company, the amount of the holding (as stated or included in the company's individual accounts) exceeds 20% of the amount of the company's assets (as so stated); or

- for the disclosures for (b) the group, the amount of the holding (as stated or included in the group accounts) exceeds 20% of the amount of the group's assets (as so stated). *[6 Sch 28, 31 (SC)].*

Where at the end of the financial year the parent company or the group has a significant holding in an undertaking which is not one of its subsidiary undertakings and does not fall within paragraph 26 (joint ventures) or paragraph 27 (associated undertakings) (see 11.4.4.C above), the following information must be stated separately for (a) the parent company and (b) the group: *[6 Sch 28-30 (SC), 6 Sch 31-33 (SC)]*

- the name of the undertaking;
- the address of the undertaking's registered office (whether in or outside the UK);
- if the undertaking is unincorporated, the address of its principal place of business;
- with respect to the shares of the undertaking held by the parent company (for the disclosures for (a) the parent) and, separately with respect to the shares of the undertaking held by the group (for the disclosures for (b) the group)
  - (i) the identity of each class of shares held;
  - (ii) the proportion of the nominal value of the shares of that class represented by those shares; and
  - (iii) if material, the aggregate amount of the capital and reserves of the undertaking as at the end of its relevant financial year and its profit or loss for that year.

    The relevant financial year is the undertaking's financial year (where this ends on the same date as the company's financial year); otherwise, it is the undertaking's financial year that ends last before the end of the company's financial year.

    This information need not be given in respect of an undertaking if the undertaking is not required by any provision of the CA 2006 to deliver a copy of its balance sheet for its relevant financial year and does not otherwise publish that balance sheet in the UK or elsewhere and the company's holding (in respect of the disclosures for (a) the parent) or group's holding (in respect of the disclosures for (b) the group) is less than 50% of the nominal value of the shares in the undertaking.

11.4.4.E   Parent company's or group's membership of qualifying undertakings

The following information must be stated where, at the end of the financial year, the parent company or group is a member of a qualifying undertaking:

- the name and legal form of the undertaking (if the information is material);
- the address of the undertaking's registered office (whether in or outside the UK) or if it does not have such an office, its head office (whether in or outside the UK) (if the information is material); and
- where the undertaking is a qualifying partnership, either:
  - (a) that a copy of the latest accounts of the undertaking has been or is to be appended to a copy of the company's accounts sent to the registrar under section 444 of the CA 2006; or
  - (b) the name of at least one body corporate (which may be the company) in whose group accounts the undertaking has been or is to be dealt with on a consolidated basis (this means full consolidation, proportional

consolidation or the equity method of accounting). This information need not be given if the notes to the company's accounts disclose that advantage has been taken of the exemption conferred by regulation 7 of the Partnerships (Accounts) Regulations 2008.

A qualifying undertaking is a qualifying partnership or an unlimited company meeting the criteria in paragraph 34(7) of Schedule 6 to the Small Companies Regulations. A qualifying partnership (and a member thereof) is as defined in the Partnerships (Accounts) Regulations 2008. Full details of these definitions are not provided here. *[6 Sch 34 (SC)]*.

11.4.4.F   *Parent undertaking drawing up accounts for a larger group*

Where the parent company is itself a subsidiary undertaking, with respect to that parent undertaking of the company which heads:

(a)   the largest group of undertakings for which group accounts are drawn up and of which that company is a member and

(b)   the smallest such group of undertakings,

the following information must be stated:

* the name of the parent undertaking;
* if the undertaking is incorporated outside the UK, the country in which it is incorporated;
* if unincorporated, the address of its principal place of business; and
* if copies of the group accounts referred to above are available to the public, the addresses from which copies of those group accounts can be obtained. *[6 Sch 35 (SC)]*.

11.4.4.G   *Identification of ultimate parent company*

Where the parent company is itself a subsidiary undertaking, the following information must be stated:

* the name of the company (if any) regarded by the directors as being the company's ultimate parent company (this may include any body corporate); and
* its country of incorporation, if outside the UK (if known to the directors). *[6 Sch 36 (SC)]*.

12   SMALL COMPANIES – STATUTORY EXEMPTIONS

There are two sets of exemptions available for small companies:

* the small companies regime – which applies to the preparation and/or filing of the financial statements; and
* the small companies exemption – which applies to the preparation and/or filing of the strategic report and directors' report.

These exemptions are available in both Companies Act accounts and IAS accounts. This section sets out the requirements in the CA 2006 and Small Companies

Regulations (as amended by SI 2015/980). The exemptions available to companies subject to the small companies regime and to companies applying the small companies exemption prior to application of SI 2015/980 are addressed in Chapter 1 at 6.5 of EY New UK GAAP 2015. The requirements for small LLPs (unless there is a subsequent change in LLP law) can be found in the equivalent paragraphs in SI 2008/1911 and the Small LLP Regulations and are similar to those described for small companies prior to application of SI 2015/980.

A company subject to the small companies regime must meet certain small size criteria and not be excluded from the small companies regime, i.e. it must not be one of the types of ineligible company nor a member of an ineligible group (see 4.3 above).

A company entitled to the small companies exemption must meet the same small size criteria as for the small companies regime and must not be an ineligible company (although it may be a member of an ineligible group). The criteria to be subject to the small companies regime are, therefore, more onerous than for the small companies exemption; companies subject to the small companies regime will also qualify for the small companies exemption. See 12.2 below.

A company that is subject to the small companies regime is entitled to apply the Small Companies Regulations, which requires fewer disclosures in the financial statements and the directors' report than the Regulations. See 12.1 below.

As noted at 6.2 above, a company that is subject to the small companies regime is not required to prepare group accounts, but may do so. This exemption from preparation of group accounts extends, where SI 2015/980 is applied, to a company that would be subject to the small companies regime (but for being a public company) and is not a traded company (meaning a company any of whose transferable securities are admitted to trading on a regulated market). *[s398, s399(1), (2A), s474(1)].*

A company that takes advantage of the small companies exemption is not required to prepare a strategic report and is entitled to certain disclosure exemptions in the directors' report. *[s414A, s415A].* See 12.2 below.

Companies subject to the small companies regime or taking advantage of the small companies exemption are also entitled to certain (but different) filing exemptions. *[s444, s444A].* See 12.3 below.

These exemptions operate independently from each other – a company entitled to both the small companies regime and the small companies exemption may choose to apply both, neither, the small companies regime only or the small companies exemption only.

If the accounts are prepared in accordance with the small companies regime (unless applying the micro-entity provisions – see Chapter 1 at 6.4), the balance sheet must contain, in a prominent position above the signature(s) of the director(s), a statement to the effect that the accounts have been prepared in accordance with the provisions applicable to companies subject to the small companies regime. *[s414(3)(b)].* See 11.2.5 above.

Where a company has taken advantage of the small companies exemption in preparing the directors' report, a statement to this effect is required in the directors' report, in a prominent place above the signature of the director or secretary, as applicable. *[s419(2)]*. Note that the statement made in the directors' report refers to the small companies exemption *even if* the company is also subject to the small companies regime.

12.1   Use of the small companies regime

Companies subject to the small companies regime (see 4.3 above), whether preparing Companies Act accounts or IAS accounts, must provide the disclosures required by the CA 2006, the Small Companies Regulations and other applicable regulations, but are exempt from certain disclosures required by companies not subject to the small companies regime.

12.1.1   *Small Companies Regulations*

SI 2015/980, where applied, significantly reduces the disclosures required by the Small Companies Regulations. However, SI 2015/980 modifies some existing disclosures and there are some new disclosures applicable to companies subject to the small companies regime in the CA 2006 and the Small Companies Regulations. The disclosures required for a company applying Section 1A are set out at 11 above (and where group accounts are voluntarily prepared, at 11.4 above).

A company preparing its accounts subject to the small companies regime must comply with the Small Companies Regulations, which (as amended by SI 2015/980) contain the following schedules:

• Schedule 1 (Companies Act individual accounts);

• Schedule 5 (Matters to be dealt with in directors' report);

• Schedule 6 (Group accounts);

• Schedule 7 (Definition of 'provision'); and

• Schedule 8 (General interpretation). *[Small Regulations 3-10]*.

Schedule 2 (Information about related undertakings where company not preparing group accounts (Companies Act or IAS individual accounts)) has been removed for a company not preparing group accounts. Part 2 of Schedule 2 contains interpretation of references to 'beneficial interest' still relevant for group accounts. Schedule 3 (Information about directors' benefits: remuneration (Companies Act or IAS accounts)) and Schedule 4 (Companies Act abbreviated accounts for delivery to Registrar of Companies) have been removed by SI 2015/980. These schedules remain in the Small LLP Regulations (unless there is a subsequent amendment to LLP law).

A company subject to the small companies regime preparing Companies Act accounts (such as FRS 101 and FRS 102 financial statements) must comply with all applicable requirements of the Small Companies Regulations. A company subject to the small companies regime preparing IAS accounts need not comply with Schedule 1 to the Small Companies Regulations (which sets out balance sheet and profit and loss account formats and other note disclosures) or Part 1 of Schedule 6 (Form and content of Companies Act group accounts). Note that both Companies Act group accounts and IAS group accounts must give the information on related undertakings (Part 2 of Schedule 6).

For Companies Act accounts, the schedules in the Small Companies Regulations provide simpler formats and reduced disclosures compared to the corresponding schedules in the Regulations applied by large and medium-sized companies and groups. However, companies are treated as complying with Schedule 1 and, in respect of group accounts, Part 1 of Schedule 6 to the Small Companies Regulations (which set out the formats for the profit and loss account and balance sheet, recognition and measurement principles, and disclosure requirements) if they comply with the corresponding provision of Schedule 1 and/or Part 1 of Schedule 6 to the Regulations. *[SC Regulations 3(3), 8(2)]*.

FRS 101 and FRS 102 (where Section 1A is not applied), which are both forms of Companies Act accounts, do not permit use of the formats included in the Small Companies Regulations. Our view is that companies subject to the small companies regime can still apply FRS 101 or FRS 102 and in doing so, are not precluded from taking advantage of *other* exemptions applicable to companies subject to the small companies regime.

Companies subject to the small companies regime are entitled to apply Section 1A of FRS 102 (see 4 above) and, if they do so, are required to use the formats in the Small Companies Regulations and provide the disclosures in Section 1A, the CA 2006 (unless not required for companies subject to the small companies regime), the Small Companies Regulations and other applicable regulations.

12.1.2   Disclosure exemptions – financial statements (IAS accounts and Companies Act accounts)

UK companies subject to the small companies regime (preparing Companies Act or IAS accounts) benefit from certain exemptions from disclosures set out in the CA 2006:

- the financial impact of off-balance sheet arrangements on the company (or if prepared, the group) is not required, although the nature and business purpose of the arrangements, to the extent necessary for enabling the financial position of the company (or where group accounts are prepared, the consolidated group) to be assessed, must be disclosed. *[s410A]*. See 11.1.5.H and 11.4.2.E above and Chapter 4 at 8.7);

- information analysing employee numbers by category and staff costs is not required, although the total average number of persons employed by the company (or where group accounts are prepared, the consolidated group) must be disclosed (see 11.1.6 and 11.4.2.C above and Chapter 4 at 8.6); *[s411]* and

- a company subject to the small companies regime is only required to disclose remuneration receivable by the company's auditor for the auditing of the annual accounts for the financial year. *[s494]*.[11] See 11.2.1 and 11.4.2.F above. Therefore, information on remuneration receivable by associates of the auditor and remuneration receivable by the company's auditor or its associates for other services, as disclosed by large companies, is not required.

In addition, the disclosures in Schedule 1 to the Small Companies Regulations (applicable to Companies Act accounts only) are significantly fewer than those required for companies applying the Regulations, and are set out in Appendix C of Section 1A (see 11.1 above).

A company preparing only individual accounts (Companies Act or IAS accounts) is not required to comply with Schedule 2 to the Small Companies Regulations, although Schedule 6 to Small Companies Regulations sets out disclosures for related undertakings that are required in the group accounts, if prepared (see 11.4.4 above).

As Schedule 3 (directors' remuneration) has been removed by SI 2015/980, the previous statutory directors' remuneration disclosures are not required; however, Section 1A (and the related statutory disclosure requirement in the Small Companies Regulations) require separate disclosure of related party transactions for the small entity's directors (or members of its governing bodies). Paragraph 1AC.35 of Section 1A clarifies that such transactions include directors' remuneration and dividends paid to directors (see 11.1.7 above). An entity applying full FRS 102, FRS 101 or IFRS would also need to comply with related party disclosures in those standards, subject to any disclosure exemptions available in FRS 101.

12.1.3   *Disclosure exemptions – directors' report and strategic report*

Where a company is subject to the small companies regime, it will also qualify for the small companies exemption. Therefore, the company is not required to prepare a strategic report and is entitled to disclosure exemptions in relation to the directors' report. See 12.2.1 and 12.2.2 below.

In addition, a company subject to the small companies regime is permitted to apply the (less onerous) requirements for the directors' report included in Schedule 5 to the Small Companies Regulations. *[5 Sch (SC)]*. Schedule 5 requires disclosure in respect of political donations and expenditure and the employment of disabled persons. However, companies subject to the small companies regime are not required to include the following disclosures in the directors' report (that are required to be given by large and medium-sized companies applying the Regulations):

- use of financial instruments – financial risk management objectives, policies and risk exposures;
- details of important post balance sheet events;
- an indication of likely future developments;
- an indication of research and development activities;
- an indication of branches outside the United Kingdom; and
- information about employee involvement.[12]

Where any of the above exemptions are taken, the required statement in the directors' report that the company has taken advantage of the small companies exemption in preparing the directors' report must be made. See 12 above.

12.2   Criteria for use of the small companies exemption

A company is entitled to the small companies exemption in relation to the directors' report (see 12.2.1 below) and the strategic report (see 12.2.2 below) for a financial year if it is entitled to prepare financial statements for the year in accordance with the small companies regime (see 4.3 above) or would be so entitled but for being or having been a member of an ineligible group. *[s415A(1), s414B]*.

The company must, therefore, meet the same small size criteria as for the small companies regime (and if the company is a parent company, it must head a small group). The company must also not have been an ineligible company itself at any time during the financial year to which the accounts relate (but may still use the small companies exemption if it was a member of an ineligible group at any time during that financial year).

The small companies exemption is available to both companies preparing Companies Act accounts and companies preparing IAS accounts (i.e. prepared using EU-adopted IFRS).

12.2.1   *Disclosure exemptions for the small companies exemption – directors' report*

There are relatively few disclosure exemptions remaining for companies entitled to the small companies exemption.

Companies entitled to the small companies exemption are exempt from including the amount recommended by the directors to be paid by way of dividend (required by section 416(3)). *[s415A(2)]*.

If a company is entitled to the small companies exemption, the directors' report must still include:

* the names of persons who were, at any time during the financial year, directors of the company; *[s416(1)(a)]* and

* the statement as to disclosure of relevant information to auditors (unless the company has taken advantage of an audit exemption). *[s418]*.

Where the company is entitled to the small companies exemption (but not subject to the small companies regime), the company must comply with the more extensive content requirements for the directors' report in Schedule 7 to the Regulations. *[para 10 and Sch 7, Regulations]*. Where the company is entitled to the small companies regime, it may comply with Schedule 5 to the Small Companies Regulations which has fewer disclosures for the directors' report, as explained at 12.1.3 above.

Where any of the above exemptions are taken, the required statement in the directors' report that the company has taken advantage of the small companies exemption in preparing the directors' report must be made. See 12 above.

12.2.2   *Small companies exemption from preparing strategic report*

A company entitled to the small companies exemption is not required to prepare a strategic report. *[s414A]*.

While there is no statutory requirement to do so, we would recommend that, where a company entitled to the small companies exemption takes advantage of the exemption not to prepare a strategic report, a statement is included in the directors' report, above the signature of the director or secretary to explain that it has done so.

12.3   Filing exemptions – small companies

Companies subject to the small companies regime (where SI 2015/980 is applied) have two choices:

- to deliver a copy of the full accounts and reports sent to members and a copy of the auditor's report (unless the company has taken advantage of an audit exemption) to the Registrar; or

- to deliver a copy of the balance sheet but choose to omit a copy of the profit or loss account and/or the directors' report. *[s444(1)]*.

This exemption not to deliver a copy of the directors' report or profit and loss account is available both to IAS accounts and Companies Act accounts.

In addition, where SI 2015/980 is applied, Companies Act group accounts delivered to the Registrar need not give the information required by paragraph 25 of Schedule 6 to the Small Companies Regulations, i.e. shares of the company held by subsidiary undertakings (see 11.4.4.B above). *[SC Regulations 11(b)]*.

SI 2015/980 removed the option to prepare separate abbreviated accounts (Companies Act individual accounts only) for filing purposes (see 12.3.1 below). The copies of the accounts and reports delivered must be copies of the annual accounts and reports. *[s444(3)]*.

Where the balance sheet or profit and loss account is abridged pursuant to paragraph 1A of Schedule 1 to the Small Companies Regulations (as amended by SI 2015/980) (see 8.1.2, 9.2 and 10.2 above), the directors must deliver to the Registrar a statement by the company that all the members of the company have consented to the abridgement. *[s444(2A)]*.

Where SI 2015/980 is applied, and the directors deliver a copy of the profit or loss account under section 444(1)(b)(i), the directors must also deliver a copy of the auditor's report (unless the company has taken advantage of an audit exemption) on the accounts (and any directors' report). *[s444(2)]*.

Where SI 2015/980 is applied and the directors do not deliver a copy of the company's profit or loss account, the copy of the balance sheet must disclose that fact. Unless the company is exempt from audit (or is a micro-entity applying the micro-entity provisions), the notes to the balance sheet must:

- state whether the auditor's report was qualified or unqualified;

- where the report was qualified, disclose the basis of the qualification (reproducing any statement under section 498(2)(a) or (b) or section 498(3), if applicable);

- where that report was unqualified, include a reference to any matters to which the auditor drew attention by way of emphasis; and

- state the name of the auditor and, where the auditor is a firm, the name of the person who signed the auditor's report as senior statutory auditor (or if the conditions in section 506 (circumstances in which names may be omitted) are met, that a resolution has been passed and notified to the Secretary of State in accordance with that section). *[s444(5A)]*.

Note that where SI 2015/980 is not applied, the directors must deliver a copy of the auditor's report on the accounts and any directors' report that are delivered. *[s444(2)]*.

Where the directors of a company subject to the small companies regime do not deliver a copy of the company's profit or loss account or directors' report, the copy of the balance sheet delivered to the Registrar must contain in a prominent position that the company's annual accounts [and reports] have been delivered in accordance with the provisions applicable to the small companies regime. *[s444(5)]*. This statement should be included above the directors' signature and printed name. See Example 3.2 below.

Example 3.2:   Example statement where filing exemptions used by companies subject to the small companies regime

These accounts [and reports] have been delivered in accordance with the provisions applicable to companies subject to the small companies regime.

This statement is required *in addition* to any statements required where the accounts for members are prepared in accordance with the small companies regime (see 12 above) or the company has taken advantage of the small companies exemption in preparing the directors' report (see 12.2.1 above).

Where SI 2015/980 is applied, the above disclosure would need to include further statements in respect of the auditor's report (as discussed above) where a copy of the profit or loss account is not delivered to the Registrar.

References to the 'profit or loss account' above include its related notes. *[s472]*. TECH 14/13 FRF – *Disclosure of auditor remuneration* – clarifies that disclosure of auditor remuneration is not regarded as a related note to the profit and loss account and therefore must be given in the copy of the accounts and reports delivered to the Registrar.[13]

In all cases, the copies of the balance sheet and any directors' report delivered to the Registrar must be signed by and state the name of the person who signed it on behalf of the board. *[s444(6), s444A(3)]*.[14]

Companies entitled to the small companies exemption only (see 12.2 above) are not required to deliver a copy of the directors' report but must deliver a copy of the balance sheet, a copy of the profit or loss account and a copy of the auditor's report on the accounts (and any directors' report that it delivers), unless the company has taken advantage of an audit exemption. *[s444A(1)-(2)]*. While there is no statutory requirement to make a statement, it may be helpful to explain that the company is taking advantage of the small companies exemption in not delivering the directors' report.

12.3.1   Abbreviated accounts

Prior to implementation of SI 2015/980, companies subject to the small companies regime preparing Companies Act individual accounts were permitted to prepare a separate set of abbreviated accounts for filing purposes to the full accounts and reports required to be prepared for the members. Abbreviated accounts were only available for Companies Act individual accounts and not for Companies Act group accounts or IAS accounts. For information on abbreviated accounts, refer to Chapter 1 at 6.5.5.A of EY New UK GAAP 2015.

SI 2015/980 withdraws the ability to file abbreviated accounts but, as discussed at 8.1 above, widens the formats available for accounts prepared for the members. The filing exemptions discussed at 12.3 are nevertheless available to small companies.

References

1 SI 2015/980, para. 2(4).
2 http://mifiddatabase.esma.europa.eu/Index.aspx?sectionlinks_id=23&language=0&pageName=REGULATED_MARKETS_Display&subsection_id=0
3 SI 2015/980, para. 2(3).
4 Statement of Recommended Practice – *Accounting by Limited Liability Partnerships*, July 2014, CCAB, paras. 30-31.
5 *Partnerships (Accounts) Regulations 2008* (SI 2008/569), para. 4 and Schedule, paras. 2 and 3.
6 *Partnerships (Accounts) Regulations 2008* (SI 2008/569), para. 4 and Schedule, paras. 2 and 3.
7 Statement of Recommended Practice – *Accounting by Limited Liability Partnerships*, July 2014, CCAB, paras. 51-52.
8 SI 2008/489, paras. 3(2)(a), 4.
9 SI 2008/489, para. 8.
10 SI 2015/980, para. 2(5).
11 SI 2008/489, paras. 3(2)(a), 4.
12 This list omits the disclosures required in the directors' report by Schedule 7 to the Regulations for quoted companies, companies with securities carrying voting rights admitted to trading on a regulated market, or public companies acquiring their own shares. Most quoted companies and companies with securities carrying voting rights admitted to trading on a regulated market are likely to be public companies and, therefore, unlikely to qualify for the small companies regime.
13 Tech 14/13 FRF, ICAEW, para. 10.3.
14 Registrars' Rules.

Chapter 4

Presentation of financial statements

Chapter 4

Chapter 4

Chapter 4

List of examples

Chapter 4

Presentation of financial statements

1 INTRODUCTION

The following sections of FRS 102 – *The Financial Reporting Standard Applicable in the UK and Republic of Ireland* – address the presentation, i.e. the form, content and structure, of financial statements:

- Section 3 – *Financial Statement Presentation*;

- Section 4 – *Statement of Financial Position*;

- Section 5 – *Statement of Comprehensive Income and Income Statement*;

- Section 6 – *Statement of Changes in Equity and Statement of Income and Retained Earnings*;

- Section 7 – *Statement of Cash Flows*; and

- Section 8 – *Notes to the Financial Statements*.

The above sections cover the content of a complete set of FRS 102 financial statements, i.e. the primary statements and notes required, as well as its concept of a true and fair view, including general principles underlying preparation of financial statements.

This Chapter deals only with Sections 3 to 6 (see 3 to 7 below) and Section 8 (see 8 below). Section 7 is addressed in Chapter 5 of EY New UK GAAP 2015. FRS 102's requirements on presentation overlap with Section 1 – *Scope* (which covers the reduced disclosure framework – see Chapter 2 of EY New UK GAAP 2015), Section 2 – *Concepts and Pervasive Principles* (see Chapter 3 of EY New UK GAAP 2015) and Section 10 – *Accounting Policies, Estimates and Errors* (see Chapter 7 of EY New UK GAAP 2015). These sections are referred to in places in this Chapter.

Small entities applying the small entities regime in FRS 102 instead follow the requirements of Section 1A – *Small Entities*, which provides for simpler presentation and disclosure requirements based on the statutory requirements for companies subject to the small companies regime (see Chapter 3). The small entities regime is only available where the FRS 102 (July 2015) amendments are applied (see effective date at 1.2 below).

Statutory accounts prepared in accordance with FRS 102 by UK companies are Companies Act accounts and must also comply with statutory requirements included in:

- the Companies Act 2006 ('CA 2006'); and

- the *Large and Medium-sized Companies and Groups (Accounts and Reports) Regulations 2008* (SI 2008/410) ('Regulations') or the *Small Companies and Groups (Accounts and Directors' Report) Regulations 2008* (SI 2008/409) ('Small Companies Regulations') and/or other applicable regulations.

In particular, Companies Act accounts are required to give a true and fair view, and to comply with the applicable regulations governing the form and content of the balance sheet and profit and loss account and additional notes. *[s396, s404]*. See Chapter 1 at 6 (and in respect of the small companies regime, Chapter 3) for information on the CA 2006 requirements for statutory accounts and reports.

FRS 102 mandates that UK companies and LLPs to comply with the requirements for a balance sheet and profit and loss account in the Regulations or the *Large and Medium-sized Limited Liability Partnerships (Accounts) Regulations 2008* (SI 2008/1913) ('LLP Regulations'). *[FRS 102.4.2, 5.5]*. Sections 4 and 5 of the standard extend this requirement to other entities except to the extent that this conflicts with the statutory frameworks that apply to their financial statements. *[FRS 102.4.1, 5.1]*.

In July 2015, the standard was further amended, *inter alia*, to introduce the small entities regime and to provide for the new 'adapted formats' introduced by SI 2015/980 (see 1.1 below). See 2.1 below for a discussion of the FRS 102 (July 2015) amendments impacting the presentation sections and the new small entities regime.

The Regulations and FRS 102 share basic principles underlying the preparation of financial statements such as going concern, prudence, accruals, materiality, aggregation, and consistency, although the Regulations restrict further when profits may be reported in the profit and loss account (see 9 below). The Regulations also set out certain requirements for recognition and measurement of assets and liabilities (see 10 below), namely the historical cost accounting rules, the alternative accounting rules and the fair value accounting rules.

1.1   Implementation of SI 2015/980

The Companies, Partnerships and Groups (Accounts and Reports) Regulations 2015 (SI 2015/980) implement Directive 2013/34/EU ('the new Accounting Directive') in the UK. SI 2015/980 amends the CA 2006, the Regulations, the Small Companies Regulations and the *Partnership (Accounts) Regulations 2008* (SI 2008/569).

The statutory instrument amends the requirements for companies and qualifying partnerships, but not Limited Liability Partnerships (LLPs), although a change to LLP law to implement the new Accounting Directive is expected to be consulted on in due course. Irish law is expected to be updated later in 2015 to implement the new Accounting Directive.

The statutory instrument makes changes to the small companies regime (see Chapter 3 at 1.1). Of particular relevance to this chapter, the statutory instrument also:

- allows UK companies and qualifying partnerships applying Schedule 1 to the Regulations to use new 'adapted formats' as an alternative to the statutory formats (which are themselves slightly amended); and

- makes certain changes to recognition, measurement and disclosure requirements in the Regulations and Small Companies Regulations.

The 'adapted formats' allow the balance sheet to distinguish between current and non-current items in a different way (to the statutory formats) and so facilitate formats closer to IAS 1 – *Presentation of Financial Statements.* 'Adapted formats' are permitted providing the information given is at least equivalent to that required had the formats not been adapted and the presentation is in accordance with generally accepted accounting principles and practice. *[1 Sch 1A].*

The Companies, Partnerships and Groups (Accounts and Reports) (No.2) Regulations 2015 (SI 2015/1672) made a further change to the Regulations and Small Companies Regulations (that had been omitted from SI 2015/980) arising from implementation of the new Accounting Directive. This statutory instrument, which has the same scope as SI 2015/980, prohibits reversal of impairments of goodwill (see 10.1.2 below).

1.2 Effective date

The amendments made by SI 2015/980 have effect for companies and qualifying partnerships (but not LLPs) in relation to financial years beginning on or after 1 January 2016 but may be early adopted for a financial year of a company beginning on or after 1 January 2015 but before 1 January 2016, if the directors of the company so decide.[1] A very few amendments, such as the changes to the small size thresholds for the audit exemption and the requirement to disclose information on related undertakings in full in the financial statements – see 5.3.4.B below – have a different effective date).[2]

As noted at 1 above, FRS 102 has been amended to implement changes arising from SI 2015/980. FRS 102 (July 2015) amendments (except for the amendment on share-based payment classification) apply for accounting periods beginning on or after 1 January 2016. Early application is permitted for accounting periods beginning on or after 1 January 2015 provided that SI 2015/980 is applied from the same date and required if SI 2015/980 is applied for a reporting period beginning before 1 January 2016. For entities not subject to company law, early application is permitted from 1 January 2015. Early application must be disclosed, unless the entity is a small entity, in which case it is encouraged to be disclosed. *[FRS 102.1.15].*

The effective dates are clearly intended to align with adoption of SI 2015/980, reflecting the fact that the standard implements company law changes included in that statutory instrument. We presume that, for entities not subject to company law, the reference to 'early application is permitted from 1 January 2015' is intended to mean for accounting periods beginning on or after 1 January 2015.

The reference to 'entities not subject to company law' is unclear. Implementation issues may arise if an LLP or Irish company adopts the amendments early and LLP law or Irish company law is subsequently changed to implement the new Accounting Directive with a different effective date.

We consider that Appendix IV – *Note on legal requirements* – to FRS 102 supports the view that LLPs may adopt early since it discusses areas of inconsistency between FRS 102 (as amended in July 2015) and LLP law (see 1.3 below).

However, in our view, the intention is that Irish companies are 'entities subject to company law' and should only early apply the amendments for a financial year beginning on or after 1 January 2015 (but before 1 January 2016) if early applying the new Accounting Directive (once this is implemented in Irish law) from the same date (i.e. a similar approach to UK companies).

1.3   Applicability to UK companies, LLPs and other entities

Except where otherwise stated, the rest of this Chapter refers to the requirements for UK companies, and therefore will refer to UK GAAP (prior to implementation of FRS 100 – *Application of Financial Reporting Requirements*, FRS 101 – *Reduced Disclosure Framework: disclosure exemptions from EU-adopted IFRS for qualifying entities* – and FRS 102) as 'previous UK GAAP'. The Chapter is relevant to all UK companies and LLPs. It covers the presentation requirements both before and after application of SI 2015/980 and highlights the changes to the presentation requirements made by the FRS 102 (July 2015) amendments. While this Chapter addresses which profit and loss account and balance sheet formats are applied by a UK banking company (applying Schedule 2 to the Regulations – see definition at 4.2.2 below), UK insurance company (applying Schedule 3 to the Regulations – see definition at 4.2.3 below) or, in group accounts, by the holding company of a banking or insurance group, it does not address the content of such formats in detail (see 4 below).

UK LLPs, qualifying partnerships and other entities preparing financial statements in accordance with Part 15 of the CA 2006 are subject to similar requirements to those for UK companies preparing Companies Act accounts, modified as necessary by the regulations that govern the content of their financial statements. The formats applicable to LLPs are addressed in this Chapter, but the main focus of the Chapter is on UK companies. The *Statement of Recommended Practice – Accounting by Limited Liability Partnerships* (July 2014) issued by Consultative Committee of Accounting Bodies (CCAB) provides additional guidance on the requirements of both FRS 102 and the LLP Regulations. This Statement of Recommended Practice is referred to, where relevant, but its requirements are not covered in detail in this Chapter.

As noted at 1.1 above, SI 2015/980 applies to companies and qualifying partnerships preparing statutory accounts but does not apply to LLPs (unless LLP law is subsequently changed). Accordingly, Appendix IV – *Note on legal requirements* – to the standard states that LLPs will be applying FRS 102 in accordance with the LLP Regulations or Small LLP Regulations. In many cases, these are similar to the Regulations or the Small Companies Regulations, but because SI 2015/980 has not been reflected in the LLP Regulations or the Small

LLP Regulations, this gives rise to some differences for LLPs. These include: the small size thresholds (and exclusions) that apply under the small LLPs regime; the flexibility to apply 'adapted formats'; and in a relatively small number of areas where SI 2015/980 made changes, recognition and measurement requirements (such as the scope of financial instruments that can be measured at fair value through profit and loss, the reversal of impairment losses in relation to goodwill, and certain other matters in relation to group accounts exemptions and the conditions for merger accounting in consolidated financial statements). If following the requirements of FRS 102 would lead to a conflict with applicable legislation, an LLP should instead apply its own legal requirements and consider whether a departure of from FRS 102 is required. *[FRS 102.A4.38, A4.43-A4.47]*. Where relevant to the content of this Chapter, such differences between the LLP Regulations and Regulations are highlighted.

Appendix VI to FRS 102 addresses Republic of Ireland Legal References, but will be updated in due course to refer to the Companies Act 2014. Irish law is expected to be updated later in 2015 to implement the new Accounting Directive.

The presentation requirements in Sections 4 and 5 apply to all entities, whether or not they report under the CA 2006. Entities that do not report under the CA 2006 should comply with these requirements and with the Regulations (or, where applicable, the LLP Regulations, where referred to, except to the extent that these requirements are not permitted by any statutory framework under which such entities report. *[FRS 102.4.1, 5.1]*.

Entities that are not UK companies need to consider carefully the statutory requirements that apply.

2   SUMMARY OF PRESENTATION REQUIREMENTS OF FRS 102

The statutory accounts of a UK company prepared in accordance with FRS 102 are Companies Act accounts. Certain other entities are also required to prepare statutory accounts in accordance with Part 15 of the CA 2006.

The discussion below relates to FRS 102, except for where Section 1A is applied by an entity subject to the small entities regime in the standard (see 2.1 below). Section 1A is discussed further in Chapter 3.

A complete set of FRS 102 financial statements contains: a statement of financial position, a statement of comprehensive income (either as a single statement or as a separate income statement and statement of comprehensive income), a statement of cash flows (unless exempt), a statement of changes in equity, and accompanying notes to the financial statements. In certain circumstances, a statement of income and retained earnings can be presented instead of the statement of comprehensive income and statement of changes in equity. Comparatives must be presented. FRS 102 permits the use of other titles – such as balance sheet or profit and loss account for the primary statements – as long as they are not misleading. See 3.5 below. *[FRS 102.3.22]*.

FRS 102 specifies the content of the primary financial statements and notes. The profit and loss account section of the statement of comprehensive income and the statement of financial position must follow the profit and loss account and balance sheet formats respectively set out in the Regulations or LLP Regulations, as applicable. An entity not subject to these requirements must also follow the same formats so long as these do not conflict with the statutory framework under which it reports. FRS 102 includes supplementary requirements on presentation of discontinued operations (see 6.8 below). The requirements for the other primary financial statements are based on (but simpler than) the requirements in IAS 1.

Financial statements must give a true and fair view of the financial position, financial performance and cash flows (when required to be presented) of the entity. This usually requires compliance with FRS 102, with additional disclosure where needed but FRS 102 provides for a 'true and fair override', consistent with the 'true and fair override' provided for in the CA 2006. See 9.2 below.

Like IAS 1 and the Regulations, FRS 102 sets out basic principles underlying the preparation of financial statements such as going concern, accruals, materiality and aggregation, and consistency. See 9 below.

A statement of compliance with FRS 102 (and, where applicable, FRS 103 – *Insurance Contracts – Consolidated and accounting reporting requirements for entities in the UK and Republic of Ireland issuing insurance contracts*) is required. FRS 102 contains certain requirements (marked 'PBE') to be applied only by public benefit entities. An entity that is a public benefit entity that applies these paragraphs must make an explicit and unreserved statement that it is a public benefit entity. See 3.8 below.

The notes to the financial statements should include: the basis of preparation; accounting policies (including judgements made and key sources of estimation uncertainty); disclosures required by FRS 102; and information relevant to understanding the financial statements that are not presented elsewhere in the financial statements. Entities applying FRS 102 may also be subject to other disclosure requirements deriving from statutory or other regulatory frameworks, e.g. a UK company's statutory accounts must be prepared in accordance with Part 15 of the CA 2006 and the Regulations. See 8 below.

FRS 102 provides for a reduced disclosure framework in the individual financial statements of qualifying entities, i.e. members of a group included in publicly available consolidated financial statements intended to give a true and fair view. In particular, a qualifying entity need not present an individual cash flow statement. See Chapter 2 at 3 of EY New UK GAAP 2015.

IFRS 8 – *Operating Segments* – is scoped in for publicly traded companies. If an entity discloses disaggregated information not complying with IFRS 8, this shall not be described as segment information. *[FRS 102.1.5]*. See 3.3.2 below.

A comparison of FRS 102 to previous UK GAAP and IFRS is presented at 11 below.

2.1 Amendments to FRS 102: Small entities and other minor amendments (July 2015)

In July 2015, *Amendments to FRS 102: Small entities and other minor amendments* ('FRS 102 (July 2015) amendments') were issued. See effective date at 1.2 above. These amendments have been included in the edition of FRS 102 issued in September 2015.

The amendments introduce a new Section 1A which sets out a new small entities regime and is addressed in Chapter 3. Small entities are not required to apply Section 1A and can instead opt to comply with full FRS 102. Small entities applying Section 1A:

• follow the recognition and measurement requirements of FRS 102 in full; and

• apply the presentation requirements of Section 1A; and

• with the exception of certain paragraphs in Section 3, are not required to apply Sections 3 to 7 (but are not precluded from applying some or all of these sections).

The principal change to the presentation sections (Sections 3 to 8) is the addition of a new 'adapted format', as an alternative to the statutory formats in Schedule 1 to the Regulations. The new 'adapted format' was introduced by SI 2015/980 (see 1.1 above) but the legislation left the detail to accounting standards. Sections 4 and 5 of FRS 102 specify the minimum line items required in the statement of financial position and statement of comprehensive income (which are based on, but not identical to, IAS 1's requirements). The statement of financial position must present separate classifications for current and non-current assets, and current and non-current liabilities. Supplementary disclosures, where 'adapted formats' are used, include:

• analyses of certain line items in the statement of financial position (required either on the face of the statement of financial position or in the notes to the financial statements); and

• a columnar analysis of continuing, discontinued and total operations on the face of the income statement/statement of comprehensive income, where there are discontinued operations (the same analysis is required where statutory formats are used).

The 'adapted format' is available as an alternative to the statutory formats where an entity applies paragraphs 1A(1)-(2) of Schedule 1 to the Regulations. This new format is therefore not available to an LLP (unless LLP law is subsequently changed), or to a company (that is a banking or insurance company, or the holding company of a banking or insurance group) applying Schedule 2 or Schedule 3 to the Regulations. However, the new format can be applied by an entity not subject to the CA 2006, except to the extent that the requirements are not permitted by any statutory framework under which such an entity reports. See 4.1.3, 5.1 and 6.5 for detailed discussion of the 'adapted formats' included in FRS 102.

Other changes to Section 3 of the standard include the removal of the concept of extraordinary item for entities applying Schedule 1 to the Regulations (see 6.7.6 below), and the replacement of the terminology of 'fair presentation' with 'true and fair view' (see 9.2 below).

A small entity (as defined at Chapter 3 at 4) need not present a cash flow statement, even if not applying Section 1A. *[FRS 102.7.1B].*

Chapter 4

3   COMPOSITION OF FINANCIAL STATEMENTS

Financial statements are a structured representation of the financial position, financial performance and cash flows of an entity. *[FRS 102.Appendix I]*. Section 2 of FRS 102 (see Chapter 3 of EY New UK GAAP 2015) explains the objective of financial statements and the conceptual and pervasive principles underlying financial statements.

Section 3 of the standard explains the requirement that financial statements give a 'true and fair view', what compliance with the standard requires and what a complete set of financial statements contains. *[FRS 102.3.1]*. Sections 4 to 8 of the standard set out the requirements in relation to the different components of financial statements. Each component of a complete set of financial statements is discussed in more detail at 5 to 8 below, with the exception of the Statement of Cash Flows (which is discussed in Chapter 5 of EY New UK GAAP 2015).

UK companies preparing Companies Act accounts must also comply with the CA 2006 and the Regulations or the Small Companies Regulations (and/or other applicable regulations) which set out further recognition, measurement and disclosure requirements. The statutory requirements in the Regulations (including the changes arising from SI 2015/980) are addressed, where appropriate, in the relevant sections below.

The general principles in the Regulations and FRS 102 (which are similar) are discussed at 9 below. See 10 below for a discussion of the three accounting models in the Regulations for the recognition and measurement of assets and liabilities:

*   historical cost accounting rules;

*   alternative accounting rules (which provide an alternative measurement basis to the historical cost rules, usually at a valuation); and

*   fair value accounting rules (which may be applied to living animals and plants, financial instruments, investment properties and certain categories of stocks (once SI 2015/980 is applied)).

FRS 102's requirements are generally consistent with but are often more restrictive than those in the Regulations. Certain areas where FRS 102's requirements are in conflict with the Regulations are highlighted in Appendix IV – *Note on legal requirements* – to the standard. The Small Companies Regulations, where applied, have the same general principles and accounting models (albeit with fewer related disclosures). See Chapter 3 at 7.2.

3.1   Key definitions

The following definitions, included in FRS 102's Glossary are relevant to presentation:

Term	Definition
Current assets (pre FRS 102 amendments (July 2015))	Assets of an entity which are not intended for use on a continuing basis in the entity's activities.
Current assets (post FRS 102 amendments (July 2015))	Assets of the entity which: (a) for an entity choosing to apply paragraph 1A(1) of Schedule 1 to the Regulations are not non-current assets; (b) for all other entities, are not fixed assets.
Current liabilities for the purposes of an entity applying paragraph 1A(1) of Schedule 1 to the Regulations (post FRS 102 amendments (July 2015))	Liabilities of the entity which: (a) it expects to settle in its normal operating cycle; (b) it holds primarily for the purpose of trading; (c) are due to be settled within 12 months after the reporting period; or (d) it does not have an unconditional right to defer settlement for at least 12 months after the reporting period.
Equity	The residual interest in the assets of the entity after deducting all its liabilities.
Expenses	Decreases in economic benefits during the reporting period in the form of outflows or depletions of assets or incurrences of liabilities that result in decreases in equity, other than those relating to distributions to equity investors.
Fair presentation (pre FRS 102 amendments (July 2015))	Faithful representation of the effects of transactions, other events and conditions in accordance with the definitions and recognition criteria for assets, liabilities, income and expenses unless the override stated in paragraph 3.4 [of the standard] applies. NB The concept of 'fair presentation' is replaced by 'true and fair view' following the FRS 102 amendments (July 2015).
Fair value	The amount for which an asset could be exchanged, a liability settled, or an equity instrument granted could be exchanged, between knowledgeable, willing parties in an arm's length transaction. In the absence of any specific guidance provided in the relevant section of the FRS, the guidance in paragraphs 11.27 to 11.32 [of the standard] shall be used in determining fair value.
Financial performance	The relationship of the income and expenses of an entity, as reported in the statement of comprehensive income.

Chapter 4

Financial position	The relationship of the assets, liabilities, and equity of an entity as reported in the statement of financial position.
Financial statements	A structured representation of the financial position, financial performance and cash flows of an entity. General purpose financial statements (generally referred to simply as financial statements) are financial statements directed to the general financial information needs of a wide range of users who are not in a position to demand reports tailored to meet their particular information needs.
Fixed assets	Assets of an entity which are intended for use on a continuing basis in the entity's activities.
Income	Increases in economic benefits during the reporting period in the form of inflows or enhancements of assets or decreases of liabilities that result in increases in equity, other than those relating to contributions from equity investors.
Income statement	Financial statement that presents all items of income and expense recognised in a reporting period, excluding the items of other comprehensive income (referred to as the profit and loss account in the CA 2006).
LLP Regulations	*The Large and Medium-sized Limited Liability Partnerships (Accounts) Regulations 2008 (SI 2008/1913).*
Material	Omissions or misstatements of items are material if they could, individually or collectively, influence the economic decisions of users taken on the basis of the financial statements. Materiality depends on the size and nature of the omission or misstatement judged in the surrounding circumstances. The size or nature of the item, or a combination of both, could be the determining factor.
Non-current assets* (post FRS 102 amendments (July 2015))	Assets of the entity which: (a) it does not expect to realise, or intend to sell or consume, in its normal operating cycle; (b) it does not hold primarily for the purpose of trading; (c) it does not expect to realise within 12 months after the reporting period; or (d) are cash or cash equivalents restricted from being exchanged or used to settle a liability for at least 12 months after the reporting period.
Non-current liabilities* (post FRS 102 amendments (July 2015))	Liabilities of the entity which are not current liabilities.
Other comprehensive income	Items of income and expense (including reclassification adjustments) that are not recognised in profit or loss as required or permitted by FRS 102.
Profit or loss	The total of income less expenses, excluding the components of other comprehensive income. In the not for profit sector, this may be known as income and expenditure (and the profit and loss account, as an income and expenditure account). *[s474(2)].*

Reporting period	The period covered by financial statements or by an interim financial report.
Regulations	*The Large and Medium-sized Companies and Groups (Accounts and Reports) Regulations 2008 (SI 2008/410).*
Small Companies Regulations	*The Small Companies and Groups (Accounts and Directors' Report) Regulations 2008 (SI 2008/409).*
Small entity (post FRS 102 amendments (July 2015))	(a) A company meeting the definition of a small company as set out in section 382 or 383 of the CA 2006 and not excluded from the small companies regime by section 384; (b) an LLP qualifying as small and not excluded from the small LLPs regime, as set out in LLP Regulations; or (c) any other entity that would have met the criteria in (a) had it been a company incorporated under company law.
Small LLP Regulations	*The Small Limited Liability Partnerships (Accounts) Regulations 2008 (SI 2008/1912).*
Statement of comprehensive income	A financial statement that presents all items of income and expense recognised in a period, including those items recognised in determining profit or loss (which is a subtotal in the statement of comprehensive income) and items of other comprehensive income. If an entity chooses to present both an income statement and a statement of comprehensive income, the statement of comprehensive income begins with profit or loss and then displays the items of other comprehensive income.
Total comprehensive income	The change in equity during a period resulting from transactions and other events, other than those changes resulting from transactions from equity participants (equal to the sum of profit or loss and other comprehensive income).
Turnover (post FRS 102 amendments (July 2015))	The amounts derived from the provision of goods and services, after deduction of: (a) trade discounts; (b) value added tax; and (c) any other taxes based on the amounts so derived.

*The definition of non-current assets and non-current liabilities is relevant where an entity applies paragraph 1A(1) of Schedule 1 to the Regulations (i.e. uses 'adapted formats').

This Chapter also makes many references to certain concepts in the Regulations. Unless otherwise indicated, these references should be interpreted as follows:

- 'General Rules to the formats' means the General Rules included in Section A of Part 1 to Schedule 1 to the Regulations;

- statutory formats means the formats in Section B of Part 1 to Schedule 1 to the Regulations; and

- 'adapted formats' means the formats permitted by paragraph 1A of Schedule 1 to the Regulations (as an alternative to the formats in Section B of Part 1 to Schedule 1 to the Regulations).

3.2   Objectives of sections in FRS 102 addressing presentation of financial statements

The objective of financial statements is to provide information about the financial position, performance and, when required to be presented, cash flows of an entity that is useful for economic decision-making by a broad range of users who are not in a position to demand reports tailored to meet their particular information needs. Financial statements also show the results of the stewardship of management – the accountability of management for the resources entrusted to it. *[FRS 102.2.2-2.3]*.

Sections 3 to 8 of the standard, which address presentation of financial statements, include the following objectives:

•   to explain that the financial statements of an entity shall give a true and fair view (prior to the FRS 102 (July 2015) amendments, a 'fair presentation'), what compliance with FRS 102 requires and what is a complete set of financial statements; *[FRS 102.3.1]*.

•   to set out the information required in the statement of financial position (referred to as the 'balance sheet' under the CA 2006) and how to present it; *[FRS 102.4.1]*

•   to require an entity to present total comprehensive income for a period, being its financial performance for the period – in one or two statements – and to set out the information required in these statements and how to present it; *[FRS 102.5.1]*

•   to set out requirements for presenting changes in an entity's equity for the period in a statement of changes in equity, or if specified conditions are met and an entity chooses, in a statement of income and retained earnings; *[FRS 102.6.1]*

•   to set out the information required in a statement of cash flows and how to present it. See Chapter 5 of EY New UK GAAP 2015 for further details; and *[FRS 102.7.1]*

•   to set out the principles underlying information required in the notes to the financial statements and how to present it. In addition, nearly every section of FRS 102 requires disclosures that are normally presented in the notes. *[FRS 102.8.1]*.

3.3   Interim financial reports and segmental reporting

3.3.1   *Interim financial reporting*

FRS 102 does not address the presentation of interim financial reports. Entities preparing such reports must describe the basis for preparing and presenting such information. FRS 104 – *Interim Financial Reporting* – sets out a basis for the preparation and presentation of interim financial reports that an entity may apply. *[FRS 102.3.25]*.

See Chapter 6 for discussion of the requirements of FRS 104.

3.3.2   *Segmental reporting*

IFRS 8 applies to an entity whose debt or equity instruments are publicly traded, or that files, or is in the process of filing, its financial statements with a securities commission or other regulatory organisation for the purpose of issuing any class of instruments in a public market, or an entity that chooses to provide information described as segment information.

If an entity discloses disaggregated information, but that information does not comply with IFRS 8's requirements, the information shall not be described as segment information. *[FRS 102.1.5]*.

3.3.2.A   *Segmental disclosures of turnover*

UK companies (except those applying the small companies regime) preparing Companies Act accounts must also give the following disclosures required by the Regulations in the notes to the accounts:

- where the company has carried on business of two or more classes during the financial year that, in the opinion of the directors, differ substantially from each other, the amount of the turnover attributable to each class, and the description of the class; and

- where the company has supplied geographical markets during the financial year that, in the opinion of the directors, differ substantially from each other, the amount of the turnover attributable to each such market.

The directors should have regard to the manner in which the company's activities are organised. Classes of business (or markets) which, in the opinion of the directors, do not differ substantially from each other must be treated as one class (or market). Amounts attributable to a class of business (or market) that are not material may be included in the amount stated in respect of another class of business (or market).

Where disclosure of any of the information required would, in the opinion of the directors, be seriously prejudicial to the interests of the company, that information need not be disclosed, but the fact that any such information has not been disclosed must be stated. *[1 Sch 68]*.

For group accounts, the disclosures are given for the company and undertakings included (i.e. consolidated) in the consolidation. *[6 Sch 1(1)]*.

Where a small company/LLP supplies geographical markets outside the UK during the financial year, the Small Companies Regulations (prior to application of SI 2015/980 only as this disclosure was removed by SI 2015/980) and the Small LLP Regulations (unless LLP law is subsequently changed) instead require a statement of the percentage of turnover that is, in the opinion of the directors, attributable to those markets, having regard to the manner in which the company's activities are organised. *[1 Sch 60 (SC), 1 Sch 58 (LLP SC)]*. See 6.6.1 below for discussion of turnover in the profit and loss account formats.

Chapter 4

3.4   Frequency of reporting and period covered

An entity must present a complete set of financial statements (including comparative information) at least annually.

When the end of an entity's reporting period changes and annual financial statements are presented for a period longer or shorter than one year, the entity shall disclose that fact, the reason for using a longer or shorter period, and the fact that comparative amounts presented in the financial statements (including the related notes) are not entirely comparable. *[FRS 102.3.10].*

Normally, financial statements are consistently prepared covering a one year period. Some entities, particularly in the retail sector, present financial statements for a 52-week period. This practice is permitted by the CA 2006 which allows companies to prepare financial statements to a financial year end, not more than 7 days before or after the end of the accounting reference period (based on the accounting reference date notified to the Registrar). *[s390(2)(b), s391].* While the standard does not explicitly address this issue, we consider that FRS 102 financial statements can be prepared to a financial year end, not more than 7 days from the end of the accounting reference period.

3.5   Components of a complete set of financial statements

A complete set of financial statements under FRS 102 (for an entity not applying Section 1A) includes all of the following, each of which should be presented with equal prominence: *[FRS 102.3.1A, 2, 17, 21]*

- a statement of financial position as at the reporting date;
- a statement of comprehensive income for the reporting period to be presented either as:
  - a single statement of comprehensive income, displaying all items of income and expense recognised during the period including those items recognised in determining profit or loss (which is a subtotal in the statement of comprehensive income) and items of other comprehensive income; or
  - a separate income statement and a separate statement of comprehensive income. In this case, the statement of comprehensive income begins with profit or loss and then displays the items of other comprehensive income;
- a statement of changes in equity for the reporting period;
- a statement of cash flows, where required, for the reporting period; and
- notes, comprising a summary of significant accounting policies and other explanatory information.

Chapter 5 at 3.1 of EY New UK GAAP 2015 sets out exemptions from preparing a cash flow statement. Qualifying entities (see Chapter 2 at 3.1 and 3.3.2 of EY New UK GAAP 2015) using the reduced disclosure framework in individual financial statements are also exempt. The FRS 102 (July 2015) amendments, where applied, further exempt a small entity (as defined at Chapter 3 at 4), whether or not applying Section 1A, from preparing a cash flow statement. *[FRS 102.7.1B].*

Sections 4 and 5 require that the balance sheet and profit and loss account formats in the Regulations (including the new 'adapted formats' available as an alternative to statutory formats under Schedule 1 to the Regulations, where SI 2015/980 is applied) or LLP Regulations are applied. *[FRS 102.4.2, 5.5, 5.7]*. See 4 below for further discussion of the formats.

Other titles for the financial statements can be used, as long as they are not misleading. *[FRS 102.3.22]*. For instance, an entity may wish to refer to a balance sheet (for the statement of financial position) or the profit and loss account (instead of an income statement).

If an entity has no items of other comprehensive income in any of the periods presented, it may present only an income statement (or a statement of comprehensive income in which the 'bottom line' is labelled profit or loss). *[FRS 102.3.19]*.

If the only changes to equity during the periods presented in the financial statements arise from profit or loss, payments of dividends, corrections of prior period errors and changes in accounting policy, the entity may present a single statement of income and retained earnings in place of the statement of comprehensive income and statement of changes in equity. *[FRS 102.3.18]*.

FRS 102 explains that notes contain information in addition to that presented in the primary statements above, and provide narrative descriptions or disaggregations of items presented in those statements and information about items that do not qualify for recognition in those statements. *[FRS 102.8.1]*.

In addition to information about the reporting period, FRS 102 also requires comparative information about the preceding period, and therefore a complete set of financial statements includes, at a minimum, two of each of the required financial statements and related notes. *[FRS 102.3.20]*.

The Regulations also require only one comparative period to be presented for the balance sheet and profit and loss account formats. *[1 Sch 7]*. The Regulations do not specifically require comparative note disclosures but, as noted above, these are required by FRS 102. Other statutory or regulatory frameworks may require further periods to be presented. Comparative information is discussed at 3.6 below.

3.6   Comparative information

Except when FRS 102 permits or requires otherwise, an entity presents comparative information in respect of the preceding period for all amounts presented in the current period's financial statements. *[FRS 102.3.14]*. This means that the requirement to present comparative information applies both to mandatory and voluntary information presented for the current period.

In certain cases, FRS 102 provides specific exemptions from presenting comparatives. For example, there is no requirement to present comparatives for the reconciliations of movements in the number of shares outstanding, or of the movements in the carrying amounts of property, plant and equipment, investment property, intangible assets, goodwill, negative goodwill, provisions or biological assets. *[FRS 102.4.12(a)(iv), 16.10(e), 17.31(e), 18.27(e), 19.26, 19.26A, 21.14, 34.7(c), 34.10(e)]*. These exemptions are addressed in the relevant chapters of this publication.

The General Rules to the formats (see 4.4 below) require that for each item presented in the balance sheet and profit and loss account, the corresponding amount for the immediately preceding financial year (i.e. the comparative) must also be shown. *[1 Sch 7(1)]*. Where an amount can be shown for an item in the formats for the immediately preceding financial year (but not the current financial year), that item must be shown under the heading or sub-heading required by the format for that item. However, if there is no amount to be shown in the current or immediately preceding financial year, the heading or sub-heading in the formats should not be included. *[1 Sch 5]*. Schedules 2 and 3 to the Regulations and the LLP Regulations have the same requirements. *[2 Sch 6, 7(1), 3 Sch 4, 5(1), 1 Sch 5, 7(1) (LLP)]*.

3.6.1   Comparative information for narrative and descriptive information

An entity shall include comparative information for narrative and descriptive information when it is relevant to an understanding of the current period's financial statements. *[FRS 102.3.14]*.

3.6.2   Consistency of, and reclassifications of comparative information

The objective of comparative information is comparability of an entity's financial statements through time to identify trends in its financial position and performance, and to enable users to compare the financial statements of different entities to evaluate their relative financial position, performance and cash flows. *[FRS 102.2.11]*.

Consequently, an entity must retain the presentation and classification of items in the financial statements from one period to the next unless: *[FRS 102.3.11]*

* it is apparent, following a significant change in the nature of the entity's operations or a review of its financial statements, that another presentation or classification would be more appropriate having regard to the criteria for selection and application of accounting policies in Section 10 (see Chapter 7 at 3.4 of EY New UK GAAP 2015); or

* where FRS 102 (or another applicable FRS or FRC Abstract) requires a change in presentation.

When entities change the presentation or classification of items in the financial statements, the comparatives must be reclassified, unless this is impracticable (in which case the reason should be disclosed). When comparative amounts are reclassified, the nature of the reclassification, the amount of each item (or class of items) reclassified and the reasons for the reclassification must be disclosed. Applying a requirement is impracticable when the entity cannot apply it after making every reasonable effort to do so. *[FRS 102.3.12-3.13, Appendix I]*.

This situation should be distinguished from a reclassification due to a change in use of an asset. An example would be a reclassification out of investment property because it ceases to meet the definition of investment property in the current period. This would be treated as a transfer arising in the current period and not lead to a reclassification of comparatives. *[FRS 102.16.9]*.

In addition, the initial application of a policy to revalue property, plant and equipment (or intangible assets, where the strict criteria are met) is treated as a revaluation in accordance with Section 17 – *Property, Plant and Equipment* – and Section 18 – *Intangible Assets other than Goodwill* – respectively. *[FRS 102.10.10A]*. This means that it is reflected as an adjustment in the period of application of the revaluation policy rather than retrospectively. This is consistent with IFRSs *[IAS 8.17]*, but differs to previous UK GAAP which required retrospective application. *[FRS 18.4, 48]*.

Restatements of comparatives may also arise from:

- changes in accounting policy (see Chapter 7 at 3.4 of EY New UK GAAP 2015);
- correction of material errors (see Chapter 7 at 3.6 of EY New UK GAAP 2015);
- presentation of discontinued operations (see 6.8 below); and
- hindsight adjustments in respect of provisional fair values of identifiable assets, liabilities and contingent liabilities arising on business combinations (see Chapter 15 at 2.1.6 of EY New UK GAAP 2015).

FRS 102 (unlike IAS 1) does not require presentation of a third balance sheet at the beginning of the preceding period when there is a retrospective restatement due to an accounting policy change, reclassification or correction of a material error. *[IAS 1.10(f), 40A-D]*. See Chapter 7 at 2.2.2 of EY New UK GAAP 2015.

Where the comparative shown in the balance sheet and profit and loss account formats is not comparable with the amount shown in the current period, the General Rules to the formats (see 4.4 below) permit a UK company preparing Companies Act accounts to adjust the comparative to make these comparable with the current period amounts. Particulars of the non-comparability and of any adjustment must be disclosed in a note to the accounts. *[1 Sch 7(2)]*. Schedules 2 and 3 to the Regulations and the LLP Regulations have the same requirements. *[2 Sch 7(2), 3 Sch 5(2), 1 Sch 7(2) (LLP)]*. These statutory requirements would allow FRS 102's requirements on restatement of comparatives to be followed. Where amounts are not restated, e.g. due to transitional provisions in accounting policies or where it is impracticable to determine the effects of a change in accounting policies on earlier periods *[FRS 102.10.11-12]*, a note to the financial statements will need to disclose the non-comparability.

3.7   Identification of financial statements

It is commonly the case that financial statements will form only part of a larger annual report, regulatory filing or other document, but FRS 102 only applies to the financial statements (including the notes). Chapter 1 at 6 addresses the content of the statutory annual report and accounts for a UK company (and Chapter 3 addresses this for a UK company applying the small companies regime). An LLP is not required to prepare a members' report, but *Statement of Recommended Practice – Accounting by Limited Liability Partnerships* (July 2014) issued by CCAB requires certain information to be disclosed which may be included in a separate members' report.[3]

Accordingly, FRS 102 requires that an entity clearly identifies the financial statements and the notes, and distinguishes them from other information in the same document. In addition, the entity must display the following information prominently, and repeat it when necessary, for an understanding of the information presented: *[FRS 102.3.23]*

- the name of the reporting entity and any change in its name from the end of the preceding reporting period;

- whether the financial statements cover the individual entity or a group of entities;

- the date of the end of the reporting period and the period covered by the financial statements;

- the presentation currency, as defined in Section 30 – *Foreign Currency Translation* (discussed in Chapter 25 at 3.7 of EY New UK GAAP 2015); and

- the level of rounding, if any, used in presenting amounts in the financial statements.

In practice, these requirements can be met through the use of appropriate headings for pages, statements, notes and columns etc., for example: the inclusion of a basis of preparation note within the accounting policies; the use of appropriate titles for the primary financial statements, distinguishing group and company; and the use of appropriate headings in the columns in the primary financial statements (and notes to the financial statements). Entities will need to consider how best to present the required information where financial statements are made available electronically.

Financial statements are usually presented to an appropriate level of rounding, such as thousands or millions of currency units. An appropriate level of rounding can avoid obscuring useful information (and hence cut clutter – see 9.4.1 below) but entities need to ensure that material information is not omitted. The level of rounding used must be clearly disclosed in the primary statements and notes to the financial statements. Entities are not precluded from using lower levels of rounding in certain notes to the financial statements. For example, where the financial statements are presented in millions of units of the presentation currency, it may be appropriate to include information on directors' remuneration at a lower level of rounding. In all cases, it is important that the units used are clearly stated.

3.8   Statement of compliance

A set of financial statements prepared in accordance with FRS 102 must contain an explicit and unreserved statement of compliance with FRS 102 in the notes to the financial statements. Financial statements must not be described as complying with FRS 102 unless they comply with *all* the requirements of the standard. *[FRS 102.3.3, FRS 100.9]*. This is similar to the requirement in IAS 1 for an entity preparing its financial statements to give an explicit and unreserved statement of compliance with IFRSs. *[IAS 1.16]*.

FRS 102 additionally requires a public benefit entity (see Chapter 29 at 6 of EY New UK GAAP 2015 for the definition of a public benefit entity) that applies the 'PBE' prefixed paragraphs to make an explicit and unreserved statement that it is a public benefit entity. *[FRS 102.PBE3.3A]*. This is because FRS 102 has specific requirements reserved for public benefit entities (prefixed with 'PBE'), which cannot be applied by analogy to other entities (other than, where specifically directed, entities within a public benefit entity group). *[FRS 102.1.2]*. See Chapter 2 at 2.4.2 of EY New UK GAAP 2015.

FRS 103 requires that an entity whose financial statements comply with FRS 103 shall, in addition to the statement of compliance made in accordance with FRS 102, make an explicit and unreserved statement of compliance with FRS 103 in the notes to the financial statements. *[FRS 103.1.12]*. An example (for an entity not applying Section 1A – see Chapter 3 at 11.2.5 and 11.3 where an entity applies Section 1A) is presented at Example 4.1 below.

Example 4.1:   Statement of Compliance – illustrative wording

These financial statements were prepared in accordance with Financial Reporting Standard 102 'The Financial Reporting Standard applicable in the UK and Republic of Ireland' [and Financial Reporting Standard 103 'Insurance Contracts']*. [The [company/entity] is a public benefit entity as defined in Financial Reporting Standard 102 'The Financial Reporting Standard applicable in the UK and Republic of Ireland']*.

*delete as applicable.

In special circumstances when management concludes that compliance with any requirement of FRS 102 or applicable legislation (only where it allows for a true and fair override) is inconsistent with the requirement to give a true and fair view, the entity shall depart from that requirement to the extent necessary to give a true and fair view, giving the required disclosures set out in paragraph 3.5 of FRS 102. *[FRS 102.3.4-3.5]*. See 9.2 below for further discussion of the 'true and fair override' under FRS 102 (and where applicable, the CA 2006) together with the implications for the statement of compliance.

3.8.1   Statement that financial statements have been prepared in accordance with applicable accounting standards

The Regulations require a UK company (that is large) preparing Companies Act accounts to state in the notes to the accounts whether the accounts have been prepared in accordance with applicable accounting standards (as defined in section 464 of CA 2006), giving particulars of any material departures from those standards and the reasons (see Chapter 1 at 4.6.1). This statement is also required in the group accounts of a medium-sized company (see Chapter 1 at 6.6.2.A) but not in its individual accounts. *[Regulations 4(2A), 1 Sch 45]*.

Where a 'true and fair override' in accordance with paragraph 3.5 of the standard (see 9.2 below) is applied in the financial statements, the above statement will need to include or refer to the disclosures of the override.

Financial statements prepared in accordance with FRS 102 are prepared in accordance with applicable accounting standards.

3.8.2   Statements of Recommended Practice (SORPs)

FRS 100 requires certain disclosures where a SORP applies to an entity, including in respect of departures from the accounting treatment or disclosure requirements of a SORP. See Chapter 1 at 4.7.

4   COMPANY LAW FORMATS

Sections 4 and 5 cover the requirements for the statement of financial position and statement of comprehensive income (and income statement, where the statement of comprehensive income is presented as two statements) respectively. These sections require that an entity presents (1) its statement of financial position (known as the balance sheet under the CA 2006), and (2) the items in the statement of comprehensive income (whether as a single statement or in two statement form) required to be included in a profit and loss account, in accordance with the requirements in Part 1 of the applicable schedule to the Regulations or the LLP Regulations. *[FRS 102.4.2, 5.5, 5.7]*. This means that FRS 102 reporters that are UK companies or LLPs will comply with the requirements for balance sheet and profit and loss account formats (statutory or, where Schedule 1 to the Regulations is applied, 'adapted formats' – see 4.1 below) in the Regulations or LLP Regulations respectively.

Sections 4 and 5 of the standard apply to *all* FRS 102 reporters, whether or not they report under the CA 2006 (apart from small entities applying Section 1A). Entities that do not report under the CA 2006 are required to comply with the requirements set out in Sections 4 and 5 and with the Regulations (or, where applicable, the LLP Regulations) where referred to in Sections 4 and 5, except to the extent that these requirements are not permitted by any statutory framework under which such entities report. *[FRS 102.1A.7, 4.1, 4.1A, 5.1, 5.1A]*.

4.1   Required formats – balance sheet and profit and loss account

4.1.1   *Individual financial statement*

An entity must present its statement of financial position; and, in the statement of comprehensive income (or in the separate income statement), the items to be included in a profit and loss account in accordance with one of the following requirements for individual financial statements: *[FRS 102.4.2, 5.5, 5.7]*

- Part 1 *General Rules and Formats* of Schedule 1 to the Regulations – applies to companies other than banking companies (defined in section 1164) and insurance companies (defined in section 1165); *[Regulations 3]*

- Part 1 *General Rules and Formats* of Schedule 2 to the Regulations – applies to banking companies; *[Regulations 5]*

- Part 1 *General Rules and Formats* of Schedule 3 to the Regulations – applies to insurance companies; and *[Regulations 6]*

- Part 1 *General Rules and Formats* of Schedule 1 to the LLP Regulations – applies to limited liability partnerships (LLPs). *[LLP Regulations 3]*.

Schedule 1 to the Regulations, where SI 2015/980 is applied, provides a choice of the statutory formats (as set out in Section B of Part 1 of that schedule – see 5.2, 5.3 and 6.6 below) or 'adapted' formats (as permitted by paragraph 1A of Schedule 1 to the Regulations – see 4.1.3, 5.1 and 6.5 below). Prior to application of SI 2015/980, Schedule 1 to the Regulations only provides for statutory formats.

Schedule 2 and Schedule 3 to the Regulations and the LLP Regulations (unless LLP law is subsequently changed) only provide for statutory formats.

While not directly relevant to formats, it is worth noting that a change introduced by SI 2015/980 is to require disclosures from paragraph 42 of Schedule 1 to the Regulations onwards to be given in the notes to the accounts (rather than in the accounts or notes to the accounts) and to specify that certain Schedule 1 disclosures are given in the note on the accounting policies rather than in the notes to the accounts. Such changes have been reflected throughout this Chapter without further reference.

4.1.2   *Consolidated financial statements*

The consolidated statement of financial position and consolidated statement of comprehensive income of a group must be presented in accordance with the requirements for a consolidated balance sheet and consolidated profit and loss account of Schedule 6 to the Regulations or Schedule 3 to the LLP Regulations. *[FRS 102.4.2, 5.5, 5.7].*

Schedule 6 to the Regulations addresses the balance sheet and profit and loss account formats applicable to group accounts of companies, modifying the formats included in the earlier schedules. The group accounts must comply, so far as practicable with the provisions of Schedule 1 to the Regulations (including the formats) as if the undertakings included in the consolidation were a single company. *[Regulations 9, 6 Sch 1(1)].*

The parent company of a group (other than a banking or insurance group) applies Part 1 of Schedule 6 to the Regulations. The parent company of a banking group (defined in section 1164(4)-(5)) applies Part 1 (as modified by Part 2) of Schedule 6 to the Regulations. The parent company of an insurance group (defined in section 1165(5)-(6)) applies Part 1 (as modified by Part 3) of Schedule 6 to the Regulations. *[Regulations 9].* The definitions of a banking company, insurance company, banking group and insurance group are at 4.2.2 and 4.2.3 below.

Schedule 3 to the LLP Regulations similarly addresses the balance sheet and profit and loss formats applicable to group accounts of LLPs. *[LLP Regulations 6, 3 Sch 1(1) (LLP), FRS 102.4.2, 5.5, 5.7].*

The modifications for group accounts for companies (excluding banking and insurance companies) and LLPs are addressed at 4.5 (presentation of non-controlling interest), 5.1 and 6.5 (adapted formats) and 5.2 and 6.6 (statutory formats) below.

4.1.3   *'Adapted formats'*

SI 2015/980 introduces a new concept of 'adapted formats' available for UK companies applying Schedule 1 to the Regulations. FRS 102 sets out the content of such formats, based on but not identical to the formats in IAS 1. These formats may therefore be attractive to certain companies, e.g. where it assists comparability with competitors or where IFRS is used for group reporting but FRS 102 has been adopted in the individual accounts of UK group undertakings.

Paragraph 1A(1) of Schedule 1 to the Regulations (as amended by SI 2015/980) allows a company's directors to adapt one of the balance sheet formats in

Section B to Schedule 1 to the Regulations (i.e. the statutory formats) so to distinguish between current and non-current items in a different way, provided that: *[1 Sch 1A(1)]*

(a)   the information given is at least equivalent to that which would have been required by the use of such format had it not been thus adapted; and

(b)   the presentation of those items is in accordance with generally accepted accounting principles or practice.

Similarly, paragraph 1A(2) of Schedule 1 to the Regulations, introduced by SI 2015/980, allows directors of a company to adapt one of the profit and loss account formats in Section B to Schedule 1 to the Regulations (i.e. the statutory formats) provided that: *[1 Sch 1A(2)]*

(a)   the information given is at least equivalent to that which would have been required by the use of such format had it not been thus adapted; and

(b)   the presentation of those items is in accordance with generally accepted accounting principles or practice.

So far as practicable, the provisions of paragraphs 2 to 9A of Section A of Part 1 of Schedule 1 to the Regulations (i.e. the General Rules to the formats – see 4.4 below) apply to the company's balance sheet or profit or loss account, notwithstanding any such adaptation pursuant to paragraph 1A. *[1 Sch 1A(3)]*.

'Adapted formats', as modified by Schedule 6 to the Regulations (see 4.1.2 above) may also be used in group accounts. *[6 Sch 1(1)]*. 'Adapted formats' are not permitted to be used by banking groups, insurance groups or LLPs (unless LLP law is subsequently changed).

Schedule 1 to the Regulations provides no further guidance on the form of 'adapted formats', leaving the detail (consistent with the statutory requirements above) to UK accounting standards, namely FRS 101 (see Chapter 2) and FRS 102 (see 5.1 and 6.5 below). Indeed, Appendix IV – *Note on legal requirements* – states that 'for entities within its scope, FRS 102 sets out a framework for the information to be presented by those entities choosing to adapt the formats'. *[FRS 102.A4.38]*.

4.2   Which formats should be applied?

This section sets out the requirements for which formats in the Regulations or LLP Regulations should be applied.

Where FRS 102 (amended July 2015) is applied, there is a choice of 'adapted formats' and statutory formats (with minor changes to the statutory formats arising from SI 2015/980) for UK companies following Schedule 1 to the Regulations. UK companies following Schedules 2 or 3 to the Regulations are not permitted to use the 'adapted formats' and must apply the statutory formats in those schedules (which are not amended). An LLP applies the statutory formats in the LLP Regulations, which are also not amended (unless there is a subsequent change to LLP law). The FRS 102 (July 2015) amendments are mandatory for accounting periods beginning on or after 1 January 2016 but with restricted early application (see effective dates at 1.2 above).

A small entity that applies FRS 102 (amended July 2015) but does not choose to apply Section 1A, must also follow the above formats in the Regulations or LLP Regulations. If Section 1A is applied, see Chapter 3 at 8.

Where FRS 102 (amended July 2015) is *not* applied, the statutory formats in the Regulations (prior to amendments by SI 2015/980) or in the LLP Regulations, as applicable, are followed. Even if the company (or LLP) applies the small companies regime (or small LLPs regime), the formats in the Small Companies Regulations or Small LLP Regulations are not followed. See Chapter 2 at 4.1 of EY New UK GAAP 2015.

4.2.1   UK companies applying FRS 102 (July 2015) amendments

UK companies (not applying Section 1A) must apply the formats in the schedule that they are required to follow under the Regulations (see 4.1 above).

If the company applies FRS 102 (amended July 2015), Schedule 1 to the Regulations allows a choice of following the statutory formats in Section B of Part 1 of Schedule 1 to the Regulations (as amended by SI 2015/980) or 'adapted formats'.

A banking or insurance company (or the parent company of a banking or insurance group) applying Schedule 2 or Schedule 3 to the Regulations must apply the statutory formats in Section B of Part 1 of the applicable schedule (which are not amended by SI 2015/980). See definitions at 4.2.2 and 4.2.3 below.

The Regulations require that the individual accounts of a banking or insurance company contain a statement that they are prepared in accordance with the provisions of the Regulations relating to banking or insurance companies, as the case may be. Similarly, the group accounts prepared by a parent of a banking or insurance group must make a statement that they are prepared in accordance with the provisions of the Regulations relating to banking groups or insurance groups, as the case may be. *[Regulations 5(3), 6(3), 9(4)].*

4.2.2   Definition of banking company and banking group

A 'banking company' means a person who has permission under Part 4A of the Financial Services and Markets Act 2000 to accept deposits, other than:

- a person who is not a company; and
- a person who has such permission only for the purpose of carrying on another regulated activity in accordance with permission under that Part.

This definition is to be read with section 22 of the Financial Services and Markets Act 2000, any relevant order under that section and Schedule 2 to the Financial Services and Markets Act 2000. *[s1164(2)-(3)].*

A 'banking group' means a group (i.e. a parent undertaking and its subsidiary undertakings) where the parent company is a banking company or where:

- the parent company's principal subsidiary undertakings are wholly or mainly credit institutions; and
- the parent company does not itself carry on any material business apart from the acquisition, management and disposal of interests in subsidiary undertakings. *[s1164(4), s1173(1)].*

For the purposes of the definition of 'banking group', the 'principal subsidiary undertakings' are the subsidiary undertakings of the company whose results or financial position would principally affect the figures shown in the group accounts and the 'management of interests in subsidiary undertakings' includes the provision of services to such undertakings. *[s1164(5)]*.

A credit institution is defined in Article 3.1 of Directive 2013/36/EC as 'an undertaking the business of which is to receive deposits or other repayable funds from the public and to grant credits for its own account.' *[s1173(1)]*.

4.2.3   *Definition of insurance company and insurance group*

An 'insurance company' means:

- an authorised insurance company (i.e. a person (whether incorporated or not) who has permission under Part 4A of the Financial Services and Markets Act 2000 to effect or carry out contracts of insurance); or

- any other person (whether incorporated or not) who:

  - carries on insurance market activity (as defined in section 316(3) of the Financial Services and Markets Act 2000); or

  - may effect or carry out contracts of insurance under which the benefits provided by that person are exclusively or primarily benefits in kind in the event of accident to or breakdown of a vehicle.

Neither expression includes a friendly society within the meaning of the Friendly Societies Act 1992. *[s1165(2)-(4)]*.

References to 'contracts of insurance' and 'to the effecting or carrying out of such contracts' must be read with section 22 of the Financial Services and Markets Act 2000, any relevant order under that section and Schedule 2 to the Financial Services and Markets Act 2000. *[s1165(8)]*.

An 'insurance group' means a group (i.e. parent undertaking and its subsidiary undertakings) where the parent company is an insurance company or where:

- the parent company's principal subsidiary undertakings are wholly or mainly insurance companies; and

- the parent company does not itself carry on any material business apart from the acquisition, management and disposal of interests in subsidiary undertakings. *[s1165(5)]*.

For the purposes of the definition of 'insurance group', the 'principal subsidiary undertakings' are the subsidiary undertakings of the company whose results or financial position would principally affect the figures shown in the group accounts and the 'management of interests in subsidiary undertakings' includes the provision of services to such undertakings. *[s1165(6)]*.

4.2.4   *LLPs (not applying Section 1A)*

LLPs must apply the formats in Section B of Part 1 of Schedule 1 to the LLP Regulations (see 4.1 above). Unless LLP law is subsequently changed, LLPs cannot apply 'adapted formats'. The amendments included in SI 2015/980 do not apply to LLPs.

4.2.5 Qualifying partnerships (not applying Section 1A)

A qualifying partnership (as defined in the *Partnerships (Accounts) Regulations 2008*) (SI 2008/569), unless exempt under regulation 7 of SI 2008/569, is required to prepare the like annual accounts and reports as would be required, if the partnership were a company under Part 15 and under the Small Companies Regulations or the Regulations, as the case may be. Part 1 of the Schedule to these regulations sets out certain modifications and adaptations to be made to the Regulations and Small Companies Regulations for these purposes.

Consequently, the requirements for qualifying partnerships preparing statutory accounts are the same (subject to the modifications and adaptations noted above) as for UK companies (see 4.2.1 above). Note that there is no requirement for the profit and loss account to show profit or loss before taxation.[4]

4.2.6 Other entities required to prepare statutory accounts in accordance with Part 15 of the CA 2006

Certain other entities are required by regulations to prepare annual accounts as if the entity is a company subject to Part 15 of the CA 2006 and these regulations specify the formats to be applied for the balance sheet and profit and loss account.

The Bank Accounts Directive (Miscellaneous Banks) Regulations 2008 (SI 2008/567) requires a 'qualifying bank' (as defined in those regulations) to prepare such annual accounts and directors' report as if it were a banking company (or the parent company of a banking group) in accordance with Schedule 2 to the Regulations (with certain adaptations or modifications set out in the Schedule to SI 2008/567).

Similarly, an insurance undertaking (as defined in *The Insurance Accounts (Directive) (Miscellaneous Insurance Undertakings) Regulations 2008* (SI 2008/565)) must prepare the like annual accounts and directors' report as if it were an insurance company (or the parent company of an insurance group) in accordance with Schedule 3 to the Regulations (with certain adaptations or modifications).

Such entities would not qualify as small entities eligible to apply Section 1A.

4.2.7 Other entities (not applying Section 1A)

Other entities must also apply one of the balance sheet (or profit or loss account) formats included in the Regulations (or, where applicable, the LLP Regulations), except to the extent that these requirements are not permitted by any statutory framework under which such entities report. *[FRS 102.4.1, 4.2, 5.1, 5.5, 5.7].* The Accounting Council Advice states that 'this would have the consequence of all entities being required to comply with the company law formats, promoting consistency amongst all those preparing financial statements intended to give a true and fair view'.[5]

As FRS 102 does not specify which format should be used, management of such entities must apply judgement in determining which is the most appropriate format to apply for the circumstances of the entity concerned.

Chapter 4

4.3   Changes in formats

The General Rules to the formats to Schedule 1 to the Regulations (or Schedule 1 to the LLP Regulations) state that once a particular format (in Section B of Part 1 to those regulations) for the balance sheet (or profit and loss account) has been adopted for any financial year, the company's directors (or the members of an LLP) must use the same format in preparing Companies Act accounts (non-IAS accounts for an LLP) for subsequent financial years, unless in their opinion there are special reasons for a change. Particulars of any such change must be given in a note to the accounts in which the new format is first used, and the reasons for the change must be explained. *[1 Sch 2, 6 Sch 1, 1 Sch 2 (LLP), 3 Sch 1 (LLP)]*. There are similar rules for changes in statutory profit and loss formats for banking companies in Schedule 2 to the Regulations. *[2 Sch 3, 6 Sch 1]*.

While the wording refers to the statutory formats, the General Rules apply so far as practicable to 'adapted formats'. *[1 Sch 1A(3)]*. Therefore, in our view, the same requirements apply to changes in the statutory format used and a change from statutory formats to 'adapted formats' in Schedule 1 to the Regulations. A change in the format applied would also be regarded as a change in accounting policy for the purposes of FRS 102 and, therefore, would be retrospectively effected. Accounting policies are defined as 'the specific principles, bases, conventions, rules and practices applied by an entity in preparing and presenting financial statements'. *[FRS 102.Appendix I, 10.2]*. See Chapter 7 at 3.4 of EY New UK GAAP 2015 for the requirements on changes in accounting policy.

4.4   General Rules to the formats

The following discussion relates to the balance sheet and profit and loss account formats included in Schedule 1 to the Regulations only. The requirements in Schedule 1 to the LLP Regulations are the same, except where noted. The General Rules to the formats applicable to Schedule 2 (banking companies) and 3 (insurance companies) to the Regulations, not addressed here, are more restrictive. See 4.3 above on changes in formats.

Subject to paragraph 1A (which provides for 'adapted formats' – see 4.1.3 above) and the following provisions, the General Rules to the formats require that every balance sheet and every profit and loss account of a company must show the items listed in the balance sheet or profit or loss format adopted. Section B of Part 1 of Schedule 1 to the Regulations, as amended by SI 2015/980, sets out a choice of two balance sheet (formats 1 and 2, only format 1 is commonly applied) and two profit or loss formats (formats 1 and 2) (referred to below as 'statutory formats'). The LLP Regulations have the equivalent requirement but there are some differences in detail in the LLP statutory formats compared to the company formats.

See Figure 4.4 at 5.2 below for the format 1 balance sheet and Figures 4.14 to 4.17 at 6.6 below for the format 1 and 2 profit and loss accounts (for a company and LLP) for the individual accounts. Each of the headings and sub-headings denoted with a capital letter or Roman numeral must be presented on the face of the balance sheet. The format 1 balance sheet includes sub-headings, denoted with an Arabic number, which have not been shown in Figure 4.4 below.

The items in the balance sheet and profit and loss account statutory formats must be shown in the order and under the headings and sub-headings given in the particular format used, but the letters or numbers assigned to that item in the format do not need to be given (and are not in practice). References to items in the formats are to the items listed in the statutory formats read together with the notes to the formats, which may also permit alternative positions for any particular items. *[1 Sch 1, 1 Sch 1 (LLP)]*. The individual line items in the statutory balance sheet and profit and loss account formats (and their related notes) are discussed respectively at 5.3 and 6.6 below.

The following provisions in the General Rules to the formats apply to the statutory formats and, so far as practicable, to the 'adapted formats'. *[1 Sch 1A(3)]*.

Every profit and loss account must show 'profit or loss before taxation' as a line item on the face of the profit and loss account. Prior to applying SI 2015/980 (and in the LLP Regulations, unless LLP law is subsequently changed), the line item required is 'profit or loss on ordinary activities before taxation'. *[1 Sch 6, 1 Sch 6 (LLP)]*. This line item is not required for a qualifying partnership preparing statutory accounts. [6]

The General Rules to the formats allow any item to be shown in the company's balance sheet or profit and loss account in greater detail than required by the particular format used. The balance sheet or profit and loss account may include an item representing or covering the amount of any asset or liability, income or expenditure not otherwise covered by any of the items listed in the format used, but preliminary expenses; the expenses of, and commission on, any issue of shares or debentures; and the costs of research may not be treated as assets in the balance sheet. *[1 Sch 3, 1 Sch 3 (LLP)]*. A qualifying partnership preparing statutory accounts is not subject to the above rules on which types of costs may not be treated as assets in the balance sheet. [7]

Where the special nature of the company's (or LLP's) business requires it, the company's directors (for an LLP, the members) *must* adapt the arrangement, headings and sub-headings otherwise required in respect of items given an Arabic number in the balance sheet or profit or loss account format used. The directors (for an LLP, the members) *may* combine items to which Arabic numbers are given in the formats if their individual amounts are not material to assessing the state of affairs or profit or loss of the company for the financial year in question; or the combination facilitates that assessment. In the latter case, the individual amounts of any items combined must be disclosed in a note to the accounts. *[1 Sch 4, 1 Sch 4 (LLP)]*. FRS 102's requirements on materiality and aggregation are discussed at 9.4 below.

FRS 102 also requires additional line items, headings and subtotals to be added where relevant to an understanding of the entity's financial position or financial performance (see 5.1, 5.2 and 6.7 below). *[FRS 102.4.3, 5.9]*. Where additional detail is provided on the face of the balance sheet or profit and loss account, it is usual to provide a subtotal for the heading. In addition, FRS 102 includes flexibility for the 'adapted formats' (see 5.1 and 6.5 below). *[FRS 102.4.2C, 5.5C]*.

Chapter 4

Where there is no amount in the current or immediately preceding financial year for a particular item in the balance sheet or profit and loss account format, that heading or sub-heading should be omitted from the balance sheet or profit and loss account, but an amount for an item relating to the immediately preceding year should be included under the required heading or sub-heading (even if there is no such item in the current financial year). *[1 Sch 5, 1 Sch 5 (LLP)]*.

A corresponding amount (i.e. comparative) must be shown for every item shown in the balance sheet or profit and loss account. Where that corresponding amount is not comparable with the amount shown in the current financial year, the corresponding amount may be adjusted. Particulars of the non-comparability and of any adjustment must be disclosed in a note to the accounts. *[1 Sch 7, 1 Sch 7 (LLP)]*. FRS 102's requirements on comparatives are discussed at 3.6 above.

Amounts in respect of items representing assets or income may not be set off against amounts in respect of items representing liabilities or expenditure (as the case may be), or *vice versa*. *[1 Sch 8, 1 Sch 8 (LLP)]*. FRS 102's requirements on offset are discussed at 9.1.1.C below.

The company's directors (for an LLP, the members) must, in determining how amounts are presented within items in the profit and loss account and balance sheet, have regard to the substance of the reported transaction or arrangement, in accordance with generally accepted accounting principles or practice. *[1 Sch 9, 1 Sch 9 (LLP)]*.

A new requirement, introduced by SI 2015/980 (see 1.1 above), not currently relevant to LLPs, is that where an asset or liability relates to more than one item in the balance sheet, the relationship of such asset or liability to the relevant items must be disclosed either under those items or in the notes to the accounts. *[1 Sch 9A]*.

Examples of situations where this may be relevant include:

- items which are partly reported in debtors: amounts falling due within one year and debtors: amounts falling due after more than one year (where reported separately on the balance sheet) in the statutory formats;
- items which are partly reported in creditors: amounts falling due within one year and creditors: amounts falling due after more than one year (in the statutory formats); and
- items which are partly reported as current and non-current assets or liabilities (in the 'adapted formats').

This disclosure requirement does not appear to extend to reporting the relationship between assets and liabilities that derive from a single transaction (e.g. an asset acquired on a finance lease has an impact both on tangible fixed assets and lease creditors) nor, say, to identifying the associated deferred tax consequences of an asset or liability. Where a *single* asset or liability is required to be reported as more than one line item in the statement of financial position, e.g. split accounting for a convertible loan between equity and liability elements, or a loan at off-market rates made by a parent to its subsidiary is split between investment and loan asset, it would seem appropriate, in our view, to disclose the relationship between these line items.

4.5   Non-controlling interests in consolidated financial statements

FRS 102, the Regulations and LLP Regulations address the presentation of non-controlling interest. These requirements are relevant to consolidated financial statements, prepared using statutory or 'adapted formats'.

Under FRS 102, non-controlling interest is defined as 'the equity in a subsidiary not attributable, directly or indirectly, to a parent'. *[FRS 102. Appendix I]*.

FRS 102 requires that non-controlling interest is presented in the consolidated statement of financial position within equity, separately from the equity of the owners of the parent (meaning holders of instruments classified as equity). *[FRS 102.9.20, 22.19, Appendix I]*.

The statement of changes in equity (see 7.1 below) presents: *[FRS 102.6.3]*

- total comprehensive income, showing separately the total amounts attributable to owners of the parent and non-controlling interests; and

- since non-controlling interest is a component of equity, a reconciliation of the changes in the carrying amount of non-controlling interest.

In addition, the statement of comprehensive income (or separate income statement, where presented) shows as allocations of profit or loss and total comprehensive income: *[FRS 102.9.21, 5.6, 5.7A-5.7C]*

- the profit or loss for the period attributable to the owners of the parent separately from the profit or loss attributable for the period to non-controlling interest; and

- the total comprehensive income attributable to the owners of the parent separately from the total comprehensive income attributable to non-controlling interest.

The definition of non-controlling interest (see Chapter 6 at 3.7 of EY New UK GAAP 2015) is wider than minority interest as used in previous UK GAAP and non-controlling interests in the Regulations (or LLP Regulations) which relate only to the amount of capital and reserves attributable to shares in subsidiary undertakings included in the consolidation held by or on behalf of persons other than the parent company (or LLP) and its subsidiary undertakings. *[FRS 2.35, 6 Sch 17, 3 Sch 17 (LLP)]*.

In most cases, the amounts shown as non-controlling interest under the standard and the amounts required by the Regulations will be the same. There is a theoretical possibility that the amounts required by the standard and the Regulations may differ. In such a case, two totals are strictly required to be presented to meet the requirements of both FRS 102 and the Regulations.

4.5.1   *Presentation requirements of non-controlling interests in the Regulations and LLP Regulations*

For group accounts of a parent company (except for banking or insurance groups), where SI 2015/980 is applied, paragraph 17 of Schedule 6 to the Regulations

Chapter 4

requires that the following are added to the formats in Schedule 1 to the Regulations: *[6 Sch 17]*

'(2)   In the balance sheet formats there must be shown, as a separate item and *under the heading "non-controlling interests"* [emphasis added], the amount of capital and reserves attributable to shares in subsidiary undertakings included in the consolidation held by or on behalf of persons other than the parent company and its subsidiary undertakings.

(3)   In the profit and loss account formats there must be shown, as a separate item and *under the heading "non-controlling interests"* [emphasis added], *the amount of any profit or loss* [emphasis added] attributable to shares in subsidiary undertakings included in the consolidation held by or on behalf of persons other than the parent company and its subsidiary undertakings.'

While paragraph 17 makes reference to the formats set out in Section B of Part 1 of Schedule 1 to the Regulations, in our view, this paragraph also applies to 'adapted formats' because any adaptations made need to be 'at least equivalent' to the information required in the statutory formats. *[1 Sch 1A, 6 Sch 1]*.

Where SI 2015/980 is not applied (and in the LLP Regulations, unless LLP law is subsequently changed), paragraph 17 states that: *[6 Sch 17, 25, 36, 3 Sch 17 (LLP)]*

'(2)   In the balance sheet formats there must be shown, as a separate item and *under an appropriate heading* [emphasis added], the amount of capital and reserves attributable to shares in subsidiary undertakings included in the consolidation held by or on behalf of persons other than the parent company (or parent LLP) and its subsidiary undertakings.

(3)   In the profit and loss account formats there must be shown, as a separate item and *under an appropriate heading* [emphasis added]:

(a)   *the amount of any profit or loss on ordinary activities, and*

(b)   *the amount of any profit or loss on extraordinary activities,* [emphasis added]

attributable to shares in subsidiary undertakings included in the consolidation held by or on behalf of persons other than the parent company (or parent LLP) and its subsidiary undertakings.'

In respect of LLPs, the modifications made in group accounts relate to the statutory formats in Schedule 1 to the LLP Regulations.

Schedule 6 to the Regulations (where applied to banking and insurance groups) includes the second version of paragraph 17 above but refers to the formats in Schedules 2 and 3, as applicable. However, where SI 2015/980 is applied, banking and insurance groups must use the heading 'non-controlling interests' rather than simply 'an appropriate heading'. Banking and insurance groups must therefore still show the two items in paragraph 17(3)(a) and (b) (although extraordinary activities are not expected in practice – see 6.7.6 below). *[6 Sch 25, 36]*.

The statutory requirements for presentation of non-controlling interests would permit a presentation consistent with the requirements of FRS 102. The heading for 'non-controlling interests' used in the balance sheet is treated as if it has a letter assigned, meaning that it must be included on the face of the balance sheet.

However, the heading used in the profit and loss account is treated as if it has an Arabic number assigned (allowing the adaptations permitted by 1 Sch 4, as described at 4.4 above). *[6 Sch 17(4), 3 Sch 17(4)(LLP)].* For banking and insurance groups, paragraph 17(4) is modified and the presentation requirements are more restrictive. *[6 Sch 25, 36].* FRS 102 requires, in any case, that non-controlling interest is presented on the face of the statement of financial position and as an allocation of profit (and total comprehensive income) on the face of the statement of comprehensive income (and separate income statement, if any).

4.5.2 *Illustrative examples of presentation of non-controlling interests*

Figure 4.1 below illustrates the presentation of non-controlling interests in the statement of financial position under FRS 102 (and consistent with the Regulations). The terminology 'non-controlling interests' in the Regulations (rather than 'non-controlling interest' in FRS 102) is used. See also Figure 4.3 at 5.1 below and Example 4.3 at 5.1.14 below for presentation of non-controlling interest in 'adapted formats'.

Figure 4.2 below illustrates the allocation of profit or loss to owners of the parent and to non-controlling interest where a separate income statement is presented (see 6.4 below). Where a separate income statement is presented, an allocation of total comprehensive income between owners of the parent and the non-controlling interest would also be presented at the end of the statement of total comprehensive income. *[FRS 102.5.6, 5.7B, 5.7C].* See also Example 4.5 at 6.5.2 below. Where a single statement of comprehensive income is presented (see 6.3 below), these allocations of profit or loss and of total comprehensive income would both be presented as two lines below the total comprehensive income for the period. *[FRS 102.5.7A-5.7C].* See Example 4.4 at 6.5.2 below.

Figure 4.1   Presentation of non-controlling interests in statement of financial position

	£'000
Capital and reserves	
Called up share capital	12,075
Share premium account	493
Capital redemption reserve	500
Merger reserve	6,250
Profit and loss account	27,882
Equity attributable to owners of the parent company	47,200
Non-controlling interests	360
	47,560

Figure 4.2   *Presentation of non-controlling interests in income statement (where presented separately)*

	£'000
Profit before taxation	7,786
Tax on profit	(3,339)
Profit after taxation and profit for the financial year	4,447
Profit for the financial year attributable to:	
Owners of the parent company	4,209
Non-controlling interests	238

Example 4.7 at 7.1.1 below illustrates the presentation of non-controlling interest in the statement of changes in equity.

5   STATEMENT OF FINANCIAL POSITION

The statement of financial position (referred to as the balance sheet in CA 2006) presents an entity's assets, liabilities and equity as of the end of the reporting period. *[FRS 102.4.1].*

Part 1 of Schedule 1 to the Regulations, where SI 2015/980 is applied, provides a choice of:

- two balance sheet statutory formats (as set out in Section B of that Part – see 5.2 and 5.3 below); or

- use of 'adapted' formats (see 5.1 below).

Schedule 2 (banking companies) and Schedule 3 (insurance companies) to the Regulations and the LLP Regulations (unless LLP law is subsequently changed) require use of the statutory formats and do not allow use of 'adapted formats'. This Chapter sets out the statutory formats for LLPs, but not for banking and insurance companies.

There may be changes in classification of line items used in the above formats from previous UK GAAP, whether statutory or 'adapted formats' are used. The line items in the statutory formats are not always aligned with the accounting requirements in FRS 102 (e.g. 'tangible fixed assets' in the statutory formats would include property, plant and equipment, investment properties and other items). Certain classification issues are highlighted in the commentary on the formats referenced above.

Note that 5.3 below addresses implementation issues with applying the statutory formats as well as highlighting some additional analyses of line items and disclosures required by the Regulations in the notes to the accounts. Disclosures in the Regulations (unless they derive directly from the notes to the statutory formats) also apply where 'adapted formats' are used. These disclosures are not separately noted in the discussion in 5.1 below on 'adapted formats'.

The consolidated statement of financial position of a group must be presented in accordance with the requirements of Schedule 6 to the Regulations (or, where applicable, Schedule 3 to the LLP Regulations). *[FRS 102.4.2].* See 4.1.2 above, and 5.1 and 5.2 below for discussion as to how the 'adapted formats' and statutory formats are applied in consolidated financial statements.

See 4.1 above for discussion as to which formats apply to which types of entity.

5.1 'Adapted formats'

An entity choosing to apply paragraph 1A(1) of Schedule 1 to the Regulations (permitted only where FRS 102 (amended July 2015) is adopted – see 1.2 and 2.1 above) and adapt one of the balance sheet formats shall, as a minimum, include in its statement of financial position the line items presented in Figure 4.3 below, distinguishing between those items that are current and those that are non-current (see 5.1.1 and 5.1.2 below). *[FRS 102.4.2A].* To comply with this requirement, an entity must present as separate classifications: current and non-current assets, and current and non-current liabilities. *[FRS 102.4.2D].*

FRS 102's presentation requirements for 'adapted formats' are similar to but not identical to formats included in IAS 1.

Figure 4.3   *Balance sheet (UK company other than a banking company or insurance company) – paragraph 1A(1) of Schedule 1 to the Regulations ('adapted formats') applied*

(a)	Property, plant and equipment
(b)	Investment property carried at fair value through profit and loss
(c)	Intangible assets
(d)	Financial assets (excluding amounts shown under (e), (f), (j) and (k))
(e)	Investments in associates
(f)	Investments in jointly controlled entities
(g)	Biological assets carried at cost less accumulated depreciation and impairment
(h)	Biological assets carried at fair value through profit and loss
(i)	Inventories
(j)	Trade and other receivables
(k)	Cash and cash equivalents
(l)	Trade and other payables
(m)	Provisions
(n)	Financial liabilities (excluding amounts shown under (l) and (m))
(o)	Liabilities and assets for current tax
(p)	Deferred tax liabilities and deferred tax assets (classified as non-current)
(q)	Non-controlling interest, presented within equity separately from the equity attributable to the owners of the parent
(r)	Equity attributable to the owners of the parent

An illustrative example statement of financial position is included in Example 4.3 at 5.1.14 below.

In general, few difficulties should arise over classification of line items since the required line items are aligned with the categories of assets and liabilities discussed in FRS 102. The above line items (and other implementation issues on classification) are discussed at 5.1.3 to 5.1.13 below. While line items (o) and (p) appear to combine liabilities and assets for current tax and deferred tax respectively, the assets will need to be shown separately from the liabilities.

Section 4 (unlike the Regulations and LLP Regulations) makes no adaptations to the line items required for consolidated financial statements, but line item (q) for non-controlling interest (see 4.5 above) is only relevant where consolidated financial statements are prepared.

So far as practicable, paragraphs 2 to 9A of the General Rules to the formats apply to the 'adapted format' balance sheet. *[1 Sch 1A(3)]*. A new requirement, introduced by SI 2015/980, so not relevant to LLPs (unless LLP law is subsequently changed), is that where an asset or liability relates to more than one item in the balance sheet, the relationship of such asset or liability to the relevant items must be disclosed either under those items or in the notes to the accounts. *[1 Sch 9A]*. See 4.4 above.

Section 4 requires that the following sub-classifications of the line items presented must be disclosed either in the statement of financial position or in the notes:

- property, plant and equipment in classifications appropriate to the entity;

- intangible assets and goodwill in classifications appropriate to the entity;

- investments, showing separately shares and loans;

- trade and other receivables showing separately amounts due from related parties, amounts due from other parties, prepayments and receivables arising from accrued income not yet billed;

- inventories, showing separately, amounts of inventories:

  - held for sale in the ordinary course of business;

  - in the process of production for such sale; and

  - in the form of materials or supplies to be consumed in the production process or in the rendering of services;

- trade and other payables, showing separately amounts payable to trade suppliers, payable to related parties, deferred income and accruals; and

- classes of equity, such as share capital, share premium, retained earnings, revaluation reserve, fair value reserve and other reserves. *[FRS 102.4.2B]*.

The descriptions of the line items in the statement of financial position used in paragraph 4.2A (listed in Figure 4.3 above) and of the sub-classifications of line items set out in paragraph 4.2B; and the ordering of items or aggregation of similar line items, may be amended according to the nature of the entity and its transactions, to provide information that is relevant to an understanding of the entity's financial position, providing the information given is at least equivalent to that required by the balance sheet format had it not been adapted. *[FRS 102.4.2C]*. The effect of paragraph 4.2C is to clarify that there is flexibility in the presentation requirements where 'adapted formats' are used (for statutory formats, the General Rules to the formats clearly set out the flexibility for Arabic numbered items, but Arabic numbered items are not used in the 'adapted formats').

An entity must present additional line items, headings and subtotals in the statement of financial position when such presentation is relevant to an understanding of the entity's financial position. *[FRS 102.4.3]*. Judgement is, therefore, needed in determining whether additional items should be presented, where material and relevant. IAS 1, which has a similar requirement, states that this judgement is based on an assessment of the nature and liquidity of assets, the function of assets within the entity, and the amounts, nature and timing of liabilities. *[IAS 1.58]*. IAS 1 further notes that use of different measurement bases (such as cost or revaluation) for different classes of assets suggests that their nature or function differs. *[IAS 1.59]*. The statement of financial position in the 'adapted formats' already shows line items for investment property and biological assets by measurement basis. An FRS 102 reporter may find IAS 1's guidance helpful but is not required to follow this; the principle is to focus on whether additional analysis is relevant to an understanding of the entity's financial position. Any amendments would need to comply with, so far as practicable, the requirements of the General Rules to the formats governing modifications of the formats (see 4.4 above).

Where 'adapted formats' are used, there is no requirement to disclose debtors: amounts falling due after more than one year or to classify creditors: amounts falling due within or after more than one year. *[FRS 102.4.4A, 4.7]*.

FRS 102, unlike IAS 1, does not require disclosure of the amount expected to be recovered or settled after more than twelve months, for each asset and liability line that combines amounts expected to be recovered or settled (a) no more than twelve months after the reporting period and (b) more than twelve months after the reporting period. *[IAS 1.61]*.

Other analyses of line items are specified by other sections of FRS 102 (refer to the relevant chapters of EY New UK GAAP 2015) or by the Regulations. Note that 5.1 and 6.5 below do not set out these disclosures, although some of the latter are highlighted at 5.2, 5.3 and 6.6 below in respect of the statutory formats. The additional disclosures required by other sections of the standard will generally be more straightforward than where the statutory formats are applied, since the line items in the 'adapted formats' are aligned with FRS 102.

The Regulations require supplementary information to be given in the notes to the accounts and these disclosures apply where statutory formats or the 'adapted formats' are used. One complexity is that the information required by the Regulations is generally in respect of headings required in the statutory formats, which may differ to the line items identified where the 'adapted formats' are used. For example, the 'adapted formats' do not refer to fixed assets, creditors: amounts falling due within one year, creditors: amounts falling due after more than one year, investments, land or buildings, or turnover. A UK company using 'adapted formats' in Companies Act accounts will, therefore, need to identify which of its assets, liabilities, revenue streams needs to be included in the required disclosures. In particular, 'adapted formats' require a classification of non-current assets and current assets which differs to the fixed assets and current assets classification required in statutory formats. For the purposes of the disclosures in the Regulations, the statutory definition of 'fixed assets' (see 5.2.2 below) is relevant.

In addition, the Regulations frequently require analyses and reconciliations to be given for Arabic-numbered sub-headings in the balance sheet statutory formats. As noted above, 'adapted formats' require various sub-classifications to be presented in the statement of financial position or notes to the financial statements. In our view, where the disclosures refer to 'in respect of each item which is or would be but for paragraph 4(2)(b) be shown' under a particular heading, it may be appropriate to give the information, for example, fixed asset reconciliations, for each of the relevant sub-classifications identified. This is because these sub-classifications in effect stand in place of the Arabic-numbered headings identified in the statutory formats. There is overlap with the reconciliations of the carrying amounts of certain assets required by FRS 102 but the Regulations require separate fixed asset reconciliations for cost and cumulative provision for depreciation and diminution. See 5.2.2 below.

5.1.1   *Definitions of current and non-current assets ('adapted formats' only)*

FRS 102 defines non-current assets, with current assets being 'assets of the entity which are not non-current assets' (i.e. the residual). *[FRS 102.Appendix I]*. This is different to IAS 1 which defines current assets with non-current assets as the residual, although the classification is aligned.

Non-current assets are defined as: 'Assets of the entity which:

(a)   it does not expect to realise, or intend to sell or consume, in its normal operating cycle (see 5.1.1.A below);

(b)   it does not hold primarily for the purpose of trading (see 5.1.1.B below);

(c)   it does not expect to realise within 12 months after the reporting period; or

(d)   are cash or cash equivalents restricted from being exchanged or used to settle a liability for at least 12 months after the reporting period'. *[FRS 102.Appendix I]*.

'Cash or cash equivalents' are defined in Appendix I of FRS 102 and should be interpreted in a manner consistent with Section 7 of the standard (see Chapter 5 at 3.3 of EY New UK GAAP 2015).

Meeting any one of (a) to (d) leads to the asset being required to be classified as non-current.

FRS 102 provides no additional guidance beyond the definition above. However, since the intention is to provide a format more aligned with IAS 1, management may consider, as permitted by the hierarchy in Section 10, the requirements of IAS 1 for further guidance. The guidance presented at 5.1.1.A to E below refers to IAS 1's requirements, where appropriate.

The current portion of non-current financial assets would be classified as current, consistent with IFRS. *[IAS 1.68]*.

5.1.1.A   *Operating cycle*

Item (a) of the definition of non-current assets above distinguishes between current and non-current based on the length of the normal operating cycle. The concept of 'operating cycle' is not further explained in FRS 102 but IAS 1 states that 'the operating cycle of an entity is the time between the acquisition of assets for processing and their realisation in cash or cash equivalents. When the entity's normal operating cycle is not clearly identifiable, it is assumed to be twelve months.' *[IAS 1.68]*.

IAS 1 further explains that when an entity supplies goods or services within a clearly identifiable operating cycle, separate classification of current and non-current assets and liabilities on the face of the statement of financial position provides useful information by distinguishing the net assets that are continuously circulating as working capital from those used in long-term operations. It also highlights assets that are expected to be realised within the current operating cycle, and liabilities that are due for settlement within the same period. *[IAS 1.62]*.

Current assets, therefore, include assets (such as inventories and trade receivables) that are sold, consumed or realised as part of the normal operating cycle even when they are not expected to be realised within twelve months after the reporting period. *[IAS 1.68]*.

5.1.1.B   Held for the purpose of trading

Current assets include assets held primarily for the purpose of trading, for example, some financial assets classified as trading in accordance with IAS 39 – *Financial Instruments: Recognition and Measurement* – or IFRS 9 – *Financial Instruments*, where these standards are applied to the recognition and measurement of financial instruments.

However, consistent with IFRS practice, a classification as 'held for trading' (e.g. as required for a derivative, that is not hedge accounted) does not necessarily mean the financial asset is 'held for the purpose of trading' for the purposes of current-non-current classification.

5.1.1.C   Assets previously classified as non-current but subsequently held for sale

FRS 102 does not include the concept in IFRS of non-current assets and disposal groups held for sale, and the 'adapted formats', therefore, do not require separate presentation for such items.

FRS 102 does not address whether items such as property, plant and equipment should be reclassified as current if expected to be realised within twelve months after the reporting period. In our view, an entity should generally continue to classify property, plant and equipment intended to be disposed of as non-current unless it is expected to be realised within 12 months after the reporting period (in which case it must be classified as current).

However, an entity that, in the course of its ordinary activities, routinely sells items of property, plant and equipment that it has held for rental to others, should transfer such assets to inventory when they cease to be rented and become held for sale, consistent with IFRS's requirements. *[IAS 16.68A]*. See Chapter 13 at 3.7.1 of EY New UK GAAP 2015. The inventory should then be classified as current or non-current in accordance with the definitions at 5.1.1, with particular reference to part (a) of the definition of non-current asset.

5.1.1.D   Deferred tax

FRS 102 specifies that deferred tax assets are classified as non-current. *[FRS 102.4.2A(p)]*.

5.1.1.E   Post-employment benefits

The question arises as to whether the current/non-current analysis needs to be made for defined benefit plan balances. IAS 19 – *Employee Benefits* – does not specify whether such a split should be made, on the grounds that it may sometimes be arbitrary. *[IAS 19.133, BC200]*.

No similar statement is included in FRS 102, but where the same concern over the arbitrary nature of a split arises, in our view, FRS 102 reporters are able to follow the practice of some IFRS reporters and report such balances as non-current.

5.1.2   *Definitions of current liabilities and non-current liabilities ('adapted formats' only)*

FRS 102, consistent with IFRS defines current liabilities, with non-current liabilities being 'liabilities of the entity which are not current liabilities' (i.e. the residual). *[FRS 102.Appendix I]*.

Current liabilities are defined as:

'Liabilities of the entity which

(a)   it expects to settle in its normal operating cycle (see 5.1.2.A below);

(b)   it holds primarily for the purpose of trading (see 5.1.2.B below);

(c)   are due to be settled within 12 months after the reporting period (see 5.1.2.C below); or

(d)   it does not have an unconditional right to defer settlement for at least 12 months after the reporting period (see 5.1.2.D below).'

Meeting any one of (a) to (d) leads to the liability being required to be classified as current.

5.1.2.A   *Operating cycle*

The concept of 'operating cycle' is explained at 5.1.1.A above.

IAS 1 explains that some current liabilities, such as trade payables and some accruals for employee and other operating costs, are part of the working capital used in the normal operating cycle, and are classified as current liabilities even if they are due to be settled more than twelve months after the reporting period. The same normal operating cycle applies to the classification of an entity's assets and liabilities and when not clearly identifiable, is assumed to be twelve months. *[IAS 1.70]*.

5.1.2.B   *Held for the purpose of trading*

Current liabilities include assets held primarily for the purpose of trading, for example, some financial liabilities classified as trading in accordance with IAS 39 or IFRS 9.

However, consistent with IFRS practice, a classification as 'held for trading' (e.g. as required for a derivative, that is not hedge accounted) does not necessarily mean the financial liability is 'held for the purpose of trading' for the purposes of current/non-current classification.

5.1.2.C   *Due for settlement within 12 months*

Some current liabilities are not settled as part of the normal operating cycle but are due for settlement within twelve months after the end of the reporting period.

Examples given by IAS 1 include bank overdrafts, the current portion of non-current financial liabilities, dividend payable, income taxes and other non-trade payables.

Financial liabilities that provide financing on a long-term basis (i.e. are not part of the working capital used in the entity's normal operating cycle) and are not due for settlement within twelve months after the end of the reporting period are non-current liabilities. *[IAS 1.71]*. Refer also to the guidance at 5.1.2.D below as there must be an unconditional right to defer settlement for at least twelve months thereafter, as at the end of the reporting date, in order for a liability to be reported as non-current.

5.1.2.D   No unconditional right to defer settlement

The assessment of a liability as current or non-current is applied strictly. IAS 1 provides further guidance on this part of the current liability definition.

The key point is that the entity has *at the end of the reporting period* an unconditional right to defer its settlement for at least twelve months thereafter. Consequently, a liability is classified as current when:

- it is due to be settled within twelve months after the end of the reporting period even if the original term was for a period longer than twelve months and an agreement to refinance or reschedule payments, on a long-term basis is completed after the reporting period and before the financial statements are authorised for issue; *[IAS 1.72, 76]*

- an entity breaches a covenant or other provision of a long-term loan arrangement on or before the end of the reporting period, with the effect that the liability becomes payable on demand (even if the lender agreed, after the reporting period and before the authorisation of the financial statements for issue, not to demand payment as a consequence of the breach); *[IAS 1.74, 76]*

   However, the liability would be classified as non-current if the lender agreed by the reporting period to provide a period of grace ending at least twelve months after the reporting period, within which the entity can rectify the breach and during which the lender cannot demand immediate repayment. *[IAS 1.75]*.

Accordingly, as explained by IAS 1, liabilities would be non-current if an entity expects and has the discretion to refinance or roll over an obligation for at least twelve months after the period end under an existing loan facility, even if it would otherwise be due within a shorter period. However, when refinancing or rolling over the obligation is not at the discretion of the entity the obligation is classified as current. *[IAS 1.73]*.

Section 11 – *Basic Financial Instruments* – requires specific disclosures where there is a breach of terms or other default in respect of a loan payable recognised at the end of the reporting period (see Chapter 8 at 8.1 of EY New UK GAAP 2015). A qualifying entity that is not a financial institution preparing individual financial statements is exempt from this disclosure (under the reduced disclosure framework), providing that the equivalent disclosures required by the standard are given in the publicly available consolidated financial statements of the group in which the qualifying entity is consolidated. *[FRS 102.1.8, 12(c), 11.47]*.

Conditions of breach or default at the end of the reporting period may, however, be material for disclosure in the financial statements (even if no specific disclosure applies) and relevant to the going concern assessment and related disclosures (see 9.3 below). A breach arising after the end of the reporting period, while not one of the examples specifically listed in Section 32 – *Events after the End of the Reporting Period*, may be a material post-balance sheet event requiring disclosure (see Chapter 27 at 3.5.2 of EY New UK GAAP 2015), *[FRS 102.32.10]*, and may also be relevant to the going concern assessment and related disclosures. These comments on disclosure are equally relevant where statutory formats are applied.

Example 4.2 below illustrates the operation of the above requirements.

Example 4.2:   Determining whether liabilities should be presented as current or non-current

Scenario 1

An entity has a long-term loan arrangement containing a debt covenant. The specific requirements in the debt covenant have to be met as at 31 December every year. The loan is due in more than 12 months. The entity breaches the debt covenant at or before the period end. As a result, the loan becomes payable on demand.

Scenario 2

Same as scenario 1, but the loan arrangement stipulates that the entity has a grace period of 3 months to rectify the breach and during which the lender cannot demand immediate repayment.

Scenario 3

Same as scenario 1, but the lender agreed not to demand repayment as a consequence of the breach. The entity obtains this waiver:

(a)   at or before the period end and the waiver is for a period of more than 12 months after the period end;

(b)   at or before the period end and the waiver is for a period of less than 12 months after the period end;

(c)   after the period end but before the financial statements are authorised for issue.

Scenario 4

An entity has a long-term loan arrangement containing a debt covenant. The loan is due in more than 12 months. At the period end, the debt covenants are met. However, circumstances change unexpectedly and the entity breaches the debt covenant after the period end but before the financial statements are authorised for issue.

As discussed at Chapter 8 at 8, Section 11 (subject to any exemption taken under the reduced disclosure framework in individual accounts of a qualifying entity) requires the following disclosures for any loans payable recognised at the reporting date, for which there is a breach of terms or default of principal, interest, sinking fund, or redemption terms that has not been remedied by the reporting date:

•   details of that breach or default;

•   the carrying amount of the related loans payable at the reporting date; and

•   whether the breach or default was remedied, or the terms of the loans payable were renegotiated, before the financial statements were authorised for issue. *[FRS 102.1.8, 1.12(c), 11.47]*.

The table below sets out whether debt is to be presented as current or non-current and whether the above disclosures are required.

	Scenario 1	Scenario 2	Scenario 3(a)	Scenario 3(b)	Scenario 3(c)	Scenario 4
At the period end, does the entity have an unconditional right to defer the settlement of the liability for at least 12 months?	no	no	yes	no	no	yes
Classification of the liability	current	current	non-current	current	current	non-current
Are the above Section 11 disclosures required?	yes	yes	no	yes	yes	no

5.1.2.E   Deferred tax

FRS 102 specifies that deferred tax liabilities are classified as non-current. *[FRS 102.4.2A(p)]*.

5.1.2.F   Post-employment benefits

Refer to the discussion at 5.1.1.E above. In our view, where the same concern over the arbitrary nature of a split arises, FRS 102 reporters are able to follow the practice of some IFRS reporters and report such balances as non-current.

5.1.3   Property, plant and equipment

FRS 102 defines 'property, plant and equipment' as tangible assets that:

- are held for use in the production or supply of goods or services, for rental to others, or for administrative purposes; and
- are expected to be used during more than one period. *[FRS 102.Appendix I]*.

Specific types of assets that may be recorded as property, plant and equipment in certain circumstances are discussed below. However, the classification may differ from that under previous UK GAAP. Chapter 13 at 3.3.1.E and 3.3.1.F of EY New UK GAAP 2015 also addresses other less common classification issues including the classification of items as inventory or property, plant and equipment where minimum levels are maintained and the production stripping costs of mines.

Where 'adapted formats' are used, FRS 102 requires that sub-classifications of property, plant and equipment that are appropriate to the entity are presented, either on the face of the statement of financial position or in the notes. *[FRS 102.4.2B(a)]*.

5.1.3.A   Heritage assets

FRS 102 sets out separate requirements for heritage assets, being tangible and intangible assets with historic, artistic, scientific, technological, geophysical or environmental qualities that are held and maintained principally for their contribution to knowledge and culture (see Chapter 29 at 5 of EY New UK GAAP 2015). *[FRS 102.Appendix I]*. Therefore, heritage assets can in principle be tangible or intangible assets; whereas under previous UK GAAP, heritage assets were defined as tangible fixed assets. *[FRS 30.2, 18]*.

5.1.3.B   *Exploration and evaluation of mineral resources*

IFRS 6 – *Exploration for and Evaluation of Mineral Resources*, which is applied by FRS 102 reporters operating in the exploration for and/or evaluation of mineral resources, *[FRS 102.34.11]*, requires entities within its scope to classify exploration and evaluation assets as either intangible or tangible assets in accordance with the nature of the assets acquired and apply the classification consistently. *[IFRS 6.15]*.

For example, drilling rights should be presented as intangible assets, whereas vehicles and drilling rigs are tangible assets. A tangible asset that is used in developing an intangible asset should still be presented as a tangible asset. However, 'to the extent that a tangible asset is consumed in developing an intangible asset, the amount reflecting that consumption is part of the cost of the intangible asset'. Therefore, the depreciation of a portable drilling rig would be capitalised as part of the intangible exploration and evaluation asset that represents the costs incurred on active exploration projects. *[IFRS 6.16, BC33]*. See Chapter 29 at 3 of EY New UK GAAP 2015.

5.1.3.C   *Service concession arrangements*

FRS 102 distinguishes two principal categories of service concession arrangements: a financial asset model and an intangible asset model. Sometimes, a service concession arrangement may contain both types *[FRS 102.34.13-15]* (see Chapter 29 at 4 of EY New UK GAAP 2015).

However, Section 35 – *Transition to this FRS* – permits first-time adopters (that are operators of service concession arrangements) to continue to use the same accounting policies as applied at the date of transition for service concession arrangements entered into before the date of transition (see Chapter 30 at 5.10 of EY New UK GAAP 2015). *[FRS 102.35.10(i)]*. FRS 5 Application Note F – *Private Finance Initiative and Similar Contracts* – distinguishes between arrangements where the property was the asset of the operator (and a tangible fixed asset was recognised) and where the property was the asset of the grantor/purchaser (and a financial asset/debtor was recognised by the operator). Where the transition exemption is taken, the previous UK GAAP classification would continue to be used.

5.1.3.D   *Software development costs*

Previous UK GAAP specifically addresses the classification of software development costs, *[FRS 10.2]*, and website development costs. *[UITF 27]*. The definition of an intangible asset within Section 18 of FRS 102 requires that it lacks physical substance. However, intangible assets can be contained in or on a physical medium such as a compact disc (in the case of computer software), legal documentation (in the case of a licence or patent) or film, requiring an entity to exercise judgement in determining whether to apply Section 17 or Section 18 of the standard. FRS 102, unlike IAS 38 – *Intangible Assets*, which has the same definition of an intangible asset, provides no further guidance. See Chapter 14 at 3.2.2 and 4.1 and Chapter 13 at 3.3.1.D of EY New UK GAAP 2015 for discussion of the classification of such costs. There is potential for reclassification of such costs under FRS 102.

5.1.3.E   Spare parts

Major spare parts and stand-by equipment are property, plant and equipment if expected to be used during more than one period. Similarly, if the spare parts can be used only in connection with an item of property, plant and equipment, they are considered property, plant and equipment. *[FRS 102.17.5]*. See Chapter 13 at 3.3.1.A.

5.1.4   Investment property

There are a number of differences between the definition of investment property under previous UK GAAP and under FRS 102; consequently, classification differences in respect of investment property may arise on transition to FRS 102. See Chapter 12 at 2.1 and 3.1 of EY New UK GAAP 2015.

Only investment property at fair value through profit and loss is required to be presented as a separate line item on the face of the statement of financial position in 'adapted formats' (see Figure 4.3 at 5.1 above). *[FRS 102.4.2A(b)]*. It is not clear whether the standard intends that investment property accounted for using the cost model (in Section 17 – *Property, Plant and Equipment*) is subsumed within the line item for property, plant and equipment or not. However, since investment property accounted for using the cost model does not strictly fall within FRS 102's definition of property, plant and equipment and has a different function, in our view, it may be appropriate, where material, to include additional line items or headings in the statement of financial position to distinguish investment property accounted for at cost. *[FRS 102.4.3]*.

5.1.5   Intangible assets

FRS 102's definition of an intangible asset (and differences to previous UK GAAP) are discussed in detail at Chapter 14 at 2.1 and 3.2 of EY New UK GAAP 2015. Specific types of assets that may be recorded as intangible assets in certain circumstances are discussed at 5.1.3.A-D above.

Where 'adapted formats' are used, FRS 102 requires that sub-classifications of intangible assets and goodwill appropriate to the entity are presented, either on the face of the statement of financial position or in the notes. *[FRS 102.4.2B(b)]*.

5.1.5.A   Goodwill and negative goodwill

FRS 102 does not specify that positive goodwill is shown as a separate line item on the face of the statement of financial position or in the notes. Goodwill does not strictly fall within the definition of an intangible asset since it is not identifiable; therefore, we would expect that entities disclose positive goodwill, if material, separately on the face of the statement of financial position. *[FRS 102.4.3]*.

Where the acquirer's interest in the net amount of the identifiable assets, liabilities and provisions for contingent liabilities recognised exceeds the cost of the business combination, FRS 102, consistent with previous UK GAAP, requires that the resulting excess (i.e. 'negative goodwill') is separately disclosed on the face of the statement of financial position, immediately below positive goodwill, and followed by a subtotal of the net amount of the positive goodwill and the excess. *[FRS 102.19.24(b), FRS 10.48]*. See Chapter 15 at 3.8.3 of EY New UK GAAP 2015.

Chapter 4

5.1.6   *Financial assets and financial liabilities*

FRS 102 requires the following line items to be presented on the face of the statement of financial position (see Figure 4.3 at 5.1 above):

(d)   financial assets (excluding items shown under (e), (f), (j) and (k)) (see Chapter 8 of EY New UK GAAP 2015);

(e)   investments in associates (see Chapter 10 of EY New UK GAAP 2015);

(f)   investments in jointly controlled entities (see Chapter 11 of EY New UK GAAP 2015);

(j)   trade and other receivables;

(k)   cash and cash equivalents (see Chapter 5 of EY New UK GAAP 2015);

(l)   trade and other payables; and

(n)   financial liabilities (excluding items shown under (l) and (m)) (see Chapter 8 of EY New UK GAAP 2015).

'Cash or cash equivalents' are defined in FRS 102 Appendix I and should be interpreted in a manner consistent with Section 7 of the standard (see Chapter 5 at 3.3 of EY New UK GAAP 2015).

FRS 102 requires that investments in associates and investments in jointly controlled entities are presented as separate line items in both individual and consolidated financial statements. Unlike IAS 1, 'investments in associates and jointly controlled entities accounted using the equity method' (only permitted in FRS 102 consolidated financial statements) are not required to be separately presented, although the 'share of the profit or loss of investments in associates and jointly controlled entities accounted for using the equity method' is a separate line item in the income statement or profit and loss section of the statement of comprehensive income (see 6.5 below). *[FRS 102.5.5B(c), 5.7A]*.

However, FRS 102 requires additional line items, headings and sub-headings (where material) to be presented in the statement of financial position, where relevant to an understanding of the financial position. *[FRS 102.4.3]*. This might be the case, for example, in consolidated financial statements where investments in associates and investments in jointly controlled entities are held as part of an investment portfolio at fair value through profit and loss. *[FRS 102.14.4A-B, 15.9A-B]*. See Chapter 10 at 3.3.1.B and Chapter 11 at 3.6.3.B of EY New UK GAAP 2015.

Where 'adapted formats' are used, FRS 102 requires that further sub-classifications are presented, either on the face of the statement of financial position or in the notes, for: *[FRS 102.4.2B(c), (d), (f)]*

(a)   investments, showing separately shares and loans;

(b)   trade and other receivables, showing separately amounts due from related parties (same definition as for Section 33 – see Chapter 28 at 3.1 of EY New UK GAAP 2015 and Chapter 5 at 12), amounts due from other parties, prepayments and receivables arising from accrued income not billed; and

(c)   trade and other payables, showing separately amounts payable to trade suppliers, payable to related parties, deferred income and accruals.

FRS 102 does not define 'investment'. Nevertheless, (a) above requires the reporting entity to disclose financial assets constituting investments, distinguishing between shares and loans. Where loans are involved, this is likely to require judgement as to whether the loan is in the nature of an investment or is an 'other receivable' (see 5.3.4.A below).

The sub-classifications at (b) and (c) are similar to but not the same as the line items required where the statutory formats are applied. See 5.1.13.B below for discussion of the classification of contract assets and liabilities. FRS 102 further requires the carrying amounts at the reporting date of the following categories of financial assets and financial liabilities, in total, to be disclosed either in the statement of financial position or in the notes:

- financial assets measured at fair value through profit or loss;

- financial assets that are debt instruments measured at amortised cost;

- financial assets that are equity instruments measured at cost less impairment;

- financial liabilities measured at fair value through profit or loss (showing financial liabilities that are not held as part of a trading portfolio and are not derivatives separately);

- financial liabilities measured at amortised cost; and

- loan commitments measured at cost less impairment. *[FRS 102.11.41].*

This analysis only applies to financial assets and liabilities that are in scope of Sections 11 or 12, or IAS 39 or IFRS 9, where applied to the recognition and measurement of financial instruments. *[FRS 102.11.2, 11.7, 12.2, 12.3-12.5].* See Chapter 8 at 8 of EY New UK GAAP 2015. The above disclosures (with the exception of those relating to measurement at fair value through profit and loss) are not required in individual financial statements of a qualifying entity that is not a financial institution, providing that the equivalent disclosures required by the standard are given in the publicly available consolidated financial statements of the group in which the qualifying entity is consolidated. *[FRS 102.1.8, 1.12(c)].*

5.1.7 Biological assets

FRS 102 defines a biological asset as 'a living animal or plant'. *[FRS 102.Appendix I].* Section 34 – *Specialised Activities* – provides an accounting policy choice, for each class of biological asset (and its related agricultural produce), to apply the fair value model or cost model (see Chapter 29 at 2 of EY New UK GAAP 2015).

Where 'adapted formats' are applied, an entity must present separately on the face of the statement of financial position:

- biological assets carried at cost less accumulated depreciation and impairment; and

- biological assets carried at fair value through profit and loss. *[FRS 102.4.2A(g), (h)].*

5.1.8 Inventories

Where 'adapted formats' are used, FRS 102 requires that inventories are shown on the face of the statement of financial position. *[FRS 102.102.4.2A(i)].* An analysis of inventories, sub-classified between (a) to (c) below, is presented either on the face of the statement of financial position or in the notes. *[FRS 102.4.2B(e)]*.

FRS 102 defines inventories as assets: *[FRS 102.Appendix I, FRS 102.13.1]*

(a)   held for sale in the ordinary course of business; or

(b)   in the process of production for such sale; or

(c)   in the form of materials or supplies to be consumed in the production process or in the rendering of services.

See Chapter 9 at 3.2 of EY New UK GAAP 2015 which addresses scope issues relevant to classification of inventories such as:

•   classification of core inventories as property, plant and equipment or inventories;

•   classification of broadcast rights as intangible assets or inventory;

•   spare parts and servicing equipment (see below); and

•   real estate inventory held for short term sale.

Inventories also include 'inventories held for distribution at no or nominal consideration' which could include advertising and promotional material (e.g. brochures not despatched) as well as items distributed to beneficiaries by public benefit entities (e.g. charities). *[FRS 102.13.4A, 18.8C(d), A4.36]*. See Chapter 9 at 3.3.11 of EY New UK GAAP 2015.

Inventories also include agricultural produce harvested from biological assets (e.g. grapes, milk or felled trees – see Chapter 9 at 3.3.12 and Chapter 29 at 2.2.1 of EY New UK GAAP 2015) and work in progress arising under construction contracts, including directly related service contracts (see 5.1.13.B below). *[FRS 102.13.2]*.

Spare parts and servicing equipment are usually carried as inventory and recognised in profit or loss as consumed. 5.1.3.E above explains in what circumstances these qualify as property, plant and equipment. *[FRS 102.17.5]*.

Sometimes assets not categorised as inventories are later transferred to inventories. An example is a property previously held as an investment property, which is transferred to inventory because it is reclassified as property under development with a view to sale. While FRS 102 is not as explicit as IFRSs, properties under development with a view to sale would fall within its definition of inventories. *[FRS 102.16.9, 16.10(e)(iv), IAS 40.57(d)]*. Another example is where a car rental company acquires vehicles with the intention of holding them as rental cars for a limited period and then selling them. Chapter 13 at 3.7.1 of EY New UK GAAP 2015 addresses the accounting for such transfer, based on the requirements of IFRS, i.e. when such items become held for sale rather than rental, they are transferred to inventory at their carrying amount when they cease to be rented. Subsequent sale of inventory is presented gross (i.e. revenue and cost of sales). *[IAS 16.68A]*.

5.1.9   Provisions

A provision is defined as a liability of uncertain timing or amount. *[FRS 102 Appendix I]*. See Chapter 17 at 3 of EY New UK GAAP 2015.

Provisions that are current and non-current will need to be reported as separate classifications in 'adapted formats' (unlike for balance sheet statutory formats, where there is a single line item for provisions for liabilities).

5.1.10   Current tax

Current tax assets and current tax liabilities must be shown as separate line items on the face of the statement of financial position, classified as appropriate as current and / or non-current. FRS 102 includes rules on offset of current tax asset and liabilities (see Chapter 24 at 10.1.1 of EY New UK GAAP 2015). *[FRS 102.29.24]*.

FRS 102 defines current tax as the amount of income tax payable (refundable) in respect of the taxable profit (tax loss) for the current period or past reporting periods. *[FRS 102.29.2, Appendix I]*. See Chapter 24 at 3 of EY New UK GAAP 2015 for discussion of what is 'income tax' under FRS 102 which is relevant to classification.

5.1.11   Deferred tax

Deferred tax assets and liabilities must be shown as separate line items on the face of the statement of financial position, but classified as non-current. *[FRS 102.4.2A]*. FRS 102 includes rules on offset of deferred tax asset and liabilities (see Chapter 24 at 10.1.1 of EY New UK GAAP 2015). *[FRS 102.29.24A]*.

Section 29 – *Income Tax* – requires deferred tax liabilities to be presented within provisions for liabilities and deferred tax assets to be presented within debtors. There is no requirement to present deferred tax separately on the face of the statement of financial position. *[FRS 102.29.23]*. This requirement was included in FRS 102 before 'adapted formats' were available for use under the Regulations and the standard. While the requirement has not been modified following the introduction of the 'adapted formats', it is inconsistent with the requirements for the 'adapted formats'. This appears to be an oversight and, in our view, paragraph 29.23 should be ignored where 'adapted formats' are used.

Certain of the statutory disclosures in the Regulations may cause particular complexity because under the statutory formats, deferred tax is included as a line item within provisions. In particular, UK companies preparing Companies Act accounts must state the provision for deferred tax separately from any other tax provisions and reconcile movements in deferred tax (as it is a line item under provisions). *[1 Sch 59-60]*. See 5.3.11 and 5.3.13.B below. In our view, this disclosure is required where 'adapted formats' (as well as statutory formats) are used, even though deferred tax is not shown as a provision in the balance sheet.

5.1.12   Equity

Equity attributable to owners of the parent, and to non-controlling interest (see 4.5 above) must be presented as separate line items within equity.

Where 'adapted formats' are used, separate sub-classifications for classes of equity such as: share capital, share premium, retained earnings, revaluation reserve, fair value reserve and other reserves are required, either on the face of the statement of financial position or in the notes. *[FRS 102.4.2B(g)]*. This list mirrors the classes of equity that are required to be shown on the face of the balance sheet (or in respect of the fair value reserve, may be presented in the notes) where the statutory formats are applied. See 5.3.12 below for further explanation of these reserves.

The amount of the revaluation reserve must be shown in the balance sheet under a separate sub-heading in the position given for the item 'revaluation reserve' under 'Capital and reserves' of the balance sheet formats. *[1 Sch 35(2)]*. While the 'adapted formats' do not include the headings set out for the statutory balance sheet in Section B of Part 1 to Schedule 1 to the Regulations (see 5.2 below), in our view, this requirement means that the revaluation reserve should be presented on the face of the statement of financial position.

In addition, where there are transfers to or from any reserves, a UK company preparing Companies Act accounts must disclose, in the notes to the accounts, a reconciliation of the aggregate of the reserves included in each item shown in the balance sheet (or would be so shown, if Arabic-numbered line items were not combined as permitted by paragraph 4(2)(b) of the General Rules to the formats). *[1 Sch 59(1)-(2)]*.

This disclosure requirement is relevant to both statutory formats and 'adapted formats' and has some similarities to FRS 102's statement of changes in equity. In our view, it would be appropriate to present the analysis of movements in reserves for the sub-classifications of classes of equity identified above. Both requirements are discussed further at 7 below.

5.1.13   *Other implementation issues*

5.1.13.A   *Lease premiums*

It was common under previous UK GAAP for lease premiums paid upfront to be classified as a tangible fixed asset. Under IFRSs, premiums relating to an operating lease over land and/or buildings are classified as a prepayment (albeit there may be a non-current element). Such payments would not be classified as property, plant and equipment under IFRSs. The definitions of property, plant and equipment in FRS 102 (and IFRSs) are similar and, consequently, in our view, it would be appropriate to report an upfront operating lease premium as a prepayment under FRS 102, classified as appropriate as current or non-current.

5.1.13.B   *Construction contracts*

The percentage of completion method is applied to construction contracts and revenue from rendering services. *[FRS 102.23.21]*. See Chapter 18 at 3.12 to 3.21 of EY New UK GAAP 2015 for further discussion of construction contracts. The presentation of construction contracts under FRS 102 may differ significantly from that for long-term contracts under previous UK GAAP. *[SSAP 9.30]*.

FRS 102 requires that, for construction contracts, an entity shall present the gross amount due from customers for contract work as an asset, and the gross amount due to customers for contract work as a liability. *[FRS 102.23.32]*.

IAS 11 – *Construction Contracts* – has a similar presentation requirement, which may provide additional clarification:

- the gross amount due from customers for contract work as an asset is the net amount of:

(a)   costs incurred plus recognised profits; less

(b)   the sum of recognised losses and progress billings

for all contracts in progress for which costs incurred plus recognised profits (less recognised losses) exceeds progress billings; and

- the gross amount due to customers for contract work as a liability is the net amount of:

(a)   costs incurred plus recognised profits; less

(b)   the sum of recognised losses and progress billings

for all contracts in progress for which progress billings exceed costs incurred plus recognised profits (less recognised losses). *[IAS 11.42-44].*

See Chapter 18 at 2.2.5 and 4.8 of EY New UK GAAP 2015.

While FRS 102 implies that a single contract asset (being the aggregate of contracts in an asset position) and/or a single contract liability (being the aggregate of contracts in a liability position) should be presented (rather than disaggregated across several lines), there is no requirement to present these on the face of the statement of financial position. This is left to the judgement of the reporting entity, but FRS 102 requires additional line items, headings and subtotals when relevant to an understanding of the entity's financial position. *[FRS 102.4.3].*

Where 'adapted formats' are used, certain sub-classifications of trade and other receivables and trade and other payables must be presented, either on the face of the statement of financial position or in the notes (see 5.1.6 above). This would also apply to contract assets and contract liabilities presented within these line items on the face of the statement of financial position. Contract assets and liabilities are akin to accrued income not billed and deferred income, but may warrant separate presentation. Where material prepayments, inventory or advance payment creditors have been included in the contract balances (see discussion below), we consider that it may be appropriate to distinguish these amounts. In addition, it would be appropriate to show separately contract balances with related parties and others.

Where it is probable that the total contract costs will exceed total contract revenue, FRS 102 requires immediate recognition of the expected loss *and a corresponding provision for an onerous contract (and cross refers to Section 21 – Provisions and Contingencies)* [emphasis added]. *[FRS 102.23.26].* The italicised words are not included in IAS 11. While these additional words could imply that the provision element of the overall contract liability is to be presented within provisions, we consider it more likely that the standard is intending a single contract asset and liability to be presented (as would be required by IAS 11). However, we would expect that full disclosures for provisions in accordance with Section 21 (and in Companies Act accounts, the Regulations) are provided, regardless of the presentation adopted.

Where the stage of completion is determined by reference to contract costs incurred for work performed to date as a proportion of estimated total costs, costs relating to future activity, such as for materials or prepayments, are excluded. *[FRS 102.23.22(a)].* Such costs are, however, recognised as an asset, where it is probable that the costs will be recovered. *[FRS 102.23.23]*. FRS 102 does not address the classification of such assets, e.g. whether part of the contract asset or liability, or as separate inventory or prepayments.

FRS 102 does not distinguish between the presentation of advances and progress billings (i.e. whether the contract asset or liability is determined after *all* payments on account – including advances – or only after progress billings) but in the Illustrative Examples to IAS 11, advances are not included in the determination of the contract asset or liability but are shown separately.

Progress billings not yet received (including any contract retentions) would be included in trade receivables.

5.1.13.C   *Assets and disposal groups held for sale*

FRS 102 does not include a concept of assets and disposal groups held for sale, comparable to that in IFRS 5 – *Non-current Assets Held for Sale and Discontinued Operations*.

The standard, therefore, does not require an entity to present a non-current asset classified as held for sale and the assets of a disposal group held for sale separately from other assets in the statement of financial position and the liabilities of a disposal group held for sale separately from other liabilities in the statement of financial position. *[IFRS 5.38, IAS 1.54]*. In addition, FRS 102 does not permit such presentation of disposal groups in the statement of financial position because the General Rules to the formats (which apply so far as practicable to 'adapted formats') do not allow the aggregation of different line items into two lines, being assets and liabilities of the disposal group, in this way. *[FRS 102.4.2C]*. This does not preclude entities presenting additional analysis in the notes to the financial statements. See also the disclosures at 5.5 below.

5.1.13.D   *Post-employment benefit assets and liabilities*

FRS 102, like IFRSs does not specify where in the statement of financial position a net asset or net liability in respect of a defined benefit plan should be presented, nor whether such balances should be shown separately on the face of the statement of financial position or only in the notes. This is left to the judgement of the reporting entity, but FRS 102 requires additional line items, headings and subtotals when relevant to an understanding of the entity's financial position. *[FRS 102.4.3]*. Classification of post-employment benefit assets and liabilities as current or non-current is discussed at 5.1.1.E and 5.1.2.F above.

Employers with more than one plan may find that some are in surplus while others are in deficit. The general rules in FRS 102 prohibit offsetting of such balances. *[FRS 102.2.52]*.

A UK company preparing Companies Act accounts (relevant to 'adapted' formats and statutory formats) must give particulars of any pension commitments included in the balance sheet, with separate particulars of any commitment relating wholly or partly to pensions payable to past directors of the company. *[1 Sch 63(5)-(6)]*. See 8.7.1 below for disclosures of guarantees and other financial commitments (including pension commitments) not included on the balance sheet.

5.1.13.E   Compound instruments

FRS 102 requires that an entity issuing a convertible or compound instrument must allocate the proceeds between the liability component and the equity component. *[FRS 102.22.13]*. This classification is permitted by the Regulations which require that, in determining how amounts are presented within items in the balance sheet, the directors of the company must have regard to the substance of the reported transaction or arrangement, in accordance with generally accepted accounting principles or practice (see 4.4 above). *[1 Sch 9]*.

Appendix 2 of TECH 02/10 *Guidance on the Determination of Realised Profits and Losses in the Context of Distributions under the Companies Act 2006* includes numerical illustrations of the treatment of compound instruments.

5.1.13.F   Government grants

FRS 102 sets out two models for recognising government grants – the accrual model (which is similar to that used under previous UK GAAP) and the performance model (see Chapter 19 of EY New UK GAAP 2015).

Where the performance model is used, FRS 102 states that grants received before the revenue recognition criteria are satisfied are recognised as a *liability* [emphasis added]. *[FRS 102.24.5B(c)]*.

Where the accrual model is used, FRS 102 requires that government grants related to assets are recognised in income on a systematic basis over the expected useful life of the asset. Where part of a grant relating to an asset is deferred, it is recognised as deferred income and not deducted from the carrying amount of the asset. *[FRS 102.24.5F-G]*. FRS 102 does not address the presentation where a grant has been received but does not meet the recognition criteria, but it would be logical to present this as a liability rather than deferred income (consistent with the requirement for the performance model).

While FRS 102 does not require government grants to be presented separately on the face of the statement of financial position, the standard specifically requires disclosure of the nature and amounts of grants recognised in the financial statements. *[FRS 102.24.6(b)]*.

5.1.14   *Illustrative statement of financial position ('adapted formats')*

Example 4.3 illustrates a statement of financial position using the 'adapted formats'. This includes some additional line items to those listed in Figure 4.3 at 5.1 above. 5.1 explains when additional line items may be or are required to be presented.

Chapter 4

Example 4.3:   *Illustrative statement of financial position*

XYZ GROUP – STATEMENT OF FINANCIAL POSITION AS AT 31 DECEMBER 2016

	£'000 2016	£'000 2015
ASSETS		
Non-current assets		
Property, plant and equipment	85,050	69,423
Investment property carried at fair value through profit or loss	20,080	19,560
Goodwill	78,003	91,200
Other intangible assets	65,270	78,000
Investments in associates	34,000	28,800
Investments in jointly controlled assets	38,050	–
Biological assets carried at cost	44,000	56,000
Deferred tax	10,563	9,765
	375,016	352,748
Current assets		
Inventories	45,080	28,333
Trade and other receivables	38,789	45,634
Cash and cash equivalents	31,200	56,445
	115,069	130,412
Total assets	490,085	483,160
Trade and other payables	63,566	44,289
Current portion of long-term borrowings	50,000	50,000
Financial liabilities – derivatives	10,200	5,436
Provisions	14,350	–
Total current liabilities	138,116	99,725
Non-current liabilities		
Deferred tax	39,679	46,555
Long-term borrowings	150,000	200,000
Financial liabilities – derivatives	20,789	18,423
Provisions	27,600	–
Defined benefit pension plan	66,341	81,977
Total non-current liabilities	304,409	346,955
Total liabilities	442,525	446,680
Net assets	47,560	36,480
EQUITY		
Share capital	12,075	10,000
Share premium	500	500
Revaluation reserve	3,300	3,100
Other reserves	5,976	(774)
Fair value reserve – cash flow hedges	1,859	2,524
Retained earnings	23,521	21,008
Equity attributable to owners of the parent	47,231	36,358
Non-controlling interests	329	122
Total equity	47,560	36,480

5.2   Statutory formats – format 1 Balance Sheet

Section B of Part 1 of Schedule 1 to the Regulations provides a choice of two 'statutory formats' for the balance sheet – format 1 is a vertical format and is adopted by virtually all UK companies. Format 2 presents assets separately from liabilities (including capital and reserves) and is rarely used.

This chapter only discusses the format 1 balance sheet applicable to companies (other than banking or insurance companies). It is beyond the scope of this chapter to discuss the formats in Schedule 2 applicable to banking companies and groups (defined in section 1164 of the CA 2006 – see definition at 4.2.2 above) or the formats in Schedule 3 applicable to insurance companies and groups (defined in section 1165 of the CA 2006 – see definition at 4.2.3 above). However, there is less flexibility to adapt the formats in Schedule 2 and Schedule 3 to the Regulations. See 4.1 above for discussion as to which formats apply to which types of entity.

The statement of financial position prepared in accordance with format 1 will look similar to one prepared under previous UK GAAP, although there is potential for reclassifications of items due to differing accounting requirements in FRS 102.

SI 2015/980 (which will apply where a UK company adopts FRS 102 (amended July 2015) – see 1.1 and 2.1 above) modifies the subheading to item K.IV.4 in format 1, which can be presented on the face of the balance sheet or in the notes. See 5.3.12 below.

Each of the headings and sub-headings denoted with a capital letter or Roman numeral, as set out in Figure 4.4 below, must be presented on the face of the format 1 balance sheet for the individual accounts in the order and under the headings and sub-headings given. The format 1 balance sheet includes sub-headings, denoted with an Arabic number, which have not been shown in Figure 4.4 as they can be (and often are) presented in the notes to the accounts. The General Rules to the formats (see 4.4 above) explain further the presentation of line items with an Arabic number. The individual line items in the format 1 balance sheet are discussed respectively at 5.3 below.

The modifications required for the group balance sheet statutory format are:

- the identification of non-controlling interests (see 4.5 above), where SI 2015/980 amended the requirements; and

- the sub-heading 'Participating interests' (at B III in Figure 4.4 below) is replaced by 'Interests in associated undertakings' and 'Other participating interests' (see 5.3.4.D and 5.3.4.E below). *[6 Sch 17, 20]*.

The General Rules to the formats (see 4.4 above) must be complied with.

Figure 4.4   *Format 1 individual balance sheet (UK company other than a banking company or insurance company)*

A	**Called up share capital not paid***	
B	**Fixed assets**	
	I	Intangible assets
	II	Tangible assets
	III	Investments
C	**Current assets**	
	I	Stocks
	II	Debtors
	III	Investments
	IV	Cash at bank and in hand
D	**Prepayments and accrued income***	
E	**Creditors: amounts falling due within one year**	
F	**Net current assets (liabilities)**	
G	**Total assets less current liabilities**	
H	**Creditors: amounts falling due after more than one year**	
I	**Provisions for liabilities**	
J	**Accruals and deferred income***	
K	**Capital and reserves**	
	I	Called up share capital not paid*
	II	Share premium account
	III	Revaluation reserve
	IV	Other reserves, including the fair value reserve**
	V	Profit and loss account

*   The notes to format 1 provide alternative positions for prepayments and accrued income, and accruals and deferred income, as sub-headings within C-II (for prepayments and accrued income) and within E and H (for accruals and deferred income). Called up share capital not paid may also be shown within C-II.

**   Where SI 2015/980 is not applied, K.IV.4 reads 'Other reserves'. See 5.3.12 below.

See 5.2.1 below for modification of the format 1 balance sheet for LLPs.

The standard requires an entity to present additional line items, headings and subtotals in the statement of financial position when such presentation is relevant to an understanding of the entity's financial position. *[FRS 102.4.3].* Judgement is needed in determining whether additional items should be presented, where material and relevant (see discussion, including relevant IAS 1 guidance at 5.1 above). Any amendments would need to comply with the General Rules to the formats (see 4.4 above).

FRS 102, like IFRS, has accounting requirements for various items that do not have separate line items in format 1, but which would be presented separately on the face of the statement of financial position under IAS 1. Such items include investment property, financial assets, biological assets, cash and cash equivalents and deferred tax. FRS 102 generally requires separate disclosures of the amounts of these items in the notes to the financial statements (and sometimes requires reconciliations of the movements in the balances of such items). As noted above, FRS 102 requires additional line items to be presented on the face of the statement of financial position where relevant to an understanding of the entity's financial position. So, for example, a property company may distinguish its investment property from other tangible fixed assets. The presentation of additional line items might require use of boxes and subtotals in order to comply with the balance sheet statutory formats.

5.2.1   Modifications of format 1 balance sheet for LLPs

The main headings in the format 1 balance sheet in the LLP Regulations differ to those in Figure 4.4 at 5.2 above in the following respects:

- A – Called up share capital is omitted so the main headings are A – Fixed Assets to I – Accruals and deferred income;

- There is an additional item J – Loans and other debts due to members. The following amounts must be shown separately under this item – the aggregate amount of money advanced to the LLP by the members by way of loan, the aggregate amount of money owed to members by the LLP in respect of profits, and any other amounts;

- In addition, K – Capital and reserves is replaced with K – Members' other interests (with sub-headings K.I – Members' capital, K.II – Revaluation reserve and K.III – Other reserves).

There are also changes to sub-headings that are highlighted in 5.3 below.

The *Statement of Recommended Practice – Accounting by Limited Liability Partnerships* (July 2014) issued by CCAB provides further guidance on members interests' and application of the statutory formats for LLPs. The SORP requires that the face of the statement of financial position shows a total for net assets attributable to members. In addition, total members' interests (being the total of items J and K less any amounts due from members in debtors) should be disclosed as a memorandum item on the face of the statement of financial position.[8] The SORP also provides illustrations of LLP balance sheets for different situations. Detailed guidance on issues specific to LLPs is outside the scope of this Chapter.

5.2.2   Fixed assets and current assets

The balance sheet statutory formats set out in the Regulations distinguish between fixed assets and current assets. Under the Regulations, fixed assets are defined and current assets are the residual. 'Fixed assets' are assets of an entity which are intended for use on a continuing basis in the company's activities, and 'current assets' are assets not intended for such use. *[10 Sch 4, 4 Sch 3 (LLP), FRS 102.Appendix I].*

Current assets include debtors, even if due after more than one year. However, where the amount of debtors due after more than one year is so material in the context of net current assets that in the absence of disclosure of the debtors due after more than one year on the face of the statement of financial position readers may misinterpret the financial statements, the amount should be disclosed on the face of the statement of financial position within current assets. In most cases, it will be satisfactory to disclose the amount due after more than one year in the notes to the financial statements. FRS 102 clarifies that this requirement does not apply where an entity chooses to apply paragraph 1A(1) of Schedule 1 to the Regulations (i.e. use 'adapted formats'). *[FRS 102.4.4A].*

Note (5) to the balance sheet statutory format in Schedule 1 to the Regulations states that the amount falling due after more than one year must be shown separately for each item included under debtors.[9]

A UK company preparing Companies Act accounts must disclose the following in the notes to the accounts, for *each* category of fixed assets shown in the balance sheet (or would be so shown, if Arabic-numbered line items were not combined as permitted by paragraph 4(2)(b) of the General Rules to the formats – see 4.4 above): *[1 Sch 51, 1 Sch 49 (LLP)]*

- the gross cost (based on the historical cost – see 10.1 below) or valuation (using the alternative accounting rules – see 10.2 below) at the beginning and end of the financial year;

- the effects on gross cost/valuation of:
    - revaluations;
    - acquisitions;
    - disposals; and
    - transfers of assets;

- the cumulative amount of provisions for depreciation or diminution in value at the beginning and end of the financial year;

- the provision for depreciation and diminution in respect of the financial year;

- adjustments to such provisions in respect of disposal of assets; and

- the amount of any other adjustments in respect of such provisions.

Where the Regulations require disclosures in respect of fixed assets or current assets, in our view, these disclosures need to be given where both statutory formats and 'adapted formats' are used. See 5.1 above for discussion on applying these requirements where 'adapted formats' are used.

The above requirement in the Regulations overlaps with FRS 102's requirements to provide reconciliations of changes in the carrying amounts for each class of property, plant and equipment, *[FRS 102.17.31]*, (see Chapter 13 at 3.8.1 of EY New UK GAAP 2015), each class of intangible asset, *[FRS 102.18.27(e)]*, (see Chapter 14 at 3.5.2 of EY New UK GAAP 2015), goodwill and negative goodwill, *[FRS 102.19.26, 26A]*, (see Chapter 15 at 4.2 of EY New UK GAAP 2015), investment property at fair value through profit or loss, *[FRS 102.16.10(e)]*, (see Chapter 12 at 3.6 of EY New UK GAAP 2015), and biological assets (separately for each class carried under the cost model and each class carried under the fair value model), *[FRS 102.34.7(c), 34.10(e)]*, (see Chapter 29 at 2.5.3 and 2.6.2 of EY New UK GAAP 2015).

The Regulations require separate fixed asset reconciliations for cost and cumulative provision for depreciation and diminution whereas FRS 102 only requires reconciliation of the carrying amounts.

The Regulations also require a UK company preparing Companies Act accounts to provide additional disclosures in the notes to the accounts where the alternative accounting rules are applied. See 10.2.4 below.

5.2.3   Creditors: amounts falling due within and after more than one year

The Regulations distinguish between:

- Creditors: amounts falling due within one year; and
- Creditors: amounts falling due after more than one year.

These two line items are shown on the face of the balance sheet in the format 1 balance sheet. In distinguishing amounts between the two categories of creditor, the deciding factor is the earliest date of payment. The Regulations state that a loan or advance (including a liability comprising a loan or advance) is treated as falling due for repayment, and an instalment of a loan or advance is treated as falling due for payment, on the earliest date on which the lender could require repayment or (as the case may be) payment, if he exercised all options and rights available to him. *[10 Sch 9, 4 Sch 6 (LLP)]*.

FRS 102 specifies that an entity (that does not choose to apply paragraph 1A(1) of Schedule 1 to the Regulations and present 'adapted formats') shall classify a creditor as due within one year when the entity does not have an unconditional right, at the end of the reporting period, to defer settlement of the creditor for at least twelve months after the reporting date. The FRS 102 (July 2015) amendments add 'for example, this would be the case if the earliest date on which the lender, exercising all available options and rights, could require repayment or (as the case may be) payment was within 12 months after the reporting date.' *[FRS 102.4.7]*. FRS 102's requirements are consistent with the statutory requirements.

IAS 1 also includes detailed guidance on the impact of refinancing liabilities that management may consider, as permitted by the hierarchy in Section 10. *[FRS 102.10.3-10.6]*. While IAS 1 requires classification between current and non-current liabilities (which is different), one part of IAS 1's definition of a current liability is that a liability is current if the entity 'does not have an unconditional right to defer settlement of the liability for at least twelve months after the reporting period'. This is consistent with the definition of a creditor due within one year in FRS 102 (and the Regulations). *[IAS 1.69(d)]*. See 5.1.2.D above.

5.3   Implementation issues – format 1 balance sheet

In most cases, it will be straightforward to identify in which line items to present assets and liabilities in the format 1 balance sheet. The discussion in this section provides a commentary on each heading and subheading included in the format 1 balance sheet and on the related notes to the statutory formats.

Where disclosures in the Regulations are discussed in this section, these are not intended to be comprehensive but to highlight additional disclosures directly related to a specific line item. The disclosures required for the line items in the notes to the accounts highlighted here are also required in the notes to the accounts where 'adapted formats' are used (unless they are required by Section B to Part 1 of Schedule 1 to the Regulations, i.e. the balance sheet statutory format or notes to the balance sheet statutory format itself). These do not cover all the related disclosures in Schedule 1 to the Regulations.

A new requirement, introduced by SI 2015/980, so not relevant to LLPs (unless LLP law is subsequently changed), is that where an asset or liability relates to more than one item in the balance sheet, the relationship of such asset or liability to the relevant items must be disclosed either under those items or in the notes to the accounts. *[1 Sch 9A]*. See 4.4 above.

5.3.1   *Called up share capital not paid*

This line item can be presented in the position of Called up share capital not paid (item A) on the face of the balance sheet. Alternatively, this line item can be presented either on the face of the balance sheet or in the notes to the accounts as item 5 within Current assets – Debtors (C II) (see 5.3.6.E below).[10]

Called up share capital (and paid up share capital) are explained at 5.3.12.A below. Called up share capital not paid can arise because calls made on the shares have not been paid, or where the share capital is 'paid up' because the amounts are payable on a specified date under the articles or terms of allotment or other arrangement for payment of shares, but has not yet been settled (and therefore is called up share capital).

5.3.2   *Intangible assets*

Figure 4.5 shows the analysis required in respect of intangible assets (on the face of the balance sheet or in the notes to the accounts – see 4.4 above) under format 1.

Figure 4.5   Analysis of intangible assets

B	Fixed assets	
I	Intangible assets	
	1	Development costs
	2	Concessions, patents, licences, trade marks and similar rights and assets
	3	Goodwill
	4	Payments on account

Intangible assets are not defined in the Regulations, but include line items denoted with an Arabic number for development costs; concessions, patents, licences, trademarks and similar rights and assets; goodwill; and payments on account. Note (2) to the balance sheet statutory formats states that amounts are only included in the balance sheet as concessions, patents, licences, trademarks and similar rights and assets if *either* the assets were acquired for valuable consideration and are not required to be shown under goodwill, *or* the assets in question were created by the company itself.[11]

FRS 102 financial statements must apply the more restrictive requirements of the standard (see 5.1.5 above and Chapter 14 of EY New UK GAAP 2015). There is potential for changes in classification compared to previous UK GAAP. The format 1 balance sheet includes a line item for payments on account, i.e. advance payments made for intangible fixed assets.

Note (3) to the balance sheet statutory formats in Schedule 1 to the Regulations states that amounts representing goodwill are only included to the extent that the goodwill was acquired for valuable consideration.[12] Therefore, consistent with FRS 102, internally generated goodwill cannot be capitalised. *[FRS 102.18.8C(f)]*.

The Regulations do not address the presentation of negative goodwill, but FRS 102's requirements on presentation of negative goodwill, which also apply to statutory formats, are addressed at 5.1.5.A above.

5.3.3   Tangible fixed assets

Figure 4.6 shows the analysis required (on the face of the balance sheet or in the notes to the accounts – see 4.4 above) in respect of tangible fixed assets under format 1.

Figure 4.6   Analysis of tangible fixed assets

B	**Fixed assets**
II	Tangible assets
	1 Land and buildings
	2 Plant and machinery
	3 Fixtures, fittings, tools and equipment
	4 Payments on account and assets in course of construction

The Regulations define fixed assets (see 5.2.2 above) but not tangible fixed assets. While FRS 102 does not define the term 'tangible assets', these differ from intangible assets in that they are assets 'with physical substance'.

The distinction between fixed assets and current assets is usually clear and the statutory definition is not normally interpreted to mean that individual assets are transferred to current assets when a decision to dispose of them has been made. See 5.3.13.C below.

The format 1 balance sheet includes a line item for payments on account, i.e. advance payments made for tangible fixed assets.

Tangible fixed assets would include property, plant and equipment, as defined in FRS 102. There is potential for changes in classification for certain assets compared to previous UK GAAP (see 5.1.3 above and Chapter 13 at 3 of EY New UK GAAP 2015). Investment property would also be classified within tangible fixed assets in the statutory formats. See 5.3.3.A below. In addition, in our view, it would be appropriate to report an upfront operating lease premium as a prepayment under FRS 102 (see 5.1.13.A above), classified as appropriate between debtors: amounts falling due within one year and debtors: amounts falling due after more than one year (although this was often classified as a tangible fixed asset in the statutory formats under previous UK GAAP).

In practice, most UK companies relegate the sub-headings within tangible assets denoted by an Arabic number to the notes to the accounts, showing only the net book value of tangible assets on the face of the balance sheet.

UK companies preparing Companies Act accounts (relevant to 'adapted formats' and statutory formats) must also disclose, in the notes to the accounts, 'land and buildings' analysed between freehold land and leasehold land, with leasehold land analysed between land held on a long lease (i.e. the unexpired term at the end of the financial year is not less than 50 years) and leasehold land held on a short lease. *[1 Sch 53, 10 Sch 7, 1 Sch 51 (LLP)]*.

5.3.3.A   Investment property

The Regulations do not require presentation of investment property on the face of the balance sheet but do permit items to be shown in greater detail. FRS 102 requires additional line items, headings and subtotals when relevant to an understanding of the entity's financial position (see 4.4 above). Therefore, some entities may consider it appropriate to present investment property as a separate line item on the face of the balance sheet.

There are a number of differences between the definition of investment property under previous UK GAAP and under FRS 102, and consequently, classification differences in respect of investment property may arise on transition to FRS 102. See Chapter 12 at 2.1 and 3.1 of EY New UK GAAP 2015.

5.3.4   Investments

Figure 4.7 shows the analysis required in respect of investments (on the face of the balance sheet or in the notes to the accounts – see 4.4 above) under format 1.

Figure 4.7   *Analysis of investments*

B	Fixed assets
III	Investments
	1 Shares in group undertakings
	2 Loans to group undertakings
	3 Participating interests†
	4 Loans to undertakings in which the company has a participating interest
	5 Other investments other than loans
	6 Other loans
	7 Own shares*
	† In group accounts, this line item is replaced by two items: 'Interests in associated undertakings' and 'Other participating interests'
	* Not included in format 1 in the LLP Regulations
C	Current assets
III	Investments
	1 Shares in group undertakings
	2 Own shares*
	3 Other investments
	* Not included in format 1 in the LLP Regulations

5.3.4.A   Current assets or fixed asset investments?

The format 1 balance sheet distinguishes between fixed asset and current asset investments. It is necessary to apply the general rule that a fixed asset is one which is 'intended for use on a continuing basis in the entity's activities' and a current asset is one not intended for such use (see 5.2.2 above). However, this is an unhelpful distinction for investments which, by their nature, are not intended for use in an entity's activities at all, whether on a continuing basis or not.

Current asset investments may include cash equivalents, meaning: short-term, highly liquid investments that are readily convertible to cash (i.e. cash on hand and demand deposits) and that are subject to an insignificant risk of changes in value *[FRS 102.Appendix I]*. Examples of current asset investments that may qualify as cash equivalents, but do not fall within the statutory heading 'cash at bank and in hand', include investments in money market funds. Current asset investments may also include investments that do not qualify as cash equivalents but are still of a short-term nature, and investments held for trading purposes.

Investments in shares in subsidiaries or associates or trade investments will generally be fixed asset investments. Indeed, FRS 102 states that, unless otherwise required under the Regulations, investments in associates should be classified as fixed assets. *[FRS 102.14.11]*. However, entities frequently make loans to subsidiaries or associates which are often on terms that are repayable on demand or where the loan has a fixed term but the entity may rollover the loan if it reaches its maturity. Management will need to exercise judgement in determining whether such items are debtors or are a fixed asset investment in nature. Where the financing is provided for the long-term, with no intention of repayment in the foreseeable future, the balance may be more of a fixed asset investment in nature, even where the balance is strictly repayable on demand.

Discussion of the different sub-headings required to be shown for investments is included below. Care must be taken not to offset amounts owed by group undertakings with amounts owed to the same group undertaking or other group undertakings where the offset criteria in the standard are not met. The same principle applies to balances with undertakings in which the entity has a participating interest. Offset requires both a legally enforceable right of set off and an intention either to settle on a net basis or to realise the asset and settle the liability simultaneously. *[FRS 102.11.38A, 12.25A]*.

UK companies preparing Companies Act accounts (relevant to 'adapted formats' and statutory formats) must disclose the following in the notes to the accounts for each line item under current asset or fixed asset investments shown in the balance sheet (or would be so shown, if Arabic-numbered line items were not combined as permitted by paragraph 4(2)(b) of the General Rules to the formats – see 4.4 above):

- the amount of listed investments included in that line item;
- the market value of the listed investments, if different from the carrying value; and
- the stock exchange value, if less than the market value so disclosed.

A listed investment is an investment which has been granted a listing on a recognised investment exchange other than an overseas investment exchange (both as defined in Part 18 of the Financial Services and Markets Act 2000) or a stock exchange of repute outside the UK. *[1 Sch 54, 10 Sch 8, 1 Sch 52 (LLP), 4 Sch 5 (LLP)]*. A list of recognised investment exchanges (and recognised overseas investment exchanges) is available on the Financial Conduct Authority website. AIM is not a recognised investment exchange.

Chapter 4

5.3.4.B   *Group undertakings, participating interests and associated undertakings*

Unlike previous UK GAAP (FRS 9 – *Associates and joint ventures*), FRS 102 does not require investments in associates and jointly controlled entities to be presented on the face of the statement of financial position in either the individual or consolidated financial statements, where the statutory formats are used.

The standard requires disclosure of the carrying amount of investments in associates and, separately, the carrying amount of investments in jointly controlled entities. *[FRS 102.14.12(b), 15.19(b)]*. This could be presented in the notes to the financial statements, although the standard requires additional line items, headings and subtotals when relevant to an understanding of the entity's financial position. *[FRS 102.4.3]*.

The line items in the balance sheet statutory formats in the Regulations refer to group undertakings, participating interests and associated undertakings. These terms are explained at 5.3.4.C to 5.3.4.E below.

UK companies preparing Companies Act accounts (relevant to 'adapted formats' and 'statutory formats') must also comply with the extensive requirements of paragraph 7 and Schedule 4 to the Regulations in relation to information about related undertakings, which must be presented in full in the financial statements.[13] See Chapter 5 at 3.4.

5.3.4.C   *Group undertakings*

A 'group undertaking' is a parent undertaking or subsidiary undertaking of the reporting entity, or a subsidiary undertaking of any parent undertaking (i.e. a fellow subsidiary undertaking) of the reporting entity. *[s1161(5)]*. Parent and subsidiary undertakings are defined in section 1162 of the Companies Act 2006. See Chapter 2 at 3.1.2 of EY New UK GAAP 2015.

FRS 102 defines a subsidiary as an entity that is controlled by the parent. Control is the power to govern the financial and operating policies of an entity so as to obtain benefits from its activities. The standard goes on to explain in what circumstances control exists or can exist. *[FRS 102.9.4-9.6A]*. These circumstances are similar but not identical to those included in the definition of a subsidiary undertaking under section 1162.

Although there are slight differences in wording emphasis between the definition of a subsidiary undertaking in section 1162 and the requirements in Section 9 – *Consolidated and Separate Financial Statements*, we would expect to see few conflicts arising in practice between Section 9 and the Companies Act 2006 (see Chapter 6 at 3.2 of EY New UK GAAP 2015).

5.3.4.D   *Participating interest*

A 'participating interest' means an interest held by, or on behalf of, an undertaking (or in group accounts, by the parent and its consolidated subsidiary undertakings) in the shares of another undertaking which it holds on a long-term basis for the purpose of securing a contribution to its activities (or in group accounts, the consolidated group's activities) by the exercise of control or influence arising from or related to that interest.

A holding of 20% or more of the shares of the undertaking is presumed to be a participating interest unless the contrary is shown. An interest in shares of another undertaking includes an interest which is convertible into an interest in shares and an option to acquire shares or any such interest, even if the shares are unissued until the conversion or exercise of the option.

In the context of the balance sheet statutory formats, 'participating interest' does not include an interest in a group undertaking (see 5.3.4.C above). *[10 Sch 11, 4 Sch 8 (LLP)]*.

5.3.4.E   Associated undertaking

An 'associated undertaking' is an undertaking in which an undertaking included in the consolidation:

*   has a participating interest (as defined at 5.3.4.D above) and over whose operating and financial policy it exercises a significant influence; and

*   which is not a subsidiary undertaking of the parent company or a joint venture dealt with in accordance with paragraph 18 of Schedule 6 to the Regulations However, the proportional consolidation permitted by this paragraph is not consistent with the requirements of FRS 102. *[FRS 102.15.9A-9B]*.

An undertaking holding 20% or more of the voting rights in another undertaking is presumed to exercise a significant influence over it unless the contrary is shown. Voting rights mean the rights conferred on shareholders in respect of their shares (or where the undertaking does not have a share capital, on members) to vote at general meetings of the undertaking on all, or substantially all matters. Paragraphs 5 to 11 of Schedule 7 to the Regulations apply in determining whether 20% or more of the voting rights are held. *[6 Sch 19, 3 Sch 19 (LLP)]*.

The term 'associated undertaking' in the Regulations will generally include both an associate (see Chapter 10 at 3.2 of EY New UK GAAP 2015) and a jointly controlled entity, *[FRS 102.14.2-3, 15.8, Appendix I]*, (see Chapter 11 at 3.3 of EY New UK GAAP 2015), as defined under FRS 102. However, FRS 102's definition of an associate does not require the existence of a participating interest so it is theoretically possible that an associate under the standard may not be an associated undertaking under the Regulations.

5.3.4.F   Own shares

While 'own shares' have a sub-heading under investments in the balance sheet formats, FRS 102 requires investments in own shares to be treated as treasury shares and deducted from equity. *[FRS 102.22.16]*. Consequently, this line item will not be used under FRS 102. The format 1 balance sheet has an alternative position 'reserve for own shares' within the capital and reserves section which will be used under FRS 102 (see 5.3.12 below).

5.3.5   *Stocks*

Figure 4.8 shows the analysis required in respect of stocks (on the face of the balance sheet or in the notes to the accounts – see 4.4 above) under format 1.

Figure 4.8   *Analysis of stocks*

C	Current assets	
I	Stocks	
	1	Raw materials and consumables
	2	Work in progress
	3	Finished goods and goods for resale
	4	Payments on account

The items reported under stocks in the balance sheet formats will generally correspond with inventories under FRS 102, which are assets: *[FRS 102.Appendix I, FRS 102.13.1]*

- held for sale in the ordinary course of business; or

- in the process of production for such sale; or

- in the form of materials or supplies to be consumed in the production process or in the rendering of services.

See also 5.1.8 above (which highlights certain classification issues over inventories) and Chapter 9 at 3.2 of EY New UK GAAP 2015.

Note (8) to the balance sheet statutory format in Schedule 1 to the Regulations states that payments on account of orders must be shown within creditors in so far as they are not shown as deductions from stocks.[14] We would not expect payments on account to be deducted from stock (or inventory) as this would not meet the offset requirements of FRS 102, and therefore all payments on account must be shown within creditors.

See 5.3.13.A below for a discussion of the presentation of construction contracts which is not specifically addressed in the Regulations and 5.1.8 above on transfers to inventories, both also relevant to classification under format 1.

5.3.6   *Debtors (including prepayments and accrued income)*

Figure 4.9 shows the analysis required in respect of debtors (on the face of the balance sheet or in the notes to the accounts – see 4.4 above) under format 1.

Figure 4.9   *Analysis of debtors*

C	**Current assets**	
II	Debtors	
	1	Trade debtors
	2	Amounts owed by group undertakings
	3	Amounts owed by undertakings in which the company has a participating interest**
	4	Other debtors
	5	Called up share capital not paid*
	6	Prepayments and accrued income*

*   Format 1 provides alternative positions for called up share capital not paid at heading A and prepayments and accrued income at heading D. In format 1 in the LLP Regulations, called up share capital is omitted and the alternative position for prepayments and accrued income is at heading C (i.e. the same as heading D in the company balance sheet formats).

**   In format 1 in the LLP Regulations, amounts owed by undertakings in which the LLP has a participating interest.

While all debtors are reported within current assets, debtors include amounts falling due within and amounts falling due after more than one year.

As discussed at 5.2.2 above, where the amount of debtors due after more than one year is so material in the context of net current assets that the financial statements might otherwise be misinterpreted, the amount should be disclosed on the face of the statement of financial position within current assets. In most cases, it will be satisfactory to disclose the amount due after more than one year in the notes to the financial statements. *[FRS 102.4.4A]*.

Note (5) to the balance sheet statutory format in Schedule 1 to the Regulations[15] states that the amount falling due after more than one year must be shown separately for each item included under debtors.

5.3.6.A   Trade debtors

Trade debtors are generally amounts receivable from customers, e.g. relating to amounts invoiced to customers, as well as debit balances owed by suppliers. The amounts in trade debtors are stated net of any bad debt provisions or write offs, and the effects of credit notes and other rebates.

Care must be taken not to offset any debit balances in trade debtors with trade creditors (and *vice versa*) where the offset criteria in the standard are not met. Offset requires both a legally enforceable right of set off and an intention either to settle on a net basis or to realise the asset and settle the liability simultaneously. *[FRS 102.11.38A, 12.25A]*.

Chapter 4

The separate line items for 'amounts owed by group undertakings' and 'amounts owed by undertakings in which the [entity] has a participating interest' will include trade debtors due from group undertakings and participating interests respectively (see 5.3.6.C below).

5.3.6.B   *Construction contracts*

There is no specific mention made in the Regulations of the presentation of construction contracts. Contract assets may include amounts receivable under contracts that have not yet been invoiced (and, therefore, are not recorded in trade debtors). See 5.3.13.A below.

5.3.6.C   *Amounts owed by group undertakings and undertakings in which the company has a participating interest*

The line items 'amounts owed by group undertakings' and 'amounts owed by undertakings in which the company has a participating interest' include all amounts owed by such undertakings e.g. loans regarded as current assets, dividends and interest receivable, trading items such as current accounts and balances with group treasury companies. The meanings of 'group undertaking' and 'participating interest' are discussed at 5.3.4.C and 5.3.4.D above.

As noted at 5.3.4.A above, management must exercise judgement in determining whether amounts owed by group undertakings or undertakings in which the entity has a participating interest are debtors or fixed asset investments. Again, care must be taken not to offset debtors and creditors where the offset criteria in the standard are not met.

5.3.6.D   *Other debtors*

This will cover debtors other than those identified in other line items, e.g. amounts receivable from a sale of property, plant and equipment.

5.3.6.E   *Called up share capital not paid*

The format 1 balance sheet permits called up share capital not paid to alternatively be shown in the position of line item A, i.e. on the face of the balance sheet (see 5.3.1 above).

5.3.6.F   *Prepayments and accrued income*

Prepayments and accrued income can alternatively be shown on the face of the balance sheet (line item D).[16]

Prepayments and accrued income are not defined in the Regulations or in FRS 102. Prepayments arise where payments are made in advance of receiving the goods or services. They must meet the definition and recognition criteria of an asset, including recoverability, in the standard (see Chapter 3 at 3.3.1 of EY New UK GAAP 2015).

FRS 102 prohibits the recognition as an intangible asset of expenditure such as internally developed brand and similar intangible assets, start-up activities, training activities, advertising and promotional activities (except for inventories held for distribution at no or nominal consideration – see Chapter 9 at 3.3.11 of EY New UK GAAP 2015), relocation and reorganisation costs and internally generated goodwill. However, the standard does not preclude recognition of a prepayment where payment is made in advance of delivery of the goods or rendering of the services. *[FRS 102.18.8C-D].*

As noted at 5.3.3 above, in our view, it would be appropriate to report an upfront operating lease premium as a prepayment under FRS 102, classified as appropriate between debtors: amounts falling due within one year and debtors: amounts falling due after more than one year (although this was often classified as a tangible fixed asset in the statutory formats under previous UK GAAP).

While the format 1 balance sheet combines prepayments and accrued income into one line item, these two items can have separate characteristics. The Financial Reporting Review Panel Annual Report 2012 indicated that a number of companies had been asked to show prepayments and accrued income separately in the notes to the financial statements as the assets differ in nature and liquidity. As noted at 4.4 above, the balance sheet formats allow any item to be shown in greater detail and FRS 102 requires additional line items, headings and subtotals when relevant to an understanding of the entity's financial position.

5.3.7   Cash at bank and in hand

The Regulations do not define cash at bank and in hand. This line item would include bank deposits with notice or maturity periods. Such bank deposits may or may not meet FRS 102's definition of 'cash' (i.e. cash on hand and demand deposits) or 'cash equivalents' (i.e. short-term, highly liquid investments that are readily convertible to known amounts of cash and that are subject to an insignificant risk of changes in value). *[FRS 102.7.2, Appendix I].* See Chapter 5 at 3.3 of EY New UK GAAP 2015 for the definition of cash and cash equivalents.

Care is needed with applying the requirements on offset of financial assets and financial liabilities, particularly in group arrangements with a bank where there are rights of offset. Offset requires both a legally enforceable right of set off and an intention either to settle on a net basis or to realise the asset and settle the liability simultaneously. *[FRS 102.11.38A, 12.25A].*

Chapter 4

5.3.8   *Creditors: amounts falling due within one year and after more than one year*

Figure 4.10 shows the analysis required in respect of creditors (on the face of the balance sheet or in the notes to the accounts – see 4.4 above) under format 1.

Figure 4.10   Analysis of creditors: amounts falling due within one year

E		Creditors: amounts falling due within one year
	1	Debenture loans
	2	Bank loans and overdrafts
	3	Payments received on account
	4	Trade creditors
	5	Bills of exchange payable
	6	Amounts owed to group undertakings
	7	Amounts owed to undertakings in which the company has a participating interest**
	8	Other creditors including taxation and social security
	9	Accruals and deferred income*
H		Creditors: amounts falling due within one year
	1	Debenture loans
	2	Bank loans and overdrafts
	3	Payments received on account
	4	Trade creditors
	5	Bills of exchange payable
	6	Amounts owed to group undertakings
	7	Amounts owed to undertakings in which the company has a participating interest**
	8	Other creditors including taxation and social security
	9	Accruals and deferred income*

*   Format 1 provides an alternative position for accruals and deferred income, at heading J. In format 1 in the LLP Regulations, the alternative position for accruals and deferred income is at heading I (i.e. the same as heading J in the company balance sheet formats).

**   In format 1 in the LLP Regulations, amounts owed to undertakings in which the LLP has a participating interest.

The same line items are required for creditors: amounts falling due within one year, and creditors: amounts falling due after more than one year. See 5.2.3 above for discussion of these two categories of creditors.

In addition, the General Rules to the formats (see 4.4 above) require that, in determining how amounts are presented within items in the balance sheet, the directors of the company (for an LLP, the members) must have regard to the substance of the reported transaction or arrangement, in accordance with generally accepted accounting principles or practice. *[1 Sch 9, 1 Sch 9 (LLP)]*. This provision facilitates the presentation of shares (such as certain preference shares) which are required to be classified as liabilities under accounting standards rather than as called up share capital under the balance sheet statutory format. See Chapter 8 at 9 of EY New UK GAAP 2015. Note however that disclosures required by the Regulations in the notes to the accounts in relation to share capital (see, for example, the disclosures listed in 5.4.2 below) still apply, even if the shares are classified as a liability.

The General Rules to the formats allow or, where the special nature of the company's business requires this, require certain adaptations to the balance sheet formats, as well as allowing line items to be shown in greater detail. The analysis of creditors is another area where entities may need to be mindful that FRS 102 requires additional line items, headings and subtotals when relevant to an understanding of the entity's financial position. For example, it may be appropriate to present preference shares classed as a liability, finance lease creditors and other items separately from other creditors.

UK companies preparing Companies Act accounts (relevant to 'adapted formats' and statutory formats) must state in the notes to the accounts, for the aggregate of all items shown under creditors, the aggregate of:

(a) the amount of any debts included in creditors which are payable or repayable otherwise than by instalments and fall due for payment or repayment after five years beginning with the day next following the end of the financial year; and

(b) for debts payable or repayable by instalments, the amount of any instalments which fall due for payment after the end of that period.

In relation to each debt which is taken into account in (a) or (b) above, the terms of payment or repayment and rate of any interest payable must be stated. If the number of debts is such that, in the opinion of the directors, the statement would be of excessive length, a general indication of these terms and the interest rates payable can be given.

For each item shown under creditors, the aggregate amount of any debts included under that item in respect of which any security has been given, and an indication of the nature (and the form, when SI 2015/980 is applied) of the securities given must also be stated. *[1 Sch 61, 1 Sch 59 (LLP)]*.

Where any outstanding loans made under the authority of section 682(2)(b), (c) or (d) (various cases of financial assistance by the company for the purchase of its own shares) are included under any item shown in the company's balance sheet, the aggregate amount of those items must be disclosed for each item in question. *[1 Sch 64(2)]*.

5.3.8.A   Debenture loans

The format 1 balance sheet has separate line items for debenture loans and bank loans and overdrafts. Therefore, bank loans and overdrafts need to be shown separately, even if they might also qualify as a debenture loan.

Note (7) to the balance sheet statutory formats in Schedule 1 to the Regulations states that the amount of any convertible loans (within debenture loans) must be shown separately.[17]

A 'debenture' is not defined in the CA 2006, except that it is stated to include 'debenture stock, bonds and other securities of a company, whether or not constituting a charge on the assets of the company.' *[s738]*. In general use, a 'debenture' is a term applying to any document evidencing a loan, and in the context of company law, it means a debt instrument issued by the company and usually giving some form of security or charge over its assets, although this is not an essential feature.

UK companies preparing Companies Act accounts (relevant to 'adapted formats' and statutory formats) must make the following disclosures in the notes to the accounts: *[1 Sch 50, 1 Sch 38 (LLP)]*

- if the company has issued any debentures during the financial year, the classes of debentures issued during the financial year, and for each class of debentures, the amount issued and consideration received by the company for the issue; and

- where any of the company's debentures are held by a nominee of or trustee for the company, the nominal amount of the debentures and the amount at which they are stated in the company's accounting records.

5.3.8.B   Bank loans and overdrafts

In relation to bank loans and overdrafts, care is needed with applying the requirements on offset of financial assets and financial liabilities, particularly in group arrangements with a bank where there are rights of offset. Offset requires both a legally enforceable right of set off and an intention either to settle on a net basis or to realise the asset and settle the liability simultaneously. *[FRS 102.11.38A, 12.25A]*.

5.3.8.C   Payments on account

As noted at 5.3.5 above we would not expect payments on account to be deducted from stock (or inventory) as this would not meet the offset requirements of FRS 102. Also see 5.3.13.A below for a discussion of how construction contract balances might be reflected in the balance sheet formats.

5.3.8.D   Trade creditors

Trade creditors are generally amounts payable to suppliers of goods and services, e.g. relating to amounts invoiced by suppliers (and could include credit balances due to trade debtors).

Care must be taken not to offset any debit balances in trade debtors with trade creditors (and *vice versa*) where the offset criteria in the standard are not met. The separate line items for 'amounts owed to group undertakings' and 'amounts owed to undertakings in which the entity has a participating interest' will include trade creditors due to group undertakings and participating interests respectively (see 5.3.8.F below).

5.3.8.E   Bills of exchange

A bill of exchange is a written instrument used mainly in international trade, where one party agrees to pay an amount to another party on demand or on a specified date. The bill can often be transferred by the holder of the bill to a bank or finance house at a discount.

5.3.8.F   Amounts owed to group undertakings and to undertakings in which the company has a participating interest

The line items 'amounts owed to group undertakings' and 'amounts owed to undertakings in which the company has a participating interest' include all amounts owed by such undertakings which could include loans, dividend and interest payable, trading items such as current accounts and balances with group treasury companies.

The meanings of 'group undertaking' and 'participating interest' are discussed at 5.3.4.C and 5.3.4.D above.

Care must be taken not to offset debtors and creditors where the offset criteria in the standard are not met.

5.3.8.G   Other creditors, including taxation and social security

Other creditors are creditors that do not belong in other line items.

Note (9) to the balance sheet statutory formats in Schedule 1 to the Regulations states that the amount for creditors in respect of taxation and social security must be shown separately from the amount for other creditors.[18] Taxation and social security creditors would include corporation tax, VAT, PAYE and National Insurance, and other taxes, including overseas taxation. This analysis can be given in the notes to the accounts.

In fact, FRS 102 does not explicitly require separate disclosure of the current tax creditor, although it requires disclosure of information that would enable users of the financial statements to evaluate the nature and financial effect of the current and deferred tax consequences of recognised transactions and other events. *[FRS 102.29.25]*.

Deferred tax liabilities are not included in this heading but in 'Provisions for liabilities' (see 5.3.11 below).

5.3.8.H   Accruals and deferred income

Accruals and deferred income can alternatively be shown the face of the balance sheet (line item J).[19] FRS 102 does not define accruals but under previous UK GAAP, the distinction presented below was drawn between accruals and provisions.

Accruals are liabilities to pay for goods or service that have been received or supplied but have not been paid, invoiced or formally agreed with the supplier including amounts due to employees (for example, amounts relating to accrued holiday pay). Although it is sometimes necessary to estimate the amount or timing of accruals, the uncertainty is generally much less than for provisions. *[FRS 12.11(b)]*.

Deferred income may arise where cash is received in advance of meeting the conditions for recognising the related revenue, e.g. rental income received in advance or where cash is received for goods not yet delivered or services not yet rendered. In addition, deferred income may arise in relation to government grants related to assets (which are recognised in income on a systematic basis over the expected useful life of the asset). *[FRS 102.24.5F-G]*. See 5.3.13.H below.

The Financial Reporting Review Panel Annual Report 2012 indicated that a number of companies had been asked to show accruals and deferred income separately in the notes to the financial statements as the liabilities differ in nature and timing.

5.3.9   Net current assets/(liabilities)

The format 1 balance sheet requires a net current assets/(liabilities) subtotal.

Note (11) to the balance sheet statutory formats in Schedule 1 to the Regulations states that any amounts shown under 'prepayments and accrued income' must be taken into account in determining net current assets/(liabilities), wherever shown (see 5.3.6.F above).[20] Therefore, net current assets/(liabilities) will represent the amounts reported at item C in the balance sheet statutory formats plus prepayments and accrued income (at item D, if shown separately) less creditors: amounts falling due within one year (at item E). See Figure 4.4 at 5.2 above.

5.3.10   Total assets less current liabilities

The format 1 balance sheet requires a subtotal for total assets less current liabilities. This subtotal would be the sum of fixed assets and net current assets/(liabilities).

While the format 1 balance sheet does not require a net assets subtotal (with a balancing subtotal for capital and reserves), most companies give this. Sometimes companies have presented a balancing subtotal for capital and reserves together with creditors: amounts falling due within one year, a practice not precluded by the Regulations.

5.3.11   Provisions for liabilities

Figure 4.11 shows the analysis required (on the face of the balance sheet or in the notes to the accounts – see 4.4 above) in respect of provisions for liabilities under format 1.

Figure 4.11   Analysis of provisions for liabilities

I	**Provisions for liabilities**	
	1	Pensions and similar obligations
	2	Taxation, including deferred taxation
	3	Other provisions

References to 'Provisions for liabilities' in the Regulations are 'to any amount retained as reasonably necessary for the purpose of providing for any liability the nature of which is clearly defined and which is either likely to be incurred, or certain to be incurred but uncertain as to amount or as to the date on which it will arise'. *[9 Sch 2, 4 Sch 9 (LLP)]*. FRS 102 defines a provision more succinctly as 'a liability of uncertain timing or amount.' *[FRS 102.Appendix I]*.

As can be seen from Figure 4.11 above, the balance sheet statutory formats include line items for pensions and similar obligations, taxation (including deferred taxation) and other provisions.

The General Rules to the formats (see 4.4 above) allow or, where the special nature of the company's business requires this, require certain adaptations to the balance sheet formats, as well as allowing line items to be shown in greater detail. The analysis of provisions is an area where entities may need to be mindful that FRS 102 requires additional line items, headings and subtotals when relevant to an understanding of the entity's financial position.

UK companies preparing Companies Act accounts (relevant to 'adapted formats' and statutory formats) must give particulars of each material provision included in the line item 'other provisions' in the notes to the accounts. *[1 Sch 59(3), 1 Sch 57(3) (LLP)]*. Particulars must also be given of any pension commitments included in the balance sheet, giving separate particulars of any commitment relating wholly or partly to pensions payable to past directors of the company (past members of the LLP). *[1 Sch 63(5)-(6), 1 Sch 60 (4) (LLP)]*.

FRS 102 requires an entity to present a reconciliation of each class of provision and requires further narrative disclosures for each class of provision. *[FRS 102.21.14].* See Chapter 17 at 3.10.2 of EY New UK GAAP 2015 and Chapter 5 at 8 (which discusses amendments to provision disclosures included in FRS 102 (amended July 2015)).

A UK company preparing Companies Act accounts (relevant to 'adapted formats' and statutory formats) must give the following disclosure for provisions required to be shown as separate line items in the balance sheet (or would be so shown, if Arabic-numbered line items were not combined as permitted by paragraph 4(2)(b) of the General Rules to the formats – see 4.4 above).

Where there have been transfers to provisions, or from any provisions for a purpose different to that for which the provision was established, the company must disclose, in the notes to the accounts, in respect of the aggregate of provisions included in the same item:

- the amount of the provisions as at the beginning and end of the financial year;

- any amounts transferred to or from the provisions during that year; and

- the source and application respectively of any amounts transferred.

Comparatives are not required. Where SI 2015/980 is applied, this information must be presented in tabular form. *[1 Sch 59(1)-(2), 1 Sch 57(1)-(2) (LLP)].*

The above reconciliation required by the Regulations is similar to that required by FRS 102. However, the requirement in the Regulations would also apply to movements in deferred tax provisions (see 5.3.13.B below) and pension provisions, as these are line items under 'provisions for liabilities'. In respect of pension provisions, FRS 102 already requires reconciliations of defined benefit obligations and plan assets, which provide similar information. *[FRS 102.28.41].* See Chapter 23 at 3.12.4 of EY New UK GAAP 2015.

5.3.12 Capital and reserves

Figure 4.12 shows the analysis required in respect of capital and reserves under format 1 for a UK company. See 5.3 above for modifications in format 1 in the LLP Regulations.

Figure 4.12   Analysis of capital and reserves

K	**Capital and reserves**	
I	Called up share capital	
II	Share premium account	
III	Revaluation reserve	
IV	Other reserves	
	1	Capital redemption reserve
	2	Reserve for own shares
	3	Reserves provided for by the articles of association
	4	Other reserves (including fair value reserve)*
V	Profit and loss account	
	* Where SI 2015/980 is not applied, the formats amend K.IV.4 'Other reserves'	

The capital and reserves section of the balance sheet includes a number of line items denoted by a Roman numeral which must be presented on the face of the balance sheet, with no adaptation of the order of the headings or description used permitted.

The analysis of other reserves may be presented in the notes to the accounts, where permitted by the General Rules to the formats (see 4.4 above).

In addition, where there are transfers to or from any reserves, a UK company preparing Companies Act accounts must disclose, in the notes to the accounts, a reconciliation of the aggregate of the reserves included in each item shown in the balance sheet (or would be so shown, if Arabic-numbered line items were not combined as permitted by paragraph 4(2)(b) of the General Rules to the formats). *[1 Sch 59(1)-(2), 1 Sch 57(1)-(2) (LLP)]*.

This disclosure requirement is relevant to both statutory formats and 'adapted formats' and has some similarities to FRS 102's statement of changes in equity (for which comparatives are required). Both requirements are discussed further at 7 below.

5.3.12.A   Called up share capital

Called up share capital, in relation to a company, means so much of its share capital as equals the aggregate amounts of the calls made on its shares (whether or not those calls have been paid) together with:

- any share capital paid up without being called; and

- any share capital to be paid on a specified future date under the articles, the terms of allotment of the relevant shares or any other arrangements for payment of those shares.

Uncalled share capital is to be construed accordingly. *[s547]*.

Shares allotted by a company, and any premium on them, may be paid up in money or money's worth (including goodwill and know-how). This does not prevent a company allotting bonus shares to its members, or from paying up, with sums available for the purpose, any amounts for the time being unpaid on any of its shares (whether on account of the nominal value of the shares or by way of premium). There are additional restrictions for payment of shares for public companies. *[s582]*.

The CA 2006 does not require that the shares issued are fully paid although a public company must not allot a share except where at least one quarter of the nominal value of the share and all of any premium on it is paid up (with an exception for shares allotted in pursuance of an employees' share scheme). *[s586]*.

A share in a company is deemed 'paid up' (as to its nominal value or any premium on it) in cash, or allotted for cash, if the consideration received for the allotment or payment up in cash is:

- cash received by the company;

- a cheque received by the company in good faith that the directors have no reason for suspecting will not be paid;

- a release of a liability of the company for a liquidated sum;

- an undertaking to pay cash to the company at a future date; or

- payment by any other means giving rise to a present or future entitlement (of the company or a person acting on the company's behalf) to a payment, or credit equivalent to payment, in cash. This can include payments made using the settlement system operated by Euroclear UK & Ireland (also known as the CREST system) – see *The Companies (Shares and Share Capital) Order 2009*.

Cash includes foreign currency. The payment of cash to a person other than the company or an undertaking to pay cash to a person other than the company is consideration other than cash. *[s583]*.

Called up share capital not paid is explained at 5.3.1 above.

FRS 102's requirements on recording issuances of equity instruments are consistent with the presentation of called up share capital in the Regulations *[FRS 102.22.7-22.12]* (see Chapter 8 at 9.6 of EY New UK GAAP 2015).

5.3.12.B   Share premium account

Share premium account is a statutory reserve that arises on the issue of share capital. It is beyond the scope of this chapter to explain the rules governing share premium in detail, but the summary below explains how share premium arises and can be applied or reduced.

If a company issues shares at a premium, whether for cash or otherwise, a sum equal to the aggregate amount or value of the premiums on those shares must be transferred to an account called the share premium account, except to the extent that merger relief (as set out in sections 612 and 613) and group reconstruction relief (as set out in section 611) apply. Chapter 6 at 4.2.1 of EY New UK GAAP 2015 discusses how these reliefs operate. Where on issuing shares, a company has transferred a sum to the share premium account, that sum can be used to write off the expenses of the issue of those shares and any commission paid on the issue of those shares. Share premium may be used to pay up new shares to be allotted to members as fully-paid bonus shares. *[s610(1)-(3), (5)]*.

Share premium also arises when treasury shares are sold for proceeds that exceed the purchase price paid by the company. The excess must be transferred to the share premium account. *[s731(3)]*. This would include sales of treasury shares to an ESOP.

The share premium account may be reduced (by special resolution supported by a solvency statement or confirmed by the court). *[s610(4), s641-651]*.

Where a limited company purchases (or redeems) shares, normally the purchase (or redemption) must be made out of distributable profits or out of the proceeds of a fresh issue made for the purposes of financing the purchase (or for the purposes of the redemption). However, any premium payable on the purchase (or redemption) must be made out of distributable profits, unless the shares were originally issued at a premium and the purchase (or redemption) is made in whole or in part out of proceeds of a fresh issue. In the latter case, the share premium account (rather than distributable profits) may be reduced up to an amount equal to the lower of (a) the aggregate of the premiums received by the company on issue of the shares purchased (or redeemed) and (b) the current amount of the share premium account (including any premiums transferred to share premium account in respect of the new shares). *[s687, s692]*.

Share premium account may also be reduced, to the extent permitted by section 734 of the CA 2006, when a private limited company makes a payment out of capital (under Chapter 5 of Part 18 of the CA 2006) that exceeds the nominal value of the shares redeemed or purchased. *[s709-723, s734]*.

Chapter 4

5.3.12.C   *Revaluation reserve*

The revaluation reserve arises where an asset is carried at valuation using the alternative accounting rules in the Regulations. *[1 Sch 35]*. See 10.2 below.

Where SI 2015/980 is not applied, the Regulations require that the amount of the revaluation reserve is presented in the position given for the item 'revaluation reserve' but, unlike the other reserves denoted with a Roman numeral, it need not be shown under that name. *[1 Sch 35(2)]*. This is also the case for LLPs (unless LLP law is subsequently changed) since the LLP Regulations were not amended by SI 2015/980. *[1 Sch 35(2) (LLP)]*.

Where SI 2015/980 is applied, the amount of the revaluation reserve is presented in the position given for the item 'revaluation reserve' under capital and reserves in the balance sheet formats and the name 'revaluation reserve' must be used. *[1 Sch 35(2)]*.

The uses of the revaluation reserve (and associated disclosures) are explained further at 10.2.3 and 10.2.4 below.

5.3.12.D   *Reserves provided for by the Articles of Association*

Where the articles specifically provide for reserves to be established, this line item is used.

5.3.12.E   *Other reserves*

The General Rules to the formats (see 4.4 above) allow or, where the special nature of the company's business requires this, require certain adaptations to the balance sheet formats, as well as allowing line items to be shown in greater detail.

The analysis of other reserves is an area where entities may need to be mindful that FRS 102 requires additional line items, headings and subtotals when relevant to an understanding of the entity's financial position. *[FRS 102.4.3]*.

5.3.12.F to 5.3.12.H below discuss the sub-headings within the 'Other reserves' category.

5.3.12.F   *Capital redemption reserve*

The capital redemption reserve is a statutory reserve which is established when: *[s733, s734]*

- the shares of a limited company are redeemed or purchased wholly out of the company's profits – the amount by which the company's issued share capital is diminished on cancellation of the redeemed or purchased shares (i.e. the nominal value of the shares redeemed or purchased) is transferred to capital redemption reserve;

- the shares of a limited company are redeemed or purchased wholly or partly out of the proceeds of a fresh issue and the aggregate amount of the proceeds is less than the aggregate nominal value of the shares redeemed or purchased – the shortfall is transferred to capital redemption reserve;

- a private company makes a redemption or purchase of own shares out of capital (under Chapter 5 of Part 18 of the CA 2006), and the permissible capital payment is less than the nominal amount of the shares redeemed or purchased – the shortfall is transferred to capital redemption reserve; and

- where treasury shares are cancelled – the share capital is reduced by the nominal amount of the shares cancelled and that amount transferred to capital redemption reserve.

It is beyond the scope of this chapter to explain the rules governing redemptions/purchases of shares, treasury shares and the capital redemption reserve in detail but the summary below explains how capital redemption reserve can be applied or reduced.

As with the share premium account, the capital redemption reserve may:

- be used to pay up new shares to be allotted to members as fully-paid bonus shares; *[s733(5)]*

- be reduced (by special resolution supported by a solvency statement or confirmed by the court); and *[s733(6), s641-651]*

- be reduced, to the extent permitted by section 734 of the CA 2006, when a private limited company makes a payment out of capital (under Chapter 5 of Part 18 of the CA 2006) that exceeds the nominal value of the shares redeemed or purchased. *[s709-723, s734].*

5.3.12.G   Reserve for own shares

The reserve for own shares is used where:

- a company issues shares to or purchases its own shares to be held by an ESOP (see Chapter 21 at 13.3 of EY New UK GAAP 2015). *[FRS 102.9.10-9.12, 9.33-9.37].*

  This applies in individual and consolidated financial statements (where the company is the sponsoring entity of the ESOP), and in consolidated financial statements that consolidate the ESOP (where the company is not the sponsoring entity of the ESOP); or

- where shares are held as treasury shares (see Chapter 8 at 9.7.3 of EY New UK GAAP 2015). *[FRS 102.22.16].*

Note (4) to the balance sheet statutory formats in Schedule 1 to the Regulations states that the nominal value of the own shares held must be shown separately in the notes to the accounts. This note strictly refers to own shares presented as an asset (which is not permitted under FRS 102) but entities commonly disclose this information even where own shares are presented in equity. Where treasury shares are held, there are further statutory disclosures (see 5.4.2 below).

5.3.12.H   Other reserves (including fair value reserve) (item K.IV.4)

Other reserves reported at item K.IV.4 would include a reserve arising where merger relief (under sections 612 and 613) or group reconstruction relief (under section 611) is taken, but the company chooses to record a reserve equivalent to the share premium that would have been recorded but for the relief (as permitted by section 615).

Chapter 4

Where a UK company prepares Companies Act accounts, the fair value accounting rules in the Regulations (see 10.3 below) have the effect that the changes in fair value:

- of the hedging instrument in respect of cash-flow hedges and hedges of net investment in foreign operations (to the extent effective);

- relating to exchange differences on monetary items forming part of the company's net investment in a foreign entity; and

- of available for sale financial assets

must or may be recognised in a separate statutory reserve (the fair value reserve). This would be an 'other reserve' in the statutory formats. The LLP Regulations have similar requirements. SI 2015/980 amends the line item K.IV.4 to read 'Other reserves (including fair value reserve)'.

FRS 102 requires that exchange differences arising on translation of a foreign operation in the financial statements that include that foreign operation (including a monetary item that forms part of the net investment in that foreign operation) are recognised in other comprehensive income and accumulated in equity. However, there is no requirement in the standard to accumulate these in a separate reserve. *[FRS 102.30.13, 30.22]*. See Chapter 25 at 3.7 of EY New UK GAAP 2015. Companies are not, however, precluded from doing so, and the fair value accounting rules imply that exchange differences on monetary items forming part of the company's net investment in a foreign entity are accumulated within the fair value reserve. See 10.3.2 below.

5.3.12.1   *Profit and loss account*

The profit and loss account reserve (or retained earnings) arises from the accumulation of the results for the year, and other items taken to other comprehensive income or to equity, but not classified in another reserve.

Where profits are unrealised, companies may prefer to report these in a reserve other than retained earnings, so as to distinguish these from other profits that are realised.

5.3.13   **Other implementation issues**

5.3.13.A   *Construction contracts*

FRS 102's requirements on presentation of construction contracts are discussed at 5.1.13.B above. This discussion is equally applicable to the statutory formats, subject to the following observations.

In our view, it would be appropriate to include the contract asset as a line item within debtors (see 5.3.6 above) and the contract liability within creditors (see 5.3.8 above). Progress billings not yet received (including any contract retentions) would be included in trade debtors (rather than trade receivables as in the 'adapted formats'). Advances, where reported separately, would be disclosed as 'payments received on account' within Creditors: amounts falling due within one year and Creditors: amounts falling due after more than one year, as appropriate. The sub-classifications required by paragraph 4.2B of FRS 102 where 'adapted formats' are used are not required where statutory formats are used.

5.3.13.B   *Deferred tax*

FRS 102 requires deferred tax liabilities to be presented within Provisions for liabilities (see 5.3.11 above) and deferred tax assets to be presented within debtors. There is no requirement to present deferred tax separately on the face of the statement of financial position. *[FRS 102.29.23]*. This is consistent with the presentation required under previous UK GAAP *[FRS 19.Appendix III.9-10]* but differs from the presentation of deferred tax under the 'adapted formats' in FRS 102 (see 5.1 above) or IFRS as a non-current asset and/or non-current liability on the face of the statement of financial position. *[IAS 1.54, 56]*.

Deferred tax assets may include amounts due after more than one year. See 5.2.2 above for the disclosure requirements for debtors: amounts falling due after more than one year in FRS 102 and the Regulations, where statutory formats are used.

UK companies preparing Companies Act accounts (relevant to 'adapted formats' and statutory formats) must state the provision for deferred tax separately from any other tax provisions. *[1 Sch 60]*.

Where there have been transfers to and from deferred tax, the amount of the provision at the beginning and end of the year, and the movements in that provision must also be disclosed in the notes to the accounts (see 5.3.11 above). *[1 Sch 59]*. This disclosure is required where statutory formats are used and in our view, may still be required where 'adapted formats' are used, even though deferred tax is not shown as a provision in the balance sheet (in order to give equivalent information).

5.3.13.C   *Assets and disposal groups held for sale*

FRS 102 does not include a concept of assets and disposal groups held for sale, comparable to that in IFRS 5. The standard, therefore, does not require an entity to present a non-current asset classified as held for sale and the assets of a disposal group held for sale separately from other assets in the statement of financial position and the liabilities of a disposal group held for sale separately from other liabilities in the statement of financial position. *[IFRS 5.38, IAS 1.54]*.

In addition, FRS 102 does not permit such presentation of disposal groups in the statement of financial position because the General Rules to the formats do not allow the aggregation of different line items into two lines, being assets and liabilities of the disposal group, in this way. *[FRS 102.4.4C]*. This does not preclude entities presenting additional analysis in the notes to the financial statements. See also the disclosures at 5.5 below.

As noted at 5.3.3 above, the statutory definition of a fixed asset is not normally interpreted to mean that individual assets are transferred to current assets when a decision to dispose of them has been made (but see 5.1.8 above which sets out some situations where we would expect a change in use of the asset to lead to reclassification as inventory). Nevertheless, some companies do make such transfers.

5.3.13.D   Post-employment benefit assets and liabilities

FRS 102 does not explicitly address the presentation of post-employment benefit assets and liabilities.

The format 1 balance sheet includes a line item 'Pensions and similar liabilities' within provisions for liabilities (see 5.3.11 above). There is no specific line item for pension surpluses but in our view, a pension asset could be presented as a separate line item within debtors. Defined benefit assets may include amounts due after more than one year. See 5.2.2 above for the disclosure requirements in FRS 102 and in the Regulations for debtors: amounts due after more than one year.

However, under previous UK GAAP, FRS 17 – *Retirement benefits* – requires presentation of the pension asset or liability (net of deferred tax) separately on the face of the balance sheet following other net assets and before capital and reserves. Where an employer has more than one scheme, the total of any defined benefit assets and the total of any defined benefit liabilities are shown separately on the balance sheet. *[FRS 17.47, 49]*. Appendix II to FRS 17 states that 'The Board has received legal advice that these requirements do not contravene the Companies Act 1985'. *[FRS 17.Appendix II.6]*.

As a result, there is likely to be divergence in practice in the presentation of defined benefit pension surpluses and deficits under FRS 102 (although the related deferred tax asset or liability should be shown separately, as offset is not permitted under the standard). Disclosure requirements for defined benefit plans are discussed at Chapter 23 at 3.12.4 of EY New UK GAAP 2015.

Disclosures in the Regulations (relevant to adapted and statutory formats) for pension commitments included in the balance sheet are discussed at 5.3.11 above and, for pension commitments not included in the balance sheet, at 8.7.1 below.

5.3.13.E   Biological assets

The format 1 balance sheet does not include a line item for biological assets, which should be reported within either tangible fixed assets (e.g. an apple orchard) or stock (e.g. farmed salmon), as appropriate.

5.3.13.F   Financial assets and financial liabilities

The format 1 balance sheet does not include specific line items for financial assets and financial liabilities. Financial assets will generally be reported within cash at bank and in hand, debtors, current asset investments or fixed asset investments, as applicable. Financial liabilities will generally be reported within creditors: amounts falling due within one year and creditors: amounts falling due after more than one year or provisions for liabilities (e.g. contingent consideration on a business combination), as applicable.

FRS 102 requires further analyses of specified categories of financial assets and financial liabilities to be disclosed either in the statement of financial position or in the notes (see 5.1.6 above for details).

5.3.13.G   Compound instruments

See 5.1.13.E above. The discussion is equally applicable to statutory formats.

5.3.13.H   Government grants

FRS 102 sets out two models for recognising government grants – the accrual model (which is similar to that used under previous UK GAAP) and the performance model (see Chapter 19 of EY New UK GAAP 2015). There is no specific line for government grants in the balance sheet statutory formats.

The discussion at 5.1.13.F above on presentation and disclosure of government grants under the two models is equally applicable to statutory formats.

5.4   Additional disclosures in respect of share capital (or equivalent)

FRS 102 (see 5.4.1 below) and the Regulations (see 5.4.2 below) require similar disclosures in respect of share capital.

5.4.1   *FRS 102 disclosures in respect of share capital (or equivalent)*

FRS 102 requires an entity with share capital to disclose the following information either on the face of the statement of financial position or in the notes: *[FRS 102.4.12]*

(a)   for each class of share capital:

    (i)   the number of shares issued and fully paid, and issued but not fully paid;

    (ii)   par value per share, or that the shares have no par value;

    (iii)   a reconciliation of the number of shares outstanding at the beginning and at the end of the period. This reconciliation need not be presented for prior periods;

    (v)   the rights, preferences and restrictions attaching to that class including restrictions on the distribution of dividends and the repayment of capital;

    (vi)   shares in the entity held by the entity or by its subsidiaries, associates or joint ventures;

    (vii)   shares reserved for issue under options and contracts for the sale of shares, including the terms and amounts; and

(b)   a description of each reserve within equity.

An entity without share capital, such as a partnership or trust, must disclose information equivalent to that required by (a) above, showing changes during the period in each category of equity, and the rights, preferences and restrictions attaching to each category of equity. *[FRS 102.4.13]*.

5.4.2   *Information required by the Regulations in respect of share capital*

Some of the FRS 102 disclosure requirements overlap with the disclosure requirements in relation to share capital included in the Regulations for UK companies preparing Companies Act accounts. The Regulations require the following disclosures in the notes to the accounts:

- the amount of allotted share capital and, separately, the amount of called up share capital which has been paid up (on the face of the statement of financial position or in the notes);[21]

- where shares of more than one class have been allotted, the number and aggregate nominal value of shares of each class allotted; *[1 Sch 47(1)(a)]*

- where shares are held as treasury shares, the number and aggregate nominal value of the treasury shares and, where shares of more than one class have been allotted, the number and aggregate nominal value of the shares of each class held as treasury shares; *[1 Sch 47(1)(b)]*.

- where any part of the allotted share capital consists of redeemable shares: *[1 Sch 47(2)]*

    - the earliest and latest dates on which the company has power to redeem those shares;

    - whether those shares must be redeemed in any event or are liable to be redeemed at the option of the company or of the shareholder; and

    - whether any (and if so, what) premium is payable on redemption.

- if the company has allotted any shares during the financial year: *[1 Sch 48]*

    - the classes of shares allotted; and

    - for each class of shares, the number allotted, their aggregate nominal value, and the consideration received by the company for the allotment.

- with respect to any contingent right to the allotment of shares in the company (i.e. any option to subscribe for shares and any other right to require the allotment of shares to any person whether arising on the conversion into shares of securities of any other description or otherwise), particulars of: *[1 Sch 49]*

    - the number, description and amount of the shares in relation to which the right is exercisable;

    - the period during which it is exercisable; and

    - the price to be paid for the shares allotted;

- if any fixed cumulative dividends on the company's shares are in arrear: *[1 Sch 62]*

    - the amount of the arrears; and

    - the period for which the dividends or, if there is more than one class, each class of them are in arrear; and

- the number, description and amount of shares in the company held by, or on behalf of, its subsidiary undertakings (except where the subsidiary undertaking is concerned as personal representative, or, subject to certain exceptions, as trustee). *[4 Sch 3]*.

The LLP Regulations do not include these disclosures (as not relevant) although the following information is required in respect of loans and other debts due to members:

- the aggregate amount of loans and other debts due to members as at the date of the financial year;

- the aggregate amounts contributed by members during the financial year;

- the aggregate amounts transferred to or from the profit and loss account during that year;

- the aggregate amounts withdrawn by members or applied on behalf of members during that year;

- the aggregate amount of loans and other debts due to members as at the balance sheet date; and

- the aggregate amount of loans and other debts due to members that fall due after more than one year. *[1 Sch 47 (LLP)]*.

The *Statement of Recommended Practice – Accounting by Limited Liability Partnerships* (July 2014) issued by CCAB provides further guidance on this disclosure and requires a reconciliation of the movement in members' interests analysed between 'Members' other interests' and 'Loans and other debts due to members' (which would meet the requirements of paragraph 4.13 of FRS 102 (see 5.4.1 above) and the statutory requirements in paragraph 47 of Schedule 1 to the LLP Regulations).[22] Detailed guidance on issues specific to LLPs is outside the scope of this Chapter.

5.5 Information on disposal groups to be presented in the notes (adapted and statutory formats)

FRS 102 requires only limited disclosures where there is, at the end of the reporting period, a disposal group. As discussed at 5.1.13.C and 5.3.13.C above, the Regulations do not permit the IFRS 5 presentation of separate line items for assets and liabilities of a disposal group held for sale in the statement of financial position.

If, at the reporting date, an entity has a binding sale agreement for a major disposal of assets, or a disposal group, the entity must disclose in the notes to the financial statements: *[FRS 102.4.14]*

- a description of the asset(s) or the disposal group;

- a description of the facts and circumstances of the sale; and

- the carrying amount of the assets or, for a disposal group, the carrying amounts of the underlying assets and liabilities.

FRS 102 defines a disposal group as 'a group of assets to be disposed of, by sale or otherwise, together as a group in a single transaction, and liabilities directly associated with those assets that will be transferred in the transaction. The group includes goodwill acquired in a business combination if the group is a cash-generating unit to which goodwill has been allocated in accordance with the requirements of paragraphs 27.24 to 27.27 of this FRS'. *[FRS 102.Appendix I]*.

6   STATEMENT OF COMPREHENSIVE INCOME

FRS 102 requires an entity to present its total comprehensive income for a period, i.e. its financial performance for period, in one or two statements. Financial performance is the relationship of the income and expenses of an entity as reported in the statement of comprehensive income. Relevant definitions of terms applicable to the statement of comprehensive income are at 3.1 above.

Section 5 of the standard applies to all FRS 102 reporters whether or not they report under the CA 2006. Entities that do not report under the CA 2006 are required to comply with the requirements set out in Section 5 and with the Regulations (or, where applicable, the LLP Regulations) where referred to in Section 5, except to the extent that these requirements are not permitted by any statutory framework under which such entities report. *[FRS 102.5.1]*.

6.1   Format of the statement of comprehensive income (applicable to both 'adapted formats' and statutory formats)

Part 1 of Schedule 1 to the Regulations, where SI 2015/980 is applied, provides a choice of:

*   two profit and loss account statutory formats (as set out in Section B of that Part – see 6.6 below); or

*   use of 'adapted' formats (see 6.5 below).

This section explains the requirements of FRS 102 to present a statement of comprehensive income in single statement form or as two statements. Items presented in other comprehensive income are discussed at 6.2 below. These items are presented outside profit or loss, whether the statement of comprehensive income is presented in single or two statement form. Supplementary requirements in FRS 102 relevant to the statement of comprehensive income are discussed at 6.7 to 6.9 below. The discussion at 6.1 to 6.4 and 6.7 to 6.9 below is relevant to both 'adapted formats' and statutory formats.

An entity must present its total comprehensive income for a period either: *[FRS 102.5.2, Appendix I]*

*   in a single statement of comprehensive income which presents all items of income and expense (and includes a subtotal for profit or loss) (see 6.3 below); or

*   in two statements – an income statement (referred to as the profit and loss account in the CA 2006) and a statement of comprehensive income, in which case the income statement presents all items of income and expense recognised in the period except those that are recognised in total comprehensive income outside of profit or loss as permitted or required by FRS 102 (see 6.4 below).

A change from the single-statement approach to the two-statement approach, or *vice versa*, is a retrospective change in accounting policy to which Section 10 applies. *[FRS 102.5.3]*. See Chapter 7 at 3.4 of EY New UK GAAP 2015.

These requirements apply both to consolidated and individual financial statements.

However, UK companies (and LLPs) preparing group accounts in accordance with the CA 2006 can take advantage of the exemption in section 408 of the CA 2006 (where the conditions are met) not to present the individual profit and loss account and certain related notes. *[s408, s472(2), Regulations 3(2), 1 Sch 65, s408 (LLP), s472(2) (LLP), LLP Regulations 3(2), 1 Sch 62-67 (LLP)]*. See Chapter 1 at 6.3.2. This exemption would not extend to individual financial statements prepared under other statutory frameworks, unless permitted by these frameworks.

SI 2015/980, where applied, has made amendments to the section 408 exemption. In particular, the company's individual balance sheet (previously the notes to the individual balance sheet) must show the company's profit for the financial year, as determined in accordance with the CA 2006, and the exemption no longer covers the disclosures on staff costs and staff numbers required in individual accounts by section 411 of the CA 2006 (see 8.6 below). These changes do not affect LLPs (unless there is a subsequent change to LLP law).

6.2 Items reported in other comprehensive income (applicable to both 'adapted formats' and statutory formats)

Other comprehensive income means items of income and expense (including reclassification adjustments), that are not recognised in profit or loss as required or permitted by FRS 102. *[FRS 102.Appendix I]*. Therefore, profit and loss is the default category; all comprehensive income is part of profit and loss unless FRS 102 permits or requires otherwise. See definitions at 3.1 above.

Tax expense / (income) is recognised in other comprehensive income where the transaction or other event that resulted in the tax is recognised in other comprehensive income. *[FRS 102.29.22]*. See Chapter 24 at 8 of EY New UK GAAP 2015.

FRS 102 requires the following items to be included in other comprehensive income:

(a) changes in revaluation surplus relating to property, plant and equipment *[FRS 102.17.15E-F]* (see Chapter 13 at 3.6.3 of EY New UK GAAP 2015) and intangible assets, *[FRS 102.18.18G-H]*, (see Chapter 14 at 3.4.2.C of EY New UK GAAP 2015);

(b) actuarial gains and losses, and the return on plan assets excluding amounts included in net interest on the net defined benefit liability (known collectively as 'remeasurements' of the net defined benefit liability) on defined benefit plans, *[FRS 102.28.23(d), 25]*, (see Chapter 23 at 3.6.8.B of EY New UK GAAP 2015);

(c) exchange gains and losses arising from translating the financial statements of a foreign operation (including in consolidated financial statements, exchange differences on a monetary item that forms part of the net investment in the foreign operation). However, under FRS 102 (unlike IAS 21 – *The Effects of Changes in Foreign Exchange Rates* – and FRS 23 – *The effects of changes in foreign exchange rates*), cumulative exchange differences accumulated in equity are not reclassified to profit and loss on disposal of a net investment in a foreign operation, *[FRS 102.9.18A, 30.13]*, (see Chapter 25 at 3.7.4 of EY New UK GAAP 2015);

(d) the effective portion of fair value gains and losses on hedging instruments in a cash flow hedge or a hedge of the foreign exchange risk in a net investment in a foreign operation. The amounts taken to equity in respect of the hedge of the foreign exchange risk in a net investment in a foreign operation are not reclassified to profit or loss on disposal or partial disposal of the foreign operation, *[FRS 102.12.23-24, 25A]*, (see Chapter 8 at 7.8 and 7.9 of EY New UK GAAP 2015);

(e)   fair value gains and losses through other comprehensive income for an investor that is not a parent measuring its interests in jointly controlled entities, *[FRS 102.15.9(c), 15.14-15A]*, and investments in associates in its individual financial statements, *[FRS 102.14.4(c), 14.9-10A]*, (see Chapter 10 at 3.3.4 of EY New UK GAAP 2015 and Chapter 11 at 3.6.2 of EY New UK GAAP 2015);

(f)   fair value gains and losses through other comprehensive income for investments in subsidiaries, associates and jointly controlled entities used by a parent in its separate financial statements or in consolidated financial statements for certain excluded subsidiaries, *[FRS 102.9.26(b), 9.26A, 9.9, 9.9A, 9.9B(b)]*, (see Chapter 6 at 3.4 and 4.2 of EY New UK GAAP 2015); and

(g)   any unrealised gain arising on an exchange of business or non-monetary assets for an interest in a subsidiary, jointly controlled entity or associate, *[FRS 102.9.31(c)]*, (see Chapter 6 at 3.8 of EY New UK GAAP 2015).

Of the above items, only the amounts taken to other comprehensive income in relation to cash flow hedges (at (d) above) may be reclassified to profit or loss in a subsequent period under FRS 102.

Where the entity applies the recognition and measurement requirements of IAS 39 or IFRS 9 to financial instruments, further items are reported in other comprehensive income (see 6.2.1 below).

Schedule 1 to the Regulations restricts when unrealised profits can be reported in the profit and loss account. Consequently, certain unrealised profits may be required to be reported in other comprehensive income (see 6.2.2 below).

6.2.1   *Items reported in other comprehensive income where an entity chooses to apply the recognition and measurement provisions of IAS 39 or IFRS 9 (and/or IAS 39)*

Where the recognition and measurement requirements of IFRS 9 (and / or IAS 39) are applied to financial instruments, as permitted by FRS 102, the following items would also be reported in other comprehensive income in accordance with the requirements of the applicable accounting standard:

(a)   gains and losses on remeasuring available-for-sale financial assets (if the entity chooses to apply IAS 39); *[IAS 39.55(b)]*

(b)   gains and losses on remeasuring investments in equity instruments designated as measured at fair value through other comprehensive income (if the entity chooses to apply IFRS 9); *[IFRS 9.4.1.4, 5.7.1(b), 5.7.5-5.7.6]*

(c)   the effective portion of gains and losses on hedging instruments in a cash flow hedge or hedge of a net investment in a foreign operation (if the entity chooses to apply IAS 39 or IFRS 9); *[IAS 39.95-102, IFRS 9.6.5.11-6.5.14]*

(d)   for liabilities designated as at fair value through profit or loss, fair value changes attributable to changes in the liability's credit risk, unless this would create or enlarge an accounting mismatch in profit and loss (if the entity chooses to apply IFRS 9). *[IFRS 9.4.2.2, 5.7.1(c), 5.7.7-5.7.9, FRS 102.A4.12C].*

This accounting treatment will usually require use of a true and fair override for a UK company or LLP since it breaches the requirements of the Regulations, Small Companies Regulations, LLP Regulations or Small LLP Regulations – see 10.3 below); and

(e) gains and losses on financial assets that are debt instruments (meeting the specified criteria) that are carried at fair value through other comprehensive income (if the entity chooses to apply IFRS 9 – see 10.3 below). *[IFRS 9.4.1.2A, 5.7.1(d), 5.7.10-5.7.11].*

Only items (a), (e) and the effective portion of gains and losses on hedging instruments in a cash flow hedge at (c) above may be reclassified to profit or loss in a subsequent period. The amounts taken to equity in respect of the hedge of the foreign exchange risk in a net investment in a foreign operation are not reclassified to profit or loss on disposal or partial disposal of the foreign operation. *[FRS 102.9.18A, 30.13].*

The requirements of IAS 39 and IFRS 9 are discussed in Chapters 47 to 49 and 51 to 52 respectively of EY International GAAP 2016.

6.2.2   Impact of realised and unrealised profits on items reported in other comprehensive income

UK companies preparing Companies Act accounts need to be mindful of the requirements of paragraph 13(a) of Schedule 1 to the Regulations that 'only profits realised at the balance sheet are to be included in the profit and loss account'. *[1 Sch 13(a), 1 Sch 13(a) (LLP)].*

Notwithstanding this restriction, paragraph 40(2) of Schedule 1 to the Regulations requires that the changes in fair value of a financial instrument, living animal or plant, or investment property measured at fair value using the fair value accounting rules (where permitted by paragraphs 36 and 39 of Schedule 1) must be reflected in the profit and loss account. This is subject to the requirements of paragraphs 40(3) and (4) of Schedule 1 for available for sale financial assets, hedge accounting and for exchange differences on monetary items forming part of the net investment in a foreign entity, which permit or require certain movements on financial instruments to be reflected in a separate reserve, the fair value reserve. While SI 2015/980 also permits stocks to be measured at fair value using the fair value accounting rules, paragraph 40(2) of Schedule 1 to the Regulations has not been amended and does not specify where fair value changes are presented. See 10.3 and 10.4 below for a discussion of the fair value accounting rules. *[1 Sch 40, 1 Sch 40 (LLP)].*

FRS 101 requires that 'an entity shall recognise all items of income and expense arising in a period in profit or loss unless an IFRS requires or permits otherwise *or unless prohibited by the Act'* [emphasis added]. *[FRS 101.AG1(k)].* Whilst FRS 102 does not include the words italicised above, there are reasons to believe that the same treatment is intended. Appendix IV – *Note on legal requirements* – to the standard highlights the above requirements of paragraphs 13 and 40 of Schedule 1 to the Regulations. *[FRS 102.A4.25-A4.29].* In addition, FRS 102's requirements for exchanges of businesses and non-monetary assets for an interest in a subsidiary, jointly controlled entity or an associate state that 'any unrealised gain arising on the exchange shall be recognised in other comprehensive income'. *[FRS 102.9.31(c)]*.

Where the standard is explicit that it requires that a particular gain must be reported in profit or loss but this would conflict with the Regulations or LLP Regulations, the entity should consider whether a 'true and fair override' of the requirements of the CA 2006 is appropriate (see 9.2 below). Where the standard is not explicit, notwithstanding that profit and loss is the default location for gains and losses, in our view, entities should look to Appendix IV to the standard, which highlights the company law requirements on realised profits. However, such considerations are only relevant to entities subject to the Regulations or LLP Regulations (or corresponding requirements in another statutory or regulatory framework that applies to the entity).

Whether profits are available for distribution must be determined in accordance with applicable law. TECH 02/10 provides guidance on the determination of the profits available for distribution (under the CA 2006). *[FRS 102.A4.29]*.

6.3   Single-statement approach (applicable to both 'adapted formats' and statutory formats)

In the single-statement approach, an entity must present the items to be included in a profit and loss account in accordance with Parts 1 of Schedules 1 to 3 (as applicable) to the Regulations, or where applicable, Part 1 of Schedule 1 to the LLP Regulations.

Part 1 of Schedule 1 to the Regulations, as amended by SI 2015/980, provides a choice of statutory formats (as set out in Section B of that Part – see 6.6 below) or 'adapted' formats (see 6.5 below).

The consolidated statement of comprehensive income of a group must be presented in accordance with the requirements of Schedule 6 to the Regulations (or, where applicable, Schedule 3 to the LLP Regulations). *[FRS 102.5.5]*.

See 4.1 above for discussion as to which formats apply to which types of entity.

A subtotal for profit or loss is included in the statement of comprehensive income. *[FRS 102.Appendix I]*.

In addition, the statement of comprehensive income must include line items that present: *[FRS 102.5.5A]*

(a)   classified by nature (excluding amounts in (b)), each component of other comprehensive income recognised as part of total comprehensive income outside profit or loss as permitted or required by the standard. These must be shown either net of related tax, or gross of related tax (with a single amount shown for the aggregate amount of income tax relating to those components);

(b)   its share of the other comprehensive income of associates and jointly controlled entities accounted for by the equity method; and

(c)   total comprehensive income.

The statement of comprehensive income must also show the allocation of profit or loss for the period and of total comprehensive income for the period attributable to non-controlling interest and owners of the parent. *[FRS 102.5.6]*. See 4.5 above for a discussion of how this allocation should be presented under the formats for the group profit and loss account.

See Example 4.4 at 6.5.2 below for an example of a single statement of comprehensive income, in this case using 'adapted formats'.

6.4 Two-statement approach (applicable to both 'adapted formats' and statutory formats)

Under the two-statement approach, an entity must present in an income statement, the items to be included in a profit and loss account in accordance with Parts 1 of Schedules 1 to 3 (as applicable) to the Regulations, or where applicable, Part 1 of Schedule 1 to the LLP Regulations. The consolidated income statement of a group must be presented in accordance with the requirements of Schedule 6 to the Regulations (or, where applicable, Schedule 3 to the LLP Regulations). *[FRS 102.5.7]*.

Part 1 of Schedule 1 to the Regulations, as amended by SI 2015/980 provides a choice of statutory formats (as set out in Section B of that Part – see 6.6 below) or 'adapted' formats. See 6.5 below.

See 4.1 above for discussion as to which formats apply to which types of entity.

The income statement must show the allocation of profit or loss for the period attributable to non-controlling interest and owners of the parent. *[FRS 102.5.7B]*.

The statement of comprehensive income (whether 'adapted formats' or statutory formats are used) begins with profit or loss as its first line and then includes, as a minimum, line items that present:

(a) classified by nature (excluding amounts in (b)), each component of other comprehensive income recognised as part of total comprehensive income outside profit or loss as permitted or required by the standard. These must be shown either net of related tax, or gross of related tax (with a single amount shown for the aggregate amount of income tax relating to those components);

(b) its share of the other comprehensive income of associates and jointly controlled entities accounted for by the equity method; and

(c) total comprehensive income.

The statement of comprehensive income must also show the allocation of total comprehensive income for the period attributed to non-controlling interest and owners of the parent. *[FRS 102.5.7A-C]*.

See 4.5 above for a discussion of how the allocations of profit or loss and total comprehensive income should be presented under the formats for the group profit and loss account.

See Example 4.5 at 6.5.2 for an example statement of comprehensive income (where a two statement approach is applied).

6.5   'Adapted formats'

An entity choosing to apply paragraph 1A(2) of Schedule 1 to the Regulations and adapt one of the profit and loss account formats (see 4.1 above for discussion as to which formats apply to which types of entity) shall, as a minimum:

- include in its statement of comprehensive income (under the single statement approach) line items that present amounts (a) to (j) for the period (as set out in Figure 4.13 below); *[FRS 102.5.5B]* and

- include in its income statement (under the two statement approach) line items that present amounts (a) to (g) for the period (as set out in Figure 4.13 below), with profit or loss as the last line. The statement of comprehensive income shall begin with profit or loss as its first line and shall display as a minimum line items (h) to (j), with total comprehensive income as its last line. *[FRS 102.5.7A]*.

The main modification required for group profit and loss account 'adapted formats' is the identification of non-controlling interests (see 4.5, 6.3 and 6.4 above). *[FRS 102.5.6, 5.7A-C]*.

Figure 4.13   *Profit and loss account (UK company other than a banking company or insurance company) – paragraph 1A(2) of Schedule 1 to the Regulations ('adapted formats') applied*

(a)	Revenue	
(b)	Finance costs	
(c)	Share of the profit or loss of investments in associates and jointly controlled entities accounted for using the equity method	
(d)	Profit or loss before taxation	
(e)	Tax expense (excluding tax allocated to items (h) and (i) below or to equity)	
(f)	A single amount comprising the total of:*	
	(i)	the post tax profit or loss of a discontinued operation, and
	(ii)	the post-tax gain or loss recognised on the remeasurement of the impairment or on the disposal of the assets or disposal group(s) constituting discontinued operations
(g)	Profit or loss	
(h)	Each item of other comprehensive income classified by nature (excluding amounts in (i))	
(i)	Share of other comprehensive income of associates and jointly controlled entities accounted for using the equity method	
(j)	Total comprehensive income	
*	As set out in paragraph 5.7E (including a column for discontinued operations – see 6.8 below)	

So far as practicable, paragraphs 2 to 9A of the General Rules to the formats – see 4.4 above) apply to the income statement (or profit and loss account section of the single statement of comprehensive income), notwithstanding any such adaptation pursuant to paragraph 1A. *[1 Sch 1A(3)]*.

An entity may include additional line items in the income statement and amend the descriptions used in the line items set out in (a) to (j) and the ordering of items, when this is necessary to explain the elements of financial performance, providing the information given is at least equivalent to that required by the profit and loss account format had it not been adapted. *[FRS 102.5.5C]*. The effect of paragraph 5.5C is to clarify that there is flexibility in the presentation requirements where 'adapted formats' are used (for statutory formats, the General Rules to the formats clearly set out the flexibility for Arabic numbered items, but Arabic numbered items are not used in the 'adapted formats'). While this requirement is included under the single statement approach, in our view, this is also intended to apply to the two statement approach. Factors to be considered, highlighted by IAS 1 (which has a similar requirement), include materiality and the nature and function of the items of income and expense. *[IAS 1.86]*.

The requirement (see 6.7.2 below) that an entity shall present additional line items, headings and subtotals in the statement of comprehensive income (and in the income statement, where presented) when such presentation is relevant to an understanding of the entity's financial performance also applies to 'adapted formats'. *[FRS 102.5.9]*.

6.5.1 Other implementation issues – 'adapted formats'

The Regulations require that the information presented in the profit and loss formats is at least equivalent to that which would have been required by the use of the statutory format had it not been thus adapted and the presentation is in accordance with generally accepted accounting principles or practice. *[1 Sch 1A(2)]*.

Beyond the minimum items required to be presented in the statement of comprehensive income (in one or two statements), the ability to adapt the headings, and the requirement to present additional line items where relevant to an understanding of financial performance (as discussed at 6.5 above), Section 5 of FRS 102 includes additional requirements relevant to the statement of comprehensive income (see 6.7 below). These include the presentation of turnover, guidance on operating profit (if presented), presentation of an analysis of expenses by nature of function, and disclosure of the nature and amount of material items included in total comprehensive income (often called 'exceptional items', although that term is not used in the standard). FRS 102's requirements for presentation of discontinued operations are discussed at 6.8 below and for earnings per share (for those entities required to or choosing to present this) are discussed at 6.9 below.

These requirements are generally self explanatory. However, 'adapted formats' must present revenue on the face of the income statement (or single statement of comprehensive income) (see 6.5 above). *[FRS 102.5.5B]*. FRS 102's requirement to present turnover on the face of the income statement (or statement of comprehensive income, if presented) (see 6.7.1 below) implies that an additional analysis of revenue between turnover and other components of revenue (if any) is required on the face of the income statement (or single statement of comprehensive income). FRS 102 also requires a detailed sub-analysis of revenue, which can be presented in the notes. *[FRS 102.23.30(b)]*. See Chapter 18 at 3.11 of EY New UK GAAP 2015.

Other sections of the standard also require supplementary analysis of certain line items presented on the face of the income statement (or profit or loss section of the statement of comprehensive income), which may be included in the notes. See relevant chapters of EY New UK GAAP 2015.

FRS 102 also includes further guidance relevant to presentation in the statement of comprehensive income. For instance,

- incoming dividends and similar income receivable must be recognised at an amount that includes any withholding tax but excludes other taxes, such as attributable tax credits. Any withholding tax suffered on incoming dividends and similar income receivable is shown as part of the tax charge. See further discussion at Chapter 24 at 8.1.2 of EY New UK GAAP 2015; and *[FRS 102.29.18]*

- Section 28 – *Employee Benefits* – does not specify how the cost of a defined benefit plan should be presented in the profit and loss account. Therefore, entities may present the cost as a single item or disaggregate the cost into components presented separately;

- Section 23 – *Revenue* – includes guidance on measurement of revenue, including principal versus agent considerations. See Chapter 18 at 3.2 of EY New UK GAAP 2015.

For UK companies preparing Companies Act accounts (relevant to 'adapted formats' and statutory formats), the Regulations require further supplementary information in respect of certain line items to be given in the notes to the accounts. One complexity is that the information required by the Regulations is generally in respect of line items required in the statutory formats (e.g. turnover), where the headings used in the formats may differ to those included where the 'adapted formats' are used. Similar considerations arise for LLPs. Further information on certain of these statutory disclosures is given in 6.6 below.

FRS 102 and the Regulations require numerous further disclosures (which may be given in the notes) concerning items recognised in profit or loss. The LLP Regulations generally include similar disclosures to the Regulations. Refer to the disclosure sections of the relevant Chapters in EY New UK GAAP 2015.

6.5.2   *Illustrative statement of comprehensive income ('adapted formats')*

Example 4.4 below illustrates a single statement of comprehensive income, where the 'adapted formats' are used. This is based on an illustrative example in IAS 1 Implementation Guidance, modified to illustrate the requirements of FRS 102. In particular,

- FRS 102 does not require separate presentation in other comprehensive income between items that will not be reclassified to profit or loss and items that may be reclassified subsequently to profit or loss;

- earnings per share information has not been illustrated (see 6.9 below for entities required to present earnings per share information); and *[FRS 102.1.4]*

- where there are discontinued operations, FRS 102 requires a line-by-line analysis with columns for continuing, discontinued and total operations (see 6.8 below). Example 4.4 shows only the 'total column' required. *[FRS 102.5.5B, 5.7E]*.

Example 4.4:   *Presentation of comprehensive income in a single statement (classification of expenses by function)*

XYZ Group – Statement of profit or loss and other comprehensive income for the year ended 31 December 2016

	2016 £'000 Total	2015 £'000 Total
Revenue	390,000	355,000
Cost of sales	(245,000)	(230,000)
Gross profit	145,000	125,000
Other income	20,667	11,300
Distribution costs	(9,000)	(8,700)
Administrative expenses	(20,000)	(21,000)
Other expenses	(2,100)	(1,200)
Finance costs	(8,000)	(7,500)
Share of profit of associates[1]	35,100	30,100
Profit before taxation	161,667	128,000
Income tax expense	(40,417)	(32,000)
Profit for the year from continuing operations	121,250	96,000
Loss for the year from discontinued operations	–	(30,500)
PROFIT FOR THE YEAR	121,250	65,500
Other comprehensive income:		
Gains on property revaluation	933	3,367
Remeasurements of defined benefit pension plans	(667)	1,333
Available-for-sale financial assets[4][5]	(24,000)	26,667
Exchange differences on translating foreign operations[4]	5,334	10,667
Cash flow hedges[4]	(667)	(4,000)
Share of gain (loss) on property revaluation of associates[2]	400	(700)
Income tax[3]	4,667	(9,334)
Other comprehensive income for the year, net of tax	(14,000)	28,000
TOTAL COMPREHENSIVE INCOME FOR THE YEAR	107,250	93,500
Profit attributable to:		
Owners of the parent	97,000	52,400
Non-controlling interests	24,250	13,100
	121,250	65,500
Total comprehensive income attributable to:		
Owners of the parent	85,800	74,800
Non-controlling interests	21,450	18,700
	107,250	93,500

Chapter 4

Alternatively, items of other comprehensive income could be presented in the statement of comprehensive income net of tax, as follows.

Statement of comprehensive income section (alternative presentation)

	2016 £'000	2015 £'000
Other comprehensive income for the year, after tax:		
Gains on property revaluation	600	2,700
Remeasurements of defined benefit pension plans	(500)	1,000
Available-for-sale financial assets[(4)(5)]	(18,000)	20,000
Exchange differences on translating foreign operations[(4)]	4,000	8,000
Cash flow hedges[(4)]	(500)	(3,000)
Share of gain (loss) on property revaluation of associates[(2)]	400	(700)
Other comprehensive income for the year, net of tax[(3)]	(14,000)	28,000

(1)   This means the share of associates' profit attributable to owners of the associates, i.e. it is after tax and non-controlling interests in the associates.

(2)   This means the share of associates' gain (loss) on property revaluation attributable to owners of the associates, i.e. it is after tax and non-controlling interests in the associates.

(3)   Unlike IAS 1, there is no requirement for the notes to disclose income tax relating to each item of other comprehensive income, although the aggregate current and deferred tax relating to items that recognised as items of other comprehensive income or equity is required in the notes. [FRS 102.29.27].

(4)   Unlike IAS 1, items in other comprehensive income are not analysed between items that will be reclassified to profit and loss and items that may be reclassified subsequently to profit and loss. Exchange differences on translating foreign operations are not subsequently reclassified under FRS 102. The change in fair value of the hedging item recognised in other comprehensive income in respect of cash flow hedges and hedges of a net investment in a foreign operation and the amounts reclassified to profit or loss in respect of cash flow hedges in the period are required to be disclosed in the notes. [FRS 102.12.29(c)-(d), 12.29A].
      FRS 102 requires an analysis of other comprehensive income by item in the statement of changes in equity or in the notes to the accounts. [FRS 102.6.3A].

(5)   An FRS 102 reporter will only have available for sale financial assets if it adopts IAS 39 for recognition and measurement of financial instruments.

Example 4.5 below shows the statement of comprehensive income using the two statement approach. This is relevant for both 'adapted formats' and statutory formats because the requirements for the statement of comprehensive income derive from the Regulations rather than FRS 102. As in Example 4.4, the items in other comprehensive income may alternatively be presented net of tax.

The separate income statement (not presented in Example 4.5) would follow the requirements for 'adapted formats' (see 6.5 above) or statutory formats (see 6.6 below), depending on the format applied and would show the allocation of profit between owners of the parent and non-controlling interest.

Example 4.5 is adapted from an illustrative example in IAS 1, but modified to illustrate the requirements of FRS 102. Example 4.5 looks the same as the latter part of the single statement of comprehensive income presented in Example 4.4 above but only shows the allocation of total comprehensive income between owners of the parent and non-controlling interest. The footnotes included in Example 4.5 relate to the same footnotes as in Example 4.4.

Example 4.5:   *Statement of comprehensive income illustrating the presentation of comprehensive income in two statements*

XYZ Group – Statement of profit or loss and other comprehensive income for the year ended 31 December 2016

	2016 £'000	2015 £'000
Profit for the year	121,250	65,500
Other comprehensive income:		
Gains on property revaluation	933	3,367
Remeasurements of defined benefit pension plans	(667)	1,333
Available-for-sale financial assets[4][5]	(24,000)	26,667
Exchange differences on translating foreign operations[4]	5,334	10,667
Cash flow hedges[4]	(667)	(4,000)
Share of gain (loss) on property revaluation of associates[2]	400	(700)
Income tax [3]	4,667	(9,334)
Other comprehensive income for the year, net of tax	(14,000)	28,000
TOTAL COMPREHENSIVE INCOME FOR THE YEAR	107,250	93,500
Total comprehensive income attributable to:		
Owners of the parent	85,800	74,800
Non-controlling interests	21,450	18,700
	107,250	93,500

6.6 Statutory profit and loss account formats

An entity must present in the statement of comprehensive income, or in the separate income statement, the items to be presented in a profit and loss account in accordance with one of the profit and loss account statutory formats in the Regulations or LLP Regulations. *[FRS 102.5.5, 5.7]*. See 4.1 above for discussion as to which formats apply to which types of entity.

The following discussion relates only to the profit and loss account statutory formats included in Schedule 1 to the Regulations. It is beyond the scope of this publication to discuss the formats in Schedule 2 applicable to banking companies and groups (defined in section 1164 of the CA 2006) or the formats in Schedule 3 applicable to insurance companies and groups (defined in section 1165 of the CA 2006) – see definitions at 4.2.2 and 4.2.3 above. However, there is less flexibility to adapt the formats in Schedule 2 and Schedule 3 to the Regulations. The profit and loss account formats for banking and insurance companies and groups (and indeed LLPs, unless there is a subsequent change in the law) continue to refer to extraordinary items, albeit these are not expected in practice.

Where not applying SI 2015/980, Section B of Part 1 of Schedule 1 to the Regulations provides a choice of four formats for the profit and loss account. Only two of these are used by the majority of companies and are discussed here, namely formats 1 and 2. Formats 3 and 4, which were rarely used, are withdrawn on adoption of SI 2015/980. There are minor adaptations to formats 1 and 2 arising from adoption of SI 2015/980, principally to remove references to ordinary and extraordinary activities and to replace the word 'charges' with 'expenses'.

Chapter 4

The format 1 and format 2 profit and loss accounts in the LLP Regulations (unless there is a subsequent change to the law) differ from the formats at Figure 4.15 and Figure 4.17 below in that the final line in the formats is 'Profit or loss for the financial year before members' remuneration and profit shares'. The *Statement of Recommended Practice – Accounting by Limited Liability Partnerships* (July 2014) issued by CCAB provides further guidance on application of the statutory formats for LLPs, and requires that 'profit or loss for the financial year before members' remuneration and profit shares', 'members' remuneration charged as an expense' and 'profit or loss for the financial year available for discretionary division among members' is presented. The basis on which each element of remuneration has been treated in the accounts should be disclosed and explained by way of note.[23] The SORP provides guidance and illustrations of LLP profit or loss account for different situations. Detailed guidance on issues specific to LLPs is outside the scope of this publication.

Format 1 analyses expenses by function and is presented at Figure 4.14 below (where SI 2015/980 has been adopted) and at Figure 4.15 below (where SI 2015/980 has not been adopted).

Figure 4.14   *Format 1 profit and loss account (UK company other than a banking company or insurance company – SI 2015/980 has been adopted)*

1	Turnover
2	Cost of sales
3	Gross profit or loss
4	Distribution costs
5	Administrative expenses
6	Other operating income
7	Income from shares in group undertakings
8	Income from participating interests†
9	Income from other fixed asset investments
10	Other interest receivable and similar income
11	Amounts written off investments
12	Interest payable and similar expenses
	Profit or loss before taxation*
13	Tax on profit or loss
14	Profit or loss after taxation
19	Other taxes not shown under the above items
20	Profit or loss for the financial year**

*   While not in format 1, every profit and loss account must show the amount of a company's profit or loss before taxation (1 Sch 6, Regulations).

†   See discussion below for modifications in group accounts.

Figure 4.15   *Format 1 profit and loss account (UK company other than a banking company or insurance company – SI 2015/980 has not been adopted, or LLP)*

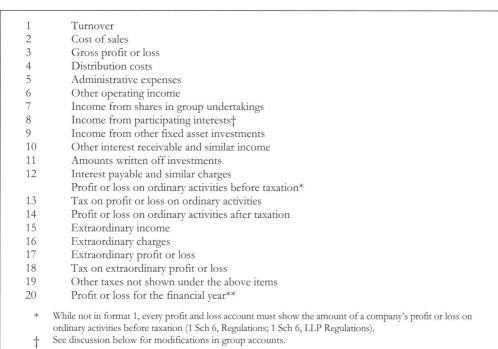

1	Turnover
2	Cost of sales
3	Gross profit or loss
4	Distribution costs
5	Administrative expenses
6	Other operating income
7	Income from shares in group undertakings
8	Income from participating interests†
9	Income from other fixed asset investments
10	Other interest receivable and similar income
11	Amounts written off investments
12	Interest payable and similar charges
	Profit or loss on ordinary activities before taxation*
13	Tax on profit or loss on ordinary activities
14	Profit or loss on ordinary activities after taxation
15	Extraordinary income
16	Extraordinary charges
17	Extraordinary profit or loss
18	Tax on extraordinary profit or loss
19	Other taxes not shown under the above items
20	Profit or loss for the financial year**

*   While not in format 1, every profit and loss account must show the amount of a company's profit or loss on ordinary activities before taxation (1 Sch 6, Regulations; 1 Sch 6, LLP Regulations).

†   See discussion below for modifications in group accounts.

**   In format 1 in the LLP Regulations, Profit or loss for the financial year before members' remuneration and profit shares.

Format 2 analyses expenses by nature and is presented at Figure 4.16 below (where SI 2015/980 has been adopted), and at Figure 4.17 below (where SI 2015/980 has not been adopted).

Figure 4.16   *Format 2 for the profit and loss account (UK company other than a banking company or insurance company – SI 2015/980 has been adopted)*

1	Turnover	
2	Change in stocks of finished goods and in work in progress	
3	Own work capitalised	
4	Other operating income	
5	(a)	Raw materials and consumables
	(b)	Other external expenses
6	Staff costs	
	(a)	wages and salaries
	(b)	social security costs
	(c)	other pension costs
7	(a)	Depreciation and other amounts written off tangible and intangible fixed assets
	(b)	Amounts written off current assets, to the extent that they exceed write-offs which are normal in the undertaking concerned
8	Other operating expenses	
9	Income from shares in group undertakings	
10	Income from participating interests†	
11	Income from other fixed asset investments	
12	Other interest receivable and similar income	
13	Amounts written off investments	
14	Interest payable and similar expenses	
	Profit or loss before taxation*	
15	Tax on profit or loss	
16	Profit or loss after taxation	
21	Other taxes not shown under the above items	
22	Profit or loss for the financial year	

*   While not in format 2, every profit and loss account must show the amount of a company's profit or loss before taxation (1 Sch 6, Regulations).

†   See discussion below for modifications in group accounts.

Figure 4.17   *Format 2 for the profit and loss account (UK company other than a banking company or insurance company – SI 2015/980 has not been adopted, or LLP)*

1	Turnover	
2	Change in stocks of finished goods and in work in progress	
3	Own work capitalised	
4	Other operating income	
5	(a)	Raw materials and consumables
	(b)	Other external charges
6	Staff costs	
	(a)	wages and salaries
	(b)	social security costs
	(c)	other pension costs
7	(a)	Depreciation and other amounts written off tangible and intangible fixed assets
	(b)	Exceptional amounts written off current assets
8	Other operating charges	
9	Income from shares in group undertakings	
10	Income from participating interests†	
11	Income from other fixed asset investments	
12	Other interest receivable and similar income	
13	Amounts written off investments	
14	Interest payable and similar charges	
	Profit or loss on ordinary activities before taxation*	
15	Tax on profit or loss on ordinary activities	
16	Profit or loss on ordinary activities after taxation	
17	Extraordinary income	
18	Extraordinary charges	
19	Extraordinary profit or loss	
20	Tax on extraordinary profit or loss	
21	Other taxes not shown under the above items	
22	Profit or loss for the financial year**	

  *   While not in format 2, every profit and loss account must show the amount of a company's profit or loss on ordinary activities before taxation (1 Sch 6, Regulations, 1 Sch 6, LLP Regulations).

  †   See discussion below for modifications in group accounts.

  **   In format 2 in the LLP Regulations, Profit or loss for the financial year before members' remuneration and profit shares.

The main modification required for group profit and loss account statutory formats is the identification of non-controlling interests (see 4.5, 6.3 and 6.4 above) and replacing 'income from participating interests' with 'income from associated undertakings' and 'income from other participating interests' (see 6.6.5 below).

The line items in the formats need to be read together with the notes to the formats. *[1 Sch 1, 1 Sch 1 (LLP)]*. The individual line items in the profit and loss account formats (together with the relevant notes to the statutory formats) are discussed at 6.6.1 to 6.6.15 below.

The General Rules to the formats (see 4.4 above) apply. As all of the line items are denoted with Arabic numbers, these allow a degree of flexibility in the profit and loss account formats. FRS 102 further requires that an entity shall present additional line items, headings and subtotals in the statement of comprehensive income (and in the income statement, where presented) when such presentation is relevant to an understanding of the entity's financial performance. *[FRS 102.5.9]*. See 6.7.2 below.

Section 5 of FRS 102 includes additional requirements relevant to the statement of comprehensive income (see 6.7 below). FRS 102's requirements for presentation of discontinued operations are discussed at 6.8 below and for earnings per share (for those entities required to or choosing to present this) are discussed at 6.9 below.

Other sections of the standard also require supplementary analysis of certain line items presented on the face of the income statement (or profit or loss section of the statement of comprehensive income), which may be included in the notes. For UK companies preparing Companies Act accounts (relevant to 'adapted formats' and statutory formats), the Regulations require further supplementary information in respect of certain line items to be given in the notes to the accounts. There are similar requirements for LLPs. Some of these disclosures are highlighted in the discussion of line items at 6.6.1 to 6.6.15 below.

FRS 102 and the Regulations require numerous further disclosures (which may be given in the notes) concerning items recognised in profit or loss. The LLP Regulations generally include similar disclosures to the Regulations. Refer to the disclosure sections of other chapters of EY New UK GAAP 2015.

6.6.1   Turnover (format 1 and format 2)

Turnover, in relation to a company, is defined as 'the amounts derived from the provision of goods and services, after deduction of:

(a)   trade discounts,

(b)   value added tax, and

(c)   any other taxes based on the amounts so derived.' *[s474(1)]*.

Where not applying SI 2015/980 and for LLPs (unless there is a subsequent change to LLP law), the definition of turnover relates to 'the amounts derived from the provision of goods and services *falling within the company's ordinary activities* [emphasis added] ....'. SI 2015/980 deletes the italicised words from the definition.

FRS 102 includes the same definition of turnover as in company law (see 3.1 above). *[FRS 102.Appendix I]*. FRS 102 (amended July 2015) also deletes the italicised words above from the definition, consistent with the company law amendments.

FRS 102 further requires that turnover is presented on the face of the income statement (or statement of comprehensive income, if presented). *[FRS 102.5.7D]*. See 6.7.1 below.

Not all income reported in the profit and loss account is turnover, nor is the concept of turnover synonymous with revenue. For example, a company may receive rental or interest income – while these would be types of revenue under FRS 102, these may or may not fall to be reported as turnover. Similarly, an entity whose business includes renting out properties to tenants would include rental income within turnover, but this may be 'other operating income' for another entity. An entity whose business is as a lessor and receives finance lease income would report that interest income in the position of the turnover line (although it may well be described as finance lease income), but a company that merely receives interest income on its bank deposits or other investments would report that interest income as 'Other interest receivable and similar income'. Where significant judgement is applied in determining which sources of revenue qualify as turnover, it may be appropriate to include an accounting policy for turnover and explain these judgements.

See 3.3.2.A above for the segmental disclosures of turnover required in Companies Act accounts.

6.6.2 Cost of sales, distribution costs and administrative expenses (Format 1)

The format 1 profit and loss account requires a functional classification of expenses – between cost of sales, distribution costs and administrative expenses. These categories of cost are not defined in the Regulations. The allocation of costs will depend on the particular circumstances of an entity's business, and should be applied consistently. Judgement may be required in allocating costs to certain functions and, where this is the case, it may be appropriate to include an accounting policy for the allocation of expenses explaining significant judgements taken (see 8.3 below). The following discussion provides guidance for the types of items that often fall within these headings.

Cost of sales for a manufacturer would generally include production costs (including direct material, payroll and other costs and direct and indirect overheads attributable to the production function) and adjustments for opening and closing inventory. For a service provider, these would include the costs of providing the service.

Distribution costs would generally include transport and warehousing costs for the distribution of finished goods. UK companies also often include selling and marketing costs (such as advertising, payroll costs of the selling, marketing and distribution functions, sales commission and overheads attributable to the selling, marketing and distribution functions) in this heading.

Administrative expenses would generally include payroll costs of general management and administrative staff, general overheads, property costs not classified within cost of sales or distribution costs, bad debts, professional fees and often goodwill amortisation and impairment.

Note (14) to the profit and loss account statutory formats (format 1) in Schedule 1 to the Regulations requires that cost of sales, distribution costs and administrative expenses are stated after taking into account any necessary provisions for depreciation or diminution in value.[24]

UK companies sometimes show other line items (e.g. research and development costs) or amend or combine other line items, taking advantage of the flexibility available in the Regulations. FRS 102 requires additional line items, headings and subtotals when relevant to an understanding of the entity's financial performance (see 6.7.2 below).

6.6.3 Gross profit (format 1)

The format 1 profit and loss account requires gross profit or loss, i.e. turnover less cost of sales, to be shown as a separate line item.

6.6.4   *Other operating income (format 1 and format 2)*

Other operating income is not defined in the Regulations. In practice, this line item would often include government grant income, operating lease income, other rental income or negative goodwill amortisation.

This line item may include exchange gains arising from trading transactions, following previous GAAP practice. While this has not been included in FRS 102, the Legal Appendix to SSAP 20 – *Foreign currency translation* – states that 'Gains or losses arising from trading transactions should normally be included under "Other operating income or expense" while those arising from arrangements which may be considered as financing should be disclosed separately as part of "Other interest receivable / payable and similar income / expense". …'. *[SSAP 20.68]*.

6.6.5   *Income from shares in group undertakings and income from participating interests (format 1 and format 2)*

The formats for the individual profit and loss account include 'income from shares in group undertakings', and 'income from participating interests'. Dividend income from shares in group undertakings and from participating interests would be included within these line items.

For the group profit and loss account statutory formats, the Regulations require 'income from participating interests' to be replaced by 'income from associated undertakings' and 'income from other participating interests'. Income from associated undertakings would usually include the share of the profit or loss of associates and jointly controlled entities. Income from shares in group undertakings will not arise in consolidated financial statements unless there are unconsolidated subsidiaries.

The meanings of group undertakings, participating interests and associated undertakings are explained at 5.3.4.C to 5.3.4.E above.

Incoming dividends and similar income receivable are recognised at an amount that includes any withholding tax but excludes other taxes, such as attributable tax credits. Any withholding tax suffered is shown as part of the tax charge. *[FRS 102.29.19]*. See 6.6.9 below.

FRS 102 requires separate disclosure of the entity's share of the profit or loss of associates accounted for using the equity method and the entity's share of any discontinued operations of such associates. *[FRS 102.14.14]*. The same information is required for jointly controlled entities. *[FRS 102.15.20]*. There is no requirement to present this information on the face of the statement of comprehensive income (or separate income statement). However, entities may consider adapting the heading 'income from associated undertakings' to show the share of the profit or loss of investments in associates and jointly controlled entities (even if the analysis of this between investments in associates and jointly controlled entities is relegated to the notes).

FRS 102 does not address where fair value movements are presented in the profit and loss account formats where investments in subsidiaries, associates and jointly controlled entities are carried at fair value through profit and loss in consolidated and/or individual financial statements. *[FRS 102.9.9-9.9B, 9.26, 9.26A, 14.4-14.4B, 15.9-15.9B]*. Chapter 6 at 3.4 and 4, Chapter 10 at 3.3.1, and Chapter 11 at 3.6.2 and 3.6.3 of EY

New UK GAAP 2015 discuss the situations where this accounting is required or permitted. In our view, entities may present fair value gains and fair value losses on such investments, where material, adjacent to income from shares in group undertakings and income from participating interests (but disclosed separately). FRS 102 would require additional line items on the face of the statement of comprehensive income (or separate income statement), where relevant to an understanding of the entity's financial performance (see 6.7.2 below).

6.6.6   Income from other fixed asset investments and Other interest receivable and similar income (format 1 and format 2)

The formats have two line items – 'income from other fixed asset investments', and 'other interest receivable and similar income'. Note (15) to the profit and loss account statutory formats (format 1 and format 2) in Schedule 1 to the Regulations states that income and interest derived from group undertakings must be shown separately from income and interest derived from other sources. For LLPs, interest receivable from members must also not be included under these line items.[25]

Incoming dividends and similar income receivable are recognised at an amount that includes any withholding tax but excludes other taxes, such as attributable tax credits. Any withholding tax suffered is shown as part of the tax charge. *[FRS 102.29.19]*. See 6.6.9 below.

In our view, entities may present fair value gains and fair value losses on other fixed asset investments, where material, adjacent to income from other fixed asset investments, but disclosed separately.

Section 28 – *Employee Benefits* – does not specify how the cost of a defined benefit plan should be presented in the profit and loss account. Therefore, entities may present the cost as a single item or disaggregate the cost into components presented separately – although it is likely many entities will want to continue with a presentation similar to that previously required by FRS 17. In our view, net interest income on defined benefit post-employment plans may be included as 'other finance income' adjacent to 'other interest receivable and similar income', i.e. consistent with the presentation required by FRS 17 for the net of the interest cost and the expected return on assets. *[FRS 17.56]*. While this has not been included in FRS 102, Appendix II to FRS 17 states that 'The Board has received legal advice that these requirements do not contravene the Companies Act 1985 but that the interest cost and expected return should be presented in a new format heading separate from "interest and similar charges". Accordingly, the FRS requires these items to be included as other finance costs (or income) adjacent to interest'. *[FRS 17.Appendix II.6]*.

'Other interest receivable and similar income' may include exchange gains arising from financing arrangements, e.g. loans, following previous UK GAAP practice. See 6.6.4 above.

The presentation of gains on settlement of financial liabilities is not addressed by FRS 102. In our view, entities may show the gains on settlement within other interest receivable and similar income, or where material, present the gains, adjacent to interest receivable and similar income but disclosed separately.

FRS 102 requires, *inter alia*, further analyses of income, expense and net gains or net losses (including fair value changes) by specified category of financial instrument. Interest expense and interest income (calculated using the effective interest method) for financial assets and financial liabilities not at fair value, and impairment losses for each class of financial asset must also be disclosed. There are also extensive disclosures for financial instruments at fair value through profit or loss (that are not financial liabilities held as part of a trading portfolio nor derivatives). These can be disclosed in the notes to the financial statements. *[FRS 102.11.48-48A, 12.26]*. See Chapter 8 at 8 of EY New UK GAAP 2015.

6.6.7   *Amounts written off investments (format 1 and format 2)*

The line item 'amounts written off investments' would be used for impairments of fixed asset investments (including investments in subsidiaries, associates and jointly controlled entities) carried at cost less impairment in the individual financial statements. It would be usual to present a write-back of a previous provision under the same heading as where the provision was originally recognised (in the same way as an adjustment to reverse a bad debt provision would also be shown within administrative expenses).

The positioning of this line item between 'other interest income receivable and similar income' and 'interest payable and similar charge' is below where many entities would position operating profit, where presented (see 6.7.3 below). Previous UK GAAP required impairments of investments in subsidiaries, joint ventures and associates in the individual financial statements to be included within operating profit. *[FRS 11.67]*. FRS 102, however, is silent on where impairments of investments should be presented so this potential for conflict between the accounting standards and the statutory formats has been removed. Nevertheless, some entities may find it appropriate, based on the nature of their business, to report 'amounts written off investments' within operating profit.

FRS 102 requires disclosure of impairment losses for each class of financial asset, i.e. a grouping appropriate to the nature of the information disclosed and that takes into account the characteristics of the financial assets. *[FRS 102.11.48(c)]*. In addition, disclosure of impairment losses and reversals of impairment losses (and the line items in which those impairment losses are included) is required separately for investments in associates and investments in jointly controlled entities. *[FRS 102.27.33(e)-(f)]*.

In addition, UK companies preparing Companies Act accounts must disclose separately in a note to the accounts (if not shown separately in the profit and loss account):

*   provisions for diminution in value; and

*   any amounts written back in respect of such provisions.

Where SI 2015/980 is not applied or for LLPs, any such provisions made and any such amounts written back must be disclosed (either separately or in aggregate) in a note to the accounts. *[1 Sch 19(3), 20(2), 1 Sch 19(3), 20(2) (LLP)]*.

These disclosures apply where the fixed asset investment is accounted for using the historical cost rules. See 10.1 below. The application of the historical cost depreciation and diminution rules (and these disclosures) to fixed assets accounted for using the alternative accounting rules (i.e. at revaluation) is explained at 10.2.2 below. The disclosures do not apply to fixed asset investments held at fair value using the fair value accounting rules (see 10.3 below).

6.6.8   *Interest payable and similar expenses (format 1 and format 2)*

Interest payable and similar expenses (prior to the SI 2015/980 amendments and in the LLP Regulations, the heading is interest payable and similar charges) would include finance costs on financial liabilities (including shares classified as a financial liability or where a component of the share is classified as a financial liability).

Note (16) to the profit and loss account statutory formats (format 1 and format 2) in Schedule 1 to the Regulations states that interest payable to group undertakings must be shown separately from income and interest derived from other sources.[26]

The presentation of losses on settlement of financial liabilities is not addressed by FRS 102. In our view, entities may show the losses on settlement within other interest payable and similar expenses, or, where material, present the losses adjacent to other interest payable and similar expenses but disclosed separately.

Section 28 does not specify how the cost of a defined benefit plan should be presented in the profit and loss account. Therefore, entities may present the cost as a single item or disaggregate the cost into components presented separately. For the same reasons as discussed in 6.6.6 above, in our view, net interest costs on defined benefit post-employment plans may be included as 'other finance costs' adjacent to 'interest payable and similar expenses'.

This line item may also include exchange losses arising from financing arrangements, such as loans, following previous UK GAAP practice. See 6.6.4 above.

FRS 102 does not address the presentation of the unwind of discounts on provisions. However, FRS 12 – *Provisions, contingent liabilities and contingent assets* – requires this to be disclosed as other finance costs adjacent to interest, following an amendment to the standard when FRS 17 was published. *[FRS 12.48]*. In our view, entities can continue to follow this previous UK GAAP presentation of the unwind of discounts under FRS 102.

FRS 102 requires, *inter alia*, further analyses of income, expense and net gains or net losses (including fair value changes) by specified category of financial instrument. Interest expense and interest income (calculated using the effective interest method) for financial assets and financial liabilities not at fair value, and impairment losses for each class of financial asset must also be disclosed. There are also extensive disclosures for financial instruments at fair value through profit or loss (that are not financial liabilities held as part of a trading portfolio nor derivatives). *[FRS 102.11.48-48A, 12.26]*. See Chapter 8 at 8 of EY New UK GAAP 2015.

In addition, UK companies preparing Companies Act accounts must state in the notes to the accounts or on the face of the profit and loss account: the amount of interest on or any similar charges in respect of (1) bank loans and overdrafts, and (2) loans of any other kind made to the company. This analysis is not required in relation to interest or charges on loans to the company from group undertakings but applies to all other loans, whether made on security of debentures or not. *[1 Sch 66, 1 Sch 63 (LLP)]*.

Chapter 4

6.6.9   *Tax on profit (or loss) (format 1 and format 2)*

Tax includes current and deferred tax. FRS 102 states that income tax includes all domestic and foreign taxes that are based on taxable profit. Income taxes also include taxes, such as withholding tax on distributions payable by a subsidiary, associate or joint venture to the reporting entity. *[FRS 102.29.1]*. In some situations, entities may need to apply judgement in determining whether a particular tax or tax credit is an income tax and whether to classify interest and penalties as tax. See Chapter 24 at 3.2 of EY New UK GAAP 2015. FRS 102 requires disclosures of judgements in applying accounting policies with the most significant effect on the financial statements – see 8.3 below.

Incoming dividends and similar income receivable are recognised at an amount that includes any withholding tax but excludes other taxes, such as attributable tax credits. Any withholding tax suffered is shown as part of the tax charge. *[FRS 102.29.19]*.

UK companies preparing Companies Act accounts must give further disclosures in respect of tax on profit or loss in the notes to the accounts. *[1 Sch 67, 1 Sch 64 (LLP)]*. FRS 102's disclosures in respect of current and deferred tax are discussed at Chapter 24 at 11 of EY New UK GAAP 2015.

Schedule 1 (prior to the SI 2015/980 amendment), Schedules 2 and 3 to the Regulations and the LLP Regulations (unless LLP law is subsequently changed) instead refer to tax on profit or loss on ordinary activities.

6.6.10   *Extraordinary income, extraordinary charges, extraordinary profit or loss, and tax on extraordinary profit or loss (Format 1 and Format 2)*

Extraordinary items are expected to be extremely rare and are not expected to be encountered in practice. FRS 102's requirements on extraordinary items are discussed at 6.7.6 below.

SI 2015/980 deletes all line items referring to extraordinary items (and associated disclosures) in Schedule 1 to the Regulations and also deletes the disclosures of particulars of any extraordinary income or charges arising in the financial year and in respect of tax on extraordinary profit or loss, in the notes to the accounts. *[1 Sch 67(2), 69(2)]*. Schedules 2 and 3 to the Regulations and the LLP Regulations (unless LLP law is subsequently changed) retain the line items relating to extraordinary items (and related disclosures). *[1 Sch 64(2), 67(2) (LLP)]*.

Figures 4.15 and 4.17 at 6.6 above present the formats (before amendment by SI 2015/980) under Schedule 1 to the Regulations and under the current LLP Regulations. The presentation of non-controlling interest in profit or loss on extraordinary activities in group accounts (where still applicable) is discussed at 4.5 above.

6.6.11   *Own work capitalised (format 2)*

The format 2 profit and loss account includes a line item for 'own work capitalised'.

Own work capitalised may arise, for example, where an entity capitalises the directly attributable costs of constructing its own property, plant and equipment. *[FRS 102.17.10]*. The costs are reported in the relevant line items and a credit item is shown in own work capitalised.

6.6.12 Staff costs (format 2)

The format 2 profit and loss account has a line item for 'staff costs', to be analysed between wages and salaries, social security costs and pension costs (see 8.6 below for the definitions). The format 1 profit and loss account does not have a line item for staff costs.

UK companies (not subject to the small companies regime – see Chapter 3 at 11.1.6 and 11.4.2.C), whether preparing Companies Act or IAS accounts, must disclose information on staff numbers and on staff costs in the notes to the accounts (insofar as not stated elsewhere in the accounts). *[s411]*. See 8.6 below.

6.6.13 Depreciation (including amounts written off assets) and Amounts written off current assets to the extent that they exceed write-offs which are normal in the undertaking concerned (format 2)

The format 2 profit and loss account has separate line items for 'depreciation (including amounts written off assets)' and 'amounts written off current assets to the extent that they exceed write offs which are normal in the undertaking concerned'.

SI 2015/980 amended the heading used on the latter line item where Schedule 1 to the Regulations is applied. The previous heading 'exceptional amounts written off current assets' is still used under Schedules 2 and 3 to the Regulations or the LLP Regulations.

Entities may also show provisions against current assets under different headings, e.g. changes in stocks / raw materials and consumables (for inventory – see 6.6.14 below) or 'other operating expenses' (e.g. this heading might be used for bad debts – see 6.6.15 below). Judgement is needed as to whether such provisions exceed write offs that are normal and fall to be presented as 'amounts written off current assets to the extent that they exceed write offs which are normal in the undertaking concerned'.

6.6.14 Changes in stocks of finished goods and work in progress and Raw materials and consumables (format 2)

The format 2 profit and loss account includes separate line items for the 'change in stocks of finished goods and work in progress' and for 'raw materials and consumables'.

'Raw materials and consumables' would include purchases of raw materials and consumables, adjusted for changes in stocks of raw materials and consumables.

6.6.15 Other external expenses and Other operating expenses (Format 2)

The format 2 profit and loss account includes separate line items for: 'other external expenses' and for 'other operating expenses' (prior to the SI 2015/980 amendments and in the LLP Regulations, the headings refer to 'other external charges' and 'other operating charges') but the Regulations do not define these terms.

There is therefore likely to be diversity in practice in the allocation of costs between these headings, but a consistent policy should be followed.

'Other operating expenses' may include exchange losses arising from trading transactions, following previous GAAP practice. See 6.6.4 above.

Chapter 4

6.7   Requirements applicable to both approaches (applicable to both 'adapted formats' and statutory formats)

FRS 102 includes supplementary requirements (beyond following the formats in the Regulations) relating to the statement of comprehensive income.

6.7.1   *Disclosure of turnover on the face of the statement of comprehensive income (or separate income statement)*

Turnover must be presented on the face of the income statement (or statement of comprehensive income, if presented). *[FRS 102.5.7D]*.

FRS 102's definition of turnover is the same as that used in the Regulations. However, not all income reported in the profit and loss account is turnover, nor is the concept of turnover synonymous with revenue. See 6.6.1 above.

The standard also requires a detailed analysis of revenue (which may be included in the notes) showing at a minimum, revenue arising from the sale of goods, the rendering of services, interest, royalties, dividends, commissions, grants and any other significant type of revenue. Contract revenue recognised as revenue must also be disclosed. *[FRS 102.23.30(b), 23.31]*.

6.7.2   *Additional line items, headings and subtotals*

An entity shall present additional line items, headings and subtotals in the statement of comprehensive income (and in the income statement, if presented) when such presentation is relevant to an understanding of the entity's financial performance. *[FRS 102.5.9]*. Judgement is needed in determining whether additional items should be presented, where material and relevant. Factors to be considered, highlighted by IAS 1 (which has a similar requirement), include materiality and the nature and function of the items of income and expense. *[IAS 1.86]*.

While any amendments to the income statement (or profit and loss section of the statement of comprehensive income) would need to comply with the General Rules to the formats (see 4.4 above), the statutory formats provide flexibility since the profit and loss account line items are denoted with Arabic numbers.

Where 'adapted formats' are used, any amendments made would need to comply so far as practicable with the General Rules to the formats. FRS 102 explains that an entity may include additional line items in the income statement and amend the descriptions used in paragraph 5.5B (i.e. for the line items (a) to (j)) (see Figure 4.13 at 6.5 above) and the ordering of items, when this is necessary to explain the elements of financial performance, providing the information given is at least equivalent to that required by the profit and loss account format had it not been adapted. *[FRS 102.5.5C]*. The effect of paragraph 5.5C is to clarify that there is flexibility in the presentation requirements where 'adapted formats' are used (for statutory formats, the General Rules to the formats clearly set out the flexibility for Arabic numbered items, but Arabic numbers do not appear in the 'adapted formats'). While this requirement is included under the single statement approach, in our view, this is intended to also apply where the two statement approach is applied.

6.7.2.A   Presentation of alternative performance measures

The Press release on additional and exceptional items issued by the FRC (see 6.7.5.B) includes guidance relevant to the presentation of additional subtotals, particularly alternative performance measures by FRS 102 reporters.

The presentation of alternative performance measures has since been considered by the IASB. While these requirements have not been included in FRS 102 and so are not mandatory, the recent amendments to IAS 1 are discussed below.

Amendments to IAS 1 – *Disclosure Initiative* – explains that when an entity presents subtotals in accordance with paragraph 85 of IAS 1 (which is similar to the requirements of paragraphs 5.5C and 5.9 of FRS 102, discussed at 6.7.2 above), those subtotals must:

- be comprised of line items made of amounts recognised and measured in accordance with IFRS;

- be presented and labelled in a manner that makes the line items that constitute the subtotal clear and understandable;

- be consistent from period to period; and

- not be displayed with more prominence than the subtotals and totals required in IFRS for the statement(s) presenting profit or loss and other comprehensive income. *[IAS 1.85A]*.

An entity shall present the line items in the statement(s) presenting profit or loss and other comprehensive income that reconcile any such 'additional subtotals' presented with the subtotals or totals required for such statements. *[IAS 1.85B]*.

In addition, in June 2015, ESMA published its final guidance on presentation of Alternative Performance Measures. This applies to regulated information and prospectuses published by issuers of securities admitted to trading on a regulated market from July 2016. The guidelines do not apply to the financial statements but would apply to the management report (e.g. the strategic report) of entities in scope. The guidance is available on the ESMA website.[27] It is likely that most entities in scope of the ESMA guidance will be applying EU-adopted IFRS.

6.7.3   Disclosure of operating profit

FRS 102 does not require disclosure of 'operating profit'. If an entity elects to disclose the results of operating activities, the entity should ensure that the amount disclosed is representative of activities that would normally be regarded as 'operating', e.g. it would be inappropriate to exclude items clearly related to operations (such as inventory write-downs and restructuring and relocation expenses) because they occur irregularly or infrequently or are unusual in amount. Similarly, it would be inappropriate to exclude items on the grounds that they do not involve cash flows, such as depreciation and amortisation expenses. *[FRS 102.5.9B]*.

The income statement (or profit and loss section of the statement of comprehensive income) identifies separate line items for the share of the profit or loss of investments in associates and jointly controlled entities accounted for using the equity method in 'adapted formats' (see 6.5 above). For entities presenting a measure of operating profit using the 'adapted formats', in our view, it is acceptable for an entity to determine which investments form part of its operating activities and include their results in that measure, with the results of non-operating investments excluded from it. Another acceptable alternative would be to exclude the results of all associates and jointly controlled entities from operating profit.

6.7.4   *Analysis of expenses by nature or function*

Unless otherwise required under the Regulations, an entity must present an analysis of expenses using a classification based on either the nature of expenses or the function of expenses within the entity, whichever provides information that is reliable and more relevant information. *[FRS 102.5.11]*.

Where classified by nature, expenses are aggregated in the statement of comprehensive income (or income statement, where presented) according to their nature (e.g. depreciation, raw materials and consumables and staff costs) and are not reallocated among various functions within the entity. Where classified by function, expenses are aggregated according to their function as part of cost of sales or, for example, the costs of distribution or administrative activities. *[FRS 102.5.11]*. This means that cost of sales must always be presented separately.

The statutory formats in Schedule 1 to the Regulations and Schedule 1 to the LLP Regulations (see 6.6 above) require an analysis of expenses by nature (where the format 2 profit and loss account is adopted) or by function (where the format 1 profit and loss account is adopted). Where the 'adapted formats' in Schedule 1 to the Regulations are used (see 6.5 above), a supplementary analysis of expenses will be required.

The reference in paragraph 5.11 of FRS 102 to 'unless otherwise required under the Regulations' presumably reflects the fact that Schedules 2 and 3 to the Regulations do not offer a choice of profit and loss account format with an analysis of expenses based by nature or function, nor do the formats in these schedules include 'cost of sales' as a line item. There is limited flexibility to adapt the formats included in Schedules 2 and 3.

The Regulations require certain information about the nature of expenses to be provided as line items in format 2 and in the notes to the accounts where format 1 is applied:

- the format 2 profit and loss account includes line items for staff costs (see 6.6.12 above) and depreciation and other amounts written off tangible and intangible fixed assets (see 6.6.13 above);

- all UK companies, except companies subject to the small companies regime, preparing Companies Act accounts (or IAS accounts) must present the analysis of staff costs in the notes to the accounts, insofar as not stated elsewhere in the accounts (see 8.6 below); and

- note (17) to the profit and loss account statutory formats in Schedule 1 to the Regulations states that the amount of depreciation and other amounts written off tangible and intangible fixed assets must be disclosed in a note to the accounts where the format 1 profit and loss account is used.[28]

In addition, UK companies preparing Companies Act accounts (relevant to 'adapted formats' and statutory formats) must disclose separately in a note to the accounts (if not shown separately in the profit and loss account) in respect of fixed assets:

- provisions for diminution in value; and

- any amounts written back in respect of such provisions. *[1 Sch 19(3), 20(2)]*.

Where SI 2015/980 is not applied or for LLPs, any such provisions made and any such amounts written back must be disclosed (either separately or in aggregate) in a note to the accounts. *[1 Sch 19(3), 20(2), 1 Sch 19(3), 20(2) (LLP)]*.

These disclosures apply where the fixed asset investment is accounted for using the historical cost rules. See 10.1 below. The application of the historical cost depreciation and diminution rules (and these disclosures) to fixed assets accounted for using the alternative accounting rules (i.e. at revaluation) is explained at 10.2.2 below. The disclosures do not apply to fixed asset investments held at fair value using the fair value accounting rules (see 10.3 below).

The statutory disclosures overlap with disclosures in FRS 102 of depreciation, amortisation and impairment charges (see Chapter 13 at 3.8, Chapter 14 at 3.5.2, Chapter 15 at 4, Chapter 22 at 8 and Chapter 29 at 2.6.2 of EY New UK GAAP 2015), *[FRS 102.17.31(e), 18.27(e), 19.26, 27.32-33, 34.10]*, defined contribution expense *[FRS 102.28.40]*, and the cost of defined benefit plans (see Chapter 23 at 3.12 of EY New UK GAAP 2015). *[FRS 102.28.41(g)]*.

6.7.5   *Presentation of 'exceptional items'*

FRS 102 does not use the phrase 'exceptional items' nor does it contain the prescriptive presentation requirements for exceptional items included in previous UK GAAP.

When items included in total comprehensive income are material, their nature and amount must be disclosed separately in the statement of comprehensive income (and in the income statement, if presented) or in the notes. *[FRS 102.5.9A]*. The level of prominence given to such items is left to the judgement of the entity concerned. Materiality is discussed at 9.4 below.

Where SI 2015/980 is applied, UK companies preparing Companies Act accounts must state the amount, nature and effect of any individual items of income and expenditure which are of exceptional size or incidence in the notes to the accounts. *[1 Sch 69(3)]*.

Where SI 2015/980 is not applied or for LLPs (unless there is a subsequent change to LLP law), disclosure is required of the effects of any transactions that are exceptional by virtue of size or incidence, though they fall within the ordinary activities of the company. *[1 Sch 69(3), 1 Sch 67(3) (LLP)]*.

Many UK companies preparing IFRS financial statements (to which 1 Sch 69 above does not apply) continue to refer to 'exceptional items' and this is likely to be the case under FRS 102 as well. Since the standard does not use the term 'exceptional items', it is important that the entity provides a definition of what items are considered to be 'exceptional items' (or other similar term used) in the accounting policies included in the financial statements. The FRC published a press release on exceptional items in December 2013 (see 6.7.5.B below).

The standard does not give examples of such items, but IAS 1 suggests that circumstances that would give rise to the separate disclosure of items of income and expense include: *[IAS 1.98]*

(a)   write-downs of inventories to net realisable value or of property, plant and equipment to recoverable amount, as well as reversals of such write-downs;

(b)   restructurings of the activities of an entity and reversals of any provisions for the costs of restructuring;

(c)   disposals of items of property, plant and equipment;

(d)   disposals of investments;

(e)   discontinued operations;

(f)   litigation settlements; and

(g)   other reversals of provisions.

FRS 102's requirements on disclosure of discontinued operations are discussed at 6.8 below.

6.7.5.A   *Presentation in the statement of comprehensive income*

As entities reporting under FRS 102 must follow the formats for the profit and loss account in the Regulations (or LLP Regulations), exceptional items will need to be included within the appropriate statutory format headings where the statutory formats are applied. In most cases, attributing exceptional items to the relevant format heading will be straightforward.

The General Rules to the formats (see 4.4 above) allow the profit and loss account to include income or expenditure not otherwise covered by any of the items listed in the statutory format, and permit or require certain adaptations to the line items given an Arabic number.

There is potentially more flexibility over presentation of exceptional items where 'adapted formats' (see 6.5 above) are presented, although (subject to any amendments permitted by paragraph 5.5C of FRS 102) the minimum items required must be presented on the face of the income statement or, where presented, the single statement of comprehensive income.

FRS 102 does not require disclosure of operating profit nor does it specify categories of exceptional items that must be reported below operating profit. However, the standard gives examples of items that should not be excluded from operating profit (see 6.7.3 above).

6.7.5.B   *FRC Press release on exceptional items*

In December 2013, the FRC issued Press Release PN 108 on the need to improve reporting of additional and exceptional items by companies and ensure consistency in their presentation. It notes that the Financial Reporting Review Panel has identified a significant number of companies that report exceptional items on the face of the income statement and include subtotals to show the profit before such items (sometimes referred to as 'underlying profit'). While the FRC stated that many companies present additional line items in the income statement to provide clear and useful information on the trends in the components of their profit in the income statement, as required by IAS 1, the FRC has identified a number where the disclosure fell short of the consistency and clarity required, with a consequential effect on the profit reported before such items.

The Financial Reporting Review Panel set out the following factors that companies should have regard to, in judging what to include in additional items and underlying profit:

- the approach taken in identifying additional items that qualify for separate presentation should be even handed between gains and losses, clearly disclosed and applied consistently from one year to the next. It should also be distinguished from alternative performance measures used by the company that are not intended to be consistent with IFRS principles;

- gains and losses should not be netted off in arriving at the amount disclosed unless otherwise permitted;

- where the same category of material items recurs each year and in similar amounts (for example, restructuring costs), companies should consider whether such amounts should be included as part of underlying profit;

- where significant items of expense are unlikely to be finalised for a number of years or may subsequently be reversed, the income statement effect of such changes should be similarly identified as additional items in subsequent periods and readers should be able to track movements in respect of these items between periods;

- the tax effect of additional items should be explained;

- material cash amounts related to additional items should be presented clearly in the cash flow statement;

- where underlying profit is used in determining executive remuneration or in the definition of loan covenants, companies should take care to disclose clearly the measures used; and

- management commentary on results should be clear on which measures of profit are being commented on and should discuss all significant items which make up the profit determined according to IFRSs.

While the press release refers to IFRSs, the same factors would apply to FRS 102 financial statements.

6.7.6 Presentation of extraordinary items

The original version of FRS 102 distinguished between ordinary activities and extraordinary items (whereas IAS 1 prohibits the presentation of extraordinary items) because these were allowed for in the statutory formats.

SI 2015/980 removes the concept of extraordinary items (and associated disclosures) from Schedule 1 to the Regulations. There is no change to Schedules 2 and 3 to the Regulations or to the LLP Regulations (unless LLP law is subsequently changed).

Accordingly, FRS 102 (amended July 2015) explains that an entity applying the 'adapted formats' or statutory formats in Schedule 1 to the Regulations (i.e. paragraphs 5.5(a) or 5.7(a) of the standard) shall not present or describe any items of income or expense as extraordinary items in the statement of comprehensive income (or in the income statement, if presented) or in the notes. *[FRS 102.5.10].*

Entities applying the formats in Schedules 2 or 3 to the Regulations and Schedule 1 to the LLP Regulations continue to apply the requirements on extraordinary items. FRS 102 states that 'extraordinary items are material items possessing a high degree of abnormality which arise from events or transactions that fall outside the ordinary activities of the reporting entity and which are not expected to recur.' The standard explains that the additional line items required to be disclosed by paragraph 5.9 (see 6.7.2 above) and material items required to be disclosed by paragraph 5.9A (see 6.7.5 above) are not extraordinary items when they arise from the entity's ordinary activities. In addition, extraordinary items do not include prior period items merely because they relate to a prior period. *[FRS 102.5.10B].*

Ordinary activities are defined as 'any activities which are undertaken by a reporting entity as part of its business and such related activities in which the reporting entity engages in furtherance of, incidental to, or arising from, these activities. Ordinary activities include any effects on the reporting entity of any event in the various environments in which it operates, including the political, regulatory, economic and geographical environments, irrespective of the frequency or unusual nature of the events'. *[FRS 102.5.10A].*

While this guidance has not been included in FRS 102, Appendix II to FRS 101 (which has similar requirements to FRS 102 in respect of extraordinary items) states that 'entities should note that extraordinary items are extremely rare as they relate to highly abnormal events or transactions'. *[FRS 101.A2.11].* Consequently, consistent with previous GAAP practice (FRS 3 – *Reporting financial performance* – includes similar definitions of extraordinary items and ordinary activities), we do not anticipate that those entities still permitted to disclose extraordinary items after SI 2015/980 is applied will do so under FRS 102.

6.8   Presentation of discontinued operations

FRS 102's definition of discontinued operations and presentation requirements differ from both IFRSs and previous UK GAAP.

FRS 102 requires an entity to disclose on the face of the income statement (or statement of comprehensive income) an amount comprising the total of:

(a)   the post-tax profit or loss of discontinued operations (see definition at 6.8.1 below); and

(b)   the post-tax gain or loss attributable to the impairment or on the disposal of the assets or disposal group(s) constituting discontinued operations (see 5.5 above for the definition of disposal group).

A line-by-line analysis must be presented in the income statement (or statement of comprehensive income), with columns for continuing operations, discontinued operations and for total operations. This is required as line item (f) in the 'adapted formats'(see 6.5 above). *[FRS 102.5.5B, 5.7E]*. This means more detailed disclosure than is commonly seen under IFRS 5, but this is to enable compliance with the profit and loss account formats in the Regulations (or, where applicable, the LLP Regulations).

There is no requirement to analyse other comprehensive income between continuing and discontinued operations.

The disclosures for discontinued operations must relate to operations discontinued by the end of the reporting period for the latest period presented, with re-presentation of prior periods where applicable. *[FRS 102.5.7F]*.

An entity must also disclose its share of the profit or loss of associates accounted for using the equity method and its share of any discontinued operations of such associates *[FRS 102.14.14]*, and the same information for jointly controlled entities. *[FRS 102.15.20]*.

6.8.1   Definition of discontinued operation

FRS 102 defines a discontinued operation as a component of an entity (i.e. operations and cash flows that can be clearly distinguished, operationally and for financial reporting purposes from the rest of the entity) that has been disposed of and: *[FRS 102.Appendix I]*

(a)   represented a separate major line of business or geographical area of operations;

(b)   was part of a single co-ordinated plan to dispose of a separate major line of business or geographical area of operations; or

(c)   was a subsidiary acquired exclusively with a view to resale.

The definition of discontinued operations in FRS 102 differs significantly from that included in FRS 3 and differs specifically to that included in IFRS 5 in that it refers to 'a component of an entity *that has been disposed of*' whereas IFRS 5 refers to a 'component of an entity that *either has been disposed of or is classified as held for sale*' [emphasis added]. As noted at 6.8 above, the presentation of discontinued operations relates to operations disposed of at the reporting date.

IFRS 5, which has the same definition of a component as in FRS 102, clarifies that 'a component of an entity will have been a cash-generating unit or a group of cash-generating units while being held for use'. *[IFRS 5.31]*. Under both IFRSs and FRS 102, a cash generating unit is 'the smallest identifiable group of assets that generates cash inflows that are largely independent of the cash inflows from other assets or groups of assets'. *[IFRS 5.Appendix A, FRS 102.27.8, Appendix I]*. See Chapter 22 at 4.2 of EY New UK GAAP 2015. Management may consider IFRS 5's guidance on a component, as permitted by the hierarchy in Section 10. *[FRS 102.10.3-10.6]*.

FRS 102 does not clarify the phrase 'has been disposed of'. In our view, the phrase 'has been disposed of' may be interpreted more widely than a sale. An entity's management must use judgement in developing and applying an accounting policy and may consider the requirements and guidance in IFRSs in this area. *[FRS 102.10.4-10.6]*. In our view, an entity could look to IFRS 5. IFRS 5's requirements would be consistent with a view that a component meeting any of the criteria (a) to (c) is discontinued if, at the end of the reporting period, the component is an abandoned operation, or the entity has partially disposed of (but lost control of) the operation or has distributed the operation. However, since the phrase 'has been disposed of' has not been explained further in FRS 102, different interpretations of what this means may be sustained.

6.8.2   *Adjustments to amounts previously presented in discontinued operations in prior periods*

FRS 102 does not address adjustments to amounts previously presented in discontinued operations. Given the absence of specific requirements in FRS 102, management may consider the requirements and guidance of IFRSs in this area. *[FRS 102.10.4-10.6]*.

IFRS 5 requires that adjustments in the current period to amounts previously presented in discontinued operations that are directly related to the disposal of a discontinued operation in a prior period are classified separately in discontinued operations. The nature and amount of such adjustments must be disclosed. Examples given by the standard of circumstances in which these adjustments may arise include the following: *[IFRS 5.35]*

- the resolution of uncertainties that arise from the terms of the disposal transaction, such as the resolution of purchase price adjustments and indemnification issues with the purchaser;

- the resolution of uncertainties that arise from and are directly related to the operations of the component before its disposal, such as environmental and product warranty obligations retained by the seller; and

- the settlement of employee benefit plan obligations, provided that the settlement is directly related to the disposal transaction.

6.8.3   *Trading between continuing and discontinued operations*

Discontinued operations remain consolidated in group financial statements and therefore, any transactions between discontinued and continuing operations are eliminated as usual in the consolidation. As a consequence, the amounts ascribed to the continuing and discontinued operations will be income and expense only from transactions with counterparties external to the group. Importantly, this means the results presented on the face of the income statement will not necessarily represent the activities of the operations as individual entities, particularly when there has been significant trading between the continuing and discontinued operations. Some might consider the results for the continuing and discontinued operations on this basis to be of little use to readers of accounts. An argument could be made that allocating external transactions to or from the discontinued operations would yield more meaningful information.

One approach would be to fully eliminate transactions for the purpose of presenting the income statement then provide supplementary information.

6.8.4   *First-time adoption*

On first-time adoption of FRS 102, an entity shall not retrospectively change the accounting that it followed under its previous financial reporting framework for discontinued operations. *[FRS 102.35.9(d)]*. Section 35 offers no further guidance on the meaning of this mandatory exception to the general transition requirements. See Chapter 30 at 4.3 of EY New UK GAAP 2015 for further discussion of the transition exception.

6.8.5   *Example of presentation of discontinued operations*

Example 4.6:   *Presentation of discontinued operations*

Statement of comprehensive income

For the year ended 31 December 2016

	2016			2015		
	Continuing operations	Discontinued operations	Total	Continuing operation (as restated)	Discontinued operations (as restated)	Total
	CU	CU	CU	CU	CU	CU
Turnover	4,200	1,232	5,432	3,201	1,500	4,701
Cost of sales	(2,591)	(1,104)	(3,695)	(2,281)	(1,430)	(3,711)
Gross profit	1,609	128	1,737	920	70	990
Administrative expenses	(452)	(110)	(562)	(418)	(120)	(538)
Other operating income	212	–	212	198	–	198
Profit on disposal of operations	–	301	301	–	–	–
Operating profit	1,369	319	1,688	700	(50)	650
Interest receivable and similar income	14	–	14	16	–	16
Interest payable and similar expenses	(208)	–	(208)	(208)	–	(208)
Profit before taxation	1,175	319	1,494	508	(50)	458
Taxation	(390)	(4)	(394)	(261)	3	(258)
Profit after taxation and profit for the financial year	785	315	1,100	247	(47)	200
Other comprehensive income						
Actuarial losses on defined benefit pension plans			(108)			(68)
Deferred tax movement relating to actuarial losses			28			18
Total comprehensive income for the year			1,020			150

The above example is taken from the Appendix to Section 5 of FRS 102 (which accompanies but is not part of that section, and provides guidance on application of paragraph 5.7E for presenting discontinued operations). Example 4.5 includes modifications to the example in that Appendix, in particular, the removal of references to 'ordinary activities' in the line items and amendment of the heading 'interest payable and similar charges', consistent with the changes to the statutory formats in Schedule 1 to the Regulations made by SI 2015/980 (see 6.6 above).

6.9   Earnings per share

IAS 33 – *Earnings per Share* (as adopted by the EU) must be followed by an entity whose ordinary shares or potential ordinary shares are publicly traded or that files, or is in the process of filing its financial statements with a securities commission or other regulatory organisation for the purpose of issuing ordinary shares in a public market. IAS 33 also applies to an entity that chooses to disclose earnings per share (EPS). *[FRS 102.1.4].*

IAS 33 requires an entity to present the basic and diluted EPS for profit or loss from continuing operations attributable to ordinary equity holders of the parent entity, and for total profit or loss attributable to ordinary equity holders of the parent entity.

This must be given for each class of ordinary share that has a different right to share in profit for the period. *[IAS 33.9, 33.66]*. Basic and diluted EPS must be presented with equal prominence in the statement of comprehensive income (or on the face of the income statement, if presented) for every period for which a statement of comprehensive income is presented. *[IAS 33.66-67A]*.

An entity may disclose basic and diluted EPS for discontinued operations *either* in the statement of comprehensive income (or on the face of the income statement, if presented) *or* in the notes. *[IAS 33.68-68A]*.

Basic and diluted EPS is presented even if the amounts are negative, i.e. a loss per share. *[IAS 33.69]*. If basic and diluted EPS are equal, dual presentation can be achieved in one line in the statement of comprehensive income. *[IAS 33.67]*.

IAS 33 provides further requirements on the calculation of basic and diluted EPS and on the accompanying disclosures. See Chapter 34 of EY International GAAP 2016 for further details.

7   STATEMENT OF CHANGES IN EQUITY

An entity must present a statement of changes in equity, or if certain conditions are met and an entity chooses to, a statement of income and retained earnings (see 7.2 below). *[FRS 102.6.1]*.

Equity is the residual interest in the assets of the entity after deducting all its liabilities. It may be sub-classified in the statement of financial position. Sub-classifications may include funds contributed by shareholders, retained earnings, and gains or losses recognised directly in equity. *[FRS 102.2.22, Appendix I]*. See Chapter 8 at 9 of EY New UK GAAP 2015 for discussion of classification of financial instruments as debt or equity.

FRS 102's requirements for the statement of changes in equity are similar to those included in IFRSs.

The Regulations and LLP Regulations do not require a statement of changes in equity to be presented. However, where there have been transfers to or from any reserves (and the reserves are shown as separate line items in the balance sheet, or would be so shown, if Arabic-numbered line items were not combined as permitted by paragraph 4(2)(b) of the General Rules to the formats – see 4.4 above), a UK company preparing Companies Act accounts must disclose, in the notes to the accounts, in respect of the aggregate of reserves included in the same item:

- the amount of the reserves at the beginning and end of the financial year;
- any amounts transferred to or from the reserve during that year; and
- the source and application respectively of any amounts transferred.

Where SI 2015/980 is applied, this information must be presented in tabular form. *[1 Sch 59(1)-(2), 1 Sch 57(1)-(2) (LLP)]*. See 5.1.12 and 5.3.12 above.

This disclosure requirement is relevant to both statutory formats and 'adapted formats'. In practice, the above analysis and reconciliation of reserves could be combined with the statement of changes in equity (for which comparatives are required).

7.1   Information to be presented in the statement of changes in equity

The statement of changes in equity presents an entity's profit or loss for a reporting period, other comprehensive income for the period, the effects of changes in accounting policies and corrections of material errors recognised in the period and the amounts of investments by, and dividends and other distributions to, equity investors during the period. *[FRS 102.6.2].*

The effects of corrections of material errors and changes in accounting policies are presented as retrospective adjustments of prior periods rather than as part of profit or loss in the period in which they arise. *[FRS 102.5.8].* This is why such errors and changes in accounting policies are reported as separate line items in the statement of changes in equity (or, if presented, the statement of income and retained earnings) *[FRS 102.6.3(b), 6.5(c), (d)].* The retrospective adjustments for material errors and changes in accounting policy are consistent with the requirements of IFRSs, but the treatment of errors differs significantly from previous UK GAAP which requires that only fundamental errors are retrospectively restated. A fundamental error is an error 'of such significance as to destroy the true and fair view and hence the validity of those financial statements'. *[FRS 3.60, 63].*

The statement of changes in equity shows: *[FRS 102.6.3-6.3A, Appendix I]*

(a)   total comprehensive income for the period (the sum of profit and loss and other comprehensive income – see 6 above) showing separately the total amounts attributable to owners of the parent and to non-controlling interests (see 4.5 above);

(b)   for each component of equity, the effects of retrospective application (of accounting policies) or retrospective restatement recognised in accordance with Section 10 of the standard; and

(c)   for each component of equity, a reconciliation between the carrying amount at the beginning and the end of the period, separately disclosing changes resulting from:

   (i)   profit or loss;

   (ii)   other comprehensive income (which must be analysed by item, either in the statement of changes in equity or in the notes); and

   (iii)   the amounts of investments by, and dividends and other distributions to, owners, showing separately issues of shares, purchase of own share transactions, dividends and other distributions to owners, and changes in ownership interests in subsidiaries that do not result in a loss of control.

It can be seen that (a) above is effectively a sub-total of all the items required by (c)(i) and (c)(ii). Items required to be recognised in other comprehensive income are listed at 6.2 above.

FRS 102 does not define a 'component of equity'. However, IAS 1, which has a similar requirement to (c) above, states that 'components of equity' include, for example, each class of contributed equity, the accumulated balance of each class of other comprehensive income and retained earnings. *[IAS 1.108].* In our view, the components presented should (at a minimum) reflect the components of capital and reserves required to be disclosed as line items in the balance sheet format followed by the entity, where statutory formats are used (see 5.3.12 above), bearing in mind that an analysis of movements in these reserves is required by the Regulations in any case. However, this is likely to be supplemented by, for example, the cash flow hedge reserve or fair value movements accumulated in equity on available for sale financial assets (where IAS 39 is applied). For UK companies, these reserves would be included within the statutory fair value reserve required by the fair value accounting rules (see 10.3 below).

Where 'adapted formats' are used (see 5.1 above), the reporting entity must present classes of equity, such as share capital, share premium, retained earnings, revaluation reserve, fair value reserve and other reserves. *[FRS 102.4.2B]*. These are likely to represent, at a minimum, components of equity for the purposes of the statement of changes in equity.

UK companies preparing Companies Act accounts (relevant to 'adapted formats' and statutory formats) are required to disclose in the notes to the accounts: *[1 Sch 43]*

- any amount set aside (or proposed to be set aside) to, or withdrawn from (or proposed to be withdrawn from) reserves;
- the aggregate amount of dividends paid in the financial year (other than those for which a liability existed at the immediately preceding balance sheet date);
- the aggregate amount of dividends that the company is liable to pay at the balance sheet date; and
- the aggregate amount of dividends that are proposed before the date of approval of the accounts, and not otherwise disclosed above.

The LLP Regulations only require the information in the first bullet to be disclosed. *[1 Sch 43 (LLP)]*.

SI 2015/980 further requires that particulars are given of the proposed appropriation of profit or treatment of loss or, where applicable, particulars of the actual appropriation of profits or treatment of the losses. *[1 Sch 72B]*.

Where an entity declares dividends to holders of its equity instruments after the end of the reporting period, those dividends are not recognised as a liability because no obligation exists at that time, but FRS 102 permits an entity to show the dividend as a segregated component of retained earnings at the end of the reporting period. *[FRS 102.32.8]*.

FRS 102 requires an entity to *disclose* the fair value of non-cash assets distributed to its owners in the reporting period (except when the non-cash assets are ultimately controlled by the same parties before and after the distribution). *[FRS 102.22.18]*.

7.1.1   *Example of statement of changes in equity*

FRS 102 does not include an illustrative statement of changes in equity. Example 4.7 illustrates the requirements below. The standard requires an analysis of other comprehensive income by item in the statement of changes in equity or in the notes to the accounts. *[FRS 102.6.3A]*. The standard does not specify the detail in which this analysis must be presented.

The *Statement of Recommended Practice – Accounting by Limited Liability Partnerships* (July 2014) issued by CCAB provides detailed guidance on the statement of changes in equity (and on the reconciliation of members' interests) for LLPs.[29]

Example 4.7: *Combined statement of changes in equity*

XYZ Group – Statement of changes in equity for the year ended 31 December 2016
(£'000)

	Called up share capital	Share premium account	Re-valuation reserve	Capital redemp-tion reserve	Own shares	Merger reserve	Fair value reserve	Profit and loss account	Equity owners of parent	Non-controll-ing interest	Total equity
Balance at 1 January 2015	10,000	500	3,000	–	(774)	–	3,098	16,849	32,673	85	32,758
Changes in accounting policy	–	–	–	–	–	–	–	600	600	–	600
Restated balance	10,000	500	3,000	–	(774)	–	3,098	17,449	33,273	85	33,358
Profit for the year	–	–	–	–	–	–	–	4,872	4,872	35	4,907
Other comprehens ive income	–	–	100	–	–	–	(574)	(541)	(1,015)	2	(1,013)
Total comprehensive income for the year (a)	–	–	100	–	–	–	(574)	4,331	3,857	37	3,894
Dividends paid	–	–	–	–	–	–	–	(1,170)	(1,170)	–	(1,170)
Share based payment expense	–	–	–	–	–	–	–	398	398	–	398
Balance at 31 December 2015	10,000	500	3,100	–	(774)	–	2,524	21,008	36,358	122	36,480
Profit for the year	–	–	–	–	–	–	–	4,674	4,674	235	4,909
Other comprehens ive income	–	–	200	–	–	–	(665)	732	267	3	270
Total comprehensive income for the year (b)	–	–	200	–	–	–	(665)	5,406	4,941	238	5,179
Dividends paid	–	–	–	–	–	–	–	(1,400)	(1,400)	(31)	(1,431)
New shares issued	2,575	100	–	–	–	6,250	–	–	8,925	–	8,925
Share issue costs	–	(100)	–	–	–	–	–	–	(100)	–	(100)
Share buy back	(500)	–	–	500	–	–	–	(1,800)	(1,800)	–	(1,800)
Share based payment expense	–	–	–	–	–	–	–	307	307	–	307
Balance at 31 December 2016	12,075	500	3,300	500	(774)	6,250	1,859	23,521	47,231	329	47,560

Chapter 4

(a)   The amount included in retained earnings for 2015 of £4,331,000 represents profit attributable to owners of the parent of £4,872,000 less remeasurement losses (net of tax) on defined benefit pension plans of £541,000 (gross £676,000 less tax £135,000).

The amount included in the cash flow hedge reserve for 2015 comprises a loss on cash flow hedges of £574,000 (£717,000 less tax £143,000) which represented losses (net of tax) transferred to cash flow hedge of £774,000 less reclassification of losses (net of tax) to profit and loss of £200,000. The amount included in non-controlling interest of £2,000 for 2015 relates to exchange translation gains (no attributable tax).

The amount included in the revaluation surplus of £100,000 for 2015 represents the share of other comprehensive income of associates of £100,000 (gross £120,000 less tax £20,000). Other comprehensive income of associates relates solely to gains or losses on property revaluation.

(b)   The amount included in retained earnings for 2016 of £5,406,000 represents profit attributable to owners of the parent of £4,674,000 plus remeasurement gains on defined benefit pension plans of £732,000 (£915,000 less tax £183,000).

The amount included in the cash flow hedge reserve for 2016 comprises a loss on cash flow hedges of £665,000 (£831,000 less tax £166,000) which represented losses (net of tax) transferred to cash flow hedge of £900,000 less reclassification of losses (net of tax) to profit and loss of £235,000. The amount included in non-controlling interest of £3,000 for 2016 relates to exchange translation gains (no attributable tax).

The amount included in the revaluation surplus of £200,000 for 2016 represents the share of other comprehensive income of associates of £200,000 (gross £240,000 less tax £40,000). Other comprehensive income of associates relates solely to gains or losses on property revaluation.

7.2   Statement of income and retained earnings

The purpose of a statement of income and retained earnings is to present an entity's profit or loss and changes in retained earnings for a reporting period.

An entity is permitted (but is not required) to present a statement of income and retained earnings in place of a statement of comprehensive income and a statement of changes in equity if the only changes to its equity in the periods for which financial statements are presented arise from: *[FRS 102.6.4]*

- profit or loss;
- payment of dividends;
- corrections of prior period errors; and
- changes in accounting policy.

In essence, this means that the statement of income and retained earnings may be presented where the entity does not have items of other comprehensive income, investments by equity investors or non-dividend distributions to equity investors in the current or comparative periods presented.

The statement of income and retained earnings (see Example 4.8 below) shows the following items in addition to the information required in the statement of comprehensive income by Section 5 of FRS 102:

- retained earnings at the beginning of the reporting period;
- dividends declared and paid or payable during the period;
- restatements of retained earnings for corrections of prior period material errors;
- restatements of retained earnings for changes in accounting policy; and
- retained earnings at the end of the reporting period. *[FRS 102.6.5]*.

Example 4.8:   Statement of income and retained earnings (extract)

	2016	2015 Restated
	£'000	£'000
Profit before taxation	1,494	458
Taxation	(394)	(258)
Profit after taxation and profit for the financial year	1,100	200
Retained earnings brought forward at 1.1.16 (1.1.15) – as originally reported	12,285	13,500
Prior period adjustment – changes in accounting policy	(1,820)	(2,235)
Prior period adjustment – correction of error	(1,900)	(1,900)
Restated earnings at 1.1.16 (1.1.15) – as restated	8,565	9,365
Dividends paid [and payable]	(1,500)	(1,000)
Retained earnings carried forward at 31.12.16 (31.12.15)	8,165	8,565

8   NOTES TO THE FINANCIAL STATEMENTS

FRS 102 sets out the principles underlying information to be presented in the notes to the financial statements, and how to present the information. Notes contain information in addition to that presented in the primary statements. Notes provide narrative descriptions or disaggregations of items presented in those statements and information about items that do not qualify for recognition in those statements. Most sections of FRS 102 require disclosures that are normally presented in the notes. *[FRS 102.8.1]*.

For UK companies preparing Companies Act accounts, the CA 2006 (principally Part 15), the Regulations and other statutory instruments require certain notes to be presented in the accounts. See, for example, Chapter 1 at 6.7. Certain of these disclosures have been commented on in the discussion of the statutory formats (because they represent additional analyses for line items) at 5.3 and 6.6 above although the disclosures generally apply where 'adapted formats' are used as well.

This section looks at, in particular, the disclosures on staff costs; off-balance sheet arrangements; guarantees, contingencies and commitments; and directors' advances, credits and guarantees. Companies Act accounts disclosures relevant to specific accounting topics are addressed in other chapters of EY New UK GAAP 2015. This publication is not intended to include a comprehensive discussion of all such disclosures.

In particular, this publication does not cover the statutory disclosures required in the notes to Companies Act and IAS accounts relating to directors' remuneration (in accordance with Schedule 5 to the Regulations), members' remuneration (and particulars of members) for LLPs, or auditors' remuneration for audit and non-audit services (in accordance with *Companies (Disclosure of Auditor Remuneration and Liability Limitation Agreements) Regulations 2008* (SI 2008/489, as amended by SI 2011/2198)). The *Statement of Recommended Practice – Accounting by Limited Liability Partnerships* (July 2014) issued by CCAB provides further guidance on members' remuneration for LLPs and TECH 14/13FRF – *Disclosure of Auditor Remuneration*, issued by the ICAEW in December 2013 provides guidance on disclosure of auditor remuneration.

Chapter 4

8.1   Structure of the notes

FRS 102 requires the presentation of notes to the financial statements that: *[FRS 102.8.2]*

(a)   present information about the basis of preparation of the financial statements and the specific accounting policies used;

(b)   disclose the information required by FRS 102 that is not presented on the face of the primary statements; and

(c)   provide information that is not presented elsewhere in the financial statements, but is relevant to an understanding of any of them.

The notes should, as far as practicable, be presented in a systematic manner. Each item in the financial statements should be cross-referenced to any related information in the notes. *[FRS 102.8.3]*.

The notes are normally presented in the following order: *[FRS 102.8.4]*

(a)   a statement that the financial statements have been prepared in compliance with FRS 102 (see 3.8 above);

(b)   a summary of significant accounting policies applied (see 8.2 below);

(c)   supporting information for items presented in the financial statements, in the sequence in which each statement and each line item is presented; and

(d)   any other disclosures.

Traditionally, entities have presented financial statements starting with the primary statements, with line items cross referred to the relevant notes to the financial statements which present a more detailed analysis of the line items. The primary statements are followed by a summary of the accounting policies applied (including the statement of compliance) and then the supporting notes to the financial statements, which usually address the line items in the order that they appear in the primary statements. This traditional order is consistent with that proposed in FRS 102.

SI 2015/980 requires that the notes (presenting the information required by Parts 3 of Schedules 1 to 3 to the Regulations) must be presented in the order in which, where relevant, the items to which they relate are presented in the balance sheet and in the profit and loss account. *[1 Sch 42(2)]*. This statutory restriction applies to UK companies preparing Companies Act accounts and applying FRS 102. This new requirement is emphasised by way of footnote to paragraph 8.4 in FRS 102 (amended July 2015) which states: 'Company law requires the notes to be presented in the order in which, where relevant, the items to which they relate are presented in the statement of financial position and in the income statement'. In our view, this restriction only applies to those entities subject to such statutory restrictions.

In recent years, a number of entities have adopted a different placement of information with the aim of ensuring that the financial statements are understandable and avoid immaterial clutter that can obscure useful information. For example, some entities have grouped the notes to the financial statements so that these deal with related accounting topics and / or integrated the accounting policies for particular items within the relevant notes. Some entities have distinguished between the most significant accounting policies and other accounting policies, which may be relegated to an appendix to the financial statements. As FRS 102 refers to 'normally presented in the following order', this allows some flexibility.

The IASB have an ongoing Disclosure Initiative looking at materiality, principles for disclosure in the notes to the financial statements and other presentation and disclosure matters which may be of interest to FRS 102 reporters.

As part of this initiative, in December 2014, the IASB published Amendments to IAS 1 – *Disclosure Initiative*. The amendments clarify, *inter alia*, that entities have flexibility over the systematic order of the notes (i.e. these do not need to be presented in the traditional order highlighted above). However, an entity must, as far as practicable, present notes in a systematic manner (and in determining this, must consider understandability and comparability). As previously, each item in the primary statements should be cross referenced to related information in the notes. The amendments give further examples of systematic ordering or grouping of notes such as:

- giving prominence to the areas of its activities that the entity considers to be most relevant to an understanding of its financial performance and position, such as grouping together information about particular operating activities;

- grouping together information about items measured similarly such as assets measured at fair value; or

- a presentation similar to that discussed in paragraph 8.4 of FRS 102.

In July 2014, the FRC Lab published a report – *Accounting policies and integration of related financial information*, following a project involving 16 companies and 19 institutional investors, analysts and representative organisations (supplemented by an online survey) which looked at:

- accounting policies: which policies are disclosed, the content of what is disclosed and their placement;

- the notes to the financial statements: the ordering, grouping and combining notes; and

- the financial review: its integration with the primary statements.

The FRC Lab report found that most investors viewed the combining of tax expense and tax balance sheet notes as logical but there was little support for combining other notes. The case for significant change in note order has not been made with some investors preferring the traditional order, some preferring company-specific ordering and some expressing no preference. Investors valued consistency of note order across companies and time; a table of contents was considered helpful, especially where notes are ordered differently. Most investors preferred the traditional approach of placing management commentary and financial statement information in separate sections of the annual report, while some saw merit in increased analysis of financial statement line items that an integrated commentary can provide.

UK companies experimenting with alternative methods of structuring the notes will need to ensure that they comply with the statutory requirements on note structure referred to above.

Chapter 4

8.2   Summary of significant accounting policies

The summary of significant accounting policies should disclose the measurement basis (or bases) used in preparing the financial statements and the accounting policies used that are relevant to an understanding of the financial statements. *[FRS 102.8.5]*. FRS 102 explains that measurement is the process of determining the monetary amounts at which assets, liabilities, income and expenses are measured in the financial statements and involves the selection of a basis of measurement. The standard specifies the measurement basis that an entity must use for many types of assets, liabilities, income or expense. Examples of common measurement bases are historical cost and fair value. *[FRS 102.2.33-2.34]*.

It is clearly necessary to apply judgement when deciding which are the significant accounting policies and the level of detail required in a summary of accounting policies. In recent years, the FRC has commented particularly on the quality of revenue recognition policies and challenged companies where the information is not company-specific; generic (including boilerplate text from accounting standards); did not reflect revenue streams described in the business review or appeared inconsistent with changes in business model. The FRC does not expect immaterial or irrelevant policies to be disclosed.[30] The FRC Lab Report – *Accounting policies and integration of related financial information*, which is available on the FRC website, highlights the views of investors and sets out 'do's and don'ts' from the FRC's Corporate Reporting Review team. Subsequently, the FRC Lab has published a report that looks at approaches taken to the presentation of significant accounting policies and other accounting policies by one listed company.[31]

Disclosure of particular accounting policies is especially useful to users when those policies are selected from alternatives allowed in the standard (e.g. the accrual or performance model for government grants in FRS 102). Indeed, as indicated below, the standard often explicitly requires accounting policies, where material, to be disclosed in such situations. In addition, disclosure is useful where it relates to significant accounting policies not specifically required by the standard that have been selected by management in accordance with the hierarchy in Section 10 *[FRS 102.10.3-10.6]*.

FRS 102 specifically requires disclosure of certain accounting policies (where material), including:

- the accounting policies adopted for the recognition of revenue (including the methods adopted to determine the stage of completion of transactions involving the rendering of services and the methods used to determine construction contract revenue recognised in the period and the stage of completion of construction contracts in progress); *[FRS 102.23.30(a), 23.31(b), (c)]*

- the measurement basis or bases used for financial instruments and the other accounting policies used for financial instruments that are relevant to an understanding of the financial statements; *[FRS 102.11.40, 12.26]*

- the accounting policies adopted in measuring inventories, including the cost formula used; *[FRS 102.13.22(a)]*

- for each class of property, plant and equipment, the measurement bases used for determining the gross carrying amount; *[FRS 102.17.31(a)]*

- a description of the methods for recognising investments in associates, jointly controlled entities and subsidiaries in the separate financial statements of a parent; *[FRS 102.9.27(b)]*

- the accounting policy for investments in associates and for investments in jointly controlled entities in individual and consolidated financial statements; *[FRS 102.14.12(a), 15.19(a)]*

- the accounting policy adopted for grants; *[FRS 102.24.6(a)]*

- the accounting policies adopted for heritage assets, including details of the measurement bases used; *[FRS 102.34.55(c)]* and

- the measurement basis used for public benefit entity concessionary loans and any other accounting policies which are relevant to the understanding of these transactions within the financial statements. *[FRS 102.PBE.34.95]*.

In addition, FRS 102 requires disclosure of methods used in applying accounting policies, including:

- for all financial assets and financial liabilities required to be measured at fair value, the basis for determining fair value e.g. quoted market price in an active market or a valuation technique (and where a valuation technique is used, the assumptions applied); *[FRS 102.11.43]*

- methods used to determine the amount of fair value change attributable to credit risk for a financial asset or liability measured at fair value through profit and loss (not required for financial liabilities held as part of a trading portfolio nor derivatives). (if the change cannot be measured reliably or is not material, that fact is stated); *[FRS 102.11.48A(b)]*

- the methods and assumptions applied in determining the fair value of each class of biological asset (where the fair value model is applied); *[FRS 102.34.7(b)]*

- the methods and significant assumptions applied in determining the fair value of investment property; *[FRS 102.16.10(a)]*

- the useful lives or the amortisation rates used and the reasons for choosing those periods, and the amortisation methods used; *[FRS 102.18.27(a)-(b)]*

- the useful life of goodwill, and if this cannot be reliably estimated, supporting reasons for the period chosen (where FRS 102 (amended July 2015) is not applied, the useful life of goodwill, and if this exceeds five years, supporting reasons); *[FRS 102.19.25(g)]*

- for each class of property, plant and equipment, the depreciation methods and useful lives or the depreciation rates used; *[FRS 102.17.31(b)-(c)]* and

- for each class of biological asset measured using the cost model, the depreciation method, useful lives or depreciation rates used; *[FRS 102.34.10(c)-(d)]*.

UK companies preparing Companies Act accounts are also required to disclose the accounting policies used in determining the amounts to be included in respect of items in the balance sheet and in determining the profit or loss of the company in the notes to the accounts. *[1 Sch 44, 1 Sch 44 (LLP)]*. The Regulations specifically require the note on accounting policies to include:

- the depreciation and diminution in value of assets; *[1 Sch 44, 1 Sch 44 (LLP)]*

- the basis of translating sums denominated in foreign currencies into sterling (or the currency in which the financial statements are drawn up); *[1 Sch 70, 1 Sch 68 (LLP)]*

- where the alternative accounting rules are used, e.g. property, plant and equipment is revalued (see 10.2 below), the items affected and the basis of valuation adopted; and *[1 Sch 34(2), 1 Sch 34(2) (LLP)]*.

- the period over which capitalised development costs are being amortised, together with the reasons for capitalising development costs (see 10.1.3 below). *[1 Sch 21, 1 Sch 21 (LLP)]*.

Where SI 2015/980 is applied, and in exceptional cases the useful life of intangible assets cannot be reliably estimated, the period over which intangible assets are amortised (which must not exceed ten years), together with the reasons for choosing that period must also be disclosed in a note to the accounts. *[1 Sch 22]*. This requirement applies to both intangible assets and goodwill and it would be usual to present this in the note to the accounting policies. SI 2015/980 has made the same amendments to Schedules 2 and 3 to the Regulations. Where SI 2015/980 is not applied, the requirement is instead to disclose the amortisation period for goodwill and the reasons for choosing that period. *[1 Sch 22(4)]*.

It is common for financial statements to disclose the accounting convention used in their preparation. An example is given below, although the nature of the departures from the historical cost convention will depend on an entity's accounting policies.

Example 4.9:   Accounting convention

The financial statements are prepared in accordance with the historical cost convention, except for the revaluation of property, plant and equipment at market value under the alternative accounting rules and application of the fair value accounting rules to derivative financial assets and liabilities and hedging relationships.

8.3   Judgements in applying accounting policies

The summary of significant accounting policies or other notes should disclose the judgements, apart from those involving estimations, that management has made in the process of applying the entity's accounting policies and that have the most significant effect on the amounts recognised in the financial statements. *[FRS 102.8.6]*.

This disclosure is not currently required by previous UK GAAP reporters, but IAS 1 has the same requirement. *[IAS 1.122]*. Examples of judgements in applying accounting policies include: whether a lease is classified as an operating or finance lease; whether a transaction is a business combination or an asset transaction; and whether the entity is acting as principal or agent in a revenue transaction.

FRS 102 specifically requires disclosure of certain judgements (although in general, there are fewer such disclosures required than under IFRSs), for example:

- the basis for concluding that control exists where the entity does not own (directly or indirectly through its subsidiaries) more than half the voting power of an investee; *[FRS 102.9.23]*

- the name of any subsidiary excluded from consolidation and the reason for exclusion; *[FRS 102.9.23]*

- the reasons for a change in functional currency; *[FRS 102.30.27]* and

- the existence of material uncertainties over going concern, or the basis of preparation and the reasons when adopting the non-going concern basis. *[FRS 102.3.8-3.9]*.

8.4   Information about estimates

The notes to the financial statements should also disclose information about the key assumptions concerning the future, and other key sources of estimation uncertainty at the reporting date, that have a significant risk of causing a material adjustment to the carrying amounts of assets and liabilities within the next financial year. In respect of those assets and liabilities, the notes shall include details of their nature and their carrying amount as at the end of the reporting period. *[FRS 102.8.7]*.

FRS 102 specifically requires disclosure of certain key assumptions, e.g. the principal actuarial assumptions used (including discount rate, expected rates of salary increases, medical cost trend rates and any other material actuarial assumption used). *[FRS 102.28.41(k)]*. See also some of the disclosures of methods and assumptions noted at 8.3 above. The Regulations also require disclosures of significant assumptions underlying valuation models and techniques used where the fair value accounting rules are applied (see 10.3.4 and 10.4.3 below).

IAS 1 has the same requirement, *[IAS 1.125]*, but with considerably more explanatory guidance that management may consider, as permitted by the hierarchy in Section 10 *[FRS 102.10.3-10.6]*, in determining how to make the above disclosure. See Chapter 3 at 5.2 of EY International GAAP 2016.

8.5   Other notes disclosures in the presentation sections of FRS 102

An entity shall also disclose in the notes to the financial statements:

- the legal form of the entity, its country of incorporation and the address of its registered office (or principal place of business, if different from the registered office); and

- a description of the nature of the entity's operations and its principal activities unless this is disclosed in the business review (or similar statement) accompanying the financial statements. *[FRS 102.3.24]*.

While the directors' report for a UK company no longer requires disclosure of the principal activities, these will often be explained in the strategic report as part of the business review.

The date the financial statements were authorised for issue and who gave that authorisation must be disclosed. If the entity's owners or others have the power to amend the financial statements after issue, the entity shall disclose that fact. *[FRS 102.32.9]*. See Chapter 27 at 3 of EY New UK GAAP 2015.

The above requirement overlaps with the requirements in the CA 2006 for the directors to approve the annual accounts and for a director, on behalf of the board, to sign the company balance sheet (with the printed name of the director stated in published and filed copies).[32] *[s414, s433, s444-447]*. For LLPs, the same requirements apply but the annual accounts are approved by the members of the LLP and signed, on behalf of the members, by a designated member. *[s414, s433, s444-447 (LLP)]*. The details on authorisation of the financial statements are also often included as a separate note to the financial statements.

In addition, where SI 2015/980 is applied, individual and group accounts (whether Companies Act or IAS accounts) must state:

- the part of the UK in which the company is registered;

- the company's registered number;

- whether the company is a public or private company and whether it is limited by shares or by guarantee;

- the address of the company's registered office; and

- where appropriate, the fact that the company is being wound up. *[s396(A1), s397(1), s404(A1), s406(1)]*.

These new statutory requirements do not apply to LLPs (unless LLP law is subsequently changed).

8.6   Staff costs

A UK company preparing Companies Act accounts or IAS accounts, unless it is subject to the small companies regime (where the required disclosures following the SI 2015/980 amendments are covered in Chapter 3 at 11.1.6 and 11.4.2.C), must disclose in the notes to the accounts:

- the average number of persons employed by the company in the financial year in total and analysed by category selected by the directors, having regard to how the company's activities are organised;

- in respect of the above persons, the aggregate amounts of:

  - wages and salaries paid or payable in respect of the year to those persons;

  - social security costs incurred by the company on their behalf; and

  - other pension costs so incurred.

The analysis of the staff costs is not required where the amounts are stated elsewhere in the company's accounts (as may be the case where the format 2 profit and loss account is used). *[s411(1), (2), (5)]*.

In group accounts, the disclosures relate to the company and its consolidated subsidiary undertakings. *[s411(7)]*. Where SI 2015/980 is not applied, where group accounts are presented, the information on employee numbers and staff costs required in the individual profit and loss account need not be given where use of the section 408 exemption is disclosed (see Chapter 1 at 6.3.2). *[s408(2)]*.

SI 2015/980 removes this exemption and therefore information is required for the consolidated group in the group accounts and for the company, in the individual accounts.

The average number of persons employed is determined by dividing the 'relevant annual number' by the number of months in the financial year. The relevant annual number is determined by ascertaining the number of persons employed under contracts of service by the company for each month (whether throughout the month or not – so including both part- and full-time employees) in the financial year and then adding together all the monthly numbers. *[s411(3)-(4)]*.

Wages and salaries, and social security costs are determined by reference to payments made or costs incurred in respect of all persons employed by the company during the financial year under contracts of service. *[s411(5), 10 Sch 14]*.

Social security costs mean any contributions by the company to any state social security or pension scheme, fund or arrangement. *[s411(6), 10 Sch 14]*.

Pension costs include any costs incurred by the company in respect of any pension scheme established for the purpose of providing pensions for current or former employees, any sums set aside for the future payment of pensions directly by the company for current or former employees, and any pensions paid directly to such persons without having first been set aside. *[s411(6), 10 Sch 14]*. These exclude contributions to a state pension scheme which are disclosed as social security costs.

Since the disclosures relate to persons employed on 'contracts of service' with the company (meaning an employment contract), these exclude self-employed people such as contractors or consultants. Executive directors generally have a contract of service, but non-executive directors may not have contracts for services and would then be excluded from the above disclosure. All directors are within the scope of statutory directors' remuneration disclosures (as noted at 8 above, these are beyond the scope of this publication).

In groups, employees with contracts of service with one company (such as the holding company or service company) may be seconded to another group company or paid by another company, sometimes with costs recharged. In such cases, we would recommend that entities supplement the statutory disclosures for persons with contracts of service with additional information on staff costs and staff numbers, explaining the particular situation, including the impact on the company's/ group's profit and loss account.

The same requirements apply to LLPs not subject to the small LLPs regime. *[s411(LLP)]*.

FRS 102 also includes disclosures in respect of share-based payment and employee benefits (see Chapter 21 at 14 and Chapter 23 at 3.12 of EY New UK GAAP 2015).

8.7 Off balance sheet arrangements

A UK company preparing Companies Act accounts or IAS accounts must disclose the following information in the notes to the accounts if, in any financial year, the company is or has been party to arrangements that are not reflected in its balance sheet and, at the balance sheet date, the risks or benefits arising from those arrangements are material:

- the nature and business purpose of the arrangements; and

- the financial impact of the arrangements on the company (unless the company qualifies for the small companies regime – where the required disclosures following the SI 2015/980 amendments are covered in Chapter 3 at 11.1.5.H and 11.4.2.E).

The information need only be given to the extent necessary for enabling the financial position to be assessed. In group accounts, the disclosures relate to the company and its consolidated subsidiary undertakings. *[s410A]*. Consequently, UK companies preparing statutory group accounts must give the information for both the company and the consolidated group.

Where SI 2015/980 is not applied, the disclosure requirement does not apply to a UK company subject to the small companies regime and a company qualifying as medium-sized under sections 465 to 467 of the CA 2006 (see Chapter 1 at 6.6) does not need to disclose the financial impact of the arrangements. SI 2015/980 extends the disclosure requirement to companies subject to the small companies regime, except that the financial impact of the arrangements need not be disclosed; medium-sized companies are now required to disclose the financial impact of the arrangements. *[s410A(1), (4)]*. This change in the scope of the disclosure has not affected LLPs (unless LLP law is subsequently changed). *[s410A (LLP)]*.

Section 410A implements the requirement for disclosure of 'off-balance sheet arrangements' included in Directive 2006/46/EC. Recital 9 to the EU Directive states:

'Such off-balance sheet arrangements could be any transactions or agreements which companies may have with entities, even unincorporated ones, that are not included in the balance sheet. Such off-balance sheet arrangements may be associated with the creation or use of one or more Special Purpose Entities (SPEs) and offshore activities designed to address, *inter alia*, economic, legal, tax or accounting objectives. Examples of such off-balance sheet arrangements include risk and benefit-sharing arrangements or obligations arising from a contract such as debt factoring, combined sale or repurchase agreements, consignment stock arrangements, take or pay arrangements, securitisation arranged through separate companies and unincorporated entities, pledged assets, operating leasing arrangements, outsourcing and the like. Appropriate disclosure of the material risks and benefits of such arrangements that are not included in the balance sheet should be set out in the notes to the accounts or the consolidated accounts.'

The examples listed in Recital 9 are not to be taken as exhaustive. FRS 102 and/or the Regulations already require disclosures about certain off-balance sheet arrangements. The Regulations also, *inter alia*, require certain disclosures including in relation to security given for debts (see 5.3.8 above) and in respect of guarantees, contingencies and other financial commitments (see 8.7.1 below).

As discussed at 8.3 above, FRS 102 requires significant judgements in applying accounting policies to be disclosed. Directors will, however, still need to consider whether the disclosures given are sufficient to meet the requirements of section 410A and whether the entity is party to material off-balance sheet arrangements not required to be disclosed by FRS 102 that should be disclosed in accordance with section 410A.

8.7.1 Guarantees, contingencies and commitments

SI 2015/980 amends the disclosure required by UK companies preparing Companies Act accounts for guarantees, contingencies and other financial commitments in Schedules 1 to 3 to the Regulations. The new disclosures mainly restate the statutory disclosures, previously in paragraphs 63 and 73 of Schedule 1 to the Regulations (and equivalent paragraphs in Schedules 2 and 3 to the Regulations). The previous disclosures are required where SI 2015/980 is not applied and remain relevant to LLPs. *[1 Sch 60, 71 (LLP)]*. The new disclosures in the Regulations additionally cover contingencies (so both contingent assets and liabilities), require disclosure of the form of valuable security given and disclosure of commitments, guarantees and contingencies undertaken on behalf of, or for the benefit of, any undertaking in which the company has a participating interest.

Where SI 2015/980 is applied, the disclosures required by the Regulations are as follows (note these have been slightly reordered from the disclosures set out in the Regulations): *[1 Sch 63]*

- particulars must be given of any charge on the assets of the company to secure the liabilities of any other person including the amount secured;

- particulars and the total amount of any financial commitments, guarantees and contingencies that are not included in the balance sheet must be disclosed, together with an indication of the nature and form of any valuable security given by the company in respect of such commitments, guarantees and contingencies;

- the total amount of any pension commitments that are not included in the balance sheet must be separately disclosed and separate particulars of any pension commitment relating wholly or partly to pensions payable to past directors of the company must be given;

- the total amount of any commitments, guarantees and contingencies that are not included in the balance sheet undertaken on behalf or for the benefit of:

  (a) any parent undertaking or fellow subsidiary undertaking of the company;

  (b) any subsidiary undertaking of the company; or

  (c) any undertaking in which the company has a participating interest

  must be separately stated and those within each of paragraphs (a), (b) and (c) must also be stated separately from those within any other of those paragraphs.

  This appears to require the totals for (a), (b), (c) (and the sum of the totals for (a) to (c)) to be separately stated.

  See 5.3.4.C and 5.3.4.D above and Chapter 2 at 3.1.2 of EY New UK GAAP 2015 for guidance on the relevant definitions; and

- particulars must also be given of pension commitments which are included on the balance sheet, with separate particulars given for any pension commitment relating wholly or partly to pensions payable to past directors of the company.

Chapter 4

In group accounts, the disclosures relate to the company and its consolidated subsidiary undertakings. *[6 Sch 1(1), 3 Sch 1(1) (LLP)]*.

8.8   Directors' advances, credits and guarantees

A UK company preparing Companies Act accounts or IAS accounts must disclose the information concerning directors' advances, credits and guarantees required by section 413 of the CA 2006. There is no equivalent disclosure for LLPs. As indicated below, SI 2015/980, where applied, has added certain disclosure requirements. Note that the disclosures set out below have been slightly reordered from the disclosures set out in the Regulations.

A company that does not prepare group accounts must disclose in the notes to its individual accounts: *[s413(1)]*

- advances and credits granted by the company to its directors; and

- guarantees of any kind entered into by the company on behalf of its directors.

A parent company that prepares group accounts must disclose in the notes to the group accounts: *[s413(2)]*

- advances and credits granted to the directors of the parent company, by that company or by any of its subsidiary undertakings; and

- guarantees of any kind entered into on behalf of the directors of the parent company, by that company or by any of its subsidiary undertakings.

The details required for an advance or credit are: *[s413(3), (5)]*

- its amount (for each advance or credit and totals in aggregate);

- an indication of the interest rate;

- its main conditions;

- any amounts repaid (for each advance or credit and totals in aggregate);

- where SI 2015/980 is applied, any amounts written off (for each advance or credit and totals in aggregate); and

- where SI 2015/980 is applied, any amounts waived (for each advance or credit and totals in aggregate).

The details required for a guarantee are: *[s413(4), (5)]*

- its main terms;

- the amount of the maximum liability that may be incurred by the company (or its subsidiary) (for each guarantee and totals in aggregate); and

- any amount paid and any liability incurred by the company (or its subsidiary) for the purpose of fulfilling the guarantee (including any loss incurred by reason of enforcement of the guarantee). Details must be given for each guarantee and also totals in aggregate.

Disclosure is required: *[s413(6)-(7)]*

- in respect of persons who were directors of the company at any time in the financial year to which the financial statements relate; and

- for every advance, credit or guarantee that subsisted at any time in the financial year:
  - whenever it was entered into;
  - whether or not the person concerned was a director of the company at the time it was entered into; and
  - in relation to an advance, credit or guarantee involving a subsidiary undertaking of the company, whether or not it was a subsidiary undertaking at the time the advance, credit or guarantee was entered into.

There are certain exemptions for banking companies (and the holding companies of credit institutions (see definitions at 4.2.2 above), as explained at 8.8.1 below.

The terms advances, credits, and guarantees are not defined in the CA 2006 itself. The rules governing the lawfulness of transactions in Part 10 of the CA 2006 refer to loans, quasi-loans (including related guarantees or provision of security) and credit transactions. While these terms do not align with the terms used in the financial statements disclosure requirements, loans and quasi-loans and credit transactions would generally be considered as advances and credits; and guarantees or provision of security would be disclosed as guarantees (of any kind).

The requirements appear to require disclosure of each advance or credit, or guarantee made. This could be arduous in some contexts, as the definition of advances and credits could include directors' current accounts or personal purchases made using a company credit card (as well as loans and outstanding credit card balances provided by banks or finance subsidiaries of certain retailers).

8.8.1   *Banking companies and holding companies of credit institutions*

Such companies are required to disclose only the details in sections 413(5)(a) and 413(5)(c), i.e. the aggregate totals of: *[s413(8)]*

- the amounts of advances or credits granted by the company (or in group accounts, by the company and its subsidiary undertakings); and
- the amounts of the maximum liability that may be incurred by the company (or its subsidiary) in respect of guarantees entered into by the company (or in group accounts, by the company and its subsidiary undertakings).

9   GENERAL PRINCIPLES FOR PREPARATION OF FINANCIAL STATEMENTS

The objective of financial statements is to provide information about the financial position, performance and, when required to be presented, cash flows of an entity that is useful for economic decision-making by a broad range of users who are not in a position to demand reports tailored to meet their particular information needs. Financial statements also show the results of the stewardship of management – the accountability of management for the resources entrusted to it. *[FRS 102.2.2-2.3]*.

FRS 102's general principles for preparation of financial statements are covered in Section 2 (see Chapter 3 of EY New UK GAAP 2015), Section 3 (covered in this chapter) and Section 10 (see Chapter 7 of EY New UK GAAP 2015) of the standard.

The selection of accounting policies is also critical in the preparation of financial statements. The requirements on selection of accounting policies and on accounting estimates are in Section 10. Disclosure of accounting policies, judgements and estimates are covered at 8.2 to 8.4 above.

This section concentrates on FRS 102's requirement for financial statements to give a true and fair view, the adoption of the going concern basis, and materiality and aggregation, i.e. the issues which are addressed in Section 3 of the standard. There are similar requirements in the Regulations, as highlighted at 9.1 below.

9.1   Requirements of the Regulations

The Regulations (and where applicable, the LLP Regulations) include:

- the requirement for accounts to give a true and fair view, and the concept of a 'true and fair override' (see 9.2 below);

- general principles for the preparation of financial statements, similar to those included in FRS 102 (see 9.1.1 below);

- recognition and measurement principles, where assets and liabilities are measured under the historical cost convention, alternative accounting rules and fair value accounting rules (see 10 to 10.4 below);

- presentation requirements for the balance sheet and profit and loss formats (see 4 to 6 above); and

- disclosure requirements (see Chapter 1 at 6.7, and the relevant Chapters of EY New UK GAAP 2015 and this supplement).

9.1.1   *General principles for preparation of financial statements*

The general principles set out in the Regulations for the preparation of financial statements are: *[1 Sch 10-15A, 40(2)]*

- the company is presumed to be carrying on business as a going concern (see 9.3 below);

- accounting policies (and measurement bases, where SI 2015/980 is applied) must be applied consistently within the same accounts and from one financial year to the next (see 3.6.2 above and Chapter 3 at 3.2.8 of EY New UK GAAP 2015);

- the amount of any item must be determined on a prudent basis, and in particular:

  - only profits realised at the balance sheet date are to be included in the profit and loss account (except where fair value changes of financial instruments, investment property or living animals or plants are required to be included in the profit and loss account by the fair value accounting rules – see 10.3 below);

  - all liabilities which have arisen in respect of the financial year to which the accounts relate or a previous financial year must be taken into account, including those which only became apparent between the balance sheet date and the date on which it is approved and signed by the Board; and

- where SI 2015/980 is applied, all provisions for diminution of value must be recognised, whether the result of the financial year is a profit or loss;

- all income and charges relating to the financial year to which the accounts relate must be taken into account without regard to the date of receipt or payment (i.e. accruals basis – see Chapter 3 at 3.8 of EY New UK GAAP 2015);

- in determining the aggregate amount of any item, the amount of each individual asset or liability that falls to be taken into account must be determined separately (i.e. no offsetting); and

- where SI 2015/980 is applied, the opening balance sheet for each financial year must correspond to the closing balance sheet for the preceding financial year.

Schedules 2 and 3 to the Regulations (and the Small Companies Regulations, which are addressed in Chapter 3) have the same requirements. The LLP Regulations have the same requirements except for the amendment made by SI 2015/980 (i.e. the final bullet above). *[1 Sch 10-15, 40(2) (LLP)]*. Only the references in Schedule 1 to the Regulations are noted below.

9.1.1.A   Substance over form

FRS 102 does not have a separate section on 'substance over form' comparable to FRS 5 – *Reporting the substance of transactions*, but requires that 'transactions and other events and conditions should be accounted for and presented in accordance with their substance and not merely their legal form. This enhances the reliability of financial statements.' *[FRS 102.2.8]* (see Chapter 3 at 3.2.5 of EY New UK GAAP 2015). In addition, where an FRS or FRC Abstract does not specifically address a transaction, management must use its judgement in developing and applying an accounting policy that results in relevant and reliable information. *[FRS 102.10.4]*. One of the characteristics of reliable information is that the financial statements 'reflect the economic substance of transactions, other events and conditions, and not merely the legal form'. *[FRS 102.10.4(b)(ii)]*. In June 2014, the FRC issued updated guidance – *True and Fair* – which refers to the above requirement and makes the point that 'if material transactions are not accounted for in accordance with their substance it is doubtful whether the accounts present a true and fair view'.

The General Rules to the formats (see 4.4 above) require that items in the balance sheet and profit and loss account formats are presented, having regard to the substance of the reported transaction or arrangement, in accordance with generally accepted accounting principles or practice. *[1 Sch 9]*. This requirement facilitates the presentation of certain shares as liabilities in accordance with FRS 102 (and previous UK GAAP).

9.1.1.B   Prudence

FRS 102 identifies prudence as 'the inclusion of a degree of caution in the exercise of the judgements needed in making the estimates required under conditions of uncertainty, such that assets or income are not overstated and liabilities or expenses are not understated. However, the exercise of prudence does not allow the deliberate understatement of assets or income, or the deliberate overstatement of liabilities or expenses. In short, prudence does not permit bias'. *[FRS 102.2.9]*. See Chapter 3 at 3.2.6 of EY New UK GAAP 2015.

However, the standard does not specifically refer to realised profits. UK companies preparing Companies Act accounts are required to prepare the profit and loss account section of the statement of comprehensive income (or separate income statement) in accordance with the Regulations. As discussed in Appendix IV – *Note on legal requirements* – to the standard, the issue of realised profits is pertinent to whether a gain is reported in profit or loss in Companies Act accounts. *[FRS 102.A4.25-A4.27]*. This interaction with the Regulations may mean that UK companies preparing Companies Act accounts must present certain gains in other comprehensive income instead. Profit or loss and other comprehensive income, including the concept of realised profits, are discussed further at 6.2 above.

FRS 102 involves more use of fair values than previous UK GAAP. In particular, UK companies should be mindful that not all gains (even if recognised in profit or loss) may be distributable. Appendix IV to the standard states that entities measuring financial instruments, investment properties, and living animals and plants at fair value should note that they may transfer such amounts to a separate non-distributable reserve, instead of a transfer to retained earnings, but are not required to do so. Presenting fair value movements that are not distributable profits in the separate reserve may assist with identification of profits available for that purpose. *[FRS 102.A4.28]*. Appendix IV further notes that the determination of profits available for distribution is a complex area where accounting and company law interface and that companies may need to refer to TECH 02/10 *Guidance on realised and distributable profits* issued by the ICAEW and ICAS to determine profits available for distribution. *[FRS 102.A4.29]*. The impact of transition on distributable profits is discussed in Chapter 1 at 5.5.

9.1.1.C   Offset

FRS 102 prohibits offset of assets and liabilities, or income and expenses, unless required or permitted by an FRS (meaning, at present, the standard itself or FRS 103, where applied). *[FRS 102.2.52]*. See Chapter 3 at 3.12 of EY New UK GAAP 2015. This is similar to the requirement in the General Rules to the formats (see 4.4 above) that amounts in respect of items representing assets or income may not be set off against amounts in respect of items representing liabilities or expenditure (as the case may be), or *vice versa*. *[1 Sch 8]*.

The standard sets out when financial assets and liabilities *[FRS 102.11.38A, 12.25A]* (see Chapter 8 at 6.7 of EY New UK GAAP 2015), employee benefits, *[FRS 102.28.3(a), 28.14, 28.30]*, (see Chapter 23 at 3.2, 3.6.7 and 3.8.2 of EY New UK GAAP 2015), current tax and deferred tax, *[FRS 102.29.24-24A]*, (see Chapter 24 at 10.1.1 of EY New UK GAAP 2015) must be offset. In these cases, the standard is effectively saying that this is a single asset or liability.

In respect of the profit and loss account, gains and losses on disposal of fixed assets are shown net of costs, where not part of normal operating activities, *[FRS 102.2.52(b)]*, and expenses for a provision are permitted to be shown net of the amount recognised for reimbursement of the provision. *[FRS 102.21.9]*. The standard also permits cash flows from operating, investing and financing activities to be presented on a net basis where specified criteria are met. *[FRS 102.7.10A-10D]*.

Appendix IV – *Note on legal requirements* – to FRS 102 explains how the standard's requirements on government grants (no offsetting), reimbursement of provisions (offsetting permitted in profit and loss only) and financial assets (offsetting when the criteria in the standard are met) are consistent with the Regulations. *[FRS 102.A4.22-A4.23]*.

9.2   True and fair view and compliance with FRS 102

The FRC's *Foreword to Accounting Standards* (March 2015) explains that accounting standards are applicable to the financial statements of a reporting entity that are required to give a true and fair view of its financial position at the reporting date and its profit or loss (or income and expenditure) for the reporting period. The whole essence of accounting standards is to provide for recognition, measurement, presentation and disclosure for specific aspects of financial reporting in a way that reflects economic reality and hence provides a true and fair view.[33]

As discussed further at Chapter 1 at 7.2.1, the FRC (and its predecessor bodies) obtained legal opinions that have confirmed the centrality of the true and fair concept to the preparation and audit of financial statements, whether prepared in accordance with UK accounting standards or international accounting standards. The FRC also issued updated guidance – *True and Fair* – in June 2014 which is referenced from its *Foreword to Accounting Standards* (March 2015).

True and Fair (June 2014) further notes, *inter alia*, that accounting standards are developed after due process and 'these processes should result in accounting standards that, in the vast majority of cases, are complied with when presenting a true and fair view'. Where the accounting standards clearly address an issue, but the requirements are insufficient to fully explain the issue, the solution is normally additional disclosure. However, a company must depart from a particular accounting standard where required in order to meet the requirement for the accounts to give a true and fair view. It notes that these circumstances are more likely to arise when the precise circumstances were not contemplated during the development of the relevant standard.

The FRC expects preparers, those charged with governance and auditors to stand back and ensure that the financial statements as a whole give a true and fair view, provide additional disclosures where compliance with an accounting standard is insufficient to give a true and fair view, to use the true and fair override where compliance with the standards does not result in the presentation of a true and fair view and to ensure that the consideration they give to these matters is evident in their deliberations and documentation.[34]

9.2.1   *True and fair view – requirements of FRS 102 and the Regulations*

FRS 102 (amended July 2015) amends the previous requirements in Section 3 on fair presentation to more closely reflect the requirements of company law. The Accounting

Council Advice accompanying the FRS 102 (July 2015) amendments explains that the change to refer to a 'true and fair view' was made to 'more closely reflect the requirements of company law. These changes are not considered to have any substantive effect as "true and fair" and "presents fairly" are synonymous, being different articulations of the same concept, as confirmed by legal opinion'.[35]

Given that the requirements are not considered to have any substantive effect, this change is largely one of terminology and UK companies (and certain other entities) were already required to follow the requirements to give a true and fair view set out in the CA 2006. Accordingly, this Chapter does not discuss the previous requirements in FRS 102 that financial statements present fairly the financial position, financial performance and cash flows of an entity or the 'fair presentation override'. Refer to Chapter 4 at 8.2 of EY New UK GAAP 2015.

FRS 102 requires that financial statements shall give a true and fair view of the assets, liabilities, financial position, financial performance and, when required to be presented, cash flows of an entity. *[FRS 102.3.2, Appendix I]*.

This requirement is consistent with the requirement of section 393 of the CA 2006 that the directors of a UK company must not approve the annual accounts unless they are satisfied that they give a true and fair view of the assets, liabilities, financial position and profit or loss of the company (and in respect of any group accounts, the undertakings included in the consolidation as a whole, so far as concerns the members of the company). *[s393]*. The 'undertakings included in the consolidation' means the parent company and its consolidated subsidiary undertakings and is referred to as 'the group' below. See also the discussion of 'true and fair' (and its relationship with accounting standards) at Chapter 1 at 7.2.1.

Companies Act accounts must include a balance sheet as at the financial year end and a profit and loss account for the financial year that give a true and fair view of the company's state of affairs (and, where applicable, the group's state of affairs, so far as concerns the members of the company) as at the end of the financial year, and of the company's profit or loss (and, where applicable, the group's profit or loss so far as concerns the members of the company) for the financial year. The accounts must comply with regulations made by the Secretary of State as to the form and content of the company's individual (and where applicable, the consolidated) balance sheet and profit and loss account, and additional information to be provided by way of notes to the accounts. *[s396(1)-(3), s404(1)-(3)]*.

Application of FRS 102, with additional disclosure when necessary, is presumed to result in financial statements that give a true and fair view of the financial position, financial performance and, when required to be presented, cash flows of entities within the scope of the standard. *[FRS 102.3.2(a)]*.

An important point here is that all paragraphs of FRS 102 have equal authority. Some sections of the standard include appendices containing implementation guidance or examples, some of which are an integral part of the standard and others provide application guidance (each specifies its status). *[FRS 102.Summary (xiv)]*. We would generally expect that entities follow such guidance unless there is a valid reason. The presumption that application of the standard (with any necessary additional disclosure) results in a true and fair view is subject to the override set out in paragraph 3.4 of the standard (and for entities preparing financial statements subject to the CA 2006, the true and fair override). *[FRS 102.3.4, Appendix I]*. See 9.2.2 below.

The additional disclosures referred to in paragraph 3.2(a) of the standard are necessary when compliance with the specific requirements in the standard is insufficient to enable users to understand the effect of particular transactions, other events and conditions on the entity's financial position and performance. *[FRS 102.3.2]*.

This is consistent with the statutory requirement that if compliance with the regulations, and any other provisions made by or under the CA 2006, as to matters to be included in a company's individual (and where applicable, group) accounts or in notes to those accounts would not be sufficient to give a true and fair view, the necessary additional information must be given in the accounts or notes to them. *[s396(4), s404(4)]*.

9.2.2   The 'true and fair view' override – requirements of FRS 102 and the Regulations

In special circumstances when management concludes that compliance with any requirement of FRS 102 or applicable legislation (only when it allows for a true and fair override) is inconsistent with the requirement to give a true and fair view, the entity shall depart from that requirement in the manner set out in paragraph 3.5 of the standard. *[FRS 102.3.4]*.

When an entity departs from a requirement of FRS 102, or from a requirement of applicable legislation, it shall disclose:

(a)   that management has concluded that the financial statements give a true and fair view of the entity's financial position, financial performance and, when required to be presented, cash flows;

(b)   that it has complied with FRS 102 or applicable legislation, except that it has departed from a particular requirement of the standard or applicable legislation to the extent necessary to give a true and fair view; and

(c)   the nature and effect of the departure, including the treatment that FRS 102 or applicable legislation would require, the reason why that treatment would be so misleading in the circumstances that it would conflict with the objective of financial statements set out in Section 2 (see 9 above), and the treatment adopted. *[FRS 102.3.5]*.

When an entity has departed from a requirement of FRS 102 or applicable legislation in a prior period and that departure affects the amounts recognised in the financial statements for the current period, it shall make the disclosures set out in (c) above. *[FRS 102.3.6]*.

These disclosures are consistent with the statutory disclosures that if in special circumstances, compliance with any of those provisions is inconsistent with the requirement to give a true and fair view, the directors must depart from that provision to the extent necessary to give a true and fair view. Particulars of the departure, the reasons for it and its effect must be given in a note to the accounts. *[s396(5), s404(5)]*.

FRS 102 does not explain what is required by the 'effect' of the departure, but in our view, this means 'financial effect'. In the absence of guidance in FRS 102, management may consider the requirements of IFRSs. Where there is a departure from IFRSs in the current period (or a departure was made in a previous period which impacts the amounts recognised in the financial statements in the current period), IAS 1 requires disclosure for each period presented, of the financial impact of the departure on each item in the financial statements that would have been reported in complying with the requirement. *[IAS 1.20(d), 21]*. Previous UK GAAP also normally required quantification of the financial effect on both the current financial year and corresponding amounts (i.e. the comparatives), except where quantification was evident from the financial statements themselves (e.g. where it was a matter of presentation rather than measurement) or where the effect cannot reasonably be quantified, in which case the directors should explain the circumstances. *[FRS 18.62-63]*.

In addition, where it appears to the directors that there are special reasons for departing from any of the general principles (see 9.1.1 above) in preparing the accounts for the financial year, the particulars of the departure, reasons and effect should be disclosed in a note to the accounts. *[1 Sch 10(2)]*. Appendix IV – *Note on legal requirements* – to FRS 102 highlights certain instances where the requirements of FRS 102 result in a departure from the requirements of the Regulations in order to give a 'true and fair view'. These examples, which are not exhaustive, are relevant to UK companies preparing Companies Act accounts (and similarly, LLPs preparing non-IAS accounts subject to the LLP Regulations).

Large- and medium-sized companies must make a statement in the notes to the accounts (see 3.8.1 above) as to whether the accounts have been prepared in accordance with applicable accounting standards, giving particulars of any material departures from those standards and the reasons. *[1 Sch 45]*. However, medium-sized companies are exempt from making this statement in individual accounts. *[Regulations 4(2A)]*. Consistent with previous UK GAAP, in our view, this statement should either include or cross refer any disclosures of the true and fair override (which are consistent with those required by FRS 102). *[FRS 18.62]*.

9.3   Going concern

FRS 102 requires management, when preparing financial statements, to make an assessment of an entity's ability to continue as a going concern. An entity is a going concern unless management either intends to liquidate the entity or to cease trading, or has no realistic alternative but to do so. In assessing whether the going concern assumption is appropriate, management takes into account all available information about the future, which is at least, but is not limited to, twelve months from the date when the financial statements are authorised for issue. *[FRS 102.3.8, Appendix I]*. This review period is a longer minimum period than that specified in IAS 1 and is consistent with that specified for management's assessment of going concern in auditing standards by ISA (UK & Ireland) 570 – *Going Concern*.

When management is aware, in making its assessment, of material uncertainties related to events or conditions that cast significant doubt upon the entity's ability to continue as a going concern, those uncertainties should be disclosed in the financial statements. *[FRS 102.3.9].*

When financial statements are not prepared on a going concern basis, that fact should be disclosed, together with the basis on which the financial statements are prepared and the reason why the entity is not regarded as a going concern. *[FRS 102.3.9].*

FRS 102 states that an entity shall not prepare its financial statements on a going concern basis if management determines after the reporting period either that it intends to liquidate the entity or to cease trading or that it has no realistic alternative but to do so. Deterioration in operating results and financial position after the reporting period may indicate a need to consider whether the going concern assumption is no longer appropriate. If the going concern assumption is no longer appropriate, the effect is so pervasive that a fundamental change in the basis of accounting rather than an adjustment to the amounts recognised within the original basis of accounting is required, and therefore the disclosure requirements in paragraph 3.9 of the standard, as described above, apply. *[FRS 102.32.7A-7B].*

FRS 102 provides no further guidance concerning what impact there should be on the financial statements if it is determined that the going concern basis is not appropriate. Accordingly, entities will need to consider carefully their individual circumstances to arrive at an appropriate basis.

FRS 102's requirements are supplemented by FRC guidance. In September 2014, the FRC issued *Guidance on Risk Management, Internal Control: and Related Financial and Business Reporting.* This guidance integrates and replaces the previous *Internal Control: Revised Guidance for Directors on the Combined Code (2005)* and *Going Concern and Liquidity Risk: Guidance for Directors of UK companies 2009* ('the 2009 Going Concern Guidance') and reflects changes made to the UK Corporate Governance Code. This new guidance is aimed primarily at entities subject to the UK Corporate Governance Code (and applies for such entities for financial years beginning on or after 1 October 2014). The FRC hopes that other entities will find it helpful but expects to issue updated guidance for unlisted entities later in 2015.

While many FRS 102 reporters will not be subject to or voluntarily applying the UK Corporate Governance Code, Section 6, Appendix A and Appendix D of *Guidance on Risk Management, Internal Control: and Related Financial and Business Reporting* include relevant guidance on adoption of the going concern basis of accounting (including disclosures on material uncertainties) in the financial statements, as well as reporting on principal risks and uncertainties (in the strategic report).

The FRC intends to issue separate, simplified guidance for companies not applying the UK Corporate Governance Code. In October 2015, the FRC issued *Exposure Draft: Guidance on the Going Concern Basis of Accounting and Reporting on Solvency and Liquidity Risks – Guidance for companies that do not apply the UK Corporate Governance Code.* The guidance, when finalised, is designed to be non-mandatory, best practice guidance for such companies required to make disclosures on the going concern basis of accounting in their financial statements and on principal risks and uncertainties in the strategic report. It replaces the 2009 Going Concern Guidance. In particular, directors should consider threats to solvency and liquidity as part of their assessment of risks and uncertainties faced by the company. The draft guidance covers factors to consider when determining whether the going concern basis of accounting is appropriate and making assessments of solvency risk and liquidity risk relevant to a company's future viability; guidance on the assessment periods for the going concern basis of accounting and risks; and a summary of the reporting requirements.

9.4   Materiality and aggregation

Financial statements result from processing large numbers of transactions or other events that are aggregated into classes according to their nature or function. The final stage in the process of aggregation and classification is the presentation of condensed and classified data, which form line items in the financial statements. *[FRS 102.3.16]*.

FRS 102 reporters must comply with the balance sheet and profit and loss account formats set out in the Regulations (or LLP Regulations) (see 4.1 above for which formats apply to which entity). FRS 102 requires an entity to present additional line items, headings and subtotals where relevant to an understanding of the financial position or financial performance. *[FRS 102.4.3, 5.5C, 5.9]*.

The extent of aggregation versus detailed analysis is clearly a judgemental one, with either extreme eroding the usefulness of the information. FRS 102 resolves this issue with the concept of materiality (see Chapter 3 at 3.2.3 of EY New UK GAAP 2015).Materiality is defined as follows: 'Omissions or misstatements of items are material if they could, individually or collectively, influence the economic decisions of users taken on the basis of the financial statements. Materiality depends on the size and nature of the omission or misstatement judged in the surrounding circumstances. The size or nature of the item, or a combination of both, could be the determining factor.' However, it is inappropriate to make, or leave uncorrected, immaterial departures from the standard to achieve a particular presentation of an entity's financial position, financial performance or cash flows. *[FRS 102.2.6, Appendix I]*.

FRS 102 requires each material class of similar items to be presented separately and items of a dissimilar nature or function to be presented separately unless they are immaterial. *[FRS 102.3.15]*. If a line item is not individually material, it is aggregated with other items either in those statements or in the notes. An item that may not warrant separate presentation in those financial statements may warrant separate presentation in the notes. *[FRS 102.3.16]*.

The General Rules to the formats (see 4.4 above) allow the directors to combine items denoted with Arabic numbers in the (statutory) balance sheet and profit and loss account formats if their individual amounts are not material to assessing the state of affairs or profit or loss of the company for the financial year in question, or where the combination facilitates that assessment (in which case, the individual amounts of the line items combined must be disclosed in the notes). *[1 Sch 4(2), 1 Sch 4(2) (LLP)]*.

FRS 102 states that an entity need not provide a specific disclosure required by the standard if the information is not material. *[FRS 102.3.16A]*. UK companies preparing Companies Act accounts must also comply with the disclosure requirements of the Regulations. The Regulations permit that 'amounts which in the particular context of any provision of Schedules 1, 2 or 3 to these Regulations are not material may be disregarded for the purposes of that provision.' *[10 Sch 10]*. The LLP Regulations have the same requirements. *[4 Sch 7 (LLP)]*.

9.4.1   'Cutting Clutter'

In recent years, there has been increased recognition that the length and complexity of annual reports and financial statements can obscure key messages and make them less understandable. This has led to a regulatory focus on 'cutting clutter' with the aim of making financial statements more concise and relevant. The FRC have published a number of papers including *Louder than Words: Principles and actions for making corporate reports less complex and more relevant* (June 2009), *Cutting Clutter: Combating clutter in annual reports* (April 2011), and *Thinking about Disclosures in a broader context: A road map for a disclosure framework* (October 2012). 'Cutting clutter' has been a recurrent message in the annual Corporate Reporting Review and a focus of the FRC Lab, for instance, Lab Insight Report – *Towards Clear and Concise Reporting* (August 2014) which contains many useful observations.

Amendment to IAS 1 – *Disclosure Initiative* (see 8.1 above) clarifies the concept of materiality and aggregation which, while not directly applicable, may be helpful for FRS 102 reporters to consider. The amendment emphasises that when applying IFRS, an entity shall decide, taking into consideration all relevant facts and circumstances, how it aggregates information in the financial statements, which include the notes. An entity shall not reduce the understandability of its financial statements by obscuring material information with other information or by aggregating material items that have different natures and functions. An entity need not provide a specific disclosure required by IFRS if the information resulting is not material, even if the IFRS contains a list of specific requirements, describing them as minimum requirements. *[IAS 1.30A-31]*.

While much of the regulatory focus has been on IFRS financial statements (and IFRS has more extensive disclosure requirements compared to FRS 102), the general messages above are also relevant for FRS 102 financial statements.

10   RECOGNITION AND MEASUREMENT, PRESENTATION AND DISCLOSURE – COMPANIES ACT ACCOUNTS

FRS 102 financial statements prepared by a UK company are Companies Act accounts and, therefore, must comply with the recognition and measurement rules included in the applicable schedule of the Regulations (or Small Companies Regulations).

FRS 102 has been modified compared to the IFRS for SMEs in order to ensure that it complies with these requirements. Appendix IV – *Note on legal requirements* – to the standard provides an overview of how FRS 102's requirements address UK company law requirements (written from the perspective of a company to which the CA 2006 applies) and highlights certain areas where following FRS 102's requirements may necessitate use of the 'true and fair override'. Appendix IV is not comprehensive and, therefore, it is useful to have an understanding of the key recognition and measurement principles included in the Regulations.

Schedules 1 to 3 to the Regulations set out fundamental accounting principles such as going concern, use of consistent accounting policies, prudence, no offsetting of assets and liabilities (or income and expense) and, where SI 2015/980 is applied, that the opening balance sheet for each financial year corresponds to the closing balance sheet for the preceding financial year. See 9.1.1 above.

The Regulations also set out the following three models for the recognition and measurement of assets and liabilities:

- historical cost accounting rules (see 10.1 below); *[1 Sch Section B]*
- alternative accounting rules (see 10.2 below); *[1 Sch Section C]* and
- fair value accounting rules (see 10.3 and 10.4 below). *[1 Sch Section D]*.

The main requirements of the three models are set out below. However, entities preparing FRS 102 financial statements also need to comply with the requirements of FRS 102, which are sometimes more restrictive than the statutory requirements.

References given below are to Schedule 1 to the Regulations only, but there are equivalent paragraphs in Schedule 2 or Schedule 3 (albeit sometimes with modifications to those in Schedule 1).

The historical cost, alternative and fair value accounting rules discussed at 10.1 to 10.4 below are the same in Schedule 1 to the Small Companies Regulations (discussed in Chapter 3), except that the related disclosures are simpler than those set out in the Regulations.

FRS 102 (amended July 2015) reflects changes, as necessary, to the three models arising from SI 2015/980. Note that, while these amendments have been driven by company law changes, they apply to all entities applying FRS 102 (but see comments on LLPs below).

Changes to the Regulations made by SI 2015/980 which have led to a change in the requirements of FRS 102 (discussed in Chapter 5) include:

- stock may no longer be measured at current cost under the alternative accounting rules but may instead be measured at fair value under the fair value accounting rules (see 10.2 and 10.4 below). Note that in most cases, stock is carried at cost under FRS 102;
- where in exceptional circumstances, the useful life cannot be reliably estimated, intangible assets (including goodwill) are amortised over their useful life, which must not exceed ten years (see 10.1.2 below);
- prohibition of reversal of a goodwill impairment loss (included in SI 2015/1672, as the change was omitted from SI 2015/980 – see 1.1 above and 10.1.2 below);
- a change to the scope of (and related disclosures required) when financial instruments can be measured at fair value under paragraph 36(4) of Schedule 1 to the Regulations (see 10.3.1 below). The same change is made in Schedule 2 and 3 to the Regulations. While not directly related to this change, Sections 11 and 12 include various amendments related to this paragraph.

Changes that have not necessitated a change to the requirements of FRS 102 include:

- where the historical cost accounting rules are applied, the purchase price is stated after subtracting any incidental reductions in the cost of acquisition (see 10.1.1 below);

- where stock is measured using a cost method, other than FIFO, LIFO (not permitted by FRS 102) or weighted average price, the cost method must reflect generally accepted accounting practice (see 10.1.1 below);

- clarifications in relation to development costs (see 10.1.3 below) and provisions (see 10.1.5 below);

- minor amendments to the requirements for provisions for diminution and related disclosure (see 10.1.2 below);

- the equity method may be applied for participating interests in individual accounts – this change, while significant, is not being implemented in FRS 102 (see 10.1.4 below);

- a requirement to show a revaluation reserve under that name in the balance sheet statutory formats (see 10.2.3 below);

- a requirement that fair value, in the context of measuring investment property, stocks and living animals and plants is fair value determined in accordance with generally accepted accounting principles or practice (previously, fair value accounting had to be permitted by international accounting standards and fair value determined in accordance with relevant international accounting standards). See 10.4.1 below; and

- an extension of the fair value disclosures in paragraph 55 of Schedule 1 to the Regulations (which previously related only to financial instruments) to cover investment property, living animals and plants (i.e. biological assets) and stocks measured using the fair value accounting rules. See 10.4.3 below.

The LLP Regulations (unless LLP law is subsequently changed) also contain the same three models, but do not reflect the amendments made by SI 2015/980. *[1 Sch 16-41 (LLP)]*. Only the references in Schedule 1 to the Regulations are noted below.

A discussion of the models prior to application of SI 2015/980 is contained in Chapter 4 at 9 of EY New UK GAAP 2015. As highlighted at 1.3 above, Appendix IV to the standard cautions that if following the requirements of FRS 102 would lead to a conflict with applicable legislation, an LLP shall instead apply its own legal requirements and consider whether disclosure of a departure from FRS 102 is required. *[FRS 102.A4.43, A46, A47]*.

Chapter 4

10.1   Historical cost accounting rules

FRS 102 makes use of the historical cost accounting rules for the following assets:

- basic financial instruments, except for: *[FRS 102.11.8, 11.14]*

    - investments in non-convertible preference shares and non-puttable ordinary shares or preference shares that are publicly traded or whose fair value can otherwise be measured reliably; or

    - debt instruments and commitments to receive a loan and to make a loan to another entity (meeting specified conditions) that are designated at fair value through profit or loss on initial recognition;

- financial instruments that are not permitted by the Regulations, Small Companies Regulations, LLP Regulations or the Small LLP Regulations to be measured at fair value through profit or loss (see 10.3.1 below); *[FRS 102.11.2A, 12.2A, 12.8(c)]*

- inventories – except for inventories measured at fair value less costs to sell through profit or loss (in active markets only) and inventories held for distribution at no or nominal consideration; *[FRS 102.13.3-13.4A]*

- property, plant and equipment – where the cost model is applied; *[FRS 102.17.15-15A]*

- investment property, where the cost model is applied since fair value cannot be measured reliably without undue cost or effort on an ongoing basis; *[FRS 102.16.1]*

- intangible assets – where the cost model is applied; *[FRS 102.18.18-18A]*

- goodwill; *[FRS 102.19.22-23]*

- biological assets; *[FRS 102.34.3A, 8-9]*

- investments in subsidiaries, associates and joint ventures in separate or individual financial statements – where the cost model is applied; *[FRS 102.9.26(a), 9.26A, 14.4(a), 14.5-14.6, 15.9(a), 15.10-15.11]* and

- investments in excluded subsidiaries in consolidated financial statements – where the cost model is applied *[FRS 102.9.9, 9.9A, 9.9B(b)]*.

Under the historical cost accounting rules,

- fixed assets are included at cost (i.e. purchase price or production cost – see 10.1.1 below) subject to any provisions for depreciation or diminution in value; *[1 Sch 17]* and

- current assets are included at the lower of cost (i.e. purchase price or production cost) and net realisable value. Where the reasons for which any provision was made have ceased to apply to any extent, the provision must be written back to the extent that it is no longer necessary. *[1 Sch 23-24]*.

Fixed assets are assets which are intended for use on a continuing basis in the company's activities, and current assets are assets not intended for such use. *[10 Sch 4]*. Note that these recognition and measurement requirements apply whether statutory formats or 'adapted formats' (which distinguish between non-current assets and current assets, defined in line with IAS 1) are used.

10.1.1 Definition of purchase price and production cost

The purchase price is the sum of the actual price paid (including cash and non-cash consideration) for the asset and any expenses incidental to its acquisition (and, where SI 2015/980 is applied, then subtracting any incidental reductions in the cost of acquisition). *[1 Sch 27(1), 10 Sch 12]*.

The production cost is the sum of the purchase price of the raw materials and consumables and directly attributable production costs. The Regulations permit the inclusion of: *[1 Sch 27(2)-(3)]*

- a reasonable proportion of costs incurred by the company which are indirectly attributable to the production of the asset (but only to the extent they relate to the period of production); and

- interest on capital borrowed to finance the production of the asset (to the extent it accrues in respect of the period of production), provided that a note to the accounts discloses that interest is capitalised in the cost of that asset and gives the amount of interest so capitalised.

Distribution costs may not be included in the production cost of a current asset. *[1 Sch 27(4)]*.

The purchase price or production cost of stocks and any fungible assets (including investments) may be determined by one of the following methods, provided that the method chosen appears to the directors to be appropriate in the circumstances of the company: *[1 Sch 28(1)-(2)]*

- last in, first out (LIFO) – this method is not permitted by FRS 102;

- first in, first out (FIFO);

- weighted average price; and

- any other method reflecting generally accepted best practice (where SI 2015/980 is not applied, this reads 'any other method similar to any of the methods mentioned above').

Fungible assets are assets which are substantially indistinguishable one from another. *[10 Sch 5]*.

Where an item shown in the balance sheet includes assets whose purchase price or production cost has been determined using any of the above methods in 1 Sch 28(1)-2), the notes to the accounts must disclose the difference (where material) between: *[1 Sch 28(3)-(5)]*

- the carrying amount of that balance sheet item; and

- the amount that would have been shown if assets of any class included under that item at an amount determined using any of the above methods had instead been included at their replacement cost as at the balance sheet date. This calculation can use the most recent actual purchase price or production cost before the balance sheet date instead of replacement cost if the former appears to the directors to be the more appropriate standard of comparison for assets of that class.

Chapter 4

Where there is no record of the purchase price or production cost (or of any price, expenses or cost relevant for determining the purchase price or production cost) or any such record cannot be obtained without unreasonable expense or delay, the purchase price or production cost of the asset must be taken to be the value ascribed in the earliest available record of its value made on or after its acquisition or production by the company. *[1 Sch 29]*.

The Regulations also permit tangible fixed assets and raw materials and consumables (within current assets) to be included at a fixed quantity and value, but only where the assets are constantly being replaced, their overall value is not material to assessing the company's state of affairs, and their quantity, value and composition are not subject to material valuation. *[1 Sch 26]*. Some companies capitalise minor items (such as tools, cutlery, small containers, sheets and towels) at a fixed amount when they are originally provided as a form of capital 'base stock' where the continual loss and replacement of stock does result in a base amount that does not materially vary. This treatment is not compliant with FRS 102 and therefore would only be acceptable where the items in question are immaterial.

Where the amount repayable on a debt owed by a company exceeds the value of the consideration received in the transaction giving rise to the debt, the Regulations allow the difference to be treated as an asset, which must then be written off by reasonable amounts each year (and must be completely written off before repayment of the debt). The current amount should be disclosed in a note to the accounts if it is not shown as a separate item in the balance sheet. *[1 Sch 25]*. This treatment would not comply with FRS 102's requirements on initial measurement of financial liabilities *[FRS 102.11.13]* (see Chapter 8 at 4.3 of EY New UK GAAP 2015).

10.1.1.A   *FRS 102 requirements on determination of cost of assets*

FRS 102's requirements for measuring cost are consistent with but more prescriptive than the Regulations. For example,

- Property, plant and equipment and intangible assets – Only costs directly attributable to bringing the asset to the location and condition necessary for it to be capable of operating in the manner intended by management are permitted to be included in the cost of property, plant and equipment and intangible assets. *[FRS 102.17.10(b), 18.10]*. Section 17 includes detailed requirements on which types of costs are capitalised. *[FRS 102.17.10-14]*. Section 17 also clarifies that the income and related expenses of incidental operations during construction or development of an item of property, plant and equipment are recognised in profit or loss if those operations are not necessary to bring the item to its intended location and operating condition. *[FRS 102.17.12]*. See Chapter 13 at 3.4 and Chapter 14 at 3.3 of EY New UK GAAP 2015.

- Borrowing costs – An entity is permitted by Section 25 – *Borrowing Costs* – to either expense borrowing costs or to adopt a policy of capitalising borrowing costs directly attributable to the acquisition, construction or production of a qualifying asset (which must be applied consistently to a class of qualifying assets). Section 25's requirements are more detailed than the Regulations and specify the period for which borrowing costs can be capitalised, and how to determine the amounts capitalised. *[FRS 102.25.1-2D]*. See Chapter 20 at 3 of EY New UK GAAP 2015.

- Inventories – The cost of inventories includes all costs of purchase, costs of conversion (direct production costs and allocated variable and fixed production overheads) and other costs incurred in bringing the inventories to their present location and condition. *[FRS 102.13.5-15]*. As noted above, the Regulations prohibit capitalisation of 'distribution costs'. FRS 102's requirements on cost (including the meaning of 'distribution costs' in this context) and the methods that can be used to determine cost *[FRS 102.13.16-18]* are discussed further at Chapter 9 at 3.3 of EY New UK GAAP 2015.

10.1.2 Depreciation and diminution of fixed assets

Where a fixed asset has a limited useful economic life, its purchase price or production cost less its estimated residual value (if any) must be reduced by provisions for depreciation to write off that amount systematically over the period of the asset's useful economic life. *[1 Sch 18]*.

SI 2015/980 amends the Regulations to further require that intangible assets must be written off over the useful economic life of the intangible asset. Where in exceptional cases the useful life of intangible assets cannot be reliably estimated, such assets must be written off over a period chosen by the directors of the company that must not exceed ten years (and that period must be disclosed, together with the reasons for choosing that period). *[1 Sch 22]*.

Where a fixed asset investment (item B.III in the balance sheet formats – see 5.3.4 above) has diminished in value, provisions for diminution in value *may* [emphasis added] be made and its carrying amount reduced accordingly. *[1 Sch 19(1)]*. Provisions for diminution in value *must* [emphasis added] be made in respect of any fixed asset which has diminished in value, if the reduction in value is expected to be permanent (whether or not the fixed asset has a limited useful life). *[1 Sch 19(2)]*.

Where the reasons for which any provision (for diminution) was made (in accordance with 1 Sch 19 to the Regulations) have ceased to apply to any extent, the provision must be written back to the extent that it is no longer necessary. *[1 Sch 20(1)]*. This paragraph is amended by SI 2015/1672 to state that provisions made in accordance with paragraph 19(2) in respect of goodwill must not be written back to any extent. There are similar amendments made in Schedule 2 and Schedule 3 to the Regulations (but no changes are made to the LLP Regulations, unless there is a subsequent change to LLP law).

SI 2015/980 does not amend 1 Sch 19(1)-(2) but adds a new general principle that 'all provisions for diminution of value must be recognised, whether the result of the financial year is a profit or loss'. *[1 Sch 13(c)]*. FRS 102's requirements for impairment of financial assets (at cost or amortised cost) and impairment of other assets in Sections 11 and 27 respectively are consistent with this new principle (see Chapter 8 at 5 and Chapter 22 respectively of EY New UK GAAP 2015).

Provisions for diminution made under 1 Sch 19(1)-(2) must be charged to and any amounts written back under 1 Sch 20(1) must be recognised in the profit and loss account. The provisions made and any write-backs must be disclosed separately in a note to the accounts, if not shown separately in the profit and loss account. *[1 Sch 19(3), 20(2)].*

Where SI 2015/980 is not applied or for LLPs, any such provisions made and any such amounts written back must be disclosed (either separately or in aggregate) in a note to the accounts. *[1 Sch 19(3), 20(2), 1 Sch 19(3), 20(2) (LLP)].*

The requirements of paragraphs 17 to 20 and 22 of Schedule 1 to the Regulations apply to any goodwill relating to an interest in an associated undertaking, e.g. an associate or jointly controlled entity, shown by the equity method of accounting. *[6 Sch 21(1)].*

10.1.2.A   FRS 102's requirements

The requirements for measuring depreciation, amortisation and impairment in FRS 102 are consistent with the Regulations but more prescriptive. For example, Section 17 contains detailed requirements on depreciation of property, plant and equipment *[FRS 102.17.16-23].* See Chapter 13 at 3.5.

Prior to the FRS 102 (July 2015) amendments, the requirements of the standard were more restrictive for goodwill and intangible asset amortisation than the Regulations (before amendment by SI 2015/980). See Chapter 14 at 3.4.3 and Chapter 15 at 3.8.2 of EY New UK GAAP 2015. FRS 102 (amended July 2015) now reflects the requirements of the Regulations (as amended by SI 2015/980). The standard's amended requirements for goodwill and intangible amortisation (see Chapter 5 at 7.1) are more restrictive than but do not conflict with the LLP Regulations (which are unchanged).

Appendix IV – *Note on legal requirements* – to FRS 102 notes that the new requirement in 1 Sch 22 to the Regulations is broadly consistent with paragraph 18.21 of FRS 102, which requires that the depreciable amount of an intangible asset is allocated on a systematic basis over its useful life, *[FRS 102.18.21],* except that FRS 102 allows for the possibility that an intangible asset will have a residual value (albeit uncommon in practice since paragraph 18.23 requires an entity to assume that the residual value is zero other than in specific circumstances). In those cases where an intangible asset has a residual value that is not zero, the amortisation of the depreciable amount of an intangible asset over its useful economic life is a departure from the requirements of 1 Sch 22 to the Regulations for the overriding purpose of giving a true and fair view, requiring the disclosures for a true and fair override (see 9.2 above). *[FRS 102.A4.37A].* See also Chapter 5 at 6.2.

FRS 102 requires amortisation of goodwill on a systematic basis over its finite useful life, so there is no residual value, consistent with the Regulations. *[FRS 102.19.23(a)].* However, there is a conflict with the requirements not to amortise goodwill in FRS 101, meaning that a true and fair override is required (see Chapter 2 at 4.1).

FRS 102 does not distinguish between temporary and permanent diminutions in value. Section 27 – *Impairment of Assets* – requires provisions for impairment of property, plant and equipment, investment property measured using the cost model, biological assets measured using the cost model, intangible assets and goodwill to be recognised when the carrying amount of the asset is not recoverable. *[FRS 102.27.5]*. Similarly, Sections 11 and 12 contain specific requirements for recognition of impairment of financial assets measured at cost or amortised cost, where there is objective evidence of impairment. *[FRS 102.11.21-11.26, 12.13]*.

FRS 102 (amended July 2015) prohibits the reversal of goodwill impairment (reflecting the change to the Regulations made by SI 2015/1672) and makes related changes to the allocation of impairment losses and reversals of impairment. *[FRS 102.27.29, 31(b)-(c)]*. See Chapter 5 at 10.

10.1.3   Development costs

SI 2015/980 states that development costs may be included in other intangible assets under fixed assets in the balance sheet statutory formats set out in Section B of Part 1 to the Regulations where this is in accordance with generally accepted accounting principles or practice. If any amount is included in a company's balance sheet in respect of development costs, the note on accounting policies must include the period over which the amount of those costs originally capitalised is being or is to be written off and the reasons for capitalising the development costs in question. *[1 Sch 21]*. These disclosures are similar to those required by FRS 102. *[FRS 102.18.27(a)]*. The reference to the statutory formats should not preclude the ability to capitalise development costs, where 'adapted formats' are used.

There were similar requirements prior to the SI 2015/980 amendments (and which remain relevant for LLPs, unless there is a subsequent change to LLP law). The Regulations then required that an amount may only be included in a company's balance sheet in respect of development costs in 'special circumstances'. The reasons for capitalising the development costs and the period over which the amount of those costs originally capitalised is being or will be written off must be disclosed in a note to the accounts. *[1 Sch 21]*. As 'special circumstances' were taken to mean where capitalisation was permitted by accounting standards (see below), this change should not have a substantive effect and no changes have been made to FRS 102's requirements.

Development costs shown as an asset are treated as a realised loss except where there are 'special circumstances' justifying the directors' decision not to treat these as a realised loss and in Companies Act accounts, the note to the accounts referred to in 1 Sch 21 to the Regulations (and for IAS accounts, any note to the accounts) states that the amount of the development costs shown as an asset is not to be treated as a realised loss, together with the circumstances relied upon to justify the directors' decision to that effect. *[s844]*. TECH 02/10 clarifies that this would be the case where the costs are carried forward in accordance with applicable accounting standards. *[s844, TECH 02/10.2.38]*. The reference to 'special circumstances' in section 844 of the CA 2006 has not changed notwithstanding the change made to the Regulations. See Chapter 14 at 3.5.3 of EY New UK GAAP 2015.

10.1.4   Equity method in respect of participating interests

SI 2015/980 introduces a new option to account for participating interests (see definition in 5.3.4.D above). The Accounting Council Advice explains that FRS 102 already includes a number of options for accounting for such investments (see paragraph 9.26) and the Accounting Council did not advise introducing this option at present.[36] Consequently, this accounting treatment is not permitted by FRS 102, although it will be available to FRS 101 reporters once the equivalent IAS 27 – *Separate Financial Statements* – amendments permitting use of the equity method in separate financial statements are adopted by the EU.

If participating interests are accounted for using the equity method:

- the proportion of profit or loss attributable to a participating interest and recognised in the profit and loss account may be that proportion which corresponds to the amount of any dividends (including dividends already paid and those whose payment can be claimed); and

- where the profit attributable to a participating interest and recognised in the profit and loss account exceeds the amount of any dividends (including dividends already paid and those whose payment can be claimed), the difference must be placed in a reserve which cannot be distributed to shareholders. *[1 Sch 29A]*.

However, the first alternative is not consistent with the equity method as applied in IFRS, FRS 101 or FRS 102, and the second alternative includes an additional statutory restriction that any excess of the amount of dividends over the profit attributable to a participating interest is to be included in a non-distributable reserve.

10.1.5   *Provisions for liabilities*

While not strictly part of the historical cost accounting rules, the Regulations define provisions for liabilities as 'any amount retained as reasonably necessary for the purpose of providing for any liability the nature of which is clearly defined and which is either likely to be incurred, or certain to be incurred but uncertain as to amount or as to the date on which it will arise'. *[9 Sch 2]*. SI 2015/980 adds that at the balance sheet date, a provision must represent the best estimate of the expenditures likely to be incurred or, in the case of a liability, the amount required to meet that liability. Provisions must not be used to adjust the value of assets. *[9 Sch 2A-2B]*.

FRS 102 defines a provision more succinctly as 'a liability of uncertain timing or amount' and also requires measurement at the best estimate of the amount required to settle the obligation at the balance sheet date. This is the amount an entity would rationally pay to settle the obligation at the end of the reporting period or to transfer it to a third party at that time. *[FRS 102.21.1, 21.7, Appendix I]*. FRS 102's requirements are, therefore, consistent with, but more detailed than, the Regulations. See Chapter 17 at 3 of EY New UK GAAP 2015.

10.2   Alternative accounting rules

Under the alternative accounting rules, assets are carried at a revalued amount (on one of the permitted bases set out in paragraph 32 of Schedule 1 to the Regulations – see 10.2.1 below). The most familiar use of the alternative accounting rules is for revaluation of property, plant and equipment, but all of the other revaluations listed below follow a similar model. Note that there is no reclassification to profit or loss (for the period) of amounts previously accumulated in equity where the alternative accounting rules are applied.

FRS 102's requirements for revaluations of the following assets make use of the alternative accounting rules:

- property, plant and equipment carried at a revalued amount, being the fair value at the date of revaluation less any subsequent accumulated depreciation and subsequent accumulated impairment losses. The revaluation model must be applied to all items in the same class (i.e. having a similar nature, function or use in the business). *[FRS 102.17.15, 17.15B-F]*. See Chapter 13 at 3.6 of EY New UK GAAP 2015;

- intangible fixed assets carried at a revalued amount, being the fair value at the date of revaluation less any subsequent accumulated amortisation and subsequent accumulated impairment losses. The revaluation model must be applied to all items in the same class, and revaluations are only permitted provided that the fair value can be determined by reference to an active market. *[FRS 102.18.18, 18.18B-H]*. In practice, it is rare to meet the criteria for revaluation of an intangible fixed asset. See Chapter 14 at 3.4.2 of EY New UK GAAP 2015;

- investments in subsidiaries, associates and jointly controlled entities, where a policy of fair value through other comprehensive income is applied in individual or separate financial statements. *[FRS 102.9.26(b), 9.26A, 14.4(c), 15.9(c)]*. See Chapter 6 at 4.2, Chapter 10 at 3.3.1 and 3.3.4, and Chapter 11 at 3.6.2 and 3.6.3.A of EY New UK GAAP 2015; and

- investments in subsidiaries excluded from consolidation carried at fair value through other comprehensive income in consolidated financial statements; *[FRS 102.9.9, 9.9A, 9.9B(b)]*. See Chapter 6 at 3.4.1 of EY New UK GAAP 2015.

- where IFRS 9 is applied, investments in equity instruments are designated as measured at fair value through other comprehensive income. *[IFRS 9.4.1.4, IFRS 9.5.7.1(b), 5.7.5-5.7.6]*.

  This accounting differs significantly from the accounting for available-for-sale financial assets under IAS 39 (which is explicitly covered by the fair value accounting rules). In particular, there is no reclassification to profit or loss of previous amounts accumulated in equity or on disposal of the financial asset. There is also no separate accounting for impairments – with the exception of dividends received, all fair value changes are recognise in other comprehensive income. Therefore, in our view, this accounting is not permitted by the fair value accounting rules but is permitted under the alternative accounting rules for fixed asset investments.

Prior to the FRS 102 (July 2015) amendments, inventories held for distribution at no or nominal consideration are measured at cost adjusted, when applicable, for any loss of service potential. When distributed, the carrying amount of these inventories is recognised as an expense. *[FRS 102.13.4A, 13.20A]*. See Chapter 9 at 3.3.11 of EY New UK GAAP 2015. Appendix IV – *Note on legal requirements* to the standard notes that although the alternative accounting rules require measurement at current cost, for inventories held for distribution at no or nominal value, there is unlikely to be a significant difference between cost and current cost. *[FRS 102.A4.36-37]*. As the Regulations, as amended by SI 2015/980, no longer permit the use of the alternative accounting rules, the accounting for such inventory has changed where the FRS 102 (July 2015) amendments are applied (see 10.2.1 and 10.4.1 below and Chapter 5 at 5).

Financial assets carried at fair value in accordance with Sections 11 and 12 or IAS 39 are generally measured using the fair value accounting rules rather than the alternative accounting rules (see 10.3 below). In our view, where financial assets are carried at fair value in accordance with IFRS 9, this also makes use of the fair value accounting rules (except for the situation discussed above).

10.2.1   Assets that may be revalued under the alternative accounting rules in the Regulations

Under the alternative accounting rules in the Regulations: *[1 Sch 32]*

- tangible fixed assets may be included at market value determined as at the date of their last valuation or at their current cost;
- fixed asset investments may be included either:
  - at a market value determined as at the date of their last valuation; or
  - at a value determined on a basis which appears to the directors to be appropriate to the company's circumstances (but in this latter case, particulars of the method of valuation adopted and of the reasons for adopting it must be disclosed in a note to the accounts); and
- intangible fixed assets (other than goodwill) may be included at current cost.

Prior to the SI 2015/980 amendments, current asset investments and stocks may also be included at current cost.

10.2.1.A   FRS 102's requirements

FRS 102's requirements for the revaluation of property, plant and equipment and intangible assets at fair value are consistent with but more prescriptive than the alternative accounting rules.

Where investments in subsidiaries, associates and joint ventures are measured at fair value through other comprehensive income in separate or individual financial statements (or investments in subsidiaries that are excluded from consolidation are measured at fair value through other comprehensive income in consolidated financial statements), a directors' valuation (that does not equate to fair value) is not permitted.

As noted at 10.2 above, other fixed asset or current asset investments included at fair value under FRS 102 generally make use of the fair value accounting rules.

Where investments in subsidiaries, associates and joint ventures are carried using the cost model in separate or individual financial statements under FRS 102, the previous GAAP carrying amount at the date of transition may be used as a deemed cost as at the date of transition. *[FRS 102.35.10(f)]*. Similarly, a first-time adopter may elect to use fair value at the date of transition (or a previous GAAP revaluation at or before the date of transition) of an item of property, plant equipment, investment property or intangible asset (which meets the recognition and revaluation criteria in Section 18) as its deemed cost at the date of transition (or the revaluation date) respectively. *[FRS 102.35.10(c), (d)]*. Where a deemed cost contains a past revaluation subject to the alternative accounting rules, the requirements of the alternative accounting rules continue to apply. See Chapter 30 at 3.5.3, 5.5 and 5.9 of EY New UK GAAP 2015.

10.2.2 Application of the depreciation and diminution rules under the alternative accounting rules

Where the alternative accounting rules are applied, the latest revalued amount used in determining the carrying amount of the asset (on any basis set out in paragraph 32 of Schedule 1 to the Regulations – see 10.2.1 above) is used, in place of the purchase price or production cost or previous revaluations, for the purposes of computing depreciation or provisions for diminution (or impairment) of the asset. *[1 Sch 33(1)]*.

With this modification, the rules in paragraphs 17 to 21, 23 to 25 of Schedule 1 to the Regulations (that are situated in Schedule B – *Historical cost accounting rules*) continue to apply. *[1 Sch 30, 33]*. This includes the disclosure requirements for provisions for diminution and write-backs of such provisions highlighted at 10.1.2 above. *[1 Sch 19(3), 1 Sch 20(2)]*.

The Regulations refer to the provision for depreciation (or diminution) calculated using the latest revalued amount as the 'adjusted amount' and the provision for depreciation (or diminution) calculated using the historical cost accounting rules as the 'historical cost amount'. *[1 Sch 33(2)]*.

The Regulations allow a company to include under the relevant profit and loss account heading the amount of provision for depreciation for a revalued fixed asset based on historical cost, provided that the difference between the historical cost amount and the adjusted amount is shown separately in the profit and loss account or in a note to the accounts. *[1 Sch 33(3)]*. However, FRS 102 requires that depreciation (based on the revalued amount) is charged to profit or loss (unless another section of the standard requires the depreciation to be recognised as part of the cost of an asset). *[FRS 102.17.18, 18.21]*.

The treatment of revaluations under the Regulations is discussed at 10.2.3 and 10.2.4 below.

10.2.3 Revaluation reserve

Under the alternative accounting rules, the initial recognition of the asset is its purchase price or production cost (as defined at 10.1.1 above). This therefore includes any expenses incidental to its acquisition (and where SI 2015/980 is applied, the cost is reduced by any incidental reductions in its cost of acquisition). *[FRS 102.A4.34, 1 Sch 27, 35(1)]*.

When an asset is subsequently revalued under the alternative accounting rules, the Regulations require that the profit or loss arising from that determination (after allowing, where appropriate, for any provisions for depreciation or diminution in value made otherwise than by reference to the value so determined and any adjustments of any such provisions made in light of that determination) must be credited or (as the case may be) debited to a separate revaluation reserve. *[1 Sch 35(1)]*. In effect, this means that the revaluation establishes a new 'base cost' for the asset and the revaluation gain or loss is based on the difference between the revalued amount and the previous carrying amount of the asset. The amount of the revaluation reserve must be shown in the balance sheet under a separate sub-heading in the position given for the item 'revaluation reserve' under 'Capital and reserves' of the balance sheet formats. Where SI 2015/980 is not applied, the amount of the revaluation reserve must be shown in this position set out in the statutory balance sheets (see 5.3.12.C above) but the name 'revaluation reserve' need not be used. *[1 Sch 35(2)]*.

FRS 102 requires that a revaluation increase is recognised in other comprehensive income and accumulated in equity, except that a revaluation increase is recognised in profit or loss to the extent it reverses a revaluation decrease of the same asset previously recognised in profit or loss. A revaluation decrease is recognised in other comprehensive income to the extent of any previously recognised revaluation increase accumulated in equity in respect of that asset, with any excess recognised in profit or loss. *[FRS 102.17.15E-F, 18.18G-H]*. FRS 102's requirements, in effect, regard a downward revaluation that reverses previously recognised revaluation increases accumulated in equity as a 'revaluation adjustment' but where a downward revaluation exceeds the previously recognised revaluation increases accumulated in equity, the excess is recognised in profit or loss (as if a diminution in value).

The statutory revaluation reserve can be applied as follows:

(a)   an amount may be transferred from the revaluation reserve to the profit and loss account, if the amount was previously charged to the profit and loss account or represents a realised profit; *[1 Sch 35(3)(a)]*

(b)   an amount may be transferred from the revaluation reserve on capitalisation. *[1 Sch 35(3)(b)]*. Capitalisation means applying an amount to the credit of the revaluation reserve in wholly or partly paying up unissued shares in the company to be allotted to the members of the company as fully or partly paid share, i.e. a bonus issue of shares; and *[1 Sch 35(4)]*

(c)   an amount may be transferred to or from the revaluation reserve in respect of the taxation relating to any profit or loss credited or debited to the reserve. The treatment for taxation purposes of amounts credited or debited to the revaluation reserve must be disclosed in a note to the accounts. *[1 Sch 35(3)(c), 35(6)]*.

The use of the revaluation reserve described in (a) is consistent with:

•   FRS 102's accounting for a revaluation increase that reverses a revaluation decrease of the same asset previously recognised in profit and loss;

•   where depreciation or an impairment has been charged based on a revalued amount (exceeding historical cost), the excess depreciation (i.e. the depreciation based on the revalued amount less that which would have been charged based on historical cost) may be debited from the revaluation reserve to the profit and loss account reserve (as a reserves transfer in equity); and

- on sale of a revalued fixed asset was sold, the amount in the revaluation reserve, where realised on the sale, could be transferred to the profit and loss account reserve (as a reserves transfer in equity).

The revaluation reserve must be reduced to the extent that the amounts transferred to it are no longer necessary for the purposes of the valuation method used and the revaluation reserve must not be reduced except as noted above. *[1 Sch 35(3), (5)]*. Although the word 'reduced' is ambiguous in the context of a reserve that may contain either debit or credit balances, the intention is to prevent companies from charging costs, e.g. valuation fees, directly to the reserve or from releasing credits to the profit and loss account, except in ways permitted by the Regulations. These provisions would also permit a company changing policy from revaluation to cost to write back the reduction in carrying value against any credit balance in the revaluation reserve.

The revaluation reserve may also be reduced, to the extent permitted by section 734 of the CA 2006, when a private limited company makes a payment out of capital (under Chapter 5 of Part 18 of the CA 2006). *[s734]*.

Care needs to be taken on transition to identify whether a statutory revaluation reserve must be created or maintained. Where an asset is carried at a deemed cost (based on a previous GAAP revaluation which would include historic revaluations grandfathered as deemed cost on transition to FRS 15 – *Tangible fixed assets*, or fair value at the date of transition), this makes use of the alternative accounting rules. This is discussed in Chapter 30 at 3.5.3, 5.5 and 5.9 of EY New UK GAAP 2015.

10.2.4 Disclosures

Where the alternative accounting rules are used for any items shown in the accounts, the items affected and the basis of valuation adopted must be disclosed in a note to the accounting policies. *[1 Sch 34(2)]*.

Where SI 2015/980 is applied, for each balance sheet item affected, the comparable amounts determined according to the historical cost accounting rules must be shown in a note to the accounts. Where SI 2015/980 is not applied, for each balance sheet item affected (except stocks), either the comparable amounts determined using the historical cost accounting rules or the differences between those amounts and the amounts actually shown in the balance sheet for that item must be shown separately in the balance sheet or in a note to the accounts. *[1 Sch 34(3)]*.

The comparable amounts required to be disclosed are: *[1 Sch 34(4)]*

- the aggregate amount (i.e. aggregate cost) which would be required to be shown for that balance sheet item if the amounts to be included in respect of all the assets covered by that item were determined using the historical cost accounting rules; and

- the aggregate amount of the cumulative provisions for depreciation or diminution in value which would be permitted or required in determining those amounts according to the historical cost accounting rules.

Where any fixed assets (other than listed investments) are included at a valuation under the alternative accounting rules, the following information is required to be disclosed in the notes to the accounts: *[1 Sch 52]*

- the years (so far as they are known to the directors) in which the assets were severally valued and the several values; and
- where the assets have been valued during the financial year,
  - the names of the persons who valued them or particulars of their qualifications for doing so; and
  - the bases of valuations used by them.

This requirement would apply to fixed assets, i.e. assets of a company which are intended for use on a continuing basis in the company's activities *[10 Sch 4 and FRS 102.Appendix I]* (see 5.2.2 above), whether 'adapted formats' or statutory formats are used.

10.3   Fair value accounting rules – financial instruments

Under FRS 102, where an entity carries financial assets or financial liabilities at fair value, or where a financial instrument is used in hedge accounting, this generally makes use of the fair value accounting rules. This is the case whatever policy choice (i.e. Section 11 and Section 12 – *Other Financial Instruments Issues*, IAS 39, or IFRS 9) the entity applies to the recognition and measurement of financial instruments.

Situations that are covered by the alternative accounting rules instead are listed at 10.2 above.

The fair value accounting rules are based on those in the new Accounting Directive (and in the predecessor 4th and 7th Company Law Directives) which are designed to be consistent with application of IAS 39 (or FRS 26 – *Financial instruments: recognition and measurement* – under previous UK GAAP). Therefore they allow for financial instruments to be accounted at fair value through profit or loss, or as available for sale financial assets.

Where financial assets or financial liabilities are measured at fair value under Sections 11 and 12, the accounting is always fair value through profit and loss (and falls within the fair value accounting rules).

Where IFRS 9 is applied, whether fair value changes are recognised in profit or loss or in other comprehensive income depends on the type of financial instrument held at fair value. Our view is that accounting for investments in equity instruments at fair value through other comprehensive income under IFRS 9 makes use of the alternative accounting rules instead of the fair value accounting rules (see 10.2 above).

However, the following situations for accounting for financial instruments at fair value under IFRS 9 do not fall neatly within the fair value accounting rules:

(a)   designation of a financial liability (other than a loan commitment or financial guarantee contract) at fair value through profit and loss; and *[IFRS 9.4.2.2, IFRS 9.5.7.1(c), 5.7.7-5.7.9]*

(b)   investments in debt instruments classified as measured at fair value through other comprehensive income which are held within a business model whose objective is achieved by both collecting contractual cash flows and selling financial assets and the contractual terms of the financial assets give rise on specified dates to cash flows that are solely payments of principal and interest on the principal amount outstanding. *[IFRS 9.4.1.2A, IFRS 9.5.7.1(d),.5.7.10-5.7.11].*

In situation (a) above, fair value changes attributable to changes in own credit risk are presented in other comprehensive income, unless that treatment would create or enlarge an accounting mismatch in profit or loss. *[IFRS 9.4.2.2, 5.7.1(c), 5.7.7-5.7.9].* Appendix IV – *Note on legal requirements* – to FRS 102 explains that entities applying IFRS 9 will need to consider a true and fair override in order to recognise fair value gains and losses attributable to changes in credit risk in other comprehensive income. *[FRS 102.A4.12C].*

Appendix IV does not discuss situation (b) above. Where investments in certain debt instruments are measured at fair value through other comprehensive income under IFRS 9, the model used for accounting for changes in the fair value of a debt instrument through other comprehensive income is similar to that for an available-for-sale asset under IAS 39 (although it is not described as 'available-for-sale'). In our view, it is inferred from the Accounting Council's silence on the matter that this model is included within the fair value accounting rules and does not therefore require the use of a true and fair override to apply.

In addition, particular care needs to be taken where Sections 11 and 12 or IFRS 9 is used, as in some situations the fair value accounting rules in the Regulations do not permit use of fair value. This conflict does not exist where IAS 39 is applied. See 10.3.1 below.

The fair value accounting rules also apply to certain commodity-based contracts (which are generally required to be accounted for as financial instruments under accounting standards). References to 'derivatives' in the fair value accounting rules include commodity-based contracts that give either contracting party the right to settle in cash or in some other financial instrument, except where such contracts: *[10 Sch 2]*

*   were entered into for the purpose of, and continue to meet the company's expected purchase, sale or usage requirements;

*   were designated for such purpose at their inception; and

*   are expected to be settled by delivery of the commodity.

Where Schedule 2 to the Regulations is applied, the definition of a derivative is in paragraph 96 of that schedule.

Chapter 4

10.3.1   Which financial instruments may be included at fair value under the Regulations?

10.3.1.A   Overview

Paragraph 36 of Schedule 1 to the Regulations permits financial instruments, whose fair values can be reliably measured (see 10.3.1.B below), to be included at fair value provided that: *[1 Sch 36]*

- the financial instrument is not of a type prohibited from being included at fair value by paragraphs 36(2) and (3) of Schedule 1 to the Regulations (unless it is a financial instrument falling within paragraph 36(4) of Schedule 1 to the Regulations (see 10.1.3.C below); *[1 Sch 36(2)-(3)]* or

- the financial instrument is of a type prohibited from being included at fair value by paragraphs 36(2) and (3) of Schedule 1 to the Regulations but the accounting is permitted by EU-adopted IFRSs (the Regulations prior to amendment by SI 2015/980 refer to EU-adopted IFRSs on or before 5 September 2006) and the disclosures required by such accounting standards are given (see 10.1.3.D below). *[1 Sch 36(4)]*.

There are equivalent paragraphs in Schedules 2 (for banking companies) and 3 (for insurance companies) to the Regulations, and the LLP Regulations (although the LLP Regulations do not reflect the change made by SI 2015/980).

It is, therefore, important to ensure that the use of fair value accounting is indeed permitted by EU-adopted IFRS. This is likely more of an issue where IFRS 9 is applied (until that standard is adopted by the EU), since the classification and measurement requirements of IFRS 9 are not identical to IAS 39, the standard currently adopted by the EU and therefore the reference point for paragraph 36(4) of Schedule 1 to the Regulations. *[FRS 102.A4.12B]*.

The FRS 102 (July 2015) amendments (see Chapter 5 at 4.1), where applied, require that an entity applying IFRS 9 as an accounting policy choice to the recognition and measurement of financial instruments must depart from IFRS 9 where the measurement of a financial asset at fair value through profit and loss in accordance with IFRS 9 is not permitted by the Regulations, Small Companies Regulations, LLP Regulations or Small Companies Regulations and instead carry the financial asset at amortised cost in accordance with paragraphs 5.4.1 to 5.4.4 of IFRS 9. *[FRS 102.11.2A, 12.2A]*.

The same issue arises where Sections 11 and 12 are applied to the recognition and measurement of financial instruments. FRS 102 similarly requires financial instruments not permitted by the Regulations, Small Company Regulations, LLP Regulations or Small LLP Regulations to be measured at fair value through profit and loss to be measured at amortised cost in accordance with paragraphs 11.15 to 11.20 of the standard. *[FRS 102.12.8(c)]*. Chapter 8 at 4.2.1 of EY New UK GAAP 2015 discusses types of financial instruments where the accounting in Sections 11 and 12 may conflict with IAS 39 (being the EU-adopted standard) and consequently with the Regulations (meaning amortised cost treatment is required under the standard).

For application of paragraph 36(4) to Schedule 1 to the Regulations under FRS 101, see Chapter 2 at 6.3.

10.3.1.B   Determination of reliable fair values

Where the fair value accounting rules are applied, financial instruments (including derivatives) may be included at fair value, only where this can be determined reliably in accordance with paragraph 37 of Schedule 1 to the Regulations. *[1 Sch 36(1), (5)]*.

The fair value of a financial instrument is determined as follows: *[1 Sch 37]*

(a)   if a reliable market can readily be identified for the financial instrument, by reference to its market value;

(b)   if a reliable market cannot readily be identified for the financial instrument but can be identified for its components of a similar instrument, by reference to the market value of its components or of the similar instrument; or

(c)   if neither (a) nor (b) apply, a value resulting from generally accepted valuation models and techniques that must ensure a reasonable approximation of the market value.

See Chapter 8 at 4.4.5 of EY New UK GAAP 2015 for FRS 102's requirements on determining fair values of financial instruments, which set out a similar (but not identically worded) fair value hierarchy. *[FRS 102.11.27]*.

10.3.1.C   Financial instruments prohibited from being included at fair value (subject to paragraph 36(4) of Schedule 1 to the Regulations)

The following types of financial instrument are prohibited from being included at fair value unless they meet the requirements of paragraph 36(4) of Schedule 1 to the Regulations (see below): *[1 Sch 36(2)-(3)]*

- financial liabilities that are neither held as part of a trading portfolio nor are derivatives;

- financial instruments (other than derivatives) held to maturity;

- loans and receivables originated by the company and not held for trading purposes;

- interests in subsidiary undertakings (as defined in section 1162 of the CA 2006), associated undertakings (as defined in paragraph 19 of Schedule 6 to the Regulations) and joint ventures (as defined in paragraph 18 of Schedule 6 to the Regulations) – see 5.3.4.C to 5.3.4.E above and Chapter 2 at 3.1.2 of EY New UK GAAP 2015 for guidance on the relevant definitions;

- equity instruments issued by the company;

- contracts for contingent consideration in a business combination; and

- other financial instruments with such special characteristics that the instruments, according to generally accepted accounting principles or practice should be accounted for differently from other financial instruments.

The Regulations were written with the application of EU-adopted IFRS in mind and terms such as 'loans and receivables', 'held to maturity' and 'held for trading' are not defined in FRS 102. The Regulations indicate that these terms are defined in Directive 2013/34/EU (the new Accounting Directive) and Directive 91/674/EEC (for insurance undertakings) and in paragraph 96 of Schedule 2 to the Regulations (for banking companies). *[10 Sch 3]*. It is not obvious where the definitions are

Chapter 4

included in the new Accounting Directive. However, it would be logical to apply the same definitions as in IAS 39.

As noted at 10.3 above, FRS 102 allows a choice of policy for the recognition and measurement of financial instruments and the situations in which financial instruments are carried at fair value differ depending on the standard applied. In relation to FRS 102, financial instruments that would fall within 1 Sch 36(2) or (3) to the Regulations would appear to include:

- financial liabilities (not held as part of a trading portfolio nor derivatives) that are designated at fair value through profit or loss; *[IAS 39.9, 11A, 12, IFRS 9.4.2.2, IFRS 9.4.3.5, FRS 102.11.14(b)]*

- financial assets held to maturity (other than derivatives) or loans and receivables originated by the company and not held for trading purposes that are:

  - designated at fair value through profit or loss (under IAS 39 or IFRS 9 or Section 11); *[IAS 39.9, IFRS 9.4.1.5, 11.14(b)]*

  - measured at fair value through profit or loss under IFRS 9; *[IFRS 9.4.1.4]*

  - debt instruments classified as measured at fair value through other comprehensive income under IFRS 9; or *[IFRS 9.4.1.2A, 5.7.1(d), 5.7.10-5.7.11]*

  - designated as available for sale assets under IAS 39; *[IAS 39.9]* or

- interests in subsidiary undertakings, associated undertakings or jointly controlled entities that are measured at fair value through profit and loss in consolidated or individual financial statements. *[FRS 102.9.9-9.9B, 9.26(c), 14.4(d), 14.4B, 15.9(d), 15.9B]*. See Chapter 6 at 3.4, 4.1 and 4.2, Chapter 10 at 3.3.1 and 3.3.4 and Chapter 11 at 3.6.2 and 3.6.3.A of EY New UK GAAP 2015.

Equity instruments issued by a company and contingent consideration in a business combination are not held at fair value under FRS 102.

See Chapter 8 of EY New UK GAAP 2015 for the requirements in relation to classification of financial instruments.

10.3.1.D   *Requirements of paragraph 36(4) of Schedule 1 to the Regulations*

The items listed in 1 Sch 36(2) or (3) to the Regulations (see 10.3.1.C above) may still be held at fair value, subject to meeting the requirements in paragraph 36(4) of Schedule 1 to the Regulations. The accounting would also need to comply with the accounting standard, FRS 101 or FRS 102, adopted.

Paragraph 36(4) of Schedule 1 to the Regulations (as amended by SI 2015/980) states that 'financial instruments which under international accounting standards may be included in accounts at fair value, may be so included, provided that the disclosures required by such accounting standards are made.' *[1 Sch 36(4)]*.

While the Regulations themselves do not define 'international accounting standards', this term means EU-adopted IFRS in accordance with the IAS Regulations. *[s474]*. This is also the meaning of 'international accounting standards' included in Article 8.6 of the new Accounting Directive.

Where SI 2015/980 is not applied, paragraph 36(4) of Schedule 1 to the Regulations states that 'financial instruments that, under international accounting standards adopted by the European Commission on or before 5 September 2006 in accordance with the IAS Regulation, may be included in accounts at fair value, may be so included, provided that the disclosures required by such accounting standards are made.' *[1 Sch 36(4)].*

The change made by SI 2015/980 has significance for accounting and disclosure. For example, it has facilitated a prospective change to the accounting for contingent consideration in a business combination in FRS 101 (see Chapter 2 at 4.4). However, the requirements of FRS 102 are based on IFRS 3 (issued 2004) and the Accounting Council did not advise amending the accounting for contingent consideration outside the context of a wider review of the accounting for contingent consideration in a business combination so no amendment was made to the standard.[37]

The amendment, where SI 2015/980 is applied, means that more financial assets may meet the requirements in paragraph 36(4) of Schedule 1 to the Regulations once IFRS 9 is adopted by the EU and this could change the accounting applied to such financial assets under FRS 102 (explained at 10.3.1.A above). Investments in subsidiaries held at fair value through profit and loss in consolidated financial statements would also meet the requirements of paragraph 36(4) of Schedule 1 to the Regulations where this would be permitted under EU-adopted IFRS (such as IFRS 10 – *Consolidated Financial Statements*) and in such situations a true and fair override would not be required.

10.3.1.E   Disclosures

Appendix IV – *Note on legal requirements* – to FRS 102 states that the disclosures required by paragraph 36(4) of Schedule 1 to the Regulations have been incorporated into Section 11. Some apply to all financial instruments held at fair value through profit and loss, while others (such as paragraph 11.48A) apply only to certain financial instruments (this does not include financial liabilities held as part of a trading portfolio nor derivatives). The disclosure requirements of paragraph 11.48A will predominantly apply to certain financial liabilities, however there may be instances where paragraph 36(3) to Schedule 1 to the Regulations requires that the disclosures must also be provided in relation to financial assets, for example, investments in subsidiaries, associates or jointly controlled entities measured at fair value (see paragraph 9.27B of FRS 102). *[FRS 102.A4.13].*

FRS 102 (amended July 2015) clarifies the scope of the disclosures in paragraph 11.48A as relating to financial instruments measured at fair value through profit or loss in accordance with paragraph 36(4) of Schedule 1 to the Regulations (and the equivalent requirements of the Small Companies Regulations, LLP Regulations and the Small LLP Regulations). This does not include financial liabilities held as part of a trading portfolio nor derivatives. The disclosures are now required by all FRS 102 reporters, whether or not companies. *[FRS 102.11.48A].* See Chapter 5 at 4.3.

The disclosures in Section 11 must be given in respect of those financial instruments held at fair value in accordance with paragraph 36(4) even where the reduced disclosure framework is applied in the individual financial statements of a qualifying entity. *[FRS 102.1.8].* FRS 102 (amended July 2015) also removes certain disclosures in

Section 11 (including paragraph 11.48A) relating to financial instruments measured at fair value through profit or loss from the disclosure exemptions where the reduced disclosure framework is applied, to ensure that they are consistent with company law disclosure requirements. *[FRS 102.1.12(c)]*. See Chapter 5 at 4.3.

Appendix II – *Note on Legal requirements* – to FRS 101, addressing the same paragraph, however, confirms that the statutory disclosures are given in relation to financial instruments measured at fair value through profit or loss (or through other comprehensive income) in accordance with paragraph 36(4) of Schedule 1 to the Regulations. *[FRS 101.A2.7B]*. In our view, care should be taken with both the scope of disclosures required by 1 Sch 36(4) to the Regulations and what disclosures are required.

In relation to scope, paragraph 11.48A's disclosures relating to financial instruments held at fair value refer only to financial instruments at fair value through profit or loss (but are also scoped in for investments in subsidiaries, associates and joint ventures that are accounted at fair value through profit or loss). *[FRS 102.9.9-9.9B, 9.26, 9.27B, 11.48A]*. In most cases under FRS 102, financial instruments held at fair value in accordance with 1 Sch 36(4) to the Regulations will be measured at fair value through profit or loss. However, entities applying IAS 39 or IFRS 9 may in principle have financial instruments held at fair value in accordance with 1 Sch 36(4) to the Regulations where fair value gains and losses are recognised in other comprehensive income (e.g. an available for sale asset or debt instrument at fair value through comprehensive income that falls within the prohibited list in paragraph 36(3)).

Where SI 2015/980 is applied, the disclosures required by 1 Sch 36(4) are those in extant IFRSs adopted by the EU, as confirmed by Appendix II – *Note on Legal requirements* – to FRS 101. *[FRS 101.A2.7, A2.20]*. The most logical interpretation of this is that an entity should make all material disclosures required by IFRS 7 – *Financial Instruments: Disclosures* – and IFRS 13 – *Fair Value Measurement* – in respect of such instruments. Where SI 2015/980 is not applied, the disclosures required are those in IFRSs adopted by the EU prior to 5th September 2006.

In any event, FRS 102 (amended July 2015) includes a new paragraph reminding reporting entities that they must ensure they comply with any relevant legal requirements applicable to it and that the standard does not necessarily contain all legal disclosure requirements. *[FRS 102.1.2A]*.

10.3.2 *Accounting for changes in fair value of financial instruments*

Notwithstanding the general requirement that only realised profits are included in the profit and loss account (from paragraph 13 of Schedule 1 to the Regulations), a change in the value of a financial instrument must be included in the profit and loss account except where:

(a)   the financial instrument accounted for is a hedging instrument under a hedge accounting system that allows some or all of the change in value not to be shown in the profit and loss account (see 10.3.3 below); or

(b)   the change in value relates to an exchange difference arising on a monetary item that forms part of a company's net investment in a foreign entity; or

(c)   the financial instrument is an available for sale financial asset (and is not a derivative). This treatment is permitted where IAS 39 is applied to the recognition and measurement of financial instruments by a FRS 102 reporter. See also the discussion at 10.3 above in respect of accounting for certain debt instruments classified as measured at fair value through other comprehensive income under IFRS 9.

In respect of (a) and (b) above, the amount of the change in value must be credited to (or as the case may be) debited from a separate reserve (the fair value reserve). In respect of (c) above, the amount of the change in value may be credited to (or as the case may be) debited from a separate reserve (the fair value reserve). *[1 Sch 40]*.

The fair value reserve must be adjusted to the extent that the amounts shown in it are no longer necessary. The treatment for taxation purposes of amounts credited to or debited to the fair value reserve must be disclosed in a note to the accounts. *[1 Sch 41]*.

FRS 102 requires that exchange differences arising on a monetary item that in substance forms part of a company's net investment in a foreign operation (which may include long-term receivables or loans, but not trade receivables or payables) are recognised in other comprehensive income (and accumulated in equity) in the financial statements that include the foreign operation and the reporting entity (e.g. consolidated financial statements). Such items are recognised in profit or loss in the separate financial statements of the reporting entity or the individual financial statements of the foreign operation, as appropriate. *[FRS 102.30.12-13]*. See Chapter 25 at 3.7 of EY New UK GAAP 2015. While not explicitly stated by the Regulations, it seems that (b) is intended to address accounts that include the foreign operation and the reporting entity.

10.3.3   Hedge accounting

10.3.3.A   Fair value hedge accounting

A company may include any assets and liabilities, or identified portions of such assets or liabilities, that qualify as hedged items under a fair value hedge accounting system at the amount required under that system. *[1 Sch 38]*.

The fair value accounting rules, therefore, permit the adjustments made to hedged items under fair value hedge accounting under IAS 39, IFRS 9 and Section 12. See Chapter 8 at 7 and Chapters 51 and 52 of EY International GAAP 2016.

10.3.3.B   Cash flow hedge and net investment hedge accounting

Where the financial instrument accounted for is a hedging instrument under a hedge accounting system that allows some or all of the change in value not to be shown in the profit and loss account, the amount of the change in value must be credited to (or as the case may be) debited from a separate reserve ('the fair value reserve'). *[1 Sch 40(3)]*.

The fair value reserve must be adjusted to the extent that the amounts shown in it are no longer necessary for the purposes of paragraph 40(3) (or 40(4)) of Schedule 1 to the Regulations. *[1 Sch 41]*.

Chapter 4

The fair value accounting rules, therefore, support hedge accounting of a net investment of a foreign operation and cash flow hedge accounting under IAS 39, IFRS 9 and Section 12. Under these forms of hedge accounting, the entity recognises in other comprehensive income only the effective portion of the hedge and amounts accumulated in equity are reclassified in profit or loss, where required by Section 12, IAS 39 or IFRS 9 for cash flow hedge accounting. FRS 102 does not permit reclassification of exchange differences accumulated in equity arising from hedges of a net investment of a foreign operation. See Chapter 8 at 7 and Chapters 51 and 52 of EY International GAAP 2016.

10.3.4   *Disclosures required by the Regulations in Companies Act accounts*

In Companies Act accounts, where financial instruments have been valued in accordance with paragraph 36 (i.e. at fair value) or paragraph 38 (i.e. adjustments to hedged items under a fair value hedge accounting system) of Schedule 1 to the Regulations, the notes to the accounts must include: *[1 Sch 55]*

- the significant assumptions underlying the valuation models and techniques used to determine the fair value of the instruments (where SI 2015/980 is not applied, this disclosure is required where the fair value of the financial instrument has been determined in accordance with paragraph 37(4) of Schedule 1 to the Regulations – but this is not a substantive change);

- where SI 2015/980 is applied, in the case of financial instruments, their purchase price, the items affected and the basis of valuation (Schedule 3 to the Regulations only);

- for each category of financial instrument, the fair value of the assets in that category and the changes in value:

  - included directly in the profit and loss account, or

  - credited to or (as the case may be) debited from the fair value reserve

  in respect of these assets.

  Where SI 2015/980 is not applied, this disclosure referred to instruments not assets. In our view, having regard to the underlying new Accounting Directive requirement, this disclosure is likely intended to apply to both financial assets and financial liabilities;

- for each class of derivatives, the extent and nature of the instruments, including significant terms and conditions that may affect the amount, timing and certainty of future cash flows; and

- where any amount is transferred to or from the fair value reserve during the financial year, there must be stated in tabular form:

  - the amount of the reserve as at the date of the beginning of the financial year and as at the balance sheet date respectively;

  - the amount transferred to or from the reserve during that year; and

  - the source and application respectively of the amounts so transferred.

Appendix IV – *Note on legal requirements* to FRS 102 notes that most of these disclosures will be satisfied by equivalent requirements of the standard but entities

Presentation of financial statements 369

will need to take care to ensure appropriate disclosure of derivatives is provided. *[FRS 102.A4.12D]*.

Where the company has derivatives that it has not included at fair value, there must also be stated for each class of derivatives, the fair value of the derivatives in that class (if such a value can be determined in accordance with paragraph 37 – see 10.3.1 above) and the extent and nature of the derivatives. *[1 Sch 56]*. This situation should rarely arise under FRS 102 since the standard requires derivatives to be recorded at fair value.

If the company has financial fixed assets that could be included at fair value under paragraph 36 of Schedule 1 to the Regulations (see 10.3.1 above) and the amount at which those items are included in the accounts is in excess of their fair value, and the company has not made provision for diminution in value of those assets in accordance with paragraph 19(1) of Schedule 1 to the Regulations (see 10.1.2 above), there must also be stated:

- the amount at which either the individual assets or appropriate groupings of those individual assets are included in the company's accounts;
- the fair value of those assets or groupings; and
- the reasons for not making a provision for diminution in value of those assets, including the nature of the evidence that provides the basis for the belief that the amount at which they are stated in the accounts will be recovered. *[1 Sch 57]*.

10.4 Investment properties, living animals and plants, and stocks

10.4.1 *Investment property, living animals and plants, and stocks – use of fair value under the Regulations*

The fair value accounting rules allow:

- investment property;
- living animals and plants; and
- where SI 2015/980 is applied, stocks

to be included at fair value, provided that, as the case may be, all such investment property, living animals and plants, and (where SI 2015/980 is applied, stocks) are so included where their fair value can reliably be determined. *[1 Sch 39(1)-(2), FRS 102.A4.26]*.

Where SI 2015/980 is applied, fair value, for these purposes, is as determined in accordance with generally accepted accounting principles or practice. *[1 Sch 39(3)]*.

Where SI 2015/980 is not applied, the fair value accounting rules only apply where, under relevant international accounting standards (which would mean EU-adopted IFRS), the asset may be included in accounts at fair value (as determined under relevant international accounting standards). *[1 Sch 39]*. A discussion of how FRS 102's accounting requirements for the above assets are consistent with relevant EU-adopted IFRS is included at Chapter 4 at 9.4 of EY New UK GAAP 2015. While the Regulations (where SI 2015/980 is not applied) state that fair value should be determined in accordance with EU-adopted IFRS (currently IFRS 13) which has a slightly different definition of fair value to FRS 102, this has not been highlighted as a potential conflict in Appendix IV – *Note on legal requirements* to the standard. We consider that the more specific guidance in FRS 102 should be referred to in determining fair value and in many circumstances, this is likely to give a fair value materially consistent with IFRS 13.

Notwithstanding paragraph 13 of Schedule 1 to the Regulations (the general requirement that only realised profits are included in the profit and loss account), a change in the value of the investment property or living animal or plant must be included in the profit and loss account. *[1 Sch 40(1), (2)]*. Paragraph 40 of Schedule 1 to the Regulations (as amended by SI 2015/980) does not specify how changes in the fair value of stock are recognised under the fair value accounting rules. However, under FRS 102 (amended July 2015), fair value gains are only recognised on inventories measured at fair value less costs to sell and these are restricted to where the entity operates in an active market, where sale can be achieved at published prices, and inventory is a store of readily realisable value. *[FRS 102.13.3]*. Where such assets qualify as 'readily convertible to cash' under the guidance in TECH 02/10, fair value gains would likely be regarded as realised and qualify for recognition in the profit and loss account under paragraph 13 of Schedule 1 to the Regulations in any event.

10.4.2   *Investment property, living animals and plants, and stocks – FRS 102's requirements for fair value accounting*

FRS 102's requirements for investment property (see Chapter 12 at 3.2 and 3.3 of EY New UK GAAP 2015) and biological assets (see Chapter 29 at 2 of EY New UK GAAP 2015) make use of the fair value accounting rules described at 10.4 above.

FRS 102 requires that investment property (including property held by a lessee under an operating lease that would otherwise meet the definition of investment property, that an entity elects (on a property-by-property basis) to treat as investment property) whose fair value can be measured reliably without undue cost or effort on an ongoing basis is measured at fair value at each reporting date with changes in fair value recognised in profit or loss. All other investment property is accounted for as property, plant and equipment using the cost model in Section 17. *[FRS 102.16.1-16.3, 16.7]*.

FRS 102 permits an entity engaged in agricultural activity a policy choice for each class of biological asset (and its related agricultural produce) to use either the fair value model or cost model. *[FRS 102.34.3A-3B]*.

Like the Regulations, FRS 102 only permits use of fair value for investment property and biological assets where it can be measured reliably. *[FRS 102.16.1, 16.8, 34.6A]*. However, FRS 102's requirements for biological assets permit a policy choice of the fair value or cost models to be applied to a class of assets whereas the Regulations would require the fair value model, if adopted, to be applied to all such biological assets, where the fair value can reliably be determined.

The FRS 102 (July 2015) amendments, where applied, change the accounting treatment in the standard for inventories held for distribution. This is now measured at the lower of cost adjusted, when applicable, for any loss of service potential and replacement cost. *[FRS 102.13.4A]*. Appendix IV – *Note on legal requirements* – to FRS 102 explains this is an application of fair value accounting and notes that for inventories, including those held for distribution at no or nominal value (particularly items distributed to beneficiaries by public benefit entities), there is unlikely to be a significant difference between replacement cost and fair value. *[FRS 102.A4.37]*.

While not noted in Appendix IV, where inventories are measured at fair value less costs to sell, *[FRS 102.13.3]*, this presumably also applies the fair value accounting rules (assuming there is unlikely to be a significant difference between fair value and fair value less costs to sell). See Chapter 5 at 5 for discussion of the FRS 102 (July 2015) amendments in relation to inventory.

10.4.3   *Disclosures required by the Regulations in Companies Act accounts*

Where the amounts included in the accounts in respect of investment property, living animals and plants (or where SI 2015/980 is applied, stocks) have been determined using the fair value accounting rules, the balance sheet items affected and the basis of valuation adopted in the case of each such item must be disclosed in a note to the accounts. *[1 Sch 58(1), (2)]*.

In respect of investment property accounted for using the fair value accounting rules, for each balance sheet item affected, the comparable amounts determined according to the historical cost accounting rules or the differences between those comparable amounts and the amounts actually shown in the balance sheet in respect of that item must be disclosed in a note to the accounts. *[1 Sch 58(3)-(4)]*. This is a similar disclosure to that required where an item is valued subject to the alternative accounting rules and is explained further at 10.2.4 above.

Where assets have been fair valued in accordance with paragraph 39 of Schedule 1 to the Regulations, the notes to the accounts must include: *[1 Sch 55]*

- the significant assumptions underlying the valuation models and techniques used to determine the fair value of the assets;
- for each category of asset, the fair value of the assets in that category and the changes in value:
    - included directly in the profit and loss account, or
    - credited to or (as the case may be) debited from the fair value reserve

    in respect of those assets; and
- where any amount is transferred to or from the fair value reserve during the financial year, there must be stated in tabular form:
    - the amount of the reserve as at the date of the beginning of the financial year and as at the balance sheet date respectively;
    - the amount transferred to or from the reserve during that year; and
    - the source and application respectively of the amounts so transferred.

These disclosures are similar to those required for financial instruments held at fair value (see 10.3.4 above).

11   SUMMARY OF DIFFERENCES

This Appendix refers to the Regulations in the context of the columns addressing FRS 102 (not applying Section 1A for small entities regime) and previous UK GAAP. The Regulations apply only to statutory accounts prepared by UK companies (not applying the small companies regime or micro-entity provisions). For simplicity, the references to the Regulations below in these two columns assume that the entity is a UK company preparing its financial statements in accordance with Schedule 1 to the Regulations. Other UK companies and certain other entities are subject to similar statutory requirements. However, the amendments made by SI 2015/980 to the CA 2006 and the Regulations do not change the requirements for LLPs. Therefore, LLPs must take particular care to determine the statutory requirements applying to them (see 1.3 above).

All relevant schedules in the Regulations apply to Companies Act accounts (such as FRS 102 financial statements and financial statements prepared under previous UK GAAP). Only certain schedules in the Regulations apply to IAS accounts, i.e. statutory accounts prepared by UK companies in accordance with EU-adopted IFRS. Therefore, many of the requirements in the Regulations referred to in the FRS 102 and previous UK GAAP columns do not apply to IAS accounts (although they do apply to FRS 101 financial statements). Except for the application of company law formats in the profit and loss account and balance sheet (explained in the table), the requirements of the Regulations only apply to entities subject to these statutory requirements.

	FRS 102	*Previous UK GAAP*	*IFRS*
Complete set of financial statements	A complete set of financial statements (see 3.5 above) includes a: • statement of financial position, • statement of comprehensive income (either as a single statement or as a separate income statement and statement of comprehensive income), • statement of cash flows (unless exempt), • statement of changes in equity, and • related notes. In certain circumstances, a statement of income and retained earnings can be presented as an alternative to a statement	A complete set of financial statements includes a: • balance sheet, • profit and loss account, • statement of recognised gains and losses, • cash flow statement (unless exempt), • reconciliation of movements in shareholders' funds (which may be presented as a primary statement or note); and • related notes. Entities with revalued assets give a statement of historical profits (where the historical cost profit is materially different to	IFRS has the same components for a complete set of financial statements as FRS 102. There is more extensive guidance on comparatives. However, there are no exemptions from presenting a cash flow statement, and a statement of income and retained earnings is not available as an alternative primary statement.

	of changes in equity and a statement of comprehensive income. Comparatives must be presented. FRS 102 includes guidance on comparatives for narrative as well as numerical information. FRS 102 permits the use of other titles – such as balance sheet or profit and loss account for the primary statements – as long as they are not misleading.	reported profit). Comparatives must be presented but there is no guidance on narrative information.	
Application of company law formats for profit and loss account and balance sheet	The income statement (or profit and loss section of statement of comprehensive income) and statement of financial position of all entities must comply with the profit and loss account and balance sheet formats set out in the Regulations, except to the extent that these requirements are not permitted by any statutory framework under which such entities report. FRS 102 (amended July 2015) permits use of 'adapted formats' as an alternative to statutory formats where Schedule 1 to the Regulations is applied. See 4.1, 5.1 and 6.5 above. Additional line items, headings and subtotals must be presented when relevant to an understanding of the financial position or financial performance (see 6.7.2 above).	The profit and loss account and balance sheet formats in the Regulations (or other applicable regulations) apply to UK companies (and other entities) subject to these statutory requirements. However, some entities (that are not subject to these requirements) preparing UK GAAP financial statements also choose to apply these formats.	The formats in the Regulations are not applicable to financial statements prepared in accordance with IFRSs (or EU-adopted IFRSs). The statement of financial position and statement of comprehensive income follow the requirements of IAS 1 which sets out minimum line items. IAS 1 requires additional line items, headings and subtotals but provides more flexibility to amend its formats compared to those in FRS 102 (which follow the Regulations).

Chapter 4

	FRS 102	*Previous UK GAAP*	*IFRS*
Definition of discontinued operations	Discontinued operations (see 6.8 above) are defined as a component of an entity that has been disposed of and: • represented a separate major line of business or geographical area of operations, or • was part of a single coordinated plan to dispose of a separate major line of business or geographical area of operations; or • was a subsidiary acquired exclusively with a view to resale. FRS 102 requires that the operations have been disposed of by the reporting date. There is no further guidance on the definition of discontinued operations.	FRS 3's definition of discontinued operation differs significantly to that in FRS 102. In particular, the sale or termination must be completed before the earlier of three months after the commencement of the subsequent period and the date of approval of the financial statements.	IFRS 5 has the same definition of discontinued operation as FRS 102, except that the definition refers to a component of an entity that either has been disposed of or is classified as held for sale. IFRS 5 includes extensive guidance on the definition. It is explicit that discontinued operations include sales of operations leading to loss of control, operations held for distribution (or distributed) and abandoned operations (in the period of abandonment).
Presentation of discontinued operations	FRS 102 requires a columnar line-by-line analysis of continuing, discontinued and total operations presented on the face of the statement of comprehensive income (or separate income statement) down to an amount that comprises the total of post-tax profit or loss of discontinued operations and the post-tax gain or loss attributed to the impairment or on the disposal of the assets or disposal group(s) comprising the discontinued operation. See 6.8.4 above.	FRS 3 requires the line items from turnover to operating profit and the non-operating exceptional items (see below) to be analysed between continuing (separately disclosing acquisitions) and discontinued operations. This is not required to be a columnar analysis. Only the analyses of turnover and operating profit (and of each of the non-operating exceptional items) are required on the face of the profit and loss account; the line items in between turnover and operating profit can be presented in the notes. An analysis of interest and tax is not required, but may be provided with the basis of allocation disclosed.	IFRS permits a one line presentation of discontinued operations comprising the total of post-tax profit or loss of discontinued operations and the post-tax gain or loss attributed to the impairment or on the disposal of the assets or disposal group(s). No columnar analysis of each line item is required. Additional analysis of this subtotal is required in the notes.

Operating profit subtotal	An operating profit subtotal is not required but FRS 102 includes guidance, where operating profit is presented. See 6.7.3 above.	FRS 3 requires an operating profit subtotal to be presented and specifies three categories of exceptional items reported outside operating profit. See 'Exceptional items' below.	Like FRS 102, IAS 1 does not require an operating subtotal to be presented and its basis of conclusions includes similar guidance to FRS 102 on operating profit, where this subtotal is presented.
Exceptional items	FRS 102 requires separate disclosure (in the notes or in the statement of comprehensive income/income statement) of the nature and amount of material items included in total comprehensive income. FRS 102 does not use the term 'exceptional items' (although the term is used in the Regulations) nor does it specify categories of exceptional item below operating profit. See 6.7.5 above. Like other profit and loss account items, exceptional items should be included in the applicable heading. However, the 'adapted formats' are less prescriptive as to the headings required than statutory formats.	FRS 3 defines exceptional items, distinguishing between operating exceptional items and non-operating exceptional items. Operating exceptional items must be presented in the appropriate format headings. They should be disclosed (and described) in a note or, where such prominence is necessary to give a true and fair view, presented on the face of the profit and loss account. FRS 3 prescribes three categories of exceptional items to be reported below operating profit on the face of the profit and loss account.	IAS 1 has the same requirements as FRS 102 (although the requirements of the Regulations do not apply).
Extraordinary items	FRS 102 (and the Regulations) include the concept of an extraordinary item but such items are not expected to occur in practice. Where FRS 102 (amended July 2015) is applied, extraordinary items are not permitted where Schedule 1 to the Regulations is applied, consistent with changes made by SI 2015/980. See 6.7.6 above.	FRS 3 has the same requirements as FRS 102 prior to application of the July 2015 amendments.	IAS 1 does not have a concept of an extraordinary item.

Chapter 4

	FRS 102	*Previous UK GAAP*	*IFRS*
Current and fixed assets (balance sheet statutory formats)	*Statutory formats* The statutory formats in Schedule 1 to the Regulations distinguish between current and fixed assets. Fixed assets are defined as assets of a company which are intended for use on a continuing basis in the company's activities, and current assets are assets not intended for such use. Current assets include debtors, even if these include items expected to be realised after more than one year. The definition of current and fixed assets differs to that for current and non-current assets in IAS 1. FRS 102 requires disclosure of the amounts of debtors due after more than one year on the face of the statement of financial position where the amounts are so material in the context of net current assets, that the financial statements may otherwise be misinterpreted. The analysis of amounts due within and after more than one year must be presented for each line item in debtors in the notes (if not on the face of the balance sheet). See 5.2.2 above.	*Statutory formats* UK companies preparing statutory accounts follow the statutory formats in the Regulations. Some entities not subject to these statutory requirements applying previous UK GAAP also follow the same formats. UITF 4 has the same requirements as FRS 102 on disclosure of debtors due after more than one year on the face of the balance sheet.	IAS 1 distinguishes between current assets (defined) and non-current assets (the residual), which are separate classifications on the statement of financial position. A presentation based on liquidity can be used where it provides reliable and more relevant information. Line items containing amounts falling due within and after more than one year must be separately analysed in the notes.

Creditors: amounts falling due within and after more than one year (balance sheet statutory formats)	*Statutory formats* The statutory formats in the Regulations distinguish between Creditors: amounts falling due within one year and Creditors: amounts falling due after more than one year. These differ from the definitions of current and non-current liabilities in IAS 1. For example, under IAS 1, an item which is not due for settlement within 12 months is reported as a current liability if the entity expects to settle it in its operating cycle. See 5.1.2 and 5.2.3 above.	*Statutory formats* UK companies preparing statutory accounts follow the statutory formats in the Regulations. Some entities not subject to these statutory requirements applying previous UK GAAP also follow the same formats.	IAS 1 distinguishes between current liabilities and non-current liabilities, which are separate classifications on the statement of financial position.. IAS 1 has detailed guidance on when a financial liability should be classified as current or non-current. A presentation based on liquidity can be used instead of a current-non-current analysis where it provides reliable and more relevant information. Line items containing amounts falling due within and after more than one year must be separately analysed in the notes.
Adapted balance sheet formats in Schedule 1 to the Regulations (where FRS 102 (amended July 2015) is applied.	*'Adapted formats'* Where 'adapted' formats in Schedule 1 to the Regulations are used, the statement of financial position must show the headings specified in Section 4 of FRS 102 (similar to IAS 1), with separate classifications for current assets, non-current assets, current liabilities and non-current liabilities (see 5.1. above). Supplementary analysis of certain headings is given in the statement of financial position or in the notes.	*Statutory formats* FRS 3 only permits the use of statutory formats (which do not use the same current-non-current classification in 'adapted formats' under FRS 102 or under IAS 1..	IAS 1 distinguishes between current assets, non-current assets, current liabilities and non-current liabilities which are separate classifications on the statement of financial position. A presentation based on liquidity can be used instead of a current-non-current analysis where it provides reliable and more relevant information. Line items containing amounts falling due within and after more than one year must be separately analysed in the notes (not required under FRS 102, where 'adapted' formats are used).

	FRS 102	Previous UK GAAP	IFRS
Provisions	*Statutory formats* There is a single heading 'provisions for liabilities' in the balance sheet statutory formats in the Regulations. See 5.3.11 above. *'Adapted formats'* Where 'adapted formats' in Schedule 1 to the Regulations are applied, the presentation is consistent with IAS 1. See 5.1 above.	*Statutory formats* UK companies preparing statutory accounts also follow the formats in the Regulations.	IAS 1 requires current and non-current provisions to be shown as separate line items.
Deferred tax	*Statutory formats* Deferred tax is shown as a debtor or within provisions for liabilities under the balance sheet statutory formats in the Regulations. See 5.3.13.B above. *'Adapted formats''* Where adapted formats in Schedule 1 to the Regulations are used, the presentation of deferred tax as a non-current asset or liability in the statement of financial position is consistent with IAS 1 See 5.1.11 above.	*Statutory formats* UK companies preparing statutory accounts also follow the formats in the Regulations.	IAS 1 requires deferred tax to be shown as a non-current asset or non-current liability.

| Retirement benefits | *Statutory formats*
The presentation of assets and liabilities under defined benefit schemes is not addressed by FRS 102. However, these would generally be presented as a debtor or provision under the Regulations. An alternative is to apply the presentation used in FRS 17 (but not net of deferred tax). See 5.3.13.D above.
'Adapted formats'
Where adapted formats in Schedule 1 to the Regulations are used, there is no specified line item for defined benefit scheme assets or liabilities. FRS 102 is silent on whether assets and liabilities under defined benefit schemes must be analysed between current and non-current. In our view, where concern over the arbitrary nature of a split arises, we believe that FRS 102 reporters are able to follow the practice of many IFRS reporters and report such balances as non-current. See 5.1.1.E above. | *Statutory formats*
FRS 17 specifies that assets and liabilities under defined benefit schemes (net of deferred tax) must be shown separately as a line item below all other net assets. | IFRS does not require assets and liabilities under defined benefit schemes to be analysed between current and non-current. |

	FRS 102	*Previous UK GAAP*	*IFRS*
Assets and disposal groups held for sale	*Statutory and 'adapted formats'* FRS 102 does not require separate presentation of assets and disposal groups held for sale and the Regulations would not permit separate presentation of disposal groups See 5.1.13.C and 5.3.13.C above. FRS 102 requires disclosures where, at the reporting date, an entity has a binding sale agreement for a major disposal of assets or a disposal group (see 5.5 above).	*Statutory formats* Like FRS 102, previous UK GAAP includes no requirements to present assets and disposal groups held for sale separately. UK companies preparing statutory accounts follow the statutory formats in the Regulations which do not permit separate presentation of disposal groups.	IAS 1 requires separate presentation in the statement of financial position of: • non-current assets and assets of disposal groups classified as held for sale; and • liabilities of disposal groups classified as held for sale Additional information is required in the notes.
Items to be reported in other comprehensive income	Items reported in other comprehensive income include *inter alia*: • revaluations of property, plant and equipment; • revaluations of investments in subsidiaries, associates and jointly controlled entities (at fair value through other comprehensive income); • remeasurement gains and losses on defined benefit schemes, • exchange gains and losses on retranslation of foreign operations, • cash flow hedges and net investment hedges. There are further categories of other comprehensive income where IAS 39 or IFRS 9 is applied. The Regulations also require that only realised profits are included in profit and loss (except for fair value movements in	Items reported in the statement of total recognised gains and losses differ to FRS 102 due principally to different accounting requirements for financial instruments. There is no reclassification of items recognised in the statement of recognised gains and losses under previous UK GAAP except where FRS 23 or FRS 26 (similar to IAS 21 and IAS 39) are applied.	Items reported in other comprehensive income may differ to FRS 102 (where Sections 11 and 12 are applied) due principally to different accounting requirements in IFRS for financial instruments. The items must be grouped between items that may be reclassified to profit and loss in a subsequent period, and items that may be reclassified subsequently to profit and loss. This is not required under FRS 102. The requirements of the Regulations on only including realised profits (with certain exceptions) in profit or loss do not apply.

	profit and loss, where the fair value accounting rules are applied). See 6.2 above. Exchange gains and losses on retranslation of foreign operations are not subsequently reclassified to profit or loss (unlike IFRS or FRS 23, where applied under previous UK GAAP).		
Statement of changes in equity (SOCIE) and Statement of Income and Retained Earnings	The SOCIE is a primary statement. Where the only movements in equity arise from profit or loss, dividends, corrections of errors or changes in accounting policy, a statement of income and retained earnings can be presented instead of the statement of changes in equity and a statement of comprehensive income. The statement of changes in equity can be combined with the analysis of movements in reserves required by the Regulations. See 7 above.	A reconciliation of shareholders' funds is presented as a primary statement or note. It can be presented in total (rather than for each component of equity). However, the Regulations require an analysis of movements in reserves (for the current period only).	IAS 1 has the same requirements as FRS 102 except that there is no alternative to present a statement of income and retained earnings. While the analysis of the reserves in the Regulations is not required, similar information is presented in the SOCIE.
Presentation of non-controlling interest in consolidated financial statements	*Statutory and 'adapted' formats* FRS 102 requires presentation of non-controlling interest as a separate component of equity in the consolidated statement of financial position.	*Statutory formats* FRS 2 – *Accounting for subsidiary undertakings* – and the Regulations require presentation of minority interest in the consolidated balance sheet.	IAS 1 has the same presentational requirement for non-controlling interest as FRS 102. The requirements of the Regulations do not apply.

Chapter 4

	FRS 102	*Previous UK GAAP*	*IFRS*
Presentation of non-controlling interest in consolidated financial statements *(Continued)*	The Regulations require presentation of non-controlling interest, meaning the amount of capital and reserves attributable to shares in subsidiary undertakings. This amount (which corresponds to minority interest under previous UK GAAP) will usually be the same as non-controlling interest under FRS 102, although in theory differences may arise. See 4.5 above.	In practice, some UK GAAP financial statements present minority interest as a line item after consolidated profit and consolidated net assets, rather than as an appropriation of consolidated profit or as a component of equity. Others use a presentation where minority interest is a component of equity.	
Presentation of associates and jointly controlled entities (where equity method is applied – i.e. in consolidated financial statements under FRS 102)	*FRS 102 requirements* *Statutory formats* FRS 102 requires the carrying amounts of investments in associates and investments in jointly controlled entities to be disclosed separately but this can be in the notes. The Regulations only require fixed asset investments to be presented as a heading on the face of the balance sheet. In group accounts, income from associated undertakings – which would generally include both associates and jointly controlled entities is a line item in the profit and loss account formats. FRS 102 requires the share of profits (and of discontinued operations) of associates and jointly controlled entities under the equity method to be separately disclosed, but this can be in the notes. The share of other comprehensive income of associates and jointly controlled entities accounted for by the	Previous UK GAAP requires • investments in associates (using the equity method) and joint ventures (using the gross equity method) to be presented separately on the face of the balance sheet; • additional analysis of the group's share of profits (or losses) of associates and, separately, joint ventures on the face of the consolidated profit and loss account, i.e. not a one line presentation as under IFRS and FRS 102. • disclosure of the group's share of joint ventures' turnover on the face of the profit and loss account, and its share of the gross assets and liabilities of joint ventures on the face of the consolidated balance sheet (the gross equity method).	IAS 1's presentational requirements for investments in associates and joint ventures on the face of the primary statements are similar to those for investments in associates and jointly controlled entities where 'adapted' formats are applied in FRS 102.

	equity method is required on the face of the statement of comprehensive income. See 5.3.4.B and 6.6.5 above. *'Adapted' formats'* Where ''adapted' formats in Schedule 1 to the Regulations are used, the presentation is consistent with IAS 1, i.e. in respect of investments in jointly controlled entities and associates accounted using the equity method, • a single line for the carrying amount of such investments is shown on the face of the statement of financial position (the analysis between investments in associates and jointly controlled entities can be in the notes); • a single line for the share of profits or losses of such investments under the equity method is shown on the face of the statement of comprehensive income (the analysis between investments in associates and jointly controlled entities, of the share of profits under the equity method (and the share of discontinued operations) can be presented in the notes); • the share of other comprehensive income for such investments is shown on the face of the statement of comprehensive income. See 5.1 and 6.5 above.		

	FRS 102	*Previous UK GAAP*	*IFRS*
Prior year adjustments	Prior year adjustments are required for retrospective correction for material errors, changes in accounting policies and reclassifications of items. The adjustment is shown as an item in the statement of changes in equity (or where presented, statement of income and retained earnings). See 3.6.2 and 7 above.	FRS 3's requirements on prior year adjustments are the same as FRS 102 except that these are required for retrospective correction of fundamental errors rather than material errors. The prior year adjustment is shown in the reconciliation of shareholders' funds and the cumulative adjustment is reported as a memorandum item at the foot of the statement of recognised gains and losses.	IAS 1's requirements are the same as FRS 102 (except there is no statement of income and retained earnings). IAS 1 additionally requires presentation of a third balance sheet at the beginning of the comparative period, where there is a restatement of comparatives.
Reduced disclosure framework (and other disclosure exemptions)	The reduced disclosure framework is available in individual financial statements of qualifying entities only, where the conditions for its use are met. Some of the disclosure exemptions require equivalent disclosures to be included in the publicly available consolidated financial statements in which the qualifying entity is consolidated. There are a number of cash flow exemptions similar to those under previous UK GAAP but these exclude small entities until the FRS 102 (July 2015) amendments are applied. These amendments extend the cash flow exemptions to small entities (whether or not applying the new small entities regime in Section 1A which allows significant disclosure reductions compared to the full FRS 102). Section 1A is addressed in Chapter 3.	Previous UK GAAP provides reduced disclosures for subsidiaries and parents in respect of financial instruments and related parties. There are also a number of cash flow exemptions. The scope of and details of these exemptions differ to FRS 102. The FRSSE provides presentation and disclosure exemptions (and simplified recognition and measurement) for small entities in its scope.	IFRSs provide no reduced disclosures for subsidiaries and parents, cash flow exemptions or exemptions for small entities.

Notes: judgements and estimation uncertainty	FRS 102 requires disclosure of • judgements, apart from those involving estimations, in applying accounting policies; and • key assumptions and sources of estimation uncertainty at the reporting date that have a significant risk of causing a material adjustment to the carrying amounts of assets and liabilities within the next financial year. See 8.3 and 8.4 above.	Disclosures of judgements and key assumptions and sources of estimation uncertainty are not required. However, FRS 18 – *Accounting policies* – requires details of significant estimation techniques.	Same requirement as FRS 102 but IAS 1 provides more guidance on disclosure of judgements and key assumptions and sources of estimation uncertainty.
Notes: sources of disclosure requirements	FRS 102 and the CA 2006, the Regulations (and other applicable regulations) include disclosure requirements for the notes. SI 2015/980 made amendments to these disclosures.	Previous UK GAAP has different (but generally more extensive) disclosure requirements to FRS 102. Disclosures in the CA 2006, Regulations (and other applicable regulations) apply as for FRS 102 financial statements.	IFRS's disclosures are more extensive than those required by FRS 102 or previous UK GAAP. The disclosures required by Schedule 1 to the Regulations do not apply to IAS accounts. However, IAS accounts must comply with disclosures in the CA 2006, and other applicable schedules of the Regulations (and other applicable regulations).

Chapter 4

	FRS 102	*Previous UK GAAP*	*IFRS*
Statement of compliance	A statement of compliance that the financial statements are prepared in accordance with FRS 102 (and where applicable, FRS 103) is required. Where an entity is a public benefit entity, a statement to this effect must also be included. The Regulations require large and medium-sized companies to state that the accounts have been prepared in accordance with applicable accounting standards, giving particulars of any departures. However, medium-sized companies do not need to give this statement in their individual accounts. See 3.8 above.	There is no requirement to give a statement of compliance, but UK companies make the statement that the accounts have been prepared in accordance with applicable accounting standards, required by the Regulations.	A statement of compliance that the financial statements are prepared in accordance with IFRSs (or EU-adopted IFRSs, where applicable) is required. The requirements of the Regulations do not apply.

References

1 *The Companies, Partnerships and Groups (Accounts and Reports) Regulations 2015*, (SI 2015/980), paras. 2 and 3.

2 The exceptions, set out in *The Companies, Partnerships and Groups (Accounts and Reports) Regulations 2015*, (SI 2015/980), para. 2 are that early adoption of the small size limits is not permitted for the purposes of the audit exemption for small companies. In addition, directors of a company cannot take advantage of section 410(2) of the Companies Act 2006 (information about related undertakings: alternative compliance) in relation to annual accounts of the company approved on or after 1 July 2015.

3 Statement of Recommended Practice – Accounting by Limited Liability Partnerships, July 2014, CCAB, paras. 30-31.

4 *Partnerships (Accounts) Regulations 2008* (SI 2008/569), para. 4 and Schedule.

5 Accounting Council Advice to FRS 102, paragraph 42.

6 *Partnerships (Accounts) Regulations 2008* (SI 2008/569), para. 4 and Schedule.

7 *Partnerships (Accounts) Regulations 2008* (SI 2008/569), para. 4 and Schedule.

8 *Statement of Recommended Practice – Accounting by Limited Liability Partnerships* (July 2014), CCAB, para. 58.

9 LLPs – Note 3 to the balance sheet formats in Section B of Part 1 of Schedule 1 to LLP Regulations (SI 2008/1913).

10 Note 1 to the balance sheet formats in Section B of Part 1 of Schedule 1 to SI 2008/410.

11 LLPs – Note 1 to the balance sheet formats in Section B of Part 1 of Schedule 1 to SI 2008/1913.

12 LLPs – Note 2 to the balance sheet formats in Section B of Part 1 of Schedule 1 to SI 2008/1913.

13 LLPs – Regulation 5 and Schedule 2 to SI 2008/1913.

14 LLPs – Note 6 to the balance sheet formats in Section B of Part 1 of Schedule 1 to SI 2008/1913.

15 LLPs – Note 3 to the balance sheet formats in Section B of Part 1 of Schedule 1 to SI 2008/1913.

16 Note 6 to the balance sheet formats in Section B of Part 1 of Schedule 1 to SI 2008/410. For LLPs, the alternative position is line item C (note 4 to the balance sheet formats in Section B of Part 1 of Schedule 1 to SI 2008/1913).

17 LLPs – Note 5 to the balance sheet formats in Section B of Part 1 of Schedule 1 to SI 2008/1913.

18 LLPs – Note 7 to the balance sheet formats in Section B of Part 1 of Schedule 1 to SI 2008/1913.

19 Note 10 to the balance sheet formats in Section B of Part 1 of Schedule 1 to SI 2008/410. For LLPs, the alternative position is line item I (note 8 to the balance sheet formats in Section B of Part 1 of Schedule 1 to SI 2008/1913).

20 LLPs – Note 9 to the balance sheet formats in Section B of Part 1 of Schedule 1 to LLP Regulations (SI 2008/1913).

21 Note 12 to the balance sheet formats in Section B of Part 1 of Schedule 1 to SI 2008/410.

22 *Statement of Recommended Practice – Accounting by Limited Liability Partnerships*, July 2014, CCAB, para. 60.

23 *Statement of Recommended Practice – Accounting by Limited Liability Partnerships*, July 2014, CCAB, paras. 51-52.

24 LLPs – Note 12 to profit and loss account format 1 in Section B of Part 1 of Schedule 1 to SI 2008/1913.

25 LLPs – Note 13 to profit and loss account formats in Section B of Part 1 of Schedule 1 to SI 2008/1913.

26 LLPs – Note 14 to profit and loss account formats in Section B of Part 1 of Schedule 1 to SI 2008/1913.

27 www.esma.europa.eu/

28 LLPs – Note 15 to profit and loss account format 1 in Section B of Part 1 of Schedule 1 to SI 2008/1913.

29 *Statement of Recommended Practice – Accounting by Limited Liability Partnerships*, July 2014, CCAB, paras. 59-60.

30 See, for example, the FRC's Corporate Reporting Review: Annual Report 2013 (October 2013), pages 15 to 17.

31 Lab case study report – William Hill: accounting policies, FRC Lab, February 2015.

32 The Registrars' Rules require that the filed copy of the annual accounts is also signed by a director.

33 *Foreword to Accounting Standards*, FRC, March 2015, paragraphs 4-5.

34 *True and Fair*, FRC, June 2014.

35 Accounting Council Advice to *Amendments to FRS 102: small entities and other minor amendments* (July 2015), paragraph 28.

36 Accounting Council Advice to *Amendments to FRS 102: small entities and other minor amendments* (July 2015), paragraph 32(a).

37 Accounting Council Advice to *Amendments to FRS 102: small entities and other minor amendments* (July 2015), paragraph 32(b).

Chapter 4

Chapter 5   Other Amendments to FRS 102

List of examples

Chapter 5   Other amendments to FRS 102

1   INTRODUCTION

This chapter covers the changes made to FRS 102 – *The Financial Reporting Standard Applicable in the UK and Republic of Ireland* – as issued in September 2015 compared to the August 2014 version of the Standard except for those changes that are not covered elsewhere in this publication (i.e. those changes which do not relate to the new small entities regime within FRS 102 – see Chapter 3 – or to the presentation changes made to financial statement presentation – see Chapter 4). References made to FRS 102 throughout this chapter are to the September 2015 edition of the Standard.

Except for the changes affecting employee benefits, the changes to FRS 102 were made by *Amendments to FRS 102 – Small entities and Other Amendments* – issued in July 2015 ('the July 2015 amendments') in order to incorporate the new small entities regime and to make other amendments necessary to maintain consistency with company law. Company law has changed as a result of the issuance of a new EU Accounting Directive and the changes have been implemented by *The Companies, Partnerships and Groups (Accounts and Reports) Regulations 2015* (SI 2015/980) which came into force on 6 April 2015.

The following subjects are covered with the headings corresponding to the equivalent chapter headings in EY New UK GAAP 2015:

* Scope of FRS 102 (see 2 below);
* Consolidated and separate financial statements (see 3 below);
* Financial instruments (see 4 below);
* Inventories (see 5 below);
* Intangible assets other than goodwill (see 6 below);
* Business combinations and goodwill (see 7 below);
* Provisions and contingencies (see 8 below);
* Share-based payment (see 9 below);

- Impairment of assets (see 10 below);
- Employee benefits (see 11 below)
- Related party disclosures (see 12 below);
- Public benefit entities (see 13 below); and
- Transition to FRS 102 (see 14 below).

The changes affecting Employee Benefits (see 11 below) and Share-based payment (see 9 below) apply for accounting periods beginning on or after 1 January 2015 with early adoption permitted.

All other changes are mandatory for accounting periods beginning on or after 1 January 2016 (which mirrors the mandatory effective date for the company law changes in SI 2015/980). Early application is:

- permitted for accounting periods beginning on or after 1 January 2015 provided that SI 2015/980 is applied from the same date; and
- required if an entity applies SI 2015/980 to a reporting period beginning before 1 January 2016.

For entities not subject to UK company law (and therefore entities to which SI 2015/980 does not apply), early application of the July 2015 amendments to FRS 102 is permitted from 1 January 2015, *[FRS 102.1.15]*, (which, in our view, means accounting periods beginning on or after 1 January 2015).

At the time of writing this publication, The Republic of Ireland is yet to issue its equivalent version of SI 2015/980 (i.e. implement the EU Accounting Directive) and we believe that entities subject to Irish company law should not implement the changes arising from the July 2015 amendments to FRS 102 linked to implementation of SI 2015/980 until this is issued. Similarly, the LLP Regulations are yet to be updated for the EU Accounting Directive and we also believe that LLPs should not implement the changes arising from the July 2015 amendments to FRS 102 until this update occurs.

If an entity applies the July 2015 amendments before 1 January 2016 it shall disclose that fact unless it is a small entity in which case it is encouraged to disclose that fact *[FRS 102.1.15]*.

2.   SCOPE OF FRS 102

2.1   Compliance with legal requirements

An entity applying FRS 102 is reminded that it must ensure it complies with any relevant legal requirements applicable to it since the standard does not necessarily contain all legal disclosure requirements. *[FRS 102.1.2A]*. A UK company preparing statutory financial statements is subject to various additional disclosure requirements in both the Act itself and in related enabling Statutory Instruments such as *The Large and Medium-sized Companies and Groups (Accounts and Reports) Regulations 2008*. Entities not subject to UK company law may need to comply with other legislative requirements.

In relation to small entities (see Chapter 3), FRS 102 contains most legal disclosure requirements but, for example, those only relevant when the financial statements have been audited are not included. *[FRS 102.1.2A]*.

2.2 Reduced disclosure framework – financial instrument disclosure exemptions

The July 2015 amendments have reduced the financial instrument disclosure exemptions available to qualifying entities that are not financial institutions. Previously, these entities, if conditions were satisfied, were exempt from the requirements of paragraphs 11.39 to 11.48A of Section 11 – *Basic Financial Instruments* – and paragraphs 12.26 to 12.29A of Section 12 – *Other Financial Instruments Issues* – provided equivalent disclosures were included in the consolidated financial statements of the group in which the entity is consolidated.

Following the July 2015 amendments, qualifying entities that are not financial institutions are exempt only from the requirements of paragraphs 11.41(b), 11.41(c), 11.41(e), 11.41(f), 11.42, 11.44, 11.45, 11.47, 11.48(a)(iii), 11.48(a)(iv), 11.48(b) and 11.48(c) of Section 11 and paragraphs 12.26 (in relation to those cross-referenced paragraphs from which a disclosure exemption is available), 12.27, 12.29(a), 12.29(b) and 12.29A of Section 12. *[FRS 102.1.12(c)]*.

These changes have been made because UK company law requires certain disclosures relating to financial instruments and therefore, a qualifying entity choosing to provide reduced disclosures will not be exempt from all the disclosure requirements of Section 11 and 12. *[FRS 102.AC Advice 31]*. It should, however, be observed that one practical impact of this change is also to increase disclosures in respect of financial instruments by qualifying entities applying FRS 102 that are not subject to UK company law.

The additional disclosures required by qualifying entities as a result of these changes are discussed in detail at 4.3 below.

2.3 Reduced disclosure framework – equivalent disclosures

The reduced disclosure exemptions in respect of financial instruments and share-based payments set out in paragraphs 1.12(c) and (d) respectively of FRS 102 are dependent on the provision of 'equivalent' disclosures in the publicly available consolidated financial statements of the parent in which the qualifying entity is consolidated. FRS 102 refers users to the Application Guidance in FRS 100 in deciding whether those disclosures are 'equivalent' to the requirements of FRS 102 (i.e. the full requirements when not applying the disclosure exemptions) from which relief is provided. *[FRS 102.1.13]*.

The Application Guidance in FRS 100 has been changed by the July 2015 amendments and is now as follows (with the key change italicised):

- it is necessary to consider whether the publicly available consolidated financial statements of the parent provide disclosures that meet the basic disclosure requirements of the relevant standard or interpretation without regarding strict conformity with each and every disclosure. This assessment should be based on the particular facts, including the similarities to and differences from the requirements of the relevant standard from which relief is provided; *[FRS 100.AG8]*

- the concept of 'equivalence' is intended to be aligned to that described in s401 of the Act; *[FRS 100.AG9]* and

- disclosure exemptions for subsidiaries are permitted where the relevant disclosure requirements are met in the consolidated financial statements, even where the disclosures are made in aggregate or abbreviated form, *or in relation to intra-group balances, those intra-group balances have been eliminated on consolidation.* If, however, no disclosure is made in the consolidated financial statements on the grounds of materiality, the relevant disclosures should be made at the subsidiary level if material in those financial statements. *[FRS 100.AG10]*.

This means that a qualifying entity must review the consolidated financial statements of its parent to ensure that 'equivalent' disclosures have been made for each of the above exemptions that it intends to use. Where a particular 'equivalent' disclosure has not been made (unless the disclosure relates to an intra-group balance eliminated on consolidation) then the qualifying subsidiary cannot use the exemption in respect of that disclosure.

3   CONSOLIDATED AND SEPARATE FINANCIAL STATEMENTS

The changes made to Section 9 – *Consolidated and Separate Financial Statements* – of FRS 102 align the wording for the exemption to prepare consolidated accounts for intermediate parents with UK company law as amended by the SI 2015/980.

3.1   Exemption from preparing consolidated financial statements by a parent entity included in EEA group accounts of a larger group (s400 exemption)

This exemption, available under s400 of the Companies Act, was discussed previously in Chapter 6 of EY New UK GAAP 2015 at 3.1.1.A. The principal changes made to FRS 102 by the SI 2015/980 deal with protection for minority shareholders (or non-controlling interest) and state that: *[FRS 102.9.3(a)-(bA)]*.

- when the immediate parent of the parent entity seeking the exemption from preparing consolidated accounts holds 90% or more of the allotted shares in the entity, the remaining shareholders must approve the use of the exemption from preparing consolidated financial statements. *[s400(1)(b)]*. This, therefore, requires a positive affirmation by all non-controlling shareholders to use the exemption which is a change from the previous requirement. There is no de-minimis limit. Previously, the exemption could be used provided notice requesting the preparation of group accounts was not served on the company by shareholders holding in aggregate more than half of the remaining allotted shares in the company or 5% of the total allotted shares in the company; and

- when the immediate parent holds more than 50% but less than 90% of the allotted share in the entity the exemption is available provided notice has not been served on the entity, requesting the preparation of group accounts, by the shareholders holding in aggregate at least 5% of the allotted shares in the company. The notice must be served at least six months before the end of the financial year to which it relates. *[s400(1)(c)]*. The previous wording also permitted minority shareholders having more than half of the remaining allotted shares in the company to object as well as shareholders holding more than 5% of the total allotted shares in the company.

The changes also clarify that the parent is not exempt from preparing group accounts if any of its transferable securities are admitted to trading on a regulated market of any EEA State within the meaning of Directive 2004/39/EC. *[FRS 102.9.3]*.

One minor change made by the SI 2015/980 not specifically identified by FRS 102 is that a parent entity using the exemption from preparing consolidated financial statements must disclose the address of the registered office of the parent that draws up the group accounts and in which it is consolidated (whether in or outside the United Kingdom). *[s400(2)(d)(i)]*. Previously, only the name of the country of incorporation was required for a parent incorporated outside the UK.

3.2 Exemption from preparing consolidated financial statements by a parent entity included in non-EEA group accounts of a larger group (s401 exemption)

This exemption, available under s401 of the Companies Act, was discussed previously in Chapter 6 of EY New UK GAAP 2015 at 3.1.1.B and 3.1.1.C. There are two principal changes made by SI 2015/980:

- those that deal with protection for non-controlling shareholders (see 3.2.1 below); and

- those that address the matter of 'equivalent' financial statements (see 3.2.2 below).

The amendments also clarify that the parent is not exempt from preparing group accounts if any of its transferable securities are admitted to trading on a regulated market of any EEA State within the meaning of Directive 2004/39/EC. *[FRS 102.9.3]*.

One minor change made by the SI 2015/980 not specifically identified by FRS 102 is that the parent entity using the exemption must disclose the address of the registered office of the parent that draws up the group accounts and in which it is consolidated (whether in or outside the United Kingdom). *[s401(2)(e)(i)]*. Previously, only the name of the country of incorporation was required for a parent incorporated outside the UK.

3.2.1 *Protection of non-controlling shareholders*

The changes made to FRS 102 as a result of the SI 2015/980 deal with protection for non-controlling interests (or minority shareholders) and state that: *[FRS 102.9.3(c)-(dA)]*

- when the parent of the parent entity seeking the exemption from preparing consolidated accounts holds more than 90% of the allotted shares in the entity, the remaining shareholders must approve the use of the exemption from preparing consolidated financial statements. *[s401(1)(b)]*. This, therefore, requires a positive affirmation by all minority shareholders to use the exemption which is a change from the previous requirement. There is no de-minimis limit. Previously, the exemption could be used provided notice

Chapter 5

requesting the preparation of group accounts was not served on the company by shareholders holding in aggregate more than half of the remaining allotted shares in the company or 5% of the total allotted shares in the company; and

- when the parent holds more than 50% but less than 90% of the allotted share in the entity the exemption is available provided notice has not been served on the entity, requesting the preparation of group accounts, by the shareholders holding in aggregate at least 5% of the allotted shares in the company. The notice must be served at least six months before the end of the financial year to which it relates. *[s401(1)(c)]*. The previous wording also permitted minority shareholders having more than half of the remaining allotted shares in the company to object as well as shareholders holding more than 5% of the total allotted shares in the company.

3.2.2   *Equivalence for the purposes of the s401 exemption*

Following amendments made to s401 of the Companies Act by SI 2015/980, the exemption from preparing consolidated financial statements for intermediate parents that are subsidiaries of non EEA parents is conditional on the higher parent's group annual report being drawn up: *[s401(2)(b)]*

- in accordance with the provisions of the Accounting Directive;
- in a manner equivalent to consolidated accounts and consolidated reports so drawn up;
- in accordance with international accounting standards adopted pursuant to the IAS Regulation (i.e. EU-adopted IFRS); or
- in accordance with accounting standards that are equivalent to EU-adopted IFRS as determined pursuant to the Commission Regulation (EC) No. 1569/2007(a) of 21 December 2007 establishing a mechanism for the determination of equivalence of accounting standards applied by third country issuers of securities pursuant to Directives 2003/71/EC and 2005/109/EC of the European Parliament and of the Council.

In practice, we believe that, in almost all circumstances, these amendments should result in no change in the ability of entities to use the exemption.

The application guidance to FRS 100 states that use of the exemption requires an analysis of a particular set of consolidated financial statements to determine whether they are drawn up in a manner equivalent to consolidated financial statements that are in accordance with the Accounting Directive. The Application Guidance exists to prevent companies and their auditors from adopting an overly cautious approach in response to uncertainty about whether exemptions can be used. *[FRS 100.AG4]*.

The Application Guidance to FRS 100 states that it is generally accepted that the reference to equivalence in s401 of the Companies Act does not mean compliance with every detail of the Accounting Directive. When assessing whether consolidated financial statements of a higher non-EEA parent are drawn up in a manner equivalent to consolidated financial statements drawn up in accordance with the Accounting Directive, it is necessary to consider whether they meet the basic requirements of the Accounting Directive; in particular, the requirement to give a true and fair view, without implying strict conformity with each and every provision. A qualitative approach is more in keeping with the deregulatory nature of the exemption than a requirement to consider the detailed requirements on a checklist basis. *[FRS 100.AG5]*.

As a result of SI 2015/980, the application guidance to FRS 100 has been amended to state that consolidated financial statements of the higher parent will meet the exemption or the test of equivalence in the Accounting Directive if they are intended to give a true and fair view and:

- are prepared in accordance with FRS 102;
- are prepared in accordance with EU-adopted IFRS;
- are prepared in accordance with IFRS, subject to the consideration of the reasons for any failure by the European Commission to adopt a standard or interpretation; or
- are prepared using other GAAPs which are closely related to IFRS, subject to the consideration of the effect of any differences from EU-adopted IFRS.

Consolidated financial statements of the higher parent prepared using other GAAPs or the IFRS for SMEs should be assessed for equivalence with the Accounting Directive based on the particular facts, including the similarities to and differences from the Accounting Directive. *[FRS 100.AG6]*.

As a result of the 2007 Commission Regulation discussed above, the EU Commission has subsequently identified the following as equivalent to IFRS: *[FRS 100.AG7]*

Equivalent GAAP	Applicable From
GAAP of Japan	1 January 2009
GAAP of the United States of America	I January 2009
GAAP of the People's Republic of China	1 January 2012
GAAP of Canada	1 January 2012
GAAP of the Republic of Korea	1 January 2012

Further, third country issuers were permitted to prepare their annual consolidated financial statements and half-yearly consolidated financial statements in accordance with the Generally Accepted Accounting Principles of the Republic of India for financial years starting before 1 January 2015. For reporting periods beginning on or after 1 January 2015, in relation to GAAP of the Republic of India, equivalence should be assessed on the basis of the particular facts. *[FRS 100.AG7]*.

3.3 Exemption from preparing consolidated financial statements for small groups

This exemption was discussed previously in Chapter 6 of EY New UK GAAP 2015 at 3.1.1.D.

The Companies Act does not require that companies that are subject to the Small Companies Regime prepare group accounts. *[s399 (1)]*. In addition, following amendments made by SI 2015/980, a company is also exempt from the requirement to prepare group accounts if (a) it would be subject to the small companies regime but for being a public company and (b) it is not a traded company. *[s399 (2A)]*. This amendment extends the scope of the exemption to a small company parent that is a public company but not a traded company. Conversely, it means that a small company parent that is a traded company but not a public company can no longer use the exemption. Similarly, s384 has been amended so that a small company parent will not be able to claim the exemption from preparing consolidated financial statements if any of the members of the group of which it is a member were a traded company (previously public company).

Consequently, Section 9 of FRS 102 exempts a parent from preparing consolidated financial statements if the parent, and group headed by it, qualify as small as set out in s383 of the Companies Act and the parent and the group are considered eligible for the exemption as determined by reference to sections 384 and 399(2A) of the Companies Act. *[FRS 102.9.3(e)]*.

The conditions for eligibility as a small company as a result of the July 2015 amendments are discussed in Chapter 3 at 4.3.

3.4   Disclosures of related undertakings (e.g. subsidiaries, associates and jointly controlled entities) required by the Regulations

For financial statements approved on or after 1 July 2015, the ability of an entity to limit the provision of information about related undertakings such as subsidiaries, associates and jointly controlled entities to the principal related undertakings if the disclosure would otherwise be of excessive length has been eliminated. This is because SI 2015/980 has removed subsection (2) of s410 of the Companies Act which provided this relief. *[SI 980/2015.2(5)]*. This means that, for example, the information required by paragraph 1 of Schedule 4 to the Regulations for each subsidiary (e.g. the name and country of incorporation, if outside the United Kingdom), including both direct and indirect subsidiaries, must be provided for *every* subsidiary.

Entities with an excessive length of related undertakings for which disclosures are required by Schedule 4 to the Regulations may be advised to consider providing this information in an appendix at the rear of the financial statements.

4   FINANCIAL INSTRUMENTS

The July 2015 amendments to FRS 102 have amended certain requirements relating to financial instruments that are or may be measured at fair value through profit or loss under either Section 11 or Section 12. This is because the new Accounting Directive permits measurement of certain financial instruments at fair value where it is in accordance with EU-adopted IFRS, whereas previously this was restricted to IFRS endorsed by 5 September 2006. In addition, the Accounting Council believes that entities applying IFRS 9 – *Financial Instruments* – will need to consider an override of the Regulations for the purposes of giving a true and fair view in order to recognise certain fair value gains and losses in other comprehensive incomer. *[FRS 102.AC Advice.30(b)]*.

The FRC has also taken the opportunity to alter the financial instrument disclosure exemptions for a qualifying entity in order to embed certain disclosures required by company law within the text of Sections 11 and 12 of FRS 102.

4.1 Entities that choose to apply IFRS 9

An entity that chooses to apply the recognition and measurement requirements of IFRS 9, as permitted by paragraphs 11.2(c) and 12.2(c) of FRS 102, must measure a financial asset at amortised cost in accordance with paragraphs 5.4.1 to 5.4.4 of IFRS 9 when that asset is not permitted to be measured at fair value through profit or loss by the Small Companies Regulations, the Regulations, the Small LLP Regulations or the LLP Regulations. *[FRS 102.11.2A]*.

The Regulations (but not the LLP Regulations or the Small LLP Regulations) have been amended to permit fair value accounting for any financial asset which under international accounting standards may be included in accounts at fair value. *[1 Sch 36(4), 2 Sch 44(4), 3 Sch 30(4)]*. However, the Note on Legal Requirements to the July 2015 amendments to FRS 102 observes that, since IFRS 9 has not yet been endorsed by the EU, IAS 39 – *Financial Instruments: Recognition and Measurement* – remains the extant reference point for determining what may be included in accounts at fair value under international accounting standards. Therefore, financial assets measured at fair value under IFRS 9 but not permitted to be measured at fair value under IAS 39 would have to be measured at amortised cost under FRS 102. *[FRS 102.A4.12B]*. The LLP and Small LLP Regulations have not yet been updated and still refer to IFRS endorsed by 5 September 2006.

The Regulations, the Small Company Regulations, the LLP Regulations and the Small Company LLP Regulations do not permit fair value gains on financial instruments measured at fair value to be recognised other than in the profit and loss account except when the financial instrument is a hedging instrument or an available-for-sale security. IFRS 9 has the following circumstances in which fair value gains or losses are recorded in other comprehensive income:

- when fair value changes in respect of financial liabilities attributable to changes in own credit risk are recorded in other comprehensive income unless that treatment would create or enlarge an accounting mismatch in profit or loss; *[IFRS 9.5.7.7-5.7.9]*;

- if, on initial recognition, an entity makes an irrevocable election to present in other comprehensive income subsequent changes in the fair value of an equity instrument that is neither held for trading nor contingent consideration; *[IFRS 9.5.7.5-6]*; and

- investment in debt instruments measured at fair value through other comprehensive income which are held within a business model whose objective is achieved by both collecting contractual cash flows and selling financial assets and the contractual terms of the financial assets give rise on specified dates to cash flows that are solely payments of principal and interest on the principal amount outstanding. *[IFRS 9.4.1.2A]*.

Chapter 5

The Note on Legal Requirements to the July 2015 amendments to FRS 102 states that accounting for fair value gains and losses on financial liabilities attributable to changes in credit risk in other comprehensive income in accordance with IFRS 9 will usually be a departure from the requirement of the Regulations and will therefore require the use of a true and fair override. *[FRS 102.A4.12C]*.

The Note on Legal Requirements is silent about the other two circumstances in IFRS 9, described above, in which accounting for fair value gains and losses are required in other comprehensive income. In our view:

- accounting for changes in the fair value of an equity instrument through other comprehensive income (without recycling of fair value changes to profit and loss) makes use of the alternative accounting rules in the Regulations, the Small Company Regulations, the LLP Regulations and the Small Company LLP Regulations and does not therefore require the use of a true and fair override (see Chapter 4 at 10.2); and

- the model used for accounting for changes in the fair value of a debt instrument through other comprehensive income is similar, but not identical, to the available-for-sale asset model under IAS 39. In our view, it is inferred from the Accounting Council's silence on the matter that this model is included within the fair value accounting rules in the Regulations the Small Company Regulations, the LLP Regulations and the Small Company LLP Regulations (see Chapter 4 at 10.3) and does not therefore require the use of a true and fair override to apply.

4.2   Disclosures for financial instruments measured at fair value through profit or loss

The July 2015 amendments to FRS 102 make changes to the disclosure requirements for financial instruments measured at fair value through profit and loss. The Note on Legal Requirements reminds entities (including qualifying entities) preparing Companies Act accounts that the disclosures required by paragraph 55 of Schedule 1 to the Regulations (and its equivalents in Schedules 2 and 3 and other Regulations) must be made. *[FRS 102.A4.12D]*. The required disclosures are:

- significant assumptions underlying any valuation models and techniques used where the fair value has been determined using generally accepted valuation techniques and models;

- the fair value of each category of financial instrument and the changes in value reported in profit and loss or credited/debited to the fair value reserve;

- for each class of derivatives, the extent and nature of the instruments including significant terms and conditions that may affect the amount, timing and uncertainty of future cash flows; and

- where any amount is transferred to or from the fair value reserve, there must be stated in tabular form, the amount of the reserve at the beginning and end of the reporting period, the amount transferred to/from the reserve in the year and the source and application of the amounts so transferred.

Most of these disclosures will be satisfied by the equivalent requirements of FRS 102 (e.g. paragraph 11.43) but entities will need to take care to ensure appropriate disclosure of derivatives is provided. *[FRS 102.A4.12D]*.

An entity applying FRS 102 and holding financial instruments at fair value, including a qualifying entity, may be required to provide the disclosures required by paragraph 36(4) of Schedule 1 to the Regulations (and its equivalents) – see Chapter 2 of EY New UK GAAP 2015 at 3.4. The Note on Legal Requirements asserts that the disclosures required by paragraph 36(4) have been incorporated into Section 11. *[FRS 102.A4.13]*.

Some of the Section 11 disclosure requirements apply to all financial instruments measured at fair value, whilst others (see below) apply only to certain financial instruments (this does not include financial instruments held as part of a trading portfolio nor derivatives). The Accounting Council believes that the disclosure requirements of paragraph 11.48A of FRS 102 (see below) will predominately apply to certain financial liabilities although there may be instances when disclosures must also be provided for financial assets, for example investments in subsidiaries, associates or jointly controlled entities measured at fair value according to paragraph 9.27B of FRS 102. *[FRS 102.A4.13]*.

Paragraph 11.48A has been amended to state that an entity, including an entity that is not a company, shall provide the following disclosures only for financial instruments measured at fair value through profit or loss in accordance with paragraph 36(4) of Schedule 1 of the Regulations (and the equivalent requirements of other Regulations). This does not include financial liabilities held as part of a trading portfolio nor derivatives. The required disclosures are:

- the amount of change, during the period and cumulatively, in the fair value of the financial instrument that is attributable to changes in the credit risk of that instrument, determined either:
  - as the amount of change in its fair value that is not attributable to changes in market conditions that give rise to market risk; or
  - using an alternative method the entity believes more faithfully represents the amount of change in its fair value that is attributable to changes in the credit risk of the instrument;
- the method used to establish the amount of change attributable to changes in own credit risk, or, if the change cannot be measured reliably or is not material, that fact;
- for a financial liability, the difference between the financial liability's carrying amount and the amount the entity would be contractually required to pay at maturity to the holder of the obligation;
- if an instrument contains both a liability and an equity feature, and the instrument has multiple features that substantially modify the cash flows and the values of those features are interdependent (such as a callable convertible debt instrument), the existence of those features;
- the aggregate difference yet to be recognised in profit and loss at the beginning and end of the period between the fair value of a financial instrument at initial

recognition and the amount determined at that date using a valuation technique, and the amount recognised in profit or loss and a reconciliation of the changes in the balance of this difference; and

- information that enables users of the entity's financial statements to evaluate the nature and extent of relevant risks arising from financial instruments to which the entity is exposed at the end of the reporting period. These risks typically include, but are not limited to, credit risk, liquidity risk and market risk. The disclosure should include both the entity's exposure to each type of risk and how it manages those risks. *[FRS 102.11.48A]*.

4.3   Disclosure exemptions for qualifying entities that are not financial institutions

The August 2014 version of FRS 102 exempted qualifying entities that were not financial institutions from all disclosures required by Sections 11 and 12 of FRS 102. However, as discussed at 4.2 above, all entities (including qualifying entities) preparing Companies Act accounts must make certain disclosures in respect of financial instruments.

To remove this inconsistency, as discussed at 2.2 above, the July 2015 amendments have removed some of the disclosure exemptions for qualifying entities that are not financial institutions. For a qualifying entity that is not a financial institution, including a qualifying entity that is not required to prepare Companies Act accounts, disclosures are now required as follows: *[FRS 102.1.12(c)]*

Disclosure requirement	*Disclosure required by a qualifying entity that is not a financial institution*
Carrying amounts of financial assets measured at fair value through profit or loss (FRS 102.11.41(a))	Yes
Carrying amounts of debt instruments measured at amortised cost (FRS 102.11.41(b))	No
Carrying amounts of equity instruments measured at cost less impairment (FRS 102.11.41(c))	No
Carrying amounts of financial liabilities measured at fair value through profit or loss. Separate disclosure of those liabilities not held as part of a trading portfolio and not derivatives (FRS 102.11.41(d))	Yes
Carrying amount of financial liabilities measured at amortised cost (FRS 102.11.41(e))	No
Carrying amount of loan commitments measured at amortised cost (FRS 102.11.41(f))	No
Information to enable users to evaluate the significance of financial instruments for its financial position and performance (FRS 102.11.42)	No
Basis for determining fair value and assumptions applied when a valuation technique is used (FRS 102.11.43)	Yes
Disclosure that reliable measure of fair value is no longer available for ordinary or preference shares measured at fair value through profit or loss (FRS 102.11.44)	No

Disclosures for transferred financial assets that do not qualify for derecognition (FRS 102.11.45)	No
Disclosures for financial assets pledged as collateral for liabilities or contingent liabilities (FRS 102.11.46)	Yes
Disclosures for loans payable at the reporting date for which there is a breach of terms or default (FRS 102.11.47)	No
Income, expense, net gains or net losses, including fair value changes, for financial assets and financial liabilities measured at fair value through profit or loss (FRS 102.11.48(a)(i)-(ii))	Yes
Income, expense, net gains or net losses, including fair value changes, for financial assets and financial liabilities measured at amortised cost (FRS 102.11.48(a)(iii)-(iv))	No
Total interest income and expense for financial assets and liabilities not measured at fair value through profit or loss (FRS 102.11.48(b))	No
The amount of any impairment loss for each class of financial asset (FRS 102.11.48(c))	No
Disclosures for financial instruments measured at fair value through profit or loss in accordance with paragraph 36(4) of Schedule 1 to the Regulations and its equivalents (FRS 102.11.48A). See 3.2 above.	Yes
Description of hedging relationships and the nature of risks being hedged and the hedged item (FRS 102.12.27)	No
Disclosures in respect of fair value hedges of changes in the fair value of the hedging instrument and hedged item recognised in profit and loss (FRS 102.12.28)	Yes
For cash flow hedges, disclosure of the periods when the cash flows are expected and a description of a forecast transaction which is no longer expected to occur (FRS 102.12.29(a)-(b))	No
For cash flow hedges, the amount of fair value change of the hedging instrument recognised in other comprehensive income, reclassified from equity to profit and loss and any excess of the fair value of the hedging instrument over the change in the fair value of the expected cash flows recognised in profit or loss (FRS 102.12.29(c)-(e))	Yes
Separate disclosure of amounts recognised in other comprehensive income and profit or loss where hedge accounting used for a net investment in a foreign operation (FRS 102.12.29A)	No

In addition to these disclosures, a qualifying entity preparing Companies Act accounts may also need to make other disclosures required by the applicable Regulations as discussed in Chapter 8 of EY New UK GAAP 2015 at 8.3.

A qualifying entity that is a financial institution is not entitled to any exemption from the disclosures required by Sections 11 and 12.

4.4   Illustrative examples of financial assets and financial liabilities

The first financial asset example and the first financial liability example of Section 11 of FRS 102 have been changed to state that a long-term receivable or payable at a market rate of interest is recognised at the amount of the cash advanced or received plus or minus transaction costs incurred. *[FRS 102.11.39-40]*. The original examples did not deal with transaction costs or mention whether the receivable/payable was originated at a market rate of interest.

5   INVENTORIES

5.1   Inventories measured at fair value less costs to sell through profit or loss

The August 2014 version of FRS 102 had no restriction on the type of inventories that could be measured at fair value less costs to sell through profit or loss and were therefore outside the scope of the measurement requirements of Section 2 – *Inventories* – of FRS 102. The July 2015 amendments: *[FRS 102.13.3]*

- state that inventories shall not be measured at fair value less costs to sell unless it is a more relevant measure of the entity's performance (i.e. more relevant than the lower of costs and estimated selling price less costs to complete and sell) because the entity operates in an active market where sale can be achieved at published prices, and inventory is a store of readily realisable value; and

- clarify explicitly that the disclosure requirements of paragraph 13.22 of Section 2 of FRS 102 apply to inventories at fair value less costs to sell through profit or loss (the August 2014 version of FRS 102 implied this via omission).

'Relevance' will be judged by the criteria in Section 2 – *Concepts and Pervasive Principles* – of FRS 102 and is discussed in Chapter 3 of EY New UK GAAP 2015 at 3.2.2.

The criteria for the use of measurement at fair value less costs in Section 2 of FRS 102 described above is different to that contained in IAS 2 – *Inventories* – which is limited to certain types of inventories (e.g. agricultural produce and inventories held by commodity broker-traders). *[IAS 2.3]*. In addition, IAS 2 contains no requirement that an entity operates in an active market or that inventory is a store of readily realisable value for fair value measurement to be applied.

5.2   Inventories held for distribution at no or nominal cost

Inventories held for distribution at no or nominal consideration includes items such as advertising and promotional material, and also items that may be distributed to beneficiaries by public benefit entities. *[FRS 102.A4.36]*.

The July 2015 amendments to FRS 102 require that inventories held for distribution at no or nominal consideration shall be measured at the lower of cost adjusted, when applicable, for any loss of service potential and replacement cost. *[FRS 102.13.4A]*. This is a change from the August 2014 version of FRS 102 which required that such inventories be measured at cost adjusted, when applicable, for any loss of service potential.

This change has been made because of changes to Schedule 1 to the Regulations by SI 980/2015 which no longer permits stocks to be included at current cost under the alternative accounting rules but instead permit stocks to be included at fair value when applying fair value accounting. *[FRS 102.A4.35]*. The Note on Legal Requirements to the July 2015 amendments to FRS 102 explains that the revised measurement basis described above (i.e. lower of cost adjusted for loss of service potential and replacement cost) is an application of fair value accounting. The Note further observes that, for inventories including those held for distribution at no or nominal value (particularly items distributed to beneficiaries by public benefit entities) there is unlikely to be a significant difference between replacement cost and fair value. *[FRS 102.A4.37]*.

Accounting issues in respect of inventories held for distribution at no or nominal consideration (e.g. unit of account) are discussed in Chapter 9 of EY New UK GAAP 2015 at 3.3.11.

6   INTANGIBLE ASSETS OTHER THAN GOODWILL

6.1   Intangible assets with a useful life that cannot be reliably estimated

The July 2015 amendments to FRS 102 state that if an entity is unable to make a reliable estimate of the useful life of an intangible asset, the life shall not exceed 10 years (previously 5 years). In addition, the revised wording explicitly states that an entity is only expected to be unable to make a reliable estimate of the useful life of an intangible asset 'in exceptional cases'. *[FRS 102.18.20]*. A similar amendment has been made in respect of goodwill (see 7.1 below).

The above change in the useful life of an intangible if an entity is unable to make a reliable estimate of that intangible and the statement that this is expected to be the case only in exceptional cases follows an equivalent change made to UK company law by SI 2015/980.

6.2   Amortisation of intangible assets with a residual value

The Note on Legal Requirements to FRS 102 has also been changed to provide guidance on the amortisation of intangible assets which have a residual value. When an intangible asset has a residual value, it is the depreciable amount that is amortised as required by paragraph 18.21 of FRS 102. In practice, the FRC believes that it is uncommon for an intangible asset to have a residual value and FRS 102 requires an entity to assume that the residual value is zero unless there is a commitment by a third party to purchase the asset at the end of its useful life or there is an active market for the asset from which to determine its residual value and it is probable that such a market will exist at the end of the assets' useful life. *[FRS 102.18.23]*.

However, in those cases where an intangible asset does have a residual life that is not zero, the amortisation of the depreciable amount of the asset over its useful economic life is a departure from the requirements of paragraph 22 of Schedule 1 to the Regulations (and its equivalents in Schedules 2 and 3 of the Regulations and the LLP Regulations) since the regulations require intangible assets to be written off over their useful economic lives. In those circumstances, the FRC states that entities must invoke a true and fair override and make the disclosures required by the Regulations for the use of a true and fair override. *[FRS 102.A4.37A]*.

7   BUSINESS COMBINATIONS AND GOODWILL

7.1   Goodwill with a useful life that cannot be reliably estimated

The July 2015 amendments to FRS 102 state that if an entity is unable to make a reliable estimate of the useful life of goodwill, the life shall not exceed 10 years (previously 5 years). In addition, the revised wording explicitly states that an entity is only expected to be unable to make a reliable estimate of the useful life of goodwill 'in exceptional cases'. *[FRS 102.19.23(a)]*. A similar amendment has been made in respect of intangible assets with an indefinite life (see 6.1 above).

The above change in the useful life of goodwill if an entity is unable to make a reliable estimate of that goodwill and the statement that this is expected to be the case only in exceptional cases follows an equivalent change made to UK company law by SI 2015/980.

A related amendment has been made to the disclosure requirements to state that if the useful life of goodwill cannot be reliably estimated, disclosure must be made of the reasons supporting the period chosen (which cannot exceed 10 years). *[FRS 102.19.25(g)]*. The previous requirement was to disclose the reasons for the useful life of goodwill if it exceeded 5 years.

7.2   The conditions for the use of merger accounting in group reconstructions

Under FRS 102, group reconstructions can be accounted for using the merger accounting method provided:

*   the use of the merger accounting method is not prohibited by company law or other relevant legislation;

*   the ultimate equity holders remain the same, and the rights of each equity holder, relative to the others, are unchanged; and

*   no non-controlling interest in the net assets of the group is altered by the transfer. *[FRS 102.19.27]*.

SI 2015/980 has changed the UK company law requirements which have to be met in consolidated financial statements before merger accounting can be applied. The new requirements for accounting for an acquisition as a merger are:

*   that the undertaking whose shares are acquired is ultimately controlled by the same party both before and after the acquisition;

*   that the control referred to above is not intended to be transitory; and

*   that adoption of the merger method accords with generally accepted accounting principles or practice. *[6 Sch 10]*.

This means that:

*   there is no longer a requirement that at least 90% of the nominal value of the relevant shares in the undertaking acquired is held by or on behalf of the parent company and its subsidiary undertakings. Now, it is required only that the undertaking is controlled by the same party both before and after the transaction;

- there is no longer a requirement that the fair value of any consideration other than an issue of equity shares given by the parent company and its subsidiary undertakings does not exceed more than 10% of the nominal value of the equity shares issued. There is now no restriction on the amount of the fair value of any consideration which is not in the form of equity shares. This will allow more group reconstructions to be accounted for using the merger accounting method; and

- a transaction in which a new parent is inserted above an existing group no longer meets the requirements for merger accounting. This is because the undertaking whose shares are acquired (e.g. the previous ultimate parent of a group) is not controlled by the same party after the acquisition since before the acquisition it was not controlled by any party. The Note on Legal Requirements to the July 2015 amendments to FRS 102 observes that paragraph 10 of Schedule 6 to the Regulations is generally consistent with paragraph 19.27 of FRS 102 (reproduced above). However, if an entity considers that, for the overriding purpose of giving a true and fair view, merger accounting should be applied in circumstances other than those set out in paragraph 10 of Schedule 6 to the Regulations, it may do so providing the relevant disclosures are made in the notes to the financial statements. *[FRS 102.A4.37A]*. The Note on Legal Requirements to the July 2015 amendments to FRS 102 does not provide any examples of such circumstances but this situation would appear to be an example of when a true and fair override might be appropriate in order to use merger accounting in the consolidated financial statements of the new parent.

SI 2015/980 has also imposed additional disclosures in the consolidated financial statements where an acquisition has taken place in the financial year and the merger method of accounting has been adopted. These are as follows:

- the address of the registered office of the undertaking acquired (whether in or outside the United Kingdom); and

- the name of the ultimate controlling party that controls the undertaking whose shares are acquired and its registered office (whether in or outside the United Kingdom). *[6 Sch 16A]*.

The scope and application of the group reconstruction requirements of FRS 102, as well as an explanation of the merger accounting method, are contained in Chapter 15 of EY New UK GAAP 2015 at 5.

8.   PROVISIONS AND CONTINGENCIES

8.1   Disclosure of provisions, contingent liabilities and contingent assets when information is seriously prejudicial

The July 2015 amendments to FRS 102 have amended paragraph 21.17 of Section 21 – *Provisions and Contingencies* – to state that when disclosure of some or all of the information required by paragraphs 21.14 to 21.16 can be expected to prejudice seriously the position of the entity in a dispute with other parties, the entity need not disclose all of the information required by those paragraphs insofar as it relates to the dispute, but shall disclose at least the following: *[FRS 102.21.17]*:

- in relation to provisions:
  - a table showing the reconciliation required by paragraph 21.14(a) in aggregate, including the source and application of any amounts transferred to or from provisions during the reporting period;
  - particulars of each provision in any case where the amount of the provision is material; and
  - the fact that, and reason why, the information required by paragraph 21.14(a) has not been disclosed
- in relation to contingent liabilities:
  - particulars and the total amount of contingent liabilities (excluding those which arise out of insurance contracts) that are not included in the statement of financial position;
  - the total amount of contingent liabilities which are undertaken on behalf of or for the benefit of:
    - any parent or fellow subsidiary of the entity;
    - any subsidiary of the entity;
    - any entity in which the reporting entity has a participating interest,

    shall each be stated separately; and
  - the fact that, and reason why, the information required by paragraph 21.15 has not been disclosed.

In relation to contingent assets, the entity shall disclose the general nature of the dispute, together with the fact that, and reason why, the information required by paragraph 21.16 has not been disclosed.

The Accounting Council's advice to the FRC to issue the July 2015 amendments to FRS 102 observes that this change was made in order to remove an inconsistency between company law and FRS 102 and to achieve consistency of disclosures by entities that are companies and those that are not. Company law does not contain a 'seriously prejudicial' exemption from the disclosure requirements of the Regulations in respect of provisions and hence the ability to use the 'seriously prejudicial' exemption has been redrafted to remind companies of the legal disclosure requirements and also to ensure that equivalent disclosures are provided by all entities applying FRS 102 including entities not required to comply with UK company law. *[FRS 102.AC Advice.30(c).July 2015 amendments]*.

The effect of this change is to significantly reduce the usefulness of any seriously prejudicial exemption. However, as the Accounting Council reminds users, the exemption applies 'only in extremely rare circumstances'.

9 SHARE-BASED PAYMENT

The July 2015 amendments to FRS 102 altered the accounting for share-based payment transactions with cash alternatives. The previous version of FRS 102 required such transactions to be accounted for as cash-settled share-based payment transactions unless either:

(a)   the entity has a past practice of settling by issuing equity instruments; or

(b)   the option has no commercial substance because the cash settlement amount bears no relationship to, and is likely to be lower in value than, the fair value of the equity instrument.

If (a) or (b) applied, paragraph 15 of FRS 102 required the transaction to be treated as equity-settled.

The amended standard looks at whether there is a choice or settlement by the entity or the counterparty. *[FRS 102.26.15]*.

When an entity has a choice of settlement of the transaction in cash (or other assets) or by the transfer of equity instruments, the entity shall account for the transaction as a wholly equity-settled share-based transaction in accordance with paragraphs 26.7 to 26.13 unless:

(a)   the choice of settlement in equity instruments has no commercial substance (e.g. because the entity is legally prohibited from issuing shares); or

(b)   the entity has a past practice or a stated policy of settling in cash, or generally settles in cash whenever the counterparty asks for cash settlement.

In circumstances (a) and (b) the entity shall account for the transaction as a wholly cash-settled transaction in accordance with paragraph 26.14. *[FRS 102.26.15A]*.

When the counterparty has a choice of settlement of the transaction in cash (or other assets) or by the transfer of equity instruments, the entity shall account for the transaction as a wholly cash-settled transaction in accordance with paragraph 26.14 unless, as per circumstance (a) above, the choice of settlement in cash (or other assets) has no commercial substance because the cash settlement amount (or value of other assets) bears no relationship to, and is likely to be lower in value than, the fair value of the equity instruments. In circumstance (a) the entity shall account for the transaction as a wholly equity-settled transaction in accordance with paragraphs 26.7 to 26.13. *[FRS 102.26.15B]*.

The amendment will mean that there will be fewer transactions accounted for as cash-settled than under the original version of FRS 102. The split accounting approach in IFRS 2 – *Share-based Payment* – has not been introduced into FRS 102 and therefore this difference between the standards remains. See EY New UK GAAP 2015 Chapter 21 at 2.5 for further details.

The accounting for cash-settled transactions under FRS 102 is discussed further in EY New UK GAAP 2015 in Chapter 21 at 10, and the accounting for equity-settled transactions at 5 to 9.

10   IMPAIRMENT OF ASSETS

The changes made to Section 27 – *Impairment of Assets* – by the July 2015 amendments to FRS 102 relate to the reversal of a goodwill impairment loss which has been prohibited by the EU Accounting Directive.

10.1   Prohibition of a reversal of a goodwill impairment loss

The following changes have been made:

- an impairment loss recognised for goodwill cannot be reversed in a subsequent accounting period; *[FRS 102.27.29]*

- if the estimated recoverable amount of a cash-generating unit exceeds its carrying amount, the excess (i.e. the impairment loss reversal) is allocated pro-rata to the assets of the cash generating unit except for goodwill; *[FRS 102.27.31(b)]* and

- any excess amount of a reversal of an impairment loss that cannot be allocated to an asset because it would increase the asset above the lower of its recoverable amount and the carrying amount that would have been determined (net of amortisation or depreciation) had no impairment loss been recognised for the asset in prior periods shall be allocated pro-rata to the other assets of the cash generating unit, except for goodwill. *[FRS 102.27.31(c)]*.

This change aligns FRS 102 with IFRS as IFRS also does not permit the reversal of a goodwill impairment loss.

11   EMPLOYEE BENEFITS

In February 2015, the FRC issued amendments to FRS 102 in respect of pension obligations. The original standard had not incorporated any of the accounting requirements of IFRIC 14 – *IAS 19 – The Limit on a Defined Benefit Asset, Minimum Funding Requirements and their Interaction.* After the publication of FRS 102 in March 2013, the FRC issued, in October 2013, a Press Notice 1 addressing the accounting in accordance with EU-adopted IFRS for a 'schedule of contributions' payable by an entity to a defined benefit pension plan.[1] Subsequently, the FRC received enquiries about the accounting for similar circumstances by entities applying FRS 102. The issue related to whether or not an entity applying FRS 102 should have regard to the principles of IFRIC 14 where it might be relevant to its circumstances. There appeared to be a diversity of views on the matter, and because the potential implications for an entity's financial statements could be significant, the FRC decided to address the matter outside the intended triennial review cycle for FRS 102.

The amendment clarified that, for entities already recognising assets or liabilities for defined benefit plans in accordance with FRS 102, no additional liabilities need to be recognised in respect of a 'schedule of contributions', even if such an agreement would otherwise be considered onerous. *[FRS 102.28.15A]*.

It also requires that disclosure should be made of the future payments to fund a deficit that have been committed. The disclosure required is a general description of the plan, including funding policy. This shall include the amount and timing of the future payments to be made by the entity under any agreement with the defined benefit plan to fund a deficit (such as a schedule of contributions). *[FRS 102.28.41(a)]*.

The amendments also clarify that the effect of restricting the recognition of a surplus in a defined benefit plan, where the surplus is not recoverable, shall be recognised in other comprehensive income, rather than profit or loss. *[FRS 102.28.25]*.

Asset ceilings and IFRIC 14 guidance are discussed further in EY New UK GAAP 2015 Chapter 23 at 2.2.2.

12   RELATED PARTY DISCLOSURES

The changes made to Section 33 – *Related Party Disclosures* – of FRS 102 by the July 2015 amendments to FRS 102 reflect an equivalent amendment made to IAS 24 – *Related Party Disclosures*, in December 2013. The changes deal with the issue of management companies that provide key management personnel services to the reporting entity or to the parent of the reporting entity. Section 33 of FRS 102 was previously silent on the matter as to whether these management companies were related parties of the reporting entity and whether staff acting for such management companies could be considered to be key management personnel of the reporting entity.

12.1   Entities, or any member of the group of which they are a part, that provide key management personnel services

An additional subparagraph has been added to the definition of a related party to state that an entity is related to the reporting entity if 'the entity, or any member of a group of which it is a part, provides key management personnel services to the reporting entity or to the parent of the reporting entity'. *[FRS 102.33.2(b)(viii)]*.

This is intended to cover situations in which an entity (described as a 'management entity'), or a member of its group, provides key management personnel services to the reporting entity. It applies to the provision of key management personnel services by the separate management entity. Staff acting for the management entity that are responsible for planning, directing and controlling the activities of the reporting entity are not considered to be key management personnel of the reporting entity. It is not necessary to look through the management entity to determine natural persons as key management personnel.

The effect of the amendment is illustrated in the following example.

Example 1:   Entities that provide key management personnel services to a reporting entity

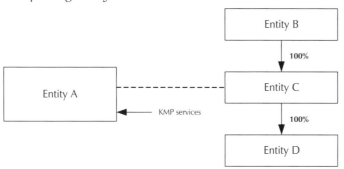

Entity C provides key management personnel (KMP) services to Entity A. For Entity A's financial statements, Entities B, C and D are all related parties. However, Entity A is not a related party of Entities B, C and D (i.e. the related party relationship between the management entity and the reporting entity is not symmetrical).

In addition, paragraph 10 of Section 33 of FRS 102 now requires an entity to disclose separately transactions with entities that provide key management personnel services. *[FRS 102.33.10(d)]*. The type of transactions that require disclosure are discussed in Chapter 28 of EY New UK GAAP 2015 at 3.2.3.

13   PUBLIC BENEFIT ENTITIES

The changes made to Section 34 – *Specialised Activities* – of FRS 102 clarify that a public benefit entity may apply merger accounting to an entity combination provided that it is permitted by the statutory framework under which it operates. If merger accounting is not permitted a combination shall be accounted for by a public benefit entity as an acquisition in accordance with Section 19 – *Business Combinations and Goodwill* – of FRS 102. *[FRS 102.PBE34.80]*. Any entity combination which is neither a combination that is in substance a gift nor a merger, or for which merger accounting is not permitted by the statutory framework under which the public entity benefit reports, shall be accounted for as an acquisition in accordance with Section 19. *[FRS 102.PBE34.81]*.

The note on legal requirements to the July 2015 amendments to FRS 102 states that the purpose of these changes is to ensure that the use of merger accounting beyond its applicability in company law, or other relevant statutory framework. If a public benefit entity that is a company considers that, for the overriding purpose of giving a true and fair view, merger accounting should be applied in circumstances other than those set out in paragraph 10 of Schedule 6 to the Regulations (see 7.2 above), it may do so, providing the relevant disclosures are made in the financial statements. *[FRS 102.A4.30A]*.

The Accounting Council's advice to the FRC to issue the July 2015 amendments to FRS 102 observes that some respondents to the original Financial Reporting Exposure Draft that proposed these changes suggested that FRS 102 should continue to require the use of merger accounting by all public benefit entity combinations meeting the definition and criteria of a merger, through requiring the use of a true and fair override. The Accounting Council noted that 'true mergers' (other than those that might be considered group reconstructions) are not likely to be common but that, as explained above, an individual public benefit entity may apply the true and fair override if it considers it appropriate to its circumstances and provides the corresponding disclosures. *[FRS 102.AC Advice.30(f). July 2015 amendments]*.

14   TRANSITION TO FRS 102

The July 2015 amendments to FRS 102 include changes to Section 35 in respect of share-based payment transactions, and provides additional exemptions for small entities in respect of financial instruments and related party transactions as detailed in Chapter 3 at 6.3.1.

14.1   Share-based payment transactions

A first-time adopter is not required to apply Section 26 – *Share-based Payment* – to equity instruments that were granted before the date of transition to FRS 102, or to liabilities arising from share-based payment transactions that were settled before the date of transition to FRS 102.

Paragraph 35.10(b) dealing with share-based payments has been amended to confirm that: [FRS 102.35.10(b)]

- A first-time adopter of FRS 102 is not required to apply Section 26 to equity instruments *(including the equity component of share-based payment transactions previously treated as compound instruments)*. This amendment takes into the account the fact that under IFRS 2 or FRS 20 an entity that had granted awards where the counterparty had a choice of settlement between cash and equity was required to apply the split accounting approach and an entity would have accounted for both a liability and equity component. See EY New UK GAAP 2015 Chapter 21 at 11 for further details on the split accounting approach. As discussed at 2.5.1 of Chapter 21, split accounting is not required under FRS 102.

- In addition, for a small entity that first adopts FRS 102 for an accounting period that commences before 1 January 2017, this exemption is extended to equity instruments that were granted before the start of the first reporting period that complies with the standard, provided that the small entity did not previously apply FRS 20 or IFRS 2.

  A small entity that chooses to apply this exemption shall provide disclosures in accordance with paragraph 1AC.31 of FRS 102 (see Chapter 3 at 6.3.1).

References

1 FRC PN 089 *Findings of the FRC in respect of the accounts of WH Smith Plc for the year ended 31 August 2012.*

Chapter 6

FRS 104 – Interim financial reporting

List of examples

Chapter 6

Chapter 6

FRS 104 – Interim financial reporting

1   INTRODUCTION

FRS 104 – *Interim Financial Reporting* – was published in March 2015 as a replacement for the Accounting Standards Board's 2007 Statement *Half-yearly financial reports*. FRS 104 does not require any entity to prepare an interim report, nor does it change the extent to which laws or regulations may require the preparation of such a report. FRS 104 is intended for use in the preparation of interim reports by entities that prepare financial statements in accordance with UK GAAP. In particular, it is intended for use by entities which apply FRS 102 – *The Financial Reporting Standard Applicable in the UK and Republic of Ireland*. Most of this chapter therefore deals with the use of FRS 104 by FRS 102 preparers. However, entities which apply FRS 101 – *Reduced Disclosure Framework* – when preparing their annual financial statements may also use FRS 104 when preparing their interim financial reports.

FRS 104 is based on the equivalent international standard IAS 34 – *Interim Financial Reporting*, but with some minor adjustments. Appendix III of FRS 104 sets out the significant differences between IAS 34 and FRS 104, mainly the omission of paragraphs which deal with presentational aspects of IAS 34 or paragraphs of IAS 34 which include disclosures not required in the annual financial statements of entities reporting under FRS 102.

1.1   Definitions

The standard defines an interim period as 'a financial reporting period shorter than a full financial year.' *[FRS 104.Appendix 1]*.

The term 'interim financial report' means a financial report for an interim period that contains either a complete set of financial statements (as described in FRS 102 Section 3 – *Financial Statement Presentation*) or a set of condensed financial statements (see 3.2 below). *[FRS 104.Appendix 1]*.

2   OBJECTIVE AND SCOPE OF FRS 104

2.1   Objective

FRS 104 sets out content, recognition and measurement principles for interim financial reports. *[FRS 104.1A].* It notes that 'timely and reliable interim financial reporting can improve the ability of investors, creditors, and others to understand an entity's capacity to generate earnings and cash flows and its financial condition and liquidity'. *[FRS 104.1].*

2.2   Scope

FRS 104 is intended for use by entities that prepare annual financial statements in accordance with FRS 102. If an entity prepares its annual financial statements under FRS 101 and applies FRS 104, it should replace references to FRS 102 in FRS 104 with the equivalent requirements in EU-adopted IFRS, as amended by paragraph AG 1 of FRS 101. *[FRS 104.2A].*

This chapter has been written primarily for entities that prepare their annual financial statements in accordance with FRS 102. However, we have included a discussion on the application of FRS 104 to FRS 101 reporters at 5 below.

FRS 104, in itself, does not require an entity to prepare interim financial reports and does not mandate, how often, or how soon after the end of an interim period an interim financial report should be issued. Where an entity is required by laws or regulations or voluntarily chooses to prepare interim financial reports it may voluntarily choose to apply FRS 104. *[FRS 104.2].*

Therefore, entities need to consider if there are any applicable laws and regulations which require them to prepare interim financial statements. For example, UK issuers that publish half-yearly reports which include a statement that a condensed set of financial statements has been prepared in accordance with pronouncements on interim reporting issued by the Financial Reporting Council (FRC) must apply FRS 104. *[FRS 104.3A].* See 2.2.1 below.

In practice, we expect a limited number of entities (primarily investment trusts and venture capital trusts) will be required to apply FRS 104. However, for entities which prepare annual financial statements under FRS 101 or FRS 102, FRS 104 may be applied voluntarily for interim reporting purposes.

2.2.1   *Issuers required to comply with the Disclosure and Transparency Rules (DTRs)*

Issuers of securities that are required to publish half-yearly financial reports in accordance with the Disclosure and Transparency Rules (DTRs) must include a responsibility statement in the report. In accordance with paragraph 4.2.10.R of the DTRs, a person making the responsibility statement will satisfy the requirement to confirm that the condensed set of financial statements gives a true and fair view of the assets, liabilities and financial position and profit or loss of the issuer (or the undertakings included in the consolidation as a whole) by including a statement that the condensed set of financial statements has been prepared in accordance with either:

- IAS 34; or

- for UK issuers not using EU-adopted IFRS, pronouncements on interim reporting issued by the FRC. *[FRS 104.A5.3]*.

FRS 104 constitutes the pronouncement on interim reporting for UK issuers not using EU-adopted IFRS as described above. The application of FRS 104 is conditional upon the person making the responsibility statement having reasonable grounds to be satisfied that the condensed set of financial statements prepared under FRS 104 is not misleading. *[FRS 104.A5.4]*.

In accordance with the DTRs, an issuer that is required to prepare consolidated accounts must prepare the condensed set of financial statements in accordance with IAS 34 and the requirements set out in FRS 104 do not apply to these issuers. *[FRS 104.A5.5]*. An issuer that is not required to prepare consolidated accounts must, as a minimum, apply the content and preparation requirements set out in paragraph 4.2.5.R of the DTRs. The content and preparation requirements of FRS 104 are consistent with those set out in the DTRs, although they are more prescriptive and detailed. *[FRS 104.A5.6]*.

2.2.2   *Unlisted entities and entities not subject to the DTRs*

While not in the scope of the DTRs, unlisted entities or entities with securities admitted to trading on an exchange not subject to the DTRs may prepare and present interim financial statements. In those circumstances, there may be no requirement to follow a particular standard on interim financial reporting. However, we would expect that where annual financial statements are prepared under either FRS 101 or FRS 102 that the interim financial statements would be prepared under FRS 104.

3   FORM AND CONTENT OF AN INTERIM FINANCIAL REPORT UNDER FRS 104

FRS 104 does not prohibit or discourage an entity from:

- publishing a complete set of financial statements (as described in Section 3 of FRS 102) in its interim financial report, rather than condensed financial statements and selected explanatory notes; or

- including in condensed interim financial statements more than the minimum line items or selected explanatory notes as set out in paragraph 8 of FRS 104.

The recognition and measurement guidance in the standard, together with the note disclosures required by the standard, apply to both complete and condensed financial statements presented for an interim period. *[FRS 104.7]*.

3.1   Complete set of interim financial statements

If an entity publishes a complete set of financial statements in its interim financial report, the form and content of those statements should conform to the requirements of Section 3 of FRS 102. *[FRS 104.9]*. A complete set of financial statements should include the following components: *[FRS 102.3.17]*

- a statement of financial position as at the reporting date;
- a statement of comprehensive income for the reporting period to be presented either as:
  - a single statement of comprehensive income for the reporting period, displaying all items of income and expense recognised during the period including those items recognised in determining profit or loss (which is a subtotal in the statement of comprehensive income) and items of other comprehensive income; or
  - a separate income statement and a separate statement of comprehensive income. In this case, the statement of comprehensive income begins with profit or loss and then displays the items of other comprehensive income;
- a statement of changes in equity for the reporting period;
- a statement of cash flows for the reporting period; and
- notes comprising a summary of significant accounting policies and other explanatory information.

The presentational requirements of Section 3 of FRS 102 are discussed in Chapter 4. In addition, the entity should make the disclosures specifically required by FRS 104 for interim financial reports (see 4 below) as well as those required by FRS 102. *[FRS 104.7]*.

An entity that will not present a statement of cash flows in its next annual financial statements is not required to include that statement in its interim financial report. *[FRS 104.9]*.

3.2   Condensed interim financial statements

In the interest of timeliness, cost, and avoiding repetition of previously reported information, an entity might be required or elect to give less information at interim dates as compared with its annual financial statements. *[FRS 104.6]*. The standard defines the minimum components of an interim report, as including condensed financial statements and selected notes, as follows: *[FRS 104.6, 8]*

(a)   a condensed statement of financial position;

(b)   a single condensed statement of comprehensive income or a separate condensed income statement and a separate condensed statement of comprehensive income;

(c)   a condensed statement of changes in equity;

(d)   a condensed statement of cash flows; and

(e)   selected explanatory notes.

Other titles for the financial statements can be used, as long as they are not misleading. *[FRS 104.8E]*.

An entity that will not present a statement of cash flows in its next annual financial statements is not required to include that statement in its interim financial report. *[FRS 104.8F]*.

Consistent with the standard's requirements for accounting policies (see 8.1 below), an entity is permitted to depart from using the same presentation as in its most recent annual financial statements if it has determined that the format will change in its next annual financial statements. *[FRS 104.8D]*.

The condensed income statement and condensed statement of comprehensive income referred to at (b) above should be presented using the same basis as the entity's most recent annual financial statements. Accordingly, if an entity presents a separate income statement in its annual financial statements, then it should also present a separate income statement in the interim financial report. Similarly, if a single statement of comprehensive income is presented in the annual financial statements, the same format is adopted in the interim financial report. *[FRS 104.8A]*.

Where the only changes to equity arise from profit or loss, payment of dividends, corrections of prior period errors or changes in accounting policies, an entity may have presented a single statement of income and retained earnings in place of the statement of comprehensive income and statement of changes in equity in its most recent annual financial statements under FRS 102. If that continues to be the case during any of the periods for which the interim financial statements are required to be presented, the entity may continue to present a single condensed statement of income and retained earnings. *[FRS 104.8B]*.

Similarly, where an entity in its most recent annual financial statements has presented only an income statement or a statement of comprehensive income in which the bottom line is labelled profit or loss (by virtue of there being no items of other comprehensive income), that entity is permitted to use the same basis of presentation in its interim financial statements if there are no items of other comprehensive income in any of the periods for which the interim financial statements are being presented. *[FRS 104.8C]*.

As a minimum, the condensed financial statements should include each of the headings and subtotals that were included in the entity's last annual financial statements. *[FRS 104.10]*.

A strict interpretation of this minimum requirement could mean that, for example, an entity is only required to present non-current assets, current assets, etc., in an interim statement of financial position. However, one of the purposes of an interim report is to help the users of the financial statements to understand the changes in financial position and performance of the entity since the end of the last annual reporting period. *[FRS 104.15]*. To that end, FRS 104 also requires additional line items or notes to be included if their omission makes the condensed interim financial statements misleading. *[FRS 104.10]*. In addition, the overriding goal of FRS 104 is to ensure that the interim report includes all information relevant to understanding of the entity's financial position and the performance during the interim period. *[FRS 104.25]*. Therefore, judgement is required to determine which line items provide useful information for decision-makers, and are presented accordingly.

Inclusion of all of the line items from the annual financial statements will often be most appropriate to help users of the interim financial statements understand the changes since the previous year-end. Nonetheless, entities may aggregate line items used in the annual financial statements, if doing so does not make the information misleading or prevent users of the interim financial statements from performing meaningful trend analysis.

Chapter 6

The following example illustrates one possible way in which an entity might choose to combine line items presented separately in the annual financial statements when preparing a condensed set of interim financial statements for an individual set of accounts prepared under Format 1 of Schedule 1 to the Regulations. However, such presentation is at the discretion of management, based on facts and circumstances, including materiality (as noted above), regulatory environment, and the overriding goal of FRS 104 to provide relevant information. *[FRS 104.25]*. Accordingly, other presentations may be appropriate.

Example 6.1:   Presenting the same headings and sub-totals in condensed interim financial statements

Statement of financial position	Annual individual financial statements ('Schedule 1 statutory format')	Condensed interim financial statements
Fixed assets		
Intangible assets	•	•
Tangible assets	•	•
Investments:		•
Investments in joint ventures	•	
Investments in associates	•	
Other investments	•	
Current assets		
Stocks	•	•
Debtors:		•
Amounts falling due within one year	•	
Amounts falling due after one year	•	
Short term deposits	•	•
Cash at bank and in hand	•	•
Creditors: amounts falling due within one year	•	•
Net current assets	•	•
Total assets less current liabilities	•	•
Creditors: amounts falling due after more than one year	•	•
Provisions for liabilities	•	•
Net assets	•	•
Capital and reserves		
Called up share capital	•	•
Share premium account	•	•
Other reserves		•
Capital redemption reserve	•	
Reserve for own shares	•	
Equity component of convertible preference shares	•	
Merger reserve	•	•
Profit and loss account	•	•
Equity attributable to owners of the parent company	•	•
Non-controlling interests	•	•
Total capital and reserves	•	•

Income statement	Annual financial statements ('Schedule 1 statutory format')	Condensed interim financial statements
Turnover	●	●
Cost of sales	●	●
Gross profit	●	●
Operating expenses		●
Distribution costs	●	
Administrative expenses	●	
Other operating expenses	●	
Other operating income	●	●
Operating profit	●	●
Income from investments:		●
Income from shares in group undertakings	●	
Income from participating interests	●	
Profit before interest and tax	●	
Interest payable	●	
Other finance costs	●	
Interest payable and similar expenses		●
Profit before tax	●	●
Tax on profit	●	●
Profit for the period	●	●

Statement of comprehensive income	Annual financial statements	Condensed interim financial statements
Profit for the period	●	●
Cash flow hedges	●	
Remeasurement gain/(loss) recognised on defined benefit pension schemes	●	
Movement on deferred tax relating to pension liability	●	
Total other comprehensive income	●	●
Total comprehensive income for the period	●	●

A statement of changes in equity and statement of cash flows are not presented in this example.

3.3   Requirements for complete and condensed interim financial information

The general principles for preparing annual financial statements are equally applicable to interim financial statements. These principles include fair presentation, going concern, materiality and aggregation. (See Chapter 4 at 8).

Furthermore, irrespective of whether an entity provides complete or condensed financial statements for an interim period, basic and diluted earnings per share should be presented for an interim period when earnings per share (EPS) information has been presented in the entity's most recent annual financial statements. *[FRS 104.11].*

Such information should be given on the face of the statement that presents components of profit or loss for an interim period. *[FRS 104.11A]*.

3.4   Management commentary

A management commentary is not explicitly required by FRS 104, but we would expect one to be included by entities in their interim financial reports along with the interim financial statements.

FRS 104 allows information required under the standard to be presented outside the interim financial statements, i.e. in other parts of interim financial report. *[FRS 104.15B, 16A.]*. Thus, some of the required disclosures may be included in a management commentary (see 4.2.1 below). The standard itself does not establish specific requirements for the content of a management commentary beyond what should be contained in (or cross-referred to) the interim financial statements.

4   DISCLOSURES IN CONDENSED FINANCIAL STATEMENTS

FRS 104 contains a number of disclosure principles:

- Entities should provide information about events and transactions in the interim period that are significant to an understanding of the changes in financial position and performance since the end of the last annual reporting period. In this context it is not necessary to provide relatively insignificant updates to information reported in the last annual financial statements (see 4.1 below). *[FRS 104.15, 15A]*.

- In addition to information to explain significant changes since the last annual reporting period, certain 'minimum' disclosures are required to be given, if not disclosed elsewhere in the interim financial report (see 4.2 below). *[FRS 104.16A]*.

- The materiality assessment for disclosure is based on the interim period data to ensure all information is provided that is relevant to understanding of the entity's financial position and its performance during the interim period (further discussed at 7 below). *[FRS 104.25]*.

Overall, applying those disclosure principles requires a considerable amount of judgement by the entity regarding what information is significant or relevant. The practice of interim reporting confirms that entities take advantage of that room for judgement, both for disclosures provided in the notes to the interim financial statements and outside.

4.1   Significant events and transactions

FRS 104 presumes that users of an entity's interim financial report also have access to its most recent annual financial report. *[FRS 104.15A]*. On that basis, an interim financial report should explain events and transactions that are significant to an understanding of the changes in financial position and performance of the entity since the previous annual reporting period and provide an update to the relevant information included in the financial statements of the previous year. *[FRS 104.15, 15C]*. The inclusion of only selected explanatory notes is consistent with the purpose of an interim financial report, to update the latest complete set of annual financial statements. Accordingly, condensed financial statements avoid repeating previously reported information and focus on new activities, events, and circumstances. *[FRS 104.6]*.

The standard requires disclosure of following events and transactions in interim financial reports, if they are significant: *[FRS 104.15B]*

(a)   write-down of inventories to net realisable value and the reversal of such a write-down;

(b)   recognition of a loss from the impairment of financial assets, property, plant, and equipment, intangible assets, or other assets, and the reversal of such an impairment loss;

(c)   reversal of any provisions for the costs of restructuring;

(d)   acquisitions and disposals of items of property, plant and equipment;

(e)   commitments for the purchase of property, plant and equipment;

(f)   litigation settlements;

(g)   corrections of prior period errors;

(h)   changes in the business or economic circumstances that affect the fair value of the entity's financial assets and financial liabilities, where those assets or liabilities are measured at fair value;

(i)   any loan default or breach of a loan agreement that is not remedied on or before the end of the reporting period;

(j)   related party transactions, unless the transaction was entered into between two or more members of a group, provided that any subsidiary which is a party to the transaction is wholly owned by such a member; and

(k)   changes in contingent liabilities or contingent assets.

The standard specifies that the above list of events and transactions is not exhaustive and the interim financial report should explain any additional events and transactions that are significant to an understanding of changes in the entity's financial position and performance. *[FRS 104.15, 15B]*. Therefore, when information changes significantly (for example, the values of non-financial assets and liabilities that are measured at fair value), an entity should provide disclosure regarding such change, in addition to the requirements listed above; the disclosure should be sufficiently detailed to explain the nature of the change and any changes in estimates.

The disclosures in the above list can be given either in the notes to the interim financial statements or, if disclosed elsewhere in the interim financial report, cross-referred to the disclosure in the notes to the interim financial statements. *[FRS 104.15B]*.

Chapter 6

4.1.1   *Relevance of other standards in condensed financial statements*

Whilst FRS 102 specifies disclosures required in a complete set of financial statements, if an entity's interim financial report includes only condensed financial statements as described in FRS 104, then the disclosures required by those other standards are not mandatory. However, if disclosure is considered to be necessary in the context of an interim report, FRS 102 provides guidance on the appropriate disclosures for many of these items. *[FRS 104.15C]*.

4.2   Other disclosures required by FRS 104

In addition to disclosing significant events and transactions as discussed at 4.1 above, FRS 104 requires an entity to include the following information either in the notes to its interim financial statements or, if disclosed elsewhere in the interim financial report, cross-referred to the information in the notes to the interim financial statements: *[FRS 104.16A]*

(a)   a statement that the same accounting policies and methods of computation are followed in the interim financial statements as in the most recent annual financial statements or, if those policies or methods have been changed, a description of the nature and effect of the change;

(b)   explanatory comments about the seasonality or cyclicality of interim operations;

(c)   the nature and amount of items affecting assets, liabilities, equity, profit or loss, or cash flows that are unusual because of their nature, size, or incidence;

(d)   the nature and amount of changes in estimates of amounts reported in prior interim periods of the current year or changes in estimates of amounts reported in prior years;

(e)   issues, repurchases, and repayments of debt and equity securities;

(f)   dividends paid (aggregate or per share) separately for ordinary shares and other shares;

(g)   certain segment disclosures as discussed at 4.3 below; but only if the entity has presented segment information in accordance with IFRS 8 – *Operating Segments* – in its most recent annual financial statements;

(h)   events after the interim period that are not reflected in the financial statements for the interim period;

(i)   the effect of changes in the composition of the entity during the interim period, including business combinations, obtaining or losing control of subsidiaries and long-term investments, restructurings, and discontinued operations. For business combinations, the entity shall disclose the information required by paragraphs 19.25 and 19.25A of FRS 102 (see Chapter 15 of EY New UK GAAP 2015 at 4.1); and

(j)   for financial instruments, certain disclosures in respect of financial instruments measured at fair value and as required by paragraphs 11.43, 11.48A(e) and 34.22 of FRS 102; but only if the entity would be required to make the disclosure in the annual financial statements, as discussed at 4.4 below.

This information is normally reported on a financial year-to-date basis (see 8 below). *[FRS 104.16A]*.

FRS 102 requires disclosures in aggregate for business combinations effected during the reporting period that are individually immaterial. *[FRS 102.19.25A]*. However, materiality is assessed for the interim period, which implies that FRS 104 may require more detailed disclosures on business combinations that are material to an interim period even if they could be aggregated for disclosure purposes in the annual financial statements under FRS 102.

If an entity has operations that are discontinued or disposed of during an interim period, these operations should be presented separately in the condensed interim statement of comprehensive income following the principles set out in Section 5 – *Statement of Comprehensive Income and Income Statement* – of FRS 102.

An entity contemplating a significant restructuring that will have an impact on its composition should follow the guidance in Section 21 – *Provisions and Contingencies* – of FRS 102 for the recognition of any restructuring cost, *[FRS 102.21.11C]*, and Section 28 – *Employee Benefits* – of FRS 102 for the recognition of any termination benefits. *[FRS 102.28.31]*. In subsequent interim periods any significant changes, including reversals, to restructuring provisions will require disclosure. *[FRS 104.15B(c)]*.

4.2.1   Location of the specified disclosures in an interim financial report

FRS 104 defines an 'interim financial report' as 'a financial report containing either a complete set of financial statements or a set of condensed financial statements for an interim period'. *[FRS 104.Appendix 1]*. Therefore, since an interim financial report *contains* the interim financial statements, it is clear that these are two different concepts. Accordingly, an entity is not required to disclose the information listed at 4.1 and 4.2 above in the interim financial statements themselves, as long as the information is included in another part of the interim financial report and is cross-referenced to the information in the notes to the financial statements. *[FRS 104.15B, 16A]*.

4.3   Segment information

If an entity has presented segment information in accordance with IFRS 8 in its most recent annual financial statements, certain segment disclosures are required in its interim financial report.

An entity applying IFRS 8 in its most recent annual financial statements should include the following information in its interim financial report about its reportable segments: *[FRS 104.16A(g)]*

(a)   revenues from external customers (if included in the measure of segment profit or loss reviewed by or otherwise regularly provided to the chief operating decision maker);

(b)   intersegment revenues (if included in the measure of segment profit or loss reviewed by or otherwise regularly provided to the chief operating decision maker);

(c)   a measure of segment profit or loss;

(d)   a measure of total assets and liabilities for a particular reportable segment if such amounts are regularly provided to the chief operating decision maker and if there has been a material change from the amount disclosed in the last annual financial statements for that reportable segment;

(e)   a description of differences in the basis of segmentation or in the basis of measurement of segment profit or loss from the last annual financial statements;

(f)   a reconciliation of the total profit or loss for reportable segments to the entity's profit or loss before income taxes and discontinued operations. However, if an entity allocates such items as income taxes to arrive at segment profit or loss, the reconciliation can be to the entity's profit or loss after those items. The entity should separately identify and describe all material reconciling items.

4.4   Fair value disclosures for financial instruments

If an entity would be required to make equivalent disclosures in its annual financial statements, FRS 104 requires that an entity should include the following in its interim financial report in order to help users evaluate the significance of financial instruments measured at fair value: *[FRS 104.16A(j)]*:

(a)   for all financial assets and financial liabilities measured at fair value, the entity shall disclose the basis for determining fair value, e.g. quoted market price in an active market or a valuation technique. When a valuation technique is used, the entity shall disclose the assumptions applied in determining fair value for each class of financial assets or financial liabilities. For example, if applicable, an entity discloses information about the assumptions relating to prepayment rates, rates of estimated credit losses, and interest rates or discount rates, *[FRS 102.11.43]*, (see Chapter 8 of EY New UK GAAP 2015 at 8.1);

(b)   for financial instruments at fair value through profit or loss that are not held as part of a trading portfolio and are not derivatives, any difference between the fair value at initial recognition and the amount that would be determined at that date using a valuation technique, and the amount recognised in profit or loss, *[FRS 102.11.48A(e)]*, (see Chapter 8 of EY New UK GAAP 2015 at 8.1);

(c)   for financial instruments held at fair value in the statement of financial position, a financial institution shall disclose for each class of financial instrument, an analysis of the level in the fair value hierarchy (as set out in paragraph 11.27) into which the fair value measurements are categorised, *[FRS 102.34.22]*, (see Chapter 8 of EY New UK GAAP 2015 at 8.2).

The inclusion of the above disclosure requirement among the items required by the Standard to be given 'in addition to disclosing significant events and transactions', *[FRS 104.16A]*, distinguishes it from the items listed at 4.1 above, which are disclosed to update information presented in the most recent annual financial report. *[FRS 104.15]*. Therefore, disclosure of the above information is required for each interim reporting period, subject only to a materiality assessment in relation to that interim report, i.e. an entity could consider it unnecessary to disclose the above information on the grounds that it is not relevant to an understanding of its financial position and performance in that specific interim period. *[FRS 104.25].* In making that judgement care would need to be taken to ensure any omitted information would not make the interim financial report incomplete and therefore misleading.

4.5   Disclosure of compliance with FRS 104

If an interim financial report complies with the requirements of FRS 104, this fact should be disclosed. Furthermore, an entity that makes a statement of compliance with FRS 104 shall comply with all of its provisions. *[FRS 104.3,19].*

5   ENTITIES REPORTING UNDER FRS 101

As noted at 2 above, FRS 104 is intended for use by entities that prepare annual financial statements in accordance with FRS 102. However it can also be used by entities that report under FRS 101, and in those circumstances references in FRS 104 to FRS 102 should be read as references to the equivalent requirements in EU-adopted IFRS as amended by paragraph AG1 of FRS 101. *[FRS 102.2A].*

The references to FRS 102 fall into three main categories:

*   disclosure of significant events and transactions (see 5.1 below);

*   business combinations (see 5.2 below); and

*   financial instruments (see 5.3 below).

While there are references to FRS 102 in other paragraphs of FRS 104, we do not expect that these will give rise to any significant differences in the application of FRS 104 between FRS 101 and FRS 102 reporters. These references are in financial statement presentation, materiality, recognition and changes in accounting policy. *[FRS 104.7, 8B-8C, 9,16B, 24, 31, 30, 33, 43-44].*

In respect of changes in accounting policies users should refer to 8.1.2 below with references to FRSs or FRC Abstracts being read as references to IFRSs or IFRIC Abstracts.

5.1   Disclosure of significant events and transactions

As discussed at 4.1 above, FRS 104 requires entities to include, in their interim financial statements, an explanation of events and transactions that are significant to an understanding of changes in the financial position and performance of the entity since the end of the previous reporting period. The standard sets out a non-exhaustive list of the types of transactions and events entities might include. *[FRS 104.15, 15B].*

The standard refers to individual sections of FRS 102 for guidance on disclosure requirements for many of the items on the list in paragraph 15B. *[FRS 104.15C].* For entities reporting under FRS 101, this reference should be amended to the relevant standard under EU-adopted IFRS as amended by FRS 101. For example, for guidance on the disclosure requirements in respect of the acquisitions and disposals of items of property, plant and equipment (paragraph 15B(d) of FRS 104), entities should refer to IAS 16 – *Property, Plant and Equipment –*

Chapter 6

rather than Section 17 – *Property, Plant and Equipment* – of FRS 102. For further discussion on any significant differences in disclosure between the relevant section of FRS 102 and the equivalent standard under EU-adopted IFRS, refer to the key differences section of the relevant chapter in EY New UK GAAP 2015.

5.2   Business combinations

Paragraph 16A(i) of FRS 104 requires entities to include in their interim financial statements details of the effect of changes in the composition of the entity during the interim period including business combinations, obtaining or losing control of subsidiaries and long-term investments, restructurings and discontinued operations. In particular, entities are required to disclose the information set out in paragraphs 25 and 25A of FRS 102 Section 19 – *Business Combinations and Goodwill.* For FRS 101 reporters we believe the equivalent requirements under EU-adopted IFRS are those set out in paragraph 16A(i) of IAS 34, which cross-refer to the requirements in paragraphs 59-63 and B64-67 of IFRS 3 – *Business Combinations.*

5.3   Financial instruments

Paragraph 16A(j) of FRS 104 requires entities to include in their interim financial statements disclosures that help users to evaluate the significance of financial instruments measured at fair value. In particular, entities are required to give the disclosures set out in paragraphs 43 and 48A(e) of FRS 102 Section 11 – *Basic Financial Instruments* – and paragraph 22 of FRS 102 Section 34 – *Specialised Activities.*

For FRS 101 reporters we believe the equivalent requirements under EU-adopted IFRS are those set out in paragraphs 91-93(h), 94, 96, 98 and 99 of IFRS 13 – *Fair Value Measurement* – and paragraphs 25, 26 and 28-30 of IFRS 7 – *Financial Instruments: Disclosures.*

The IFRS 13 disclosures above will only be required if an entity has financial instruments which (after initial recognition) are measured at fair value on a recurring or non-recurring basis.

FRS 101 allows qualifying entities that are not financial institutions (see Chapter 2 at 2.1 and 6.4 for the definitions of a qualifying entity and a financial institution, respectively) to take advantage of exemptions to disclose information required by IFRS 7 and paragraphs 91 to 99 of IFRS 13 in their annual financial statements provided that equivalent disclosures are included in the consolidated financial statement of the group in which the entity is consolidated. If such disclosure exemptions are reasonably expected to be taken by the qualifying entity when preparing its annual financial statements, there is no requirement to disclose such information in the entity's interim financial report.

6. PERIODS FOR WHICH INTERIM FINANCIAL STATEMENTS ARE REQUIRED TO BE PRESENTED

Irrespective of whether an entity presents condensed or complete interim financial statements, the components of its interim financial reports should include information for the following periods: *[FRS 104.20]*

(a) statements of financial position as of the end of the current interim period and a comparative statement of financial position as of the end of the immediately preceding financial year;

(b) statements of profit or loss and other comprehensive income for the current interim period and, if different, cumulatively for the current financial year-to-date, with comparative statements of profit or loss and other comprehensive income for the comparable interim periods (current and, if different, year-to-date) of the immediately preceding financial year;

(c) statements of changes in equity cumulatively for the current financial year-to-date period, with a comparative statement for the comparable year-to-date period of the immediately preceding financial year; and

(d) statements of cash flows cumulatively for the current financial year-to-date, with a comparative statement for the comparable year-to-date period of the immediately preceding financial year.

The requirement in paragraph (d) does not apply to entities that will not present a statement of cash flows in their next annual financial statements.

An interim financial report may present for each period either a single statement of 'profit or loss and other comprehensive income', or separate statements of 'profit or loss' and 'comprehensive income', consistent with the basis of preparation applied in its most recent annual financial statements. Accordingly, if the entity presents a separate statement for items of profit or loss in its annual financial statements, it should present a separate condensed statement of profit or loss in the interim financial report. *[FRS 104.8A]*. If an entity's business is highly seasonal, then the standard encourages reporting additional financial information for the twelve months up to the end of the interim period, and comparative information for the prior twelve-month period, in addition to the financial statements for the periods set out above. *[FRS 104.21]*.

An entity that presents a single condensed statement of income and retained earnings in place of the statement of comprehensive income and statement of changes in equity in accordance with paragraph 8B of FRS 104, shall present a single condensed statement of income and retained earnings for the periods set out in paragraph 20(b). *[FRS 104.20A]*.

An entity that presents an income statement, or a statement of comprehensive income in which the 'bottom line' is labelled 'profit or loss' in accordance with paragraph 8C of FRS 104, shall present an income statement or a statement of comprehensive income on that basis for the periods set out in paragraph 20(b). *[FRS 104.20B]*.

Chapter 6

The examples below illustrate the periods that an entity is required and encouraged to disclose under FRS 104. *[FRS 104.Appendix II: Illustrations and examples]*.

Example 6.2:   Entity publishes interim financial reports half-yearly

If an entity's financial year ends on 31 December (calendar year), it should present the following financial statements (condensed or complete) in its half-yearly interim financial report as of 30 June 2016:

Half-yearly interim report	*End of the current interim period*	*End of the comparative interim period*	*Immediately preceding year-end*
	30/6/2016	30/6/2015	31/12/2015
Statement of financial position	●		●
Statement(s) of profit or loss and other comprehensive income			
– Current period and year-to-date (6 months) ending	●	●	
– 12 months ending	○	○	
Statement of changes in equity			
– Year-to date (6 months) ending	●	●	
– 12 months ending	○	○	
Statement of cash flows			
– Year-to-date (6 months) ending	●	●	
– 12 months ending	○	○	

● Required   ○ Disclosure encouraged if the entity's business is highly seasonal

If an entity publishes a separate interim financial report for the final interim period (i.e. second half of its financial year), it presents the following financial statements (condensed or complete) in its second half-yearly interim financial report as of 31 December 2016:

Second half-yearly interim report	*End of the current interim period*	*End of the comparative interim period*
	31/12/2016	31/12/2015
Statement of financial position	●	●
Statement(s) of profit or loss and other comprehensive income		
– Current period (6 months) ending	●	●
– Year-to-date (12 months) ending	●	●
Statement of changes in equity		
– Year-to-date (12 months) ending	●	●
Statement of cash flows		
– Year-to-date (12 months) ending	●	●

● Required

Example 6.3:   *Entity publishes interim financial reports quarterly*

If an entity's financial year ends on 31 December (calendar year), it should present the following financial statements (condensed or complete) in its quarterly interim financial reports for 2015:

First quarter interim report	End of the current interim period	End of the comparative interim period	Immediately preceding year-end
	31/3/2016	31/3/2015	31/12/2015
Statement of financial position	●		●
Statement(s) of profit or loss and other comprehensive income			
– Current period and year-to-date (3 months) ending	●	●	
– 12 months ending	○	○	
Statement of changes in equity			
– Year-to-date (3 months) ending	●	●	
– 12 months ending	○	○	
Statement of cash flows			
– Year-to-date (3 months) ending	●	●	
– 12 months ending	○	○	

● Required   ○ Disclosure encouraged if the entity's business is highly seasonal

Second quarter interim report	End of the current interim period	End of the comparative interim period	Immediately preceding year-end
	30/6/2016	30/6/2015	31/12/2015
Statement of financial position	●		●
Statement(s) of profit or loss and other comprehensive income			
– Current period (3 months) ending	●	●	
– Year-to-date (6 months) ending	●	●	
– 12 months ending	○	○	
Statement of changes in equity			
– Year-to-date (6 months) ending	●	●	
– 12 months ending	○	○	
Statement of cash flows			
– Year-to-date (6 months) ending	●	●	
– 12 months ending	○	○	

● Required   ○ Disclosure encouraged if the entity's business is highly seasonal

Chapter 6

Third quarter interim report	End of the current interim period	End of the comparative interim period	Immediately preceding year-end
	30/9/2016	30/9/2015	31/12/2015
Statement of financial position	●		●
Statement(s) of profit or loss and other comprehensive income			
– Current period (3 months) ending	●	●	
– Year-to-date (9 months) ending	●	●	
– 12 months ending	○	○	
Statement of changes in equity			
– Year-to-date (9 months) ending	●	●	
– 12 months ending	○	○	
Statement of cash flows			
– Year-to-date (9 months) ending	●	●	
– 12 months ending	○	○	

● Required   ○ Disclosure encouraged if the entity's business is highly seasonal

If an entity publishes a separate interim financial report for the final interim period (i.e. fourth quarter of its financial year), it presents the following financial statements (condensed or complete) in its fourth quarter interim financial report as of 31 December 2015:

Fourth quarter interim report	End of the current interim period	End of the comparative interim period
	31/12/2016	31/12/2015
Statement of financial position	●	●
Statement(s) of profit or loss and other comprehensive income		
– Current period (3 months) ending	●	●
– Year-to-date (12 months) ending	●	●
Statement of changes in equity		
– Year-to-date (12 months) ending	●	●
Statement of cash flows		
– Year-to-date (12 months) ending	●	●

● Required

6.1   Other comparative information

For entities presenting condensed financial statements under FRS 104, there is no explicit requirement that comparative information be presented in the explanatory notes. Nevertheless, where an explanatory note is required by the standard (such as for inventory write-downs, impairment provisions, segment revenues etc.) or otherwise determined to be needed to provide useful information about changes in the financial position and performance of the entity since the end of the last annual reporting period, [FRS 104.15], it would be appropriate to provide information for each period presented. However, in certain cases it would be unnecessary to provide comparative information where this repeats information that was reported in the notes to the most recent annual financial statements. *[FRS 104.15A]*. For example, it would only be necessary to provide information about business combinations in a comparative period when there is a revision of previously disclosed fair values. See Chapter 15 of EY New UK GAAP 2015 at 4.1.

For entities presenting complete financial statements, whilst FRS 104 sets out the periods for which components of the interim report are included, it is less clear how these rules interact with the requirement in FRS 102 to report comparative information for all amounts in the financial statements. *[FRS 102.3.14]*. In our view, a complete set of interim financial statements should include comparative disclosures for all amounts presented.

6.2 Change in financial year-end

A change in an entity's annual financial reporting period-end impacts the periods presented for interim reporting. For example, an entity changing its reporting date from 31 December to 31 March would have to change its half-year reporting date from 30 June to 30 September. As FRS 104 requires comparative information for 'the *comparable* interim periods (current and year-to-date) of the immediately preceding financial year', the entity would also have to change the comparative interim periods presented. *[FRS 104.20]*.

Example 6.4: Entity changes financial year-end

If an entity changes its financial year-end from 31 December (calendar year) to 31 March, and first reflects the change in its annual financial statements for the period ended 31 March 2016, it should present the following financial statements (condensed or complete) in its half-yearly interim financial reports for 2016:

Half-yearly interim report	End of the current interim period	End of the comparative interim period	Immediately preceding year-end
	30/9/2016	30/9/2015	31/03/2016
Statement of financial position	●		●
Statement(s) of profit or loss and other comprehensive income			
– Current period and year-to-date (6 months) ending	●	●	
– 12 months ending	○	○	
Statement of changes in equity			
– Year-to date (6 months) ending	●	●	
– 12 months ending	○	○	
Statement of cash flows			
– Year-to-date (6 months) ending	●	●	
– 12 months ending	○	○	

● Required ○ Disclosure encouraged if the entity's business is highly seasonal

The entity in the example above should not show information for half-year ended 30 June 2015 as the comparative period, notwithstanding the fact that this period was the reporting date for the last published half-yearly report.

7   MATERIALITY

In making judgements on recognition, measurement, classification, or disclosures in interim financial reports, the overriding goal in FRS 104 is to ensure that an interim financial report includes all information relevant to understanding of an entity's financial position and performance during the interim period. *[FRS 104.25]*. The standard draws from Section 2 – *Concepts and Pervasive Principles* – of FRS 102, which defines an item as material if its omission or misstatement could influence the economic decisions of users of the financial statements, but does not contain quantitative guidance on materiality. *[FRS 102.2.6]*. FRS 104 requires materiality to be assessed based on the interim period financial data. *[FRS 104.23]*.

Therefore, decisions on the recognition and disclosure of unusual items, changes in accounting policies or estimates, and errors are based on materiality in relation to the interim period figures to determine whether non-disclosure is misleading. *[FRS 104.25]*.

Neither the previous year's financial statements nor any expectations of the financial position at the current year-end are relevant in assessing materiality for interim reporting. However, the standard adds that interim measurements may rely on estimates to a greater extent than measurements of annual financial data. *[FRS 104.23]*.

8   RECOGNITION AND MEASUREMENT

The recognition and measurement requirements in FRS 104 arise mainly from the requirement to report the entity's financial position as at the interim reporting date, but also require certain estimates and measurements to take into account the expected financial position of the entity at year-end, where those measures are determined on an annual basis (as in the case of income taxes). Many preparers misinterpret this approach as representing some form of hybrid of the discrete and integral methods to interim financial reporting. This could cause confusion in application.

In requiring the year-to-date to be treated as a discrete period, FRS 104 prohibits the recognition or deferral of revenues and costs for interim reporting purposes unless such recognition or deferral is appropriate at year-end. As with a set of annual financial statements complying with FRS 102, FRS 104 requires changes in estimates and judgements reported in previous interim periods to be revised prospectively, whereas changes in accounting policies and corrections of material prior period errors are required to be recognised by prior period adjustment. However, FRS 104 allows looking beyond the interim reporting period, for example in estimating the tax rate to be applied on earnings for the period, when a year-to-date approach does not.

The recognition and measurement requirements of FRS 104 apply regardless of whether an entity presents a complete or condensed set of financial statements for an interim period, *[FRS 104.7]*, and are discussed below.

8.1   Same accounting policies as in annual financial statements

The principles for recognising assets, liabilities, income and expenses for interim periods are the same as in the annual financial statements. *[FRS 104.29]*. Accordingly, an entity uses the same accounting policies in its interim financial statements as in its most recent annual financial statements, adjusted for accounting policy changes that will be reflected in the next annual financial statements. However, FRS 104 also states that the frequency of an entity's reporting (annual, half-yearly or quarterly) do not affect the measurement of its annual results. To achieve that objective, measurements for interim reporting purposes are on a year-to-date basis. *[FRS 104.28A]*.

8.1.1   Measurement on a year-to-date basis

Measurement on a year-to-date basis acknowledges that an interim period is a part of a full year and allows adjustments to estimates of amounts reported in prior interim periods of the current year. *[FRS 104.29]*.

The principles for recognition and the definitions of assets, liabilities, income and expenses for interim periods are the same as in annual financial statements. *[FRS 104.29, 31]*. Therefore, for assets, the same tests of future economic benefits apply at interim dates as at year-end. Costs that, by their nature, do not qualify as assets at year-end, do not qualify for recognition at interim dates either. Similarly, a liability at the end of an interim reporting period must represent an existing obligation at that date, just as it must at the end of an annual reporting period. *[FRS 104.32]*. An essential characteristic of income and expenses is that the related inflows and outflows of assets and liabilities have already occurred. If those inflows or outflows have occurred, the related income and expense are recognised; otherwise they are not recognised. *[FRS 104.33]*.

The standard lists several circumstances that illustrate these principles:

- inventory write-downs, impairments, or provisions for restructurings are recognised and measured on the same basis as at a year-end. Later changes in the original estimate are recognised in the subsequent interim period, either by recognising additional accruals or reversals of the previously recognised amount; *[FRS 104.30(a)]*

- costs that do not meet the definition of an asset at the end of an interim period are not deferred in the statement of financial position, either to await information on whether it meets the definition of an asset, or to smooth earnings over interim periods within a year. *[FRS 34.30(b)]*. For example, costs incurred in acquiring an intangible asset before the recognition criteria in FRS 102 are met are expensed under Section 18 – *Intangible Assets other than Goodwill* – of FRS 102. Only those costs incurred after the recognition criteria are met can be recognised as an asset; there is no reinstatement as an asset in a later period of costs previously expensed because the recognition criteria were not met at that time; *[FRS 102.18.17]* and

- income tax expense is 'recognised in each interim period based on the best estimate of the weighted-average annual income tax rate expected for the full financial year, using the tax rates and laws that have been enacted or substantively enacted at the end of an interim reporting period. Amounts accrued for income tax expense in one interim period may have to be adjusted in a subsequent interim period of that financial year if the estimate of the annual income tax rate changes'. *[FRS 104.30(c)]*.

Chapter 6

8.1.2   New accounting standards and other changes in accounting policies

As noted above, under FRS 104, an entity uses the same accounting policies in its interim financial statements as in its most recent annual financial statements, adjusted for accounting policy changes that will be in the next annual financial statements, and to determine measurements for interim reporting purposes on a year-to-date basis. *[FRS 104.28-28A]*.

FRS 104 requires that a change in accounting policy, other than where the transition rules are specified by FRS 102, should be reflected by: *[FRS 104.43]*

(a)   restating the financial statements of prior interim periods of the current year and the comparable interim periods of any prior financial years that will be restated in the annual financial statements under Section 10 – *Accounting Policies, Estimates and Errors* – of FRS 102; or

(b)   when it is impracticable to determine the cumulative effect at the beginning of the year of applying a new accounting policy to all prior periods, adjusting the financial statements of prior interim periods of the current year and comparable interim periods of prior years to apply the new accounting policy prospectively from the earliest date practicable.

Therefore, regardless of when in a financial year an entity decides to adopt a new accounting policy, it has to be applied from the beginning of the current year. *[FRS 104.44]*. For example, if an entity that reports on a quarterly basis decides in its third quarter to change an accounting policy, it must restate the information presented in earlier quarterly financial reports to reflect the new policy as if it had been applied from the start of the annual reporting period.

8.1.2.A   Accounting policy changes becoming mandatory during the current year

One objective of the year-to-date approach, described at 8.1.2 above, is to ensure that a single accounting policy is applied to a particular class of transactions throughout a year. *[FRS 104.44]*. To allow accounting policy changes as of an interim date would mean applying different accounting policies to a particular class of transactions within a single year. This would make interim allocation difficult, obscure operating results, and complicate analysis and understandability of the interim period information. *[FRS 104.45]*.

Accordingly, when preparing interim financial information, consideration is given to which amendments to FRSs or FRC Abstracts are mandatory in the next (current year) annual financial statements. The entity generally adopts these amendments in all interim periods during that year.

While FRS 104 generally prohibits an entity from adopting a new accounting policy during an interim period, it makes an exception for those for which FRS 102 specifically requires transition during the financial year. *[FRS 104.43]*.

The disclosure requirements with respect to amendments which are effective for the entity's next annual financial statements, but which do not contain specific disclosure requirements under FRS 104, are not clear. In some cases, it might be determined that an understanding of an amendment is material to an understanding of the entity, in which case the entity discloses this fact, as well as information relevant to assessing the possible impact of the amendment on the entity's financial statements. *[FRS 102.10.13]*. In other cases, an entity might conclude that a particular amendment is not material to an understanding of its interim financial report, and thus not disclose information about the issuance of the amendment, or its possible impact on the entity.

8.1.2.B   Voluntary changes of accounting policy

An entity can also elect at any time during a year to apply an amendment to an FRS or an FRC Abstract before it becomes mandatory, or otherwise decide to change an accounting policy voluntarily. However, before voluntarily changing an accounting policy, consideration should be given to the interaction of the requirements of Sections 2 and 10 of FRS 102 which only permit an entity to change an accounting policy if the information results in information that is 'reliable and more relevant' to the users of the financial statements. *[FRS 102.10.8(b)]*.

When it is concluded that a voluntary change in accounting policy is permitted and appropriate, its effect is generally reflected in the first interim report the entity presents after the date on which the entity changed its policy. The entity generally restates amounts reported in earlier interim periods as far back as is practicable. *[FRS 104.44]*. The restatement of information reported in previous interim periods is also discussed at 11 below.

One exception to this principle of retrospective adjustment of earlier interim periods is when an entity changes from the cost model to the revaluation model under Section 17 or Section 18 of FRS 102. These are not changes in accounting policy that are covered by FRS 102 in the usual manner, but instead are required to be treated as a revaluation in the period. *[FRS 102.10.10A]*. Therefore, the general requirements of FRS 104 do not override the specific requirements of Section 10 of FRS 102 to treat such changes prospectively.

However, to avoid using two differing accounting policies for a particular class of assets in a single financial year, consideration should be given to changing from the cost model to the revaluation model at the beginning of the financial year. Otherwise, an entity will end up depreciating based on cost for some interim periods and based on the revalued amounts for later interim periods.

8.1.3   Change in going concern assumption

Another situation in which an entity applies different accounting policies in its interim financial statements as compared to its most recent annual financial statements is when the going concern assumption is no longer appropriate.

Although FRS 104 does not specifically address the issue of going concern, the general requirements of Section 3 of FRS 102 apply to both a complete set and to condensed interim financial statements. Section 3 states that when preparing financial statements, management assesses an entity's ability to continue as a going concern, and that the financial statements are prepared on a going concern basis unless management either intends to liquidate the entity or cease trading, or has no realistic alternative but to do so. *[FRS 102.3.8]*. The going concern assessment is discussed in more detail in Chapter 4 of EY New UK GAAP 2015 at 8.3.

Chapter 6

Under Section 3 of FRS 102, the going concern assessment is made based on all available information about the future, which at a minimum is twelve months from the *end of the reporting period. [FRS 102.3.8]*. Therefore, with respect to interim reporting under FRS 104, the minimum period for management's assessment is also at least twelve months from the interim reporting date; it is not limited, for example, to one year from the date of the most recent annual financial statements.

Example 6.5:   Going concern assessment

An entity's financial year-end is 31 December (calendar year) and its annual financial statements as of 31 December 2015 are prepared on a going concern basis. In assessing the going concern assumption as at 31 December 2015, management considered all future available information through to 31 December 2016.

In preparing its quarterly interim financial statements (condensed or complete) as at 31 March 2016, management should evaluate all future available information to at least 31 March 2017.

If management becomes aware, in making its assessment, of material uncertainties related to events or conditions that may cast significant doubt upon the entity's ability to continue as a going concern, the entity should disclose those uncertainties. If the entity does not prepare financial statements on a going concern basis, it should disclose that fact, together with the basis on which it prepared the financial statements and the reason why the entity is not regarded as a going concern. *[FRS 102.3.9]*.

8.1.4   *Voluntary changes in presentation*

In some cases, the presentation of the interim financial statements might be changed from that used in prior interim reporting periods. However, before changing the presentation used in its interim report from that of previous periods, management should consider the interaction of the requirements of FRS 104 to include in a set of condensed financial statements the same headings and sub-totals as the most recent annual financial statements *[FRS 104.10]* and to apply the same accounting policies as the most recent or the next annual financial report, *[FRS 104.28]*, and the requirements of Section 3 of FRS 102 as they will relate to those next annual financial statements. Section 3 states that an entity should retain the presentation and classification of items in the financial statements, unless it is apparent following a significant change in the nature of operations or a review of the financial statements that another presentation is more appropriate, or unless the change is required by FRS 102, or another applicable FRS or FRC Abstract. *[FRS 102.3.11]*.

If a presentation is changed, the entity should also reclassify comparative amounts for both earlier interim periods of the current financial year and comparable periods in prior years. *[FRS 104.43(a)]*. In such cases, an entity should disclose the nature of the reclassifications, the amount of each item (or class of items) that is reclassified, and the reason for the reclassification. *[FRS 102.3.12]*.

8.2   Seasonal businesses

Some entities do not earn revenues or incur expenses evenly throughout the year, for example, agricultural businesses, holiday companies, domestic fuel suppliers, or retailers who experience peak demand at Christmas. The financial year-end is often chosen to fit their annual operating cycle, which means that an individual interim period would give little indication of annual performance and financial position.

An extreme application of the integral approach would suggest that they should predict their annual results and contrive to report half of that in the half-year interim financial statements. However, this approach does not portray the reality of their business in individual interim periods, and is, therefore, not permitted under the year-to-date approach adopted in FRS 104. *[FRS 104.28A]*.

8.2.1   Revenues received seasonally, cyclically or occasionally

The standard prohibits the recognition or deferral of revenues that are received seasonally, cyclically or occasionally at an interim date, if recognition or deferral would not be appropriate at year-end. *[FRS 104.37]*. Examples of such revenues include dividend revenue, royalties, government grants, and seasonal revenues of retailers; such revenues are recognised when they occur. *[FRS 104.38]*.

FRS 104 also requires an entity to explain the seasonality or cyclicality of its business and the effect on interim reporting. *[FRS 104.16A(b)]*. If businesses are highly seasonal, FRS 104 encourages reporting of additional information for the twelve months up to the end of the interim period and comparatives for the prior twelve-month period (see 6 above). *[FRS 104.21]*.

8.2.2   Costs incurred unevenly during the year

FRS 104 prohibits the recognition or deferral of costs for interim reporting purposes if recognition or deferral of that type of cost is inappropriate at year-end, *[FRS 104.39]*, which is based on the principle that assets and liabilities are recognised and measured using the same criteria as at year-end. *[FRS 104.29, 31]*. This principle prevents smoothing of costs in seasonal businesses, and the recognition of assets or liabilities at the interim date that would not qualify for recognition at the end of an annual reporting period.

For direct costs, this approach has limited consequences, as the timing of recognising these costs and the related revenues is usually similar. However, for indirect costs, the consequences are greater, and depend on which section of FRS 102 an entity follows, as an entity may not recognise or defer such costs under FRS 104 in an interim period if such a policy is not appropriate at year-end.

For example, manufacturing entities that use fixed production overhead absorption rates should recognise variances and unallocated overheads in the interim period in which they are incurred. *[FRS 102.13.9]*. In contrast, under the hierarchy in Section 10 of FRS 102, construction contractors that use the percentage of completion method may recognise as an asset indirect contract costs that are attributable to contract activity in general, if it is probable that they will be recovered. *[IAS 11.27]*. IAS 11 – *Construction Contracts* – does not provide any guidance on how to determine if it is probable that a cost will be recovered when it relates to contract activity in general.

The implications are unclear for professional service companies that recognise revenue under Section 23 – *Revenue* – of FRS 102 using the percentage of completion method. On one hand, Section 23 includes the same guidance on the percentage of completion method for both construction contracts and service provision, *[FRS 102.23.21]*, implying that both entities can defer costs and the related variances at the end of an interim reporting period. On the other hand, service providers might also follow the guidance in Section 13 – *Inventories* – FRS 102 which also gives guidance for the cost of inventories of a service provider, and which results in expensing such costs and variances at the end of the reporting period. *[FRS 102.13.14]*. However, these are issues that an entity would also face at the end of an annual reporting period. What is clear is that an entity should not diverge from these requirements just because information is being prepared for an interim period.

This application of the discrete approach reflects the reality of that interim period's performance, but also emphasises the limited usefulness of the interim report for a seasonal business, because it shows that the results of that period mean little in isolation. Conversely, allocating costs to interim periods in proportion to the expected levels for the year, which FRS 104 does not allow, might show the results in context, but is subjective and requires forecasting, rather than reporting on the results of the interim period. Probably for this reason, FRS 104 recommends that entities wishing to give the results in context include additional year-to-date disclosures for seasonal businesses, as discussed at 6 above.

9   EXAMPLES OF THE RECOGNITION AND MEASUREMENT PRINCIPLES

Appendix II of FRS 104 provides several examples that illustrate the recognition and measurement principles in interim financial reports. *[FRS 104.40]*.

9.1   Property, plant and equipment and intangible assets

9.1.1   *Depreciation and amortisation*

Depreciation and amortisation for an interim period is based only on assets owned during that interim period and does not consider asset acquisitions or disposals planned for later in the year. *[FRS 104.A2.26]*.

An entity applying a straight-line method of depreciation (amortisation) does not allocate the depreciation (amortisation) charge between interim periods based on the level of activity. However, under Sections 17 and 18 of FRS 102, an entity may use a 'unit of production' method of depreciation, which results in a charge based on the expected use or output (see EY New UK GAAP 2015 Chapter 13 at 3.5.6.C and Chapter 14 at 3.4.3.B). An entity can only apply this method if it most closely reflects the expected pattern of consumption of the future economic benefits embodied in the asset. The chosen method should be applied consistently from period to period unless there is a change in the expected pattern of consumption of those future economic benefits. Therefore, an entity cannot apply a straight-line method of depreciation (amortisation) in its annual financial statements, while allocating the depreciation (amortisation) charge to interim periods using a 'unit of production' based approach.

9.1.2   *Impairment of assets*

Section 27 – *Impairment of Assets* – of FRS 102 requires an entity to recognise an impairment loss if the recoverable amount of an asset declines below its carrying amount. *[FRS 104.A2.37]*. An entity should apply the same impairment testing, recognition, and reversal criteria at an interim date as it would at year-end. *[FRS 104.A2.38]*.

However, FRS 104 states that an entity is not required to perform a detailed impairment calculation at the end of each interim period. Rather, an entity should perform a review for indications of significant impairment since the most recent year-end to determine whether such a calculation is needed. *[FRS 104.A2.38]*. Nevertheless, the standard does not exempt an entity from performing impairment tests at the end of its interim periods. For example, an entity that recognised an impairment charge in the immediately preceding year, may find that it needs to update its impairment calculations at the end of subsequent interim periods because impairment indicators remain.

9.1.3   Recognition of intangible assets

An entity should apply the same definitions and recognition criteria for intangible assets, as set out in Section 18 of FRS 102, in an interim period as in an annual period. Therefore, costs incurred before the recognition criteria are met should be recognised as an expense. *[FRS 104.A2.10]*. Expenditures on intangibles that are initially expensed cannot be reinstated and recognised as part of the cost of an intangible asset subsequently (e.g. in a later interim period). *[FRS 102.18.17]*. Furthermore, 'deferring' costs as assets in an interim period in the hope that the recognition criteria will be met later in the year is not permitted. Only costs incurred after the specific point in time at which the criteria are met should be recognised as part of the cost of an intangible asset. *[FRS 104.A2.10]*.

9.2   Employee benefits

9.2.1   Employer payroll taxes and insurance contributions

If employer payroll taxes or contributions to government-sponsored insurance funds are assessed on an annual basis, the employer's related expense should be recognised in interim periods using an estimated average annual effective rate, even if it does not reflect the timing of payments. A common example contained in Appendix II to FRS 104 is an employer payroll tax or insurance contribution subject to a certain maximum level of earnings per employee. Higher income employees would reach the maximum income before year-end, and the employer would make no further payments for the remainder of the year. *[FRS 104.A2.3]*.

9.2.2   Year-end bonuses

The nature of year-end bonuses varies widely. Some bonus schemes only require continued employment whereas others require certain performance criteria to be attained on a monthly, quarterly, or annual basis. Payment of bonuses may be purely discretionary, contractual or based on years of historical precedent. *[FRS 104.A2.7]*. A bonus is recognised for interim reporting if, and only if: *[FRS 104.A2.8]*

(a)   the entity has a present legal or constructive obligation to make such payments as a result of past events; and

(b)   a reliable estimate of the obligation can be made.

Chapter 6

A present obligation exists only when an entity has no realistic alternative but to make the payments. *[FRS 102.21.6]*. Section 28 of FRS 102 gives guidance on accounting for profit sharing and bonus plans (see EY New UK GAAP 2015 Chapter 23 at 3.3).

In recognising a bonus at an interim reporting date, an entity should consider the facts and circumstances under which the bonus is payable, and determine an accounting policy that recognises an expense reflecting the obligation on the basis of the services received to date. Several possible accounting policies are illustrated in Example 6.6 below.

Example 6.6:   Measuring interim bonus expense

An entity pays an annual performance bonus if earnings exceed £10 million, under which 5% of any earnings in excess over £10 million will be paid up to a maximum of £500,000. Earnings for the six months ended 30 June 2016 are £7 million, and the entity expects earnings for the full year ended 31 December 2016 to be £16 million.

The following table shows various accounting policies and the expense recognised thereunder in the interim financial statements for the six months ended 30 June 2016.

	Expense (£)
Method 1 – constructive obligation exists when earnings target is met	Nil
Method 2 – assume earnings for remainder of year will be same	200,000
Method 3 – proportionate recognition based on full-year estimate	131,250
Method 4 – one-half recognition based on full-year estimate	150,000

Method 1 is generally not appropriate, as this method attributes the entire bonus to the latter portion of the year, whereas employees provided service during the first six months to towards earning the bonus.

Likewise, Method 2 is generally not appropriate, as the expense of £200,000 [(£14 million – £10 million) × 5%] assumes that the employees will continue to provide service in the latter half of the year to achieve the bonus target, but does not attribute any service to that period.

In contrast to Methods 1 and 2, Method 3 illustrates an accounting policy whereby an estimate is made of the full-year expense and attributed to the period based on the proportion of that bonus for which employees have provided service at 30 June 2016. The amount recognised is calculated as (£7 million ÷ £16 million) × [5% × (£16 million – £10 million)].

Similar to Method 3, Method 4 also takes the approach of recognising an expense based on the full year estimate, but allocates that full-year estimate equally to each period (which is similar to the approach used for share-based payment transactions). The amount recognised is calculated as [50% × 5% × (£16 million – £10 million)].

In addition to Methods 3 and 4, which might be appropriate, depending on the facts and circumstances, an entity might determine another basis on which to recognise bonus that considers both the constructive obligation that exists as of 30 June 2016, and the services performed to date, which is also appropriate.

9.2.3   Pensions

Section 28 of FRS 102 requires an entity to determine the present value of defined benefit obligations and the fair value of plan assets at the end of the reporting period. While Section 28 does not require an entity to involve a professionally qualified actuary in the measurement of the obligations, nor to undertake a comprehensive annual actuarial valuation, we expect that in practice most entities will do so.

For interim reporting purposes, the defined benefit obligation can often be reliably measured by extrapolation of the latest actuarial valuation adjusted for changes in employee demographics such as number of employees and salary levels. *[FRS 104.A2.42]*.

If there are significant changes to pension arrangements during the interim period (such as changes resulting from a material business combination or from a major redundancy programme) then entities may wish to consider whether they should obtain a new actuarial valuation of scheme liabilities. Similarly, if there are significant market fluctuations, such as those arising from changes in corporate bond markets, the validity of the assumptions in the last actuarial estimate, such as the discount rate applied to scheme liabilities, should be reviewed and revised as appropriate.

Market values of plan assets as at the interim reporting date should be available without recourse to an actuary and in normal circumstances, companies will not necessarily go through the full process of measuring pension liabilities at interim reporting dates, but rather will look to establish a process to assess the impact of any changes in underlying parameters (e.g. through extrapolation). As with all estimates, the appropriateness in the circumstances should be considered.

9.2.4 Vacations, holidays and other short-term paid absences

Section 28 of FRS 102 distinguishes between accumulating and non-accumulating paid absences. *[FRS 102.28.6-7]*. Accumulating paid absences are those that are carried forward and can be used in future periods if the current period's entitlement is not used in full. Section 28 requires an entity to measure the expected cost of and obligation for accumulating paid absences at the amount the entity expects to pay as a result of the unused entitlement that has accumulated at the end of the reporting period (see EY New UK GAAP 2015 Chapter 23 at 3.3). FRS 104 requires the same principle to be applied at the end of interim reporting periods. Conversely, an entity should not recognise an expense or liability for non-accumulating paid absences at the end of an interim reporting period, just as it would not recognise any at the end of an annual reporting period. *[FRS 104.A2.12]*.

9.3 Inventories and cost of sales

9.3.1 Inventories

An entity should apply the recognition and measurement requirements of Section 13 of FRS 102 for interim financial reporting in the same way as it does for annual reporting purposes, despite the problems of determining inventory quantities, costs and net realisable values. However, FRS 104 does comment that to save cost and time, entities often use estimates to measure inventories at interim dates to a greater extent than at annual reporting dates. *[FRS 104.A2.27]*.

Net realisable values are determined using selling prices and costs to complete and dispose at the end of the interim period. A write-down should be reversed in a subsequent interim period only if it would be appropriate to do so at year-end (see EY New UK GAAP 2015 Chapter 9 at 3.4.2). *[FRS 104.A2.28].*

9.3.2   *Contractual or anticipated purchase price changes*

Both the payer and the recipient of volume rebates, or discounts and other contractual changes in the prices of raw materials, labour, or other purchased goods and services should anticipate these items in interim periods if it is probable that these have been earned or will take effect. However, discretionary rebates and discounts should not be recognised because the resulting asset or liability would not meet the recognition criteria in FRS 102. *[FRS 104.A2.25].*

9.3.3   *Interim period manufacturing cost variances*

Price, efficiency, spending and volume variances of a manufacturing entity should be recognised in profit or loss at interim reporting dates to the same extent that those variances are recognised at year-end. It is not appropriate to defer variances expected to be absorbed by year-end, which could result in reporting inventory at the interim date at more or less than its actual cost. *[FRS 104.A2.30].* See 8.2.2 above for a discussion on this topic as it applies to costs incurred by service providers.

9.4   Taxation

Taxation is one of the most difficult areas of interim financial reporting, primarily because FRS 104 does not clearly distinguish between current income tax and deferred tax, referring only to 'income tax expense.' This causes tension between the approach for determining the expense and the asset or liability in the statement of financial position. In addition, the standard's provisions combine terminology, suggesting an integral approach with guidance requiring a year-to-date basis to be applied. The integral method is used in determining the effective income tax rate for the whole year, but that rate is applied to year-to-date profit in the interim financial statements. In addition, under a year-to-date basis, the estimated rate is based on tax rates and laws that are enacted or substantively enacted by the end of the interim period. Changes in legislation expected to occur before the end of the current year are not recognised in preparing the interim financial report. The assets and liabilities in the statement of financial position, at least for deferred taxes, are derived solely from a year-to-date approach, but sometimes the requirements of the standard are unclear, as discussed below.

9.4.1   *Measuring interim income tax expense*

FRS 104 states that income tax expense should be accrued using the tax rate applicable to expected total annual earnings, by applying the estimated weighted-average annual effective income tax rate to pre-tax income for the interim period. *[FRS 104.A2.14].* However, this is not the same as estimating the total tax expense for the year and allocating a proportion of that to the interim period (even though it might sometimes appear that way), as demonstrated in the discussion below.

Because taxes are assessed on an annual basis, using the integral approach to determine the annual effective income tax rate and applying it to year-to-date actual earnings is consistent with the basic concept in FRS 104, that the same recognition and measurement principles apply in interim financial reports as in annual financial statements. *[FRS 104.A2.15]*.

In estimating the weighted-average annual income tax rate, an entity should consider the progressive tax rate structure expected for the full year's earnings, including changes in income tax rates scheduled to take effect later in the year that are enacted or substantively enacted as at the end of the interim period. *[FRS 104.A2.15]*. This situation is illustrated in Example 6.7 below.

Example 6.7:   Measuring interim income tax expense [FRS 104.A2.17]

An entity reporting quarterly expects to earn 10,000 pre-tax each quarter and operates in a jurisdiction with a tax rate of 20% on the first 20,000 of annual earnings and 30% on all additional earnings. Actual earnings match expectations. The following table shows the income tax expense reported each quarter:

	Pre-tax earnings	Effective tax rate	Tax expense
First quarter	10,000	25%	2,500
Second quarter	10,000	25%	2,500
Third quarter	10,000	25%	2,500
Fourth quarter	10,000	25%	2,500
Annual	40,000		10,000

10,000 of tax is expected to be payable for the full year on 40,000 of pre-tax income (20,000 @ 20% + 20,000 @ 30%), implying an average annual effective income tax rate of 25% (10,000 / 40,000).

In the above example, it might look as if the interim income tax expense is calculated by dividing the total expected tax expense for the year (10,000) by the number of interim reporting periods (4). However, this is only the case in this example because profits are earned evenly over each quarter. The expense is actually calculated by determining the effective annual income tax rate and multiplying that rate to year-to-date earnings, as illustrated in Example 6.8 below.

Example 6.8:   Measuring interim income tax expense – quarterly losses
           [FRS 104.A2.18]

An entity reports quarterly, earns 15,000 pre-tax profit in the first quarter but expects to incur losses of 5,000 in each of the three remaining quarters (thus having zero income for the year), and operates in a jurisdiction in which its estimated average annual income tax rate is 20%. The following table shows the income tax expense reported each quarter:

	Pre-tax earnings	Effective tax rate	Tax expense
First quarter	15,000	20%	3,000
Second quarter	(5,000)	20%	(1,000)
Third quarter	(5,000)	20%	(1,000)
Fourth quarter	(5,000)	20%	(1,000)
Annual	0		0

Chapter 6

The above example shows how an expense is recognised in periods reporting a profit and a credit is recognised when a loss is incurred. This result is very different from allocating a proportion of the expected total income tax expense for the year, which in this case is zero.

If an entity operates in a number of tax jurisdictions, or where different income tax rates apply to different categories of income (such as capital gains or income earned in particular industries), the standard requires that to the extent practicable, an entity: *[FRS 104.A2.16]*

- estimates the average annual effective income tax rate for each taxing jurisdiction separately and applies it individually to the interim period pre-tax income of each jurisdiction; and

- applies different income tax rates to each individual category of interim period pre-tax income.

This means that the entity should perform the analysis illustrated in Example 6.8 above for each tax jurisdiction and arrive at an interim tax charge by applying the tax rate for each jurisdiction to actual earnings from each jurisdiction in the interim period. However, the standard recognises that, whilst desirable, such a degree of precision may not be achievable in all cases and allows using a weighted-average rate across jurisdictions or across categories of income, if such rate approximates the effect of using rates that are more specific. *[FRS 104.A2.16]*.

Example 6.9:   Measuring interim tax expense – many jurisdictions *[FRS 104.A2.16]*

An entity operates in 3 countries, each with its own tax rates and laws. In order to determine the interim tax expense, the entity determines the effective annual income tax rate for each jurisdiction and applies those rates to the actual earnings in each jurisdiction, as follows:

(All values in £)	Country A	Country B	Country C	Total
Expected annual tax rate	25%	40%	20%	
Expected annual earnings	300,000	250,000	200,000	750,000
Expected annual tax expense	75,000	100,000	40,000	215,000
Actual half-year earnings	140,000	80,000	150,000	370,000
Interim tax expense	35,000	32,000	60,000	127,000

By performing a separate analysis for each jurisdiction, the entity determines an interim tax expense of £127,000, giving an effective average tax rate of 34.3% (£127,000 ÷ £370,000). Had the entity used a weighted-average rate across jurisdictions, using the expected annual earnings, it would have determined an effective tax rate of 28.7% (£215,000 ÷ £750,000), resulting in a tax expense for the interim period of £106,190 (370,000 @ 28.7%). Whether the difference of nearly £21,000 lies within the range for a reasonable approximation is a matter of judgement.

9.4.2   Changes in the effective tax rate during the year

9.4.2.A   Enacted changes for the current year that apply after the interim reporting date

As noted above, the estimated income tax rate applied in the interim financial report should reflect changes that are enacted or substantively enacted as at the end of the interim reporting period, but scheduled to take effect later in the year. *[FRS 104.A2.15]*. The Glossary in FRS 104 explains that tax rates can be regarded as substantively enacted when the remaining stages of the enactment process historically have not affected the outcome and are unlikely to do so. In particular, a UK tax rate is regarded as having been substantively enacted if it is included in:

*   a Bill that has been passed by the House of Commons and is awaiting only passage through the House of Lords and Royal Assent; or

*   a resolution having statutory effect that has been passed under the Provisional Collection of Taxes Act 1968.

A Republic of Ireland tax rate can be regarded as having been substantively enacted if it is included in a Bill that has been passed by the Dáil.

For example, assume that the 30% tax rate (on earnings above 20,000) in Example 6.7 was substantively enacted as at the second quarter reporting date and applicable before year-end. In that case, the estimated income tax rate for interim reporting would be the same as the estimated average annual effective income tax rate computed in that example (i.e. 25%) after considering the higher rate, even though the entity's earnings are not above the required threshold at the half-year.

If legislation is enacted only after the end of the interim reporting period but before the date of authorisation for issue of the interim financial report, its effect is disclosed as a non-adjusting event. *[FRS 102.32.11(h)]*. Under Section 32 – *Events after the End of the Reporting Period* – of FRS 102 estimates of tax rates and related assets or liabilities are not revised. *[FRS 104.32.6]*.

9.4.2.B   Changes to previously reported estimated income tax rates for the current year

FRS 104 requires an entity to re-estimate at the end of each interim reporting period the estimated average annual income tax rate on a year-to-date basis. *[FRS 104.A2.15]*. Accordingly, the amounts accrued for income tax expense in one interim period may have to be adjusted in a subsequent interim period if that estimate changes. *[FRS 104.30(c)]*. FRS 104 requires disclosure in interim financial statements of material changes in estimates of amounts reported in an earlier period or, in the annual financial statements, of material changes in estimates of amounts reported in the latest interim financial statements. *[FRS 104.16A(d)]*.

Accordingly, just as the integral approach does not necessarily result in a constant tax charge in each interim reporting period, it also does not result in a constant effective tax rate when circumstances change.

Chapter 6

Example 6.10:   Changes in the effective tax rate during the year

Taking the fact pattern in Example 6.7 above, an entity reporting quarterly expects to earn 10,000 pre-tax each quarter; from the start of the third quarter the higher rate of tax on earnings over 20,000 increases from 30% to 40%. Actual earnings continue to match expectations. The following table shows the income tax expense reported in each quarter:

	Period pre-tax earnings	Pre-tax earnings: year to date	Effective tax rate	Tax expense: year to date	Period tax expense
First quarter †	10,000	10,000	25%	2,500	2,500
Second quarter †	10,000	20,000	25%	5,000	2,500
Third quarter	10,000	30,000	30%	9,000	4,000
Fourth quarter	10,000	40,000	30%	12,000	3,000
Annual	40,000				12,000

† As previously reported from Example 6.7 using an effective tax rate of 25%.

The increase in the tax rate means that 12,000 of tax is expected to be payable for the full year on 40,000 of pre-tax income (20,000 @ 20% + 20,000 @ 40%), implying an average annual effective income tax rate of 30% (12,000 / 40,000). With cumulative pre-tax earnings of 30,000 as at the end of the third quarter, the estimated tax liability is 9,000, requiring a tax expense of 4,000 (9,000 – 2,500 – 2,500) to be recognised during that quarter. In the final quarter, earnings of 10,000 result in a tax charge of 3,000, using the revised effective rate of 30%.

9.5.2.C   Enacted changes applying only to subsequent years

In many cases, tax legislation is enacted that takes effect not only after the interim reporting date but also after year-end. Such circumstances are not addressed explicitly in the standard. Indeed, because FRS 104 does not clearly distinguish between current income tax and deferred tax, combined with the different approaches taken in determining the expense recognised in profit or loss compared to the statement of financial position, this can lead to confusion in this situation.

On the one hand, the standard states that the estimated income tax rate for the interim period includes enacted or substantively enacted changes scheduled to take effect later in the year. *[FRS 104.A2.15].* This implies that the effect of changes that do not take effect in the current year is ignored in determining the appropriate rate for current tax. On the other hand, FRS 104 also requires that the principles for recognising assets, liabilities, income and expenses for interim periods are the same as in the annual financial statements. *[FRS 104.29].* In annual financial statements, deferred tax is measured at the tax rates expected to apply to the period when the asset is realised or the liability is settled, based on tax rates (and tax laws) enacted or substantively enacted by the end of the reporting period, as required by FRS 102. *[FRS 102.29.12].* Therefore, an entity should recognise the effect of a change applying to future periods if this change is enacted by the end of the interim reporting period.

These two requirements seem to be mutually incompatible. FRS 104 makes sense only in the context of calculating the effective *current* tax rate on income earned in the period. Once a deferred tax asset or liability is recognised, it should be measured under Section 29 – *Income Tax* – of FRS 102. Therefore, an entity should recognise an enacted change applying to future years in measuring deferred tax assets and liabilities as at the end of the interim reporting period. One way to treat the cumulative effect to date of this remeasurement is to recognise it in full, by a credit to profit or loss or to other comprehensive income, depending on the nature of the temporary difference being remeasured, in the period during which the tax legislation is enacted, in a similar way to the treatment shown in Example 6.10 above, and as illustrated in Example 6.11 below.

Example 6.11:   Enacted changes to tax rates applying after the current year

An entity reporting half-yearly operates in a jurisdiction subject to a tax rate of 30%. Legislation is enacted during the first half of the current year, which reduces the tax rate to 28% on income earned from the beginning of the entity's next financial year. Based on a gross temporary difference of 1,000, the entity reported a deferred tax liability in its most recent annual financial statements of 300 (1,000 @ 30%). Of this temporary difference, 200 is expected to reverse in the second half of the current year and 800 in the next financial year. Assuming that no new temporary differences arise in the current period, what is the deferred tax balance at the interim reporting date?

Whilst the entity uses an effective tax rate of 30% to determine the tax expense relating to income earned in the period, it should use a rate of 28% to measure those temporary differences expected to reverse in the next financial year. Accordingly, the deferred tax liability at the half-year reporting date is 284 (200 @ 30% + 800 @ 28%).

Alternatively, if the effective *current* tax rate is not distinguished from the measurement of deferred tax, it could be argued that FRS 104 allows the reduction in the deferred tax liability of 16 (300 – 284) to be included in the estimate of the effective income tax rate for the year. Approach 2 in Example 6.14 below applies this argument. In our view, because FRS 104 does not distinguish between current and deferred taxes, either approach would be acceptable provided that it is applied consistently.

9.4.3   Difference in financial year and tax year

If an entity's financial year and the income tax year differ, the income tax expense for the interim periods of that financial year should be measured using separate weighted-average estimated effective tax rates for each of the income tax years applied to the portion of pre-tax income earned in each of those income tax years. *[FRS 104.A2.19]*. In other words, an entity should compute a weighted-average estimated effective tax rate for each income tax year, rather than for its financial year.

Example 6.12:   Difference in financial year and tax year [FRS 104.A2.20]

An entity's financial year ends 30 June and it reports quarterly. Its taxable year ends 31 December. For the financial year that begins 1 July 2016 and ends 30 June 2017, the entity earns 10,000 pre-tax each quarter.

The estimated average annual income tax rate is 30% in the income tax year to 31 December 2016 and 40% in the year to 31 December 2017.

Quarter ending	Pre-tax earnings	Effective tax rate	Tax expense
30 September 2016	10,000	30%	3,000
31 December 2016	10,000	30%	3,000
31 March 2017	10,000	40%	4,000
30 June 2017	10,000	40%	4,000
Annual	40,000		14,000

Chapter 6

9.4.4   Tax loss and tax credit carrybacks and carryforwards

Appendix II to FRS 104 repeats the requirement in Section 29 of FRS 102 that for carryforwards of unused tax losses, a deferred tax asset should be recognised to the extent that it is probable that they will be recovered against the reversal of deferred tax liabilities or other future taxable profits. *[FRS 104.A2.23]*. In assessing whether future taxable profit is available, the criteria in Section 29 are applied at the interim date. If these criteria are met as at the end of the interim period, the effect of the tax loss carryforwards is included in the estimated average annual effective income tax rate.

Example 6.13:   Tax loss carryforwards expected to be recovered in the current year
[FRS 104.A2.24]

An entity that reports quarterly has unutilised operating losses of 10,000 for income tax purposes at the start of the current financial year for which a deferred tax asset has not been recognised. The entity earns 10,000 in the first quarter of the current year and expects to earn 10,000 in each of the three remaining quarters. Excluding the effect of utilising losses carried forward, the estimated average annual income tax rate is 40%. Including the carryforward, the estimated average annual income tax rate is 30%. Accordingly, tax expense is determined by applying the 30% rate to earnings each quarter as follows:

	Pre-tax earnings	Effective tax rate	Tax expense
First quarter	10,000	30%	3,000
Second quarter	10,000	30%	3,000
Third quarter	10,000	30%	3,000
Fourth quarter	10,000	30%	3,000
Annual	40,000		12,000

This result is consistent with the general approach for measuring income tax expense in the interim report, in that any entitlement for relief from current tax due to carried forward losses is determined on an annual basis. Accordingly, its effect is included in the estimate of the average annual income tax rate and not, for example, by allocating all of the unutilised losses against the earnings of the first quarter to give an income tax expense of zero in the first quarter and 4,000 thereafter.

In contrast, the year-to-date approach of FRS 104 means that the benefits of a tax loss carryback are recognised in the interim period in which the related tax loss occurs, *[FRS 104.A2.22]*, and are not included in the assessment of the estimated average annual tax rate, as shown in Example 6.8 above. This approach is consistent with Section 29 of FRS 102 which requires the benefit of a tax loss that can be carried back to recover current tax already incurred in a previous period to be recognised as an asset. *[FRS 102.29.4]*. Therefore, a corresponding reduction of tax expense or increase of tax income is also recognised. *[FRS 104.A2.22]*.

Where previously unrecognised tax losses are expected to be utilised in full in the current year, it seems intuitive to recognise the recovery of those carried forward losses in the estimate of the average annual tax rate, as shown in Example 6.12 above. However, where the level of previously unrecognised tax losses exceeds expected taxable profits for the current year, a deferred tax asset should be recognised for the carried forward losses that are now expected to be utilised, albeit in future years.

The examples in FRS 104 do not show how such a deferred tax asset is created in the interim financial report. In our view, two approaches are acceptable, as shown in Example 6.14 below.

Example 6.14:   Tax loss carryforwards in excess of current year expected profits

An entity that reports half-yearly has unutilised operating losses of 75,000 for income tax purposes at the start of the current financial year for which no deferred tax asset has been recognised. At the end of its first interim period, the entity reports a profit before tax of 25,000 and expects to earn a profit of 20,000 before tax in the second half of the year. The entity reassesses the likelihood of generating sufficient profits to utilise its carried forward tax losses and determines that the FRS 102 recognition criteria for a deferred tax asset are satisfied for the full amount of 75,000. Excluding the effect of utilising losses carried forward, the estimated average annual income tax rate is the same as the enacted or substantially enacted rate of 40%.

As at the end of the current financial year the entity expects to have unutilised losses of 30,000 (75,000 carried forward less current year pre-tax profits of 45,000). Using the enacted rate of 40%, a deferred tax asset of 12,000 is recognised at year-end. How is this deferred tax asset recognised in the interim reporting periods?

Approach 1

Under the first approach, the estimate of the average annual effective tax rate includes only those carried forward losses expected to be utilised in the current financial year and a separate deferred tax asset is recognised for those carried forward losses now expected to be utilised in future annual reporting periods.

In the fact pattern above, using 45,000 of the carried forward tax losses gives an average effective annual tax rate of nil, as follows:

Estimation of the annual effective tax rate – Approach 1

Expected annual tax expense before utilising losses carried forward (45,000 @ 40%)	18,000
Tax benefit of utilising carried forward tax losses (45,000 @ 40%)	(18,000)
Expected annual tax expense before the effect of losses carried forward to future annual periods	0
Expected annual effective tax rate	0%
Effect of tax losses carried forward to future periods (75,000 – 45,000 @ 40%)	(12,000)
Tax income to be recognised in the interim period	(12,000)

The remaining tax losses give rise to a deferred tax asset of 12,000, which is recognised in full at the half-year, to give reported profits after tax as follows:

	First half-year	*Second half-year*	*Annual*
Profit before income tax	25,000	20,000	45,000
Income tax (expense)/credit			
– at expected annual effective rate	0	0	0
– recognition of deferred tax asset	12,000	0	12,000
Net profit after tax	37,000	20,000	57,000

Approach 2

Under the second approach, the estimate of the average annual effective tax rate reflects the expected recovery of all the previously unutilised tax losses from the beginning of the period in which the assessment of recoverability changed. In the fact pattern above, recognition of the unutilised tax losses gives an average effective annual tax rate of –26.67%, as follows:

Estimation of the annual effective tax rate – Approach 2

Expected annual tax expense before utilising losses carried forward (45,000 @ 40%)	18,000
Tax benefit of recognising unutilised tax losses (75,000 @ 40%)	(30,000)
Expected annual tax credit after recognising unutilised tax losses	(12,000)
Expected annual effective tax rate (–12,000 ÷ 45,000)	–26.67%

This approach results in reported profits after tax as follows:

	First half-year	*Second half-year*	*Annual*
Profit before income tax	25,000	20,000	45,000
Income tax (expense)/credit – at expected annual effective rate	6,667	5,333	12,000
Net profit after tax	31,667	25,333	57,000

Approach 1 is consistent with the requirements of Section 29 of FRS 102 as it results in recognising the full expected deferred tax asset as soon as it becomes 'probable that they will be recovered against the reversal of deferred tax liabilities or other future taxable profits'. *[FRS 102.29.7]*. However, given that FRS 104 does not specifically address this situation, and is unclear about whether the effective tax rate reflects changes in the assessment of the recoverability of carried forward tax losses, we also believe that Approach 2 is acceptable.

9.4.5   Tax credits

FRS 104 also discusses in more detail the treatment of tax credits, which may for example be based on amounts of capital expenditures, exports, or research and development expenditures. Such benefits are usually granted and calculated on an annual basis under tax laws and regulations and therefore are reflected in the estimated annual effective income tax rate used in the interim report. However, if tax benefits relate to a one-time event, they should be excluded from the estimate of the annual rate and deducted separately from income tax expense in that interim period. *[FRS 104.A2.21]*.

9.5   Foreign currency translation

9.5.1   *Foreign currency translation gains and losses*

An entity measures foreign currency translation gains and losses for interim financial reporting using the same principles that Section 30 – *Foreign Currency Translation* – of FRS 102 requires at year-end (see Chapter 25 of EY New UK GAAP 2015). *[FRS 104.A2.31]*. An entity should use the actual average and closing foreign exchange rates for the interim period (i.e. it may not anticipate changes in foreign exchange rates for the remainder of the current year in translating at an interim date). *[FRS 104.A2.32]*. When Section 30 requires translation adjustments to be recognised as income or expense in the period in which they arise, the same approach should be used in the interim report. An entity should not defer some foreign currency translation adjustments at an interim date, even if it expects the adjustment to reverse before year-end. *[FRS 104.A2.33]*.

9.5.2   *Interim financial reporting in hyperinflationary economies*

Interim financial reports in hyperinflationary economies are prepared using the same principles as at year-end. *[FRS 104.A2.34]*. Section 31 – *Hyperinflation* – of FRS 102 requires that the financial statements of an entity that reports in the currency of a hyperinflationary economy be stated in terms of the measuring unit current at the end of the reporting period, and the gain or loss on the net monetary position be included in profit or loss. In addition, comparative financial data reported for prior periods should be restated to the current measuring unit (see Chapter 26 of EY New UK GAAP 2015). *[FRS 104.A2.35]*. As shown in Examples 6.2 and 6.3 above, FRS 104 requires an interim report to contain many components, which are all restated at every interim reporting date.

The measuring unit used is the same as that as of the end of the interim period, with the resulting gain or loss on the net monetary position included in that period's net income. An entity may not annualise the recognition of gains or losses, nor may it estimate an annual inflation rate in preparing an interim financial report in a hyperinflationary economy. *[FRS 104.A2.36]*.

While it is highly unlikely for a UK company to have the functional currency of a hyperinflationary economy, a UK based group may prepare consolidated financial statements under FRS 102 with a subsidiary that operates in, and has a functional currency of, a country subject to hyperinflation.

Chapter 6

9.6   Provisions, contingencies and accruals for other costs

9.6.1   *Provisions*

FRS 104 requires an entity to apply the same criteria for recognising and measuring a provision at an interim date as it would at year-end. *[FRS 104.A2.6]*. Hence, an entity should recognise a provision when it has no realistic alternative but to transfer economic benefits because of an event that has created a legal or constructive obligation. *[FRS 104.A2.5]*. The standard emphasises that the existence or non-existence of an obligation to transfer benefits is a question of fact, and does not depend on the length of the reporting period. *[FRS 104.A2.6]*.

The obligation is adjusted upward or downward at each interim reporting date, if the entity's best estimate of the amount of the obligation changes. The standard states that any corresponding loss or gain should normally be recognised in profit or loss. *[FRS 104.A2.5]*. However, an entity applying IFRIC 1 – *Changes in Existing Decommissioning, Restoration and Similar Liabilities* – under the hierarchy in Section 10 of FRS 102 (see Chapter 13 of EY New UK GAAP 2015 at 3.4.3) might instead need to adjust the carrying amount of the corresponding asset rather than recognise a gain or loss.

9.6.2   *Other planned but irregularly occurring costs*

Many entities budget for costs that they expect to incur irregularly during the year, such as advertising campaigns, employee training and charitable contributions. Even though these costs are planned and expected to recur annually, they tend to be discretionary in nature. Therefore, it is generally not appropriate to recognise an obligation at the end of an interim financial reporting period for such costs that are not yet incurred, as they do not meet the definition of a liability. *[FRS 104.A2.13]*.

As discussed at 8.2.2 above, FRS 104 prohibits the recognition or deferral of costs incurred unevenly throughout the year at the interim date if recognition or deferral would be inappropriate at year-end. *[FRS 104.39]*. Accordingly, such costs should be recognised as they are incurred and an entity should not recognise provisions or accruals in the interim report to adjust these costs to their budgeted amount.

9.6.3   *Major planned periodic maintenance or overhaul*

The cost of periodic maintenance, a planned major overhaul, or other seasonal expenditures expected to occur after the interim reporting date should not be recognised for interim reporting purposes unless an event before the end of the interim period causes the entity to have a legal or constructive obligation. The mere intention or necessity to incur expenditures in the future is not sufficient to recognise an obligation as at the interim reporting date. *[FRS 104.A2.4]*. Similarly, an entity may not defer and amortise such costs if they are incurred early in the year, but do not satisfy the criteria for recognition as an asset as at the interim reporting date.

9.6.4   *Contingent lease payments*

Contingent lease payments can create legal or constructive obligations that are recognised as liabilities. If a lease includes contingent payments based on achieving a certain level of annual sales (or annual use of the asset), an obligation can arise in an interim period before the required level of annual sales (or usage) is achieved. If the entity expects to achieve the required level of annual sales (or usage), it should recognise a liability as it has no realistic alternative but to make the future lease payment. *[FRS 104.A2.9].*

9.6.5 Levies charged by public authorities

When governments or other public authorities impose levies on entities in relation to their activities, as opposed to income taxes, it is not always clear when the liability to pay a levy arises and a provision should be recognised. As there is no specific guidance on accounting for such provisions under FRS 102, entities may, under the hierarchy set out in Section 10 of FRS 102, refer to the guidance in IFRIC 21 – *Levies* – in formulating an appropriate accounting policy for these obligations.

9.7 Earnings per share

As noted at 3.3 above, FRS 104 requires that where an entity has presented EPS information in accordance with IAS 33 – *Earnings per Share* (as adopted in the EU) in its most recent annual financial statements, then it will present basic and diluted EPS in its interim financial statements. *[FRS 104.11].* EPS in an interim period is computed in the same way as for annual periods. However, IAS 33 does not allow diluted EPS of a prior period to be restated for subsequent changes in the assumptions used in those EPS calculations. *[IAS 33.65].* This approach might be perceived as inconsistent to the year-to-date approach which should be followed for computing EPS for an interim period. For example, if an entity, reporting quarterly, computes diluted EPS in its first quarter financial statements, it cannot restate the reported diluted EPS subsequently for any changes in the assumptions used. However, following a year-to-date approach, the entity should consider the revised assumptions to compute the diluted EPS for the six months in its second quarter financial statements, which, in this case would not be the sum of its diluted EPS for first quarter and the second quarter.

10 USE OF ESTIMATES

FRS 104 requires that the measurement procedures followed in an interim financial report should be designed to ensure that the resulting information is reliable and that all material financial information that is relevant to an understanding of the financial position or performance of the entity is appropriately disclosed. Whilst estimation is necessary in both interim and annual financial statements, the standard recognises that preparing interim financial reports generally requires greater use of estimates than at year-end. *[FRS 104.41].* Consequently, the measurement of assets and liabilities at an interim date may involve less use of outside experts in determining amounts for items such as provisions, contingencies, pensions or non-current assets revalued at fair values. Reliable measurement of such amounts may simply involve updating the previously reported year-end position. The procedures may be less rigorous than those at year-end. The example below is based on Appendix II to FRS 104. *[FRS 104.A2.39-47].*

Example 6.15:   Use of estimates

Inventories	Full stock-taking and valuation procedures may not be required for inventories at interim dates, although it may be done at year-end. It may be sufficient to make estimates at interim dates based on sales margins.
Classifications of current and non-current assets and liabilities	Entities may do a more thorough investigation for classifying assets and liabilities as due within one year or after more than one year (or an equivalent classification between current and non-current assets and liabilities) at annual reporting dates than at interim dates.
Provisions	Determining the appropriate provision (such as a provision for warranties, environmental costs, and site restoration costs) may be complex and often costly and time-consuming. Entities sometimes engage outside experts to assist in the annual calculations. Making similar estimates at interim dates often entails updating of the prior annual provision rather than the engaging of outside experts to do a new calculation.
Pensions	Section 28 of FRS 102 requires an entity to determine the present value of defined benefit obligations and the fair value of plan assets at the end of each reporting period. Section 28 does not require an entity to involve a professionally qualified actuary in measurement of the obligations nor does it require an annual comprehensive actuarial valuation. As discussed at 9.2.3 above, market values of plan assets as at the interim reporting date should be available without recourse to an actuary, and reliable measurement of defined benefit obligations for interim reporting purposes can often be extrapolated from the latest actuarial valuation adjusted for changes in employee demographics such as number of employees and salary levels.
Income taxes	Entities may calculate income tax expense and deferred income tax liability at annual dates by applying the tax rate for each individual jurisdiction to measures of income for each jurisdiction. Paragraph A2.16 of Appendix II (see 9.4.1 above) acknowledges that while that degree of precision is desirable at interim reporting dates as well, it may not be achievable in all cases, and a weighted-average of rates across jurisdictions or across categories of income is used if it is a reasonable approximation of the effect of using more specific rates.
Contingencies	The measurement of contingencies may involve the opinions of legal experts or other advisers. Formal reports from independent experts are sometimes obtained for contingencies. Such opinions about litigation, claims, assessments, and other contingencies and uncertainties may or may not also be needed at interim dates.
Revaluations and fair value accounting	Section 17 of FRS 102 allows an entity to choose as its accounting policy the revaluation model whereby items of property, plant and equipment are revalued to fair value. Similarly, Section 16 of FRS 102 requires an entity to measure the fair value of investment property. For those measurements, an entity that relies on professionally qualified valuers at annual reporting dates is not required to rely on them at interim reporting dates.
Specialised industries	Because of complexity, costliness, and time, interim period measurements in specialised industries might be less precise than at year-end. An example is calculation of insurance reserves by insurance companies.

Attention is given to items that are recognised at fair value. Although an entity is not required to use professionally qualified valuers at interim reporting dates, and may only update the previous year-end position, the entity is required to recognise impairments in the appropriate interim period.

11   RESTATEMENT OF PREVIOUSLY REPORTED INTERIM PERIODS

As discussed at 8.1 above, an entity should apply the same accounting policies as applied in the most recent annual financial statements as adjusted for accounting policy changes that are to be reflected in the next annual financial statements. *[FRS 104.28]*. One objective of FRS 104's rules on the adoption of new accounting policies is to ensure that a single accounting policy is applied to a particular class of transactions throughout the year. Another objective is to ensure consistency with Section 10 of FRS 102, under which a change in accounting policy is adopted retrospectively and prior period financial data are restated as far back as practicable. *[FRS 104.44]*.

In the absence of any specified transitional provisions in FRS 102, FRS 104 requires a change in accounting policy to be reflected: *[FRS 104.43]*

(a)   by restating the financial statements of prior interim periods of the current year, and the comparable interim periods of any prior years that will be restated in the annual financial statements under Section 10 of FRS 102; or

(b)   when it is impracticable to determine the cumulative effect at the beginning of the year of applying a new accounting policy to all prior periods, by:

(i)   adjusting the financial statements of prior interim periods of the current year; and

(ii)   applying the new accounting policy prospectively from the earliest date practicable in comparable interim periods of prior years.

The Glossary to FRS 104 states that application of a requirement is 'impracticable' when the entity cannot apply it after making every reasonable effort to do so. *[FRS 104.Glossary]*.

Therefore, as discussed at 8.1.2 above, a new accounting policy has to be applied from the beginning of the current year (regardless of when in a financial year an entity decides to adopt that policy) and prior interim periods are restated unless it is impracticable to do so. *[FRS 104.44]*.

12   FIRST-TIME PRESENTATION OF INTERIM REPORTS COMPLYING WITH FRS 104

The standard defines 'interim period' as a financial reporting period shorter than a full financial year *[FRS 104.Glossary]* and requires the format of condensed financial statements for an interim period to include each of the headings and subtotals that were included in the entity's most recent annual financial statements. *[FRS 104.10]*.

However, FRS 104 provides no guidance for an entity that chooses to issue condensed interim financial statements before it has prepared a set of FRS 102 compliant annual financial statements. This situation will arise in the entity's first year of its existence or in the year in which the entity converts from previous UK

Chapter 6

GAAP to FRS 102. Whilst the standard does not prohibit the entity from preparing a condensed set of interim financial statements, it does not specify how an entity would interpret the minimum disclosure requirements of FRS 104 when there are no annual financial statements to refer to.

The entity should consider making additional disclosures to recognise that a user of this first set of interim financial statements does not have the access otherwise assumed by the standard to the most recent annual financial report of the entity. Accordingly, the explanation of significant events and transactions and changes in financial position in the period should be more detailed than the update normally expected in FRS 104. *[FRS 104.15]*. In the absence of any specific regulatory requirements to which the entity is subject, the following are examples of additional considerations that would apply:

- since it is not possible to make a statement that the same accounting policies and methods of computation have been applied, *[FRS 104.16A(a)]*, the entity should disclose all those accounting policies and methods of computation in the same level of detail as it would in a set of annual financial statements. When the entity issues interim reports on a quarterly basis, the first quarter interim report should provide the abovementioned details; subsequent quarterly reports could refer to the details included in the first quarter report;

- similarly, the disclosure of the nature and amount of changes in estimates of amounts reported in prior periods will have to go into more detail than just the changes normally required to be disclosed; *[FRS 104.16A(d)]*

- more extensive disclosure than simply the changes since the last report date will be required for contingent liabilities and contingent assets; *[FRS 104.15B(m)]* and

- in the absence of a complete set of annual financial statements complying with FRS 102, the entity should include each of the headings and subtotals in the condensed financial statements that it would expect to include in its first financial statements prepared under FRS 102.

Entities that have converted another financial reporting framework to FRS 102 and have not yet published FRS 102 annual financial statements are required to make additional disclosures when presenting interim reports in accordance with FRS 104: *[FRS 104.16B]*

- a description of the nature of each change in accounting policy;

- a reconciliation of its equity determined in accordance with its previous financial reporting framework to its equity determined in accordance with the new financial reporting framework for the following dates:

  - the date of transition to the new financial reporting framework; and

  - at the end of the comparable year to date period of the immediately preceding financial year; and

- a reconciliation of profit or loss determined in accordance with its previous financial reporting framework for the comparable interim period (current and if different year-to-date) of the immediately preceding financial year.

If an entity becomes aware of errors made under its previous financial reporting framework, the reconciliations above shall, to the extent practicable, distinguish the correction of those errors from changes in accounting policies. For an entity converting to FRS 102 in their next annual financial statements, the requirements of Section 35 – *Transition to this FRS* – of FRS 102 should be applied. Those requirements, which include the reconciliations above, are discussed in Chapter 30 of EY New UK GAAP 2015.

Chapter 6

Index of standards

FRS 102

FRS 103

FRS 104

The Limited Liability Partnerships (Accounts and Audit) (Application of Companies Act 2006) Regulations 2008

TECH 02/10

Large and Medium-sized Companies and Groups (Accounts and Reports) Regulations 2008

Small Companies and Groups (Accounts and Directors Report) Regulations 2008

Large and Medium-sized Limited Liability Partnerships Regulations 2008

Small Limited Liability Partnerships (Accounts) Regulations 2008

FRSSE

Foreword to Accounting Standards

Index

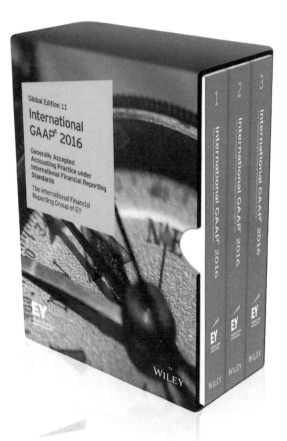